THE
THIRD PARISH REGISTERS
OF
BELIZE
1828-1841

St. George's Caye Cemetery
Yarborough Cemetery

The 1832, 1835, and 1839 Censuses of Belize

Births, Marriages, and Deaths in British Newspapers

The Belize Advertiser, 1839-1841

Compiled by
Sonia Bennett Murray

CLEARFIELD

Reprinted for Clearfield Company by
Genealogical Publishing Company
Baltimore, Maryland
2012

ISBN 978-0-8063-5580-1

Made in the United States of America

To

the People of Belize –

Past, Present, and Future.

Acknowledgements

The writer owes a very great debt of gratitude to her husband, Gilbert Murray, who accompanied her on so many trips to Belize over the years, photographed the tombstones in Yarborough Cemetery, and checked digital pictures downloaded into the laptop at the Bullfrog Inn while she worked at the Archives in 2008 and 2010. Without his love and his patient support, this book would not have been possible. Leon Chelette of the Gulfport L.D.S. Church has kept the Family History Library open for researchers for decades, making it possible to check census transcripts against LDS microfilm; Alvina Bristow and Louise York, who gave much good advice, are gone but never forgotten. Rosa M. Chambless translated Spanish names; Beth Berry, Sheila Woods, and Al and Judy Gill all strained their eyes in puzzling over doubtful names on film.

Dr. James Garber, of Texas State University, contributed a report on the dig at the cemetery on St. George's Caye, including a map made in 1872 by Rob Humes, locating and identifying a number of the tombs. Sister Eustochium, the bursar of St. Cecilia's Abbey on the Isle of Wight, shared her knowledge of the Bennetts and Hydes who owned Appley House there. Mera Gisela Johnson gave information on Marcus Belisle and some of his descendants. May Ann Thompson Adams traced George Runnals' first wife, Sophia Augusta Barnes, back to English roots. Lizet Thompson Hegar and her staff at the Belize National Archives could not have been more helpful during my visits to Belmopan; Mary Alpuche has been invaluable, not only by answering innumerable questions but by sending a scan of a page when my photograph proved too badly out of focus to be transcribed. Michael Wooten, then a graduate student at USM, kindly obtained film of the Belize Advertiser on interlibrary loan from the University of South Carolina, making it possible to access the many items of genealogical value in this 19th century newspaper.

The records in this book were photographed at the Archives at Belmopan and at Yarborough Cemetery, for transcription at home. Transcripts of baptisms and burials were checked against the pictures and checked a second time; census transcripts were rechecked against LDS films; transcripts of newspaper extracts were rechecked against the film. With all the care in the world, there will inevitably be mistakes – though hopefully, fewer than in the first two volumes, drawn from earlier records in far worse condition. Old handwriting, even that of ministers and Keepers of Records, who were educated men, may not be fully legible. Records that got wet during hurricanes became stained and blackened by mold, with ink washed out, blurred, or faded. In cases of uncertainty, readers are advised to go to the Archives and examine the record for themselves, or to write to the Archives to purchase a photocopy of the entry in question.

Many people have helped in the compilation of this book – but there will inevitably be errors. All mistakes and errors are entirely my own.

Introduction

Tracing ancestry in Belize requires comparison of evidence from all available sources: baptismal and burial registers, every census taken from 1816 to 1839, monumental inscriptions in the cemeteries, old newspapers, and information from descendants who have family histories. The Belize genealogical forum connects searchers with cousins all over the world, people who have information to share and compare.

A great deal of information about the early records of Belize appears in the introductions to the First and the Second Parish Register of Belize, and will not be repeated here. Information specific to records in the present volume is given at the commencement of each section of the book. However, some peculiarities must be pointed out. Belize was largely founded by Scots, who brought the custom of the patronymic, by which women kept their maiden names throughout life. St. John's marriage records have apparently not survived. Couples with different surnames who appear in censuses with children are described in the writer's notes as husband and wife; some would have married in a church, while others joined Bay-fashion in a consensual union. Wills and gravestones may clarify marital status by describing a woman as a wife. Tropical fevers and diseases were endemic; many people died in their twenties or thirties, leaving children in need of a breadwinner or caregiver, so quick remarriage was the norm. This is why the censuses show so many put-together families with children of different surnames.

A surprising number of decedents who were recorded in the burial register do not appear in censuses. Some may have been children born after a census date, either not baptized at St. John's or baptized in a year for which records are missing, and dead before the next census took place. Others would have been businessmen, petty traders, and drifters from Central America and the islands who came to Belize, fell ill, and died. Efforts to identify decedents with difficult and partially visible names in censuses and other records were made. James ?ocle, for example, was identified as James Toole, but other attempts failed: a search for Thomas with a partial surname, .ich....., showed possibilities such as Nicholson and Richardson, but the given name did not appear in any of these families. A search of newspapers digitized by the British Library showed people who died in Belize but were not in any other record found to date.

The land for Yarborough Cemetery was donated by Capt. James D. Yarborough in 1796; burials took place there until 1891, but in the 1880's the ground was almost full, so new cemeteries were established farther out of town. The killer hurricane of 1931 brought a wall of water laden with wreckage to smash through the graveyard and damage the tombs. Photos of the destruction can be seen on the internet; estimates of death vary from 1500 to 2500, so many that victims were buried in mass graves. The storm surge rose over St. George's Key and washed the tombs in the disused cemetery there into the bay. In 1961, Hurricane Hattie devastated and flooded the city and its burial grounds again. "Yarbra," as the locals called it, was abandoned and neglected, growing up in weeds. When the writer and her husband searched for family tombs in 1982 we had to wade through undergrowth, and were warned about snakes. There was extensive vandalism (locals said broken pieces of marble were used as washboards, ballast in crab traps, shelves to keep food cool, etc) before the cemetery was cleaned up for the millennium.

The rector of St. John's (at this time Matthew Newport) recorded color in his registers by the initials W, C, or B, and paupers as P. He did this because the fees he and his clerk received were fixed by law and based on social status. The Almanac of 1839 shows the fee for baptism of whites and persons of colour of all ages was £2 for the minister and 10/- for the clerk; for blacks, £1/6/8 and 6/8. The burial fee for whites and persons of colour over the age of 10 was £2/13/4 for the minister and 13/- for the clerk; for whites under 10, £1/6/8 and 6/8; for blacks over 10, £1/13/4 and 8/4, and under 10, £1 and 5/-. Fees for paupers of all classes, paid from public funds, were 13/4d for adults and 3/4d for children. The minister recorded government military pensioners as G.M. P., or pens'r, or pens; fees for their burial services are not shown in the Almanac. The minister served as chaplain to the garrison, and the military paid to bury pensioners.

The handwriting of ministers, clerks, and Keepers of Records was not always clear, and Keepers compiled censuses from lists given in by settlers whose writing varied from good to abominable. Books that got wet during hurricanes had ink washed out, and were stained and blackened by mold. A question mark indicates a doubtful word or name. In cases of uncertainty, readers are advised to go to Belmopan and examine the record for themselves, or to write to the Archives to purchase a photocopy of the entry in question.

If you find your ancestor with a surname in the 1839 census but not in the 1835, or in the 1839 and '35 but not in the '1832, he or she may have been in the same family but with only a given name; many people took the family's surname on emancipation. What a pity that in the censuses after 1832, no ages were given!

While some people lacking surnames were blessed with unusual given names such as Devonshire or Olive, dozens had very common names – John, Mary, Thomas, Sarah, Eliza, etc., and were close in age. One family in the 1832 census included two children named Sarah, one aged 11, the other aged 4, and two named John, one aged 8 and the other aged 3. Another family had two boys named Thomas, one 11 and the other 10; another, two Williams, aged 14 and 15; another, Allick, 11, and Allick, 10. The more common the name the more difficult it will be to pick out an individual from the crowd. An oral or written family history is almost essential to tracing slave ancestry in a time and place in which so few records have survived.

If you are new to genealogy, ask your oldest living relatives to tell you about their grandparents and great-grandparents, aunts, uncles, and cousins; write down everything they remember, and share the information on the internet; others may be able to help.

Good luck, and happy hunting!

Errata and Updates, *First* **and** *Second Parish Registers of Belize:*

Catherine CUNNINGHAM, who had children with Marshal BENNETT ca. 1825-28 and died in November 1833, was misidentified in Vols. 1 and 2 as Catherine TILLETT Cunningham. In fact, she was the daughter of Andrew Cunningham and Sarah KEEFE, and the sister in law of Catherine Tillett Cunningham, who had married her brother, Charles Keefe Cunningham. Charles K. (adult and wealthy in the 1816 census, i.e born pre- 1795) and Catherine "Kitty" TILLETT, 1789- 1832 (interred 8 Jan 1832 aged 43, second daughter of Capt. William TILLETT and Mary WHITE,) had children including Catherine Tillett Cunningham, born in 1826, who married Thomas ROBINSON and died in 1859.

Sophia Augusta RUNNALS, the first wife of George Runnals or Runnels, was born 9 Dec 1801 and baptized 3 Jan 1802 at St John, Hackney, Middlesex to Thomas and Jane BARNES. Susanna Elizabeth Runnals was assumed to have been George and Sophia's daughter; it now appears that she was George's daughter by his second wife, Elizabeth Ramsay WADE.

1826 Census: p. 209 #501: James, 31. p. 219 #509: Charley, 35. p. 222 #515: Tracy (not Mary) STEWART. p. 226 #529: Elizabeth FELIX Jr is adult. p. 228 #533: the name is BELLNOE.

1829 Census: p. 242 #4: William SMITH Jr., 000-100-000-000 was omitted. p. 262 #48: Arabian (not Andrew) MYVITT. p. 276, #91: John (not Joseph) GAMBOA. p. 287 #123, Eager (not Edgar) appears as Hagar in other censuses. p. 290 #129: Enumerator's error: in other records, Anne Maria/AnnMaria/Mariann POTTS. p. 304. #181: Francis (not Frances) WILSON. p. 312 #223, John GORDON, 000-000-110-100. p. 313 #224: Isabella GRAHAM (not GORDON.) p. 357 (#324 continued,) Richmond (not Richard.) p. 383 #396 should read Catherine SMITH, 000-241-020-000. p. 392 #428: Andria (not Andrew.) p. 399 #442, William ANDERSON, 28. p. 408 #484: David (not Daniel) EDWARDS.

Table of Contents:

1. Introduction, page iii.

2. Errata and Updates, *First* and *Second Parish Register of Belize*, p. v.

3. Table of Contents, p. vi.

4. St. John's Baptismal Register, 1828-29 and 1835-36, p. 1.

5. St. John's Burial Register, 1828-1841, p. 24.

6. St. George's Caye Cemetery, p. 75.

7. The Church Street Cemetery, p. 78.

8. Yarborough Cemetery, p. 79.

9. The 1832 Census, p. 100.

10. The 1835 Census, p. 174.

11. The 1839 Census, p. 223.

12. Births, Marriages, and Deaths in Family Records and British Newspapers, 309.

13. The Belize Advertiser, 1839-41, p. 314.

14. Index to People, p. 378.

15: Index to Shipping, p. 414.

THE THIRD BAPTISMAL REGISTER OF ST JOHNS,
1828-1829 and 1835-1836

Much of this register is clearly written, but some names are scribbled and uncertain; these are indicated by a question mark. The record has considerable damage. Hurricanes broke windows and tore at the roof of the church; rainwater puddled on shelves and soaked the bottom of the book, washing out ink so that the lowest entry on many pages is lost to us; and in a humid climate, mold proliferated on damp paper. Color is noted in the margin as W, C, or B, but on many pages the margins are so browned and rotted that the initials are lost or uncertain; only those which are clearly visible are given below. At some future date, chemical techniques may make it possible to bring out faded lettering and missing names. Months are abbreviated. Abode is copied only if other than Belize. The Rev. Matthew Newport, who officiated, signed each entry as shown in #1.

Baptisms in 1828:

p. 1:
#1: Jan 1, Betsy to John RABAN & Ann CRAWFORD, Convention Town, Wood
        Cutter, C. M. Newport, Chaplain.

#2: " " Catherine to John RABAN & Ann CRAWFORD, ditto.

#3: " " John to John RABAN & Ann CRAWFORD, ditto.

#4: " " Margaret to John RABAN & Ann CRAWFORD, ditto.

#5: " " Samuel to John & Rosanna TWEENY, New Town Barracks,
        Serg't in the 2nd W. I. Reg't.

#6: Jan 2, Maria HAMILTON to *blank* & Kate DOUGLAS, Free Black.

#7: " " John Stanley CHERRINGTON to William T. CHERRINGTON & Phoebe
        FLOWERS, Mahogany Cutter.

#8: " " George to Willm... *washed out and illegible.*

p. 2:
#9: Jan 2, William to William BERNARD & Joana WILLIAM, Fisherman, B.

#10: " " Charles to William BERNARD & Joana WILLIAM, Fisherman, B.

#11: " " Thomas to William BERNARD & Joana WILLIAM, Fisherman, B.

1

#12: Jan 3, Fanny ROBINSON to Polydore BIRD & Dorcas ROBINSON, Bakers,
Planter, B.

#13: " " Alexander to John GREEN & Maria FLOWERS, Lime Walk, Planter, B.

#14: " " Diana to John JOHNSON & Amelia HINKS, Shop Keeper.

#15: " " Mary Elizabeth to George HUME & Mary COLQUHOUN, Mahogany
Cutter.

#16: *Ink washed out* to George HUME & Mary COLQUHOUN, Mahogany *illegible*.

p. 3:
#17: Jan 3, Mary HICKEY HUME MEIGHAN to Francis MEIGHAN & Elizabeth
HUME, Mahogany Cutter, C.

#18: " " Alfred to John YOUNG & Ann HUNT, Physician, C.

#19: Jan 4, William HAMMOND to John HAMMOND & Cleanther ARTHUR, Bakers,
Planter, C.

#20: " " Ann to George FRAZER & Ann McVIE, Clerk, C.

#21: Jan 5, Quamina BURGESS to James LAMB & Sarah BURGESS, Free Black, B.

#22: Jan 7, b. 1827 25 Nov, Ann to John & Sarah ADAM, Merchant, W.

#23: " " John CARD to Willm CARD & Sarah McKENZE, C.

#24: Susannah to *washed out and illegible*.

p. 4:
#25: Jan 7, Thomas Joseph to Joseph LAMB and Elizabeth POLYDORE, Free Black.

#26: " " John PITTS, Free Black Adult.

#27: " " William GRANT, Free Black Adult.

#28: Jan 10, b. 3 Jun 1826, Mary Jane to Michael GAVIN & Elizabeth SWACEY, [sic],
Provost Marshal.

#29: Jan 13, b. 16 Sep 1822, William LEWIS to John M. CUNNINGHAM & Margaret,
Mahogany Cutter, C.

#30: " " b. 5 Oct 1827, Margaret to John M. CUNNINGHAM & Margaret,
Mahogany Cutter, C.

2

#31: Jan 14, John to John Edwd HENDERSON & *illegible* BROSTER, *(=Eliza A.)*
Mahogany Cutter, C.

#32: *Washed out and illegible.*

p.5:
#33: Jan 16, Margaret MEANY to Colin CAMPBELL & Eliza DAVIS, Mahogany
Cutter, C.

#34: Jan 17, Thomas PARKS to Joshua GABOUREL & Margaret TATE, Mahogany
Cutter, C.

#35: Jan 19, b. 28 Nov 1826, Elizabeth to Frederick COFFIN & Phoebe TUCKER,
Store Keeper, C.

#36: " " b. 19 Jan 1827, Charles JEFFERIES [*sic*] to John JEFFREYS [*sic*] &
Eleanor GRANT, Carpenter, C.

#37: " " George HUGHS, Northern River, Free Black adult, B.

#38: Jan 27, b. 30? Jan 1827, Charles Henry to Benjamin VERNON & Rachel JONES,
Pilot, C.

#39: Jan 28, b. 3 Jan 1828, Mary Ann to James & Ann WAIGHT, Church Clerk &
Warden, W.

#40: " " b. 21 *illegible* Frances Anne to David BETSON & Ann GABOUREL, C.

p. 6:
#41: Jan 29, NOWELL Michael to Joseph VERNON & Marg^t NEALE, Pilot, C.

#42: Feb 5, b. 2 Aug 1827, John Samuel to John Samuel & Sarah AUGUST,
Mahogany Cutter, W.

#43: Feb 5, John TURNBULL to Robert TURNBULL & Lucinda DIXON,
Mahogany Cutter, C.

#44: Feb 9, b. 5 Jul 1827, Marshal BENNETT to Marshall BENNETT & Catherine W.
CUNNINGHAM, Merchant, C.

#45: Feb 14, b. 14 Nov 1827, Elizabeth Ann CROFT to William James CROFT &
Catherine ASKEW, Carpenter, C.

#46: Feb 20, Polly SMITH, adult black woman.

#47: Feb 26, b. 5 Jan 1828? Lucy Catherine to Rich'd & Betsy DeBAPTIST, Trader.

3

#48:   *Washed out and illegible.*   Private, late Corporal -----

p. 7:

#49: Mar 8,   Elizabeth Evelina to Ebenezer SHAW & Jane AUGUST. Father at
Boston, U.S., mother at Belize.
Master Mariner. C.

#50: Mar 9,   William BISHOP, adult, Newtown Barracks, Private, 2nd W.I.R., B.

#51:   "   "   Thomas PINDER, adult, Newtown Barracks, Private, 2nd West Ind. Reg't.

#52:   "   "   Caroline to Peter & Mary PANGLOSS, Newtown Barracks, Private, W.I.R.

#53: Mar 16, Mary Ann to James GRENOUGH & Maria WARNER, Stan Creek,
Labourer.

#54: Mar 25, b. 8 Oct 1826, Frances Amelia to John HUGHES & Adelaide VERNON,
Merchant, C.

#55: Mar 27, Jessy SANCHO, adult F.... *(= Free Black.)*

#56: Apr ? *Washed out and illegible.*

p. 8:

#57: Apr 6,   John DITMAS, adult, Newtown Barracks, Private 2 W. I. Reg't.

#58:   "   "   John JAHSEY, adult, Newtown Barracks, Private 2 W. I. Reg't.

#59: Apr 7,   Charlotte to July & Joana McNISH, ditto, Drummer, 2nd W. I. Reg't.

#60:   "   "   Mary Jane CODD to Phillip CODD & Matilda SMITH, late Secretary to
His Mgst's Superintendant, C.

#61: Apr 10, Edward CAMPBELL to Nicholas CAMPBELL & Catherine LEWIS,
Triangles, Mariner, C.

#62: May 3,   Sarah DeSSOUS to Romane? DeSSOUS & Quasheba FLOWERS,
Shop Keeper, C.

#63: May 5,   Charles William to Frederick Albert & Jean Alexandra LOINSWORTH,
Newtown Barracks, Staff Surgeon.

#64: May ?   John WRIGHT to John WALDRON WRIGHT & Ann YOUNG, Merchant.

p. 9:

#65: May 25, John NOAT, Newtown Barracks, Private, 2nd W. I. Reg't, B.

4

#66: Jun 16, Henry GORDON to Luisa SHAW, Barracks, Free Black,
unmarried woman, B.

#67: Jun 24, b. 23 Feb 1827, John Alexander LINDSAY to John LINDSAY &
Duncanette CAMPBELL, Ass't
Commissary General, C.

#68: Jul 7, John GIDDY to Thomas GIDDY & Rosa HUGHS, Newtown Barracks,
Serg't, 2nd W. I. Reg't, B.

#69: Jul 25, b. 13 Sep 1827, William GIBSON to William GIBSON & Betsy
ANDERSON, Wee Wee Key,
Turtler, W.

#70: Aug 9, Eve to *blank* & Ann MAZER, Newtown Barracks, Private 2nd W. I. Reg't.

#71: Aug 10, b. 19 May 1828, Richard John to James & Patience McDONALD, Merch't.

#72: " " Maria to Matthew & Catherine NEWPORT, St. Johns Parsonage,
Clergyman.

p. 10:
#73: Aug 21, George DUBRAIL to Christian & Mary Ann DUBRAIL, Newtown
Barracks, Priv't, 2nd W. I. R., C.

#74: Aug 30, Henry Thomas to Prince CADELL & Mary THOMAS *(entry crossed out.)*

#75: " " Henry Thomas to Prince CADLE [*sic*] & Maria THOMAS, Free
Black woman.

#76: Sep 7, b. 8 Feb 1828, Charles to Charles LOINSWORTH & Charlotte TINKER,
Free Black.

#77: Sep 15, b. 17 May 1827, Mary Caroline to Charles & Anne Frances SCHAW,
Cat [*sic*] 32^{d} Res., Major of Brigade.

#78: Sep 21, b. 26 Nov 1827, John Freiweather to James BELISLE & Charlotte
HYDE, Carpenter.

#79: *illegible* b. 30 Aug 1828, Catherine GARNETT to George GARNETT & Rebecca
YOUNG, Carpenter.

#80: *Washed out and illegible.*

p. 11:
#81: Sep 29, George to Edward CODD & Jane GORDON, Government House, Major
General and Superintendant, C.

5

#82: Sep 29, Ann Elizabeth to Edward CODD & Jane GORDON, Government House, Major Gen'l and Superintendant, C.

#83: Oct 7, b. 19 Jun 1828, Clarissa CLARK to Thomas CLARK & Aurora CHANDLER, Commissariat, Deputy Ass't Commiss'y Gen'l, W.

#84: Oct 9, Robert MILLAR ARTHUR to James MILLAR & Lavinia WILLIAMS, Carpenter, C.

#85: Oct 28, b. 6 Jun 1828, Jane Elizabeth to Philip MEIGHAN & Janette SWACEY,* Branch Pilot, C. *= *SWASEY.*

#86: Nov 16, Hamilton TUCKBURY, adult Black man, B.

#87: Nov 18, b. 30 Jan 1828, Margaret WHITE to Lennard WHITE & Ann CUMMINS, Free Black.

#88: *illegible* Harriet ..... to Joseph GRANT & ..... *illegible, ink washed out.*

p. 12:
#89: Dec 16, Isabella to John & Sarah ADAM, Merchant, W.

#90: Dec 21, William Francis YOUNG to Francis YOUNG & Samentee, Clerk, C.

#91: " " John Alexander COPELEY to Patrick COPELEY & Phillis CURRANT, Carpenter, C.

#92: " " Jane BRISTOW to Serg't BRISTOW & Maria WATERS, Serg't 2nd West Indies Reg't, B.

#93: Dec 28, Robert to James POTTS & Clarinda TRAPP, Free Black, B.

#94: " " Alexander RENAU to Joseph RENAU & Mary KENNEDY, Ship Carpenter, C.

#95: " " b. 19 Oct 1837, Fanny to William GODFREY & Jane BESS, Carpenter.

#96: " " Robert? to Robert HAYLOCK? & ... *illegible,* Carpenter.

p. 13:
#97: Dec 29, Mary WOOD to Daniel BRYAN & Tina SUTHERLAND, Mahogany Cutter.

#98: Dec 30, b. 26 Oct 1827, John CANAUN? to John & Elizabeth WAGNER, Carpenter.

6

#99: Dec 31, Francis to John Henry STAIN & Elizabeth LOWRY, Mahogany Cutter, C.

#100: " "   *blank* Ellice? to Remie? & Rosette LAVINE? Free Black.

The remainder of this page is blank, with a swirling flourish drawn across it.

Baptisms in 1829:

p. 14:
#101: Jan 1: Charles DASH to Charles & Elizabeth FELIX, Gov't Mil'y Pensioner.

#102: " "   Elizabeth CRAIG FOREMAN to Robert FORMAN & Eliza GLADDEN,
Baker, C.

#103: " "   Augusta to Laurence LOWRY & Fanny HUGHES, child Free Black, B.

#104: Jan 3, William Archibald to Archibald William & Mary FLOWERS,
Logwood Cutter.

#105: " "   b. 28 Jul 1828, Rosanne BAILEY to Toney BAILEY & Maria BAILEY,
Fisherman, B.

#106: Jan 4, b. 10 Mar 1828, Richard Francis O'BRIEN to Joseph PETER & Maria
BRIEN, [*sic*] Free Black, B.

#107: *illegible* Jacob   *(This entry crossed out.)*

#108:   *Washed out and illegible* ----LY, Free Black.

p. 15:
#109: Jan 4, Benjamin SPROAT to Edward SPROAT & Phoebe HEWS, Labourer, B.

#110: Jan 6, Mary Ann to John Thomas FLOWERS & Elizabeth STANE,
Fisherman, B.

#111: " "   Agnes REBAN to John REBAN & Ann CRAWFORD, Convention Town,
Logwood Cutter, C.

#112: " "   William Henry to Henry LOWE & Ann LONGSWORTH, Mahogany
Cutter, C.

#113: " "   b. 6 Apr 1827, Caroline Wilhemina TOOTH to W. B. TOOTH & Elizabeth
JACKSON, Cattle Keeper, C.

#114: Jan 7, b. 15 Aug 1828, Elizabeth EWING HAMILTON to Joseph HAMILTON
& Elizabeth DOMINGO,
Mahogany Cutter, C.

#115: " " MORLAND? HUGHES BLYTH to Samuel BLYTH & Mary BLYTH,
Mahogany Cutter.

#116: Jan 11, John Alexander GERETSON to John HARRIS & Elizabeth ROBINSON,
Carpenter.

p. 16:
#117: Jan 11, b. 23 Nov 1828, Amelia CUNNINGHAM to Billy CUNNINGHAM &
Mary Adney BROSTER,
Cattle Keeper, C.

#118: " " b. 2 Feb 182?, Anne CRABB to John CRABB & Sarah FAIRWEATHER,
Carpenter, C.

#119: Jan 17, b. 23 Dec 1827, Maria HAYLOCK to Francis HAYLOCK & Catherine
COFFLE, Settee, Carpenter, C.

#120: Jan 21, b. 30 Jun 1828, Eve to Fame BELISLE & Anna PRIO, Mahog'y Cutter, C.

#121: " " b. 22 Aug 1824, Anne GENTLE to William GENTLE & Eve BELISLE,
Mahogany Cutter, C.

#122: " " 4 months old, Aberdeen BELISLE to Thomas BELISLE & Rose
FLOWERS, Mahogany Cutter, B.

#123: " " 3 months old, William TILLET to William TILLET & Sarah JONES,
Mahogany Cutter, C.

#124: *Washed out and illegible* to Edward BOWMAN & Free Black.

There are only 48 pages of these registers in the folder at Belmopan. Page 16 ends with baptism #124 on 21 January 1829; the next page extant commences with #781 on 14 March 1835, so it appears that 657 baptisms between these dates are lost to us.

While the first 16 pages are clearly numbered, the remaining 32 are so badly blackened at the top that their original page numbers cannot be made out. Over time, at least two people added numbers, one in pencil and the other in ink, but in no clear sequence. In the transcript which follows these pages are identified as 17- 48, 17 being the 17ᵗʰ page counting back from page 1 in the folder at the Archives. Date order can always be used to locate an entry. Some of the baptisms in the original record lack entry numbers; to facilitate referencing the transcript, the missing numbers have been filled in.

Baptisms in 1835:

p. 17:
#781:   Mar 14, Elizabeth LOVELL to William LOVELL & Betsy GENTLE.

#782:   "   "   James to William GENTLE & Chloe GENTLE.

#783:   "   "   b. 16 Sep 1834, Anne COCHRAN to Richard COCHRAN & Georgina
                                    WARDLOW, Mahogany Cutter, C.

Note: R. C. and Georgina are shown as given names; the surname is WARDLOW.

#784:   Mar 15, Andrew CUNNINGHAM to Ralph CUNNINGHAM & Leonara
                                    MITCHELL, C.

#785:   Mar 16, William Henry MITCHELL to George MITCHELL & Margaret
                                    HEWLETT, C.

#786:   Mar 18, Catherine Elizabeth to William GIBSON & Sarah Ann CASTLE,
                                    Carpenter.

#787:   "   "   Ann Amelia to William GIBSON & Sarah Ann CASTLE, Carpenter.

#788:   "   "   Betsy to Benjamin G.......? (or F.......?) and... *Washed out and illegible.*

p. 18:
#789:   Mar 21, Ann Maria LOCK to John LOCK & Frances YOUNG, Half Moon Key,
                                    Pilot.

#790:   Mar 25, Sarah Maria to John & Lydia ERSKINE, Clerk.

#791:   Apr 12, William JEFFERSON, Gov't Mil'y Pensioner.

#792:   Apr 26, b. 30 Feb? 1825, Louisa Frances to Robert & Maria LUCAS, Newtown
                                    Barracks, Serg't , 2nd W. I. Reg't.

#793:   May 3, Frances NEAL to George NEAL & Rachel WARREN, Carpenter, C.

#794:   May 17, John Henry to John & Catherine O'CONNOR, Seaman, C.

#795:   "   "   Elizabeth to John & *illegible* YORK, Newtown Barracks, Serg't,
                                    2nd W. I. Reg't.
#796:   *Washed out and illegible.*   Ship

p. 19:   42 is penciled at the top of this page.
#797:   Jun 22, Alexander to Joseph Emanuel & Nisida SWASEY, Merchant.

9

#798:   Jul 5,   Betsey HEWLETT to George HEWLETT & Catherine WAGNER, Seaman.

#799:   Jul 8,   Margaret to George & Margaret MENZIES, Watch Maker.

#800:   Jul 12,   William WALLACE GARDINER to Henry GARDINER & Elizabeth HEWLETT, Clerk, C.

#801:   Jul 18,   Susanne DUMAS to Cassimer & Amelia DeBRIEN, Clerk.

#802:   "   "   Maria to James FELLOWS? & Mary Ann ROBINSON, Apprenticed Labourer.

#803:   Jul 19,   William   *washed out and illegible*   Adult.

#804:   Jul 22,   Margaret to Joseph ...   *Washed out and illegible.*

p. 20:   (50 is written in ink over the original, washed out page number.)
#805:   Jul 27,   Nicholas to Nicholas CAMPBELL & Catherine LEWIS, Spanish Key, Mariner.

#806:   Jul 30,   Rose to Joseph YARNESS & Flora JONES, C.

#807:   "   "   Edward to Jose ALBINO & Anna BENNETT, Wood Cutter.

#808:   Aug 8,   b. 12 Jun 1833, Richard SMITH to Philip SMITH alias DAVIS & Catherine FLOWERS, Servant.

#809:   "   "   William JOHNSON to Francis JOHNSON & Integrity *blank,* Labourer.

#810:   Aug 9,   b. 21 Dec 183-?, Sarah to John CARMICHAEL & Nancy GLADDEN, Merchant.

#811:   *illegible* Gerald to Gerald FITZGIBBON & ...... C...... *washed out*   Fisherman.

#812:   *Washed out and illegible.*   Mahogany

p. 21:
#813:   Aug 13,   John BECK to John BECK & Maria LONGSWORTH, Turtler.

#814:   Aug 14,   Richard SMITH to Thomas SMITH & Eve WARRIOR.

#815:   "   ·   "   Cesar FULLER, Adult.

#816:   Aug 15,   Betsy to *blank* SIMPSON & Sally ELRINGTON, Serg't 2nd W. I. Reg't.

#817:   " "   Nancy to *blank* SIMPSON & Sally ELRINGTON, Serg't 2nd W. I. R.

#818:   Aug 16, John GRIFFITHS to John GRIFFITHS & Sarah JONES, Mariner.
(Jones is the surname of both.)

#819:   Aug 18, Margaret POTTS, adult.

#820:   Aug 24, Mary?   to John   *Washed out and illegible.*

p. 22: (In the original record, only #821 is numbered.)
#821:   Aug 24, Louisa to John & Rosanna TWEENY, Freetown, Gov't Mil'y Pens'r.

#822:   Aug 27, Henry CADEL, Muscle Creek, Adult Black.

#823:   Aug 30, John to Charles BLADEN & Ann EVERITT, Wood Cutter.

#824:   " "   b. 30 May 1833, Madoc to Henry ARNOLD & Jane DOUGLAS,
Carpenter.

#825:   " "   Jane Priscilla SMITH to Thomas SMITH & Eve WARRIOR, Shoe Maker.

#826:   " "   Abraham SMITH to Thomas SMITH & Eve WARRIOR, Shoe Maker.

#827:   " "   Thomas SMITH to Thomas SMITH & Eve WARRIOR, Shoe Maker.

#828:   *Washed out and illegible.*   ---chant

p. 23:
#829:   Sep 4, Benjamin WILSON to Will'm WILSON & Marg't HEWLETT, Tailer.

#830:   Sep 5, Angelina Camilla SAVERY to Joseph SAVERY & Betsy BENNETT,
Ship Carpenter.

#831:   Sep 6: John to Henry Jno. SMITH & Maria BATES, Carpenter, C.

#832:   " "   Augusta to Morgan BROSTER & Phillis BAILY, Labourer, B.

#833:   " "   George KENNEDY to Rodney KENNEDY & Gamboa, Labourer, B.

#834:   " "   b. 20 Oct 1833, John BLYTHE to William & Margaret LEWIS,
Mahogany Cutter, C.

#835:   " "   b. 21 Nov 1833, John FONCERA to Raimundo FONCERA & Mary Ann
CONNOR.

#836:   Sep 7, George Isaac? to George ...   *Washed out and illegible.*

p. 24: *(54 inked in at the top, and in pencil, 102.)*

#837:   Sep 10, Sarah NEAL to Duncan NEAL & Mary Ann O'CONNOR, Black.

#838:   Sep 12, b. 3 Apr 1835, Rebecca to James CASTELLAN & Monimia JONES,
        Merchant.

#839:   Sep 14, Maria Bernartha ESCALAN to Dr. CAMAYANA & Juana Antonia
        ESCALAN, Merchant, C.

#840:   Sep 17, Christian to John FERGUSON & Marg^t ROY, Store Keeper, C.

#841:   Sep 18, Francis AUGUSTA to John AUGUSTA & Leonora MITCHEL,
        Carpenter.

#842:   Oct 1,   Robert to William BURNS & Lydia CADEL, Grazier.

#843:   *illegible* Francis *illegible* to John JOSEPH & *illegible* J...(JACKSON?) Carpenter.

#844:   *Illegible, ink washed out, torn and rotted.*

p. 25:

#845:   Oct 17, Mary Ann to John GARBUTT & Jane PITTS, Turtler.

#846:   Oct 18, Daniel GIDEON to John GIDEON & Sarah FLOWERS, Carpenter.

#847:   Oct 24, Charlotte to John GIBSON & Louisa GRACIA, Queen Charlotte Town,
        Labourer.

#848:   " "   Helen to Fred^k COFFIN & Phoebe TUCKER, Victualler, C.

#849:   Oct 25, Christian to Joseph LONGSWORTH & Eleanor YOUNG, Pilot.

#850:   Oct 28, Nina Malvina KENNEDY to James & Elizabeth WOODS, Jailer.

#851:   Nov 1, Terence James to Terence? & Ann CASSIDY, Newtown... Serg't in 2nd...

#852:   Nov 4, James to Ed....   *Illegible, ink washed out, torn and rotted.*

p. 26:

#853:   Nov 8, Aramina to Peter & Amelia BONHAM, Newtown Barracks, Serg't
        in the 2nd West Ind. Reg't.

#854:   Nov 15, Elizabeth DIXON to Thos. DIXON & Mary ROBINSON, Labourer.

#855:   Nov 16, James to Benjamin WHITEHEAD & Angelina JONES, Labourer.

#856: Nov 21, Robert HAYLOCK to Francis HAYLOCK & Catherine COFFILL, Settee River, Turtler, C.

#857: " " Joseph HAYLOCK to Francis HAYLOCK & Catherine COFFILL, Settee River, Turtler, C.

#858: Nov 26, b. 16 Sep 1835, Sarah BURNS to George BURNS & Eliza WILLIAMS, Carpenter, C.

#859: *illegible* Jane? to Joseph RENEAU & *illegible* Carpenter.

#860: *Illegible, ink washed out, torn and rotted.*

p. 27:
#861: Dec 6, Alicia to George WARREN* & Eve HINKS, Mahogany Cutter, C.
Son of George Knox Warren & Mrs. Ann Elrington? See will of Marcus Belisle.

#862: Dec 12, John to William GILL & Catherine GLADDEN, Pilot, C.

#863: Dec 15, b. 16 Nov 1834, Anthony Richard John YOUNG to Patrick YOUNG & Jane WILLIAMS, Freetown, Black.

#864: Dec 18, b. 11 Jun 1834, James CHAPMAN QUILTER to James QUILTER & Agnes WALL, Surgeon, C.

#865: " " CAMPBELL AUGUST, Apprentice Labourer, B.

#866: Dec 19, Sarah to John GIDEON & Jane POTTS, Carpenter, B.

#867: Dec 22, William Henry GRIFFITHS to William GRIFFITHS & Letetia COFFIN, Sailer.

#868: Dec 25, George ..... to George? *Illegible, ink washed out, torn and rotted.*

p. 28:
#869: Dec 26, Richard DeBAPTISTE to John DeBAPTISTE & Lucy PARKS, Seaman.

#870: Dec 28, Elizabeth to Francisco and Phoebe PITTS, a Churchman & Apprenticed Labourer.

#871: Dec 30, Nathaniel WESTBY to George WESTBY & Ariadne SMITH, Carpenter.

#872: " " Mary Ann FERRALL to Duncan CAMPBELL & Clara GOFF, Labourer.

#873: Dec 31, b. 26 Dec 1835, Caroline AUDINETT to Peter AUDINETT & Emma POTTS, Carpenter.

#874: Jan 1, Harry COUTTEUSE to George COUTTEUSE & Betsy BROSTER,
            Carpenter.

#875: " " b. 14 Feb 1835, John Henry to Henry TUCKER & *illegible* Labourer.

#876:   *Illegible, ink washed out, torn and rotted.*

p. 29: (47 penciled at top of page)
#877: Jan 1, Jame [*sic*] to William LONGSWORTH & Betsy ROBINSON,
            Mahogany Cutter.

#878: " " Eliza DeBAPTISTE to John DeBAPTISTE & Elizabeth WILLIAMS,
            Sailer.

#879: Jan 2, Isabella PRATT to Richard PRATT & Phoebe THOMSON, Turtler.

#880: " " Susanna GARRETT to William GARRETT & Diana LAMB, Carpenter, B.

#881: Jan 3, William USHER to William USHER & Cath. BENNET, Mahogany
            Cutter, C.
#882: " " Elizabeth BIRD, Adult, B.

#883: " " George FORT to Charles McLEAN & Elizabeth CRAFT? *illegible*
            Apprentice Labourer.

#884: " " Simon   *Illegible, ink washed out, torn and rotted.*

p. 30:
#885: Jan 3, Daniel FORD to James ROBURN & Elizabeth BIRD, Apprentice Lab'r.

#886: " " Harry FORD to James ROBURN & Elizabeth BIRD, App. Lab.

#887: " " Richard FORD to James ROBURN & Elizabeth BIRD, App. Lab.

#888: " " Charles WINTER to Fran^s WINTER & Jane BIRD, App. Lab.

#889: " " Frank FORT [*sic*] to Jn° GREEN & Maria FORD, [*sic*], Logwood Cutter, C.

#890: " " Sophia FORD to Jn° GREEN & Maria FORD, Logwood Cutter, C.

#891: " " Thomas *washed out* to Robert NELLIS & *illegible* App. Lab, B.

#892:   *Illegible, ink washed out, torn and rotted.*

14

#893: 3 Jan, Joseph Alexander to Alick McKAY & Susan WARRIER, Labourer.

#894: " " Nancy FORD to Jas. ROBURN & Elizabeth BIRD, App. Lab.

#895: " " Maria FORD, Apprentice Labourer.

#896: " " Amelia Richard to Richard BROSTER & Phillis LORD,
                                        Apprentice Labourer, B.

#897: " " John WRIGHT, Apprentice Labourer, B.

#898: " " John to Peter & Elizabeth NAIRN, Fort George, Corp'l, Royal Artill'y, W.

#899: Jan 4, John Charles Frederick BEVINS to William BEVINS & Sarah POTTS,
                                        T... *Illegible, probably Turtler.*

#900: " " Joseph to B?..... *Illegible, ink washed out, torn and rotted.*

#901: Jan 4, Jane WILLIAMS to Charles MINNEY & Elizabeth ARTHURS,
                                        Wood Cutter.

#902: " " Archibald GRANT to George GRANT & Sarah HALL, Sailer.

#903: " " Sarah FAIRWEATHER to Benjamin FAIRWEATHER & Eleanor GOFF,
                                        Sailer.

#904: " " b. 10 May 1835, Elizabeth Samuel to Samuel POTTS & Anne BURGESS,
                                        Labourer, B.

#905: " " William CADELL, Apprentice Labourer, B.

#906: " " Cudjoe POTTS, Apprentice Labourer, B.

#907: " " *Illegible* POTTS, Apprentice Labourer, B.

#908: *Illegible, ink washed out, torn and rotted.*

#909: Jan 5, b. 3 Aug 1832, Ellen MATHER to George MATHER & Amelia
                                        COURTNEY, Clerk.

#910: " " b. 20 Oct 1835, Eliza Ann ROBERT to Virgin ROBERT & Elizabeth
                                        LAMB, Carpenter.

#911: Jan 5, Sophia GILLETT to Robert GILLETT & Eleanor CADELL,
                                    Logwood Cutter.

#912: " " b. 12 Jul 1835, Lucinda DeMACK to Joseph DeMACK & Elleanor
                                    GENTLE, Logwood Cutter.

#913: " " Edward PORTER, Apprentice Labourer.

#914: Jan 6, b. 31 Oct 1832, Rachel NEAL to William & Catherine NEAL, Carpenter.

#915: " " b. 5 Jan 1835, Peter Frederick Adolphus to William & Catherine NEAL,
                                    Carpenter.

#916: " " Edward to *possibly Sam'l? Illegible, ink washed out, torn and rotted.*

p. 34:
#917: Jan 6, Catherine WESTBY to George WESTBY & Anna BENNETT, Carpenter.

#918: " " Leah HUME. *No other information given.*

#919: " " Thomas BURK to Peter RAYBON & Sylvia BURNS.

#920: " " William James to James EARNEST & Araminta LAMB, Wood Cutter.

#921: Jan 7, William Henry BRADDICK to George BRADDICK & Sarah WINTER,
                                    Carpenter.

#922: Jan 8, Margaret WAGNER to Francis WAGNER & Catherine BONYEAR,
                                    Laborer.

#923: Jan 9, William LEWIS, an African.

#924:   *Illegible, ink washed out, torn and rotted.*   Wood

p. 35:
#925: Jan 10, Rebecca CUNNINGHAM to Llewellen CUNNINGHAM & Ann TUCKE,
                                    Wood Cutter.

#926: " " Sarah HALL to John HALL & Sylvia PARKS, Wood Cutter.

#927: " " Robert HEWLETT to Robert HEWLETT & Patty CUNNINGHAM,
                                    Wood Cutter.

#928: " " Marcia HEWLETT to Robert HEWLETT & Patty CUNNINGHAM,
                                    Wood Cutter.

16

#929: Jan 10, Emily Maria JONES to James JONES & Margaret HULSE, Wood Cutter.

#930: " " George MARTIN to Thos. MARTIN & Sabina BENNET, Wood Cutter.

#931: " " Jeanette MARTIN to Thos. MARTIN & Sabina B... *Illegible, washed out.*

#932: Jan 11, *Illegible, ink washed out, torn and rotted.*

p. 36:
#933: " " Sarah GRISTOCK to George L. GRISTOCK & Eliza GIBSON, Merchant.

#934: " " George Henry GRISTOCK to Richard GRISTOCK & Mary BURRELL, Mahogany Cutter.

#935: " " Adam ROBINSON to Benjamin ROBINSON & Agnes GOFF, Convention Town, Wood Cutter.

#936: Jan 12, Mary ROBINSON to Benjamin ROBINSON & Agnes GOFF, Convention Town, Wood Cutter.

#937: " " b. 8 Dec 1834, John DAVIS to David BAKER & Peggy CRAMER, Free Town, Gov't Mil'y Pensioner.

#938: Jan 13, George Andrew to Andrew BENNETT & Maria ANTONIA.

#939: *Illegible,* to DOMINGUEZ & *illegible* Carpenter.

#940: *Illegible, ink washed out, torn and rotted.*

Note: The minister was required to fill in the date and entry number of each baptism he recorded, but as time passed his numbering became sporadic, and at #941, he stopped. Entry numbers from this point on have been added to facilitate referencing the transcript. Date order should be used to locate entries in the original record.

p. 37:
#941: Jan 14, Eleana DOMINGUEZ to Joseph O'BRIEN DOMINGUEZ & Ann Rose DOMINGUEZ, Carpenter.

#942: Jan 15, James MEIGHAN, Labourer.

#943: Jan 17, Jane RENEAU to Joseph RENEAU & Mary KENNEDY, Carpenter.

#944: " " George LEWIS BILLERY to Andrew BILLERY & Catherine LEWIS, Wood Cutter.

17

#945: Jan 17, b. 29 Sep 1834, Amelia Henry GIBSON to Joseph FRANCIS &
         Jean GIBSON, Sailer.

#946: " " Catherine RABAN to William RABAN & Elizabeth FLOWERS,
         Wood Cutter.

#947: " " Kate ENNIS to George ENNIS & Eve *blank*   Wood... *Illegible.*

#948: " " Elizabeth ....   *Illegible, ink washed out, torn and rotted.*

p. 38:
#949: Jan 17, Mary STAIN to Peter STAIN & Betsy GRANT, Wood Cutter.

#950: " " b. 16 Mar 1835, Samuel GRAEME to Edward & Louisa HATTEN,
         Free Town, Mil'y Pensioner.

#951: " " Mary to Joseph FRANCIS & Joan GIBSON, Sailor.

#952: Jan 18, b. 24 Jun 1833, Richard GABOUREL to Joshua GABOUREL & Margaret
         WINTER, Mahogany Cutter, C.

#953: " " b. 8 Jun 1835, Benjamin CRAFT GABOUREL to Joshua GABOUREL
         & Margaret WINTER,
         Mahogany Cutter, C.

#954: Jan 19, b. 22 Dec 1835, Phoebe GLADDEN to Michael GLADDEN & Maria
         LEWIS, Wood Cutter, B.

#955: " " b.14 Jun 1833, Henrietta to John GLASS & ... *illegible* Labourer.

#956:   *Illegible, ink washed out, torn and rotted.*

p. 39:
#957: Jan 20, b. 26 Dec 1835, Elizabeth COLQUHOUN to Archibald COLQUHOUN
         & Mary JOHN, Wood Cutter.

#958: Jan 21, Maria..? *(Marina?)* PATTINETT to John PATTINETT & Polly PINDER,
         Convention Town, Wood Cutter.

#959: " " Ann PATTINETT to John PATTINETT & Polly PINDER, Convention
         Town, Wood Cutter.

#960: " " John PATTINETT to John PATTINETT & Polly PINDER, Convention
         Town, Wood Cutter.

#961:   Jan 21, Rosanne PATTINETT to John PATTINETT & Polly PINDER,
Convention Town, Wood Cutter, B.

#962:   Jan 22, Ann Amelia GIBSON to William GIBSON & Sarah Ann CASTLE,
Carpenter, C.

*Note: The child of the same name baptized on 18 March 1835 to this couple must have
died. Was William's mother or Sarah's mother named Ann Amelia?*

#963:   " "   A.... *(possibly Adult or Aged?)*   Nancy MILES.

#964:   Jan 24, *Illegible, ink washed out, torn and rotted.*

p. 40:
#965:   Jan 24, Charles MOODY to Thomas MOODY & Rebecca SMITH, Northern
River, Logwood Cutter.

#966:   Jan ?   Eliza Ann SAVERY to George SAVERY & Amelia JACKSON,
Carpenter.

#967:   Jan 27, b. 29 May 1835, Samuel FLOWERS to Henry FLOWERS & Rose
LOUIS, Ship Carpenter, B.

#968:   " "   b. 29 Mar 1833, Catherine FLOWERS to Henry FLOWERS & Rose
LOUIS, Ship Carpenter.

#969:   Jan 29, Jn° MASKALL, Apprentice Labourer, B.

#970:   " "   Diana, Apprentice Labourer.

#971:   Jan 31, James to Lewis & ... *illegible* WILLIAMS, Jeweller.

#972:   *Illegible, ink washed out, torn and rotted.*

p. 41:
#973:   Feb 1,   James Jose to Louis HYDE & Margery POTTS, Wood Cutter.

#974:   Feb 4,   George MOODY to Edward MOODY & Prue POTTS, Carpenter.

#975:   Feb 6,   Cynthia, Apprentice Labourer.

#976:   " "   Adelaide to Tony VITTORINE & Cynthia DIAMOND, Fisherman.

#977:   " "   Sarah BURGESS, Adult, B.

#978: Feb 7, b. 19 Apr 1835, Alice NEAL to William NEAL & Elizabeth GODFREY, Carpenter, C.

#979: " " b. 8 Aug 1835, William FRANCIS to Joseph FRANCIS & Susan ... *illegible,* Wood Cutter.

#980: " " John to George? .... *illegible, ink washed out, torn and rotted.*

p. 42:
#981: Feb 7, b. 16 Aug 1833, John GOFF to Joseph GOFF & Catherine BENNETT, Black Smith.

#982: " " b. 25 Oct 1835, Edward GOFF to Joseph GOFF & Catherine GOFF, Black Smith.

#983: Feb 7, b. 6 Dec 1834, James Henry to Henry PIPERSBURG & Ann his wife, Carpenter.

#984: " " Eliza MILES to *blank* MILES & Amelia HINKS, Commander of the Gov't Schooner.

#985: " " Maria BLANCO to Jose BLANCO & Sue WARRIOR, Wood Cutter, C.

#986: " " b. 18 Aug 1835, Isabella Chaisa? to John CRAIG & Eliza GODFREY, Clerk in the Record Office, C.

#987: El...?... HEMMING? *illegible, ink washed out* Adult.

#988: *Illegible, ink washed out, torn and rotted.*

p. 43: *The top of this page has a hole where paper has rotted away.*
#989: Feb 14, b.6 May 1832,Eliza to James & Ann WAIGHT, Master of the Free School.

Note: *James also served as organist at St. John's, and as a churchwarden.*

#990: *The line for this entry is blank.*

#991: Feb 16, b. 22 Oct 1835, Helen HYDE to Robert & Francis TURNBULL, Mahogany Cutter.

#992: Feb 19, Clarissa POTTS to David POTTS & Nelly POTTS, Labourer.

#993: Feb 27, Robert Charles CUNNINGHAM to Andrew CUNNINGHAM & Grace MILLER, Mahogany Cutter, C.

#994: " " Thomas GRISTOCK to George GRISTOCK & Sarah PITTS,
Merchant, C.

#995: Mar 3, b. 8 Aug 1834, John McCOLLUCK to William Mc'CULLUCH &
Dolly BURN, Ship -----, C.

#996: *Illegible, washed out and rotted.*

*p. 44: The top of this page has "Year 1835" written in - from baptism of a child born in
1836, the enumerator's error - and a hole where paper has rotted away.*

#997: Mar 4, b. 19 Dec 1831, William MIDDLETON to John MIDDLETON & Harriet
KEEFE, Labourer, C.

#998: " " b. 1 Jul 1836? Adam to John MIDDLETON & Harriet KEEFE,
Labourer, C.

#999: Feb 26, [*sic*], b. May 1832, Charlotte to John & Luisiana KNOTE, New Town
Barracks, Private, 2nd W. I. Reg't.

#1000: Mar 6, b. 20 Jan 1836, Eliza RAN [*sic*] to William TILLET & Sarah JONES,
Wood Cutter.

#1001: " " Henrietta Maria to John & Sarah COLLINS, Mahogany Cutter.

#1002: " " Ellen to John & Sarah COLLINS, Mahogany Cutter.

#1003: " " Eliza to John & Sarah COLLINS, Mahogany Cutter.

#1004: *Illegible, washed out and rotted.*

p. 45:
#1005: Mar 6, John Alexander PARKER, C, to Richard PARKER & Flora CAMPBELL,
Carpenter.

#1006: " " William PARKER to Richard PARKER & Flora CAMPBELL, Carpenter.

#1007: " " b. 19 Dec 1835, Thomas ROBINSON to John ROBINSON & Tabia
BENNETT, Carpenter.

#1008: " " Francis SLUSHER to Simon SLUSHER & Rebecca GENTLE, Carpenter.

#1009: Mar 7, Ann Eliza to John & Mary DACIE? New Town Barracks,
Private, 2nd W. I. Reg't.

#1010: Mar 8, William HYDE, Apprentice Labourer.

21

#1011: Mar 12, Ann Julia NICHOLSON to George NICHOLSON & Amelia *illegible.*

#1012: "   "   *Illegible, ink washed out, torn and rotted.*

p. 46:
#1013: Mar 19, Robert to Richard ANDERSON & Diana ANDERSON, Merchant, C.

#1014: "   "   William to Francis ACHISON & Mary GORDON, Ship Wright, C.

#1015: Mar 20, b. 10 Oct 1835, Stewart LIDDEL to Thomas YOUNG LIDDEL &
                         Ann GOFF, Clerk, C.

#1016: "   "   Edward POTTS to James POTTS & Amelia BENNETT, Labourer, B.

#1017: Mar 25, David WHITE to Lennon WHITE & Lydia TRAPP, Labourer.

#1018: Apr 21, Josiah to David BRITTEN & Margaret LOCKWARD, Chief
                         Officer of Police.

Note: Britten is a second given name: the family's surname is Lockward.

#1019: Apr 24, b. 25 Nov 1835, Ann --- to Sam'l TUCKER & *illegible* Servant.

#1020:   *Illegible, ink washed out, torn and rotted.*

p. 47:
#1021: May 22, b. --- -- 1836, Ann BLACK to William BLACK & Catherine GORDON,
                         Fisherman.

#1022: Jun 3,   b. 7 Sep 1835, Eliza Mary GOFF to Roger GOFF & Marina GILLETT,
                         Pilot.

#1023: Jun 15, Robert to Robert TUCKER & Elizabeth USHER, Carpenter.

#1024: Jul 3,   b. 26 Dec 1834, Maria SANCHEZ to Antonio SANCHEZ & Diana
                         STAIN, Sailer.

#1025: Jul 5,   Thomas SLADE to Thomas SLADE & Mary CLAPPER, Clerk.

#1026: "   "   Ralph DeBRIEN to Julius DeBRIEN & Elizabeth FLOWERS, Carpenter.

#1027: Jul 10, John Alexander Douglas to William ROBINSON & Ann COLE?

#1028: "   "   *Illegible, ink washed out, torn and rotted.*

22

p. 48:
#1029: Jul 26, Philip HINKS, Adult, Apprentice Labourer.

#1030: Jul 28, Frank CRAWFORD, Adult, Apprentice Labourer.

#1031: Jul 31, Alfred to Johr. & Sarah USHER, Mahogany Cutter.

#1032: Aug 1, John Leslie GREYSON to James Leslie GREYSON & Jeanetta YOUNG,
Commander of the Barque *Anteus.*

#1033: " " Jane Elizabeth MIDDLETON to Charles MIDDLETON & Jane Elizabeth
LONGSWORTH, Merchant.

#1034: " " Benjamin CROFT to Benjamin CROFT & Rachel JONES, Carpenter.

#1035: Aug 4, Jen... *illegible,* to George HEMSLEY & ... *Washed out and illegible.*

#1036: *Illegible, ink washed out, torn and rotted.*

---oOo---

THE BURIAL REGISTER OF ST JOHN'S, BELIZE, 1828-1841.

Burials in 1828: *Initials following the names stand for colour; P stands for Pauper.*

p. 1:
#1:   Henry BRADFORD, B, Government Military Pensioner, died in the Hospital at
       Newtown Barracks, Jan 1.
#2:   Jacob O'BRIEN, B, Jan 1, 30 years.
#3:   Apollo PLOWDEN, B, Gov't Mil'y Pens'r, 3 Jan, *(age)* not known.
#4:   Thomas LEE, B P, died in the Public Hospital, 3 Jan, aged.
#5:   Mary TUCKER alias Mary GADES, C P, 6 Jan, 103 years.
#6:   Richard HARRISON, W, 9 Jan, 31 years.
#7:   *Illegible* ...WORTH, 10 Jan, Newtown Barracks, 3 years.
#8:   *Washed out, tattered, and illegible.*

p. 2:
#9:   James LESLIE, B, Newtown Barracks, 28 Jan, about 60 years.
#10:   William GRANT, B, 3 Feb, 18 years.
#11:   ----- [*sic*] MIDDLETON, C, 7 Feb, not known.
#12:   Harry ----- [*sic*], B, 9 Feb, not known.
#13:   Thomas FRAIN, W, 16 Feb, 48 years.
#14:   Thomas JONES, W, 16 Feb, supposed about 30 years.
#15:   George? B. BENOIT, B, 18 Feb, 18 years.
#16:   *Washed out, tattered, and illegible.*

p. 3:
#17:   Thos. GREY, W, 9 Mar, not known.
#18:   Jessamy CORNITT, B, Pens'r, Queen Charlotte Town, 24 Mar, not known.
#19:   Marcus BELISLE, B, 24 Mar, about 19 or 20.
#20:   William HULSE, C, 28 Mar, infant.
#21:   Timothy GARCIA, B, Gov't Mil'y Pens'r, 4 Apr, not known.
#22:   John FARRELL, C, 10 Apr, not known.
#23:   John GRAHAM, B, *illegible,* Pens'r, 13 Apr, not known.
#24:   *Illegible* GRAHAM, B, 14 Apr, about *illegible.*

p. 4:
#25:   Thos. MARTIN, W P, 15 Apr, not known.
#26:   Crispin BOSTOCK, B, Gov't Mil'y Pens'r, 22 Apr, not known.
#27:   John DAVIDSON, B, Newtown Barracks, 27 Apr, not known.
#28:   Sophia HUGHES, C, 27 Apr, infant.
#29:   Rachel HOARE, B, 1 May, not known.
#30:   Jane HALL, B, Freetown, 3 May, not known.

#31: Stepney HALL, B, 3 May, about 4 years.
#32: *Washed out and illegible. The decedent was probably Thomas BARNES.*

p. 5:
#33: Maria ALEXANDER, B, 16 May, not known.
#34: John FREEMAN, B, New Orleans, 18 May, about 17 years.
#35: Phoebe McAULAY, B, 27 May, not known.
#36: Name not known, P, died in the Public Hospital, 30 May, not known.
#37: Nicholas, B, a Carib, 30 May, not known.
#38: ----- [*sic*] DURHAM, B, Soldiers wife, Newtown Barracks, 30 May, not known.
#39: Cuffee? LEBRO, B, 7 Jun, not known.
#40: *Washed out and illegible.* B, 13 Jun, 21 years.

p. 6:
#41: Thomas JOHNSON, W, 15 Jun, 22 years.
#42: Fanny McDONALD, B, 15 Jun, 11 years.
#43: Name not known, W, Ship *Nautilus*, 17 Jun, not known.
#44: John CAMPBELL, C, 30 Jun, 2 days.
#45: Thomas GLADDEN, C, 1 Jul, 33 years.
#46: Figaro GUBREN, B, Newtown Barracks, 4 Jul, not known.
#47: *Illegible* CAMPBELL alias CALDWELL? C, 9 Jul, female infant 11 days old.
#48: Maria SAFERY, B, *illegible,* 9 Jul, not known.

p. 7:
#49: Laurent DESPIAGES? B, Pens'r, 14 Jul, not known.
#50: Charles John ALLEN, W, 16 Jul, 3 years.
#51: Eliza Matilda ALEXANDER, W, 18 Jul, 15 years.
#52: John SHAKESPEARE, B, Pens'r, 19 Jul, not known.
#53: Thos. PHILLIPS, C, 24 Jul, 1 year.
#54: John COOPER, W P, 25 Jul, not known.
#55: MACBETH, B, Pens'r, 28 Jul. not known.
#56: *Washed out and illegible.*

p. 8:
#57: Jean CLAUD, B, Gov't Mil'y Pens'r, 6 Aug, not known.
#58: Margaret LONGSWORTH, C, 8 Aug, 12 years.
#59: Eve MAZER, B, Newtown Barracks, 10 Aug, 1 month.
#60: Jaon? PIERRE, B, Newtown Barracks, 11 Aug, not known.
#61: Elizabeth COFFIN, C, 14 Aug, 21 months.
#62: William BALFOUR, B, Gov't Mil'y Pens'r, Queen Charlotte Town, 15 Aug, not known.
#63: John POWEL, Sailer in the Brig *Ark*, 15 Aug, not known.
#64: *Washed out and illegible.*

p. 9:
#65: Maria BROHAIR, C, 16 Aug, 4 years and 2 months.

#66:   Maria NEWPORT, W, St. John's Parsonage, 16 Aug, 18 days. By John W.
       WRIGHT, Magistrate. *(The minister and his wife had lost their baby.)*
#67:   Joseph BROWN, W, 18 Aug, not known.
#68:   Spaniard, B, 19 Aug, not known.
#69:   A Soldier, B, Newtown Barracks, 20 Aug, not known.
#70:   William McMILLAN, W, Brig *Margaret,* 21 Aug, not known.
#71:   *Illegible* NOTT, *illegible,* 21 Aug, not known.
#72:   *Washed out and illegible.*

p. 10:
#73:   Sergeant ---- [*sic*] SHEA, W, 2nd W. I. Reg't, Newtown Barracks, 24 Aug, not
       known.
#74:   Sarah HAYLOCK, C, 28 Aug, 18 months.
#75:   Thomas BISHOP, W, 28 Aug, 16 years.
#76:   James CRUIKSHANK, W, 22 Aug, not known.

*Note: James Cruickshank published Belize's first newspaper, the Honduras Gazette &
Commercial Advertiser, but lost it in November 1827 as a result of a lawsuit by Manfield
W. Bowen. Extracts from this paper, given in the Second Parish Register, tell the story.
Bowen died the following year. No tombstone has survived for either of these men.*

#77:   Diana JOHNSON, C, 1 Aug, 2 years.
#78:   ----- FITZGERALD, W, daughter of Serg't FITZGERALD, Newtown Barracks,
       1 Sep, about 8 years.
#79:   Ann FITZGERALD, W, Newtown Barracks, 6 Feb, 33 years.
#80:   *Washed out and illegible.*

p. 11:
#81:   Edward BIGGIN? B P, 8 Sep, not known.
#82:   Helen YOUNG, C, 9 Sep, not returned.
#83:   John TURNBULL, C, 9 Sep, 2 ½ years.

*Note: Entries #84 - 88 do not exist. The Chaplain overwrote the 3 of 83, misread it as 88,
and made the next number 89.*

#89:   Henry WORSLEY, B, Newtown Barracks, 11 Sep, aged.
#90:   Elizabeth ALLEN, W, 13 Sep, 2 years.
#91:   Catherine DERRY, W, Freetown, 15 Sep, 2 years.
#92:   Mrs. Sarah? SWAN, W, 18 Sep, not known, supposed about 45 years.
#93:   *Washed out and illegible.* 22 Sep, 6 *illegible*

p. 12:
#94:   Name not given, a Spaniard, C P, died in the Public Hospital, 23 Sep, not known.
#95:   Joseph BROSCHER, 25 Sep, very old.

Note: Both the entries above and below are numbered #95.

#95:   Name not sent by the Constable, P, died in Public Hospital, 26 Sep, not known.
#96:   John HOARE, B, 25 Sep, child.
#97:   John CLEMENT, W, 26 Sep, not known.
#98:   Name not sent by the Constable, W P, died in the Public Hosp., 28 Sep, not known.
#99:   James GRANT, *illegible*, 29 Sep, 20 years. *(Son of Mr. J. Grant of Newcastle.)*
#100: *Washed out and illegible.*

p. 13:
#101: Ann LOCKWARD, W, 4 Oct, 64 years. *(Her MI gives her age as 62.)*
#102: Sally GRAHAM, C, 7 Oct, about 50 years.
#103: Samuel BURN, W, 12 Oct, not known.
#104: Charles IRVINE, B, Newtown Barracks, 15 Oct, not known.
#105: David BERTY, W, died in the Public Hospital, 18 Oct, not known.
#106: Charles BULL, C, 19 Oct, 15 years.
#107: Lucretia MILES, *illegible*, 19 Oct, aged.
#108: *Washed out and illegible.* Newtown *(Barracks.)*

p. 14:
#109: James DODSON, C, 20 Oct, about 55 years.
#110: ---- [*sic*] McLEAN, a Soldier's wife, 23 Oct, not known.
#111: Rachel CARR, B, 26 Oct, 10 years.
#112: William DOYLE alias DARNEL, W P, 26 Oct, not known.
#113: James USHER, C, 30 Oct, infant.
#114: David FLOWERS, B, 31 Oct, 14 months.
#115: John GOURDEN, W, 17 Nov, not known.
#116: *Illegible* PETTIT? *illegible – possibly Gov't Mil'y Pens'r?* 19 *(Nov)*

p. 15:
#117: William MACKAY, W P, 19 Nov, not known.
#118: Harriet GRETTON, W, 20 Nov, 32 years.
#119: Charles MORRELL, B, 1 Nov, 5 years.
#120: John CASSELS alias John CHARLES, W P, 21 Nov, not known.
#121: Sarah GOFF, C, 22 Nov, 70 years.
#122: Daniel McRITCHEY, W, Brig *Margaret*, 23 Nov, 24 years.
#123: Penelope JONES, *illegible*, 25 Nov, not known.
#124: *Illegible,* Second Mate of *illegible,* 27 Nov, about 55 years.

p. 16:
#125: Jonas DECENCY, B, Pens'r, 9 Dec, not known.
#126: BERTRAND, B, Pens'r, 9 Dec, not known.
#127: Corp'l POOL, B, Pens'r, 13 Dec, not known.
#128: Sarah ADAM, W, 14 Dec, 33 years. *(MI: aged 35, wife of John Adam.)*
#129: *Blank*, W, Seaman belonging to the Barque *Vittoria*, 16 Dec, not known.
#130: Charles BLACKBOURN, W P, Seaman in a coasting vessel, 17 Dec, not known.
#131: Thomas BLOCKLEY, W, 23 Dec, about 23 years.
#132: Spaniard, *illegible,* 27 Dec, not known.

p. 17:
#133:   Josa [*sic*] LOPEZ, B P, 28 Dec, not known.
#134:   A Spaniard, C, 29 Dec, not known.
#135:   James SHANKLIN, W, Seaman of the Brig *Margaret,* 30 Dec, about 35 years.
#136:   George GRAVES, B, Soldier, Newtown Barracks, 31 Dec, not known.

The remainder of this page is blank; the minister started the New Year on a new page.

Burials in 1829:

p. 18:
#137:   Rafiel, C P, a Spaniard, 2 Jan, not known.
#138:   Daniel MAHONY, W P, 2 Jan, not known.
#139:   Soldier, B, Newtown Barracks, 6 Jan, not known.
#140:   Sailer, W, Brig *Margaret,* 11 Jan, not known.
#141:   John Louis GOUDECOURT, B, Pens'r, Queen Charlotte, 14 Jan, not known.
#142:   Name not given, B P, dead in the Public Hospital, 17 Jan, not known.
#143:   William PATNETT, C, 21 Jan, about 28 years.
#144:   *Washed out and illegible.*   25 Jan

p. 19:
#145:   ----- [*sic*] ROGERS, W P, found drowned, 27 Jan, not known.
#146:   William BERNARD, B, 27 Jan, aged.
#147:   Rosanna BAILEY, B, 28 Jan, 6 months.
#148:   Thomas MOULD, B, a Soldier, Newtown Barracks, 30 Jan, not known.
#149:   ----- [*sic*] JOHNSON, W P, 7 Feb, not known.
#150:   Edward FLOWERS, B, 7 Feb, not known.
#151:   ----- [*sic*] LUCAS, B, Soldier's wife, 8 Feb, not known.
#152:   *Washed out and illegible.* 8 Feb, 4 *illegible.*

p. 20:
#153:   Maria FRANCISCO, B, 11 Feb, not known.
#154:   Julian YELA, W, Guatimala [*sic*], 13 Feb, 65 years.
#155:   James WILSON, W, Brig *Dawn,* 16 Feb, 22 years.
#156:   Walter HUGO, B, Soldier, Newtown Barracks, 17 Feb, not known.
#157:   John HARTY (*or HARTZ?*) B, 18 Feb, not known.
#158:   Charles GILL, C, 19 Feb, 4 years.
#159:   Sklyr? Le CROIX, Pens'r, 20 Feb, not known.
#160:   *Washed out and illegible,* Brig *Dawn,* 22 Feb, 57

p. 21:
#161:   James GREEN, B, Pensioner, Mar 1, not known.
#162:   Noah, B, Soldier 2nd W. I. R., Newtown Barracks, Mar 10, not known.
#163:   Jane BESS, C, Mar 19, 30 years.

28

#164: A Black man, B P, name and condition unknown, he was found drowned, Mar 22, not known.
#165: Ann MEIGHAN, B, 24 Mar, 2 years.
#166: A Spaniard, B P, name unknown, *(abode)* not known, 25 Mar, not known.
#167: Lucy STEWART, B, 18 Mar, 7 years.
#168: *Illegible,* Mussle [*sic*] Creek, 1st, not known.

p. 22:
#169: Elizabeth Mary BLOCKLEY, W, 17 Apr, 27 years.
#170: Mary Ann GRANT, B, Newtown Barracks, 18 Apr, 7 years.
#171: A Soldier whose name was not returned, B, Newtown Barracks, 29 Apr, not known.
#172: Joseph TONEY, B, 5 May, about 60 years.
#173: Lucretia CARD, B, 5 May, not known.
#174: Jane HOWEL BLAKE, C, 7 May, 18 months.
#175: John TUXIE, C, 19 May, about 40 years.
#176: Edmund DUORMILL, B, Gov't Mil'y Pens'r, Queen Charlotte Town, 19 May, not known.

p. 23:
#177: Mary COHEN, C, 17 Jul, age not returned.
#178: A Soldier, B, name not returned, Newtown Barracks, 1 Jun, not returned.
#179: James WALDRON, W, 4 Jun, supposed about 54 years.
#180: William Henry MASKALL, W, 7 Jun, 6 years.
#181: George NOBLE, Pens'r, B, 10 Jun, not known.
#182: Henry LOWE, W, 12 Jun, about 23 years.
#183: *Illegible,* B, Gov't Mil'y Pens'r, Queen Charlotte, 18 Jun, not known.
#184: *Illegible,* C, 19 Jun, 1 year.

p. 24:
#185: A Soldier, B, name not returned, Newtown Barracks, 19 Jun, not known.
#186: A Soldier, B, name not returned, Newtown Barracks, 26 Jun, not known.
#187: Francis WOOD, W, 27 Jun, not returned.
#188: Edward BENNETT, C, 30 Jun, not returned.

Note: *Both the entries above and below are numbered 188.*

#188: A Free Black woman, late the property of Wm. GENTLE, Esq., name not returned, 3 Jul, not known.
#189: George HARRIS, B, 4 Jul, not known.
#190: Lucretia GABOUREL, B, 7 Jul, not known.
#191: *Paper holed and illegible,* W P, 12 Jul, not known.

p. 25:
#192: Thomas HARRIS, W P, 15 Jul, not known.
#193: James MORGAN, W P, 20 *(or 26?)* Jul, 19 years.

29

#194: Joseph FISHER, B, 27 Jul, not known.
#195: Byon [*sic*] COATQUELVIN, B, 28 Jul, about 42 years.
#196: Antonio LOPEZ, W, a Dominican Friar, Guatimala, 30 Jul, 60 years.
#197: Jose MARIA, C P, 12 Aug, not known.
#198: Sarah TRAPP, B, 14 Aug, aged.
#199: *Illegible,* 28 Aug, about *illegible.*

p. 26:
#200: Emanuel, C, 2 Sep, not known.
#201: Gov't Mil'y Pensioner, B, 6 Sep, not known.
#202: A Soldier, B, Newtown Barracks, 10 Sep, not known.
#203: James PITT, B, Queen Charlotte, 12 Sep, 11 years.
#204: Estaban YNCLAN [*sic*], W, Spanish refugee from Guatimala, 15 Sep, 32 years.
#205: Catherine LAMB, W, 20 Sep, 76 years. *(Widow of David Lamb, Loyalist.)*
#206: Gov't Mil'y Pensioner, B, 21 Sep, not known.
#207: *Illegible,* 22 Sep, not known.

p. 27:
#208: *Blank* B, Gov't Mil'y Pens'r, Queen Charlotte, 24 Sep, not known.
#209: Catherine SAVERY, B, 22 Sep, 82 years.
#210: Charles MORGAN, W P, 30 Sep, not known.
#211: Sig'r [*sic*] DEMAS, C, Central America, 7 Oct, not known.
#212: Mary GAVIN, W, 8 Oct, about 3 months.
#213: James DAVIE, W, 9 Oct, about 27 years.
#214: Mary Elizabeth DOWSETT, B, 9 Oct, 2 years.
#215: John *illegible,* W P, 10 Oct, not known.

p. 28:
#216: A Soldier, name not returned, B, Newtown Barracks, 13 Oct, not known.
#217: Dick EDWARDS, B, Queen Charlotte Town, 16 Oct, not known.
#218: Thomas BATES, C, 19 Oct, about 60.
#219: Abraham LAFILLE, B, Gov't Mil'y Pens'r, 20 Oct, not returned.
#220: James DOUGLE, W, Brig *Mariner,* 21 Oct, about 20.
#221: Richard FLOWERS, B, 21 Oct, 1 year and 9 months.
#222: Maria RANN, B, 24 Oct, about 56 years.
#223: *Illegible,* Gov't Mil'y Pens'r, Newtown Barracks, 28 Oct, about 50?

p. 29:
#224: Athanasia RODRIGUEZ, C, Guatimala, 31 Oct, 40 years.
#225: *Blank* Spaniard, C P, Refugee from Guatimala, 4 Nov, not known.
#226: A pensioner's wife, B, name not returned from the Brigade Major's Office,
        Queen Charlotte, 5 Nov, not returned.
#227: A pensioner, B, name not returned from the Brigade Major, Newtown,
        6 Nov, not returned.
#228: Pens'r, B, Queen Charlotte, 10 Nov, not known.
#229: Isabella ADAM, W, 19 Nov, 1 year.

30

#230: John YOUNG, W, 25 Nov, not known.
#231: *Washed out and illegible.* 25 Nov, belie... 28?

p. 30:
#232: Clarinda PITTS, B, 25 Nov, very old.
#233: Thomas BAILEY, B, 27 Nov, 4 months.
#234: *Blank* TURBULL, C, 28 Nov, 1 year.
#235: Maria TRANWHO? B, 29 Nov, 30.
#236: Name not returned, W, Fort George, 29 Nov, not returned.
#237: Augustus Henry ELSTER, W, London, 5 Dec, 36 years.
#238: Alex' N. HOUSTON, W, late of Scotland, 12 Dec, supposed about 35 years.
#239: George *washed out and illegible,* 19 Dec

p. 31:
#240: Sarah FOGARTY, C, 19 Dec, not known.
#241: George USHER, C, 20 Dec, *blank.*
#242: George MARTIN, W, R. A., Fort George, 21 Dec, not returned.
#243: George HULBERT, W F, 27 Dec, not known.
#244: Elizabeth FLOWERS, B, 27 Dec, 6 days.
#245: George NORRISON, W F, died in the Public Hospital, 28 Dec, not known.

Note: The last two lines are blank. The minister started the New Year on a new page.

Burials in 1830:

p. 32:
#246: Eleanor DeBRIEN, C, 3 Jan, 19 years.
#247: Juan FRANCISCO, B, 6 Jan, about 22 years.
#248: William GRAFHEAD? B, 8 Jan, not known. *(D is doubtful.)*
#249: Jose Maria PLACIDO, C P, 13 Jan, not known.
#250: Mary JONES, B, 15 Jan, about 57 years.
#251: Thomas DESIRE', B, Gov't Mil'y Pens'r, 24 Jan, not known.
#252: Maria LARIA, B, 25 Jan, 10 days.
#253: *Washed out and illegible.* 27 Jan, *illegible* days

Note: There are no entries numbered 254-258. Page 32 ends on 27 January with #253, and page 33 begins on 1 February with #259.

p. 33:
#259: James ATKINSON, W, Chief Mate of the Barque *Ocean,* 1 Feb, 28 years.
#260: James PASLOW, B, 1 Feb, very old.
#261: Charles BULL, W, 1 Feb, about 39 years.
#262: James COLQUHOUN, C, 1 Feb, about 5 years.
#263: John BELISLE, C, 6 Feb, 16 months.
#264: Man not named, B, a Soldier, Newtown Barracks, 14 Feb, not known.

#265: Manfield William BOWEN, W, 21 Feb, about 50 years.
#266: *Washed out and illegible.* 23 Feb not *illegible (=not known.)*

p. 34:
#267: Elizabeth GARNETT, C, 24 Feb, 18 months.
#268: Simon PHILON, B, Pens'r, 24 Feb, not known.
#269: John WILSON, B, 1 Mar, not known.
#270: Alexander ANDERSON, C, 2 Mar, about 30 years.
#271: William REDDING, B, Pens'r, 6 Mar, not returned.
#272: Barnes HUME, B, 6 Mar, old.
#273: Jenny McNIST, B, Newtown Barracks, 8 Mar, very old.
#274: Thos. *illegible,* Freetown, 9 Mar, old.

p. 35:
#275: NICHOLAS, W, a Spanish gentleman, Havanna, 12 Mar, not known.
#276: ----- STEWART, B, Pens'r, 15 Mar, not known.
#277: Amelia POTTS, B, 1 Mar, about 41 years.
#278: Mark DRUMMOND, B, Pens'r, 25 Mar, not returned.
#279: James DAVIDSON, B, Pens'r, 25 Mar, not returned.
#280: Willm WAGNER, C, Pens'r, Serg't, 26 Mar, not returned.
#281: A Soldier in the 2nd W. I. R., B, Newtown Barracks, 26 Mar, not returned.
#282: *Washed out and illegible.* Freetown 28 Mar

p. 36:
#283: Elizabeth SHAW, C, 27 Mar, supposed 3 years.
#284: Jean MARI, W P, 1 Apr, not known.
#285: ----- GUNNING *(or GUNNERY?)* B, Soldier, Newtown Barracks, 1 Apr,
        not returned.
#286: *Blank* MILES, W, 15 Apr, about 36 years.
#287: Mary SIERS, B, 18 Apr, not returned.
#288: Thomas BACCHUS, B, Gov't Mil'y Pens'r, Freetown, 29 Apr, not returned.
#289: John FIFE, B, Gov't Mil'y Pens'r, 29 Apr, not returned.
#290: *Washed out and illegible.* Died in the Public *illegible,* 4 *(May,)* not

p. 37:
#291: Clarissa POTTS, C, 5 May, about 65 years.
#292: James BURN, W, 6 May, 23 years.
#293: Serg't GUISSANT, B, Gov't Mil'y Pens'r, 7 May, not returned.
#294: Jack REDASS, B, Gov't Mil'y Pens'r, 14 May, not returned.
#295: Jane TUCKER, B, 18 May, 9 months.
#296: ---- JAMES, Pens'rs wife, Freetown, 26 May, not returned.
#297: Private MOORE, B, Pens'r, died in the jail, 26 May, not returned.
#298: *Washed out and illegible.* Freetown, 6 Jun, not

p. 38:
#299: Jose GABRIEL, B, 6 Jun, not known.

#300: James STIBBINS, C, 12 Jun, 42 years.
#301: William SMITH, W, 19 Jun, supposed about 36 years.
#302: John HAMILTON SMITH alias THOMPSON, W, 22 Jun, not known.
#303: William KOLLER, B, Priv't 2nd W. I., Newtown Barracks, 5 Jul, about 25 years.
#304: Thomas HEWLETT, C, 7 Jul, 1 year and 4 months.
#305: Ciperion BONGARD, B? Pens'r, 12 Jul, not known.
#306: *Washed out and illegible,* died in *illegible,* 27 *(Jul)* not known.

p. 39:
#307: Mary HAYES GAVIN, W, 28 Jul, about 30 years. *(Wife of Michael Gavin, Esq.)*
#308: Charles USHER, C, 1 Aug, 18 months.
#309: Eliza KAUNTZ, W, 6 Aug, not known.
#310: Robert FOSTER, W, Brig *Janette Dunlop,* 7 Aug, about 26 years.
#311: Thomas BENNETT, C, 7 Aug, 8 years.
#312: Valentine ESCARFIT, B, Pensioner, Freetown, 15 Aug, not known.
#313: *Illegible,* Soldier, B, Newtown Barracks, 16 Aug, *blank.*
#314: *Washed out and illegible.*

Note: Pages 40-59 do not exist. The minister apparently misread p. 39 as 59, and numbered the next page 60.

p. 60:
#315: Antonio D'ACUSTA, W, Omoa, 18 Aug, not known.
#316: Elizabeth TUCKER, C, 17 Aug, about 70 years.
#317: Thomas WOOD, W, 25 Aug.
#318: Frances Amelia HUGHS [*sic*], 31 Aug, 4 years.
#319: James Edward WELSH, W, 9 Sep, 19 months.
#320: Euphemia GANNON, B, 10 Sep, 6 days.
#321: ----- GLOVER, B, a Soldier, Newtown Barracks, 12 Sep, not returned.
#322: *Illegible* WANSLEY? alias *illegible,* C, *illegible.*

p. 61:
#323: Richard MILLER ANDREW, W, 21 Sep, 10 months.
#324: Susanna WELSH, W, 5 Oct, 3 weeks.
#325: Henry LEY HANNAM, W, 4 Oct, 52 years.
#326: *Blank* JENNER, W, 4 Oct.
#327: John CLEMENT, C, 8 Oct, 8 years.
#328: Joseph LEWREY? *(or LINSEY?)* W, 9 Oct, 75 years.
#329: John DAVIDSON, W, 12 Oct, about 55 years.
#330: *Washed out and illegible,* 15 Oct, very aged.

p. 62:
#331: Mary BAKER, B, Newtown Barracks, 16 Oct, 16 years.
#332: Gabriel GORDON, B, Newtown Barracks, 16 Oct, aged.
#333: ----- MONDAY, B, a Soldier in the 2nd W. I. R., Newtown Barracks, 20 Oct, not returned.

#334:   Name unknown, C P, died in the Public Hospital, 26 Oct, not returned.
#335:   Mary FLOWERS, B, 27 Oct, 7 years.
#336:   C. L. D. W. CROMPTON, W, Newtown Barracks, 31 Oct, supposed about
          27 years.
#337:   *Blank,* a Spaniard, B, 2 Nov, not known.
#338:   *Washed out and illegible,* 4 Nov, 30 *(years.)*

p. 63:
#339:   Charles MONK, C, 9 Nov, *blank.*
#340:   George LIND, B, Disch'd Soldier 5th W. I. Reg't, 14 Nov, 44 years.
#341:   Elizabeth HARDY, C, 16 Nov, *blank.*
#342:   John William WHITE, B, 18 Nov, 3 months.
#343:   John HAY, B, Discharged Soldier, 19 Nov, about 46.
#344:   John TATE, B, Discharged Soldier, 15 Nov, *blank.*
#345:   William ROY, C, 28 Nov, 80 years.
#346:   *Washed out and illegible.* 29 Nov, 5 years

p. 64:
#347:   Barbara MOLINA, C, 1 Dec, supposed about 45 years.
#348:   Robert McINTYRE, B, Disb' Soldier, 8 Dec, aged.
#349:   William RADCLIFFE, W, died in the Public Hospital, 14 Dec, not known.
#350:   Amelia FAXARDO, W, 15 Dec, 3 years. *(Note: No Faxardo in censuses.)*
#351:   John PETIE, B, Disbanded Soldier, Queen Charlotte Town, 18 Dec, 57 years.
#352:   *Blank,* Spaniard, C, Belize late Omoa, 24 Dec, not known.
#353:   *Blank,* a Spaniard, C P, 28 Dec, not known.
#354:   William LEWIS CUNNINGHAM, *(illegible - C in censuses)* 30 Dec, 8 years.

p. 65:
#355:   John HAMLYN, W, Jamaica, 31 Dec, 24 years.

Note: The remainder of this page is blank. The minister commenced the New Year on a new page.

Burials in 1831:

p. 66:
#356:   Chloe PARKES, B, 1 Jan, very old.
#357:   Robert F. COURTNEY, C, 2 Jan, 10 days.
#358:   William FLOWERS, B, Freetown, 6 Jan, about 96 years.

Note: William Flowers, who came to Belize from the Mosquito Shore in 1788, was one of the brave men who voted to fight the Spanish rather than evacuate the settlement in 1798. There should be a monument at Yarborough Cemetery to him and all the others buried there who risked their lives, their families, their freedom, and everything else they had in the world, in choosing to do battle against an enemy of overwhelming strength.

#359: Maria CORNI, C, 11 Jan, not known.
#360: Mathia [*sic*] SULIVA, C, 12 Jan, not known.
#361: Linn FOOT, Peten Indian, C P, Peten, 3 Jan, not known.
#362: John HAMILTON, B, Gov't Pensioner, 4 Feb, *blank.*
#363: *Washed out and illegible.* 4 Feb.

p. 67:
#364: Amelia CAMPBELL, B, 12 Feb, infant.
#365: Josepha FLORENTINE, C, 20 Feb, supposed about 30 years.
#366: Joseph GIDEON, B, Queen Charlotte Town, 23 Feb, 9 years.
#367: Richard MOWBRAY MASKALL, W, 7 Mar, 5 years.
#368: Robert HODDER, B, Pnv't, 2nd W. I. R't, Newtown Barracks, 9 Mar, not known.
#369: James SWASEY, C, 11 Mar, 3 days.
#370: Charles HYDE, B, 13 Mar, very old.
#371: Vulcan? FONT? B, Freetown, 13 Mar, not known. *(Names are almost illegible.)*

p. 68:
#372: Elizabeth ANDREW, W, 20 Mar, 28 years. *(Wife of Richard J. See MI.)*
#373: *Blank,* a Pensioner, B, 28 Mar, not known.
#374: Mary M. McKAY, C, 28 Mar, 2 years.
#375: Mary HUGHES, B, 30 Mar, 1 year.
#376: Joseph BELILE, C, 5 Apr, about 40 years.
#377: Caroline SPENCER, B, Newtown Barracks, 5 Apr, 7 days.
#378: Corp'l Mc'CREA, B, Military Pens'r, 12 Apr, very aged.
#379: John KENYON WAGNER, *(color illegible - census shows C)* 27 Apr, 4 years.

p. 69:
#380: Ann PATERSON, W, 30 Apr, about 70 years.
#381: Alexander TATE, W, 30 Apr, about 28 years.
#382: Devonshire MEIGHAN, B, 3 May, about 45 years.
#383: *Blank,* soldier, B, Newtown Barracks, 6 [*sic*] May, not returned.
#384: *Blank,* pensioner, B, Queen Charlotte Town, 11 May, not returned.
#385: John MARLOW, B, Newtown Barracks, 18 May, *blank.*
#386: Emma BELISARE, C, 19 May, *blank.*
#387: *Washed out and illegible.* 19 May

p. 70:
#388: Maria Julia WESTBY, C, 19 May, 5 months.
#389: John LEON, B P, 2 Jun, not known.
#390: OXEA, a Spaniard, W P, Mauger Key, supposed about 32 years.
#391: J. MALETTE, B, a Soldier, Newtown Barracks, 15 Jun, not returned.
#392: Marg^t ARCHY, C, Triangles, 20 Jun, about 38 years.
#393: Anthony JOSEPH, B, Mil'y Pens'r, 22 Jun, not returned.
#394: Pens'rs wife, B, Freetown, 26 Jun, not known.
#395: John SIMPSON, B, 29 Jun, 44 years.

p. 71:
#396: Sarah USHER, W, 30 Jun, *blank.*
#397: Elizabeth GRANT, B, 6 Jul, 40 years.
#398: James SMITH, W P, died in the Hospital, 8 Jul, about 45 years.
#399: Sarah MOODY, C, 13 Jul, about 5 years.
#400: Ann CRABB, C, 14 Jul, about 2 years.
#401: Pablo MANSANO, C P, a Spaniard, 19 Jul, about 48 years.
#402: George FRAZER, C, 27 Jul, 27 years.
#403: *Washed out and illegible.*

p. 72:
#404: Luke STAFFORD, W, Ship *Merlin,* 31 Jul, not known.
#405: Sarah GALLINO, C, 31 Jul, not known.
#406: Mary FRANCIS, B, 2 Aug, 40 years.
#407: Catherine GARNETT, C, 7 Aug, 11 months.
#408: Thomas SMITH, W, Capt. 2nd W. I. Reg't, Newtown Barracks, 7 Aug, *blank.*
#409: W. S. EVE, Lieut. 2nd W. I. Reg't, Newtown Barracks, 7 Aug, *blank.*
#410: John LURGAN, B, Garrison Hospital, 12 Aug, not returned.
#411: John MARSHAL, W P, died in the public hospital, 14 Aug, about 45 years.

p. 73:
#412: Hugh O'NEIL, B, Newtown Barracks, 16 Aug.
#413: David LONGSWORTH, C, 20 Aug, 70 years.
#414: Maria HINEY, C, 23 Aug, not known.
#415: Peter ROBARTS, W P, Sailer, died in the Public Hospital, 27 Aug, about 45 yrs.
#416: James GLADDEN, C, 28 Aug, 99 years.
#417: *Blank* O'BRIEN, W, Newtown Barracks, 28 Aug, *blank.*
#418: Mary PRICE, B, 3 Sep, about 56 years.
#419: *Washed out and illegible,* Gov't Mil'y Pens'r, 11 Sep

p. 74:
#420: Sigario, C P, 16 Sep, about 21 years.
#421: John MARSHALL, W P, 16 Sep, *blank.*
#422: W. H. WALL, W, Ass't. Surgeon 2 W. I. R, Newtown Barracks, 19 Sep, *blank.*
#423: *Blank,* Pens'r, B, 25 Sep, *blank.*
#424: Eleanor HOARE, B, 25 Sep, 60 years.
#425: Kate WAGNER, B, 27 Sep, 46 years.
#426: *Illegible* LOGAN, W P, 27 Sep, *blank.*
#427: Rodney *illegible,* B, 29 Sep, *blank.*

p.75:
#428: James WAIGHT, W, 3 Oct, 45 years. *(Schoolmaster, organist, churchwarden.)*
#429: *Illegible* C, 8 Oct, *blank.*
#430: Don BISENT, C, a Spaniard, 10 Oct, *blank.*
#431: Joseph CURRANT, B, River Sibun, 11 Oct, 18 years.

36

#432: Sarah JACKSON, C, 12 Oct, 60 years.
#433: Charles CRAWFORD, B, 13 Oct, *blank*.
#434: Ellen ROBINSON, B, 13 Oct, 1 month.
#435: Elizabeth Susanna TOOTH, C, 13 Oct, 45 years.

p. 76:
#436: Thos. FIRBY, B, Pens'r, 14 Oct, *blank*.
#437: Marshal BENNETT, C, 18 Oct, 4 years.
#438: George HILL, B, Newtown Barracks, 21 Oct, *blank*.
#439: Wm SPENCER, B, Newtown Barracks, 28 Oct.
#440: Maria BAYLY, B, 22 Oct, 35 years.
#441: Dr. Jose Maria GUIROLA? Guatimala, 1 Nov.
#442: Juliana LAMB, C, 4 Nov, *blank*.
#443: *Washed out and illegible*, 5 Nov.

p. 77:
#444: *Blank*, a Soldier, B, Newtown Barracks, 6 Nov, *blank*.
#445: Edmund WESTBY, C, 7 Nov, 11 months.
#446: Robert, B, 9 Nov, 4 years.
#447: Edward KING, B, Pens'r, 11 Nov, *blank*.
#448: Robert HUGHES, B, 11 Nov, 11 days.
#449: Catherine DeBAPTIST, C, 16 Nov, *blank*.
#450: Jacob DORSET, B, Freetown, 7 Nov, 32 years.
#451: *Washed out and illegible*, 18 Nov, 37 years.

p. 78:
#452: Nich^s DAWSON, C, New River, 20 Nov, about 19 years.
#453: Corp'l EDWARDS, B, Pens'r, Queen Charlotte Town, 21 Nov, *blank*.
#454: Margaret POTTS, C, 22 Nov, aged.
#455: David DIXON, C P, 23 Nov, 85.
#456: Lillias NELLIN, C, 25 Nov, about 80.
#457: Maria EMERY, C, 25 Nov, 6 years.
#458: Maria ANDERSON, B, 7 Nov, *blank*.
#459: ..lse..? *illegible* CRAWFORD, B, 2 Dec, 33.

p. 79:
#460: George ADOLPHUS, C, 3 Dec, *blank*.
#461: Sarah NEAL, C, 12 Dec, *blank*.
#462: Bartholomew EDWARDS, C, 13 Dec, infant, 5 days.
#463: John HOWARD, W, 17 Dec, *blank*.
#464: *Blank* HOSKIN, W, Lieut 2nd W. I. Reg't, 18 Dec.
#465: Isaac JENKINS, W P, Died in the Public Hospital, 20 Dec.
#466: Jean Pierre DeRIVEAU, B, Pens'r, 23 Dec.
#467: Thomas CRABB, B? 24 Dec, 56.

p. 80:
#468:   Sophia MOYERS, C, Freetown, 26 Dec, *blank.*
#469:   Betsy FLOWERS, B, 28 Dec, 2 months.

Note: The minister was closing out the year. The remainder of this page is blank, with a swirling flourish drawn across it.

Burials in 1832:

p. 81:
#470:   A Soldier, B, Newtown Barracks, 1 Jan, *blank.*
#471:   Jose MARTIN, C P, 3 Jan, 28 years.
#472:   Hagar BREWYER, B, 7 Jan, 90 years.
#473:   Kitty TILLETT, C, 8 Jan, 43 years.

Note: Kitty Tillett was born ca. 1789 to Capt. William and Mary White Tillett: the list of 1790 shows Elizabeth and Kitty as children in their household. MI's on the tombs of other family members have survived, but hers is missing. Her children by Charles Keefe Cunningham were William, Sarah Keefe, and Catherine Tillett Cunningham.

#474:   John LOCK, W P, 8 Jan, 40 years.
#475:   Mary MOYERS, C, 10 Jan, 50 years.
#476:   Rose WALL, B, Queen Charlotte Town, 11 Jan.
#477:   Mary Jane? ----MAN, *illegible,* B, Queen Charlotte Town, 15 Jan.

p. 82:
#478:   Thos. FITZGERALD, W, Fort George, 17 Jan, *blank.*
#479:   Desborough SWAN, B, Pens'r, Freetown, 18 Jan, *blank.*
#480:   Petrona ALBINA, C P, 20 Jan, 40 years.
#481:   Ann MOODY, C, 20 Jan, 19 years.
#482:   Joseph MORRIS, B, 20 Jan, 1 year.
#483:   *Blank,* Pens', B, Freetown, 21 Jan, *blank.*
#484:   Smart BELILE, B, 25 Jan, 14 years.
#485:   Joseph GARIET, B, 26 Jan, 21 years.

p. 83:
#486:   John CHARLEMAN, B, 2 Feb, *blank.*
#487:   Figaro, B, Pens'r, 3 Feb, *blank.*
#488:   Caesar, B, Pens'r, 6 Feb, *blank.*
#489:   R. J. ANDREW, W, 14 Feb, *blank. (Rich'd James d. 13th – Caledonian Mercury.)*
#490:   *Blank,* Pens', B, 17 Feb, *blank.*
#491:   John FAIMO, B, Pens'r, Queen Charlotte Town, 22 Feb.
#492:   John RANN, B, 25 Feb.
#493:   *Washed out and illegible,* 3 Mar.

p. 84:
#494: Adam LOWRIE, B, 3 Mar, 70 years.
#495: Mary THOMAS, B, Queen Charlotte, 12 Mar, aged.
#496: *Blank,* P, 13 Mar, *blank.*
#497: Rita FAXARDO, W, 14 Mar, 22.
#498: Nero GIBSON, B, 16 Mar, about 40.
#499: John? C P, 23 Mar, *blank.*
#500: Manuel VISCADO, C, Seaman of the *Vapois,* a Spanish Brig, 24 Mar, *blank.*
#501: *Washed out and illegible,* 27 Mar.

p. 85:
#502: Catherine GADDES, B, 3 Apr, aged.
#503: Cato WINTER, B, 8 Apr, 55.
#504: BESCENTE', B P, 16 Apr, 29.
#505: Thos. HOWARD, B, Newtown Barracks, 23 Apr, *blank.*
#506: Don Francisco DE LA RIOS, W, Central America, 28 Apr, *blank.*
#507: BEARD, B, Soldier, Newtown Barracks, 5 May, *blank.*
#508: Thos. TUCKER, B, 7 May, child.
#509: *Washed out and illegible,* 15 May.

p. 86:
#510: George BURK, B, 18 May, old.
#511: Pens', B, 19 May, *blank.*
#512: Julian ORNANDEZ, B, 20 May, 32.
#513: *Blank,* Pens', B, 21 May, *blank.*
#514: Unknown, C P, unknown as he was found drowned, not recognized, 23 May.
#515: *Blank,* soldier's wife, B, Newtown Barracks, 24 May, *blank.*
#516: George GRANT, B P, 24 May, *blank.*
#517: James? JENKS? *illegible,* 28 May, 20?

p. 87:
#518: John VAUGHAN, C, 17 Jun, 11 months.
#519: John GREEN, W, Ship *Stan Rumney,* 21 Jun, 44.
#520: Benj'n WALTON HALFHIDE, W, 24 Jun, 5 years.
#521: Marina HOARE, B, 27 Jun, aged.
#522: John S. DALGETY, W, 2 Jul, 83. *(Memorial plaque: John SMALE DALGETTY.)*
#523: Judith, B, 2 Jul, *blank.*
#524: COOKE, Private 2nd W. I. Reg't, B, Newtown Barracks, 14 Jul.
#525: *Washed out and illegible,* C, Central *illegible,* 14 Jul, aged.

p. 88:
#526: Manuel PIRRONTIL? W, Truxillo, 16 Jul, 45.
#527: Geronimo LEZAYA, W, Central America, 18 Jul, blank.
#528: Florence VERNON, B, Pers'r, 19 Jul, blank.
#529: James LIVINGSTON, W P, 21 Jul, blank.
#530: Henry GRISTOCK, C, 22 Jul, 1 year.

#531: Thomas MARSHAL, W, 25 Jul, 26 years.
#532: James BEDFORD, B, Pens'r, 26 Jul, blank.
#533: Gerald HILL, B, 26 Jul, *illegible or blank.*

p. 89:
#534: Charles PARDREN, B, Pens'r, 27 Jul, *blank.*
#535: Wellington Burt CROSKEY, W, United States of America, 30 Jul, 19 years.
#536: Maria YALUPA, C, 6 Aug, 2 years.
#537: John Robert SHAW, W, 6 Aug, 27 years.
#538: A Soldier whose name was not returned, B, Newtown Barracks, 11 Aug, *blank.*
#539: *Blank* PASLOW, C P, 13 Aug, *blank.*
#540: Wm Jas. WAGNER, C, 16 Aug, 6 years.
#541: *Washed out and illegible,* C, 17 Aug.

p. 90:
#542: Antonia, C, 19 Aug, *blank.*
#543: Maria LUCAS LINDSAY, W, 23 Aug, 28. *(MI: wife of John Lindsay.)*
#544: George WARREN, *illegible,* 24 Aug, child.
#545: Eleanor ROSS, C, 25 Aug, 1 year.
#546: William SCOTLAND, W P, 29 Aug, about 32 years.
#547: Thos. SEBASTIAN, W P, 29 Aug, about 40 years.
#548: Lydia TRAPP, B, 4 Sep, very old.
#549: John HOOK, C, 4 Sep, *blank.*

p. 91:
#550: Etienne CASTLE, B, Pens'r, 5 Sep.
#551: Lorenzo DESSONS, B, 7 Sep.
#552: Jose MARIA, C, Truxillo, 3 years.
#553: John PAUL, B, Pens'r, 11 Sep, 54 years.
#554: Isabella SMITH GUNN, C, 11 Sep, 14 months.
#555: *Blank,* Pens', B, 14 Sep, *blank.*
#556: Richard PHILLIPS, C, 19 Sep, 9 days.
#557: *Washed out and llegible* ----BELL, C, 19 Sep, 9 *illegible.*

p. 92:
#558: John BENNETT, C, 19 Sep, 9 days.
#559: Willm Ja^s CROFT, C, 19 Sep, 32 years.
#560: Nancy PORTAL, C, Central America, 21 Sep, about 6 years.
#561: John LAYARD, B, 24 Sep, about 53 years.
#562: Augustus YOUNG, B, 27 Sep, about 40 years.
#563: Susan SMITH, C, 4 Oct, 7 days.
#564: Charles STOCKDALE, B, Newtown Barracks, 10 Oct, infant.
#565: *Washed out and illegible,* Newtown Barracks, 13 Oct

p. 93:
#566: Ann OSMAN, C, 16 Oct, *blank.*

#567: Frank AVILLA, W, 16 Oct, *blank.*
#568: Philip MANUEL, B, 19 Oct, 1 year.
#569: Juan ANTONIA, W, 27 Oct, aged.
#570: COLUMBINE, W P, 27 Oct, 37.
#571: Tho[s] HUGHES, W P, died in the Public Hospital, 29 Oct, about 40.
#572: Will[m] Amos HAYLOCK, C, 29 Oct, 2 months.
#573: *Washed out and illegible, badly stained.*   30 Oct.

p. 94:
#574: Manuel BETANCEN, W, 3 Nov, about 30.
#575: Polly DeBECK, B, 4 Nov, *blank.*
#576: *Blank,* Pens', B, Queen Charlotte, 5 Nov, *blank.*
#577: William GILL, C, 6 Nov, 3 years.
#578: John DIBDIN, B, Newtown Barracks, 6 Nov.
#579: Benjamin CRAFT, C, 8 Nov, 6 years.
#580: Bernard BELISLE, B, 11 Nov.
#581: *Washed out and illegible*

p. 95:
#582: Ann Eve McNISH, B, Newtown Barracks, 16 Nov, 3 years.
#583: Maria WILLIAMS, B, Newtown Barracks, 18 Nov, 3 years.
#584: Hannah SIDDON, C, 23 Nov.
#585: Andrew GRAHAM, B, 24 Nov, old.
#586: Andrew BAYNTON, W, 23 Nov, *blank.*
#587: Joseph WILLIAMS, C, 30 Nov, 9 years.
#588: Peter Le FOY, W P, died in the Public Hospital, 30 Nov, about 30 years.
#589: Joseph *illegible,* 1 Dec, 9 *illegible.*

Note: Joseph's surname, like many that have been washed out, is tantalizing: the letters are so close to being visible! Hopefully, in time, chemical techniques will be made available to darken the surviving molecules of ink.

p. 96:
#590: James FULLICK, W, Newtown Barracks, 1 Dec, *blank.*
#591: Elizabeth GREENOCK, B, 1 Dec, *blank.*
#592: Sam[l] YOUNG, B P, 11 Dec, 35.
#593: Thomas, B, G. M. P.*, 13 Dec, aged. *(*Government Military Pensioner.)*
#594: William SPENCER, B, Newtown Barracks, 14 Dec, 10 days.
#595: John GILL, C, 16 Dec, 3 years.
#596: James BAGSHAW NEAL, C, 16 Dec, 4 years.
#597: *Washed out and illegible.*

p. 97:
#598: Emily WHITING, C, 22 Dec, 10 months.
#599: Widow ----- [*sic*] MOYERS, B, 25 Dec, *blank.*

#600:   Ann DeBAPTIST, C, 25 Dec, 10 *(or 16?)* months.
#601:   Esther, B, 31 Dec, *blank.*

Burials in 1833:

#602:   *Blank,* B, Newtown Barracks, 1 Jan 1833, *blank.*
#603:   *Blank,* A Spaniard, B, 2 Jan, *blank.*
#604:   Maria, C, 2 Jan, *blank.*
#605:   *Washed out and illegible.*

Note: At this point in the register, the Chaplain stopped numbering his entries. The writer continued numbering in order to facilitate referencing the transcript.

p. 98:
#606:   Josepha M. RODRIGUEZ, C P, 6 Jan, 38.
#607:   *Blank,* B, 7 Jan, *blank.*
#608:   Clarinda NEAL, C, 8 Jan, 3? years.
#609:   Jose MARIA, C, 8 Jan, 45.
#610:   James JOHNSON, C, 17 Jan, 13.
#611:   Nicholas RINTON, B, 20 Jan, 7.
#612:   *Blank, illegible,* Newtown Barracks, 20 Jan, *blank.*
#613:   *Washed out and illegible.*

p. 99:
#614:   Abraham LAWRIE, B, 15 Feb, upwards of 104 years.
#615:   Nicholas BRUNO, B, 16 Feb, *blank.*
#616:   Peter STRUTT, Pens'r, B, 16 Feb, *blank.*
#617:   Charles Thomas HUGHS [*sic*], W, 16 Feb, 1 year.
#618:   Willm COKER, C, 16 Feb, *blank.*
#619:   John James HUGHES, C, 18 Feb, infant. *(Son of John Hughes/Adelaide Vernon.)*
#620:   John Roger EVANS, W, 19 Feb, infant.
#621:   *Washed out and illegible.*

p. 100:
#622:   Herbert STANTON, B, Pens'r, 25 Jan, aged.
#623:   Marina MARTIN, B, Newtown Barracks, 29 Jan, *blank.*
#624:   Abraham HEIGH, W P, 3 Feb, *blank.*
#625:   Eleanor Susanna CROFT, C, 4 Feb, 18 months.
#626:   Robert WALDRON WOOD, C, 13 Feb, 13.
#627:   Charles CAMPBELL, C, 13 Feb, infant.
#628:   Mary FYLIY [*sic*], Newtown Barracks, B, 13 Feb, *blank.*
#629:   *Washed out and illegible.*

p. 101:
#630:   Jean BAPTISTE, C P, 28 Feb, blank.

#631: *Blank,* W, Fort George, 1 Mar, blank.
#632: Maria McDONALD, B, Freetown, 4 Mar, blank.
#633: Henry SMITH, B, 6 Mar, blank.
#634: Jose, C P, 13 Mar, about 29.
#635: Mary HAWKINS EVINS, C, 19 Mar, blank.
#636: James NEIL, C, 20 Mar, infant.
#637: *Washed out and illegible.*

p. 102:
#638: *Blank,* C P, 25 Mar, *blank.*
#639: Maria LOSANCA, B, 4 Apr, *blank.*
#640: Peter SMITH, C, 11 Apr, *blank.*
#641: Louisa Ann HOWARD, W, 15 Apr, 10 months.
#642: John WILD, W, Fort George, 18 Apr, *blank.*
#643: George McLOUGHLIN, W, Brig *Catherine,* 21 Apr, about 40.
#644: Pascal BRACELOW, B, Queen Charlotte Town, 28 Apr, *blank.*
#645: *Washed out and illegible.*

p. 103:
#646: Louis BERNARD, B, Freetown, 5 May, *blank.*
#647: Richard BAKER, W, 6 May, *blank.*
#648: *Blank,* B, Freetown, 6 May, *blank.*
#649: Peter O'SAY, B, 20 May, *blank.*
#650: A Musquito Man, C P, 30 May, *blank.*
#651: Philip FALLS, W, 3 Jun, *blank.*
#652: Jane HEWLETT, C, 4 Jun, *blank.*
#653: *Washed out and illegible.*

p. 104:
#654: *Blank,* B, Queen Charlotte Town, 16 Jun, *blank.*
#655: Pablo MONTALANO, C, 17 Jun, child.
#656: Pascale, B, Queen Charlotte Town, 28 Jun, *blank.*
#657: Joseph MUSLAAR, W, 28 Jun, 5.
#658: George KANE, B, 10 Jul, 2 years.
#659: William TUSSEY, B P, Musquito Shore, 1 Jul, *blank.*
#660: Gregorio BASQUEZ, B P, 13 Jul, *blank.*
#661: *Washed out and illegible.*

p. 105:
#662: Jean PIERRE, B, 21 Jul, *blank.*
#663: Venus SLUSHER, B, 22 Jul, *blank.*
#664: Peggy, C, Freetown, 23 Jul, *blank.*
#665: George HASTING GREY, C, 31 Jul, 12 days.

Note: Burials #666 - 670 took place in August. The minister continued to write "July" until 18 August, when he realized his mistake.

43

#666: James WELSH, C, 7 Jul [*sic*], 16 days.
#667: Mrs. DESOYCE, B, Queen Charlotte Town, 13 Jul. *blank.* *(= DeSOURCE.)*
#668: St. GEO, B, 14 Jul, *blank.*
#669: Pierre LOMAN, B, Queen Charlotte, 15 Jul, *blank.*

p. 106:
#670: James MILLAR, B, 18 Jul *(overwritten)* Aug, *blank.*
#671: George SUNTON, B, 18 Aug, *blank.*
#672: Duncan CONNOR, B, 19 Aug, *blank.*
#673: Frances PAREOJEAN, C, 21 Aug, *blank.*
#674: Edward BERTIE, C, 21 Aug, *blank.*
#675: *Blank,* B, 23 Aug, *blank.*
#676: *Blank,* B, 25 Aug, *blank.*
#677: Charles A..... *remainder of surname illegible,* C, 26 Aug, *blank.*

p. 107:
#678: William MURRAY, C, 27 Aug, *blank.*
#679: Ann NICHOLSON, C, 29 Aug, *blank.*
#680: London CRAFT, C, 30 Aug, *blank.*
#681: James HALES, W, Seaman of the *Elizabeth,* 1 Sep, *blank.*
#682: Hannah MARTIN, C, 2 Sep, 1 month.
#683: Mary SUTTLE, W, 9 Sep, 12 years.
#684: Paul WORKMAN, B, 15 Sep, *blank.*
#685: *Washed out and illegible.*

p. 108:
#686: John YOUNG, B P, 19 Sep, *blank.*
#687: Ann THOMAS, B, 23 Sep, *blank.*
#688: Juan GAMBOA, C, 13 Sep, *blank.*
#689: Helen DAN, W, Fort George, 15 Oct, 41.
#690: Charles COOKE, C, 22 Oct, *blank.*
#691: Jose COOK [*sic*], C, 24 Oct, *blank.*
#692: Francis LEIGH BALFOUR, W, 30 Oct, 28. *(Keeper of the Records in 1832.)*
#693: Willm *illegible,* W, 30 Oct, *blank.* (MI: William B. BAKER, d.29 Oct, aged 19.)

p. 109:
#694: James Joseph JOHNSON, C, 7 Nov, 3 years.
#695: Jose, C P, 11 Nov, 20.
#696: Laura PITKETHLY, C, 17 Nov, *blank.*
#697: Catherine CUNNINGHAM, 19 Nov, 32.
#698: Duncan McLARTY, W, 22 Nov, *blank.*
#699: James MURRAY, W P, 25 Nov, *blank.*
#700: Manuel ANTONIO, C P, 26 Nov, *blank.*
#701: Alexander *illegible,* B, 27 Nov, *blank.*

44

p. 110:
#*702:*   Thomas WHITTER, B, 5 Sep, aged.
#*703:*   Richard PARKS, B, 5 Dec, *blank.*
#*704:*   Laurence MEIGHAN, C, 13 Dec, *blank.*
#*705:*   Robert SAVERY, C, 17 Dec, 7.
#*706:*   Martha PETZOLD, *blank or too faint to be made out,* 23 Dec, 7 months.
#*707:*   Christopher, B, 23 Dec, *blank.*
#*708:*   Pedro CHRISTIAN, C P, 26 Dec, *blank.*
#*709:*   *Washed out and illegible.*

Burials in 1834:

p.111:
#*710:*   James LINTO, W P, 1 Jan, about 29 years.
#*711:*   Philip SMITH, C, 5 Jan, 5 days.
#*712:*   Isabella JOHNSON, C, 5 Jan, *blank.*
#*713:*   Ann GADDES, C, 6 Jan, *blank.*
#*714:*   *Blank,* C P, 8 Jan, *blank.*
#*715:*   William H. CATES, W, 13 Jan, *blank.*
#*716:*   C^s VALANCY, B, 13 Jan, *blank. (Carlos? Charles was abbreviated as Chas.)*
#*717:*   David JOHNSON, W, 20 Jan, *blank.*

p. 112:
#*718:*   Carlos GAMBOA, C P, 21 Jan, *blank.*
#*719:*   KINGSTON, B, 23 Jan, 4 years.
#*720:*   BONCHANCE, B, 24 Jan, *blank.*
#*721:*   Ben. GRAHAM, B, 25 Jan, 60.
#*722:*   Patrick SIMON, B, 27 Jan, *blank.*
#*723:*   James HARVEY, W, 1 Feb, *blank.*
#*724:*   *Blank* EVANS, W, 2 Feb, *blank.*
#*725:*   William T. CHERRINGTON, W, 7 Feb, *blank.*

p. 113:
#*726:*   *Blank,* B, Newtown Barracks, 10 Feb, *blank.*
#*727:*   Mary WHITE, C, 18 Feb, *blank. (See MI: Mrs. Mary TILLETT, 68, children.)*
#*728:*   Thomas DALE, B, 28 Mar [*sic*], very aged.
#*729:*   John ALEXANDER, C, 28 Feb, *blank. (1832 census p. 197: W.)*
#*730:*   James SCOTT, W, 5 Mar, *blank.*
#*731:*   George PITKETHLY, C, 6 Mar, 1 year.
#*732:*   St. Mark LaCASS, B, 3 Apr, *blank.*
#*733:*   Simon MOULE, B, 6 Apr, *blank.*

p. 114:
#*734:*   Bryan PHILIP, B, 6 Apr., *blank*
#*735:*   Eleanor DIXON B, 11 Apr, *blank.*

45

#736: Rose CRAWFORD, B, 15 Apr, *blank.*
#737: Francis HICKEY, B, 23 Apr, aged.
#738: Amelia TENA, B, 26 Apr, *blank.*
#739: John WILLIAMS, Mosquito Shore, 27 Apr, *blank.*
#740: Seferino RETIS, W, Spain, 29 Apr, 76 years.
#741: Fanny, B, 1 May, 2 years.

p. 115:
#742: *Blank* WOODS, W, 2 May, 4 months.
#743: John HECTOR, B, 3 May, aged.
#744: William COOKE, W, 3 May, *blank.*
#745: E. BLOOMFIELD, B, 7 May, *blank.*
#746: Amos SWAN, B, 7 May, *blank.*
#747: Sarah HAMMOND, C, 14 May, *blank.*
#748: Manuel JOSE, C P, 27 May, *blank.*
#749: Joseph JOSEP, C P, 28 May, *blank.*

p. 116:
#750: William AOSNER C, 1 Jun, 28. *(Mishearing of HOSNER?)*
#751: William HALE, W, Brig *Coquet,* 2 Jun, *blank.*
#752: Sam FLUIDEO, B, 13 Jun, *blank.*
#753: Augusta BAILY, C, 19 Jun, *blank.*
#754: Maria Des NIEVES, C, 22 Jun, *blank.*
#755: Mary CUMMINS, B, 23 Jun, *blank.*
#756: James POTTS CUNNINGHAM, C, 28 Jun, 17.
#757: Charles STEWART, W, Ship *Cares,* 30 Jun, about 30.

p. 117: *This and the next two page numbers are washed out.*
#758: Eliza HULSE, C, 6 Jul, *blank.*
#759: Henry Hugh BRENNAN, W, Newtown Barracks, 8 Jul, *blank.*
#760: Barbara CYPIE *(or CYPIC?)* B, Freetown, 22 Jul, *blank.*
#761: *Blank,* B, 24 Jul, *blank.*
#762: Judith, B, 25 Jul, *blank.*
#763: Jose Maria LOPEZ, C, 4 Aug, *blank.*
#764: Prince, B, 4 Aug, *blank.*
#765: Mary COLQUHOUN, W, 25 Aug, 46. *(Widow of Archibald Colquhoun, Esq.)*

p. 118:
#766: George HYMER, B, Newtown Barracks, 28 Aug, *blank.*
#767: Agnes CRAIG, C, 1 Sep, *blank.*
#768: John Le CROIX, C, Musquito Shore, 2 Sep, *blank.*
#769: James BIRKHARD, B, Newtown Barracks, 2 Sep, *blank.*
#770: William OTTLEY, C, Newtown Barracks, 4 Sep, *blank.*
#771: Pedro JOSEPH, C, 5 Sep, 18.
#772: Clara? B, 8 Sep, *blank.*
#773: Mary M. QUILTER, C, 8 Sep, *blank.*

p. 119:
#774:   George NORMAN, W, 10 Sep, *blank*.
#775:   Bernardo FLORES, C. St. [*sic*] Salvador, 12 Sep, 1 year.
#776:   James WALTERS, W, Barque *Excellent*, 15 Sep, 15.
#777:   Lucretia DUGARD, B. Newtown Barracks, 16 Sep, *blank*.
#778:   John BURKE Mc'KAY, C, 22 Sep, 17 months.
#779:   Ann GENTLE, B, 22 Sep, 5 years.
#780:   A Spanish woman, C, late of Omoa, 23 Sep, *blank*.
#781:   Rosanna SAMSON, B, 28 Sep, infant.

p. 120:
#782:   Robert SMITH, C, 28 Sep, infant.
#783:   Ellen Le CASS, B, 28 Sep, infant.
#784:   Colin McDONALD, W P, 30 Sep, *blank*.
#785:   Spanish female child, C, 1 Oct, 3 days.
#786:   *Blank*, B P, died in hospital, 3 Oct, *blank*.
#787:   William HEMSLEY, W, 4 Oct, 84.
#788:   Joseph PIPERSBURG, B, 5 Oct, 5.
#789:   Michael ROGERS, W, Fort George, 16 Oct, *blank*.

p. 121:
#790:   Margaret SILVA, B, Queen Charlotte Town, 18 Oct, *blank*.
#791:   Lucretia POTTS, C, 23 Oct, *blank*.
#792:   Rose GRANT, B, 23 Oct, *blank*.
#793:   Charles ALEXANDER, W, 27 Oct, *blank*.
#794:   James PARKER, W, 29 Oct, 54.
#795:   Pamella [*sic*] TOOTH, W, 30 Oct, *blank*.
#796:   Nathaniel HULSE, W, 5 Nov, *blank*.
#797:   Volumnia McNISH, B, 7 Nov, *blank*.

p. 122:
#798:   Juana CATALINA, B, 11 Nov, 7.
#799:   Emily KENYON, W, Newtown Barracks, 17 Nov, child.
#800:   David ENNIS, B, Freetown, 18 Nov, *blank*.
#801:   Alexander GILCHRIST, W, 18 Nov, *blank*.
#802:   James CLARKE, W P, died in the public hospital, 18 Nov, *blank*.
#803:   Thomas FLOWERS, B, 22 Nov, *blank*.
#804:   Rachel PICKSTOCK, B, 22 Nov, 7 years.
#805:   Maria HOARE, *illegible*, 28 Nov, *blank*.

p. 123:
#806:   Mary MORRIS, W, 4 Dec, infant.
#807:   James ROGERS, W, 7 Dec, child.
#808:   George HILL, B, 7 Dec, *blank*.
#809:   Ann SMITH, C, 12 Dec, about 32.

#810: John P. BRENNER, W, Newtown Barracks, 9 [*sic*] Dec, *blank.*
#811: James WILSON, B, Queen Charlotte Town, 17 Dec, *blank.*
#812: Francisco, B, died in the public hospital, 18 Dec, *blank.*
#813: William JEFFREY, W, died in the public hospital, 21 Dec, *blank.*

p. 124:
#814: Francisco ASCAIYO, C? 25 Dec, 23.
#815: *Blank,* C? 28 Dec, *blank.*
#816: Pedro ARAENGAS, C, 29 Dec, *blank.*
#817: Jenny *blank,* W, 29 Dec, *blank.*
#818: Mary HEMMINGS, W, 31 Dec, *blank.*

Burials in 1835:

#819: Sylvia PICKSTOCK, B, 1 Jan, *blank.*
#820: SAAR [*sic*], B, G.M.P., 2 Jan, *blank.*
#821: Jane GARDNER, C, 5 Jan, *blank.*   (1832 census p. 10: Jane H. Gardner, child.)

p. 125:
#822: Pablo MARTINEZ, C, 5 Jan, *blank.*
#823: Constantia YOUNG, C, 6 Jan, *blank.*
#824: Philip MARTIN, B, 7 Jan, *blank.*
#825: William HUGHS, B, 7 Jan, *blank.*
#826: William THOMSON, C, 8 Jan, *blank.*
#827: Rosanna NOTT, C, 9 Jan, *blank.*
#828: Mary WALCOTT, C, 17 Jan, 15. *blank.*
#829: Francis RODD, B? 23 Jan, *blank.*

p. 126:
#830: Jose ANSELMO, C, 25 Jan, *blank.*
#831: John BELILE, B, 26 Jan, *blank.*
#832: John UTER, C, 31 Jan, infant.
#833: Charles APRISE, B, G.M.P., 12 Feb, *blank.*
#834: Emily Eliza WILLIAMS, C, 16 Feb, 4 years.
#835: John DUAMI, B, Newtown Barracks, 18 Feb, *blank.*
#836: Qua, B, 19 Feb, *blank.*
#837: William VASQUEZ, *illegible,* 22 Feb, 4 days.

p. 127:
#838: John WEDDY, B, Newtown Barracks, 24 Feb, *blank.*
#839: Sam[l] GRAVES, B, 24 Feb, *blank.*
#840: Betsy DeBAPTISTE, B, 24 Feb, 45.
#841: Fanny DeLaHOUSIE, B, 12 Mar, *blank.*
#842: Fred[k] PORTER, B, Freetown, 13/14 (*overwritten*) Mar, *blank.*
#843: Oliver OSCAR, C, 14 Mar, *blank.*

#844: Ann Susanna HARPER, W, Newtown Barracks, 16 Mar, *blank.*
#845: Z. HUBBARD, B, 16 Mar, *blank.*

p. 128:
#846: Philip EGERTON, B, 16 Mar, *blank.*
#847: Betsy FAIRWEATHER, B, 19 Mar, *blank.*
#848: Eleanor WALL, B, 21 Mar, *blank.*
#849: William SPENCE, B, Newtown Barracks, 1 Apr, *blank.*
#850: Eliza W. McPHERSON, W, Newtown Barracks, 3 Apr, *blank.*
#851: Sharper HYDE, B, 6 Apr, *blank.*
#852: James TRAPP USHER, C, 5 Apr, 44.
#853: *Washed out and illegible, with brown streaks through the space.*

p. 129:
#854: Christian YOUNG, C, 12 Apr, *blank.*
#855: Sally DALY, B, Newtown Barracks, 25 Apr, 5.
#856: Hannah TUCKER, C, 29 Apr, 90.
#857: William SUTHERLAND, B, 4 May, *blank.*
#858: William FLOWERS, B, 7 May, *blank.*
#859: Charles Thomas SMALL, C, 9 May, *blank.*
#860: Catherine GOFF, B, 12 May, aged.
#861: Robert ROBERTS, C, 14 May, *blank.*

p. 130:
#862: Bristow CARD, B, 15 May, *blank.*
#863: John FLOWERS, B, 15 May, *blank.*
#864: George SPROAT, C, 20 May, 45.
#865: Bill HOPE, B, 1 Jun, aged. *blank.*
#866: Claude DESOYNER, B, Queen Charlotte Town, 2 Jun, aged.
#867: Marshal BENNETT Junr., W, 3 Jun, *blank.*

Note: Marshal Jr., ca. 1799 – 1835, the writer's GGG-Grandfather, was a merchant. If his tomb has survived, its slab with the MI is missing. He was a son of John and Sarah Warburton Bennett of Sheffield, England; a nephew of the magistrate Marshal Bennett Sr.; and a grandson of Thomas and Elizabeth Cooper Bennett, merchants of Sheffield. He had children by Catherine Meighan, the daughter of Edmund Meighan and Bess Ewing, and by Catherine Cunningham, a daughter of Andrew Cunningham and Sarah Keefe. See the wills of Edmund Meighan (died 1813 Belize, will probated 1815 in London,) and of John Bennett (died 1846 at Sheffield, will probated in 1847 at York.)

#868: J. MITCHEL, C, 8 Jun, *blank.*
#869: E. EVANS, B? 9 Jun, *blank.*

p. 131:
#870: Thomas SLESHER [*sic*], B, 12 Jun, 28.
#871: George DEWAR, W, Barque *Orestes,* 14 Jun, *blank.*

#872: Robert CHAREL? B, 17 Jun, *blank.*
#873: Rebecca SHARP, B, Newtown Barracks, 18 Jun, *blank.*
#874: A Spaniard, name unknown, C, died in the public hospital, 23 Jun, *blank.*
#875: Henry PATERSON, W, Barque *Fair Arcadian,* 25 Jun, *blank.*
#876: John Alexander HEMMETT, C, 28 Jun, *blank.*
#877: Mrs. E? *(or C?)* CARD? *(washed out,)* W, Newtown Barracks, 2 Jul, *blank.*

p. 132:
#878: Patience BROWN, B, 2 Jul, very old.
#879: Fred^k McBEAN, B, Newtown Barracks, 3 Jul, *blank.*
#880: Margaret MENZIES, W, 8 Jul, 18 months.
#881: John MASON, B, Freetown, 10 Jul, 14 years.
#882: Peter CHILD, B, Newtown Barracks, 19 Jul, *blank.*
#883: John CONNOR, C, 19 Jul, 5 months.
#884: Elizabeth BLAKE, W, Barque *Orestes,* 19 Jul, 35.
#885: Duncan CANNOR [*sic*], B, 20 Jul, 15 months.

p. 133:
#886: Laughlin McLEAN, W, Brig *Europa,* 24 Jul, *blank.*
#887: William TEWKSBURY, W, Barque *Orestes,* 27 Jul, *blank.*
#888: Nicholas CAMPBELL, C, Spanish Key, 28 Jul, *blank.*
#889: Cornelius MURPHY, W, 29 Jul, *blank.*
#890: Spanish Indian, name unknown, C, found drowned, 30 Jul, *blank.*
#891: Jose MARIA, C, 31 Jul, *blank.*
#892: Henry BALLARINE, C, 1 Aug, *blank.*
#893: Elizabeth COLQUHOUN, B, 2 Aug, *blank.*

p. 134:
#894: Patience ROBINSON, B, 2 Aug, *blank.*
#895: Mark Le CAS, B, Queen Charlotte Town, 5 Aug, *blank.*
#896: Mary PHILLIPS, C, 7 Aug, *blank.*
#897: Rose St. GERMAN, B, 8 Aug, *blank.*
#898: Robert GAMBLE, B, 9 Aug, 18 months.
#899: Catherine SAVERY, B, 10 Aug, 8 years.
#900: Jesse BURKE, B, 13 Aug, 70.
#901: John BECK, C, 14 Aug, 5 days.

p. 135:
#902: Richard SMITH, C, 15 Aug, 5 years.
#903: Moise St.VILLE, B, 16 Aug, *blank.*
#904: T. DURHAM, B, 17 Aug, *blank.*
#905: Nora HEWLETT, B, A. L.* 22 Aug, 20. *(*Apprentice Labourer.)*
#906: Maria BURNS, W, 24 Aug, aged.
#907: Averino, C, Peten, 31 Aug, 4.
#908: Lucas, B, 6 Sep, *blank.*
#909: Benjamin *washed out and illegible* 9 Sep, *blank.*

p. 136:
#*910:*   Pompey, B, A. L., 11 Sep, *blank.*
#*911:*   Adelaide VERNON, C, 13 Sep, *blank.* *(Wife of John HUGHES?)*
#*912:*   Joseph COLLINGS [*sic*] GRIGG, R. N., W, Special Magistrate, 13 Sep, *blank.*
#*913:*   Kate MONROE, B, A. L., 14 Sep, *blank.*
#*914:*   Raphael Antonio PANDI, C, 18 Sep, *blank.*
#*915:*   J. WILLIAMS, G. M. P, B, 21 Sep, *blank.*
#*916:*   Sarah WALKER GIBSON, C, 21 Sep, 5.
#*917:*   John TRABB [*sic*], B? 21 Sep, *blank.* *(= TRAPP)*

p. 137:
#*918:*   Matthias MEIGHAN, C, 22 Sep, *blank.*
#*919:*   Thomas HAGAN, W, late of Barque *Miriam & Jane,* 22 Sep, *blank.*
#*920:*   Isaac BURNELL, B, 25 Sep, *blank.*
#*921:*   Alick BURNELL, A. L, *color not given,* 25 Sep, *blank.*
#*922:*   Elizabeth SIDDEN, C, 25 Sep, *blank.* *(MI: Elizabeth SEDDONS GENTLE.)*
#*923:*   Manuel YNISTRELLA, C, 26 Sep. *blank.*
#*924:*   F. CHRISTIE, C, 28 Sep, *blank.*
#*925:*   QUARTERMASTER, C, Mosquito Shore, 29 Sep, *blank.*

p. 138:
#*926:*   Juan JOSE, C P, 29 Sep, *blank.*
#*927:*   Juan PEOQUINTO BORGES, B, 30 Sep, 1 year.
#*928:*   James GILL, C, 9 Oct, 3 years.
#*929:*   Ingoald [*sic*] CHRISTENSEN, W P, Norway, 5 Oct, *blank.*
#*930:*   Sarah CRUMP, C, Freetown, 5 Oct, *blank.*
#*931:*   Samuel GABOUREL, B, A. L., 8 Oct, *blank.*
#*932:*   John DOYLE, W, 14 Oct, *blank.*
#*933:*   William BYRON, W, 16 Oct, 17. *(Joint MI with brother.)*

p. 139:
#*934:*   William JOHNSON, W P, 16 Oct, *blank.* *(margin note:)* a Swede.
#*935:*   Terence CASSIDY, W, Newtown Barracks, 17 Oct, *blank.*
#*936:*   Anarichy? VERNEY, B, G. M. P., 21 Oct, *blank.*
#*937:*   James H. CARMICHAEL, W, 23 Oct, *blank.*
#*938:*   Isaac DARNALL, W, Brig *Lyon,* Scotland, 24 Oct, *blank.*
#*939:*   J. MIDDLEBURY, B, G. M. P., 25 Oct, *blank.*
#*940:*   Helen COFFIN, C, 25 Oct, 3.
#*941:*   Charlotte GIBSON, C, 25 Oct, 9 days.

p. 140:
#*942:*   Christian LONGSWORTH, C, 30 Oct, 20 months.
#*943:*   S. FRANON *(or FRANOIS?)* B, 31 Oct, *blank.*
#*944:*   Matilda CASSIDY, W, Newtown Barracks, 2 Nov, 6.
#*945:*   James BOWMAN, B, Freetown, 5 Nov, 9 days.

#946: J. FINDLING, B, G. M. P., Freetown, 8 Nov, *blank.*
#947: James BULL, C, 10 Nov, *blank.*
#948: Lydia FORBES, C, 10 Nov, 2.9
#949: Harriet PATINETT, C, 10 Nov, *blank.*

p. 141/142: *This number is overwritten. Dates indicate there is no missing page.*
#950: Jean AUGISTE, B P, Jail, 13 Nov, *blank.*
#951: Mary Elizabeth HAMPSHIRE, C, 13 Nov, 25. (MI: wife of W. E. Hampshire, 26.)
#952: Angelina JONES, B, 19 Nov, 19.
#953: G. DICK, B, G. M. P., 21 Nov, *blank.*
#954: Susan MYVETT, B, 28 Nov, about 22.
#955: Sam[l] JENKINS, B, Craboo Ridge, 2 Dec, *blank.*
#956: Benjamin CROFT, C, 6 Dec, about 38 years.
#957: James CHAPMAN QUILTER, W, 7 Dec, 33.

p. 143:
#958: Jane HINKS, B, 13 Dec, *blank.*
#959: Quashaba CUNNINGHAM, B, 13 Dec, *blank.*
#960: Dick, B, 14 Dec, *blank.*
#961: John BOND, B, Newtown Barracks, 16 Dec, *blank.*
#962: Campbell AUGUST, B, A. L., 19 Dec, *blank.*
#963: James WHITEHEAD, B, 20 Dec, 1 month.
#964: Anancio CHANN, B, 27 Dec, *blank.*
#965: Clarissa SAVERY, *illegible,* 27 Dec, 3 years.

p. 144:
#966: Jupiter, B, 28 Dec, *blank.*
#967: Joseph Gabriel GONZALES, C, abode unknown, 29 Dec, *blank.*
#968: Jose Maria CHARVIS, C P, 31 Dec, *blank.*
#969: John JOHNSON, C, 31 Dec, *blank.*
#970: Daniel McAULAY, B, 31 Dec, *blank.*
#971: Betsy, B, 31 Dec, 7 days.

Burials in 1836:

#972: Jose NARCISSA, C P, 1 Jan, *blank.*
#973: Catherine Elizabeth GIBSON, *illegible,* 4 Jan, *blank.*

p. 145:
#974: Benjamin GROVES, W, Brig *Belize,* 5 Jan, 25.
#975: Jose MARCELLO, C P, 6 Jan, *blank.*
#976: Primus, B, A. L., 6 Jan, *blank.*
#977: Hamlet POTTS, B, 7 Jan, *blank.*
#978: LANGDON DWYER, W, 8 Jan, *blank.*
#979: Manuel? JOSE, C P, 13 Jan, *blank.*

#980: George WALKER, W P, 18 Jan, *blank.*
#981: Mary FRANCIS, *illegible,* 18 Jan, 3 days.

p. 146:
#982: John JOHNSON, W, 22 Jan, about 50.
#983: Bebian? PETER, B, 29 Jan, 70.
#984: Betsy LANG, B, Queen Charlotte Town, 4 Feb, *blank.*
#985: Eliza GIBSON, C, 4 Feb, *blank.*
#986: Henrietta POTTER, C, 5 Feb, *blank.*
#987: Aberdeen BELILE, B, 8 Feb, very old.
#988: Joseph MYVETT, B, 12 Feb, child.
#989: Rebecca JAY, *illegible,* 13 Feb, child. (1835 census #115: Rebecca JAYE, B.)

p. 147:
#990: Joseph VERNON, C, 13 Feb, *blank.*
#991: Augusta LAWRIE, C, 15 Feb, *blank.*
#992: Grace THOMSON, B, 22 Feb, *blank.*
#993: George SHEPARD, W, Schooner Isabella, 26 Feb, *blank.*
#994: Thomas BROSTER, B, A. L. 29 Feb, *blank.*
#995: John HURN, B A. L., 2 Mar, *blank.*
#996: John DAVIS, W, 4 Mar, *blank.*
#997: Juana, a Spanish child, 6 Mar, *blank.*

p. 148:
#998: Phoebe, B P, A. L., 9 Mar, *blank.*
#999: John O'CONNOR, W, 8 Mar, *blank.*
#1000: John LOCK, B, 12 Mar, *blank.*
#1001: Mary WILLIAMS, C, 12 Mar, *blank.*
#1002: Venus MIDDLETON, B, 15 Mar, *blank.*
#1003: Guy HUNT, B, Queen Charlotte Town, 18 Mar, *blank.*
#1004: *Blank* B, 18 Mar, *blank.*
#1005: Mary FLOWERS, B, 18 Mar, 49.

p. 149:
#1006: Edward POTTS, B, 21 Mar, 1 day.
#1007: James CROZIER, *blank,* 24 Mar, *blank.* (1832 census: James H. Crozier, W.)
#1008: David WHITE, B, 27 Mar, 11 days.
#1009: Benjamin BENNETT, *blank,* A. L., 16 Apr, *blank.*
#1010: Lucy BOLT, C, 2 May, *blank.*
#1011: William HARRIS, *illegible,* 7 May, *blank.*
#1012: Margaret PERRY, *illegible,* 19 May, *blank.*
#1013: Jose CAPAH? *illegible* 23 May, 18.

p. 150:
#1014: Jane HALL, B, 24 May, *blank.*
#1015: John, B, 6 Jun, 5 years.

#1016: John DARLING, G. M. P., 10 Jun, *blank.*
#1017: Willm LUCAS, W, 13 Jun, *blank.*
#1018: Lennon WILSON, B, A. L., 14 Jun, *blank.*
#1019: Rose, P, Freetown, 15 Jun, *blank.*
#1020: Robert TUCKER, B, 16 Jun, 7 days.
#1021: Rosette CADET, B, Queen Charlotte Town, 18 Jun, *blank.*

p. 151:
#1022: Jose, B, 24 Jun, 4 years.
#1023: Name unknown, B? P, 26 Jun,
#1024: John MITCHEL, C, 26 Jun, 6 months.
#1025: Maria GRANT, B, 1 Jul, 6 years.
#1026: Bill, P, 6 Jul, *blank.*
#1027: John DIXON TINA, B, 12 Jul, *blank.*
#1028: George *washed out – possibly blank,* B, 15 Jul, *blank.*
#1029: John IRVING, Brig *Susan,* 16 Jul, *blank.*

p. 152:
#1030: Elizabeth AGNEW, W, 18 Jul, 35.
#1031: *Blank,* W, Schooner *Henry,* 20 Jul, *blank.*
#1032: Lucy PASLOW, B, 23 Jul, 83.
#1033: John Leslie GREYSON, C, 2 Aug, 9 days.
#1034: John COX, W, Dragger *Eliza,* 2 Aug, *blank.*
#1035: James HEMSLEY, C, 9 Aug, 6 days.
#1036: Felix, C, 12 Aug, *blank.*
#1037: Maria GRAMIZES, C, 14 Aug, *blank.*

p. 153: *In the first three entries, color is not given.*
#1038: Lucas, P, abode unknown, 15 Aug, *blank.*
#1039: Spaniard, name unknown, abode unknown, 15 Aug, *blank.*
#1040: Mary MARTIN, A. L., 19 Aug, *blank.*
#1041: Leonard BYRON, W, 20 Aug, *blank. (Joint MI with brother.)*
#1042: James GARBUTT, C, 20 Aug, 3 years.
#1043: Henry WHITE, W, Brig *Mary Ann,* 23 Aug, *blank.*
#1044: *Blank,* 26 Aug, *blank. In the margin:* X
#1045: Philip OXLEY, W, Mate of Barque *Hecule?* 26 Aug, *blank.*
        The Newcastle Journal gives his age as 42 and names the ship as the Herald.
p.154:
#1046: Maria, 26 Jul, *blank. In the margin:* +
#1047: *Blank,* 26 Jul, *blank. In the margin:* +
#1048: Mustapha MULLINS, B, 27 Aug, *blank.*
#1049: Joseph MILES, B, 27 Aug, *blank.*
#1050: George Henry LeGEYT, W, 28 Aug, *blank.*
#1051: Robert JONES, B, 28 Aug, 21, *blank.*
#1052: Francis GADDIS, B, 28 Aug, *blank.*
#1053: Susanna BENNETT, B, 28 Aug, *blank.*

p. 155:
#*1054:* *Blank,* A. L., 29 Aug, *blank.*
#*1055:* Betsy JAMES, A. L., 30 Aug, *blank.*
#*1056:* James McGENNETT, W, 1 Sep, *blank.*
#*1057:* John Maurice CUNNINGHAM, C, 6 Sep, *blank.*
#*1058:* John MENZIES, W, 2 Sep, 20 *(or 26?)*
#*1059:* James WILLIAMS, C, 14 Sep, 3.
#*1060:* Elizabeth FORBES, C, 16 Sep, child.
#*1061:* Robert WALDRON, B? 17 Sep, *blank.*

p. 156:
#*1062:* Joshua GABOUREL, C, 18 Sep, *blank.*
#*1063:* Colin McARTHER, W, 19 Sep, *blank.*
#*1064:* James SPINKS, B, 21 Sep, *blank.*
#*1065:* Joseph VERNON, C, 23 Sep, *blank.*
#*1066:* Elizabeth SMITH, W, 2 Oct, 3 months.
#*1067:* Frederick COFFIN, W, 4 Oct, *blank.*
#*1068:* Georgiana COX, W, Isle of Wight, 6 Oct, *blank.*
#*1069:* B....aparte, 7 Oct, *blank.* *(= Buonaparte?)*

p.157:
#*1070:* Henry BURNAN, C, 7 Oct, *blank.*
#*1071:* Spaniard, name unknown, C, abode unknown, 10 Oct, *blank.*
#*1072:* Juana ARBISA, C, 13 Oct, 26.
#*1073:* Jeter SMITH, B, A. L., 16 Oct, *blank. (Peter with unlooped P?)*
#*1074:* Thomas MILLER, W, 16 Oct, 32.
#*1075:* *Blank* MILES, W, Government Schooner, 18 Oct, *blank.*
#*1076:* Samuel RABATEAU, C, 19 Oct, 6 weeks.
#*1077:* Salome, C P, 20 Oct, *blank.*

p. 158:
#*1078:* David CUMMING, W, 20 Oct, *blank.*
#*1079:* *Blank* ALEXANDER, W, 22 Oct, *blank.*
#*1080:* Francis DYER, C, 23 Oct, 13 months.
#*1081:* Joanna CARD, B, 24 Oct, 56.
#*1082:* William LOCKWARD, C, 24 Oct, *blank.*
#*1083:* An Indian woman, name unknown, C, abode unknown, 28 Oct, *blank.*
#*1084:* Ann ROGERS, W, 9 Nov, 28 years.
#*1085:* Jane Harriet BEATTY, *illegible,* 10 Nov, *blank.*

p. 159:
#*1086:* Jane Elizabeth ARTHERS, C, 12 Nov, 2 years.
#*1087:* Maria BAILY, B, 12 Nov, aged.
#*1088:* Lydia ERSKINE, C, 18 Nov, *blank.*
#*1089:* *Blank,* ERSKINE, C, 18 Nov, infant.

#*1090:* Jane BIRD, B, A. L., 19 Nov, *blank.*
#*1091:* Manuel PASTON, P, 22 Nov, *blank.*
#*1092:* Seaman, name unknown, W P, 26 Nov, *blank.*
#*1093:* P?........a? *washed out* CARD, C, 28 Nov, *blank.*

p. 160:
#*1094:* Eliza MILES, C, 7 Dec, 2 years.
#*1095:* Joann *(or Joana?)* DOMINGUEZ, B, 10 Dec, 3 years.
#*1096:* Willm BIBBY, B, 10 Dec, *blank.*
#*1097:* Michael A. HERON, W, 11 Dec, *blank.*
#*1098:* Alexander FRANCE, *illegible,* P, 11 Dec, *blank.*
#*1099:* William LAUGHTON, W, Brig *Nestor,* 12 Dec, *blank.*
#*1100:* Elizabeth JACOBS SUSMEIZEN, W, 16 Dec, 70? *(0 uncertain.)*
#*1101:* Jane SUTHERLAND, C, 16 Dec, 75.

p. 161:
#*1102:* Walter WALTERS, W P, 23 Dec, *blank.*
#*1103:* Susanna CROPPER, B, 25 Dec, *blank.*
#*1104:* Elizabeth Ann GOUGH, W, 25 Dec, 7.
#*1105:* Thomas WILSON JENNINGS, C, 29 Dec, *blank.*
#*1106:* Jose, B, 30 Dec, *blank.*
#*1107:* William GILL, C, 31 Dec, 7 months.

Burials in 1837:

#*1108:* Joseph Charles JOYNER, W, 1 Jan, 4 years
#*1109:* George HYDE, C? 1 Jan, *blank.*

p. 162:
#*1110:* Juan SANDERS, B, 2 Jan, *blank.*
#*1111:* John SPROAT, B, 3 Jan, *blank.*
#*1112:* Maria JOYNER, W, 4 Jan, 39.
#*1113:* Batty SPROAT, B, 4 Jan, *blank.*
#*1114:* Richard WARDLOW, C, 10 Jan, 7 months. *(MI: Son of Richard & Georgiana.)*
#*1115:* Sancho, B, A. L., 13 Jan, *blank.*
#*1116:* Manuel MORAZON, 13 Jan, 15.
#*1117:* El... TILLETT, 13 Jan, *blank. (MI: aged 52; names Elizabeth's 6 children.)*

p. 163:
#*1118:* Robert DOUGLAS, W, 16 Jan, 60.   *(This family came from Scotland.)*
#*1119:* Samuel HOWARD, W, 22 Jan, *blank.*
#*1120:* John ALLEN, B, 26 Jan, *blank.*
#*1121:* Abigail HENSLEY, B, 29 Jan, 71.
#*1122:* Margaret GENIOUS, 1 Feb [*sic*], 39.
#*1123:* Betsy GOFF, B, 30 Jan [*sic*], *blank.*

#1124: Ellen FITZGERALD, W, 30 Jan [*sic*], *blank.*
#1125: Chas JEFFRIES, *illegible,* 8 Feb, *blank.*

p. 164:
#1126: Fanny SPENCER, W, Mullins River, 15 Feb, very old.
#1127: Frank HYDE, B, A. L., 16 Feb, *blank.*
#1128: Jose AVARIZA, C, 18 Feb, 6 months.
#1129: Margaret GRANT, B, 18 Feb, *blank.*
#1130: Mrs. Mc`LEAN, B, Freetown, 20 Feb, aged.
#1131: Margaret McSWEENY, W, 21 Feb, 4.
#1132: Mary WALLIS, W, 24 Feb, 48. *blank.*
#1133: Su.......h LYNCH, C, 25 Feb, *blank.* *(Susannah?)*

p. 165:
#1134: James AUGUST, W, 27 Feb, *blank.*
#1135: Santiago LOPEZ, W, Central America, 6 Mar, *blank.*
#1136: David TWEENY, W P, 8 Mar, *blank.*
#1137: Elizabeth, B, Queen Charlotte, 9 Mar, *blank.*
#1138: William UTER, C, 10 Mar, 3 weeks.
#1139: Emma COOKE, W, 14 Mar, infant. *(b. 9 Mar to W.R S. & Emma Byron Cooke.)*
#1140: Chefa JOSEPA MAYAN, *(MAYAN in name column)* abode Belize, B, 17 Mar,
#1141: *Washed out and illegible,* 17 Mar, 2?

p. 166:
#1142: *Blank,* W P, 23 Mar, *blank.*
#1143: John HULL, W, *abode left blank,* 26 Mar, *blank.*
#1144: Thomas GIDDY, B, 29 Mar, *blank.*
#1145: Fidelia LOWLY, B, 31 Mar, *blank.*
#1146: Benjamin Jas.? POTTS, B, 31 Mar, *blank.*
#1147: George WHITNEY, C, 5 Apr, 2 days.
#1148: Fanny MOODY, B, 5 Apr, *blank.*
#1149: Georgiana *illegible,* 7 Apr, 5?

p. 167:
#1150: Catherine SLUSHER, B, 14 Apr, *blank.*
#1151: Edward ELGAR, B, 17 Apr, 2.
#1152: A Spaniard, name unknown, B, died in Public Hospital, 20 Apr, *blank.*
#1153: Eleanor POTTS, B, 21 Apr, *blank.*
#1154: Clarissa POTTS, B, 21 Apr, *blank.*
#1155: Quashie KEEFFE, B, A. L , 26 Apr, *blank.*
#1156: Executed for murder, C, 26 Apr, *blank.*
#1157: *Washed out and illegible,* 29 Apr, *blank.*

p. 168:
#1158: Elizabeth HEWLETT, W, 30 Apr, *blank.*
#1159: Sally STEWART, B, Freetown, 13 May, *blank.*

#1160: Quamina EDWARDS, B, Queen Charlotte Town, 13 May, *blank.*
#1161: Dido LAMB, B, 14 May, *blank.*
#1162: Olive, B, 14 May, *blank.*
#1163: Fanny DeBRIEN, C, 27 May, *blank.*
#1164: Catherine PITTS, *illegible,* 28 May, 17.
#1165: M.... *illegible* BAYNTUN, 1 May [*sic*], *blank.*

p. 169:
#1166: Charlotte WAGNER, B, 4 Jun, *blank.*
#1167: Louisa WOLFENSTEIN, W, 6 Jun, *blank.*
#1168: Elizabeth CONNOR, C, 12 Jun, 3 days.
#1169: *blank* JACKSON, W, 15 Jun, *blank.*
#1170: John JOHNSON, W, 19 Jun, *blank. (Caledonian Mercury: Esq., merchant.)*
#1171: William SMITH, B, 29 Jun, *blank.*
#1172: Spaniard named Jose ELIAS, B P, Hospital, 30 Jun, *blank.*
#1173: Edward? BROASTER, *illegible,* 2 Jul, *blank.*

p. 170:
#1174: Willm Mc`CULLOCH, C, 2 Jul, *blank.*
#1175: Willm WARRIOR, B, 2 Jul, very old.
#1176: Samuel HOFFMAN, W, Barque *Calcutta,* 16 Jul, *blank.*
#1177: Catherine ROBINSON, W, 17 Jul, 82.
#1178: Martha ARMSTRONG, W, 14 [*sic*] Jul, *blank.*
#1179: Spanish child, B, 19 Jul, *blank.*
#1180: Charles, an African, B, 24 Jul, *blank.*
#1181: John BARROW, *illegible,* 25 Jul, *blank.*

p. 171:
#1182: Found dead, name of the man unknown, B P, abode unknown, 31 Jul, *blank.*
#1183: William Mc`KENZIE, W, Cutter *Elizabeth,* 2 Aug, *blank.*
#1184: Modest GIDEON, B, Queen Charlotte, 6 Aug, *blank.*
#1185: Priscilla, B, 7 Aug, 7 months.
#1186: Pensioner, name not returned, B, buried at Barracks, 8 Aug, *blank.*
#1187: Catherine CONALLY, W P, 12 Aug, *blank.*
#1188: John RAMSAY, B? 13 Aug, *blank.*
#1189: Spaniard, *illegible,* Truxillo, 20 Aug, *blank.*

p. 172:
#1190: London, A. L. 22 Aug, *blank.*
#1191: Ohanio CORDERO, B P, 26 Aug, *blank.*
#1192: Pedro MALACHI, B P, 27 Aug, *blank.*
#1193: Spanish woman, name unknown, B, abode *blank,* 27 Aug, *blank.*
#1194: Rebecca SMITH, W, 29 Aug, 18.
#1195: ----- TAYLOR, W, died in the Pub' Hosp., 15 [*sic*] Aug, *blank.*
#1196: John JOSEPH, C, 1 Sep, 2 days.
#1197: Pensioner? *washed out and illegible,* Newtown   9 Sep

p. 173:
#*1198:* John POLLARD, B, 9 Sep, *blank.*
#*1199:* James HENRY, Brig *Davida Witton,* 9 Sep, *blank.*
#*1200:* Ellen MEATHER [*sic*], C, 10 Sep, *blank. (Dau. Geo. Mather & Eliz. Courtney?)*
#*1201:* Louisa LAWRIE, C. 15 Sep, 45.
#*1202:* Michael CARTY, W, 16 Sep, *blank.*

Note: Was this the drunken brute whose vicious abuse of a slave girl became a cause célèbre for the abolition movement? Or his son? Or another man of the same name?

#*1203:* Lewis McLENAN, W. 18 Sep, *blank.*
#*1204:* James MAJOR ROGERS, W, 21 Sep, *blank.*
#*1205: Washed out and illegible,* 21 Sep, *blank.*

p. 174:
#*1206:* James TURNER CASSIDY, W, Newtown Barracks, 24 Sep, child.
#*1207:* Andrew HUME, B, 26 Sep, child.
#*1208:* Otway, B, A. L., 27 Sep, *blank.*
#*1209:* John THOMSON, W, Barque *Caleb Angus,* 3 Oct, *blank.*
#*1210:* Name unknown, W P, found dead, 4 Oct, *blank.*
#*1211:* David SHAW, B, Newtown Barracks, 4 Oct, *blank.*
#*1212:* Mary Jane GILCRIST, W, 7 Oct, *blank.*
#*1213:* Scipio SPROAT, A L., 11 Oct, *blank.*

p. 175:
#*1214:* Rose SPROAT, B, 12 Oct, aged.
#*1215:* John H. FLOWERS, B, 14 Oct, *blank.*
#*1216:* A Gov't Mil'y Pensioner, B, name not given, 15 Oct, *blank.*
#*1217:* A Gov't Mil'y Pensioner, B, name not given, 16 Oct, *blank.*
#*1218:* George WAIGHT, alias WHITE, B, A. L., 19 Oct, *blank.*
#*1219:* Mary BENNETT, B, A. L., 19 Oct, *blank.*
#*1220:* James R? LIVINGSTONE, W, 31 Oct, *blank.*
#*1221: Illegible* HENRY, *illegible,* 4 Nov, *blank.*

p. 176:
#*1222:* William CRAIG, B, 7 Nov, *blank.*
#*1223:* Susanna DUNCANETTE, B, A. L., 14 Nov, *blank.*
#*1224:* Louis AUDINET, B, 17 Nov, *blank.*
#*1225:* James STAIN, C, 19 Nov, *blank.*
#*1226:* Duncanette CAMPBELL, B. 19 Nov, *blank.*
#*1227:* Francis LONG, B, 19 Nov, 3.
#*1228:* Ann DAVIS, B, 24 Nov, 1 month.
#*1229: Illegible* WILLIAMS, *illegible,* 26 Nov, *blank.*

p. 177:
#*1230:* Francisco SILVERRIA, B, 28 Nov, 18 months.

#1231: Edward John EAGLETON, W, 29 Nov, *blank*.
#1232: Susanna SIMPERT *(or LIMPERT?)* B, 1 Dec, 13 months.
#1233: William BOWMAN, B, 12 Dec, 9.
#1234: Sarah RENNY DeSOURCE, 15 Dec, 7. (1835 census p. 35: Sarah REMIE.)
#1235: A Gov't Mil'y Pensioner, name not returned, B, Queen Charlotte Town, 19 Dec, *blank*.
#1236: Juan, B, Central America, 20 Dec, *blank*.
#1237: JACKSON, *illegible,* Newtown Barracks, 22 Dec, *blank*.

p. 178:
#1238: Susanna, illegible, 23 Dec, infant.
#1239: ----- SMITH [*sic*], W P, 23 Dec, *blank*.   *(Mother and child?)*
#1240: Lucas NUNN? B, Newtown Barracks, 26 Dec,
#1241: Joe KEENE, B, 27 Dec, *blank*.

Burials in 1838:

#1242: Betsy MONDAY, B, 2 Jan, *blank*.
#1243: Juan KENNER? *(or KENNIE?)* C, 3 Jan, *blank*.
#1244: John DEERE, W, Brig *Lois,* 5 Jan, about 20.
#1245: Francisco SEGUNDE, B? 6 Jan, *blank*.

p. 179:
#1246: Mary Anne HOWARD, W, 6 Jan, *blank*.
#1247: Rachel BRIEN, B, 7 Jan, *blank*.
#1248: Frank MEIGHAN, B, A. L., 9 Jan, *blank*.
#1249: GONDISCOURT, Newtown Barracks, 10 Jan, *blank*.
#1250: Andrew NEELE, W, 10 Jan, *blank*.
#1251: Charlotte MOFFIT, W, Fort George, 3 years.
#1252: Margaret CUMMINGS, B, 15 Jan, *blank*.
#1253: George? PATINETT, C, 21 Jan, infant.

p. 180:
#1254: James GARNETT, B, 26 Jan, *blank*.
#1255: Mary McMANUS, W, 26 Jan, 40.
#1256: A Gov't Mil'y Pensioner, name not returned, B, 29 Jan, *blank*.
#1257: Orlando SUTTLE, W, 30 Jan, *blank*.
#1258: George MOODIE, C, 3 Jan, [*sic*], 6.
#1259: James RUMBOD [*sic*], C, 6 Feb, *blank*. *(= RUMBOLD)*
#1260: A Gov't Mil'y Pensioner, Newtown Barracks, 6 Feb, *blank*.
#1261: Mary PITT, *illegible,* 7 Feb, *blank*.

p. 181:
#1262: Tom HEWLETT, B, A. L., 8 Feb, *blank*.
#1263: Peter ANDERSON, B, A. L., 11 Feb, *blank*.

#1264: John MIDDLETON, B, 11 Feb, *blank*.
#1265: John GIBSON, B, 14 Feb, *blank*.
#1266: Christian THOMAS, C, 15 Feb, infant.
#1265: A pensioner, name not returned, B? 19 Feb, *blank*.
#1268: George GIBSON, B, 21 Feb, *blank*.
#1269: Adam, B, 22 Feb, *blank*.

p. 182:
#1270: William Henry HANSEN, W, Barque *Wanstead*, 26 Feb, *blank*.
#1271: London, B, A. L., 27 Feb, *blank*.
#1272: George HEOMITAYO [*sic*], W, barque *Lotus*, 28 Feb, 12.
#1273: Joseph MILES, B. 3 Mar, infant.
#1274: John VERRYHAN? C, 4 Mar, *blank*.
#1275: Laurence, B, 4 Mar, *blank*.
#1276: Catherine Patricia WHEELER, W, 4 Mar, 34.
#1277: Charles MUCKLEHANY, B, 6 Mar, *blank*.

p. 183: *The page number has been overwritten in ink*, 186.
#1278: Keith CATTO, B, 6 Mar, *blank*.
#1279: Mary USHER, B, A. L., 7 Mar, *blank*.
#1280: Choucoo *(or Choncos?)* BENNETT, B, 9 Mar, from 95 to 100 years old.

Note: Was Choucoo or Choncos an African tribal name, pointing to this man's birthplace?

#1281: William WHITE, B, 9 Mar, *blank*.
#1282: Rose FITZGIBBON, B, 9 Mar, 9 months.
#1283: Stephen STAIN, C, 10 Mar, 57.
#1284: Mary ROBINSON, W, 11 Mar, *blank*.
#1285: Frederick *illegible*, W. 12 Mar, *blank*.

p. 184:
#1286: Deborah NEWMAN, B, 13 Mar, 2, *blank*.
#1287: John GLASS, B, 15 Mar, infant.
#1288: George HEWLETT, B. 15 Mar, 7.
#1289: Ann TOOTH, W, 15 Mar, *blank*.
#1290: Gov't Mil'y Pensioner, B, Newtown Barracks, 18 Mar, *blank*.
#1291: Simon TAYLOR ANDERSON, W, 19 Mar, *blank*.
#1292: Lucia BEDHILL, B, 22 Mar, 2 months.
#1293: Catherine FRANCIS, *illegible*, 25 Mar, 18 months.

p. 185:
#1294: Henry GRANT, B, 26 Mar, *blank*.
#1295: William ROGERS, B, 6 Apr, 30.
#1296: James GOOLBURN, W, England, 6 Apr, *blank*.
#1297: Baptiste ROUQUE', W, 10 Apr, 27.

#1298: John HOOKER, C P, 11 Apr, *blank.*
#1299: Lucretia BILLERY, B, 21 Apr, infant.
#1300: Maria WADE, B, 24 Apr, *blank.*
#1301: John WARREN, B, 27 Apr, *blank.*

p. 186:
#1302: Victoriana MENDOZA, C, 27 Apr, *blank.*
#1303: John LAING, W P, 29 Apr,
#1304: Pensioner, name not given, *blank,* 30 Apr, *blank.*
#1305: Eliza NEAL *(or NEALE?)* B, I May, *blank.*
#1306: Jane ANDERSON, B, 1 May, *blank.*
#1307: Pedro ALCANTRA, B, 1 May, 4 months.
#1308: Prince HYDE, B, 4 May, *blank.*
#1309: Clarissa PASLOW, C, 4 May, *blank. (Widow of Thomas Paslow. See MI.)*

p. 187:
#1310: John H. PETZOLD, W, 4 May, *blank.*
#1311: Sabrina ELRINGTON, B, 5 May, *blank.*
#1312: Peggy HYDE, B, 11 May, *blank.*
#1313: Thomas DEYRUCHE', W, 15 May, about 21. *(= De RUCHE'.)*
#1314: Mary JONES, B P, G.M.? [sic], 15 May, *blank.*
#1315: Catherine CARROLL, W, 27 May, 47.
#1316: Benjamin WOLFENSTEIN, W, 27 May, *blank.*
#1317: Mary E. LEWIS, C, 1 Jun, *blank.*

p. 188:
#1318: Alfred YOUNG, C, 4 Jun, *blank.*
#1319: Michaela, a Spanish girl, 6 Jun, *blank.*
#1320: *Blank* ROBINSON, W, 8 Jun, *blank.*
#1321: Andrew, B, 16 Jun, *blank.*
#1322: John HOWARD alias COWARD, W, 24 Jun, *blank.*
#1323: Patience MOYER, B, 30 Jun, *blank.*
#1324: Mary WARRIOR, B, 2 Jul, *blank.*
#1325: Sally LESTER *(or LISTER?)* B P, 3 Jul, *blank.*

p. 189:
#1326: Pierre LOUIS, B P, 4 Jul, *blank.*
#1327: Ellen McARTHY, W P, 6 Jul, 5.
#1328: Dorinda HUME, B P, 6 Jul, *blank.*
#1329: Thomas BENNETT, B, 9 Jul, *blank.*
#1330: Mary McARTHY, W, 10 Jul, *blank.*
#1331: Ignetz WEIBELHAUSER, W, Germany, 10 Jul, *blank.*
#1332: John GIDEON, B, 18 Jul, 2 ½ years.
#1333: *Blank* MASON, W, 19 Jul, *blank.*

p. 190:
#*1334:* Charles MIDDLETON, W, 19 Jul, *blank.*
#*1335:* Maria PATRONA, C, 19 Jul, *blank.*
#*1336:* John McMANUS, W P, 26 Jul, *blank.*
#*1337:* Maria BURGESS, B, 26 Jul, *blank.*
#*1338:* Dominique LaCUSSAGNE, W, 27 Jul, *blank.*
#*1339:* Mary HAMILTON, B, 4 Aug, *blank.*
#*1340:* Francis HENRY, B, 8 Aug, *blank.*
#*1341:* Mary LYNCH, W, 11 Aug, *blank.*

p. 191:
#*1342:* Nancy, B P, 11 Aug, *blank.*
#*1343:* Philip VALPY, W, 12 Aug, 16.
#*1344:* John CARROLL, W, 13 Aug, 17.
#*1345:* William CARROLL, W, 16 Aug, 57.
#*1346:* George CARMICHAEL, C, 16 Aug, 7.
#*1347:* *Illegible* MURRAY, W P, 19 Aug, *blank.*
#*1348:* Joseph POTTS GIBSON, B, 20 Aug, 1 year.
#*1349:* James PRICE, W, 21 Aug, *blank.*

p. 192:
#*1350:* James JAMIESON, W, 21 Aug, *blank.*
#*1351:* Juan FARRO, W, 23 Aug, *blank.*
#*1352:* Elizabeth CARROLL, W P, 25 Aug, 19.
#*1353:* Frederick William MARTINY, W, 25 Aug, 38.
#*1354:* PHILIPS, W, 25 Aug, buried with Jewish Rites, *blank.*
#*1355:* Elizabeth CARROLL, W, 25 Aug. *(This entry crossed out.)*
          Interlined: Registered twice by mistake.
#*1356:* Rebecca MASKALL, W, 27 Aug, *blank.*
#*1357:* Eliza GALLIMORE, B, 27 Aug, *blank.*

p. 193:
#*1358:* Ann SWEENEY, W P, 28 Aug, *blank.*
#*1359:* James E. LaMOTTE, B, 31 Aug, *blank.*
#*1360:* Sam¹ HAWES, W P, 2 Sep, *blank.*
#*1361:* Emily JANNETT, C, 5 Sep, *blank.*
#*1362:* Jose MACCA NIASSA, W P, 8 Sep, *blank.*
#*1363:* Mary Ann WARREN, C, 9 Sep, *blank.*
#*1364:* Joshua BROSTER, C, 10 Sep, *blank.*
#*1365:* Sarah ERSKINE, C, 12 Sep, *blank.*

p. 194:
#*1366:* Elizabeth AGNER, W, 12 Sep, 14.
#*1367:* James HICKEY, B, 13 Sep, *blank.*
#*1368:* Richard ARNSTEL, C, 15 Sep, *blank.*
#*1369:* William QUILTER, C, 17 Sep, *blank.*

#1370:	Jose CUBOE, B, 21 Sep, *blank.*
#1371:	Success BAILEY, B, 21 Sep, *blank.*
#1372:	Sam¹ BAILEY, B, 30 Sep, *blank.*
#1373:	Margaret YOUNG, C, 30 Sep, *blank.*

p. 195:

#1374:	*Blank* NEEDHAM, W, 30 Sep, *blank.*
#1375:	Name not returned, P, 1 Oct, *blank.*
#1376:	Betsy HEWLETT, B, 6 Oct, 4 years.
#1377:	Eleanor PITKETHLY, C, 11 Oct, *blank.*
#1378:	John McGILL, W, Barque *Egyptian,* 14 Oct, *blank.*
#1379:	Violet SMITH, B, 24 Oct, aged.
#1380:	William GOW, W, 30 Oct, *blank.*
#1381:	Charles USHER, C, 30 Oct, *blank. (Son of John & Sarah. MI: aged 5.)*

p. 196:

#1382:	Charles ANDREWS, C, 3 Nov, 2.
#1383:	Margaret JAMISON WILLS, C, 3 Nov, 2.
#1384:	John LAWTON, W, Barque *Hebe,* 15 Nov, *blank. (MI: Captain, aged 49.)*
#1385:	John STAIN, C, 15 Nov, 18 months.
#1386:	Margaret TUCKER, B, 16 Nov, 2 ½ years.
#1387:	Mary Ann BROWN, C, 21 Nov, 15 months.
#1388:	Henry JOHNSON, W, 22 Nov, *blank.*
#1389:	John Alexander CROFT, C, 24 Nov, *blank.*

p. 197:

#1390:	Elizabeth CROFT, C, 24 Nov, *blank.*
#1391:	Sarah CURRANTS, B, 25 Nov, *blank.*
#1392:	John ALEXANDER, W, 25 Nov, *blank.*
#1393:	Peter ROBERTSON, W, 28 Nov, *blank.*
#1394:	Elizabeth TILLETT WADE, C, 28 Nov, *blank. (Dau. of R.F. or of W.A.Wade?)*
#1395:	Amelia BROSTER, B, 30 Nov, *blank.*
#1396:	John PANTING, C, 30 Nov, 9.
#1397:	Augustine, B, 1 Dec, *blank.*

p. 198:

#1398:	Aaron SARRY, B, an African, 3 Dec, *blank.*
#1399:	William CARR, B, Freetown, 5 Nov [*sic*], *blank.*
#1400:	James PORTER, W P, 6 Dec, *blank.*
#1401:	James MEIGHAN, C, 7 Dec, *blank.*
#1402:	Mary ELLIS, B, 14 Dec, *blank.*
#1403:	Mary AVILLA, B, 17 Dec, 6.
#1404:	*Blank* Pensioner, B, 17 Dec, *blank.*
#1405:	Sue BENNETT, B, 22 Dec, *blank.*

p. 199:

#*1406:* Stephen, B, 24 Dec, *blank.*
#*1407:* Mr. C. ERSKINE, W, Glasgow, 25 Dec, *blank.*
#*1408:* Jeremiah SPROAT, B, 29 Dec, 18.
#*1409:* Lucy EDWARDS, B. 30 Dec, *blank.*
#*1410:* Philip BENNETT, B, 30 Dec, *blank.*
#*1411:* William HEMMINGS, B, 31 Dec, *blank.*

Burials in 1839:

#*1412:* Edward FOX STRANGEWAY, W, Government House, 1 Jan, *blank.*
#*1413:* William ESTRADA, C, 4 Jan, 22.

p. 200:
#*1414:* Margaret HENDERSON, C, 6 Jan, 2 years.
#*1415:* William GENTLE, C, 9 Jan, *blank.*
#*1416:* Robert COLQUHOUN, C, 10 Jan, *blank.*
#*1417:* Venus, B, 10 Jan, *blank.*
#*1418:* Eliza BENNETT, B, 12 Jan, *blank.*
#*1419:* John FOREMAN, C, 19 Jan, *4 months.*
#*1420:* Quamina CARD, B, 20 Jan, *blank.*
#*1421:* Arthur ANDERSON, B, 20 Jan, *blank.*

p. 201:
#*1422:* Elizabeth THOMSON, B, 21 Jan, *blank.*
#*1423:* James LaFLEUR, B, Queen Charlotte Town, 22 Jan, 3.
#*1424:* George VITTORIA, B, 23 Jan, 14.
#*1425:* Elsee [*sic*] HUME, B, 23 Jan, *blank.*
#*1426:* Olive ARMSTRONG, B, 28 Jan, *blank.*
#*1427:* Isaac SIMONS, W, 30 Jan, 22.
#*1428:* Eleanor La ROI, B, 30 Jan, 23.
#*1429:* Peter, B, 4 Feb, *blank.*

p. 202:
#*1430:* Pablo JOSE, C, 7 Feb, 7 days.
#*1431:* John JAYE, B, Newtown Barracks, 7 Feb, *blank.*
#*1432:* Joseph UTER, C, 8 Feb, *blank.*
#*1433:* Jose, C, 15 Feb, *blank.*
#*1434:* John GAMBER, B, Newtown Barracks, 18 Feb, *blank.* *(= GAMBOA?)*
#*1435:* Erskine Maria CATO, C, 18 Feb, *blank.*
#*1436:* Adam, an African, B, 18 Feb, *blank.*
#*1437:* Jose Maria MARTINEZ, Campeachy, *23 Feb, 54.*

p. 203:
#*1438:* Ann GENTLE, C, 25 Feb, *blank.*

#*1439:* *Blank* BROWN, W P, 28 Feb, *blank.*
#*1440:* Catherine MEIGHAN, B P, 1 Mar, *blank.*
#*1441:* Mary Ann BENNETT, B P, 1 Mar, *blank.*
#*1442:* Maria Josepha NUFIO, B P, 2 Mar, *blank. Margin note:* a Spanish woman.
#*1443:* Phillipa MITCHEL, B, 3 Mar, *blank.*
#*1444:* Jane BAILEY, B, 6 Mar, 44.
#*1445:* George ..... *surname and color illegible,* 6 Mar, 10 days.

p. 204:
#*1446:* Betsy PASLOW, B, 6 Mar, *blank.*
#*1447:* James DAVIS, B, 8 Mar, *blank.*
#*1448:* Eleanor FACEY, B, 19 Mar, *blank.*
#*1449:* Jarvis SPRAY, C P, 21 Mar, *blank.*
#*1450:* Cupid ANDERSON, B P, 22 Mar, blank.
#*1451:* James GOFF, C, 22 Mar, *blank.*
#*1452:* Emma BLANCHFORD, C, 27 Mar, 12 days.
#*1453:* Robert TYLER, B, 29 Mar, *blank.*

p. 205:
#*1454:* Thomas CUNNINGHAM, W P, 1 Apr, *blank.*
#*1455:* John ANDERSON, W P, Barque *Ceylon,* 3 Apr, *blank.*
#*1456:* Juliana WILLIAMS, C, 4 Apr, 2 weeks.
#*1457:* John HILL, B P, 8 Apr, *blank.*
#*1458:* DOMINGUEZ, B P, 21 Apr, *blank.*
#*1459:* Janette GARBUTT, C, 27 Apr, 7.
#*1460:* Fanny WILLIAMS, B P, 6 May, *blank.*
#*1461:* Joseph *surname illegible,* W, 8 May, 36.

p. 206:
#*1462:* A Pensioner, B, Freetown, 10 May, *blank.*
#*1463:* William LEWIS, W, 10 May, *blank.*
#*1464:* William HEWLETT, B, 15 May, *blank.*
#*1465:* EGLEBY [*sic*] FRAZER, W P, 23 May, *blank.*
#*1466:* John McDONALD, W P, 26 May, *blank.*
#*1467:* Timothy HAYES, W, 26 May, 16.
#*1468:* Ann NEIL, B, 31 May, *blank.*
#*1469:* John STOREY, W, Barque *Mere,* 7 Jun, *blank.*

p. 207:
#*1470:* Francisco MENDOZA, C, Peten, 17 Jun, *blank.*
#*1471:* William WALKER, W, Barque *La Bonne Mere,* 17 Jun, *blank.*
#*1472:* Elmira MAXWELL, C, 18 Jun, *blank.*
#*1473:* James GIBDON (or GIBSTON?) W, Barque *Le Bonne Mere,* 1 Jun, *blank.*
#*1474:* Charlotte, B, 23 Jun, *blank.*
#*1475:* James RATCLIFF, W, 25 Jun, *blank.*

#1476: John ADAEAR [sic], W, 27 Jun, *blank.*
#1477: Secundino .....LER? *illegible,* 29 (Jun,) *blank.*

p. 208:
#1478: John WILLIAMS, W, Brig *Joseph Hume,* 1 Jul, *blank.*
#1479: Nancy HOARE, C, 1 Jul, 4 days, *blank.*
#1480: William ROGERS, C P, 5 Jul, *blank.*
#1481: Philip BAYLEY, B, 6 Jul, *blank.*
#1482: Sarah LYNCH, B, 7 *(this entry crossed out with large X' s.)*
#1483: Francisca, B P, 12 Jul, *blank.*
#1484: Mrs. BURTEY *(or BURTING?)* B, Freetown, 16 Jul, *blank.*
#1485: Francis *surname and color illegible,* 16 Jul, *blank.*

p. 209:
#1486: Swift, B, Freetown, 18 Jul, *blank.*
#1487: Fernando CATALAN, W, Truxillo, 20 Jul, *blank.*
#1488: Samuel SAMSON, B, 21 Jul, 9 days, *blank.*
#1489: John De BAPTISTE, C, 26 Jul, *blank.*
#1490: Sharper GRANT, B, 28 Jul, *blank.*
#1491: STRICKLAND, Gov't Mil'y Pens'r, 29 Jul, *blank.*
#1492: Alexander BRYNNER, W, 6 Aug, *blank.*
#1493: *Washed out and illegible,* Newtown *illegible,* 7 (Aug,) *blank.*

p. 210:
#1494: Isaak LEAH, W, 8 Aug, *blank.*
#1495: Eve HUGHES, B P, 18 Aug, *blank.*
#1496: Thomas WELSH, W, 18 Aug, *blank.*
#1497: Hannah Fushina [sic] O'GEERY, 22 Aug, 6 months. *(Faustinia, misspelled.)*
#1498: Elizabeth GIBSON, 22 Aug, *blank.*
#1499: Sarah GOODROW, C, 25 Aug, infant.
#1500: Conrand? HENDERSON, P B, 25 Aug, *blank.*
#1501: William *surname and colour washed out,* 29 Aug, *blank.*

p. 211:
#1502: William DAVY, W P, 6 Sep, *blank.*
#1503: William RHYS, 12 Sep, 9 days. *In margin:* X
#1504: Catherine PETZOLD, 19 Sep, C, *blank.*
#1505: Frances GRANT, B, 20 Sep, 6 days.
#1506: Betsy DUNN, C, 26 Sep, *blank.*
#1507: George LIBERTY, W, 27 Sep, *blank.*
#1508: John Henry WOOLMAN, W, 27 Sep, 17.
#1509: *Washed out, illegible,* 27 (Sep) *illegible.*

p. 212:
#1510: Jose JULITTE? C P, 29 Sep, *blank.*
#1511: John SMITH, W P, 2 Oct, *blank.*

67

#1512:   Marshall BENNETT, W, 4 Oct, *blank.*

Note: Baptized in 1763 at Sheffield, England, M. B. (Sr.) was a son of Thomas and Elizabeth Cooper Bennett, factors and merchants. He was in Jamaica by 1784, settled in Belize four years later, and became a wealthy merchant. He served as an officer in the militia and as a magistrate for many years, ending as Senior Magistrate and Chief Justice. He married Elizabeth Cooke in England in 1803 and had a son, Marshal Cooper Bennett, born in 1810, who died in 1814 in London. His will, probated in England, left his widow, who lived at Appley House on the Isle of Wight, an annuity, and made bequests to his brothers John and Charles, his nephews and grandnephews (some in Belize,) his lifelong friend and employee Charles Knoth, and Juta (= Juba,) a black woman who nursed him in old age. His obituary is given in the Belize Advertiser. Sadly, his tomb has not survived.

#1513:   Andrew BLYGH, B, 5 Oct, *blank.*
#1514:   George GRANT, B, 11 Oct, 14 months.
#1515:   Gov't Mil'y Pensioner, B, 12 Oct, *blank,*
#1516:   Philippe, C P, 12 Oct, *blank.*
#1517:   John HA...... *surname and color washed out,* 14 Oct, *illegible.*

p. 213:
#1518:   Jose MARIA, C P, 16 Oct, *blank.*
#1519:   George HYDE, B P, 16 Oct, *blank.*
#1520:   Nancy JEFFRIES, B, 17 Oct, *blank.*
#1521:   Juan JOSE, C P, 19 Oct, *blank.*
#1522:   Ramin, C P, 19 Oct, *blank.*
#1523:   Catherine DOUGLAS, B, 21 Oct, *blank.*
#1524:   Charles ABEL, B P, 22 Oct, *blank.*
#1525:   Philippe .... *washed out and illegible.*

p. 214:
#1526:   George BIDDOCK, W P, 22 Oct, *blank.*
#1527:   Juan MANUEL, W P, 23 Oct, *blank.*
#1528:   George MARTINY, B P, 30 Oct, *blank. (Drowned – see Belize Advertiser.)*
#1529:   Robert DUNSTAN, *color not given,* P, 2 Nov, *blank.*
#1530:   Michael CARROLL, W, 6 Nov, 22,
#1531:   Jane HART, W, 6 Nov, 17.
#1532:   George RICHARDSON, B, 10 Nov, *blank.*
#1533:   Thomas .... *washed out and illegible,* 10 Nov, *illegible.*

p. 215:
#1534:   John THOMSON, B, Newtown Barracks, 11 Nov, *blank.*
#1535:   Ralph WARDLOW, C, 11 Nov, 1 month.
#1536:   Jose MARCO, C P, 11 Nov, *blank.*
#1537:   William SMITH, W, 13 Nov, *blank.*
#1538:   John KELLY, B? 14 Nov, 3.
#1539:   Jose Maria GUIROLA, W, Guatimala, 17.

#1540: Philip RICHARDSON, B, 17 Nov, *blank.*
#1541: *Washed out and illegible,* 17 *(Nov,) illegible.*

p. 216:
#1542: Matthew QUAVE, W P, 18 Nov, *blank.*
#1543: Charles KNOTH, W, Central America, 22 Nov, *blank.*

Note: Charles Knoth and Marshal Bennett Sr. were both in Jamaica in 1784. Charles was enumerated in Marshal's household in censuses, had charge of his mine at Guayabillas in Honduras, and was an executor of his will. Charles died in Belize only a few weeks after his friend and employer passed away.

#1544: *Blank,* W, Barque *Elizabeth & Jane,* 22 Nov, *blank.*
#1545: *Blank,* W, Barque *Elizabeth & Jane,* 22 Nov, *blank.*
#1546: *Blank, abode blank,* 2? Nov, *blank.*
#1547: Andrew GALAGHER, W, 24 Nov, *blank.*
#1548 Charles CHAPMAN, W P, Brigantine *Alice,* 25 Nov, *blank.*
#1549: Jane S...... *washed out, illegible,* 29 *(Nov,) illegible.*

p. 217:
#1550: William WILLIAMSON, W, 3 Nov, *blank.*
#1551: James GARNETT, B P. 1 Dec, *blank.*
#1552: David SMITH, W, 1 Dec, 58.
#1553: Scotland RICHARDS, B, 4 Dec, *blank.*
#1554: Henry PRESTON, W P, 5 Dec, *blank.*
#1555: Maria PATTEN, W, Manatee Lagoon, 8 Dec, *blank.*
#1556: Juan IGLESIA, C P, 9 Dec, *blank.*
#1557: William .... *surname and color illegible,* Guatimala, 12 *(Dec,) blank.*

p. 218:
#1558: Charles GABOUREL, B P, 12 Dec, *blank.*
#1559: Jose LOCARIO, B P, 16 Dec, 7 days.
#1560: R. DARYLEMENT, B, G M. P., Newtown Barracks, 14 [sic] Dec, *blank.*
#1561: G. LIND, B, G. M. P., Newtown Barracks, 16 Dec, 7? *illegible.*
#1562: Edward, an African, B, 20 Dec, *blank.*
#1563: Manuel, C, 26 Dec, *blank.*
#1564: John GRANT, B, 30 Dec. *blank.*
#1565: William .... *surname and color illegible,* 31 *(Dec,) blank.*

Burials in 1840:

p. 219:
#1566: Benjamin MYVETT, B, 1 Jan, *blank.*
#1567: Manuel ROMARO, B P, 6 Jan, *blank.*
#1568 John BRADLEY, B, a Pensioner, 6 Jan, *blank.*

69

#1569: Daniel TILDESLY, W, 7 Jan, *blank.*
#1570: William Alexander CRAMMAND, C, 7 Jan, *blank. (Obit. in Belize Advertiser.)*
#1571: Mary GARRETT, B P, 7 Jan, *blank.*
#1572: William RABATEAU, C, 8 Jan, *blank.*
#1573: *Washed out, stained, mildewed and illegible,* 8 *(Jan,) illegible.*

Note: At some time in the past a hurricane breached the church; this register got wet, and in the aftermath was stood up and fanned out to dry. The center pages dried quickly, but the outer pages stayed damp longer. As moisture drained to the bottom, molds colonized the wet paper, causing stains and blackening. The pages at the back are by far the worst.

p. 220:
#1574: Ann MORRIS, W, 11 Jan, 31.
#1575: Daniel SPENCER, B, 13 Jan, *blank.*
#1576: William CRABB, C, 16 Jan, *blank.*
#1577: Fernando GOMEZ, C, 16 Jan, *blank.*
#1578: Diana TRAPP, B, 20 Jan, *blank.*
#1579: Judy TUCKER, B, 21 Jan, *blank.*
#1580: Jose Manuel BYAS, B, 22 Jan, *blank.*
#1581: Ruffien? *color illegible,* 24 Jan, *blank..*

p. 221:
#1582: William GABOUREL, C, 26 Jan, *blank.*
#1583: Glasgow, B P, 3 Feb, *blank.*
#1584: John DAY BETSON, W, 8 Feb, *blank.*
#1585: Matthew ERNEST, B, 12 Feb, *blank.*
#1586: Jose RUBEN, C P, 12 Feb, *blank.*
#1587: Jose ANTONIO, C, 21 Feb, *blank.*
#1588: James TOOLE, C, 25 Feb, *blank.*
#1589: G...... *washed out and illegible,* 26 *(Feb,) illegible.*

p. 222:
#1590: Maria Louise HENDERSON, C, 28 Feb, *blank.*
#1591: Jane HEWLETT, B, 6 Mar, 4.
#1592: Thomas MOON, W, 11 Mar, *blank.*
#1593: Barney, B P, 23 Mar, *blank.*
#1594: Maria JOSEPHA, C, 25 Mar, *blank.*
#1595: Manuel, C P, 29 Mar, *blank.*
#1596: Margaret GURNEY, B P, 9 Apr, *blank.*
#1597: *Mildewed and washed out,* 16 Apr, *illegible.*

p. 223:
#1598: Thomas CURRAN, W P, from the Brig *Penelope,* 24 Apr, *blank.*
#1599: *Blank* Gov't Mil' Pensioner, B, Freetown, 25 Apr, *blank.*
#1600: Mary PARK, B, 26 Apr, *blank.*
#1601: George COX, W, Brig *Penelope,* 28 Apr, 22.

#1602: John N. SMITH, W. American Schooner *Custer Braxton*, 4 May, *blank*.
#1603: James McARTHY, W P, Died in Hospital, from the Brig *Penelope*, 5 May, *blank*.
#1604: Michael COLEMAN. W P, From the Brig *Penelope*, 5 May, *blank*.
#1605: *Mildewed and washed out, 7 (May,) blank.*

p. 224:
#1606: Henry HUNT, W P, died in the Public Hospital, 12 May, *blank*.
#1607: Leah GEORGE, B, 14 May, *blank*.
#1608: James GANN [*sic*], W. 27 May, *blank*.
#1609: Mary MAGDELENE, B, 30 May, *blank*.
#1610: Robert PRIC [*sic*], B P, 6 Jun, *blank*. (= *PRICE.*)
#1611: William JOHN, B. G. M. P., 12 Jun, *blank*.
#1612: John FERGUSON. W P, 15 Jun, *blank*.
#1613: Thomas A. *illegible*, W P, Brig *illegible*, 17 Jun, *illegible*.

p. 225:
#1614: Thomas COX, W, 18 Jun, *blank*.
#1615: Elizabeth ANDERSON, B, 26 Jun, *blank*.
#1616: George GOREY, W, 29 Jun, about 29.
#1617: John BRITT, W P, 29 Jun, *blank*.
#1618: James CLEMENT, W P, *abode blank*, 2 Jul, *blank*.
#1619: ANESTECA [*sic*], C P, 3 Jul, *blank*.
#1620: Simon GRANT, B, 4 Jul, *blank*.
#1621: Edward *surname and color illegible*, 7 (*Jul*,) *illegible*.

p. 226:
#1622: Mary Ann SPROAT, W, 7 Jul, 25.
#1623: Elleaner [*sic*] GARBUTT, C, 7 Jul, *blank*.
#1624: Eve BARNARD, B, 9 Jul, *blank*.
#1625: Eleanor JAMES, B, 11 Jul, *blank*.
#1626: Margaret DYER, W P, 12 Jul, *blank*.
#1627: Samuel PERRY, B P, 17 Jul, *blank*.
#1628: Elizann? C P, 17 Jul, *blank*.
#1629: Thomas? MILLER? W P, 18 Jul, *illegible*.

p. 227:
#1630: Jacob RUST, W P. 18 Jul, *blank*.
#1631: Thomas EVANS, W P, 18 Jul, *blank*.
#1632: A Musquito Indian. name unknown, C P, Mosquito Nation, 19 Jul, *blank*.
#1633: Name unknown, C P, abode unknown, 19 Jul, *blank*.
#1634: Harriet HUGHES, B, Newtown Barracks, 19 Jul, *blank*.
#1635: Phillis BURGESS, C, 20 Jul, 10 days.
#1636: Lydia BULL, *illegible*, 22 Jul, *blank*.
#1637: Maria, a *illegible* Ind.... *illegible*, 24 Jul, *illegible*.

p. 228:
#1638: Juan MANUEL, C P, 26 Jul, *blank.*
#1639: Jose CABASAR, C, 27 Jul, *blank.*
#1640: George KENNY, W, Fort George, 28 Jul, *blank.*
#1641: Frederick FORBES, C, 29 Jul, *blank.*
#1642: John McGILLIVRAY, W P, *abode blank,* 1 Aug, *blank.*
#1643: John Mc`LEAN, W P, *abode blank,* 1 Aug, *blank.*
#1644: Jose PETRANA, *illegible, abode blank,* 1 Aug, *blank.*
#1645: Elizabeth *surname and color illegible,* 2 *(Aug,) age given but illegible.*

p. 229:
#1646: William GENTLE, C, 3 Aug, 29. *(MI in Yarborough Cemetery.)*
#1647: Ann MUSLAAR, W, 7 Aug, 7.
#1648: Janette GILLETT, C, Boom, 8 Aug, 4.
#1649: John SPIKES, B, G. M. P., Queen Charlotte Town, 8 Aug, *blank.*
#1650: *blank,* B, Newtown Barracks, 9 Aug, *blank.*
#1651: John WEATHERBY, W, Barque *Trinidad,* 9 Aug, *blank.*
#1652: Charles FAYARD? W? Brig *Britannia,* 9 Aug, *blank.*
#1653: *Mildewed, stained, washed out and illegible.*

p. 230:
#1654: Margaret GREEN, C, 11 Aug, *blank.*
#1655: Margaret STEWART, W P, 14 Aug, *blank.*
#1656: CHICHINACUS [*sic*], C P, 14 Aug, *blank.*
#1657: *Blank,* C P, 15 Aug, *blank.*
#1658: Alexander ABRAMS, C, 15 Aug, *blank.*
#1659: Eleanor LONGSWORTH, C, 15 Aug, 6.
#1660: Benjamin *surname and color illegible,* 16 Aug, *illegible.*
#1661: *Blackened and illegible.*

p. 231:
#1662: Name not known, C, 19 Aug, *blank.*
#1663: Susanna DYER, W P, New Liverpool Emigrant, 21 Aug, *blank.*
#1664: John CONNOR, W P, 28 Aug, *blank.*
#1665: Henry PARKER, W, Dragger *Eliza,* 29 Aug, *blank.*
#1666: Peter SCOTT, Brig *Netreach?* 31 Aug, *blank.*
#1667: Agnes OCHITA, C, 1 Sep, *blank.*
#1668: George MORRISON, W 3 Sep, 23.
#1669: *Blackened and illegible.*

p. 232:
#1670: Dorcas GABOUREL, B P, 10 Sep, *blank.*
#1671: *Blank,* MADDOC, W, 11 Sep, *blank.*
#1672: Thomas JAX, W, 12 Sep, *blank.*
#1673: James JOSEPH, B, Newtown Barracks, 13 Sep, infant.
#1674: Richard NELSON, B P, 13 Sep, *blank.*

#1675: Jose ANTONIO, C P, 17 Sep, *blank.*
#1676: Philip L. FANTISSY, *illegible,* 18 Sep, *age given but illegible.*
#1677: *Blackened and illegible.*

p. 233:
#1678: John BROWN, W P, died in the Public Hospital, 20 Sep, *blank.*
#1679: James LIBERTY, W, 23 Sep, *blank.*
#1680: Edward BERTIE, C, 23 Sep, 2 years and 9 months.
#1681: Mary HEMSLEY, C, 27 Sep, 3 days.
#1682: Alexander HOPE, B, Gov't Mil'y Pensioner, 2 Oct, *blank.*
#1683: Thomas LEE, W P, 6 Oct, *blank.*
#1684: Mary *surname and color illegible,* 6 Oct *blank.*
#1685: *Blackened and illegible. The surname starts with B. .*

p. 234:
#1686: Sarah BENNETT, C, 10 Oct, 10.
#1687: Henry BRENNAN, C, 15 Oct, 6.
#1688: ----- [*sic*] DICKSON, B P, 15 Oct, *blank.*
#1689: Benjamin McCOLLOCH, C, 18 Oct, child.
#1690: Selina Leonora DeBRIEN, C, 19 Oct, child.
#1691: Emma Lavinia CRAIG, C, 20 Oct, child.
#1692: Thomas –ICH-----, *illegible,* 21 Oct, *blank.*
#1693: *Blackened and illegible.*

p. 235:
#1694: Peter MOYER, C, 21 Oct, 3.
#1695: Elizabeth GARRETT, C, 22 Oct, 45.
#1696: Manuel, C P, 23 Oct, *blank.*
#1697: Daniel JONES, B, 24 Oct, 8.
#1698: James PORTER, *illegible or blank,* P, 25 Oct, *blank.*
#1699: Henry HICKEY, B, 29 Oct, aged.
#1700: *Blackened and illegible,* W, 2 Oct, *illegible.*
#1701: *Blackened and illegible.*

p. 236:
#1702: Ann YOUNG, C, 10 Nov, *blank. (Shopkeeper; wife of John W. WRIGHT, Esq.)*
#1703: Joseph GIBSON, B, 13 Nov, 6 days.
#1704: Elizabeth DUGARD, B, 25 Nov, child.
#1705: Frances ALEXANDER, C, 26 Nov, 1 year.
#1706: *Blank,* W, H. M. Ship *Comus,* 1 Dec, *blank.*
#1707: Elizabeth WADE, C, 1 Dec, 9. *(Whose daughter, Robert's or Williams?)*
#1708: *Blackened and illegible,* 1 Dec, *illegible.*
#1709: *Blackened and illegible.*

p. 237:
#1710: *Blank,* Gov't Mil'y Pensioner, B, 7 Dec, *blank.*

73

#*1711:*	Mary NEVILLE, B, 13 Dec, aged.
#*1712:*	Matilda Caroline BOWEN, C, 15 Dec, 29.
#*1713:*	William TWIGG, B, G. M. P., 18 Dec, *blank.*
#*1714:*	Deanna ARTHUR, B, 19 Dec, *blank.* *(Given name overwritten.)*
#*1715:*	Henry PASCAL, B, 25 Dec, *blank.*
#*1716:*	Richard PICKET, *illegible,* 25 Dec, *blank.*
#*1717:*	*Blackened and illegible.*

p. 238:
#*1718:*	Archibald LIDDELL, W, 28 Dec, infant.
#*1719:*	Robert BETSON, B, 28 Dec, *blank.*
#*1720:*	Thomas ALEXANDER, C, 30 Dec, 4 months.

Burials in 1841:

#*1721:*	PIMMELON, C, 1 Jan, *blank.*
#*1722:*	Mary Ann YARBOUROUGH [*sic*], B, 6 Jan, *blank.*
#*1723:*	Rose HYDE, B, 7 Jan, very aged.
#*1724:*	*Blackened and illegible.*
#*1725:*	*Blackened and illegible.*

p. 239:
#*1726:*	Ellen HAYES, C, 20 Jan, 8.
#*1727:*	Henry WHITNEY, C, 21 Jan, 3.
#*1728:*	Andrew BELL, W, 23 Jan, *blank.*
#*1729:*	John McLEOD, W, 28 Jan, *blank.*
#*1730:*	Edward TULLY, B, G. M. P., 1 Feb, *blank.*
#*1731:*	Thomas MORRIS, W P, 1 Feb, *blank.*
#*1732:*	Joseph .....S, *blackened and illegible,* W, 3 Feb, *blank.*
#*1733:*	*Blackened and illegible.*

p. 240:
#*1734:*	John LUIS, B, G. M. P., 12 Feb, *blank.*
#*1735:*	George CLARKE, C, 13 Feb [*sic*], *blank.*
#*1736:*	Ann HINCKS, B, Sibun Point, 3 Mar [*sic*], aged.
#*1737:*	John KNOT [*sic*] JENKINS, B, G. M. P., 4 Mar, *blank.* *(= KNOTH)*
#*1738:*	Ned EWING, B P, 5 Mar, aged.
#*1739:*	Elizabeth LeGEYT, 10 Mar, 6.
#*1740:*	*Blackened and illegible.* 18 Mar, 101 (or 104?)
#*1741:*	*Blackened and illegible.*

---o0o---

ST. GEORGE'S CAYE CEMETERY

The cemetery on St. George's Caye was a final resting place for two centuries and more before it filled up towards the end of the 19th century. The tombs and burials near the surface were washed away by storm surge in the hurricane of 1931; probing shows layers of mahogany coffins underneath. Selected inscriptions copied by John Purcell Usher at this and other cemeteries were published in 1907 as Memorial Inscriptions and Epitaphs: Belize, British Honduras. Dr. Thomas Gunn visited the caye in 1926 and described tombs in his book, Ancient Cities and Modern Tribes. In 1985 Mary Check-Pennell, a Peace Corps volunteer, compiled a history of the cemeteries. Dr. James Garber of Texas State University and Dr. Jaime J. Awe of the Institute of Archeology at Belmopan are conducting an archeological investigation at the site; Dr. Garber kindly gave the writer reports which include a plan made in 1872 by Rob Humes, locating and identifying tombs.

A map of "Caio Cosina," the Spanish name for St. George's Caye, made in 1764 and published in Cartografia de Ultramar in 1780, lists as residents Mrs. MAUD, Mr. GIEL (= GILL,) Mr. DOCIL (= GENTLE?) Mr. CAME; Dr. GALES, Capt. TOL, Mr. MACALE (= McAULAY,) Mr. HARRAL (= HARROLD,) Mr. SAM, Mr. MILIQUITA (a Spanish surname,) Mrs. MACQUINCE (= McKENZIE,) Mrs. GAROCI (= GRACE?) Mr. YISQUIBIS, Capt. HILL, Capt. REYT (= WRIGHT,) Mr. ORFIL (= ORGILL?) and Sr. RICALDE. The evacuation of the Shore brought more people to the caye; almost a hundred settlers taken prisoner when the Spanish attacked in 1779 and freed in 1784 are named in a petition now held at the British National Archives (CO/123/2.2 pp. 83-84.) It appears that most of the petitioners moved to town, as in August 1798, when the caye was evacuated and burned to prevent the Spanish from using it as a base to attack the settlement, Magistrates' Minutes name only seventeen residents who claimed for losses: Mary ARMSTRONG, Mary BATES, Charles BRITTEN, Estate of O'BRIEN, Mary BRYAN, Robert DOUGLAS, James EDWARDS, Ann GRACE, Joseph HINKS, James P. LAWRIE, Edward JONES, Leah McAULAY, John POTTS, Thomas POTTS, James USHER, Hugh WILSON, and Benjamin WORMEL. Many of these people and their families lived out their lives and were buried on the caye.

The following inventory combines information from Rob Humes' plan, St. John's burial registers, John Purcell Usher's transcripts, Dr. Thomas Gunn's book, Magistrates' Minutes, Colonial records, and Belize wills and newspapers. Dates are abbreviated and Bible verses and poems summarized as Verse.

St. John's burial register: Mary ARMSTRONG, B, buried at St. George's Key, 10 Aug 1822.

Sacred to the memory of William Henry AUGUST, who departed this life 19 Sep 1824 aged 12 months and 10 days. *Verse.*

To the memory of James BARTLET, Esq., native of Aberdeen, many years inhabitant of this settlement, who faithfully discharged the duties of the several offices to which he was chosen, and employed wth unremitting assiduity his superior talents to promote the welfare of the community, departed this life on 24 Jan 1800, in the 47th year of his age.

Capt. Marcus BELISLE died shortly before 6 Feb 1810, when his will, desiring burial "on St. George's Bay, as close as possible to my late respected friend, Jno. EMMONS HILL," was proved.

In memory of Joseph BEVANS, died Sep 5 1889, aged 89. *Verse.*

Sacred to the memory of Eve BROASTER, a native of Mandingo in Africa, who departed this life 28 July 1821, aged 65 years, whose inoffensive primeval conduct endeared her to all with whom she was acquainted, and as a tribute to departed worth, this stone is erected to her memory by her disconsolate daughter, Ariadne Broaster. This rude stone, what few superb marbles can, may truly boast, here lies an honest woman.

Sacred to the memory of SELWYN HODGE COX, son of Austin and Mary COX, who departed this life Apr 16 1861 aged 14 years. *Verse.*

Sacred to the memory of Theodor Austin William CRAMER, born Aug 27 1868, died Feb 25 1869.

In loving memory of Agnes Mary, daughter of Sydney and Amy Jane CUTHBERT, born 9 Jan, died 26 Jun 1892. Baby Nan. *Verse.*

Sacred to the memory of Mrs. Mary ESTILL, daughter of Mrs. Catherine FERRALL of this settlement, born Jul 1 1784, departed this life 23 Feb 1818 in the 34th year of her age.

Here are deposited the remains of Thomas GALE, Esq., a native of Greenock, who died on 2 Aug 1813 in the 29th year of his age, endeared to his family and friends... This stone is erected by disconsolate parents. St. John's burial register: Thomas GOLT, [sic] W, Aug 3 1813, at St. George's Kay. Tablet at St. John's: Thomas GALT, [sic] Esq. *Magistrates' Minutes show Thomas' name spelled both Gale and Galt.*

St. John's Burial Register: Henry August GREY, buried on St. George's Key 15 Nov 1846.

Mary Check-Pennell found: E. HALLIDAY, died Mar 27 1888.

Sacred to the memory of John EMMONS HILL, Esq, who departed this life 11 May 1808 aged 37 years. *Verse. Marcus Belisle's will mentions Sarah Hill, Richard Hill, Louisa Hill, and an unnamed female child, John Emmons Hill's children by Ann ARMSTRONG.*

In reverent memory of George HUME, Mahogany Cutter and Bayman, but God-fearing. *George Hume was a merchant at Black River in the 1760's and 1770's.*

Here lies the body of Edward JONES, Esq., who departed this life on Monday 9 Apr 1804, aged 49 years.

St. John's burial register: Ellis KELLY, W, Mate of the Bark *Stockton*, Mar 6, about 48. *Margin note:* I had rec'd no notice to have gone to St. George's Kay. *Apparently the the minister was not present at the burial, and felt it necessary to explain his absence.*

J. P. LAWRIE appears to be named on a tomb on Rob Hume's map. *In the report on the dig, this map has been so greatly reduced to fit the page that some writing is unclear.*

Sacred to the memory of Elmira Elizabeth McDONALD, who died of cholera on 13 Sep 1836 at St. George's Key aged 3 years 2 months and 9 days. *Verse.*

In memory of James McNAB, born at St. Petersburg in Russia May 21 1833, and departed this life at St. George's Kaye Sep 14 1863. This tomb was erected by his wife, Mary Jane McNAB.

The Honduras Gazette & Commercial Advertiser, Vol 1 #23, 22 Dec 1826: Deaths: On Tuesday morning last at St. George's Key, Mrs. MAIDEN. *One would think she was the wife of Dr. John Maiden, and was buried on the caye. There is no entry for her in St. John's burial register, suggesting that another minister officiated.*

In memory of Rev'd John C. MONGAN, M.A., incumbent of St. Mary's Church, who departed this life on 22 Aug 1860, aged 60 years. *A plaque in his church adds:* Garrison chaplain, vicar of Dishane and rector of Kilnemartory, Cork, Ireland, aged 60.

Sacred to the memory of Robert PERRY, who departed this life 14 Oct 1787, aged 45 years. *Rob Humes read this name as EMERY; J. P. Usher described the stone as "very much worn and hard to decipher," but copied it as PERRY. The writer believes the decedent was Robert PERRY, who went to the Caye in 1784 and obtained a Spanish title to his land in 1787.*

St. John's burial register: Catherine FERRAL POTTS, C, St. George's Key, Sep 22 1823. *Catherine was the beloved companion of Thomas Potts, who died in 1806. The 1816 census shows her in the household of her nephew, John Potts Sr.*

Sacred to the memory of John POTTS Senior, Esq., who departed this transitory world 15 Oct 1821 at St. George's Key, aged 66 years. He filled the situation of a Magistrate for many successive years. Upright in his principles, he always acted the part of an independent and honest man, a most benevolent friend to the distressed, and an affectionate father whose loss will be irreconcilable to those who have survived him.

Adjacent:

Sacred to the memory of Sarah POTTS, who departed this life 7 Nov 1787 aged 6 years, and to Ann GRACE, who departed this life 5 Oct 1800 aged 33 years, and to Catherine, daughter of Sarah POTTS, who departed this life 5 Nov 1800, aged 8 years. *J. P. Usher noted "the stone is badly worn and the first age may be different." If Catherine was born ca. 1792, Sarah had to have been adult and living at that time. Was she Sally Baldwin?*

Sacred to the memory of Thomas POTTS, Esq., of Durham, Senior Magistrate of this settlement, who died 8 Nov 1806, aged 66, having resided chiefly in this country upwards of 40 years... He was a zealous and active magistrate, and in social life his amiable qualities were happily blended with his laborious habits and unwearied pursuit of business. He closed his useful life lamented as a public and private loss, respected and beloved by his friends and venerated as the father of the community. *Dr. Gunn's book includes a photograph and a detailed description of the elaborate, footed sarcophagus.*

St. John's burial register: Mary TADD [*sic*] *(= TODD?)* W, buried at St. George's Key, Aug 15 1819, about 26 Years.

The *Clarion*, Mar 22 1906: Harold George USHER, Mar 16 1806, 2 years 7 ½ months, youngest son of John Purcell and Ethel Blanch USHER, interred at St. George's Caye.

In loving memory of Mary WHITE USHER, died 3 Aug 1894, aged 71 years. *Mary was a daughter of John and Sarah Purcell Usher, and a great-aunt of John Purcell Usher.*

Mary Check-Pennell found two modern burials: John QUALLO, 1 Nov 1954 *(Belize Billboard)* and Alice Frances CUTHBERT PEARCE, 1895-Dec 1984, ashes scattered in 1985.

THE CHURCH STREET CEMETERY

In August 1787 (Magistrate's Minutes, copied in CO/123/5 p. 158) a burial ground extending 210' adjacent to the small church being built on Church Street was laid off, and used until 1796, when a new cemetery was opened at Yarborough plantation. The Church Street graveyard was enclosed in 1804 by order of the Magistrates, "out of respect for our departed friends, and for the protection of their graves from the Hoggs." The land was low, so flooding during storms moved markers and made location of the graves uncertain; and as the population increased, all downtown land became more valuable. At a meeting on 27 June 1809 it was agreed that "the vacant ground on the South side, formerly the burial place, be sold at public sale, and the Magistrates authorized to lay the same out in lots best calculated to increase the public interest, from Church Street to Bishop Street along Albert Street." The tombstones, if any exist, lie buried in the soil beneath the stores of downtown Belize City.

MONUMENTAL INSCRIPTIONS IN YARBOROUGH CEMETERY
and ST. JOHN's CATHEDRAL

The land for Yarborough Cemetery, donated in 1796 by Capt. James Dandridge Yarborough, a Loyalist from South Carolina and evacuee from the Mosquito Shore, was in use until 1891. The cemetery was once more extensive than it is today; land was added, but proved too low for burials, and an area was cleared for housing. Many graves were never marked, and over the centuries hurricanes and vandals destroyed the marble slabs on many of the tombs. Memorial plaques in the church and some, though not all, burial registers have survived. Selected monumental inscriptions (MI's) were published by J. P. Usher in 1907; if only he had copied every stone extant at that time! Mary Check-Pennell's history and inventory of Yarborough and other cemeteries, made in the 1980's, is invaluable, locating family plots and giving information on some stones that have not survived. The writer and her husband photographed every MI we could find in 2004, and will gladly e-mail pictures of ancestral graves.

While a few of the tombs are highly elaborate, most are simple rectangles of brick or concrete, covered with concrete and topped with a stone, marble, or granite slab giving the name and dates of the deceased. Those described as finely worked have an ogee edge or other carving. The first inscription is given in full, as an exemplar; thereafter, dates have been abbreviated. Illegible or missing information is indicated by a line of dots; Bible and other verses are summarized as Verse. Wives whose maiden names are given in MI's are alphabetized by their husbands' surnames.

Tablets at St. John's show: The first stone of this church was laid by Lt. Col. John NUGENT SMYTH, Superintendent, on 20th July 1812, at the request of the Magistrates and Committee of Public Works, Marshal BENNETT, Thomas PASLOW, John POTTS, James GORDON, William GENTLE, Edward MEIGHAN, Thomas FRANCE, Peter C. WALL, Thomas GALT, and William LECKIE, Esquires, and the Reverend John ARMSTRONG, Chaplain.

The tablets on the east end of the church were presented by Marshal BENNETT Esq., A.D. 1814. The communion plate was presented by George ARTHUR, Esq., A.D. 1815. The silver baptismal basin was the bequest of Mary ARMSTRONG of this settlement, A.D. 1825. The interior was embellished by the Rev'd Matthew NEWPORT under the direction of John W. WRIGHT, Esq., Magistrate and Church Warden, 1824-25. The organ was erected in 1826. Tablets were placed in 1827 during the government of Major-Gen. Edward CODD, H. M.'s Superintendent, and Marshal BENNETT, Charles EVANS, Thomas PICKSTOCK, David BETSON, Charles CRAIG, James McDONALD, and Alexander FRANCE, Esq's, Magistrates. Reverend M. NEWPORT, B.M., of Trinity College, Dublin, Chaplain. James McDONALD and George WESTBY Esq's, Church Wardens.

Sacred to the memory of Sarah, wife of John ADAM, Merchant, Belize, who departed this life 13th Dec[r] 1828, aged 35 years, and of their infant daughter Isabella, born 10th Dec[r] 1828 died 18th Nov[r] 1829, aged 11 months and 22 days. *Grey stone slab.*

Note: Sarah died three days after giving birth. Was she among the countless victims of infection caused by doctors who went from treating suppurating wounds to women in childbirth? Her baby did not long survive her.

In memory of Harriet, wife of William BRYAN AIKMAN, Clerk-assistant to the Clerk of Assembly and Clerk of Courts in this colony, died Apr 11 1861, aged 34 years. *Verse.* This tablet was erected... by her afflicted husband as a testimony to the peculiar grace which adorned her, even the ornament of a meek and quiet spirit... *White marble slab.*

To the memory of Alexander ANDERSON Esq., Merchant, who was born at Muirside in the County of Forfar, North Britain, and died in this settlement, respected and regretted, on 21 May 1811, aged 44 years. *Grey stone slab. Will at the British National Archives.*

M. L. F. A. In loving memory of my mother, Frances ANDERSON, died Sep 1 1888, aged 60.

Mary Check Pennell's history of the cemetery includes "possibly R. M. ANDERSON." The writer and her husband did not find this stone.

Broken stone, inscribed in French, divided by a vertical line. Left side: ......e ANDRE... mort le .... er 1845... *Right side:* Marie A... bonne mere e bonne epouse... l'education des enfans de son village... Ils se sont maries en 1839 et ont... le malheur de perdre tous leurs enfans... bas age. Ils ont arrives a Belize 6 Dec 1844. *White marble slab.*

A century ago, when this stone was whole, John Purcell Usher copied: Philip ANDRE, ne a Thones in Savoie, etais Sarde age de 47 ans. Mort 14 Jan 1845, vivement regrette de sus epouse et de sus amis. Il a ete bon mari et bon pere et tourjours bien honore de ses ceux qui l'on connu.... MARIE ANDRE, nee en Villard sur Thones Savoie, agee de 35 ans. Morte 30 Jan 1845.... a donne tout son bien aux pauvres a l'education des enfans de son village et a'la Englise.

In memory of Elizabeth, wife of .... *(marble missing)* ANDREW, ...settlement, ...Mar 1831... years. *White marble slab. When the stone was whole, J. P. Usher read the name as R. J. Andrew. The 1829 census, household #249, shows Richard J. and Elizabeth Andrew. R. J. was a merchant. Some records show the name as ANDREWS.*

A plaque in the church reads: The silver baptismal basin is the bequest of Mary ARMSTRONG of this settlement, 1825. *Was she the Mary buried on the caye in 1822?*

In loving memory of William Oswald (Willie,) the beloved son of the Rev. William H. and Jane Isabella ATKIN, born Oct 6 1881, died Jan 21 1882. *Finely worked white marble slab.*

Sacred to the memory of John Samuel AUGUST, Esq., a respectable inhabitant of this settlement, one of the Magistrates and Colonel to the Militia, who left this country in 1838 after a residence of early 50 years, and died in England on 29 Aug 1839, in the 67th year of his age. Also in memory of his sons, Samuel Frederick AUGUST and James AUGUST, and of his sons in law, Leonard BYRON and William BYRON, who died in this colony. *Plaque in the church.*

Georgeo M. AVARRO, S. J. *J. P. Usher copied a plaque at the Catholic church showing this man was Italian and died in August 1873. The memorial at Yarborough names both Avarro and Avemann, below, but the writer and her husband did not find the stones.*

In memory of Louis AVEMANN, born Aug 8 1840, died of yellow fever Jul 6 1860.

Sacred to the memory of William B. BAKER, who departed this life Oct 29 1833, aged 19 years. *Mottled white marble slab.*

J. P. Usher copied: Francis LEIGH BALFOUR, of Townley Hall, Co. Leath, Ireland, who died aged 28, of the country fever, on 29 Oct 1833. *Verse. The tomb has not survived.*

Sacred to the memory of Bessie, beloved daughter of Mr. John BANKS, Edinburgh, Scotland, who died of yellow fever at Belize, Honduras, 29 Aug 1869, aged 22 years. *Verse. Domed grey granite slab.*

Sacred to the memory of Thomas BARNES… who departed this life on ? May 1828, aged 37 years. He was …. a member of the committee appointed…? the building of the Church… to this Settlement… *Dark grey slab. A history of the cemetery describes him as a bricklayer who built St. John's. Descendants say he and his wife, Jane, came from London to build the church.*

….. 8 Jun…. Aged 25 years… Children of Thomas and …. BARNES, formerly of London… *Lower half of a broken dark grey slab. The baptismal register shows Thomas' wife was Jane.*

The history of the cemetery includes an index showing with the same number, indicating a family plot, George Frederick BARNES, Amelia Sophia COATES, Sarah HOLTON COATES, and Sophia Augusta RUNNALS, whose MI has survived, and who descendants say was a daughter of Thomas and Jane BARNES.

J. P. Usher copied: Sacred to the memory of Henry BAYFIELD, Midshipman of H.M.S. S. Leopard, son of Rear-Admiral Bayfield, R.N., who died of yellow fever at Belize, 15 Apr 1858, aged 17 years. *Verse. The tomb has not survived.*

Mr. F. G. BEDFORD, Midshipman of H. M. S. Blossom, who, with Lt. William WILSON, R. N. and others, died of yellow fever in Aug 1830 and was interred on Goff's Key. *Memorialized on a plaque in the church.*

Sacred to the memory of Mrs. Elizabeth RAMSAY BENNETT, died 29 Mar 1849, aged 35 years, deeply regretted by her affectionate husband, Marcus Charles BENNETT. *White marble slab. Elizabeth was baptized in 1814 to Capt. Peter Adolphus Wade and Elizabeth Tillett, whose tomb is adjacent. Her first husband was George Runnels. Marcus Charles Bennett was baptized in Belize in 1820 to Marshal Bennett Jr. and Catherine Meighan, and served as a lieutenant in the militia in 1838. He went to Guatemala to hire lawyers to reclaim land stolen from his great-uncle, Marshal Sr., and was murdered there in October or November 1849. His mother and her second husband, Archibald Handyside, brought up his four orphaned children until they were old enough to be sent to school in England. Marshal Bennett Jr., died 1835, Sr., died 1839, Archibald Handyside, died 1866, and Catherine Handyside were all buried at Yarborough, but their tombs have not survived. John Bennett, below, was Marcus' half brother.*

In memory of John BENNETT Esq., who departed this life Sep 10 1849, aged 25 years, much lamented by all who knew him. *White marble slab, cracked across.*

Joint stone: To the memory of Capt. John BIDDLE, a native of Spain, who departed this life Mar 2 1886, aged 60? years. Edwin FORREST FALLS, born at New Orleans Sep 20 1866, died Jan 26 1874. *White marble slab.*

In loving memory of Amy Bertha, infant daughter of Fred. & Christabel BLOCKLEY, who fell asleep on 22 Aug 1881, aged 8 months. *Verse. White marble slab.*

In affectionate remembrance of George HUME BOWEN, who was drowned on 21 Mar 1886, aged 21 years. This tablet was erected by his sorrowing friends. *Tablet in the church. The tomb has not survived.*

In affectionate remembrance of Jane GROVER BOWEN, died 19 Sep 1881, aged 33 years, beloved wife of W. M. C. BOWEN. I leave the world without a tear, save for the friends I held so dear... *White marble slab. An adjacent tomb has lost its MI.*

Sacred to the memory of Matilda Caroline BOWEN, d. 15 Dec 1840 aged 29, and Sophia SEARLE BOWEN, d. 6 Dec 1840 aged 32. *Plaque in the church. Their father,* Manfield BOWEN, *listed in Mary Check-Pennell's history, was probably interred beside their mother, Mary Hickey, but the writer and her husband did not find these tombs.*

In memory of George M. BRADDICK, born at Long Island, Bahama, 24 Dec 1802. Arrived in this colony in the year 1823. Died 1 Apr 1869, aged 66 years. A sinner saved by grace. *Verse. Gray stone slab.*

Sacred to the memory of *(stone broken away)*.........ine BRINTON,.......... Malborough County, Mass., ...st 17 1806, died in Belize, British Honduras, Nov 5 1856, aged 70 years, 2 months and 19 days. *Verse. The MI, on the side of the concrete tomb, was intact when J. P. Usher copied:* Sacred to the memory of Mrs. Caroline BRINTON, New Malborough, Berkshire County, Mass, born Aug 17 1806.

Sacred to the memory of Mary BURRELL, who on 1 Nov 1800 two hours after she was safely delivered of a daughter who survived her, was seized by a frenzy, and after 13 successive paroxysms, was snatched into eternity in the 43rd year of her age. ... the mournful writer of this, Robert SPROAT, M.D. Also of Elizabeth LESTRANGE GRAY, her daughter, who died of a malignant fever in the 20th year of her age. Also James Robert the son of the said Elizabeth who died on 20 Nov in the 6th year of his age. *Verse. White marble slab. The year of James Robert's death is not given on the stone.*

Sacred to the memory of William MASKALL BYRON,* who departed this life on 15 Oct 1835 aged 17 years, also Leonard MASKALL BYRON who departed this life on 19 Aug 1836 aged 22 years. This tablet is placed over the remains of two dutiful sons by their affectionate & disconsolate Mother. *White marble slab. *Leeds Intelligencer:* Late of York.

The index to Mary Check Pennell's history shows, "possibly A. CAMPBELL." The writer and her husband did not find this grave.

In memory of George Benjamin CARTER, who departed this life on 13 Apr 1825, aged 37 years. This monument was erected by Catherine CARTER, in testimony of her regard and esteem. *Finely worked grey granite slab.*

Sacred to the memory of Angelo CHAPPELL, a native of New York, born 11 Mar 1818, died at Belize, Honduras, 9 Sep 1856. *White marble slab.*

Sacred to the memory of Edward William CLARKE, B.A., Rector of Great Yeldham and Chaplain to the Garrison of Honduras, who departed this life 24 Apr 1843, aged 37 years. *Verse. Large stone, not in the walled cemetery, but in the garden of the church. Bury & Norwich Post:* Eldest son of the late Dr. Edward Daniel Clarke.

This stone is placed in memory of James CLARK, a native of the county of Cumberland, who died at Belize on 24 Aug 1855, in the 41st year of his age. *White marble slab.*

Sacred to the memory of Eliza COFFIN, born 30 Sep 1796, died 4 Mar 1877. *White marble slab.*

The index to Mary Check-Pennell's history shows next to Eliza: William Henry COFFIN. *J. P. Usher found a record showing W. H. Coffin died 28 Jun 1892, and described the stone as illegible. It is now missing.*

Sacred to the memory of my dear mother, Margaret Letitia COLLINS, who departed this life on 1 Apr 1888? Aged 58 years. *Upright stone with curved top.*

Sacred to the memory of Archibald COLQUHOUN, who departed this life on Jan 19 1824, in the 41st year of his age. *Verse. White marble slab. A tablet in the church adds:* Esquire, several years one of the Magistrates of this Settlement. Also Mary his wife, died 24 Aug 1834, aged 46 years.

... memory of.. .... Mary COX, ...ter of .... Mary COX, ... le of Wight, ...ted this life ... Oct 1836 ... years. *When the stone was whole, J. P. Usher copied:* Sacred to the memory of Georgiana Mary COX, daughter of William and Mary COX of Ryde, Isle of Wight, who departed this life on 6 Oct 1836 aged 21 years. *Right half of a grey slab, level with the grass; the left half is missing.*

In memory of Gerhard Heinrich Anton CRAMER, born Apr 10 1821, died Feb 6 1868. *White painted tomb with inscription on the side.*

Sacred to the memory of Rev. James Walter CROOK, Senior Canon of St. John's Cathedral, who fell asleep in Jesus May 24, 1905, aged 37. *Verse. Tablet in the church; the tomb has not survived.*

In memory of ....FFE ... formerly of.... died Mar 2.. ... CUNLIFF... *Mottled granite. This is the tomb of Frank CUNLIFFE, whose name is on a tablet at the memorial, and of another person of the same surname. The inscription is low down on the side, and very difficult to read.*

G. S. D., Jan 16 1859. *Small, erect white painted stone on a base of bricks.*

Small stone cross, on a similar brick base, without any inscription.

L. M. D., Aug 26 1829. *Small, erect white painted stone on a slab.*

Sacred to the memory of John SMALE DALGETTY, late Provost Marshal General of Honduras, died 1 Jul 1832, aged 34 years. This monument is erected by his deeply sorrowing friends. *Plaque in the church.*

In affectionate remembrance of John McKINNEY DALY, a native of Kingston, Jamaica, who died Jan 13 1870, aged 58 years. *Verse. White marble slab*

Sacred to the memory of Tiburicio ROSADO ESTEVEZ, a resident of this colony of British Honduras upwards of 20 years, who died on 10 Mar 1869, aged 50 years. Requiescat in pace. *Grey, slightly convex granite slab.*

...Charles the son of Charles E.... died... *Fragment of white marble, in the grass. More than a century ago, J. P. Usher described this stone as severely damaged. He thought the surname might be EVANS, and the date of death 24 ...... Charles and Sarah Evans' son Charles, born in 1825, was in their household in the 1826 census, but was missing in 1829. For further information on this family see the writer's earlier books, The First Parish Register and The Second Parish Register of Belize.*

Georgiana Victoria HALL, eldest daughter of Benjamin and Virginia Clarissa FAIRWEATHER, who fell asleep in Jesus Mar 15 1890 in her 33rd year. Erected by her father. *Tablet in the church. The tomb has not survived.*

Mary Check Pennell found: William TATHAM FARQUHARSON, of Spring Vale in the Island of Jamaica, for many years Clerk of Court and Keeper of Records in this settlement, died 13 Feb 1861, aged 40 years and 10 months. Universally regretted.

Sacred to the memory of Juan RAMON FERRO, a native of Gualan in Central America, born 9 Mar 1820 and departed this life 22 Aug 1838, aged 18 years 5 months and 15 days, ... very much belov'd by his sorrowful friends. *Verse.* Also in loving memory of Philip TOLEDO, born Aug 23 1818? and departed this life 30 May 1884. At rest. *Finely worked white marble slab.*

Erected by John FORRESTER in memory of his beloved wife Margaret STEWART M. NIVEN, who died Mar 12 1868. Her end was peace. *Grey granite slab.*

Sacred to the memory of Elizabeth SEDDONS GENTLE, who departed this life on 25 Sep 1835 in the 45th year of her age, leaving behind her a disconsolate family to mourn her early loss. *White marble slab. The burial register names her as Elizabeth SIDDON, C. Her son and grandson are adjacent:*

In memory of William GENTLE Jr., who died 3 Aug 1840, in the 29th year of his age. Reader, boast not thyself of tomorrow, for thou knowest not what a day may bring forth. *White marble slab. A plaque in the church describes him as Esq., and adds,* In the midst of life we are in death.

Sacred to the memory of my beloved husband, William GENTLE, Merchant, Belize, Honduras, who died 20 Feb 1875, aged 39 years. ... From all his love, his care, and smile, divided for a little while. *The stones below identify his wife as Agnes. Convex white marble slab.*

In memory of Willie BANKS, the beloved child of William and Agnes GENTLE, died 15 May 1868, aged 10 months and 10 days. In loving remembrance of Little Willie and Baby. Of such is the Kingdom of Heaven. *Two small erect white marble stones, on graves one behind the other.*

To the memory of Henry GIFFORD, Clerk of H. M.'s Ship *Hyacinth,* who died May 10 1845, aged 21 years, universally regretted by his brother officers. *J. P. Usher copied this and the MI below; the stones have not survived.*

Sacred to the memory of John GOUGH, Public Treasurer of this settlement, who departed this life ... 13 1855, universally beloved and lamented. *Verse. In 1839 his wife was Emily.*

In memory of John GRANT. nephew to James GRANT, Senior Engineer, who departed this life June 18 1855, aged 24 years. *Verse. White marble slab; 24 clearly inscribed. He was the oldest son of Mr. J. F. Grant of Newcastle; the Courant says "in his 21st year."*

Gretta *is listed both on the memorial and in Mary Check Pennell's history. The name must have been on a fragment of stone; the writer and her husband could not find it.*

Sacred to the memory of John GRAY, Esq., Captain in the Royal Honduras Militia and Public Treasurer of this Settlement, whose integrity in his public and whose manners in his private character gained him universal approbation and esteem. This tablet, as a token of love and duty towards a dear and lamented husband, was placed by Rebecca, his faithful and affectionate widow. He was born in London Mar 3 1787 and died at Belize Feb 3 1817 in his 30th year. *Verse. White marble slab.*

In memory of my dear husband, Thomas Walter GRAY, who departed this life on 18 Oct 1876, aged 36. *Verse.*

In Memory of MELBOURNE Joseph GRIFFITHS, Surveyor General of this colony, born Mar 9 1815, died ... 13 1887. This tablet has been erected by the friends who loved him in life, and who mourn their loss... *Verse. Tablet in the church. The tomb has not survived.*

In affectionate memory of Charles Henry HADLEY, Civil Engineer, third son of Henry George and Rosina Hadley of Lee, London. He died Oct 26 1885, while marking out the western boundary of this country, aged 30 years. *Tablet in the church. Was he buried in the west? If his body was brought back, the tomb has not survived.*

Sacred to the memory of Capt. Andrew HALLIDAY HALL, late 20th, 41st, and 2nd W. I. Regiments, who died at Belize on 17 Mar 1787, in the 50th year of his age. Much loved, respected, and deeply lamented. *Erect dark grey stone with light grey surround.*

Sacred to the memory of Mary Elizabeth, the wife of W. E. HAMPSHIRE, who departed this life on 13 Nov 1835 in the 26th year of her age. *Burial register: aged 25. White marble slab.*

In memory of Ellen HARPER, youngest daughter of the late Mrs. S. C. HARPER of Cheltenham, England, late Head Mistress of the Central Schools, who was drowned in the Belize River on 12 May 1860, aged 26. *Verse. White marble upright stone with curved top.*

Sacred to the memory of Asst. Surgeon HARRIS of H. M.'s 2nd West India Regt., who fell victim to yellow fever on 31 Dec 1860, leaving a young widow to regret the loss of an affectionate husband. This tablet erected by the officers and chaplain of the garrison, in sad rememberance of his death. *The tomb has not survived.*

Sacred to the memory of Thomas GIBBES HARVEY, eldest son of Thomas CHAPMAN HARVEY and Elizabeth his wife, born at Mons, Belgium Dec 13 1847, died at Belize Mar 26 1854. *Peaked white marble with triangular ends, in the grass.*

Mary Check Pennell found: To the memory of George Emanuel HAYLOCK, who departed this life on the night of Dec 31? 1876, in the 66th year of his age. *Verse.* This stone is erected by his son George, in token of deep affection.

Sacred to the memory of Christopher HEMPSTEAD, a native of Connecticut, United States of America, for 30? *(or 36?)* years a resident of this colony, died 8 Apr 1875, aged 63 years and 6 months. *Mottled brown marble, convex. Mary Check Pennell described Christopher Hempstead as the American Consul to Belize, and an auctioneer.*

Sacred to the memory of Mrs. Mary HICKEY, many years an inhabitant of this settlement, who departed this life after a few days' sickness on 15 July 1826, leaving children Francis HICKEY MEIGHAN, Elizabeth Mary GRANT, Sophia Searle BOWEN, Catherine Amelia BOWEN, Matilda Caroline BOWEN, Richard Henry BOWEN, James William BOWEN, and Charles HICKEY BOWEN. This monument is erected by her affectionate friend, Manfield William BOWEN, Esq., the father of the six last named children, as a tribute of regard to the memory of his affectionate and beloved companion during a happy union of fifteen years. *The writer and her husband copied this interesting MI in 1982, but did not find it when photographing in 2004.*

....liam.... .... HICKEY ... arted... 17 Aug... the ag... *Fragment of white marble, in the grass.*

In fond rememberance of Rev. William Spencer HODGSON, who died Nov 1889, aged 30 years. *Verse. White marble slab.*

Blanche Ida, second daughter of Otto and Blanch Ida* HOFIUS, born in Belize 7 June 1890, died in Belize 8? 1890. A little angel. *Plaque at St. Mary's; we did not find the tomb. *Nee Farquharson, according to a GGrandson of her brother George Percy Farquharson.*

To the memory of George Nathaniel HULSE, Esq., the beloved husband of Susan Elizabeth HULSE, died in Belize 25 Jan 1889, aged 60 years. William MUNRO HULSE, their eldest and loving son, who was born in Belize 29 Mar 1854, and died 6 Jun 1879, aged 25 years. Not lost, but gone before. *The elaborate white marble tomb, at the front of the cemetery, resembles a twin bed with a high Victorian headboard.*

In loving remembrance of my dear husband, Rev. John JACKSON, Presbyterian Church, Belize, who died at Belize on 13 Sep 1888. *Upright brown stone with ivy leaf design.*

Sacred to the memory of Deborah, wife of Willm JECKELL, who departed this life on Oct 5 1824, aged 30 years... *Grey stone slab.*

In memory of Charles JEFFREYS, who departed this life 22 Oct 1827, aged 36 years. This tablet is placed here by his affectionate and dutiful children, being the last tribute of respect due to the remains of a kind and tender parent. *Grey stone slab.*

Mary Check Pennell found: William JEX, born at Brinton in the county of Norfolk, England, in 1815. Died in Belize Dec 28 1865 after suffering with great Christian fortitude, aged 50 years, leaving a large family of children in tender years to lament, deplore, and mourn their loss.

... ory of John JOHNSTON, native of Campbelltown, Argyllshire, Scotland, who resided in Belize eight years, and died 20 Jun 1827, aged 29. Erected by his friends. *Grey stone slab, partly broken away.*

Sacred to the memory of Edward Thomas JONES, who died at Southampton on 17 July 1860, aged 32 years. *Tablet at St. Mary's.*

Sacred to the memory of Andrew KENNEDY, Esq., Merchant and Agent for Lloyds, who departed this life May 26 1842, in the 37th year of his age. Sincerely lamented by all who knew his worth. *White marble slab, broken across.*

Mary Check-Pennell copied a partial MI: Elizabeth KEN... 6 April. *The writer and her husband did not find this stone.*

In loving memory of Alfred SEAMAN KINDRED, who fell asleep Jun 8 1887 aged 49. *Verse. Brown granite tomb, peaked with triangular ends.*

Adjacent: In memory of Edward VAUGHAN KINDRED, born 25 Aug 1871, died 23 May 1872. Not lost but gone before. *Convex grey granite tomb.*

Sacred to the memory of Mrs. Catherine LAMB, who departed this life Sep 19 1829, aged 75 years. This tombstone is placed over her remains as a mark of that sincere friendship that subsisted between the deceased and the subscriber for upwards of forty years. Clarissa PASLOW. *White marble slab. Widow of Capt. David Lamb, Loyalist.*

Sacred to the memory of Capt. John LAWTON, of the Merchant Service, who departed this life 13 Nov 1838, in the 49th year of his age, leaving a widow and five children deeply lamenting his loss. He was universally respected by all who knew him. *Verse. Grey stone slab, cracked lengthwise. Censuses do not show his family in Belize.*

Erected to the memory of the late William LESLIE, of North Shields, Commander of the British barque *Hopewell*, who died of fever at Belize ... Jun 1843. *Erect whitewashed or white painted stone, very hard to read.*

In memory of John LEVER, Esq., 3rd West India Reg't, son of the late Charles LEVER Esq. of Tavistock Squre, London, who died at Belize, British Honduras on 5 Jun 1861, aged 27. *Verse. Brown granite convex slab. J. P. Usher copied a plaque in the Church of St. Mary the Virgin, giving the same information.*

Sacred to the memory of Thomas YOUNG LIDDAL, a native of Irvine, Scotland, and many years a merchant of this town, who departed this life on 2 Sep 1844, deeply lamented by his family and friends, aged 42 years. *Verse.* His widow has caused this stone to be erected as a slight tribute of her affection and respect for his memory. *White marble slab.*

Adjacent:

Sacred to the memory of William, son of Thos. Y. and Elizabeth LIDDAL, who departed this life 14 Nov 1841, aged 4 years. *Verse. Small dark grey stone slab.*

Sacred to the memory of Asst. Com^y Genl John LINDSAY, who departed this life Dec 6 1835, aged 45 years. *White marble slab.*

In memory of Maria LUCAS, wife of John LINDSAY, who died Aug 22 1832, aged 28 years. *White marble slab.*

Sacred to the memory of Ann LOCKWARD, who died 3 Oct 1828, aged 62. *Upright stone, white marble with a swirl design at the top. The burial register gives her age as 64.*

The history of the cemetery includes a map showing "possibly D. B. LOCKWARD;" this man appears in newspaper and other records as David B. Lockward. Bricks protruding from the grass may mark the site of this and other tombs that have crumbled away.

In memory of Robert Henry LOGAN, B.A. Oxon, Barrister at Law, Middle Temple, a member of the legislative council of this colony and a past ranger of the ancient order of foresters, born in the parish of Earlston on 14 Feb 1858. For 13 years a prominent inhabitant of this colony. A true friend, an able lawyer, a wise and upright man. He died on 12 Oct 1898, universally esteemed and lamented. Erected by his friends. *Tablet in the church. The tomb has not survived.*

Sacred to the memory of James McDONALD, Esq., a native of Stirling, Scotland, who resided in this country nearly 50 years. Born 22 Mar 1793, died 11 Mar 1861. *Verse. Finely worked white marble slab.*

Adjacent: Sacred to the memory of Patience Susannah, widow of the late James McDONALD, Esq., whom she survived eight months. Born 15 Nov 1800, died 10 Nov 1861. *Verse. Finely worked white marble slab.*

Sacred to the memory of James MACDONALD, of Inverness, Scotland, born Oct 19 1847, died Aug 15 1885. From all his love and care and smile, divided for a little while. *Grey granite slab. Tombs inches away on each side have lost their inscriptions.*

Sacred to the memory of Valencourt Henry McDONALD, died Oct 26 1884 aged 54. Come unto me, all ye that labour and are heavy laden, and I will give you rest. *White marble slab. Adjacent:*

Sacred to the memory of VALENCOURT LLEWELLYN, beloved son of Valencourt Henry & Ellen LEWELLYN McDONALD, born 6 Mar 1859, died 24 Sep 1863. *Verse. Finely worked white marble slab, with carved roses.*

J. P. Usher copied plaques in the Church of St. Mary the Virgin, one duplicating the information above, the other showing Sacred to the memory of Herbert RHYS

89

McDONALD, son of Valencourt Henry & Ellen LEWELLYN McDONALD, born 28 Nov 1860, died 23 Aug 1887. Erected in affectionate remembrance by members of the Belize Wanderers Cricket Club. *If the tomb exists, it has lost the slab with the MI.*

Erected by the Rev. D. S. McEACHRAN, Cromarty, Scotland, in memory of his brother, Archibald McEACHRAN, Merchant, Belize, who died 7 Feb 1855. *Finely worked white marble slab.*

Sacred to the memory of *(marble missing)* McSWEANY, a native of Ireland, died at Belize 20th Jan 1865 aged 32 years. This stone is placed over his remains by his sorrowing widow, Margaret. *White marble slab with multiple breaks.*

J. P. Usher copied: In memory of Frederick William MARTINY, a native of Hamburg, who expired Aug 24 1838 in the 39th year of his age. He was a sincere and devout Christian, a most kind and indulgent husband, and an affectionate father. Beloved by all who knew him. *The tomb was not found when the cemetery was cleaned.*

Sacred to the memory of Mrs. Mary MASKALL, who departed this life Mar 1 1819, aged 61 years. Erected to her memory by her affectionate son, John Samuel AUGUST, Esq. *Grey stone slab. Mary was the widow of Henry Maskall, who died in 1805. John Samuel August was her son in law; his wife was her daughter, Sarah Maskall.*

Sacred to the memory of Rev'd HARMAN MASON, Wesleyan Missionary, who departed this life Jan 3 1853, in the 27th year of his age, and the second of his ministry. Deeply regretted... for his zeal and devotion for the conversion of men to God. *Verse. White marble slab.*

There is no memorial at Yarborough for Francis MEIGHAN, reported as murdered by A. LOPEZ at Omoa, Spanish Honduras during the last week of August, 1848. Lopez fled from Honduras to Belize and the Superintendent and Magistrates offered a reward of $300 local currency for his capture. If the murdered man was Francis Hickey Meighan, son of Edmund Meighan and Mary Hickey, Lopez had leapt from frying pan to fire by going to Belize. Was he arrested, and what became of him?

In memory of Marion Louise Geraldine, the beloved infant of Carlos and Florence MELHADO, born 15 Dec 1886, died 13 July 1887. *The small grey slab is level with and half buried in the grass. The surname is not listed on the memorial.*

In loving memory of Margaretta the wife of William MILLER, Asst. Surveyor General of this colony, died Aug 1886, aged 22 years. *Tablet in the church. The tomb has not survived.*

Erected by Rev. John MUCKERSIE, in loving memory of Margaret WILKINSON, his wife, who fell asleep 17 Dec 1889. *Upright grey granite stone, with a pointed top.*

J. P. Usher copied: Charlotte Ethel Marguerite MURRAY, "Daisy," entered into rest July 11 1893, aged 18. *Plaque at St Mary's. Her tomb has not survived.*

The Reverend Matthew NEWPORT, DD, who fell asleep in the Lord 22 Apr 1860, having been Rector of this Parish for 35 years. *Verse. Plaque in the church.*

In loving memory of Rev.d Edwin NICHOLSON, who died January 20 1890, aged 26 years. *Verse. White marble slab.*

In memory of Leonard Von OEHLHAFFEN, born at Liverpool, England, 1859, died at Caledonia, British Honduras 1870, and Eugene Edward Benedict Von OELHAFFEN, born at Liverpool, England 1855, died at Caledonia, British Honduras, 1871. *Tablet in the church. Considering the difficulty of travel at that time, these men were probably buried at Caledonia. If they were interred at Yarborough their tombs have not survived.*

Sacred to the memory of Spencer COBBOLD PAGE, Esq., son of the Rev'd F. L. PAGE of Woolpit Rectory, Suffolk. He departed this life at Belize, British Honduras, March 15 1857, in the 24th year of his age. *Large erect white stone with floral bas relief, and a cross on a marble slab; S. C. P. 1857 on footstone; enclosed in black iron palings.*

Sacred to the memory of Clarissa PASLOW, who departed this life 3 May 1838 aged 74 years. *Finely worked white marble slab. Widow of Thomas, adjacent.*

Sacred to the memory of Thomas PASLOW, Esq., Lt. Col. Commanding the P.R. R. H. Royal Artillery. For forty years an inhabitant of Honduras, where his character was well known for firmness, justice, and integrity. A Magistrate and a Man. He was one of those gallant spirits who so gloriously fought and successfully defended the colony when attacked by the Spaniards on 10 September 1798. He was a native of Ireland, and died on 11 Feb 1825. This stone was placed over his remains in respect to his talents and his virtues by his Nephew, William WALSH. *Finely worked white marble slab, adjacent to the tomb of the Hon. William Walsh.*

Sacred to the memory of Thomas PHILLIPS, a native of Yorkshire in England, who died on 15 May 1865, aged 64 years. *White marble slab.*

Alfred Cecil PRICE, died 24 Dec 1876, aged 42 years. *Verse. Mottled grey granite slab.*

J. P. U. copied: Sacred to the memory of James CHAPMAN QUILTER, Surgeon, a native of England but many years resident in this town, who departed this life after a few days illness on 6 Dec 1835 in the 32nd year of his age, sincerely regretted by a large circle of family and deeply lamented by his affectionate widow. *Verse. Bury & Norwich Post:* the 2nd son of the late Samuel SACKER QUILTER Esq., formerly of Walton, Suffolk.

Sacred to the memory of Jane QUILTER, who died Feb 21 1856 aged 21 years and 7 days, also Georgiana, her daughter, who died 16 May 1856, aged 4 months and 2 days. *White marble slab. The tomb of James Chapman Quilter was not found.*

In eternal remembrance of Sarah, beloved partner? of Benjamin RENEAU, Belize, British Honduras, who died of dysentery on Saturday, 18 Jun 1879 in the 56th year of her age. She was a faithful wife, a loving parent, and a sincere friend. *Verse. Convex brown granite slab.*

Sacred to the memory of Isac REYES, a native of Tihosuco of Yucatan, and for many years a resident in the town of Belize, who died 11 Jun 1868, aged 65 years and 8 days, much respected and deeply regretted. Requiescat in pace. *White marble slab.*

Sacred to the memory of Thomas RHYS, Surgeon, a native of South Wales, born 2 Nov 1792, departed this life 19 Mar 1855. *White marble slab.*

In memory of ..a^s Wm DECKNER ROBERTSON, born 30 Nov 1843, died 28 Nov 18... *Fragment of white marble, in the grass. The index to the cemetery shows the given name as Chas. The spacing suggests Ja^s.*

Sacred to the memory of Catherine TILLETT CUNNINGHAM, the beloved wife of Thomas ROBINSON, Shipmaster, Belize, who departed this life on 26 July 1859 in the 33rd year of her age. *White marble slab, between Tillett tombs and that of her first cousin, Robert Forsyte Wade. Daughter of Charles Keith Cunningham and Catherine Tillett.*

Juaquin RODRIGUEZ, hijo, nacido en esta cuidad de Trujillo, murio asasinado insidiousamente a las 9 de la noche 27 de Marzo 1851 a los 28 anos 11 meses 4 dias de edad. *Same tomb:* Aqui yacen los restos de Juaquin RODRIGUEZ, natural de Cadiz, murio el dia 4 de diciembre de 1840, de los 59 anos 11 meses y 6 dias de edad. Dedicarles este funebre recuerdo su desconsolada familia. *A large and highly elaborate raised white marble tomb, with carved swags and urns.*

Aqui yacent los humanos desposios de Doña Angela ONGAY De ROSADO, su virtud volo al cielo. Novio en Bacalar Nov 10 1851. Murio in Belize May 16 1881. Fieles, rogad por su eterno descanso. J. M. ROSADO. *Finely worked grey granite slab. At the Catholic Cathedral of the Holy Redeemer, J. P. Usher found plaques memorializing Doña Nicolada CALVO de ONGAY, native of Cataluna, died in Corazon on 25 Aug 1872 leaving a desolate son, and Da. Valeriana ROSADO de ROSADO, died 9 Sep 1873 aged 50, wife and mother. No tomb was found at Yarborough for Valeriana.*

Sacred to the memory of Sophia Augusta RUNNALS, who departed this life for a happier on 18 Jan 1824 aged 22 years. This last tribute of affection is most respectfully dedicated by her beloved affectionate and disconsolate husband, George RUNNALS. *Verse...* Her dwelling is that house the living flies. Plucked from the earth just like an op'ning flower ... before lov'd George half her sweetness knew. *Finely worked white marble slab. A daughter of Thomas and Jane BARNES.*

In memory of Harriet SCHAISE, born 23 Jul 1791, died 23 Aug 1865. And in memory of John E. STAIN who was drowned in the Belize River on 28 Jun 1872, aged 32 years and 9 months. *White marble slab.*

J. P. Usher copied: In memory of Julius Henry SCHRIEVER, a native of Germany, who died 2 Jun? 1860 aged 21. This tablet was erected by a few of his friends in testimony of their regard? and esteem. *The tomb has not survived.*

Sacred to the memory of Emma Maria, wife of Henry SCHURER, who died Jul 5 1859, aged 34 years and 6 months, deeply deplored by sorrowing friends. Also in memory of her stillborn son. *Finely worked white marble slab.*

This stone is placed here by George H., Emma F. and Amy D. SCHURER, in memory of their father Henry Rudolph SCHURER, a native of Libau, Courland, Russia and for many years a resident in this town of Belize, British Honduras, who died 3 May 1868, aged 61 years and 33 days. Much respected and deeply regretted. *White marble slab.*

In memory of Mrs. C. H. SCOTT, daughter of the late Major James ROBERTSON, of Cray, Perthshire, Scotland, who died here 24 Feb 1855 aged 33 years. *White marble slab.*

In remembrance of Henry SHAW of Scarboro, late carpenter on the *Viceroy* of London, who died here of yellow fever, Sep 23 1860, aged 22 years. *Verse. Grey stone slab.*

J. P. Usher copied: To the memory of the Rev'd Edward FOX STRANGEWAYS, Rector of Melbury in the county of Dorset, fifth son of the Hon. & Rev'd Charles REDLYNCH STRANGEWAYS, born Apr 2 1806, died at the Government House, Belize, Dec 31 1838. *Verse. The stone has not survived.*

In loving memory of Norah Muriel SWEET-ESCOTT, born at Rose Hill, Mauritius, 14 May 1885, died of yellow fever at Government House, Belize, 28 May 1905, second daughter of Sir BICKHAM SWEET-ESCOTT, K. C. M. G., Governor of British Honduras. *Tablet in the church. The tomb has not survived.*

To the memory of George Mc'KENZIE ROSS, son of Thomas STUART, Esq., Merchant of this Settlement, who died 5 Feb 1852, aged 14 months. *Verse. White marble slab.*

To the memory of Isabella BALFOUR, daughter of Thomas STUART, Merchant in this Settlement, who departed this life 28 May 1852, aged 4 years. *Verse. White marble slab.*

Sacred to the memory of Thomas STUART, a native of the parish of Resolis, Ross-shire, Scotland, and for many years a merchant in this settlement, who departed this life 20 Jun 1857, aged 54 years. This stone is placed over his remains by his disconsolate and sorrowing widow, Isabella BALFOUR STUART. *Verse. Finely worked white marble slab.*

In memory of Emma Lavinia, eldest daughter of James and Lavinia Elizabeth THOMSON, born 9 Feb 1859, died 4 Feb 1864. Suffer little children, and forbid them not to come unto me, for such is the kingdom of heaven. *Grey stone slab.*

Sacred to the memory of Mary THOMSON, who departed this life Mar 5 1877, at the age of 27 years and 44 days. Her precious form entombed with prayer... *Verse. White marble slab.*

Sacred to the memory of Doctor John THORNTON, a native of Scotland, who departed this life suddenly Oct 31 1824 aged 35 years. He had practiced in this settlement most successfully for upwards of ten years... *White marble slab.*

J. P. Usher copied: To the memory of William THURSTON, of Surlingham, Norfolk, who died Aug 20 1863 aged 30 years. This tablet was erected as a token of gratitude by P. E. WODEHOUSE, Esq., Superintendent of Honduras, in whose family he served faithfully for many years. *The tomb has not survived.*

Sacred to the memory of Mrs. Elizabeth TILLETT, who departed this life 13 Jan 1837, aged 52 years, and to whose memory this tomb is erected as a testimony of the affection of her children, Sarah USHER, Robt F. WADE, Ann M. WADE, Elizth R. WADE, Willm A. WADE, Cath^n WILLS, and Mary Ann POTTS. *Finely worked white marble slab, between her mother and her brother.*

Note: Elizabeth was the writer's GGG-grandmother. The list of 1790 shows her as a child with her parents, Capt. William and Mary White Tillett. The marriages of her children are given in The First Parish Register & First Four Censuses of Belize. Sarah was her daughter by Capt. Purcell; the three Wades by Capt. Peter Adolphus Wade of Bristol and Belize; and Catherine Ferrill and Mary Ann (or Marianne) by John Potts Jr. Do any of her children have descendants in Belize today?

Adjacent: Beneath this tomb are interred the remains of Mrs. Mary TILLET, who departed this life 17 Feb 1834, aged 68 years, and to whose memory this tomb is erected as a testimony of the affection of her children, Elizabeth, George, and William Tillett. *White marble slab, to the left of Elizabeth and William.*

Note: Mary appears in the burial record as Mary White, C, and in censuses as white and as coloured. She was a daughter of Capt. William White and Elizabeth --?--, and the widow of Captain William Tillett, who is said to have been buried on their land at Bakers, 6 miles west of Ladyville. Her younger daughter, Kitty Tillett - Catherine Tillett Cunningham, wife of Charles K. Cunningham - was interred 8 Jan 1832 aged 43, probably in one of the nearby tombs with missing slabs. In 1832 Mary was living with Daniel Tillett – her grandson? The tombs of her three surviving children and her son George's wife Sarah --?-- (BIRD?) are adjacent.

Here lie the earthly remains of Sarah TILLETT, the beloved wife of George TILLETT, Esq., Bakers, born 27 Jul 1800, joined the Baptist Church 6 Aug 1840, and after fourteen years consistent walk in her holy profession fell asleep in Jesus on 24 Feb 1854. *Finely worked white marble slab. Her husband would have been buried nearby, but his MI is missing; 13 tombs in the immediate area have lost their marble slabs.*

Sacred to the memory of William TILLETT Esq., departed this life 8 Jan 1848 aged 53 years. This monument was erected as a token of affection by his brother, George Tillett. *White marble slab; his sister Elizabeth lies between him and his mother, Mary White Tillett. The MI of his wife, Sarah Jones, has not survived. His will shows they had twelve children.*

Sacred to the memory of Mrs. Jane TRAPP, who departed this life on Thursday, 21 Jun MDCCCVVVII, *(=1827,)* aged 80 years. This stone was laid down as a tribute of affection by her loving children, Catherine HUME, James USHER, and John USHER. *Finely worked white marble slab.*

Sacred to the memory of Master Charles BEACH USHER, born Sep 5 1833, departed this life Oct 29 1838, aged 5 years 1 month and 24 days. *Small white marble slab.*

Note: Charles Beach Usher was a son of John and Sarah Purcell Usher. The tombs of his uncle and aunt, Robert Forsyth Wade and Elizabeth Ramsay Wade Runnals Bennett, are adjacent. His brother is interred nearby:

Sacred to the memory of John HUME USHER, born Saturday, Dec 20 1828, who was cruelly murdered in cold blood by numerous gunshot wounds inflicted on Friday Jan 21 1848 by a Spaniard named Marcello SEVERIA, a native of Central America, who left him to perish at Manatee, but was miraculously rescued by his brother, and after undergoing excruciating agonies in his perfect senses, departed this life on Sunday Jan 30 1848, aged 19 years 1 month and 10 days. *White marble slab with rounded corners. To the left, the photograph shows marble half buried in the grass; this needs to be investigated.*

A plaque in the church memorializes their parents: Sacred to the memory of John USHER, Esq., Assistant Judge of the Supreme and Summary Courts of British Honduras, born at St. George's Cay and died at Belize 23 Apr 1869 aged 74 years; for many years a member of the public meeting and assistant judge of the supreme and summary courts of British Honduras. Sarah his wife died on 16 Jul 1859. Jane Elizabeth their second daughter died on 26 Nov 1867 aged 41 years. Thy will be done. *The writer and her husband could not find these tombs. They may have been buried on St. Georges Caye; their daughter Mary White Usher, who never married, was buried there.*

Information on St. John's brass lectern and a plaque may show roots in England: Ethel Louise USHER, the only and dearly loved child of Henry and Louisa H. USHER, born at Welhouse, Golcar near Huddersfield, Yorkshire on 28 Apr 1874, died at Birchington, Kent 15 Jun 1890. Interred at Birchington churchyard. *Did the Ushers have family at Welhouse? Ethel was a scholar at Cuddington, Bucks in 1881, and at a school in Kent when she fell ill; she was being educated in England, as was customary. The eagle lectern was given in her memory by Henry C. Usher, a member of the Executive Council.*

A la memor... de Don Valeriano VIDEZ, nacio in Santa A.... el 15 de Dici... *(= Diciembre)* Fallecio en Belize el 10 de.... *Verse. Broken slab, pieces missing.*

95

Sacred to the memory of Mary Jane WADE, daughter of Robert Forsyth WADE, born 6 Oct 1839, died 13 Mar 1859, and of her mother Mrs. Jane BRADDICK, who departed this life 11 Oct 1873, aged 56 years. *Verse. Mary Check-Pennell found this MI.. Jane, but not her daughter, is listed on a tablet at the Yarborough memorial.*

In memory of Robert FORSYTH WADE, of Belize, Honduras, who departed this life 26 Aug 1848, aged 41 years. *White marble slab.*

Note: Robert's tomb lies between that of his first cousin, Catherine Tillett Cunningham Robinson, and his sister, Elizabeth Ramsay Wade Runnals Bennett. He was named for his maternal G-grandfather, Robert Forsyth or Forsyte; his grandmother was Susanna Forsyte Wade and his grandfather Capt. Peter Wade of Bristol, who died in 1803. His wife, Jane Braddick Wade, his daughter Mary Jane, and his brother, William Augustus Wade, are probably in nearby tombs that have lost their slabs. His will is available at the Belize and at the British National Archives.

In memory of George WAGNER, a native of this colony, who departed this life 31 Aug 1873, aged 49 years 10 months and 7 days. *Verse. Mottled brown convex granite slab.*

In loving memory of James WAGNER, who died 15 Nov 1883, aged 57 years. *Verse. Raised, elaborate white marble tomb, with high peaked roof. A plaque in the church adds,* Also of Sarah his beloved wife, who died 19 Mar 1893, aged 63 years. This tablet is erected by their loving children.

James WAIGHT, the master of the Free School, church warden, and organist, died 3 October 1831, aged 45 years, and was buried at the far end of the cemetery, beyond the present cemetery wall. Descendants prevented his grave from being taken for a housing development, and marked it with a cross, but were forced to remove the cross for safekeeping due to repeated acts of vandalism.

In memory of William WALKER, of Middleton, Nigg, Kincardineshire, who died at Belize 2 Nov 1883, aged 27 years. Erected by his brothers and sisters. *Upright grey granite with scalloped top and elaborate engraved design.*

Sacred to the memory of Peter CHESTER WALL, many years an inhabitant, and repeatedly a Magistrate in this settlement. This monument is erected by the grateful affection of his Wife. In his life he was simple in his manners, sincere in his professions, and cordial in his friendship. In his sickness the word of God was his comfort, Christ was his hope… He finished the course Jul 12 1820. *White marble slab. See the First Parish Register and the Second Parish Register for further information.*

The Hon. William WALSH departed this life on 3 Feb 1843. *A tablet in the church adds:* Member of the Executive Council, Magistrate, and upwards of 17 years Treasurer of this settlement, aged 55 years. *Finely worked white marble slab, adjacent to Thos. Paslow.*

Richard, infant son of R. C. & Georgiana WARDLOW, died 9 Jan 1837, aged 7 months and 20 days. *Small, finely worked white marble slab.*

Here are interred the remains of James Edward WELSH, born 17 Feb 1829, died 8 Sep 1830, and of Susannah WELSH, born 9 Sep 1830, died 3 October following, the infant children of James WELSH. *White marble slab.*

A map of the cemetery showing numbered graves includes:
Possibly H. C. and J. G. H. WILLIAMSON. *The tomb may be among the many that have been destroyed or vandalized; the writer and her husband did not find it.*

The last interment at Yarborough was not, as widely believed, that of Catherine WILLS, buried in the family plot on Feb 26 1891; Sarah WAGNER, who died in 1893, was buried with her husband. *Catherine Ferrill Potts, a daughter of John Potts and Elizabeth Tillett, married Dr. James A. Wills ca. 1834-5. No MI was found for her or for her husband; their names are not on the memorial.*

In loving memory of Charles Henry WILSON, M.A., F.G.S., son of the Revd. Edward WILSON, Vicar of Nocton, Lincolnshire, born Apr 16 1851, scholar of Eton and King's College Cambridge, after faithful service at Rugby, Tennessee, and in this colony, died in Belize Sep 9 1887. *Verse. Tablet in the church. The tomb has not survived.*

Sacred to the memory of Lieutenant William WILSON, R. N, Mr. F. G. BEDFORD, Midshipman, the Sergeant of Marines and nine seamen, all of H. M. S. Blossom, who died of yellow Fever in Aug 1830 and were interred on Goff's Key. This tablet is erected by Capt. OWEN and the officers of the ship as a tribute of affection and esteem. *Verse. Tablet in the church.*

Here lies the body of Elizabeth WITEMAN, aged 28, born at Yarmouth, deceased at Belize 30 Oct 1844, extremely regretted by all who knew her. *Finely worked white marble slab.*

Sacred to the memory of Mrs. Louisa WOLFENSTAN, who died Jun 5 1837, aged 32? years. A tender mother and a faithful wife... *Verse. Grey stone slab. The burial register spells her name Wolfenstein.*

Sacred to the memory of Sydney WOODS, born 20 Feb 1832, died 6 May 1866. *White marble slab.*

William Henry WOODS, born 29 Jan 1830, died 21 Jun 1864. *White marble slab.*

Here lieth the body of Peter YOUNG, son of John YOUNG of Burntisland, North Britain, who departed this life 18 Dec 1803, aged 79? years and 4 months. *Worn grey slab. In 1831, a schoolmaster at Burntisland in Fifeshire wrote an account of the population in which he described the Messrs. Young as heritors, gentry owning land and manor houses.*

Inscriptions on broken fragments in the grass:

...Justice of Honduras died .... 24 1818... years & month... *White marble.*

...and Jane... ...ded this life... after a ling... eighteen months.....nth year of... *Grey stone.*

Plaques at the Catholic, Wesleyan, and Ebenezer Church copied by John Purcell Usher name priests and others who died after 1877, when Yarborough cemetery was officially closed. (Rose Elizabeth TRUMBACH, who died in 1889, could have been buried in a family plot, but no stone has been found for her.) Inscriptions on the plaques, memorials to people who died overseas, MI's in the Contagious Disease cemetery, and MI's at the Military Cemetery are all available in J. P. Usher's book.

The Belize Tourism Board cleaned up Yarborough Cemetery for the millennium as a historic attraction, and constructed a semi-circular memorial of dark green tile with five white tablets, listing names of people buried there, at the farther end. Surnames not given on this memorial but found in the cemetery are added below in brackets. The tablets read:

William Bryan AIKMAN; Alexander ANDERSON, Esq; Frances ANDERSON; Mary ANDRE; Philippe ANDRE; Louis AVEMAN; Georgio M. AVARRO, S. J.; William B. BAKER; Bessie BANKS; Willie BANKS; George Frederick BANES; Thomas BARNES; John BENNETT; Mrs. Elizabeth RAMSAY BENNETT; Capt. John BIDDLE; Amy Bertha *(MI: BLOCKLEY;)* Caroline BOWEN; Jane GROVER BOWEN; Sophia SEARLE BOWEN; Mrs. Jane BRADDICK; Mrs. Caroline BRITON; Thomas J. BROWN; Charles BULL; Mary BURRELL; Leonard MASKALL BYRON; William MASKALL BYRON; S. B.; George Benjamin CARTER; Angelo CHAPPELL; James CLARK; Eliza COFFIN; William Henry COFFIN; Sarah HOLTON COATES;

Amelia Sophia COATES; Archibald COLQUHOUN; Catherine TILLETT CUNINGHAM; [*sic*], Margaret Lititia [*sic*] COLLIN; William Thomas COLLINS JR.; Mary COX; Frank CUNLIFFE; J. B. C John Mc`KINNEY DALY; G. S. D..; L. M. D.; Marie Eleanna; Mary Elizabeth; Tiburicio ROSADO ESTAVEZ; Charles E.; Elizabeth; Edwin FORREST FALLS; William TATHAM FARQUHARSON; Juan ROMAN FERRO; John FORRESTER; Elizabeth SEDDON GENTLE; William GENTLE; William GENTLE Jr.; Marion Louise Geraldine *(MI: MELHADO;)* John GRANT; John GRAY; Thomas Walter GRAY; Gretta;

Capt. Andrew HALLIDAY HALL; Ellen HAPPER *(MI: HARPER;)* Thomas GIBBES HARVEY; George Emanuel HAYLOCK; Christopher HEMPSTEAD; Mrs. Mary HICKEY; Rev. William SPENCER HODGSON; Markus HUGO; George Nathaniel HULSE, Esq; William MUNRO HULSE; Harriet; Charlotte Ida; Isabella; Rev. John JACKSON; Deborah JECKELL; Charles JEFFREYS; William JEX; Euphergene Mary De JIMINEZ; John JOHNSTON; Elizabeth KEE; Andrew KENNEDY; Alfred SEAMAN

KINDRED; Edward VAUGHN KINDRED; Mrs. Catherine LAMB; Capt. John
LAWTON; John LEVER; William LESLIE; Thomas YOUNG LIDDAL; John LINSAY;

Ana *(MI: Ann)* LOCKWARD; Maria LUCAS; John JOHNSTONE MACLACHLAN;
James MacDONALD – Susannah Patience; Emma Maria; Mary MASKALL; Rev Edwin
NICHOLSON; William OSWALD; Spencer COBBALD PAGE, Esq; Clarissa PASLOW;
Thomas PASLOW, Esq; Thomas PHILLIPS; Alfred Cecil PRICE; Sarah RENEAU; Dr.
Thomas RENWICK; Isac REYES; Thomas RHYS; James ROBERT; Charles W. M.
DECKNER ROBERTSON; Juaquin RODRIGUEZ Sr.; Juaquin RODRIGUEZ Jr; Doña
Angela ONGAY de ROSADO; George Mc'KENZIE ROSS; Sophia Augusta RUNNALS;
Richard; Georgiana QUILTER;

Jane QUILTER; Harriet SCHAISE; Henry Rudolph SCHURER; Mrs. C. H. SCOTT;
Henry SHAW; John E. STAINE; Mary THOMSON; Doct. John THORNTON; Mrs.
Elizabeth TILLETT; Sarah TILLETT; William TILLETT, Esq; Mrs. Jane TRAPP; John
HUME USHER; Don Valeriano VIDEZ; Robert FORSYTH WADE; James WAGANER
(MI: WAGNER;) George WAGNER; James Harold WRIGHT; William WALKER; Peter
CHESTER WALL; Hon. William WALSH; Richard WARDLOW; James Edward
WELSH; Susannah WELSH; Frances WILLIAMS; Elizabeth WITEMAN; Mrs. Louisa
WOLFENSTAN; Sydney WOODS; William Henry WOODS; Peter YOUNG.

*As noted earlier, Yarborough Cemetery was closed in 1877 except for burials in family
plots. By that time other cemeteries were in temporary use: the Contagious Disease
cemetery for victims of cholera and yellow fever, and the Vaults, above ground tombs
which were disliked because they were too vulnerable to hurricanes, and were soon
abandoned. In 1885 the Lord's Ridge cemetery, on high ground on the outskirts of town,
was opened. The Wesleyans, Methodists, and Baptists established private burial grounds,
but these were little used, and according to locals were totally destroyed in the hurricanes
and storm surge of 1931 and 1961. In the spirit of "leaving no stone unturned," however,
the writer intends to visit these forgotten graveyards to see if anything of interest remains.*

---o0o---

THE 1832 CENSUS OF BELIZE

This record is in bad condition, foxed, mildewed, and water stained; the first few pages have multiple small holes and missing edges. The headings are White, Coloured, Free Black, and Slave, with columns for total numbers in each category; but instead of three columns showing the number of men, women, and children in each category, as in previous censuses, there are four columns, for men, women, and male and female children. Since given names normally show gender, male and female children are lumped together as one column in the transcript. In each category, total numbers are given by gender; these numbers were consulted to resolve doubtful names such as Francis/ Frances. Each household commences with "Family of ...," in almost all cases duplicating the name of the first person listed. Therefore, "Family of..." was only copied if the head of household was absent, subsumed, or deceased. Spelling and abbreviations vary as in the original record: William, for example, was written as William, Wm., Willm, and W^m.

p. 1: *(Ink on this page is blurred; 3's and 5's are difficult to read.)*
#1: George NICHOLSON, 1 0 0 – 0 0 0 – 0 0 0 – 1 1 0:
John DOYLE, 1 0 0 – 0 0 0 – 0 0 0 – 0 0 0
　　Clara, 40; George, 17.

#2: Property of John W. WRIGHT, 8 0 0:
　　Joe BANKS, 30; March, 35; John SULIMAN, 38 *(or 58?)*; Friday, 37;
　　Lennan, 40; Walker, 50; Willm NEAL, 22; John HINKS, 21.

#3: John YOUNG, 1 0 0 – 0 0 0 – 0 0 0 – 1 2 3:
Adriana YOUNG, 0 1 0 – 0 0 0 – 0 0 0 – 0 0 0
Louisa F. L. YOUNG, 0 0 1 – 0 0 0 – 0 0 0 – 0 0 0
Georgina M. YOUNG, 0 0 1 – 0 0 0 – 0 0 0 – 0 0 0
George C. YOUNG, 0 0 1 – 0 0 0 – 0 0 0 – 0 0 0
Frederick, 0 0 0 – 0 0 1 – 0 0 0 – 0 0 0 *(Surname not given.)*
Richard PARK, 0 0 0 – 0 0 0 – 1* 0 0
　　Philip, 20; Emma YOUNG, 28; Honor, 51; Richard, 9 months, Mary Ann, 4;
　　Bessey, 5. *Paper missing. No black child: totals show one black male.*

#4: William GENTLE, 1 0 0 – 0 0 0 – 0 0 0 – 35 17 24 (16 males, 9 females)
Jane M. GENTLE, 0 0 0 – 0 0 1 – 0 0 0 – 0 0 0
　　London, 41; John MEENY, 46; John HERCULES, 52; Sandy, 44; Jacob, 34;
　　William LOVELL, 56; Robt GENTLE, 44; Wm GENTLE, 36; Long Ben,
　　51; Peter GENTLE, 44; Edwd LEWIS, 56; Jack THOMAS, 44;

p. 2:　　Clarke GRAHAM, 43; Middleton, 44; Congo Edward, 44; Cardigan, 44;
　　Morgan, 54; John, 56; Tom (aged); Commodore, ditto. *(Ages not given.)*

100

William BOYLE, 48; Tom GENTLE, 20; Sutherland GENTLE, 22; Toby GOFF, 22; William GOFF, 20; William WOOD, 14.
Runaways: Billy, 41; Sam, 41; James, 42; Moses, 56; Henry, 30; Ned, 41; Harry, 42; London, 44; Romeo, 46.
Women: Betty, 46, Betsey, 27; Mary GRAHAM, 48; Camilla, 44; Polly, 44; Kitty, 42; Elsey, 42; Margaret, 41;

p. 3: Sophia GENTLE, 25; Juno GENTLE, 25; Eleanor GENTLE, 24; Jeany DOUGLAS, 32; Mary DOUGLAS, 28; Eliza DOUGLAS, 23; Rebecca GENTLE, 22; Jane GENTLE, 21; Peggy GENTLE, 18; Aaron GENTLE, 10; Philip GENTLE, 9; Abel GENTLE, 13; Frederick GENTLE, 10; Robert GENTLE, 14; Thomas GENTLE, 12; Henry GENTLE, 8; Ben GENTLE, 5; James GENTLE, 10; Charles GENTLE, 4; George GENTLE, 5; Andrew GENTLE, 2; Francis GENTLE, 2; Donald GENTLE, 2; William GENTLE, 1½; James GENTLE, 1; Judy GENTLE, 13; Cassandra GENTLE, 15; Rachel GENTLE, 13; Chloe GENTLE, 16; Caroline GENTLE, 9; Christian GENTLE, 4; Elizabeth GENTLE, 2; Anney GENTLE, 2; Letitia GENTLE, 2.

p. 4:
#5: William GENTLE Junr., 0 0 0 – 1 0 0 – 0 0 0 – 0 1 4:
Clementine, 33; March, 8; Bob, 4; Eve, 12; David, 2.

#6: John CADDLE, 0 0 0 – 1 0 0 – 0 0 0 – 1 1 0:
Patty ENDIN, 0 0 0 – 0 1 0 – 0 0 0 – 0 0 0
William CADDLE, 0 0 0 – 0 0 1 – 0 0 0 – 0 0 0
George, 27; Peggy, 24.

#7: John POTTS, 0 0 0 – 1 0 0 – 0 0 0 – 24 1 1:
Cath^n F. POTTS, 0 0 0 – 0 0 1 – 0 0 0 – 0 0 0
Marianne POTTS, 0 0 0 – 0 0 1 – 0 0 0 – 0 0 0
George GIBSON, 0 0 0 – 1 0 0 – 0 0 0 – 0 0 0
Chance WRIGHT, 59; Ebo James, 47; Ebo HERCULES, 47; Ben POPHAM, 47; John PUPO, 26; Richmond, 48; James FLOWERS, 47; John DESMO, 26; Charles WALL, 42; Tom REDUGEN, 34; Sam PARKER, 47; Bat.YOUNG, 38.
Runaways: Ebo John, 47; Holland, 57; Tyger Joe, 37; Jack SNOWDEN, 57.
Property of Cath^n F. POTTS:
Ned BERK, 29; Robert WETHERBY, 26; Robt LAMB, 24.
Property of Mariana POTTS:
Frederick, 26; John HERCULES, 14.
Property of George GIBSON:
John GIBSON, 36;

p. 5: John JOHN, 32; Nelson, 29; George, 36; Violet, 56.

101

Note: There were three closely related men named John Potts living in Belize in the same time period. The will of John Potts Sr., dated 10 Oct 1821, names John Potts Jr. (the head of household above) as his son, and Catherine and Marian Potts as his granddaughters. The will of Thomas Potts, dated 5 Oct 1806, names, among children by Catherine Ferrill, a son John Potts (b. 1786;) several children by Susanna Burrell; and a nephew, John Potts (Sr.) So John Potts Jr. and John Potts b. 1786 were cousins once removed. After Thomas died Catherine Ferrill lived with her nephew John Potts Sr, whose son John Potts Jr. named a daughter for her. Catherine Ferrill's property, Ferrill's Landing, descended to John Potts Jr's children; in a deed made in 1866 it was described as having burned. John Potts Jr. and Elizabeth Tillett, parents of Catherine F. and Marian/Mary Ann Potts, were enumerated separately, as both owned many slaves. George Gibson was enumerated with John Potts Jr. Was he related, and if so, how?

#8:   Elizabeth TILLETT, 0 0 0 – 0 1 0 – 0 0 0 – 9 7 8:
           Charles MUCKLEHANY, 52; Joe WILSON, 47; Roderick; Joseph
           PURCELL, 19; Harry BURNHAM; Hunter, 47; Ratcliffe; Old Jock;
           Present, 42; Patty, 40; Claudia, 29; Caroline, 21; Dorcas, 25;
           Frances; Hannah, 36; Phoebe, 10; Elenor, 9; Amelia; Catherine; John
           COOLIN, 12; Henry; Thomas; Richard. *(Ages not shown are not given.)*
           Runaway: Joe HEMSLEY, 44.

#9:   Mary WHITE, 0 0 0 – 0 1 0 – 0 0 0 – 20 9 6:
        Daniel TILLETT, 0 0 0 - 1 0 0 – 0 0 0 – 0 0 0
        Catherine TILLETT, 0 0 0 – 0 0 1 – 0 0 0 – 0 0 0
        London, 36; Joseph; Maryatt; Mintin, 38;

p. 6:   Will, 29; Peter WHITE, 36; Old George; Peter GORDON; Tuslar; Busso;
        Jemmy, 61; Rum and Water, 21; Robert; James; Joe; Thomas; Adam, 36,
        Luckie, 58; Jane, 31; Margaret, 26; Betsey; Louisa; Nancy, 41; Jenny; Peggy;
        Rachel. Runaways: Ben BULL; Handle, 42; Jupiter, 46; Prince, 46;
        Felix, 37; Philip, 46; Peter, 51; Betsey, 40; Kitty DUNCAN.
        (Ages not shown are not given.)

#10:   Jane PANTING, 0 0 0 – 0 1 0 – 0 0 0 – 0 0 0
       Peter YOUNG, 0 0 0 – 0 0 1 – 0 0 0 – 0 0 0

p. 7:   Alice C. HAMPSHIRE, 0 0 0 – 0 0 1 – 0 0 0 – 0 0 1
        The property of Alice C. HAMPSHIRE: Eleanor, 12.

#11:   William TILLETT, 0 0 0 – 1 0 0 – 0 0 0 – 1 2 2:
       Sarah JONES, 0 0 0 – 0 1 0 – 0 0 0 – 0 0 0
       Elizabeth TILLETT, 0 0 0 – 0 0 1 – 0 0 0 – 0 0 0
       Solomon TILLETT, 0 0 0 – 0 0 1 – 0 0 0 – 0 0 0
       John TILLETT, 0 0 0 – 0 0 1 – 0 0 0 – 0 0 0
       George TILLETT, 0 0 0 – 0 0 1 – 0 0 0 – 0 0 0
       Robert TILLETT, 0 0 0 – 0 0 1 – 0 0 0 – 0 0 0

David TILLETT, 0 0 0 – 0 0 1 – 0 0 0 – 0 0 0
William TILLETT, 0 0 0 – 0 0 1 – 0 0 0 – 0 0 0
Mary WHITE TILLETT, 0 0 0 – 0 0 1 – 0 0 0 – 0 0 0
    Dan, 3C; James, 2; Henry, 4 months; Jessy, 22.
Property of Sarah JONES:
    Present, 36.

Note: William Tillett, head of household above, and his sibs Elizabeth, Catherine, and George Tillett were children of Captain William and Mary White Tillett. The child Mary White Tillett, above, was named for her grandmother.

#12:   George TILLETT, 0 0 0 – 1 0 0 – 0 0 0 – 1 1 1:
        Nelson, 43; Sue, 18; Daniel, Infant.

#13:   Sarah BIRD, 0 1 0 – 0 0 0 – 0 0 0 – 0 1 0: *(Was Sarah Bird George's wife?)*
        Jane, 18.

#14:   Mary Ann UTER, 0 0 0 – 0 1 0 – 0 0 0 – 1 3 4:
    Clara UTER, 0 0 0 – 0 0 1 – 0 0 0 – 0 0 0
    John UTER, 0 0 0 – 1 0 0 – 0 0 0 – 0 0 0
    Joseph UTER, 0 0 0 – 0 0 1 – 0 0 0 – 0 0 0
    Florencio, 0 0 0 – 0 0 0 – 0 0 1 – 0 0 0 *(Surname not given.)*
        George, 21; Johnny, 1 ½; William, 2 weeks; Monimia, 22; Margaret, 26;
        Phillis, 18; Jane, 6; Rebecca, 2.

p. 8:
#15:   Sarah KEEFE, 0 1 0 – 0 0 0 – 0 0 0 – 10 10 12:
    S. K. CUNNINGHAM, 0 0 1 – 0 0 0 – 0 0 0 – 0 0 0
        Peter, 71; Quashee, 66; George, 51; November, 36; Britain, 47; Bennett, 44;
        William, 30; Peter, 30; Adam, 27; Brister, 20; Sylvia, 56; Cynthia, 51;
        Venus, 36; Harriet, 34; Ariadne, 33; Diana, 28; Rebecca, 24; Patty, 31; Bella,
        21; Eve, 20; John, 6; Frederick, 15; Middleton, 6; Henry, 4; Edwin, 2;
        Robert, 6; Toby, 1; Francis, 1; Phillis, 9; Margaret, 5; Mary, 5; Sabina, 8.

Note: Sarah Keefe Cunningham was 25 in 1832; she is marked here, incorrectly, as a child. She was born 26 Sep 1807 to Andrew Cunningham, Esq. and Sarah Keefe. Britain was aged 44 in Charles Cunningham's household in 1829.

p. 9
#16:   William GENTLE, 0 0 0 – 1 0 0 – 0 0 0 – 0 0 0
    Catherine Elizabeth, 0 0 0 – 0 0 1 – 0 0 0 – 0 0 0 *(Surname not given.)*

#17:   Abigail BENNETT, 0 0 0 – 0 1 0 – 0 0 0 – 1 1 0:
    Mary DAWSON, 0 0 0 – 0 1 0 – 0 0 0 – 0 0 0
        Aberdeen, 40; Rachel, 60.

103

#18: D. B. LOCKWARD, 1 0 0 – 0 0 0 – 0 0 0 – 0 0 0
      Margaret EMERY, 0 0 0 – 0 1 0 – 0 0 0 – 0 0 0
      Cornelia LOCKWARD, 0 0 0 – 0 0 1 – 0 0 0 – 0 0 0
      John LOCKWARD, 0 0 0 – 0 0 1 – 0 0 0 – 0 0 0
      Ann LOCKWARD, 0 0 0 – 0 0 1 – 0 0 0 – 0 0 0
      Manuel, 0 0 0 – 0 0 0 – 1 0 0 – 0 0 0 *(Surname not given.)*
      Jose MANUEL, 0 0 0 – 0 0 0 – 1 0 0 – 0 0 0

#19: Edward SHIEL, 1 0 0 – 0 0 0 – 0 0 0 – 0 1 0:
      Nanny *(Age not given.)*

#20: John S. AUGUST, 1 0 0 – 0 0 0 – 0 0 0 – 24 7 6:
      Sarah AUGUST, 0 1 0 – 0 0 0 – 0 0 0 – 0 0 0
      Ann MASKALL, 0 1 0 – 0 0 0 – 0 0 0 – 0 0 0
      Mary BYRON, 0 1 0 – 0 0 0 – 0 0 0 – 0 0 0 *(m. Wm Robt Smith Cooke ca. 1836)*
      George AUGUST, 0 0 1 – 0 0 0 – 0 0 0 – 0 0 0
          Handy, 37; Bristow, 35; Bob, 48; Charles, 45; John, 35; Primus, 55;
          Polydore, 60; Taylor, 40; Simon, 32; Simon BROASTER, 39; George, 30;
          Ned WALDRON, 34;

p. 10:   Daniel, 18; Abel, 16; Middleton, 12; William, 8; Nelson, 4; Charles, 3;
          Harry, 14; Rosette, 50; Rose, 35; Sally PEACHY, 35; Sarah, 24; Hannah,
          20; Sarah EVE, 37; Margaret, 45; Sophia, 10.
          Runaways: John STEPHEN, 53; Smart, 50; Alick, 50; Duncan, 35; Alick
          KIDD, 45; Frank, 38; Harry, 31; Harry MARTIN, 35; Tommy, 35; Ned
          AUGUST, 30.

#21: Edward WALKER, 1 0 0 – 0 0 0 – 0 0 0 – 0 0 0

#22: Henry GARDINER, 0 0 0 – 1 0 0 – 0 0 0 – 0 0 0
      Eliza A. HEWLETT, 0 0 0 – 0 1 0 – 0 0 0 – 0 0 0
      Jane H. GARDNER, 0 0 0 – 0 0 1 – 0 0 0 – 0 0 0

p. 11:
#23: Charles CRAIG, 1 0 0 – 0 0 0 – 0 0 0 – 11 4 2:
      Agnes CRAIG, 0 0 0 – 0 1 0 – 0 0 0 – 0 0 0
      Louisa HILL, 0 0 0 – 0 1 0 – 0 0 0 – 0 0 0
      Jane A. CRAIG, 0 0 0 – 0 0 1 – 0 0 0 – 0 0 0
      Elizabeth CRAIG, 0 0 0 – 0 0 1 – 0 0 0 – 0 0 0
          Charles, 33; Lewis, 39; Jem, 46; John, 34; Lucy, 69; Princess, 64; Stella, 38;
          Sarah, 24; George, 4; Eliza, 1 ½.
          Runaways: Daniel, 44; Charles, 69; Duke, 62; Sam, 46; Boston, 52; Mingo,
          52.
      Property of A. CRAIG:
          Jack, 46.

#24: John ALEXANDER, 1 0 0 – 0 0 0 – 0 0 0 – 0 0 0
      Mary ALEXANDER, 0 0 0 – 0 0 1 – 0 0 0 – 0 0 0

#25: Edward BOWMAN, 0 0 0 – 0 0 0 – 1 0 0 – 0 0 0
      John BOWMAN, 0 0 0 – 0 0 0 – 0 0 1 – 0 0 0
      Edward BOWMAN, 0 0 0 – 0 0 0 – 0 0 1 – 0 0 0
      Maria BOWMAN, 0 0 0 – 0 0 0 – 0 0 1 – 0 0 0
      William H. BOWMAN, 0 0 0 – 0 0 0 – 0 0 1 – 0 0 0
      George BOWMAN, 0 0 0 – 0 0 0 – 0 0 1 – 0 0 0
      Jean BOWMAN, 0 0 0 – 0 0 0 – 0 0 1 – 0 0 0
      Amelia BOWMAN, 0 0 0 – 0 0 0 – 0 0 1 – 0 0 0
      Thomas C. BOWMAN, 0 0 0 – 0 0 0 – 0 0 1 – 0 0 0
      William FANTASSY, 0 0 0 – 0 0 0 – 0 0 1 – 0 0 0
      Margaret FANTASSY, 0 0 0 – 0 1 0 – 0 0 0 – 0 0 0
      Elizabeth FANTASSY, 0 0 0 – 0 0 0 – 0 0 1 – 0 0 0

p. 12:
#26: James FORRESTER, 1 0 0 – 0 0 0 – 0 0 0 – 1 2 4:
      Sarah FORRESTER, 0 1 0 – 0 0 0 – 0 0 0 – 0 0 0
          Venus, 28; Rose, 15; Maria, 8; Sarah, 5; Elizabeth, 2; Frederick, 5; Charles
          EVE, 28.

#27: Property of Messrs. HYDE & FORBES, 2 1 0:
          Sharper HYDE, 48; Jack NEAL, 45; Venus, 40.

#28: Alexander FORBES, 1 0 0 – 0 0 0 – 0 0 0 – 0 1 0:
      James H. CAMPBELL, 1 0 0 – 0 0 0 – 0 0 0 – 0 0 0
          Christiana BROASTER, 50.

#29: Amelia GORDON, 0 1 0 – 0 0 0 – 0 0 0 – 6 3 0:
      Isabella SUTHERLAND, 0 1 0 – 0 0 0 – 0 0 0 – 0 0 0
          Warwick, 44; Bill, 44; Richard, 36; Kitty, 29; Mary, 14.
          Runaway: Davy, 44; Ramsay, 48; Charles, 48.
      Property of Isabella SUTHERLAND:
          Jane, 22

#30: James McDONALD, 1 0 0 – 0 0 0 – 0 0 0 – 4 0 0:
      Patience McDONALD, 0 1 0 – 0 0 0 – 0 0 0 – 0 0 0
      George WALTERS, 1 0 0 – 0 0 0 – 0 0 0 – 0 0 0
          Joe, 41; Quamino, 56.
          Runaway: Billy GOFF, 51; Peter, 18

p. 13: Richard McDONALD, 0 0 1 – 0 0 0 – 0 0 0 – 0 0 0
        Valancourt McDONALD, 0 0 1 – 0 0 0 – 0 0 0 – 0 0 0

#31:   Property of Amelia Catherine McDONALD, 0 0 1:
       St John the Baptist, 5.

#32:   Property of James R. McDONALD, 1 1 0:
       Walter, 13; Betty, 17.
       Runaway: William, 39.

#33:   Property of George W^m McDONALD, 1 1 1:
       John HANDY, 28; Henry WALTERS, 6; Betty MASKALL, 26.

#34:   Family of Margaret PERRY, 2 3 2:
       Catherine WHEELER, 0 1 0 – 0 0 0 – 0 0 0 – 0 0 0
       James BERTIE, 1 0 0 – 0 0 0 – 0 0 0 – 0 0 0
       Margaret PERRY, 0 1 0 – 0 0 0 – 0 0 0 – 2 3 2:
       George PEDDIE, 1 0 0 – 0 0 0 – 0 0 0 – 0 0 0
           Samuel SNELLINGS, 22; Cyrus, 30; George NICHOLSON, 4;
           Nancy SNELLING [*sic*], 40; Celby HARRIS, 30; Diana, 28; Nancy, 2.

#35:   James H. CROZIER, 1 0 0 – 0 0 0 – 0 0 0 – 0 0 0
       Harriet EVERITT, 0 0 0 – 0 1 0 – 0 0 0 – 0 0 0
       James R. CROZIER, 0 0 0 – 0 0 1 – 0 0 0 – 0 0 0
       Jacob H. CROZIER, 0 0 0 – 0 0 1 – 0 0 0 – 0 0 0

#36:   George RUNNALS, 0 0 0 – 1 0 0 – 0 0 0 – 1 0 0
       Elizth R. RUNNALS, 0 0 0 – 0 1 0 – 0 0 0 – 0 0 0

p. 14:   Susanna E. RUNNALS, 0 0 0 – 0 0 1 – 0 0 0 – 1 0 0
         Property of Susanna E. RUNNALS:
         Daniel BROASTER, 28.

Note: It appears that Susanna E. was the child of George and his second wife, Elizabeth Ramsay Wade - not his first, Sophia Augusta Barnes, b. Dec 9 1801 and bapt. Jan 3 1802 at St John, Hackney, Middlesex, to Thomas and Jane Barnes. There was no child Susanna living with George, or with widowed Jane Barnes, in 1826 and 1829. Elizabeth R. Wade, born in 1814, was in her mother's household in 1829. In 1830 George purchased and manumitted Memba Bode; the 1835 census shows Memba with a child Maria Bode. Was Maria George's daughter? George and Elizabeth separated – when? She remarried to Marcus Charles Bennett and had four children by him, Charles Marshal, Catherine, Emma Louisa, and Marshal Bennett. George probably moved to his plantation on Sibun River, as he does not appear in later censuses. He died in 1849; his will names Susanna E. his daughter, Joshua, George Jr., Horatio, and Richard Runnels (who was their mother?) and Mrs. Trapp, Isabella McKinney, Margaret Stain, Maria Runnals (Memba Bode's daughter?) and his servant, Joseph Iles.

#37:   John ARMSTRONG, 0 0 0 – 1 0 0 – 0 0 0 – 0 0 0
       Martha ARMSTRONG, 0 1 0 – 0 0 0 – 0 0 0 – 0 0 0

Agnes ARMSTRONG, 0 0 0 – 0 1 0 – 0 0 0 – 0 0 0
Walter R. ARMSTRONG, 0 0 0 – 0 0 1 – 0 0 0 – 0 0 0
Martha S. ARMSTRONG, 0 0 0 – 0 0 1 – 0 0 0 – 0 0 0
The property of E. M. CARMICHAEL, 1 0 0:
  Prince, 38.

#38: John PARKS, 0 0 0 – 1 0 0 – 0 0 0 – 1 0 0:
      Abby FLOWERS, 0 0 0 – 0 0 0 – 0 1 0 – 0 0 0
        Prince, 55.

#39: William USHER, 1 0 0 – 0 0 0 – 0 0 0 – 0 0 0
      Sarah USHER, 0 1 0 – 0 0 0 – 0 0 0 – 0 0 0
      William C. USHER, 0 0 1 – 0 0 0 – 0 0 0 – 0 0 0
      Frederick W. USHER, 0 0 1 – 0 0 0 – 0 0 0 – 0 0 0
      The property of F. R. USHER, G. M. USHER, Emma USHER, Wm C. USHER,
      and F. W. USHER: 12 7 10:
        Philip JACKSON, 36; Joe McKEE, 16; Jack JACKSON, 20; Jack, 36;
        Dasher, 20; Tom PASLOW, 22; Tom LONGSWORTH, 25; Ellick, 45;
        Dublin, 60; Ellick, 50; Hamlet, 40; Billy, 45; Richard, 15;

p. 15: John, 16; William, 12. Henry, 14; Tom, 15; George, 12; Benjamin, 10; Leah,
        26; Child, 2; Mimba, 55; Clarinda, 30; Grace, 8; Phoebe, 25; Susan, 8; Jenny,
        15; Nelly, 15; Fanny, 50.

#40: Samuel F. AUGUST, 0 0 0 – 1 0 0 – 0 0 0 – 13 6 0:
      Ann R. AUGUST, 0 0 0 – 0 1 0 – 0 0 0 – 0 0 0   *(Ann ROSS AUGUST)*
      Elizabeth AUGUST, 0 0 0 – 0 0 1 – 0 0 0 – 0 0 0
      Anne R. AUGUST, 0 0 0 – 0 0 1 – 0 0 0 – 0 0 0   *(Ann ROSS AUGUST Jr.)*
      Saml F. AUGUST, 0 0 0 – 0 0 1 – 0 0 0 – 0 0 0   *(Samuel F. AUGUST Jr.)*
      Simon M. K. AUGUST, 0 0 0 – 0 0 1 – 0 0 0 – 0 0 0
      Richard AUGUST, 0 0 0 – 0 0 1 – 0 0 0 – 0 0 0
      Elizabeth AUGUST, 0 0 0 – 0 0 0 – 0 1 0 – 0 0 0
        Andrew, 46; Campbell, 37; Charley, 43; Jackey, 30; Nelson, 27; Port Royal,
        58; Richard, 22; Scotland, 38; Toby, 22.
        Runaway: Sampson, 48; Tom, 51; Tom, 40; William, 38; Fanny, 31; Fanny,
        28;

p. 16: Penelope, 22; Eleanor, 21; Cloe, 37; Amelia, 19.

#41: John USHER, 0 0 0 – 1 0 0 – 0 0 0 – 11 2 2:
      Sarah USHER, 0 0 0 – 0 1 0 – 0 0 0 – 0 0 0   *(Sarah PURCELL USHER)*
      Joseph H. USHER, 0 0 0 – 0 0 1 – 0 0 0 – 0 0 0
      Edward P. USHER, 0 0 0 – 0 0 1 – 0 0 0 – 0 0 0   *(Edward PURCELL? USHER)*
      John H. USHER, 0 0 0 – 0 0 1 – 0 0 0 – 0 0 0
      Robert USHER, 0 0 0 – 0 0 1 – 0 0 0 – 0 0 0   *(Robert BEACH USHER)*
      Mary W. USHER, 0 0 0 – 0 0 1 – 0 0 0 – 0 0 0   *(Mary WHITE USHER)*

107

Jane E. USHER, 0 0 0 – 0 0 1 – 0 0 0 – 0 0 0
   Joseph USHER, 35; Edward USHER, 38; Peter USHER, 40; Ned USHER,
   25; Prince USHER, 45; Jacob USHER, 48; Lord USHER, 50; John USHER,
   39; Charles USHER, 26; Coffee USHER, 32; Jenny USHER, 40; Caroline
   USHER, 45; Francis USHER, 12; Charley USHER, 3.
   Runaway: David USHER, 36.

Note: A tablet in St. John's Cathedral memorializes John Usher, Esq. His wife, Sarah Purcell Usher, was baptized in 1806, the only known child of Capt. Purcell and Elizabeth Tillett. Robert Beach Usher, above, married Mary Anne Cochrane and had children including John Purcell Usher, whose transcript of cemetery MI's was published in 1907. Descendants had strong ties of friendship; the writer's aunt, Winifred Bennett Keddy Reddyrough, spoke of Arthur Norman Usher, son of John Purcell and Sarah Blanch Usher, visiting her father, Elizabeth Tillett's great-grandson Marshal Handyside Bennett, in England during WWI before leaving for France. Norman Usher was awarded the Military Cross for valor, but was killed in action on 4 Nov 1918, just a week before the Armistice. His brother or cousin? Hubert Wardlow Usher was killed in France in 1816. Both men are buried in France.

#42:   Mary WINTER, 0 0 0 – 0 1 0 – 0 0 0 – 0 0 0
       C. R. BALDWIN, 0 0 1 – 0 0 0 – 0 0 0 – 0 0 0
       Nancy GEDDES, 0 0 0 – 0 0 0 – 0 1 0 – 0 0 0
       Ann J. MEIGHAN, 0 0 0 – 0 0 1 – 0 0 0 – 0 0 0

#43:   Property of R. J. ANDREW & Co., 15 4 2:
       George, 35; Edward, 30; Adam, 40; London, 40; Ben, 41; Scotland, 27;

p. 17:   William, 28; Ned, 30; Nelson, 36; Archie, 17; Cupid, 30; Harry, 36; Peter, 37;
         Tom, 38; Charley, 34; Thomas, 12; Jenny, 30; Jackey, 40; Lucretia, 16;
         Clarissa, 14; Mary, 18 months.

#44:   Joseph SWASEY, 0 0 0 – 1 0 0 – 0 0 0 – 7 2 5:
       John SWASEY, 0 0 0 – 0 0 1 – 0 0 0 – 0 0 0
       Nisida SWASEY, 0 0 0 – 0 1 0 – 0 0 0 – 0 0 0
       Maria SWASEY, 0 0 0 – 0 0 1 – 0 0 0 – 0 0 0
       Frances SWASEY, 0 0 0 – 0 0 1 – 0 0 0 – 0 0 0
       Jane SWASEY, 0 0 0 – 0 0 1 – 0 0 0 – 0 0 0
       James M. SWASEY, 0 0 0 – 0 0 1 – 0 0 0 – 0 0 0
           Henry SWASEY, 17; Joe BULL, 52; Ireland, 47; Billy CUNNINGHAM, 26;
           Llewellen, 22; Parkes, 33; Davy, 53; March SWASEY, 14; Joe YOUNG, 14;
           Nancy, 22; Sukey, 34; Amelia, 2; Bella, 6; Caroline, 1.

#45:   John Alexr. La CROIX, 0 0 0 – 1 0 0 – 0 0 0 – 0 0 0
       Diana M. MILLER, 0 0 0 – 0 1 0 – 0 0 0 – 0 0 0

p. 18: Ann M. La CROIX, 0 0 0 – 0 1 0 – 0 0 0
Isabella La CROIX, 0 0 0 – 0 0 1 – 0 0 0 – 0 0 0
Margaret R. La CROIX, 0 0 0 – 0 0 1 – 0 0 0 – 0 0 0

#46: Elizabeth SWASEY, 0 0 0 – 0 1 0 – 0 0 0 – 0 1 0:
George HAYLOCK, 0 0 0 – 1 0 0 – 0 0 0 – 0 0 0
John WRIGHT, 0 0 0 – 1 0 0 – 0 0 0 – 0 0 0
Selina ORGILL, 0 0 0 – 0 1 0 – 0 0 0 – 0 0 0
Mary Jane GAVIN, 0 0 0 – 0 1 0 – 0 0 0 – 0 0 0
Susan SWASEY. *(Age not given.)*

#47: James R. CUNNINGHAM, 0 0 0 – 1 0 0 – 0 0 0 – 0 1 0:
Catherine SMITH, 0 0 0 – 0 0 0 – 0 1 0 – 0 0 0
John Nic^s CROFT, 0 0 0 – 1 0 0 – 0 0 0 – 0 0 0
Edward CROFT, 0 0 0 – 0 0 1 – 0 0 0 – 0 0 0
Indian CUNNINGHAM, 0 0 0 – 0 0 1 – 0 0 0 – 0 0 0
Sally CUNNINGHAM, 20.

#48: James WELSH, 1 0 0 – 0 0 0 – 0 0 0 – 1 3 0:
William E. HAMPSHIRE, 1 0 0 – 0 0 0 – 0 0 0 – 0 0 0
S. M. MUNRO, 0 1 0 – 0 0 0 – 0 0 0 – 0 0 0
Philip DAVIS, 0 0 0 – 1 0 0 – 0 0 0 – 0 0 0)
John WELSH, 0 0 0 – 0 0 0 – 1 0 0 – 0 0 0) Indented Servants.
Billy MASKALL; Elizabeth STOBO; Belle; Kate. *(Ages not given.)*

p. 19:
#49: William WILSON, 0 0 0 – 1 0 0 – 0 0 0 – 0 0 0
Elizabeth WILSON, 0 0 0 – 0 0 0 – 0 1 0 – 0 0 0
John HENRY, 0 0 0 – 0 0 1 – 0 0 0 – 0 0 0

#50: Family of JOHNSTON, CARMICHAEL & Co.:
John JOHNSTON, 1 0 0 – 0 0 0 – 0 0 0 – 0 0 0
Duncan MacLARTY, 1 0 0 – 0 0 0 – 0 0 0 – 0 0 0
Amado ARGUELLAS, 1 0 0 – 0 0 0 – 0 0 0 – 0 0 0
Arch^d MONTGOMERY, 1 0 0 – 0 0 0 – 0 0 0 – 0 0 0 *(m. Miss Saunders 1847*
at St. James Westminster)

#51: Joseph LORD, 0 0 0 – 1 0 0 – 0 0 0 – 0 0 0

#52: Ann WAIGHT, 0 1 0 – 0 0 0 – 0 0 0 – 1 0 0:   *(Widow of James Waight,*
James WAIGHT, 0 0 1 – 0 0 0 – 0 0 0 – 0 0 0   *master of the Free School,*
John W. WAIGHT, 0 0 1 – 0 0 0 – 0 0 0 – 0 0 0   *churchwarden and*
Mary A. WAIGHT, 0 0 1 – 0 0 0 – 0 0 0 – 0 0 0   *organist.)*
Eliza WAIGHT, 0 0 1 – 0 0 0 – 0 0 0 – 0 0 0
George WHITE [*sic*], 32.

#53:   Richard SMITH, 0 0 0 – 0 0 0 – 1 0 0 – 0 0 0
Joanna BATTISTA, 0 0 0 – 0 0 0 – 0 1 0 – 0 0 0

#54:   Eleanor CADDLE, 0 0 0 – 0 1 0 – 0 0 0 – 4 1 0:
Edward CODD, 0 0 0 – 0 0 1 – 0 0 0 – 0 0 0
    Billy, 45; Joe, 42; George, 53; Prince, 31; Olive, 29.

p. 20:
#55:   Menimer JONES, 0 0 0 – 0 1 0 – 0 0 0 – 0 0 0
Eliza, 0 0 0 – 0 0 1 – 0 0 0 – 0 0 0
Margaret, 0 0 0 – 0 0 1 – 0 0 0 – 0 0 0
Susanna, 0 0 0 – 0 0 1 – 0 0 0 – 0 0 0
Henrietta, 0 0 0 – 0 0 1 – 0 0 0 – 0 0 0
Mary Ann, 0 0 0 – 0 0 1 – 0 0 0 – 0 0 0 *(Surnames not given.)*

#56:   Matthew NEWPORT, 1 0 0 – 0 0 0 – 0 0 0 – 0 0 0 *(Rector of St. John's.)*
Catherine NEWPORT, 0 1 0 – 0 0 0 – 0 0 0 – 0 0 0
Eliza Mary NEWPORT, 0 0 1 – 0 0 0 – 0 0 0 – 0 0 0
Henry M. NEWPORT, 0 0 1 – 0 0 0 – 0 0 0 – 0 0 0
Eaton EDWARDS, 0 0 0 – 0 0 0 – 1 0 0 – 0 0 0
John CARD, 0 0 0 – 0 0 0 – 0 0 1 – 0 0 0
    (blank)   0 0 0 – 0 0 0 – 0 1 0 – 0 0 0

#57:   Robert HOARE, 0 0 0 – 0 0 0 – 1 0 0 – 0 0 0
Daphne Eliz[th] HINKS, 0 0 0 – 0 0 0 – 0 1 0 – 0 0 0

#58:   Henry BAILEY, 0 0 0 – 0 0 0 – 1 0 0 – 1 0 0:
Jane GRANT, 0 0 0 – 0 0 0 – 0 1 0 – 0 0 0
Wm. ANDERSON, 0 0 0 – 0 0 0 – 0 0 1 – 0 0 0
    Rodney, 21.

p. 21:
#59:   Joseph RENAUD, 0 0 0 – 1 0 0 – 0 0 0 – 0 0 0
Mary KENNEDY, 0 0 0 – 0 0 0 – 0 1 0 – 0 0 0
Elizabeth PANTING, 0 0 0 – 0 0 1 – 0 0 0 – 0 0 0
Harriet RENAUD, 0 0 0 – 0 0 1 – 0 0 0 – 0 0 0
Benjamin RENAUD, 0 0 0 – 0 0 1 – 0 0 0 – 0 0 0
Alexander RENAUD, 0 0 0 – 0 0 1 – 0 0 0 – 0 0 0
Lucy RENAUD, 0 0 0 – 0 0 1 – 0 0 0 – 0 0 0
Joseph RENAUD, 0 0 0 – 0 0 1 – 0 0 0 – 0 0 0

#60:   James ROBINSON, 0 0 0 – 0 0 0 – 1 0 0 – 0 0 0

#61:   Family of Lawrence CRAWFORD, 0 1 0:
Susannah PRICE, 0 0 0 – 0 1 0 – 0 0 0 – 0 0 0
Eliza CRAWFORD, 0 0 0 – 0 1 0 – 0 0 0 – 0 0 0

John CRAWFORD, 0 3 0 – 1 0 0 – 0 0 0 – 0 0 0
William CRAWFORD, 0 0 0 – 1 0 0 – 0 0 0 – 0 0 0
Jane CRAWFORD, 0 0 0 – 0 0 1 – 0 0 0 – 0 0 0
Ann CRAWFORD, 0 C 0 – 0 0 1 – 0 0 0 – 0 0 0
George CRAWFORD, 0 0 0 – 0 0 1 – 0 0 0 – 0 0 0
Nicholas DAWSON, 0 0 0 – 0 0 1 – 0 0 0 – 0 0 0
Lawrence CRAWFORD, 0 0 0 – 1 0 0 – 0 0 0 – 0 0 0
    Patty CRAWFORD, 65.

Note: Was Lawrence omitted from the start of the list by error, then added at the end?

#62:   George R. PITKETHLY, 1 0 0 – 0 0 0 – 0 0 0 – 0 0 0
    Laura PITKETHLY, 0 C 0 – 0 1 0 – 0 0 0 – 0 0 0

p. 22:
#63:   William MASKALL, 1 0 0 – 0 0 0 – 0 0 0 – 14 4 6:
    Rebecca MASKALL, 0 1 0 – 0 0 0 – 0 0 0 – 0 0 0
    Maria Elizth GRAY, 0 1 0 – 0 0 0 – 0 0 0 – 0 0 0
    Margaret M. MASKALL, 0 0 1 – 0 0 0 – 0 0 0 – 0 0 0
    Frederick N. MASKALL, 0 0 1 – 0 0 0 – 0 0 0 – 0 0 0
    Leonard M. BYRON, 1 C 0 – 0 0 0 – 0 0 0 – 0 0 0
    William M. GRAY, 1 0 C – 0 0 0 – 0 0 0 – 0 0 0
        John DRACKSON*, 41; Peter BAKER, 24; Edward, 25; Cherry, 43; Ned, 40;
        Fortune, 48; Tom, 42; Duncan, 44; Joe, 51; Old John, 72; Jem GRAY, 38;
        Nicholas, 18; Charles, 11; Mary Ann, 20; Frances, 17; James (her child,) 2;
        John, 14; Edward, 9; Mary Ann DAVIS, 30; Jane (her child,) 7; Marinah, 36;
        James (her child,) 6; Anne, ditto, 3; Sue, 9. *= DERIXON, DRAKSON.*

#64:   Sarah MASKALL, 0 0 0 – 0 1 0 – 0 0 0 – 0 0 0
    Catherine McKINNEY, 0 0 0 – 0 1 0 – 0 0 0 – 0 0 0
    Isabella McKINNEY, 0 0 C – 0 0 1 – 0 0 0 – 0 0 0
    Property of the Estate of Isa^a GRAHAM, Dec'd: 1 1 2:
        Hannah GRAHAM, 33; Thomas GRAHAM, 19; Sarah GRAHAM, 2;
        Ellen GRAHAM, 1.

p. 23:
#65:   George CLARKE, 0 0 0 – 1 0 0 – 0 0 0 – 0 0 0

#66:   Mary McKAY, 0 1 0 – 0 0 0 – 0 0 0 – 0 1 0:
    Janette, 17.

#67:   Alexander HOOK, 0 0 0 – 0 0 0 – 1 0 0 – 0 0 0

#68:   William CROSBIE, 0 0 0 – 1 0 0 – 0 0 0 – 0 0 0

#69:   Wm. WILLIAMSON, 1 0 0 – 0 0 0 – 0 0 0 – 0 0 0

#70:   Clashmore LAWLESS, 0 0 0 – 0 0 0 – 1 0 0 – 0 0 0
       Penelope LAWLESS, 0 0 0 – 0 0 0 – 0 1 0 – 0 0 0

#71:   Charles RABAN, 0 0 0 – 1 0 0 – 0 0 0 – 0 0 0
       Elizabeth WILLIAMS, 0 0 0 – 0 1 0 – 0 0 0 – 0 0 0

#72:   Geo. Ure. SKINNER, 1 0 0 – 0 0 0 – 0 0 0 – 0 0 0
       C. S. MIDDLETON, 1 0 0 – 0 0 0 – 0 0 0 – 0 0 0
       Jose, 0 0 0 – 1 0 0 – 0 0 0 – 0 0 0
       Modesta, 0 0 0 – 0 1 0 – 0 0 0 – 0 0 0
       Child, 0 0 0 – 0 0 1 – 0 0 0 – 0 0 0 *(Surnames not given.)*

p. 24:
#73:   William H. COATES, 1 0 0 – 0 0 0 – 0 0 0 – 1 0 0:
       Edward MAIDEN, 0 0 1 – 0 0 0 – 0 0 0 – 0 0 0 *(Son of Dr. & Mrs. Maiden?)*
       Maria GUEST, 0 0 0 – 0 1 0 – 0 0 0 – 0 0 0
       Elizabeth TYLER, 0 0 0 – 0 1 0 – 0 0 0 – 0 0 0
       Eleanor DAW, 0 0 0 – 0 1 0 – 0 0 0 – 0 0 0
           Daniel, 65.

#74:   Robert TURNBULL, 1 0 0 – 0 0 0 – 0 0 0 – 0 0 0
       Frances TURNBULL, 0 1 0 – 0 0 0 – 0 0 0 – 0 0 0
       David TURNBULL, 0 0 0 – 0 0 1 – 0 0 0 – 0 0 0
       Maria TURNBULL, 0 0 0 – 0 0 1 – 0 0 0 – 0 0 0

#75:   Francis HAYLOCK, 0 0 0 – 1 0 0 – 0 0 0 – 0 0 0
       Catherine COFFIN, 0 0 0 – 0 1 0 – 0 0 0 – 0 0 0
       Francis HAYLOCK, 0 0 0 – 0 0 1 – 0 0 0 – 0 0 0
       James HAYLOCK, 0 0 0 – 0 0 1 – 0 0 0 – 0 0 0
       Maria HAYLOCK, 0 0 0 – 0 0 1 – 0 0 0 – 0 0 0
       Robert HAYLOCK, 0 0 0 – 0 0 1 – 0 0 0 – 0 0 0

#76:   Richard BULL, 0 0 0 – 1 0 0 – 0 0 0 – 0 0 0
       Lydia Mary BULL, 0 0 0 – 0 1 0 – 0 0 0 – 0 0 0
       Harriet BULL, 0 0 0 – 0 1 0 – 0 0 0 – 0 0 0

#77:   Stephen STAIN, 0 0 0 – 1 0 0 – 0 0 0 – 0 0 0
       Catherie TUCKER, 0 0 0 – 0 0 0 – 0 1 0 – 0 0 0
       Mary Ann STAIN, 0 0 0 – 0 0 0 – 0 0 1 – 0 0 0
       Eliza STAIN, 0 0 0 – 0 0 0 – 0 0 1 – 0 0 0

p. 25:
#78:   John WAGGNER, 0 0 0 – 1 0 0 – 0 0 0 – 0 0 0
       Elizabeth WAGGNER, 0 0 0 – 0 1 0 – 0 0 0 – 0 0 0
       Francis WAGGNER, 0 0 0 – 0 0 1 – 0 0 0 – 0 0 0
       Robert WAGGNER, 0 0 0 – 0 0 1 – 0 0 0 – 0 0 0

Sarah WAGGNER, 0 0 0 – 0 0 1 – 0 0 0 – 0 0 0
Louisa WAGGNER, 0 0 0 – 0 0 1 – 0 0 0 – 0 0 0
Catherine WAGGNER, 0 0 0 – 0 0 1 – 0 0 0 – 0 0 0

#79:   John WARRIOR, 0 0 0 – 0 0 0 – 1 0 0 – 0 0 0
Mary WOOD, 0 0 0 – 0 0 0 – 0 1 0 – 0 0 0
Quasheba WARRIOR, 0 0 0 – 0 0 0 – 0 1 0 – 0 0 0
Ann S. WARRIOR, 0 0 0 – 0 0 0 – 0 1 0 – 0 0 0

#80:   James BELISLE, 0 0 0 – 1 0 0 – 0 0 0 – 0 0 0
Charlotte BELISLE, 0 0 0 – 0 0 0 – 0 1 0 – 0 0 0
Joseph BELISLE, 0 0 0 – 0 0 1 – 0 0 0 – 0 0 0
Margaret BELISLE, 0 0 0 – 0 0 1 – 0 0 0 – 0 0 0
Elizabeth BELISLE, 0 0 0 – 0 1 0 – 0 0 0 – 0 0 0
Hannah BELISLE, 0 0 0 – 0 0 1 – 0 0 0 – 0 0 0
Jane BELISLE, 0 0 0 – 0 0 1 – 0 0 0 – 0 0 0
Eliza BELISLE, 0 0 0 – 0 0 0 – 0 1 0 – 0 0 0

#81:   John McKINNEN, 0 0 0 – 1 0 0 – 0 0 0 – 0 0 0
Margaret McKINNEN, 0 0 0 – 0 1 0 – 0 0 0 – 0 0 0
Alex^r McKINNEN, 0 0 0 – 0 0 1 – 0 0 0 – 0 0 0

p. 26:
#82   Family of Cath^n TILLETT, Dec'd, 1 5 5:
William CUNNINGHAM, 0 0 0 – 0 0 1 – 0 0 0 – 0 0 0
Sarah K. CUNNINGHAM, 0 0 0 – 0 0 1 – 0 0 0 – 0 0 0
Cath^n T. CUNNINGHAM, 0 0 0 – 0 0 1 – 0 0 0 – 0 0 0
     Robert, 23; Dolly, 26; Kitty, 34; Sue, 34; Quasheba, 50; Rachel, 18; Eleanor,
     14; Betsey, 6; Sarah, 3; Alick, 10; Alick, 11.

*Note: Catherine "Kitty" Tillett, b. ca. 1789 to William Tillett and Mary White, was
buried on 8 Jan 1832, aged 43. She married Charles Keefe Cunningham; William was
born in 1822, Sarah Keefe in 1823, and Catherine Tillett in 1826; the latter married
Thomas Robinson and died in 1859.*

#83:   William H. COFFIN, 1 0 0 – 0 0 0 – 0 0 0 – 8 2 0:
Eliza JOHNSON, 0 0 0 – 0 1 0 – 0 0 0 – 0 0 0
     John HEMSLEY; Brown; Toby NEAL; Harry; Peter; Ben; Jack; Sancho;
     Olive; Lucretia. *(Ages not given.)*

#84:   Property of the Estate of Eliz. M. BLOCKLEY, 0 3 6:
     Jenny, 29; Peggy, 39; Elizabeth, 14; Phillis, 12; Jane, 9; Mary, 5; Bella, 2;
     Prue, 61; George 12.
p. 27:
#85:   Joseph Jas. RABATEAU, 0 0 0 – 1 0 0 – 0 0 0 – 3 0 0:
George W. RABATEAU, 0 0 0 – 0 0 1 – 0 0 0 – 0 0 0

James BULL, 0 0 0 – 0 0 1 – 0 0 0 – 0 0 0
Mary SAVORY, 0 0 0 – 0 1 0 – 0 0 0 – 0 0 0
    Lawrence LAWRIE, 45; Edmund LOVELL, 35; John SAVORY, 33.

#86:   Joseph VERNON, 0 0 0 – 1 0 0 – 0 0 0 – 4 1 0:
    Margaret NEALE, 0 0 0 – 0 1 0 – 0 0 0 – 0 0 0
    Janette VERNON, 0 0 0 – 0 0 1 – 0 0 0 – 0 0 0
    John VERNON, 0 0 0 – 0 0 1 – 0 0 0 – 0 0 0
    William VERNON, 0 0 0 – 0 0 1 – 0 0 0 – 0 0 0
    Joshua VERNON, 0 0 0 – 0 0 1 – 0 0 0 – 0 0 0
    Michael VERNON, 0 0 0 – 0 0 1 – 0 0 0 – 0 0 0
    Benjamin VERNON, 0 0 0 – 0 0 1 – 0 0 0 – 0 0 0
    Alexander VERNON, 0 0 0 – 0 0 1 – 0 0 0 – 0 0 0
    Moses, 65; Punch, 60; Dan, 20; Joe, 17; Catherine, 16.

#87:   Elizabeth SMITH, 0 0 0 – 0 0 0 – 0 1 0 – 2 2 0:
    Simon, 23; Jack, 20; Diana, 48; Eve, 17.

#88:   John DARLING, 0 0 0 – 0 0 0 – 1 0 0 – 1 0 0:
    Nancy PITT, 0 0 0 – 0 0 0 – 0 0 1 – 0 0 0
    Derry DARLING. *(Age not given.)*

#89:   Charles SMITH, 0 0 0 – 1 0 0 – 0 0 0 – 1 0 0:
    Maria SMITH, 0 0 0 – 0 0 0 – 0 1 0 – 0 0 0
    John J. SMITH, 0 0 0 – 1 0 0 – 0 0 0 – 0 0 0
    Limehouse SMITH, 31.

p. 28:
#90:   The Estate of Mary HICKEY, Dec'd, under charge of F. W. MARTINY, 31 9 2:
    London, 29; Peter, 43; Venture, 45; Charley, 50; Joe, 50; Harry Corromantee,
    55; Mongola Adam, 55; Jemmy MEANY, 55; Anthony, 55; Moco Jack, 55;
    Henry, 55; Hazard, 55; Quam, 60; Sandy, 60; William PITT, 65; Stepney, 73;
    Mandingo Harry, 80; Moco Scotland, 90; James, 21; Louisa, 29; Patience, 50;
    Mary, 50; Nancy, 75; Araminta, 39; Grace, 14; Ben, 29; Alexander
    ANDERSON, 41.
    Legacies: Jenny, 18; Mimba, 21; Esther, 21; Nora, 20; William, 15;

p. 29:   John, 23; Monday, 23.
    Runaways: Shakespear, 45; Parker, 45; Goodluck 45; Sampson, 45; Richard,
    45; Quashie GOFF, 50; Bob, 55; Ned WILSON, 71.

#91:   Frederick Wm. MARTINY, 1 0 0 – 0 0 0 – 0 0 0 – 1 3 2:
    Eliza MARTINY, 0 1 0 – 0 0 0 – 0 0 0 – 0 0 0
    Fred^{k} B. MARTINY, 0 0 1 – 0 0 0 – 0 0 0 – 0 0 0
    Henry H. MARTINY, 0 0 1 – 0 0 0 – 0 0 0 – 0 0 0
    Emily MARTINY, 0 0 1 – 0 0 0 – 0 0 0 – 0 0 0

114

Old Jemmy, 70; Sam, 5½; Robert, 3; Sylvia, 50; Jessy GOOD, 37; Emily FRANCES, 8.

#92:   James USHER, 0 0 0 – 1 0 0 – 0 0 0 – 2 1 0: *(Brother of John.)*
        Abigail USHER, 0 0 0 – 0 1 0 – 0 0 0 – 0 0 0
        Jane LONGSWORTH, 0 0 0 – 0 1 0 – 0 0 0 – 0 0 0
        Marcus EWING, 0 0 0 – 1 0 0 – 0 0 0 – 0 0 0
        Helena LE ROY, 0 0 0 – 0 1 0 – 0 0 0 – 0 0 0
        Property of Jane LONGSWORTH:
            Maria, 60; Benjamin, 28; Quamina, 45.

Note: Abigail Ewing Usher and Marcus Ewing were children of John and Elizabeth Ewing. Jane was their half-sib, child of Elizabeth Ewing and William Longsworth. John Ewing died in 1797. Elizabeth and Edmund Meighan had a daughter, Catherine Meighan, baptized in 1806. Elizabeth later had more children with William Longsworth. The children's baptisms are recorded: See the First Parish Register of Belize.

#93:   Richard JONES, 0 0 0 – 0 0 0 – 1 0 0 – 0 0 0
        Barbara JONES, 0 0 0 – 0 0 0 – 0 1 0 – 0 0 0

p. 30:
#94:   Nathaniel HULSE, 1 0 0 – 0 0 0 – 0 0 0 – 3 3 7:
        Margaret HULSE, 0 0 0 – 0 1 0 – 0 0 0 – 0 0 0
        Thomas ORD, 0 0 0 – 0 0 1 – 0 0 0 – 0 0 0
        Mary Ann HULSE, 0 0 0 – 0 0 1 – 0 0 0 – 0 0 0
        Eliza HULSE, 0 0 0 – 0 0 1 – 0 0 0 – 0 0 0
        George HULSE, 0 0 0 – 0 0 1 – 0 0 0 – 0 0 0 *(George Nathaniel HULSE.)*
        Hannah HULSE, 0 0 0 – 0 0 1 – 0 0 0 – 0 0 0
            Robert WILLIS, 30; Robert EVE, 45; Pompey, 46; Patience, 35; Tabitha, 22;
            Pala, 18; Pope, 16; Sarah, 13; Sarah, 4; John, 3; Joseph, 1; Maria, 1; John, 8.

Note: George Nathaniel Hulse is named in a Deed of Lease and Release dated 1866 as attorney and guardian of Emma Louisa Bennett, a minor in his houehold. He was settling the estate of her father, Marcus Charles Bennett, d. 1849, after the death of her father's executor, her step-grandfather Archibald Handyside. Who did Emma Louisa marry? Did she have children?

#95:   Family of John NORO, 6 1 0:   *(John is not present in the household.)*
        William GUILD, 1 0 0 – 0 0 0 – 0 0 0 – 0 0 0
        Thomas FERNIE, 1 0 0 – 0 0 0 – 0 0 0 – 0 0 0
        Richard HAWKINS, 1 0 0 – 0 0 0 – 0 0 0 – 0 0 0
        John HUNTER, 0 0 0 – 0 0 1 – 0 0 0 – 0 0 0
        J. J. SABIO, 0 0 0 – 0 0 0 – 1 0 0 – 0 0 0
            Robert COLQUHOUN; Robert GARBUT; John ILES; James; Richard
            LONGSWORTH; Spanish Joe; Nanny. *(Ages not given.)*

#96:   Mary HUME, 0 0 0 – 0 1 0 – 0 0 0 – 11 4 1:
       Margaret ALTEREITH, 0 0 0 – 0 1 0 – 0 0 0 – 0 0 0
       Rebecca J. USHER, 0 0 0 – 0 0 1 – 0 0 0 – 0 0 0
       Eleanor E. CRABBE, 0 0 0 – 0 0 1 – 0 0 0 – 0 0 0
       Abraham DICKSON, 0 0 0 – 1 0 0 – 0 0 0 – 0 0 0
            Sampson, above 50; Knight, above 50; Adam, above 50; William, 46;
            Charles, 40; Richard, 40; Francis, 37; Robert, 36; Lawrence, 28; Edward, 21;
            Nelson, 21;

p. 31:   Grace, 50; Clara, 40; Fatima, 33; Sophia, 25; Sarah Anne, 1½.

#97:   Richard C. WARDLAW, 1 0 0 – 0 0 0 – 0 0 0 – 3 3 2: *(C. = COCHRANE.)*
       Georgiana WARDLAW, 0 0 0 – 0 1 0 – 0 0 0 – 0 0 0   *(=Georgiana McAULAY)*
       Mary HUME WARDLAW, 0 0 0 – 0 0 1 – 0 0 0 – 0 0 0
            John, 25; Emma, 21; Betsey, 24; Daniel, 19; George FREDERICK, 17; Phillis
            alias Mary, 16; James, 9; Thomas, 6.

#98:   Virgin ROBERTS, 0 0 0 – 0 0 0 – 1 0 0 – 1 0 0:
       Caesar ANDREW, 0 0 0 – 0 0 0 – 1 0 0 – 0 0 0
       Phyllis DORSET, 0 0 0 – 0 0 0 – 0 1 0 – 0 0 0
       Clarissa HOPE, 0 0 0 – 0 0 0 – 0 0 1 – 0 0 0
       James HOPE, 0 0 0 – 0 0 0 – 0 0 1 – 0 0 0
            Cooper Ned, 50.

#99:   Ann GOFF, 0 0 0 – 0 1 0 – 0 0 0 – 0 2 0:
       Thomas GIBSON, 0 0 0 – 0 0 1 – 0 0 0 – 0 0 0
       Robert GIBSON, 0 0 0 – 0 0 1 – 0 0 0 – 0 0 0
       William GIBSON, 0 0 0 – 0 0 1 – 0 0 0 – 0 0 0
            Monemia, 45; Juliana, 21.

#100: William McKAY, 0 0 0 – 1 0 0 – 0 0 0 – 0 1 0:
       Mary MORGAN, 0 0 0 – 0 1 0 – 0 0 0 – 0 0 0
       Margaret E. McKAY, 0 0 0 – 0 0 1 – 0 0 0 – 0 0 0
       Edward McKAY, 0 0 0 – 0 0 1 – 0 0 0 – 0 0 0
            Anna, 44.

p. 32:
#101: Benjamin VERNON, 0 0 0 – 1 0 0 – 0 0 0 – 0 1 1:
       Rachel JONES, 0 0 0 – 0 1 0 – 0 0 0 – 0 0 0
       Joseph E. VERNON, 0 0 0 – 0 0 1 – 0 0 0 – 0 0 0
       George F. VERNON, 0 0 0 – 0 0 1 – 0 0 0 – 0 0 0
       Thomas VERNON, 0 0 0 – 0 0 1 – 0 0 0 – 0 0 0
       Mary E. VERNON, 0 0 0 – 0 0 1 – 0 0 0 – 0 0 0
       Margaret A. VERNON, 0 0 0 – 0 0 1 – 0 0 0 – 0 0 0
       Charles H^y VERNON, 0 0 0 – 0 0 1 – 0 0 0 – 0 0 0

116

Catherine F. VERNON, 0 0 0 – 0 0 1 – 0 0 0 – 0 0 0
Rose, 26; Janette, 6 months.

#102: Mary HEMMINGS, 0 0 0 – 0 1 0 – 0 0 0 – 5 2 0:
Sarah FRAIN, 0 0 0 – 0 1 0 – 0 0 0 – 0 0 0
Henrietta PRICE, 0 0 0 – 0 0 0 – 0 1 0 – 0 0 0
Lewis, 50; Billy, 40; Ben, 30; Jack, 18; William, 16; Fatima, 60; Eleanor, 20.

#103: Jervis HARRISON, 1 0 0 – 0 0 0 – 0 0 0 – 2 1 5:
William M. HARRISON, 0 0 0 – 0 0 1 – 0 0 0 – 0 0 0
Elizabeth POTTS, 0 0 0 – 0 1 0 – 0 0 0 – 0 0 0
Robert COLQUHOUN, 0 0 0 – 1 0 0 – 0 0 0 – 0 0 0
Wm. HARRISON, 0 0 0 – 0 0 1 – 0 0 0 – 0 0 0
Hannah, 26; William, 9; Jem, 5; Maria, 6.
Property of E. POTTS:
Quashie, 14; Angelina, 11.
Runaways: Muntucko, 45; Charles, 40.

p. 33:
#104: George HYDE, 0 0 0 – 1 0 0 – 0 0 0 – 65 9 19:
Phoebe, 19; Sabina, 17; Rosanna, 16; Elizabeth, 9; Jane, 9 months; Jenny, 40; Amelia, 18; Janet, 30; Hannah, 10; Lucretia, 8; Charlotte, 4; Mary, 40; Rachel, 10; Catherine, 5; Rose, 66; Rina, 10; Charlotte, 24; Jane, 6; Jean, 4; Julia, 10; William, 12; Daniel, 4; Charles, 3; Frederick, 2; Toby, 36; Francis, 3; Jem POTTS, 28; Tom, 24; Jeffrey, 18; Papa George, 45; Mandingo Harry, 42; Hunter, 66; William HYDE, 41;

p. 34:
Hercules, 51; Nago Hazard, 44; William HUNT, 46; Mungola Hazard, 35; Tom HOME, 21; Jack, 34; Jeffrey ILES, 20; Louis, 20; Tom LAWRIE, 34; Monday, 15; McLachlan, 42; Nelson, 49; Mungola Ned, 40; Nicholas, 42; Rodney PASLOW, 50; Mungola Prince, 39; Mundingo Prince, 39; Charles PARKER, 35; Bony [sic] Quashie, 43; Papa Quashie, 44; Quamino, 46; Robert, 17; Eado [= Eabo] Rodney, 42; Tom ROVER, 36; Peter RUMFORD, 42; Toby, 19; Townsend, 52; Congo Thomas, 36; Eabo Tom, 58; Philip TAIT, 29; Tommy, 41. John WOOD, 19; Edmond WALL, 44;

p. 35:
William, 13; Old Simon, 75; Ellice, 5; George, 15; Harry, 16; Hamlet ANDERSON, 41; Arran, 23; Black Adam, 50; Adam ANDERSON, 40; Sam BELISLE, 62; Breetchie, 58; George BULL, 39; Bogle, 42; Cato, 66; William CADDLE, 31; Caesar, 46; Daniel, 39; Davy, 20; Old Daniel, 66; Edmond, 34; Frank, 62. Frederick, 18; Philip GARNETT, 52; Coromantee George, 52; Bob GAPPER, 52; Congo George, 34; Infant Girl.

Note: George Hyde was baptized in 1795, son of James Hyde and Ariadne Broaster. Ariadne's mother, Eve Broaster, once belonged to Marcus Belisle; he freed her and bequeathed property to George Hyde, suggesting he was George's maternal grandfather.

#105:   Polydore HAMER, 0 0 0 – 0 0 0 – 1 0 0 – 0 1 0:
        Sally PRICE. *(Age not given)*

p. 36:
#106:   Prince HENRY, 0 0 0 – 0 0 0 – 1 0 0 – 0 0 0
        Catherine BURKE, 0 0 0 – 0 0 0 – 0 1 0 – 0 0 0
        Betsey FLOWERS, 0 0 0 – 0 0 0 – 0 1 0 – 0 0 0
        Sue FLOWERS, 0 0 0 – 0 0 0 – 0 1 0 – 0 0 0
        George FLOWERS, 0 0 0 – 0 0 0 – 0 0 1 – 0 0 0
        William FLOWERS, 0 0 0 – 0 0 0 – 0 0 1 – 0 0 0

#107:   Peter JOHNSON, 0 0 0 – 0 0 0 – 1 0 0 – 0 0 0
        Charles JOHNSON, 0 0 0 – 0 0 0 – 0 0 1 – 0 0 0
        James JOHNSON, 0 0 0 – 0 0 0 – 1 0 0 – 0 0 0
        John BAIN, 0 0 0 – 1 0 0 – 0 0 0 – 0 0 0
        Margaret MURRAY, 0 0 0 – 0 0 0 – 0 1 0 – 0 0 0
        Lucy SMITH, 0 0 0 – 0 0 0 – 0 1 0 – 0 0 0

#108:   John GORDON, 0 0 0 – 0 0 0 – 1 0 0 – 0 1 0:
        Juliana GORDON, 0 0 0 – 0 0 0 – 0 1 0 – 0 0 0
        Jemima, 13.

#109:   Jose GREGORIO, 0 0 0 – 0 0 0 – 1 0 0 – 0 0 0
        Manuel CIORE, 0 0 0 – 0 0 0 – 1 0 0 – 0 0 0

#110:   James TURNER, 0 0 0 – 0 0 0 – 1 0 0 – 0 2 0:
        John, 0 0 0 – 0 0 0 – 1 0 0 – 0 0 0 *(Surname not given.)*
        Patty; Susannah. *(Ages not given.)*

#111:   John LAWRIE, 0 0 0 – 0 0 0 – 1 0 0 – 0 1 0:
        Jane TUCKER, 0 0 0 – 0 0 0 – 0 1 0 – 0 0 0
        Jean BERN, 0 0 0 – 0 0 0 – 0 1 0 – 0 0 0
        Rosanna TUCKER, 60.

p. 37:
#112:   John WILLIAMS, 0 0 0 – 0 0 0 – 1 0 0 – 0 0 0
        Joanna BREWER, 0 0 0 – 0 0 0 – 0 1 0 – 0 0 0
        Ann WILLIAMS, 0 0 0 – 0 0 0 – 0 1 0 – 0 0 0
        Eleanor WILLIAMS, 0 0 0 – 0 0 0 – 0 1 0 – 0 0 0
        Agar [*sic*] WILLIAMS, 0 0 0 – 0 0 0 – 0 1 0 – 0 0 0
        Rosanna WILLIAMS, 0 0 0 – 0 0 0 – 0 1 0 – 0 0 0
        Elizabeth WILLIAMS, 0 0 0 – 0 0 0 – 0 1 0 – 0 0 0
        James WILLIAMS, 0 0 0 – 0 0 0 – 1 0 0 – 0 0 0
        John WILLIAMS, 0 0 0 – 0 0 0 – 1 0 0 – 0 0 0
        Joseph WILLIAMS, 0 0 0 – 0 0 0 – 0 0 1 – 0 0 0
        Robert WILLIAMS, 0 0 0 – 0 0 0 – 0 0 1 – 0 0 0

118

Henry WILLIAMS, 0 0 0 – 0 0 0 – 0 0 1 – 0 0 0
Thomas WILLIAMS, 0 0 0 – 0 0 0 – 0 0 1 – 0 0 0

#113: Family of Wm. VAUGHAN, 9 1 4:
Catherine GRIZZLE, 0 0 0 – 0 1 0 – 0 0 0 – 0 0 0
Wm. VAUGHAN, 1 0 0 – 0 0 0 – 0 0 0 – 0 0 0
Clarissa CARTER, 0 0 0 – 0 0 1 – 0 0 0 – 0 0 0
Mary CARTER, 0 0 0 – 0 0 1 – 0 0 0 – 0 0 0
Sarah A. VAUGHAN, 0 0 0 – 0 0 1 – 0 0 0 – 0 0 0
Mary H. VAUGHAN, 0 0 0 – 0 0 1 – 0 0 0 – 0 0 0
Dorset, 38; John FREEMAN, 40; John LAMB, 19; Nelson, 18; Robert LAMB, 32; Temple, 18; Phillis, 27; Emily, 11; Catherine, 2; David, 5; Simon, 2.
Runaways: Port Royal, 38; Sampson, 30; Thomas, 14.

p. 38:
#114: George CARD, 0 0 0 – 0 0 0 – 1 0 0 – 0 0 0
Joanna CARD, 0 0 0 – 0 0 0 – 0 1 0 – 0 0 0
Betsey BARNARD, 0 0 0 – 0 0 0 – 0 1 0 – 0 0 0
Charles BARNARD, 0 0 0 – 0 0 0 – 1 0 0 – 0 0 0
Thomas BARNARD, 0 0 0 – 0 0 0 – 1 0 0 – 0 0 0
James BARNARD, 0 0 0 – 0 0 0 – 0 0 1 – 0 0 0
Joseph BARNARD, 0 0 0 – 0 0 0 – 0 0 1 – 0 0 0
Richard BARNARD, 0 0 0 – 0 0 0 – 0 0 1 – 0 0 0
George BARNARD, 0 0 0 – 0 0 0 – 0 0 1 – 0 0 0

#115: William HARRIS, 0 0 0 – 0 0 0 – 1 0 0 – 1 0 0:
Mrs. HARRIS, 0 0 0 – 0 0 0 – 0 1 0 – 0 0 0
Jessy SANCHO, 0 0 0 – 0 0 0 – 0 1 0 – 0 0 0
William SMITH, 0 0 0 – 0 0 0 – 1 0 0 – 0 0 0
John MEIGHAN, 0 0 0 – 0 0 0 – 1 0 0 – 0 0 0
Elizabeth FULLER, 0 0 0 – 0 0 0 – 0 1 0 – 0 0 0
Samuel FULLER, 0 0 0 – 0 0 0 – 1 0 0 – 0 0 0
J. D. MEIGHAN, 0 0 0 – 0 0 0 – 1 0 0 – 0 0 0
E. HARRIS, 0 0 0 – 0 0 0 – 0 0 1 – 0 0 0 *(Female.)*
Simon MORELL, 0 0 0 – 0 0 0 – 1 0 0 – 0 0 0
Joseph GIDEON, 0 0 0 – 0 0 0 – 1 0 0 – 0 0 0
Sancho, 25.

#116: Jack GEORGE, 0 0 0 – 0 0 0 – 1 0 0 – 1 0 0:
Mary GEORGE, 0 0 0 – 0 0 0 – 0 1 0 – 0 0 0
John GEORGE, 0 0 0 – 0 0 0 – 1 0 0 – 0 0 0
Gabriel GEORGE, 0 0 0 – 0 0 0 – 1 0 0 – 0 0 0
Bill GEORGE, 0 0 0 – 0 0 0 – 1 0 0 – 0 0 0
Betsey GEORGE, 0 0 0 – 0 0 0 – 0 1 0 – 0 0 0

119

Mary MAGDALEN, 0 0 0 – 0 0 0 – 0 1 0 – 0 0 0
Andrew, 65.

p. 39:

#117: Ann ELRINGTON, 0 1 0 – 0 0 0 – 0 0 0 – 2 3 3:
Ann E. ELRIGHTON, 0 1 0 – 0 0 0 – 0 0 0 – 0 0 0
George E. WARREN, 1 0 0 – 0 0 0 – 0 0 0 – 0 0 0
William J. PEEBLES, 1 0 0 – 0 0 0 – 0 0 0 – 0 0 0
Property of G. WARREN:
  Sally, 32; Sabina, 25; Andrew, 5; Matilda, 3; Sarah, 70; Lucretia,
  7 months; Dick, 23; Francis, 20.

#118: James GILLETT, 0 0 0 – 1 0 0 – 0 0 0 – 0 0 0
George GILLETT, 0 0 0 – 1 0 0 – 0 0 0 – 0 0 0
Mary BURRELL, 0 0 0 – 0 1 0 – 0 0 0 – 0 0 0
Maria GILLETT, 0 0 0 – 0 1 0 – 0 0 0 – 0 0 0
Nancy GILLETT, 0 0 0 – 0 1 0 – 0 0 0 – 0 0 0
George GILLETT, 0 0 0 – 0 0 1 – 0 0 0 – 0 0 0
Mary GILLETT, 0 0 0 – 0 0 1 – 0 0 0 – 0 0 0

#119: Archibald FLOWERS, 0 0 0 – 0 0 0 – 1 0 0 – 2 0 0:
Mary ARCHIBALD, 0 0 0 – 0 0 0 – 0 1 0 – 0 0 0
Margaret FLOWERS, 0 0 0 – 0 0 0 – 0 0 1 – 0 0 0
Norah FLOWERS, 0 0 0 – 0 0 0 – 0 0 1 – 0 0 0
William FLOWERS, 0 0 0 – 0 0 0 – 0 0 1 – 0 0 0
Fanny FLOWERS, 0 0 0 – 0 0 0 – 0 0 1 – 0 0 0
Statira FLOWERS, 0 0 0 – 0 0 0 – 0 0 1 – 0 0 0
John GILLETT, 0 0 0 – 0 0 0 – 1 0 0 – 0 0 0
  Lunnun; Joseph. *(Ages not given.)*

#120: Joseph KEANE, 0 0 0 – 0 0 0 – 1 0 0 – 0 0 0
Josefa JUAN, 0 0 0 – 0 0 0 – 0 1 0 – 0 0 0
Jose, 0 0 0 – 0 0 0 – 0 0 1 – 0 0 0
Seriaco, 0 0 0 – 0 0 0 – 0 0 1 – 0 0 0 *(Both male; surnames not given.)*

p. 40:

#121: Henrietta GODFREY, 0 0 0 – 0 1 0 – 0 0 0 – 3 0 1:
Henrietta JOHNSTON, 0 0 0 – 0 1 0 – 0 0 0 – 0 0 0
Mary JOHNSTON, 0 0 0 – 0 0 1 – 0 0 0 – 0 0 0
Isabella JOHNSTON, 0 0 0 – 0 0 1 – 0 0 0 – 0 0 0
Agnes JOHNSTON, 0 0 0 – 0 0 1 – 0 0 0 – 0 0 0
John JOHNSTON, 0 0 0 – 0 0 1 – 0 0 0 – 0 0 0
James JOHNSTON, 0 0 0 – 0 0 1 – 0 0 0 – 0 0 0
Jane JOHNSTON, 0 0 0 – 0 0 1 – 0 0 0 – 0 0 0
  Cyrus, 34; Peter, 38; Dick, 49; Edith, 11.

#122: John Thomas FLOWERS, 0 0 0 – 0 0 0 – 1 0 0 – 0 0 0
        Joseph FLOWERS, 0 0 0 – 0 0 0 – 0 0 1 – 0 0 0
        Thomas FLOWERS, 0 0 0 – 0 0 0 – 0 0 1 – 0 0 0
        Stephen FLOWERS, 0 0 0 – 0 0 0 – 0 0 1 – 0 0 0
        Charles FLOWERS, 0 0 0 – 0 0 0 – 0 0 1 – 0 0 0
        John CARD, 0 0 0 – 0 0 0 – 0 0 1 – 0 0 0
        Peter CARD, 0 0 0 – 0 0 0 – 0 0 1 – 0 0 0
        Elizabeth STAIN, 0 0 0 – 0 1 0 – 0 0 0 – 0 0 0
        Mary A. FLOWERS, 0 0 0 – 0 0 0 – 0 0 1 – 0 0 0

#123: John FLOWERS, 0 0 0 – 0 0 0 – 1 0 0 – 0 0 0
        Joseph FLOWERS, 0 0 0 – 0 0 0 – 0 0 1 – 0 0 0
        George FLOWERS, 0 0 0 – 0 0 0 – 0 0 1 – 0 0 0
        Hamilton FLOWERS, 0 0 0 – 0 0 0 – 0 0 1 – 0 0 0
        Cretin [sic] NEAL, 0 0 0 – 0 0 0 – 0 1 0 – 0 0 0

#124: Isaac BURRELL, 0 0 0 – 0 0 0 – 1 0 0 – 0 0 0

p. 41:
#125: Alexander FRANCE, 1 0 0 – 0 0 0 – 0 0 0 – 30 15 31:
        Ariadne BRASTER, 0 0 0 – 0 1 0 – 0 0 0 – 0 0 0 *(= BROASTER)*
            Joe, 72; John, 52; Davey, 52; Charles, 52; Bacchus, 50; Charles GIBSON,
            43; Andrew, 49; Bill, 44; Frederick, 42; Toby, 36; Adam, 38; Peter, 31;
            Jackey, 28; Tom, 28; Martin, 27; Mangan[sic], 27; James CADDLE, 27;
            Glasgow, 44; James, 26; Robert, 24; Richard, 22; George, 22; Morrison, 22;
            Brown, 21; Richmond, 21; Harry, 20; Hamlet, 20; Otway, 19; Joe, 14; Sam,
            10; Edward, 14; Marcus, 11; Thomas, 8.

p. 42:
            Johnston, 11; Nelson, 7; Jury, 6; Caesar, 6; Hercules, 4; Robert, 7;
            Alexander, 6; Devonshire, 5; Prince, 5; Joshua, 3; Diamond, 10 months;
            Anthony, 2 years; Mary, 56; Sylvia, 47; Kitty, 43; Arabella, 26; Betsey, 34;
            Nelly, 29; Louisa, 23; Emma, 22; Molly, 23; Maria, 23; Patience, 21; Jeanie,
            19; Diana, 20; Nancy, 19; Prudence, 16; Harriet, 8; Evelina, 7; Emily, 7;
            Elizabeth, 7; Phyllis, 5; Jessie, 5;

p. 43:
            Mary Frances, 5; Edie, 2; Rosette, 2; Christiana, 3 months; Georgiana, 6;
            Emmaline, 12.
            Runaways: Jacob, 44; Jack, 44; Edward, 36.
            Bristol (omitted above) 6 months.

#126: Catherine ROBINSON, 0 0 0 – 0 1 0 – 0 0 0 – 9 4 5:
        P.[sic] J. STEWART, 0 0 0 – 0 1 0 – 0 0 0 – 0 0 0 *(In 1829, Bridget J. STEWART.)*
        James STEWART, 0 0 0 – 1 0 0 – 0 0 0 – 0 0 0
            Chance alias Henry, 47; Josey, 34; James alias York, 38; Mellago alias
            Robert, 36; Devonshire, 31; Peter, 28; Henry, 20; Edwin, 18; George, 14;
            John, 12; Chloe, 30; Grace, 24; Phoebe, 21; Mary Ann, 15; Priscilla, 1;

121

Betsey, 6 months; Maria, 3 months.
Runaway: Quamina, 44.

#127: Francis JOHNSON, 0 0 0 – 0 0 0 – 1 0 0 – 0 0 0

p. 44:
#128: Ann BODE, 0 0 0 – 0 1 0 – 0 0 0 – 7 5 3:
       Martha MEIGHAN, 0 0 0 – 0 1 0 – 0 0 0 – 0 0 0
       Peter STAIN, 0 0 0 – 0 0 1 – 0 0 0 – 0 0 0
       Sarah PITTS, 0 0 0 – 0 1 0 – 0 0 0 – 0 0 0
       Edmund MEIGHAN, 0 0 0 – 0 0 1 – 0 0 0 – 0 0 0
       Thomas GRISTOCK, 0 0 0 – 0 0 1 – 0 0 0 – 0 0 0
             Joseph BODE, 44; James BODE, 24; John BODE, 22; Hamlet BODE, 18;
             Blandford, 17; Jeffrey, 10; Elizabeth, 41; Lucy, 25; Catherine, 18; Fanny, 18;
             Diana, 22; John, 18; Berry, 13; Henry, 20; Maria, 16 days.

#129: Stephen GERRARD, 0 0 0 – 0 0 0 – 1 0 0 – 0 0 0
       Ann GERRARD, 0 0 0 – 0 0 0 – 0 1 0 – 0 0 0
       Elizabeth GERRARD, 0 0 0 – 0 0 0 – 0 0 1 – 0 0 0

#130: Antonio GOMEZ, 0 0 0 – 0 0 0 – 1 0 0 – 0 0 0
       Tomas GOMEZ, 0 0 0 – 0 0 0 – 1 0 0 – 0 0 0
       Remundo GOMEZ, 0 0 0 – 0 0 0 – 1 0 0 – 0 0 0
       Domingo GOMEZ, 0 0 0 – 0 0 0 – 1 0 0 – 0 0 0
       Juana IMPOTETO, 0 0 0 – 0 0 0 – 0 1 0 – 0 0 0

Note: The entries above and below are both numbered 130.

#130: Elizabeth PERRY, 0 0 0 – 0 0 0 – 0 1 0 – 0 0 0
       Ann GLADDEN, 0 0 0 – 0 0 0 – 0 1 0 – 0 0 0

#131: Property of B. J. STEWART, 1 0 0: *(In 1829, Bridget J. STEWART.)*
       William, 50. *(In 1829, William THOMSON, 47.)*

p. 45:
#132: George COATQUELVIN, 0 0 0 – 0 0 0 – 1 0 0 – 0 0 0

#133: Jacob MUSLAAR, 1 0 0 – 0 0 0 – 0 0 0 – 0 0 0
       Joseph F. MUSLAAR, 0 0 1 – 0 0 0 – 0 0 0 – 0 0 0
       Margaret MUSLAAR, 0 1 0 – 0 0 0 – 0 0 0 – 0 0 0
       Sarah KENNEDY, 0 0 0 – 0 0 1 – 0 0 0 – 0 0 0

#134: John Edw[d] HENDERSON, 0 0 0 – 1 0 0 – 0 0 0 – 5 2 0:
       Eliza A. BROSTER, 0 0 0 – 0 1 0 – 0 0 0 – 0 0 0
       John E. HENDERSON Jr., 0 0 0 – 0 0 1 – 0 0 0 – 0 0 0
       George HENDERSON, 0 0 0 – 0 0 1 – 0 0 0 – 0 0 0

Eliza Ann HENDERSON, 0 0 0 – 0 0 1 – 0 0 0 – 0 0 0
    Moland, 45; Thomas, 39; George, 53; Kelly, 48; Dick, 45; Diana, 25; Fanny, 21.

#135: John GIDEON, 0 0 0 – 0 0 0 – 1 0 0 – 0 0 0
    Modest GIDEON, 0 0 0 – 0 0 0 – 1 0 0 – 0 0 0
    Joseph GIDEON, 0 0 0 – 0 0 0 – 1 0 0 – 0 0 0
    Daniel GIDEON, 0 0 0 – 0 0 0 – 0 0 1 – 0 0 0
    Sarah GLADDEN, 0 0 0 – 0 0 0 – 0 1 0 – 0 0 0

#136: Thomas BELISLE, 0 0 0 – 0 0 0 – 1 0 0 – 0 0 0
    Rosanna FLOWERS, 0 0 0 – 0 0 0 – 0 1 0 – 0 0 0
    Aberdeen FLOWERS, 0 0 0 – 0 0 0 – 0 0 1 – 0 0 0
    Jane FLOWERS, 0 0 0 – 0 0 0 – 0 0 1 – 0 0 0

p. 46:
#137: Harry GRANT, 0 0 0 – 0 0 0 – 1 0 0 – 0 0 0
    Caroline DOUGLAS, 0 0 0 – 0 0 0 – 0 1 0 – 0 0 0
    Chloe DOUGLAS, 0 0 0 – 0 0 0 – 0 1 0 – 0 0 0
    Eliza DOUGLAS, 0 0 0 – 0 0 0 – 0 0 1 – 0 0 0
    Sarah DOUGLAS, 0 0 0 – 0 0 0 – 0 0 1 – 0 0 0
    Ancilla DOUGLAS, 0 0 0 – 0 0 0 – 0 1 0 – 0 0 0

#138: Flora GOFF, 0 0 0 – 0 0 0 – 0 1 0 – 0 0 0
    Margaret FERRELL, 0 0 0 – 0 1 0 – 0 0 0 – 0 0 1:
    Property of ditto:
        Margaret, 10.
    Mary Ann FERRELL, 0 0 0 – 0 1 0 – 0 0 0 – 0 1 0:
    Property of ditto:
        Susannah, 18.

#139: Catherine SAVORY, 0 0 0 – 0 1 0 – 0 0 0 – 0 0 0
    Susan WOOD, 0 0 0 – 0 0 1 – 0 0 0 – 0 0 0

#140: James GILLETT, 0 0 0 – 1 0 0 – 0 0 0 – 0 2 0:
    S. BURRELL, 0 0 0 – 0 1 0 – 0 0 0 – 0 0 0
    Elizabeth GILLETT, 0 0 0 – 0 0 1 – 0 0 0 – 0 0 0
    William GILLETT, 0 0 0 – 0 0 1 – 0 0 0 – 0 0 0
    Robert GILLETT, 0 0 0 – 0 0 1 – 0 0 0 – 0 0 0
    Alexander GILLETT, 0 0 0 – 0 0 1 – 0 0 0 – 0 0 0
    George GILLETT, 0 0 0 – 0 0 1 – 0 0 0 – 0 0 0
    Ann GILLETT, 0 0 0 – 0 0 1 – 0 0 0 – 0 0 0
        Peggy, 20; Rabien, 19.

#141: James BANKES, 1 0 0 – 0 0 0 – 0 0 0 – 0 0 0
    Philip TOLEDO, 1 0 0 – 0 0 0 – 0 0 0 – 0 0 0

p. 47:

#142: Joseph NOEL, 0 0 0 – 1 0 0 – 0 0 0 – 0 0 0
Dorlisca NOEL, 0 0 0 – 0 0 1 – 0 0 0 – 0 0 0

#143: James KELLY, 0 0 0 – 0 0 0 – 1 0 0 – 0 0 0
Frederick WALL, 0 0 0 – 0 0 0 – 1 0 0 – 0 0 0
Robert GEDDICE [sic], 0 0 0 – 0 0 0 – 1 0 0 – 0 0 0
Maria HARRIS, 0 0 0 – 0 1 0 – 0 0 0 – 0 0 0

#144: Sarah PARKS, 0 1 0 – 0 0 0 – 0 0 0 – 3 2 4:
Charles PARKS, 0 0 1 – 0 0 0 – 0 0 0 – 0 0 0
Bob PARKS, 60; Richmond, 18; Moley, 40; Sylvia, 35; Betsey, 20; Mary, 9;
Fidelia, 4; Amanda, 7; Edward, 5.

#145: Family of Mt WINTER:
Joshua GABOUREL, 0 0 0 – 1 0 0 – 0 0 0 – 0 0 0
Margaret WINTER, 0 0 0 – 0 1 0 – 0 0 0 – 0 0 0
Mary J. GABOUREL, 0 0 0 – 0 0 1 – 0 0 0 – 0 0 0
Catherine GABOUREL, 0 0 0 – 0 0 1 – 0 0 0 – 0 0 0
Amos GABOUREL, 0 0 0 – 0 0 1 – 0 0 0 – 0 0 0
Thomas GABOUREL, 0 0 0 – 0 0 1 – 0 0 0 – 0 0 0
Robert D. GABOUREL, 0 0 0 – 0 0 1 – 0 0 0 – 0 0 0
Margaret GABOUREL, 0 0 0 – 0 0 1 – 0 0 0 – 0 0 0

#146: John Aaron LAWSON, 1 0 0 – 0 0 0 – 0 0 0 – 0 0 0

p. 48:

#147: William T. CHERRINGTON, 1 0 0 – 0 0 0 – 0 0 0 – 1 0 0:
Clarinda WILLIAMS, 0 0 0 – 0 1 0 – 0 0 0 – 0 0 0
Phoebe FLOWERS, 0 0 0 – 0 1 0 – 0 0 0 – 0 0 0
Eleanor CHERRINGTON, 0 0 0 – 0 1 0 – 0 0 0 – 0 0 0
William CHERRINGTON, 0 0 0 – 0 0 1 – 0 0 0 – 0 0 0
Sarah CHERRINGTON, 0 0 0 – 0 0 1 – 0 0 0 – 0 0 0
Elizabeth CHERRINGTON, 0 0 0 – 0 0 1 – 0 0 0 – 0 0 0
Emma CHERRINGTON, 0 0 0 – 0 0 1 – 0 0 0 – 0 0 0
Henry CHERRINGTON, 0 0 0 – 0 0 1 – 0 0 0 – 0 0 0
John CHERRINGTON, 0 0 0 – 0 0 1 – 0 0 0 – 0 0 0
James CHERRINGTON, 0 0 0 – 0 0 1 – 0 0 0 – 0 0 0
Jack HUNT, 70.

#148: John TWEENY, 0 0 0 – 0 0 0 – 1 0 0 – 0 0 0
Alexander TWEENY, 0 0 0 – 0 0 0 – 0 0 1 – 0 0 0
John TWEENY, 0 0 0 – 0 0 0 – 0 0 1 – 0 0 0
Samuel TWEENY, 0 0 0 – 0 0 0 – 0 0 1 – 0 0 0
Henry TWEENY, 0 0 0 – 0 0 0 – 0 0 1 – 0 0 0
Joseph TWEENY, 0 0 0 – 0 0 0 – 0 0 1 – 0 0 0

124

Rose TWEENY, 0 0 0 – 0 0 0 – 0 1 0 – 0 0 0
Pollenor TWEENY, 0 0 0 – 0 0 0 – 0 0 1 – 0 0 0 *(Female.)*
Eleanor TWEENY, 0 0 0 – 0 0 0 – 0 0 1 – 0 0 0
Mrs. DOBSON, 0 0 0 – 0 1 0 – 0 0 0 – 0 0 0

#149: William FAIRFAX, 0 0 0 – 0 0 0 – 1 0 0 – 0 0 0
Thomas FAIRFAX, 0 0 0 – 0 0 0 – 0 0 1 – 0 0 0
Maria FAIRFAX, 0 0 0 – 0 1 0 – 0 0 0 – 0 0 0
Lucina FAIRFAX, 0 0 0 – 0 0 1 – 0 0 0 – 0 0 0
Benjamin FAIRFAX, 0 0 0 – 0 0 1 – 0 0 0 – 0 0 0

p. 49:
#150: Estate of Sarah GOFF under charge of Nathaniel HULSE, Esq., 10 8 9:
Sammy, 35; Somerset, 34; Harry, 24; Jem, 28; William, 19; John, 16;
Sambo, 26; Peggy, 34; Hannah, 32; Molly, 33; Fanny 30; Agnes, 31; Clara,
23; Elizabeth, 22; Adolphus, 13; William, 16; Quashie, 4; Derry, 13; Robert,
8; Richard, 5; Joseph, 4; Hannah, 1; Catherine, 4; Valentine, 10; Nelly, 13;
Rhoda, 10; Rose, 6.

#151: Maria FLOWERS, 0 0 0 – 0 1 0 – 0 0 0 – 0 0 0
Catherine PRATT, 0 0 0 – 0 0 1 – 0 0 0 – 0 0 0
Sarah PRATT, 0 0 0 – 0 0 1 – 0 0 0 – 0 0 0
Mary PRATT, 0 0 0 – 0 0 1 – 0 0 0 – 0 0 0

p. 50:
#152: Elizabeth HEMSLEY, 0 0 0 – 0 1 0 – 0 0 0 – 0 0 0
Thomas NEAL, 0 0 0 – 1 0 0 – 0 0 0 – 0 0 0
Joseph HEMSLEY, 0 0 0 – 0 0 1 – 0 0 0 – 0 0 0
Rebecca HOARE, 0 0 0 – 0 0 0 – 0 0 1 – 0 0 0
Beatrice HOARE, 0 0 0 – 0 0 0 – 0 0 1 – 0 0 0
Bella HOARE, 0 0 0 – 0 0 0 – 0 0 1 – 0 0 0
James HOARE, 0 0 0 – 0 0 0 – 0 0 1 – 0 0 0
Daniel HOARE, 0 0 0 – 0 0 0 – 0 0 1 – 0 0 0
Richard GARDINER, 0 0 0 – 0 0 0 – 1 0 0 – 0 0 0

#153: Francisco CHICO, 0 0 0 – 0 0 0 – 1 0 0 – 0 0 0
Maria DOMINGO, 0 0 0 – 0 0 0 – 0 1 0 – 0 0 0
Pedro ANGO, 0 0 0 – 0 0 0 – 1 0 0 – 0 0 0
Katano [sic] MARIA, 0 0 0 – 0 0 0 – 0 0 1 – 0 0 0 *(Female.)*
Juana PANTALION, 0 0 0 – 0 0 0 – 0 0 1 – 0 0 0

#154: Chance GRANT, 0 0 0 – 0 0 0 – 1 0 0 – 0 0 0

#155: James PRICE, 1 0 0 – 0 0 0 – 0 0 0 – 1 1 0:
George LAMB, 27; Lizzy, 33.

125

#156: John M'KINNEY DALY, 0 0 0 –1 0 0 – 0 0 0 – 0 0 0

#157: Rogers GOFF, 0 0 0 – 1 0 0 – 0 0 0 – 0 0 0
Marino [sic] INLET, 0 0 0 – 0 1 0 – 0 0 0 – 0 0 0

p. 51:
#158: Ann HOME, 0 0 0 – 0 1 0 – 0 0 0 – 10 2 0:
Margaret CLEMENT, 0 0 0 – 0 0 1 – 0 0 0 – 0 0 0
    William ROGERS, 60; Dick GUTHRIE, 40; Anthony DAWKINS, 35;
    Prince CAMPBELL, 37; William STANFORD, 47; William STANFORD
    Jr., 22; Henry STANFORD, 20; Alexander HOME, 33; John STANFORD,
    50; Blucher HOME, 14; Maria HOME, 50; Rose HOME, 37.

#159: Mary BATES, 0 0 0 – 0 1 0 – 0 0 0 – 0 1 1:
Margaret RABATEAU, 0 0 0 – 0 1 0 – 0 0 0 – 0 0 0
Isaac RABATEAU, 0 0 0 – 0 0 1 – 0 0 0 – 0 0 0
Alfred RABATEAU, 0 0 0 – 0 0 1 – 0 0 0 – 0 0 0
Caroline PANTING, 0 0 0 – 0 0 1 – 0 0 0 – 0 0 0
William WINTER, 0 0 0 – 0 0 0 – 1 0 0 – 0 0 0
John MYVETT, 0 0 0 – 1 0 0 – 0 0 0 – 0 0 0
    Adriana; Cecilia. *(Ages not given.)*

#160: John COLLINS, 0 0 0 – 0 0 0 – 1 0 0 – 0 0 0
Diana SMITH, 0 0 0 – 0 0 0 – 0 1 0 – 0 0 0

#161: George LE GEYT, 1 0 0 – 0 0 0 – 0 0 0 – 0 1 0:
Elizabeth LE GEYT, 0 1 0 – 0 0 0 – 0 0 0 – 0 0 0
Mary Ann LE GEYT, 0 0 1 – 0 0 0 – 0 0 0 – 0 0 0
Eliza LE GEYT, 0 0 1– 0 0 0 – 0 0 0 – 0 0 0
Elizabeth LE GEYT, 0 0 1 – 0 0 0 – 0 0 0 – 0 0 0
    Janette, 25.

p. 52:
#162: Henry DUNBAR, 0 0 0 – 1 0 0 – 0 0 0 – 0 0 0
Catherine DUNBAR, 0 0 0 – 0 1 0 – 0 0 0 – 0 0 0
Henry USE [sic], 0 0 0 – 1 0 0 – 0 0 0 – 0 0 0

#163: Pascal VASE, 0 0 0 – 0 0 0 – 1 0 0 – 0 0 0
Antonia FLORENCE, 0 0 0 – 0 0 0 – 0 1 0 – 0 0 0

#164: Margaret GREEN, 0 0 0 – 0 1 0 – 0 0 0 – 1 2 1:
Emma LE GEYT, 0 0 0 – 0 0 1 – 0 0 0 – 0 0 0
    John, 50; Amelia, 40; Sophia, 16; Jem. *(Child. Paper missing, torn away.)*

#165: Betsey STANFORD, 0 0 0 – 0 0 0 – 0 1 0 – 0 0 0
Grace STANFORD, 0 0 0 – 0 0 0 – 0 1 0 – 0 0 0

Flora STANFORD, 0 0 0 – 0 0 0 – 0 1 0 – 0 0 0
Sylvia STANFORD, 0 0 0 – 0 0 0 – 0 1 0 – 0 0 0
Peggy STANFORD, 0 0 0 – 0 0 0 – 0 0 1 – 0 0 0
Isabella STANFORD, 0 0 0 – 0 0 0 – 0 0 1 – 0 0 0
Anne STANFORD, 0 0 0 – 0 0 0 – 0 0 1 – 0 0 0
Mary STANFORD, 0 0 0 – 0 0 0 – 0 0 1 – 0 0 0
Amanda STANFORD, 0 0 0 – 0 0 0 – 0 0 1 – 0 0 0
Amy ROBERTS, 0 0 0 – 0 0 0 – 0 0 1 – 0 0 0
Mary WILLIAMS, 0 0 0 – 0 0 0 – 0 0 1 – 0 0 0
John WILLIAMS, 0 0 0 – 0 0 0 – 0 0 1 – 0 0 0
James GIBSON, 0 0 0 – 0 0 0 – 0 0 1 – 0 0 0
Diamond GORDON, 0 0 0 – 0 0 0 – 0 0 1 – 0 0 0 *(Female.)*
Maria GORDON, 0 0 0 – 0 0 0 – 0 0 1 – 0 0 0

p. 53:
#166: Tinah BEATTIE, 0 0 0 – 0 1 0 – 0 0 0 – 3 2 5:
Eleanor POTTS, 0 0 0 – 0 1 0 – 0 0 0 – 0 0 0
Rose POTTS, 0 0 0 – 0 1 0 – 0 0 0 – 0 0 0
Marianne POTTS, 0 0 0 – 0 0 1 – 0 0 0 – 0 0 0
Benjamin POTTS, 0 0 0 – 0 0 1 – 0 0 0 – 0 0 0
George, 35; Andrew, 26; William, 36; Jenny, 26; Patty, 8; Charley, 7;
John JOHNSTON, 1; Margaret, 18; Clarissa, 5; James, 1.

#167: William N. SMITH, 0 0 0 – 1 0 0 – 0 0 0 – 0 0 0
Fanny BURRELL, 0 0 0 – 0 1 0 – 0 0 0 – 0 0 0
Thomas SMITH, 0 0 0 – 0 0 1 – 0 0 0 – 0 0 0
James SMITH, 0 0 0 – 0 0 1 – 0 0 0 – 0 0 0

#168: David BETSON, 1 0 0 – 0 0 0 – 0 0 0 – 2 0 0:
John D. BETSON, 1 0 0 – 0 0 0 – 0 0 0 – 0 0 0
Samuel BLAKE, 26.
Runaway: John ELLICE, 40.

#169: Jane E. ROSS, 0 0 0 – 0 1 0 – 0 0 0 – 0 0 0
"   ROSS, 0 0 0 – 0 0 1 – 0 0 0 – 0 0 0

#170: James C. QUILTER, 1 0 0 – 0 0 0 – 0 0 0 – 0 1 0
Kate. *(Age not given.)*

#171: Hannah MYVETT, 0 0 0 – 0 0 0 – 0 1 0 – 3 0 0:
Jeremiah MYVETT, 0 0 0 – 1 0 0 – 0 0 0 – 0 0 0
Eleanor MYVETT, 0 0 0 – 0 1 0 – 0 0 0 – 0 0 0
Prince, 15; Tom PEPPER, 20; Neptune, 60.

p. 54:
#172: Maria EMORY, 0 0 0 – 0 1 0 – 0 0 0 – 7 9 9:

Adam, 38; Joe, 29: Quaw, 24; John, 22; Harry, 70; Tom, 80; Bathsheba, 44;
Eve, 35; Clara, 48; Bess, 47; Lucy, 30; Bess, 17; Elizabeth, 15; Agnes, 24;
Charles, 13; Thomas, 11; William, 8; Thomas, 10; James, 6; Daniel, 2;
Francis, 3½; Amelia, 5; Prue, 6 months; Nanny, 85; Prince MEIGHAN, 68.

#173: Sarah BATES, 0 0 0 – 0 1 0 – 0 0 0 – 0 1 1:
Eliza Frances EVE, 0 0 0 – 0 1 0 – 0 0 0 – 0 0 0
Mary PRICE, 0 0 0 – 0 1 0 – 0 0 0 – 0 0 0
Edward ROSS, 0 0 0 – 0 0 1 – 0 0 0 – 0 0 0
Maria CARTER, 0 0 0 – 0 0 1 – 0 0 0 – 0 0 0
Bathsheba, 40; Grace, 7.

p. 55:
#174: John McKEE, 0 0 0 – 0 0 0 – 1 0 0 – 0 0 0
Susannah POOLE, 0 0 0 – 0 0 0 – 0 1 0 – 0 0 0

#175: Casimir J. DE BRIEN, 0 0 0 – 1 0 0 – 0 0 0 – 0 0 0
Amelia DE BRIEN, 0 0 0 – 0 0 0 – 0 1 0 – 0 0 0
Anne M. DE BRIEN, 0 0 0 – 0 0 1 – 0 0 0 – 0 0 0
Georgina DE BRIEN, 0 0 0 – 0 0 1 – 0 0 0 – 0 0 0

#176: Thomas JENNINGS, 0 0 0 – 1 0 0 – 0 0 0 – 1 2 1
Cath^n P. JENNINGS, 0 0 0 – 0 1 0 – 0 0 0 – 0 0 0
Rebecca LINDO, 0 0 0 – 0 1 0 – 0 0 0 – 0 0 0
Lavinia E. JENNINGS, 0 0 0 – 0 0 1 – 0 0 0 – 0 0 0
Cath^n P. JENNINGS, 0 0 0 – 0 0 1 – 0 0 0 – 0 0 0
Angelina P. JENNINGS, 0 0 0 – 0 0 1 – 0 0 0 – 0 0 0
Property of ditto, 0 1 0:
Judith JONES, 50.
Property of R. LINDO, 0 1 1:
Susannah SMART, 18; Child of S. SMART, 1 month.
Property of L. JENNINGS, 1 0 0:
Alexander CALERMON, 14.

#177: Mary WALL, 0 1 0 – 0 0 0 – 0 0 0 – 3 2 1:
Mary Ann RICHARDSON, 0 1 0 – 0 0 0 – 0 0 0 – 0 0 0
Cecilia, 35; Leonora, 69; Dublin, 46; James, 17; Morris, 12½; Richard, 61.

#178: Phoebe McAULAY, 0 0 0 – 0 0 0 – 0 1 0 – 0 0 0
Robt Hen^y McAULAY, 0 0 0 – 0 0 0 – 0 0 1 – 0 0 0
Margaret L. DYER, 0 0 0 – 0 0 0 – 0 0 1 – 0 0 0

p. 56:
#179: Thomas RHYS, 1 0 0 – 0 0 0 – 0 0 0 – 1 1 0:
Eleanor RHYS, 0 0 0 – 0 1 0 – 0 0 0 – 0 0 0
Ethlin [*sic*] RHYS, 0 0 0 – 0 0 1 – 0 0 0 – 0 0 0

Ellen RHYS, 0 0 0 – 0 0 1 – 0 0 0 – 0 0 0
Petrona, 0 0 0 – 0 1 0 – 0 0 0 – 0 0 0 *(Surname not given.)*
Johnson; Mary. *(Ages not given.)*

#180: Henry FLOWERS, 0 0 0 – 0 0 0 – 1 0 0 – 0 0 0
Rose LOUI, 0 0 0 – 0 0 0 – 0 1 0 – 0 0 0 *(= LOUIS. Mary ROSE in 1826?)*
Ann FLOWERS, 0 0 0 – 0 0 0 – 0 0 1 – 0 0 0
Henry FLOWERS, 0 0 0 – 0 0 0 – 0 0 1 – 0 0 0
Joseph B. FLOWERS, 0 0 0 – 0 0 0 – 0 0 1 – 0 0 0

#181: William MUCKLEHANY, 0 0 0 – 1 0 0 – 0 0 0 – 1 1 0:
Mary GOFF, 0 0 0 – 0 1 0 – 0 0 0 – 0 0 0
Elizabeth ARTHUR, 0 0 0 – 0 1 0 – 0 0 0 – 0 0 0
Thomas TOOTH, 0 0 0 – 0 0 1 – 0 0 0 – 0 0 0
Sarah CASE, 0 0 0 – 0 0 1 – 0 0 0 – 0 0 0
Ann E. MUCKLEHANY, 0 0 0 – 0 0 1 – 0 0 0 – 0 0 0
Richman GOFF, 45; Patience GOFF, 43.

#182: Anne MEIGHAN, 0 1 0 – 0 0 0 – 0 0 0 – 4 1 0: *(Anna GAPPER MEIGHAN)*
Thomas J. BLOCKLEY, 0 0 1 – 0 0 0 – 0 0 0 – 0 0 0
Maria, 18; Joe, 74; Philip, 51; Prince, 41; Henry, 21.

#183: Charles BENNETT, 0 0 0 – 0 0 0 – 1 0 0 – 0 0 0
Rose GRANT, 0 0 0 – 0 0 0 – 0 1 0 – 0 0 0
Juliana BENNETT, 0 0 0 – 0 0 0 – 0 0 1 – 0 0 0

p. 57:
#184: John H. STAIN, 0 0 0 – 1 0 0 – 0 0 0 – 7 4 7:
Elizabeth STAIN, 0 0 0 – 0 1 0 – 0 0 0 – 0 0 0
James STAIN, 0 0 0 – 1 0 0 – 0 0 0 – 0 0 0
Janet STAIN, 0 0 0 – 0 1 0 – 0 0 0 – 0 0 0
Stephen STAIN, 0 0 0 – 1 0 0 – 0 0 0 – 0 0 0
John STAIN, 0 0 0 – 0 0 1 – 0 0 0 – 0 0 0
Francis STAIN 0 0 0 – 0 0 1 – 0 0 0 – 0 0 0
Toney, 60 Alexander, 60; Scotland, 50; Quamina, 26; Pallmall, 24;
Thomas, 18; William, 14; William, 15; Edward, 11; George, 5; Henry 3;
Mary, 48; Lucretia, 45; Amanda, 30; Eliza, 28; Elizabeth, 12; Lucretia, 10;
Henrietta, 8.

Note: This entry, showing two boys named William in the same household and only a year apart in age, demonstrates the difficulty of tracing slave ancestry in this time period, and the use of other records to solve problems. See this family, #40 in the 1835 census!

#185: Lewis McLENAN, 1 0 0 – 0 0 0 – 0 0 0 – 1 0 0:
Catherine McLENAN, 0 1 0 – 0 0 0 – 0 0 0 – 0 0 0
Marcia ALEXANDER, 0 1 0 – 0 0 0 – 0 0 0 – 0 0 0

129

Cath^n Elizabeth McLENAN, 0 0 1 – 0 0 0 – 0 0 0 – 0 0 0
Fred^k COUSE[*sic*] McLENAN, 0 0 1 – 0 0 0 – 0 0 0 – 0 0 0
Henry Alex^r McLENAN, 0 0 1 – 0 0 0 – 0 0 0 – 0 0 0
  Fame, 36

Note: Marcia Alexander, bapt. 1790 to Lawrence Meighan Sr. and Marcia Davis
Meighan, married 1) Capt. John O'Connor and 2) in 1804, Capt. Alexander Alexander,
who died at Halifax in 1814. Her son Henry Leslie Alexander became an engineer and
married Marie Elizabeth Cockerill in London in 1834; they had ten children, and lived
and died in Leige, Belgium. Was Catherine McLenan her sister, Catherine Meighan?

#186: John H. PETZOLD, 1 0 0 – 0 0 0 – 0 0 0 – 1 1 1:
    Margaret PETZOLD, 0 0 0 – 0 0 1 – 0 0 0 – 0 0 0
    Francis PETZOLD, 0 0 0 – 0 0 1 – 0 0 0 – 0 0 0
    Elizabeth PETZOLD, 0 0 0 – 0 0 1 – 0 0 0 – 0 0 0
    Catherine AVILLA, 0 0 0 – 0 1 0 – 0 0 0 – 0 0 0
      Eady, 25; Patrick, 55; Henry, 12.

p. 58:
#187: Richard ANDERSON, 0 0 0 – 1 0 0 – 0 0 0 – 33 7 7:
    Estate of Alex^r ANDERSON, Dec'd, under charge of Richd ANDERSON:
    Cudjoe, 59; Scipio, 46; Wattle, 49; Glasgow, 38; Murphy, 49; Hero, 49;
    Cupid, 54; Alfred 49; Scotland, 49; Quashie, 49; November, 54; Charlie, 49;
    Hardwicke, 54; Cato, 49; Neale, 44; Bobby, 44; Jem, 54; Cuffie, 47; Peter,
    57; Robert, 49; Charlie, 25; Daniel, 23; Duncan, 59; John, 59; Johnson, 55;
    Toby, 58; Blackwick, 59; Neptune, 64; Jacob, 44; Caesar, 69;

p. 59:   Bill HOPE, 79; Cobus, 74; Nelson, 23; Byron, 12; Davy, 10; Henry, 6;
    Cato, 2; Sophia, 49; Mary Anne, 49; Maria, 49; Sarah, 49; Peggy, 59;
    Friendship, 19; Charlotte, 17; Patience, 13; Peggy, 7; Grace, 5.

#188: Joseph GOFF, 0 0 0 – 1 0 0 – 0 0 0 – 0 1 0:
    Catherine BENNETT, 0 0 0 – 0 0 0 – 0 1 0 – 0 0 0
      Harriet, 50.

#189: Robert F. WADE, 1 0 0 – 0 0 0 – 0 0 0 – 3 0 0: *(b. 7 May 1806 to Capt. Peter*
      Belford, 25; Thomas, 27; Jose, 15.   *(Adolphus Wade and Elizabeth Tillett.)*

#190: John B. ERSKINE, 0 0 0 – 1 0 0 – 0 0 0 – 1 0 0:   *(Son of Margaret Hewlett - see*
    Margaret HEWLETT, 0 0 0 – 0 1 0 – 0 0 0 – 0 0 0   *Leah McAulay's will.)*
    Selina HEWLETT, 0 0 0 – 0 1 0 – 0 0 0 – 0 0 0
    George D. HEWLETT, 0 0 0 – 0 0 1 – 0 0 0 – 0 0 0
    Daniel HEWLETT, 0 0 0 – 0 0 1 – 0 0 0 – 0 0 0
    Wm. Henry MITCHELL, 0 0 0 – 0 0 1 – 0 0 0 – 0 0 0
      George Keith McAULAY, 19

p. 60:

#191:   Estate of Cath. GEDDES, deceased, 1 2 2:
          Benjamin CARTER; Betsey; Evelina; Ann GRACE; Eustatia.
          (Ages not given.)

#192:   Property of Edw. SHIEL and George A. USHER, 17 0 0:
          B. JONES; B. LONGSWORTH; Billy LONGSWORTH;
          Dick COLQUHOUN; Francis; George FRAZER; Jack FORSYTH; George
          MEIGHAN; Guildford; Henry COLQUHOUN; Hector; Jem
          LONGSWORTH; Nelson; Peter McLELLAN; Sam TONY; Simon; Hill.
          (Ages not given.)

#193:   John JOHNSON, 0 0 0 – 1 0 0 – 0 0 0 – 2 0 0:
          William JOHNSON, 0 0 0 – 0 0 1 – 0 0 0 – 0 0 0
            Sam, 50; Limus, 40.

#194:   Susannah POTTS, 0 0 0 – 0 1 0 – 0 0 0 – 0 3 1:
          Janet DUNWELL, 0 0 0 – 0 1 0 – 0 0 0 – 0 0 0
          P. DELTORO, 0 0 0 – 1 0 0 – 0 0 0 – 0 0 0
            Patience; Anne; Jenny *(ages not given;)* Emily, 2.

p. 61:

#195:   John HUGHES, 1 0 0 – 0 0 0 – 0 0 0 – 0 1 0:
          Adelaide J. VERNON, 0 0 0 – 0 1 0 – 0 0 0 – 0 0 0
          Mary Ann HUGHES, 0 0 0 – 0 0 1 – 0 0 0 – 0 0 0
          Ann Eliz[th] HUGHES, 0 0 0 – 0 0 1 – 0 0 0 – 0 0 0
          Edward Hugh HUGHES, 0 0 0 – 0 0 1 – 0 0 0 – 0 0 0
          John James HUGHES, 0 0 0 – 0 0 1 – 0 0 0 – 0 0 0
            Chloe, 22.
          Property of A. J. VERNON, 0 1 0:
            Phoebe, 63.
          Property of P. F. & J. De ST. CROIX of Jersey, 1 0 0:
            Runaway: Rob[t] MILLER, 39.

#196:   John HUNT, 0 0 0 – 1 0 0 – 0 0 0 – 0 0 0
          Elizabeth CASTLE, 0 0 0 – 0 1 0 – 0 0 0 – 0 0 0
          Thomas HUNT, 0 0 0 – 0 0 1 – 0 0 0 – 0 0 0
          John HUNT, 0 0 0 – 0 0 1 – 0 0 0 – 0 0 0

#197:   Lucy PATINETT, 0 0 0 – 0 1 0 – 0 0 0 – 3 0 0:
          Catherine MARTIN, 0 0 0 – 0 0 1 – 0 0 0 – 0 0 0
          Ann TINKHAM, 0 0 0 – 0 0 1 – 0 0 0 – 0 0 0
          George TINKHAM, 0 0 0 – 0 0 1 – 0 0 0 – 0 0 0
          Joe, 50; John, 28; Peter, 50.

131

#198: Amelia ARTHURS, 0 0 0 – 0 1 0 – 0 0 0 – 4 1 2:
John JONES, 0 0 0 – 1 0 0 – 0 0 0 – 0 0 0
Elizabeth ARTHURS, 0 0 0 – 0 1 0 – 0 0 0 – 0 0 0
>Peter ARTHURS, 50; Johnny, 40; Tommy, 24; Billy, 27; Sarah, 50; Ann, 13; Elinor, 9.

#199: Phoebe TRAPP, 0 0 0 – 0 0 0 – 0 1 0 – 0 0 0

p. 62:
#200: Marshall BENNETT, 1 0 0 – 0 0 0 – 0 0 0 – 138 49 66:
W. COOKE, 1 0 0 – 0 0 0 – 0 0 0 – 0 0 0
David BENNETT, 0 0 0 – 0 0 1 – 0 0 0 – 0 0 0 *(Who were his parents?)*
William BARTLETT, 1 0 0 – 0 0 0 – 0 0 0 – 0 0 0
Tabia, 0 0 0 – 0 0 0 – 0 1 0 – 0 0 0 *(Surname not given.)*
Thomas WILLIAMS, 1 0 0 – 0 0 0 – 0 0 0 – 0 0 0
Hugh URQUHART, 1 0 0 – 0 0 0 – 0 0 0 – 0 0 0
>Philip; Bob HIBBERT; Charles; Bob; Davy WATSON; Quawm [*sic*]; Murphy COURTNEY; Johnson; George GRAHAM; Stafford; George ELLICE; Duncan; Middleton; Moco Frank; Marcus; Monday; William BODEN; London; Tom JONES; Guildford; Jamaica Jem; Bill; Thomas BENNETT; Titus; Rodney; Julius; Mack; Duckworth; William MARTIN; Little Jack; Abel; Chatham;

p. 63: Robin Mandingo; Alick MIDDLETON; Duke; Devonshire MEIGHAN; Jem WHITE; Robin (Captain); Jupiter; George SLATER; Tom DOUGLAS; George CRAWFORD; Cyrus; Andrew KEENE; George MORAVIA; Batty HARRIS; Peter WALDRON; Otway; Dick; Cudjoe YOUNG; Harry GIBSON; Dick ALEXANDER; John BAPTIST; John (Mulatto); Richard WALDRON; Prince POTTS; Time PASLOW; Cudjoe YOUNG; Ocro [*sic*]; Fortune; Benjamin BENNETT; Adam; Sampson POTTS; John BENNETT; James;

p. 64: Francis BENNETT; David BENNETT; Richard BARRETT; Richard WALKER; Johnson BENNETT; Tom JOHNSON; Tom MARTIN; Bristol; Joseph; Adam JACKSON; Thomas EVE; Giddy; Tom HEWLETT; Tom BRENNAN; Alex^r BENNETT; Robert GALLIMORE; Alick MARTIN; Delvit; London DOUGLAS; Michael MARTIN; Joseph TRAPP; Philip BRENNAN; Jem FERGUSON; John MOODY; Thomas; George FERGUSON; Joseph POTTS; Cork; Sampson HUME; John YOUNG; Kingsale; Richard POTTS; Henry FERGUSON;

p. 65: W. BENNETT; John SMITH; Thomas TOWNSEND; Archibald POTTS; George POTTS; William; Joseph; John HEWLETT; Adam; Peter; Robert; Francis; Thomas; Murphy; Quaw; Chelsea STAINE; Prince BENNETT; Jamaica Robert; Gift; Davy TUNDO; Sue O'BRIEN; Jessy; Mary

BARRETT; Juba. Stella; Mary MARTIN; Statira; Delia; Eve; Hannah; Susannah; Mary CHARLES; Ruth;

p. 66:   Sabina; Patty CRAWFORD; Bella; Jenny POTTS; Sarah POTTS; Betsey POTTS; Polly POTTS; Mary JACKSON; Diana STAINE; Helena; Eleanor EVE; Prudence; Margaret MOODY; Amelia; Betty POTTS; Mary ELLIS; Betsy PRICE; Bessy; Joanna CARD; Theresa; Amelia; Betsey BENNETT; Amelia POTTS; Tabia; Judy; Patience; Kate JONES; Flora; Henrietta; Elizabeth; Catherine FLOWERS; Sarah; Mimba;

p. 67:   Elizabeth EVE; Mary EVE; Margaret; Catherine GOFF; Margaret GOFF; Patty FERGUSON; Jane SMITH; Elizabeth SMITH; Clara; Sarah; Sarah TOWNSEND; Abbe; Marion FRAZER; Princess; Diana; Catherine; Diana; [sic]; Frances SMITH; Maria; Catherine; Jane; Maria; Marina; Sarah CRABBE; Bill, 12; Marshal; Quaco; Toby BUTCHER; Pompey; Kingston; Ned; Caesar; Sandy.

p. 68:   Francis (or Frances?) 2; Anne, 2; Helen, 2; Elizabeth, 2; Margaret, 1; Edward, 3; Thomas, 3; John, 2; Olivia, 1; Mary, 6; Kate, 6; James, 9; Janet, 1½; Joe, 3; James, 2½; John SAVORY, 2½; James, ½; Helen FRAZER, 2½; Augusta, 2½; Sylvia, 2½; Margaret STAINE, 3; Abigail STAINE, 2; Sarah STAINE, 1; Joe KEENE; Taylor Ben; Hector; Susannah; Bennaba; Mary.
           Runaways: Jervis; Bristol; Neptune ALEXANDER;

p. 69:   Mondingo Tom; Chamba Jack; Kingsale; Joe ELLIOTT; Smart KEENE; Edinburgh; Kent; Mongola Jack; Jem Mondingo; Greenwich; Damon; George YATES; Polydore; John CASSIMERE; Nelson PASLOW; Hamilton; Ginger; Tom PASLOW; Toby GRAHAM; Moco Peter; Tom Indian; George ELRINGTON; Richard YATES; Jack KEENE.

#201: Benjamin CARTER, 0 0 0 – 1 0 0 – 0 0 0 – 0 0 0
       Mary B. PRICE, 0 0 0 – 0 1 0 – 0 0 0 – 0 0 0
       Edward S. ROSS, 0 0 0 – 0 0 1 – 0 0 0 – 0 0 0
       Maria F. CARTER, 0 0 0 – 0 0 1 – 0 0 0 – 0 0 0

p. 70:
#202: Joseph DAVIS, 0 0 0 – 1 0 0 – 0 0 0 – 0 0 0
       Eleanor DAVIS, 0 0 0 – 0 0 0 – 0 1 0 – 0 0 0

#203: James LAMB, 0 0 0 – 0 0 0 – 1 0 0 – 0 0 0
       Abigail LAMB, 0 0 0 – 0 0 0 – 0 1 0 – 0 0 0
       Quamina BURGESS, 0 0 0 – 0 0 0 – 0 0 1 – 0 0 0

#204: Prince WINTER, 0 0 0 – 0 0 0 – 1 0 0 – 0 0 0
       Catherine MIDDLETON, 0 0 0 – 0 0 0 – 0 1 0 – 0 0 0

#205: Thomas MOODIE, 0 0 0 – 1 0 0 – 0 0 0 – 0 0 1:
Rebecca SMITH, 0 0 0 – 0 1 0 – 0 0 0 – 0 0 0
Margaret MOODIE, 0 0 0 – 0 0 1 – 0 0 0 – 0 0 0
James MOODIE, 0 0 0 – 0 0 1 – 0 0 0 – 0 0 0
William, 7.

#206: Richard S. ALLEN, 1 0 0 – 0 0 0 – 0 0 0 – 0 0 0
Eliza ALLEN, 0 1 0 – 0 0 0 – 0 0 0 – 0 0 0
Jane Marg^t ALLEN, 0 0 1 – 0 0 0 – 0 0 0 – 0 0 0

#207: Robert FLOWERS, 0 0 0 – 0 0 0 – 1 0 0 – 0 0 0

#208: Robert PRICE, 0 0 0 – 0 0 0 – 1 0 0 – 0 0 0

#209: Joseph JONES, 0 0 0 – 0 0 0 – 1 0 0 – 1 0 0
John JONES, 16.

p. 71:
#210: Charles FLOWERS, 0 0 0 – 1 0 0 – 0 0 0 – 0 0 0
Margaret FLOWERS, 0 0 0 – 0 1 0 – 0 0 0 – 0 0 0
Fanny FLOWERS, 0 0 0 – 0 0 1 – 0 0 0 – 0 0 0
Caesar FLOWERS, 0 0 0 – 0 0 1 – 0 0 0 – 0 0 0
Richard FLOWERS, 0 0 0 – 0 0 1 – 0 0 0 – 0 0 0
Joseph FLOWERS, 0 0 0 – 0 0 1 – 0 0 0 – 0 0 0
Prue FLOWERS, 0 0 0 – 0 0 1 – 0 0 0 – 0 0 0
Richd Step. FLOWERS, 0 0 0 – 0 0 1 – 0 0 0 – 0 0 0

#211: John RABATEAU, 0 0 0 – 1 0 0 – 0 0 0 – 0 0 0
Elizabeth NEALE, 0 0 0 – 0 1 0 – 0 0 0 – 0 0 0
Sophia RABATEAU, 0 0 0 – 0 0 1 – 0 0 0 – 0 0 0

#212: Phyllida LAMB, 0 0 0 – 0 0 0 – 0 1 0 – 0 0 0
Joe LAMB, 0 0 0 – 0 0 0 – 0 0 1 – 0 0 0

#213: William EMERY, 0 0 0 – 1 0 0 – 0 0 0 – 0 0 0
Eleanor EMERY, 0 0 0 – 0 0 1 – 0 0 0 – 0 0 0

#214: Patience GORDON, 0 0 0 – 0 1 0 – 0 0 0 – 0 2 3:
William CADDLE, 0 0 0 – 0 0 1 – 0 0 0 – 0 0 0
Emily, 35; Elizabeth, 2; Amelia, 30; William, 4; James, 2½.

#215: Benjamin TUCKER, 0 0 0 – 0 0 0 – 1 0 0 – 0 0 0
Arabella LOWRY, 0 0 0 – 0 0 0 – 0 1 0 – 0 0 0

p. 72:
#216: Patrick C. DE BRIEN, 0 0 0 – 1 0 0 – 0 0 0 – 10 2 5:

Mrs. J. BARNES, 0 1 0 – 0 0 0 – 0 0 0 – 0 0 0
Mrs. P. C. DE BRIEN, 0 1 0 – 0 0 0 – 0 0 0 – 0 0 0
Pamela BARNES, 0 1 0 – 0 0 0 – 0 0 0 – 0 0 0
Maria MACKAY, 0 0 0 – 0 1 0 – 0 0 0 – 0 0 0
Elizabeth KEENE, 0 1 0 – 0 0 0 – 0 0 0 – 0 0 0
Jane COATES, 0 0 1 – 0 0 0 – 0 0 0 – 0 0 0
Lucretia ANDERSON, 0 0 0 – 0 0 0 – 0 0 1 – 0 0 0
Anne VERNON, 0 0 0 – 0 0 1 – 0 0 0 – 0 0 0
George KEENE, 1 0 0 – 0 0 0 – 0 0 0 – 0 0 0
    Joe MASCALL, 27; Harry De BRIEN, 40; James DE BRIEN, 38; Dick
    LAMB, 32; David DAVIS, 28; Tom DAVIS, 33; William LAMB, 39;
    Sampson KEENE, 50; John BULL, 50; James DE BRIEN, 2; Jack BARNES,
    60; Maria DAVIS, 40; Isabella DE BRIEN, 4; Louisa DE BRIEN, 27;
    Evelina DE BRIEN, 4; Maria DE BRIEN, 7; John DE BRIEN, 2.

*Note: Mrs. Barnes was Jane, the widow of Thomas Barnes, the master bricklayer who
built St. John's. Two of their daughters, Amelia Sophia and Sarah Holton, married
Coates. Who were the parents of Jane P. S. Coates?*

#217: William SMITH, 1 0 0 – 1 0 0 [*sic*] – 0 0 0 – 5 1 3:
      Josiah SMITH, 0 0 0 – 0 0 1 – 0 0 0 – 0 0 0
      Obadiah SMITH, 0 0 0 – 0 01 – 0 0 0 – 0 0 0
      Francis SMITH 0 0 0 – 0 0 1 – 0 0 0 – 0 0 0
      Stephen SMITH, 0 0 0 – 0 0 1 – 0 0 0 – 0 0 0
      R. SMITH, 0 0 0 – 0 0 0 – 0 0 0 – 0 0 0 *(No mark. Female, = Rebecca.)*
        Jack SMITH, 25; Sampson SMITH, 23; William SMITH, 21; Benj[n] SMITH,
        19; Harry SMITH, 17; Abel SMITH, 14; Mary SMITH, 12; Nanny SMITH,
        8; Sarah SMITH, 43.

*Note: Totals show one white man, four coloured male children, and one coloured female
child - R., from the names and naming sequence. The 1835 census, #64, shows William
Smith with children Rebecca, Francis, and Stephen.*

#218: Edwin COFFIN, 1 0 0 – 0 0 0 – 0 0 0 – 0 0 0
      M. A. COFFIN, 0 1 0 – 0 0 0 – 0 0 0 – 0 0 0
      William BAKER, 1 0 0 – 0 0 0 – 0 0 0 – 0 0 0
      H. E. BAKER, 0 1 0 – 0 0 0 – 0 0 0 – 0 0 0

p. 73:
#219: Harriet SMITH, 0 0 0 – 0 0 0 – 0 1 0 – 0 0 0
      Caesar FULLER, 0 0 0 – 0 0 0 – 1 0 0 – 0 0 0

#220: William GODFREY, 0 0 0 – 1 0 0 – 0 0 0 – 0 0 0
      John GODFREY, 0 0 0 – 0 0 1 – 0 0 0 – 0 0 0
      Maria GODFREY, 0 0 0 – 0 0 1 – 0 0 0
      E. GODFREY, 0 0 0 – 0 0 1 – 0 0 0 – 0 0 0

#221: Catherine HUME, 0 0 0 - 0 1 0 – 0 0 0 – 0 1 1:
Frances H. WALDRON, 0 0 0 – 0 0 1 – 0 0 0 – 0 0 0
Jane R. WALDRON, 0 0 0 – 0 0 1 – 0 0 0 – 0 0 0
Brasilla, 35; Joseph, 5.

#222: John HEMMONDS, 0 0 0 – 1 0 0 – 0 0 0
Cath^n TONOSTON, 0 0 0 – 0 1 0 – 0 0 0 – 0 0 0
James JONES, 0 0 0 – 1 0 0 – 0 0 0 – 0 0 0
Mary JONES, 0 0 0 – 0 1 0 – 0 0 0 – 0 0 0
George JONES, 0 0 0 – 1 0 0 – 0 0 0 – 0 0 0
Nancy JONES, 0 0 0 – 0 1 0 – 0 0 0 – 0 0 0
Cleantes ARTHURS, 0 0 0 – 0 1 0 – 0 0 0 – 0 0 0
Joan HEMMONDS, 0 0 0 – 0 1 0 – 0 0 0 – 0 0 0
William HEMMONDS, 0 0 0 – 0 0 1 – 0 0 0 – 0 0 0
John HEMMONDS, 0 0 0 – 0 0 1 – 0 0 0 – 0 0 0
Thomas HEMMONDS, 0 0 0 – 0 0 1 – 0 0 0 – 0 0 0

#223: John A. NEWMAN, 0 0 0 – 0 0 0 – 1 0 0 – 0 0 0

p. 74:
#224: James WAGNER, 0 0 0 – 1 0 0 – 0 0 0 – 0 0 0
Catherine JOSEPH, 0 0 0 – 0 0 0 – 0 1 0 – 0 0 0
George WAGNER, 0 0 0 – 0 0 1 – 0 0 0 – 0 0 0
James WAGNER, 0 0 0 – 0 0 1 – 0 0 0 – 0 0 0
William NEAL, 0 0 0 – 0 0 1 – 0 0 0 – 0 0 0

#225: Nancy MILES, 0 0 0 – 0 0 0 – 0 1 0 – 0 0 0
Lucretia MILES, 0 0 0 – 0 0 0 – 0 1 0 – 0 0 0
Joseph MILES, 0 0 0 – 0 0 0 – 0 0 1 – 0 0 0
Juliana MILES, 0 0 0 – 0 0 0 – 0 0 1 – 0 0 0
Henrietta MILES, 0 0 0 – 0 0 0 – 0 1 0 – 0 0 0

#226: Thomas PHILLIPS, 1 0 0 – 0 0 0 – 0 0 0 – 0 0 0
Sarah BURNS, 0 0 0 – 0 1 0 – 0 0 0 – 0 0 0
Caroline PHILLIPS, 0 0 0 – 0 0 1 – 0 0 0 – 0 0 0
James PHILLIPS, 0 0 0 – 0 0 1 – 0 0 0 – 0 0 0
Anne G. GRAY, 0 0 0 – 0 1 0 – 0 0 0 – 0 0 0
Martha TUCKER, 0 0 0 – 0 0 0 – 0 1 0 – 0 0 0
Lewis, 0 0 0 – 0 0 0 – 1 0 0 – 0 0 0 *(Surname not given.)*

#227: William DAWSON, 1 0 0 – 0 0 0 – 0 0 0 – 0 0 0
Elizabeth RAYBON, 0 0 0 – 0 1 0 – 0 0 0 – 0 0 0
Daniel DAWSON, 0 0 0 – 0 0 1 – 0 0 0 – 0 0 0
Sarah, 0 0 0 – 0 0 1 – 0 0 0 – 0 0 0 *(Surname not given.)*

#228: William HENRY, 0 0 0 – 1 0 0 – 0 0 0 – 0 0 0
John HENRY, 0 0 0 – 0 0 1 – 0 0 0 – 0 0 0

p. 75:
#229: John CLARK, 0 0 0 – 0 0 0 – 1 0 0 – 0 0 0
Sabina CLARK, 0 0 0 – 0 0 0 – 0 1 0 – 0 0 0
William CLARK, 0 0 0 – 0 0 0 – 0 0 1 – 0 0 0
Lucretia CLARK, 0 0 0 – 0 0 0 – 0 0 1 – 0 0 0
Lucy CLARK, 0 0 0 – 0 0 0 – 0 0 1 – 0 0 0

#230: Violet CARD, 0 0 0 – 0 0 0 – 0 1 0 – 0 0 0
Betsey CARD, 0 0 0 – 0 0 0 – 0 0 1 – 0 0 0
Rachel CARD, 0 0 0 – 0 0 0 – 0 0 1 – 0 0 0
Matilda CARD, 0 0 0 – 0 0 0 – 0 0 1 – 0 0 0
Mary Ann CARD, 0 0 0 – 0 0 0 – 0 0 1 – 0 0 0
John CARD, 0 0 0 – 0 0 0 – 0 0 1 – 0 0 0
Robert CARD, 0 0 0 – 0 0 0 – 0 0 1 – 0 0 0
Hagar CARD, 0 0 0 – 0 0 0 – 0 0 1 – 0 0 0
Lenan CARD, 0 0 0 – 0 0 0 – 0 0 1 – 0 0 0

#231: Elizabeth GODFREY, 0 0 0 – 0 1 0 – 0 0 0 – 0 0 0
Selina BENNETT, 0 0 0 – 0 0 1 – 0 0 0 – 0 0 0
George MONKS, 0 0 0 – 0 0 1 – 0 0 0 – 0 0

Note: Selina Bennett was born in 1815 to Elizabeth Godfrey and Marshal Bennett,
Merchant (Sr. or Jr. not shown - probably Sr., as Sr. was a merchant and Jr. was in his
mid teens at the time.) George Monks was born in 1818 to Elizabeth Godfrey and James
J. Moncks, Store Keeper. See the Second Baptismal Register. In 1835, #218, Selina was
listed as Eliza, and in 1839, #320, as Celina.

#232: Elizabeth SPROAT, 0 0 0 – 0 0 0 – 0 1 0 – 0 0 0

#233: Nancy MEANY, 0 0 0 – 0 0 0 – 0 1 0 – 0 0 0
Catherine GRANT, 0 0 0 – 0 0 0 – 0 1 0 – 0 0 0
Rachael GRANT, 0 0 0 – 0 0 0 – 0 0 1 – 0 0 0
Simon GRANT, 0 0 0 – 0 0 0 – 0 0 1 – 0 0 0

p. 76:
#234: Samuel FORBES, 1 0 0 – 0 0 0 – 0 0 0 – 0 0 0
Jane AUGUST, 0 0 0 – 0 1 0 – 0 0 0 – 0 0 0
Elizabeth FORBES, 0 0 0 – 0 0 1 – 0 0 0 – 0 0 0

#235: Anne SMITH, 0 0 0 – 0 0 0 – 0 1 0 – 0 0 0
Tabia SMITH, 0 0 0 – 0 0 0 – 0 0 1 – 0 0 0
Marion SMITH, 0 0 0 – 0 0 0 – 0 0 1 – 0 0 0

#236: John Wm BARROW, 0 0 0 – 1 0 0 – 0 0 0 – 0 0 0
Mimba BARROW, 0 0 0 – 0 1 0 – 0 0 0 – 0 0 0
William T. BARROW, 0 0 0 – 0 0 1 – 0 0 0 – 0 0 0
Elizth Ann BARROW, 0 0 0 – 0 0 1 – 0 0 0 – 0 0 0
Mary Jane BARROW, 0 0 0 – 0 0 1 – 0 0 0 – 0 0 0
George H^y BARROW, 0 0 0 – 0 0 1 – 0 0 0 – 0 0 0
Edward BARROW, 0 0 0 – 0 0 1 – 0 0 0 – 0 0 0

#237: Jane GORDON, 0 0 0 – 0 1 0 – 0 0 0 – 1 2 4:
Hannah GORDON, 0 0 0 – 0 0 0 – 0 1 0 – 0 0 0
Ann Elizth CODD, 0 0 0 – 0 0 1 – 0 0 0 – 0 0 0
Diana GORDON, 13; Henry GORDON, 7; Toby GORDON, 40; Elizabeth
GORDON, 26; Margaret, 25; James, 7; Jane Elizabeth, 4.

#238: Adeline MASKALL, 0 0 0 – 0 0 0 – 0 1 0 – 0 0 0

#239: James BUCKNOR, 0 0 0 – 1 0 0 – 0 0 0 – 0 0 0

p. 77:
#240: Eyre COOTE, 0 0 0 – 0 0 0 – 1 0 0 – 0 0 0
Betty FALL, 0 0 0 – 0 0 0 – 0 1 0 – 0 0 0

#241: Joseph FLOWERS, 0 0 0 – 0 0 0 – 1 0 0 – 0 0 0
Caesar FLOWERS, 0 0 0 – 0 0 0 – 1 0 0 – 0 0 0
Mary FLOWERS, 0 0 0 – 0 0 0 – 0 0 1 – 0 0 0

#242: Priscilla HICKEY, 0 0 0 – 0 1 0 – 0 0 0 – 0 0 0
Thisbe HICKEY, 0 0 0 – 0 0 0 – 0 1 0 – 0 0 0
Quaw CAREL, 0 0 0 – 0 0 0 – 1 0 0 – 0 0 0
Fanny GODFREY, 0 0 0 – 0 0 1 – 0 0 0 – 0 0 0
Willm HAMILTON, 0 0 0 – 1 0 0 – 0 0 0 – 0 0 0
Caesar HICKEY, 0 0 0 – 0 0 0 – 1 0 0 – 0 0 0

#243: William LEWIS 0 0 0 – 1 0 0 – 0 0 0 – 2 3 1:
Margaret LEWIS, 0 0 0 – 0 1 0 – 0 0 0 – 0 0 0
William T. LEWIS, 0 0 0 – 0 0 1 – 0 0 0 – 0 0 0
Mary Emma LEWIS, 0 0 0 – 0 0 1 – 0 0 0 – 0 0 0
Ann Julia LEWIS, 0 0 0 – 0 0 1 – 0 0 0 – 0 0 0
Prince, 40; Sarah, 18; Elizabeth, 12; Jenny, 38; John Adam, 4.
Runaway: Adam, 21.

#244: Susannah GORDON, 0 0 0 – 0 0 0 – 0 1 0 – 1 1 0:
Susannah MYVETT, 0 0 0 – 0 0 0 – 0 1 0 – 0 0 0
Fanny; Sam. *(Ages not given.)*

#245: Philip RICHARDSON, 0 0 0 – 0 0 0 – 1 0 0 – 0 0 0

p. 78:
#246: George SAVORY, 0 0 0 – 1 0 0 – 0 0 0 – 0 0 0
Amelia JACKSON, 0 0 0 – 0 0 0 – 0 1 0 – 0 0 0
Stephen SAVORY, 0 0 0 – 0 0 1 – 0 0 0 – 0 0 0

#247: James WHITE, 0 0 0 – 1 0 0 – 0 0 0 – 0 0 0
Peter FLOWERS, 0 0 0 – 0 0 0 – 1 0 0 – 0 0 0

#248: Joseph BOURN, 1 0 0 – 0 0 0 – 0 0 0 – 0 0 0 *(The Baptist missionary.)*
Mehetiable BOURN, 0 1 0 – 0 0 0 – 0 0 0 – 0 0 0
Eliza GIBSON, 0 0 0 – 0 1 0 – 0 0 0 – 0 0 0

#249: Ann SMITH, 0 0 0 – 0 1 0 – 0 0 0 – 6 3 7:
William SWASEY, 26; James SWASEY, 22; Robert SWASEY, 21;
Maligo SWASEY, 18; Henry SWASEY, 13; George SWASEY, 16;
Francis SWASEY, 12; Benjamin SWASEY, 13; Nancy, 42; Charity, 46;
Eve, 29; Maria, 12; Cuba, 10½; Daphne, 14.
Runaway: Christmas SWASEY, 24; Toby SWASEY, 35.

#250: Thomas BAILEY, 0 0 0 – 0 0 0 – 1 0 0 – 0 0 0

p. 79:
#251: Archibald COLQUHOUN, 0 0 0 – 0 0 0 – 1 0 0 – 0 0 0
Eady COLQUHOUN, 0 0 0 – 0 0 0 – 0 1 0 – 0 0 0
Charles COLQUHOUN, 0 0 0 – 0 0 0 – 0 0 1 – 0 0 0
Elizabeth COLQUHOUN, 0 0 0 – 0 0 0 – 0 0 1 – 0 0 0
Nancy HUME, 0 0 0 – 0 0 0 – 0 1 0 – 0 0 0
William HUME 0 0 0 – 0 0 0 – 0 0 1 – 0 0 0

#252: George D. ADOLPHUS, 1 0 0 – 0 0 0 – 0 0 0 – 1 2 0:
Batt LOWRIE; *(age not given,)* Samuel ROBERTSON, 38; William JEYES,
17; Helen DAVIS, 25; Billy PITT, 37; Linder, 45.

Note: Was G. D. Adolphus related to Capt. Peter Adolphus Wade, and if so, how?

#253: John CONNOR, 1 0 0 – 0 0 0 – 0 0 0 – 0 0 0
Elizabeth HEWLETT, 0 0 0 – 0 1 0 – 0 0 0 – 0 0 0
Charles ROGERS, 0 0 0 – 0 0 1 – 0 0 0 – 0 0 0
Susannah ROGERS, 0 0 0 – 0 0 1 – 0 0 0 – 0 0 0

#254: Maria F. UVE, 0 0 0 – 0 1 0 – 0 0 0 – 0 0 0
Juana ESTEVE UVE, 0 0 0 – 0 1 0 – 0 0 0 – 0 0 0
Maria L. MUSINGE, 0 0 0 – 0 1 0 – 0 0 0 – 0 0 0
Maria J. UVE, 0 0 0 – 0 1 0 – 0 0 0 – 0 0 0

#255: John LEANDRO, 0 0 0 – 1 0 0 – 0 0 0 – 0 0 0
Jose NACHULETT, 0 0 0 – 1 0 0 – 0 0 0 – 0 0 0
Maria PETURINA, 0 0 0 – 0 1 0 – 0 0 0 – 0 0 0

p. 80:
#256: Duncanette CAMPBELL, 0 0 0 – 0 1 0 – 0 0 0 – 1 5 2:
John A. LINDSAY, 0 0 0 – 0 0 1 – 0 0 0 – 0 0 0
Susannah; Molly; Kitty; Amelia; Eleanor; Mary; Major; William.
(Ages not given.)

#257: George Wm. RICHARDSON, 0 0 0 – 0 0 0 – 1 0 0 – 0 0 0
Susannah POOLE, 0 0 0 – 0 0 0 – 0 1 0 – 0 0 0

#258: James SAVORY, 0 0 0 – 1 0 0 – 0 0 0 – 1 0 0:
Lucretia POTTS, 0 0 0 – 0 1 0 – 0 0 0 – 0 0 0
Robert SAVORY, 0 0 0 – 0 0 1 – 0 0 0 – 0 0 0
Mary Ann SAVORY, 0 0 0 – 0 0 1 – 0 0 0 – 0 0 0
Catherine SAVORY, 0 0 0 – 0 0 1 – 0 0 0 – 0 0 0
Chelsea. *(Age not given.)*

#259: Edith LAMB, 0 0 0 – 0 0 0 – 0 1 0 – 0 0 0
Henrietta LAMB, 0 0 0 – 0 0 0 – 0 0 1 – 0 0 0
Dido LAMB, 0 0 0 – 0 0 0 – 0 1 0 – 0 0 0

#260: Cecilia CADDLE, 0 0 0 – 0 1 0 – 0 0 0 – 0 0 0
Nancy AUGUST, 0 0 0 – 0 0 1 – 0 0 0 – 0 0 0
Margaret TUCKER, 0 0 0 – 0 0 1 – 0 0 0 – 0 0 0
Thomas PASLOW, 0 0 0 – 0 0 1 – 0 0 0 – 0 0 0
Andrew SAY, 0 0 0 – 1 0 0 – 0 0 0 – 0 0 0

p. 81:
#261: Isabella MEANY, 0 0 0 – 0 0 0 – 0 1 0 – 0 0 1:
Priscilla MOHEAR, 0 0 0 – 0 0 0 – 0 0 1 – 0 0 0
Mary MEANY, 12.

#262: John M. CUNNINGHAM, 0 0 0 – 1 0 0 – 0 0 0 – 2 1 0: *(See baptism in the First*
Margaret CUNNINGHAM, 0 0 0 – 0 1 0 – 0 0 0 – 0 0 0   *Register of Belize.)*
James CUNNINGHAM, 0 0 0 – 0 0 1 – 0 0 0 – 0 0 0   *(James Potts Cunningham*
Mary H. CUNNINGHAM, 0 0 0 – 0 0 1 – 0 0 0 – 0 0 0   *d. June 1834, aged 17.)*
John M. CUNNINGHAM, 0 0 0 – 0 0 1 – 0 0 0 – 0 0 0
William CUNNINGHAM, 0 0 0 – 0 0 1 – 0 0 0 – 0 0 0
Runaway: Frank; Chance; Mary. *(Ages not given.)*

#263: Francis FORT, 0 0 0 – 1 0 0 – 0 0 0 – 2 3 3:
Betinah FORT, 0 0 0 – 0 1 0 – 0 0 0 – 0 0 0

140

Sarah DAWSON, 0 0 0 – 0 1 0 – 0 0 0 – 0 0 0
George, 23; James, 18; Daniel, 12; Harry, 11; Richard, 5; Betty, 42; Maria, 20; Nancy, 16.

#264: Margaret FLOWERS, 0 0 0 – 0 0 0 – 0 1 0 – 0 0 0
George GLADDEN, 0 0 0 – 0 0 0 – 1 0 0 – 0 0 0
Royal GLADDEN, 0 0 0 – 0 0 0 – 1 0 0 – 0 0 0
Nancy GLADDEN, 0 0 0 – 0 0 0 – 0 1 0 – 0 0 0
Catherine GLADDEN 0 0 0 – 0 0 0 – 0 1 0 – 0 0 0
Jane C. GLADDEN, 0 0 0 – 0 0 0 – 0 0 1 – 0 0 0

#265: Charles M. DANCE, 0 0 0 – 1 0 0 – 0 0 0 – 0 0 0

p. 82:
#266: William FLOWERS, 0 0 0 – 0 0 0 – 1 0 0 – 0 0 0
Grace WINTER, 0 0 0 – 0 0 0 – 0 1 0 – 0 0 0
Elizabeth FLOWERS, 0 0 0 – 0 0 0 – 0 0 1 – 0 0 0
Benjamin FLOWERS, 0 0 0 – 0 0 0 – 0 0 1 – 0 0 0
Maria FLOWERS, 0 0 0 – 0 0 0 – 0 0 1 – 0 0 0

#267: George GARNETT, 0 0 0 – 1 0 0 – 0 0 0 – 5 2 1:
Elizabeth GARNETT, 0 0 0 – 0 0 1 – 0 0 0 – 0 0 0
Jessy BOURKE, 0 0 0 – 0 0 0 – 0 1 0 – 0 0 0
George PITKETHLY, 0 0 0 – 0 0 1 – 0 0 0 – 0 0 0
James CATOUCHE, 0 0 0 – 0 0 0 – 0 0 1 – 0 0 0
George CATOUCHE, 0 0 0 – 0 0 0 – 1 0 0 – 0 0 0
Charles AUGUSTIN, 0 0 0 – 0 0 0 – 1 0 0 – 0 0 0
James McPHERSON, 1 0 0 – 0 0 0 – 0 0 0 – 0 0 0
Scotland; James LAMB; Jonathan; Jasper WALDRON; Monday; James DUNN; Elizabeth GRAY; Fanny MOODIE.

#268: Ellen ROBINSON, 0 0 0 – 0 0 0 – 0 1 0 – 0 0 0
Thomas ROBINSON, 0 0 0 – 0 0 0 – 1 0 0 – 0 0 0
John ROBINSON, 0 0 0 – 0 0 0 – 1 0 0 – 0 0 0
Louisa ROBINSON, 0 0 0 – 0 0 0 – 0 1 0 – 0 0 0

#269: Eve BELISLE, 0 0 0 – 0 0 0 – 0 1 0 – 0 0 0
Sarah BELISLE, 0 0 0 – 0 0 1 – 0 0 0 – 0 0 0
Mary BELISLE, 0 0 0 – 0 0 1 - 0 0 0 – 0 0 0
Sarah BELISLE, 0 0 0 – 0 0 0 – 0 1 0 – 0 0 0
Aberdeen BELISLE, 0 0 0 – 0 0 0 – 1 0 0 – 0 0 0

#270: John CHARLES, 0 0 0 – 0 0 0 – 1 0 0 – 0 0 0

p. 83:
#271: John GIDDY, 0 0 0 – 0 0 0 – 1 0 0 – 0 0 0

141

Thomas GIDDY, 0 0 0 – 0 0 0 – 1 0 0 – 0 0 0
Louisa HUGHES, 0 0 0 – 0 0 0 – 0 1 0 – 0 0 0
Patience HUGHES, 0 0 0 – 0 0 0 – 0 0 1 – 0 0 0
Nancy HUGHES, 0 0 0 – 0 0 0 – 0 0 1 – 0 0 0
William HUGHES, 0 0 0 – 0 0 0 – 0 0 1 – 0 0 0
Susannah GIDDY, 0 0 0 – 0 0 0 – 0 0 1 – 0 0 0
Jane GIDDY, 0 0 0 – 0 0 0 – 0 0 1 – 0 0 0
John GIDDY, 0 0 0 – 0 0 0 – 0 0 1 – 0 0 0
Betsey GIDDY, 0 0 0 – 0 0 0 – 0 0 1 – 0 0 0

#272: Behavior TUCKER, 0 0 0 – 0 0 0 – 0 1 0 – 0 0 0
Ann TUCKER, 0 0 0 – 0 0 0 – 0 1 0 – 0 0 0
Wm S. TUCKER, 0 0 0 – 0 0 0 – 1 0 0 – 0 0 0
Francis O. TUCKER, 0 0 0 – 0 0 0 – 1 0 0 – 0 0 0
James TUCKER, 0 0 0 – 0 0 0 – 0 0 1 – 0 0 0

#273: Fidelia TUCKER, 0 0 0 – 0 0 0 – 0 1 0 – 0 0 0
Robert TUCKER, 0 0 0 – 0 0 0 – 1 0 0 – 0 0 0
Amelia TUCKER, 0 0 0 – 0 0 0 – 0 1 0 – 0 0 0
Lucy TUCKER, 0 0 0 – 0 0 0 – 0 1 0 – 0 0 0
Sophia TUCKER, 0 0 0 – 0 0 0 – 0 0 1 – 0 0 0

#274: Joseph FLOWERS, 0 0 0 – 0 0 0 – 1 0 0 – 0 0 0
Lucretia FLOWERS, 0 0 0 – 0 0 0 – 0 1 0 – 0 0 0
Cyrus FLOWERS, 0 0 0 – 0 0 0 – 0 0 1 – 0 0 0
Joseph T. FLOWERS, 0 0 0 – 0 0 0 – 0 0 1 – 0 0 0
John FLOWERS, 0 0 0 – 0 0 0 – 0 0 1 – 0 0 0

p. 84:
#275: Peter STANN, 0 0 0 – 1 0 0 – 0 0 0 – 0 3 3:
Elizabeth CARD, 0 0 0 – 0 0 0 – 0 1 0 – 0 0 0
Richard S. STANN, 0 0 0 – 1 0 0 – 0 0 0 – 0 0 0
Catherine STANN, 0 0 0 – 0 1 0 – 0 0 0 – 0 0 0
Maria STANN, 0 0 0 – 0 1 0 – 0 0 0 – 0 0 0
Dorothy STANN, 0 0 0 – 0 1 0 – 0 0 0 – 0 0 0
Aurelia STANN, 0 0 0 – 0 1 0 – 0 0 0 – 0 0 0
Sophia STANN, 0 0 0 – 0 1 0 – 0 0 0 – 0 0 0
Susannah STANN, 0 0 0 – 0 0 1 – 0 0 0 – 0 0 0
John STANN, 0 0 0 – 0 0 1 – 0 0 0 – 0 0 0
Henry STANN, 0 0 0 – 0 0 1 – 0 0 0 – 0 0 0
Maria STANN, 0 0 0 – 0 0 1 – 0 0 0 – 0 0 0
Elizabeth ALEXANDER, 0 0 0 – 0 0 1 – 0 0 0 – 0 0 0
　　　Rosanna, 22; Joanna, 19; Jane, 18; Stephen, 4; John, 10 mo's; Delia, 1½ yrs.

#276: Michael FLOWERS, 0 0 0 – 1 0 0 – 0 0 0 – 0 0 0
Mary STANE [sic], 0 0 0 – 0 1 0 – 0 0 0 – 0 0 0

142

#277: James TRAPP, 0 0 0 – 1 0 0 – 0 0 0 – 0 0 0
        Elizabeth TRAPP, 0 0 0 – 0 0 0 – 0 1 0 – 0 0 0
        William HUME, 0 0 0 – 0 0 0 – 1 0 0 – 0 0 0

#278: William HEMSLEY, 0 0 0 – 1 0 0 – 0 0 0 – 0 0 0
        Catherine HEMSLEY, 0 0 0 – 0 1 0 – 0 0 0 – 0 0 0
        Sarah ERSKINE, 0 0 0 – 0 1 0 – 0 0 0 – 0 0 0

#279: George MASKALL, 0 0 0 – 1 0 0 – 0 0 0 – 1 0 0:
        Elizabeth MASKALL, 0 0 0 – 0 0 0 – 0 1 0 – 0 0 0
            Francis MASKALL, 57.

p. 85:
#280: William BERNARD, 0 0 0 – 0 0 0 – 1 0 0 – 0 0 0
        John BERNARD, 0 0 0 – 0 0 0 – 0 0 1 – 0 0 0
        Daniel BERNARD, 0 0 0 – 0 0 0 – 0 0 1 – 0 0 0
        Mary Ann BERNARD, 0 0 0 – 0 0 0 – 0 0 1 – 0 0 0

#281: William McCULLOCH, 0 0 0 – 1 0 0 – 0 0 0 – 0 0 0
        Dorothy BURNS, 0 0 0 – 0 1 0 – 0 0 0 – 0 0 0
        Thomas McCULLOCH, 0 0 0 – 0 0 1 – 0 0 0 – 0 0 0
        William McCULLOCH, 0 0 0 – 0 0 1 – 0 0 0 – 0 0 0

#282: Rachael JEFFRIES, 0 0 0 – 0 0 0 – 0 1 0 – 1 1 0:
        Emanuel ANTONIO, 1 0 0 – 0 0 0 – 0 0 0 – 0 0 0
        Archibald HANDYSIDE, 1 0 0 – 0 0 0 – 0 0 0 – 0 0 0
        Richard HANDYSIDE, 1 0 0 – 0 0 0 – 0 0 0 – 0 0 0
        James RUMBOLD, 0 0 0 – 1 0 0 – 0 0 0 – 0 0 0
        George JEFFREYS, 0 0 0 – 0 0 1 – 0 0 0 – 0 0 0
        Charles JEFFREYS, 0 0 0 – 0 0 1 – 0 0 0 – 0 0 0
        William JEFFREYS, 0 0 0 – 0 0 1 – 0 0 0 – 0 0 0
        Henrietta JEFFREYS, 0 0 0 – 0 0 1 – 0 0 0 – 0 0 0
            John, 30; Betsey, 28.

#283: Ado FLOWERS, 0 0 0 – 0 0 0 – 1 0 0 – 0 0 0
        Harriet TINAH, 0 0 0 – 0 0 0 – 0 1 0 – 0 0 0
        James FLOWERS, 0 0 0 – 0 0 0 – 0 0 1 – 0 0 0
        John FLOWERS, 0 0 0 – 0 0 0 – 0 0 1 – 0 0 0

#284: William HARDY, 0 0 0 – 0 0 0 – 1 0 0 – 0 0 0
        Elizabeth FLOWERS, 0 0 0 – 0 0 0 – 0 1 0 – 0 0 0

p. 86:
#285: Marshal BENNETT, 1 0 0 – 0 0 0 – 0 0 0 – 1 1 2: *(Marshal Jr.)*
        Catherine MEIGHAN, 0 0 0 – 0 1 0 – 0 0 0 – 0 0 0
        Catherine MEIGHAN, 0 0 0 – 0 0 1 – 0 0 0 – 0 0 0

143

Ann McKEE, 0 0 0 – 0 1 0 – 0 0 0 – 0 0 0 *(Was she Ann LONGSWORTH?)*
    Benjamin, 28.
Property of C. MEIGHAN:
    Eliza, 25; Mary Ann, 4; Edward, 2.

#286: George BILLERY, 0 0 0 – 0 0 0 – 1 0 0 – 0 0 0
       Charles BILLERY, 0 0 0 – 0 0 0 – 1 0 0 – 0 0 0
       Peter BILLERY, 0 0 0 – 0 0 0 – 1 0 0 – 0 0 0
       Nonoon [*sic*] BILLERY, 0 0 0 – 0 0 0 – 0 1 0 – 0 0 0
       Jane BILLERY, 0 0 0 – 0 0 0 – 0 0 1 – 0 0 0

#287: Sarah HICKEY, 0 0 0 – 0 0 0 – 0 1 0 – 0 0 0
       John CARD, 0 0 0 – 0 0 1 – 0 0 0 – 0 0 0
       James GRANT, 0 0 0 – 0 0 0 – 0 0 1 – 0 0 0

#288: James WOODS, 1 0 0 – 0 0 0 – 0 0 0 – 1 0 0:
       Elizabeth WOODS, 0 1 0 – 0 0 0 – 0 0 0 – 0 0 0
       Mehetiable WOODS, 0 1 0 – 0 0 0 – 0 0 0 – 0 0 0
       William H. WOODS, 0 0 1 – 0 0 0 – 0 0 0 – 0 0 0
       Sidney M. WOODS, 0 0 1 – 0 0 0 – 0 0 0 – 0 0 0
       Rachael, 25.

#289: John COURTNEY, 0 0 0 – 1 0 0 – 0 0 0 – 0 0 0

#290: Francisco JOSE, 0 0 0 – 0 0 0 – 1 0 0 – 0 0 0

p. 87:
#291: George BEAKE, 1 0 0 – 0 0 0 – 0 0 0 – 0 0 0
       John BEAKE, 0 0 0 – 1 0 0 – 0 0 0 – 0 0 0
       Betty BEAKE, 0 0 0 – 0 1 0 – 0 0 0 – 0 0 0
       Maria BEAKE, 0 0 0 – 0 1 0 – 0 0 0 – 0 0 0
       Margaret SMITH, 0 0 0 – 0 1 0 – 0 0 0 – 0 0 0
       Charles LIGHT, 0 0 0 – 1 0 0 – 0 0 0 – 0 0 0
       Jane OGLES, 0 0 0 – 0 1 0 – 0 0 0 – 0 0 0 *(= ORGILL?)*
       Joseph MARTIN, 0 0 0 – 1 0 0 – 0 0 0 – 0 0 0
       Francis MARTIN, 0 0 0 – 1 0 0 – 0 0 0 – 0 0 0
       John MARTIN, 0 0 0 – 1 0 0 – 0 0 0 – 0 0 0

#292: Franklin MEIGHAN, 0 0 0 – 0 0 0 – 1 0 0 – 0 0 0
       Elizabeth CURRANT, 0 0 0 – 0 0 0 – 0 1 0 – 0 0 0
       Sarah FRANKLIN, 0 0 0 – 0 0 0 – 0 1 0 – 0 0 0
       Chloe FRANKLIN, 0 0 0 – 0 0 0 – 0 1 0 – 0 0 0
       Peter FRANKLIN, 0 0 0 – 0 0 0 – 0 0 1 – 0 0 0
       William FRANKLIN, 0 0 0 – 0 0 0 – 0 0 1 – 0 0 0
       Fanny FRANKLIN, 0 0 0 – 0 0 0 – 0 0 1 – 0 0 0
       Susannah FRANKLIN, 0 0 0 – 0 0 0 – 0 0 1 – 0 0 0

#293: Thomas SMITH, 0 0 0 – 1 0 0 – 0 0 0 – 0 0 0
        Eve CURRANT, 0 0 0 – 0 0 0 – 0 1 0 – 0 0 0
        Isabella SMITH, 0 0 0 – 0 0 1 – 0 0 0 – 0 0 0
        Abraham SMITH, 0 0 0 – 0 0 1 – 0 0 0 – 0 0 0
        Priscilla SMITH, 0 0 0 – 0 0 1 – 0 0 0 – 0 0 0
        Richard SMITH, 0 0 0 – 0 0 1 – 0 0 0 – 0 0 0

#294: Benjamin ROBINSON, 0 0 0 – 1 0 0 – 0 0 0 – 0 0 0

p. 88:
#295: Louisa FRANCIS, 0 0 0 – 0 1 0 – 0 0 0 – 0 0 0
        John GREEN, 0 0 0 – 0 0 0 – 1 0 0 – 0 0 0
        Francis ARTHUR, 0 0 0 – 0 0 0 – 1 0 0 – 0 0 0

#296: William B. TOOTH, 1 0 0 – 0 0 0 – 0 0 0 – 1 3 2:
        Thomas TOOTH, 0 0 0 – 0 0 1 – 0 0 0 – 0 0 0
        Ann TOOTH, 0 0 0 – 0 0 1 – 0 0 0 – 0 0 0
        Eliza TOOTH, 0 0 0 – 0 0 1 – 0 0 0 – 0 0 0
        Susan TOOTH, 0 0 0 – 0 0 1 – 0 0 0 – 0 0 0
        Elizabeth TOOTH, 0 0 0 – 0 0 1 – 0 0 0 – 0 0 0
        Caroline TOOTH, 0 0 0 – 0 0 1 – 0 0 0 – 0 0 0
        Clarissa C. TOOTH, 0 0 0 – 0 0 1 – 0 0 0 – 0 0 0
            Nelson TOOTH, 17; Daniel TOOTH, 2; Pamela TOOTH, 2½; Mary ELLIS,
            40; Fanny TOOTH, 21; Molly GOFF, 30.

Note: The 1823, 1826, and 1829 censuses show William's wife was Elizabeth JACKSON.

#297: Simon THOMPSON, 0 0 0 – 0 0 0 – 1 0 0 – 0 0 0
        Elizabeth THOMPSON, 0 0 0 – 0 0 0 – 0 1 0 – 0 0 0
        Edward SPROAT, 0 0 0 – 0 0 0 – 1 0 0 – 0 0 0
        Adam SPROAT, 0 0 0 – 0 0 0 – 1 0 0 – 0 0 0
        Grace SPROAT, 0 0 0 – 0 0 0 – 0 1 0 – 0 0 0
        Jeremiah SPROAT, 0 0 0 – 0 0 0 – 0 0 1 – 0 0 0
        Elizabeth SPROAT, 0 0 0 – 0 0 0 – 0 0 1 – 0 0 0
        Rose SPROAT, 0 0 0 – 0 0 0 – 0 0 1 – 0 0 0
        Richard SPROAT, 0 0 0 – 0 0 0 – 0 0 1 – 0 0 0
        Benjamin HUGHES, 0 0 0 – 0 0 0 – 0 0 1 – 0 0 0

#298: William QUAYMAN, 0 0 0 – 0 0 0 – 1 0 0 – 0 0 0
        Sarah PITTS, 0 0 0 – 0 0 0 – 0 1 0 – 0 0 0
        Abraham QUAYMAN, 0 0 0 – 0 0 0 – 0 0 1 – 0 0 0

p. 89:
#299: Family of C. CUNNINGHAM, 3 4 4:
        Sarah BENNETT, 0 0 1 – 0 0 0 – 0 0 0 – 0 0 0

145

Henry BENNETT, 0 0 1 – 0 0 0 – 0 0 0 – 0 0 0
Catherine CUNNINGHAM, 0 1 0 – 0 0 0 – 0 0 0 – 0 0 0
    Sam, 38; Caesar, 43; John HILL, 35; Peg NICHOLSON, 56; Sukey, 31;
    Jane, 13; Joe, 8; Allan, 6; James, 4; Eve, 23; John, 8 months.

*Note: Did Sarah, the oldest child, make out the return because her mother was too ill to
do so? Her mother was interred on 19 November 1832.*

#300: John JACOB, 0 0 0 – 1 0 0 – 0 0 0 – 0 0 0

#301: Joe GOFF, 0 0 0 – 1 0 0 – 0 0 0 – 2 4 4:
      Celia GOFF, 0 0 0 – 0 1 0 – 0 0 0 – 0 0 0
          Eleanor GOFF, 30; Betsey, 19; William, 15; Cuffee, 34; Jonah, 5; Sarah, 4;
          Simon, 2.
          Runaways: Polly, 37; Behavior, 35; Ben, 10.

#302: David JOHNSON, 1 0 0 – 0 0 0 – 0 0 0 – 0 0 0
      Mary Ann JOHNSON, 0 1 0 – 0 0 0 – 0 0 0 – 0 0 0

#303: Mary C. THOMPSON, 0 0 0 – 0 1 0 – 0 0 0 – 0 0 0

p. 90:
#304: Margaret JONES, 0 0 0 – 0 1 0 – 0 0 0 – 2 1 2:
      Mary Ann EVE, 0 0 0 – 0 1 0 – 0 0 0 – 0 0 0
      Jane VALPY, 0 0 0 – 0 0 1 – 0 0 0 – 0 0 0
      James VALPY, 0 0 0 – 0 0 1 – 0 0 0 – 0 0 0
      Richard VALPY, 0 0 0 – 0 0 1 – 0 0 0 – 0 0 0
      Penelope JONES, 0 0 0 – 0 0 0 – 0 1 0 – 0 0 0
          Romeo; Harry. *(Ages not given.)*
      Property of M. A. EVE:
          Charlotte; Hannah; an Infant. *(Ages not given.)*

#305: John SLUSHER, 0 0 0 – 1 0 0 – 0 0 0 – 0 0 0
      Nancy LOWRIE, 0 0 0 – 0 0 0 – 0 1 0 – 0 0 0
      Fanny LOWRIE, 0 0 0 – 0 0 0 – 0 1 0 – 0 0 0
      Lucy PARKS, 0 0 0 – 0 1 0 – 0 0 0 – 0 0 0
      Thomas PARKS, 0 0 0 – 0 0 1 – 0 0 0 – 0 0 0
      Peter PARKS, 0 0 0 – 0 0 1 – 0 0 0 – 0 0 0
      William PARKS, 0 0 0 – 0 0 1 – 0 0 0 – 0 0 0
      Elizabeth GRANT, 0 0 0 – 0 1 0 – 0 0 0 – 0 0 0
      Infant, 0 0 0 – 0 0 1 – 0 0 0 – 0 0 0

#306: Juan SALVADOR, 0 0 0 – 0 0 0 – 1 0 0 – 0 0 0
      Paula JOSEFE, 0 0 0 – 0 0 0 – 0 1 0 – 0 0 0
      Jose SALVADOR, 0 0 0 – 0 0 0 – 1 0 0 – 0 0 0
      Chica F. SALVADOR, 0 0 0 – 0 0 0 – 0 1 0 – 0 0 0

Maria SALVADOR, 0 0 0 – 0 0 0 – 0 1 0 – 0 0 0
Luciana SALVADOR, 0 0 0 – 0 0 0 – 0 1 0 – 0 0 0

#307:   James HOARE, 0 0 0 – 0 0 0 – 0 0 0 – 1 0 0

p. 91:
#308:   Simon T. ANDERSON, 1 0 0 – 0 0 0 – 0 0 0 – 0 1 0:
        Malea L. CALDERONA, 0 0 0 – 0 1 0 – 0 0 0 – 0 0 0
        Antonia RAMONA, 0 0 0 – 0 0 1 – 0 0 0 – 0 0 0
        Lorenzo JACOBO, 0 0 0 – 0 0 0 – 0 0 1 – 0 0 0
            Charlotte, 25.

#309:   Elizabeth SEDDONS, 0 0 0 – 0 1 0 – 0 0 0 – 4 2 2:
            William, 42; Toby SEDDONS, 38; Old March, 38; Mary, 41; Maria, 32;
            Richard, 4; Isabella, 2.
            Runaway: Boatswain, 56.

#310:   Phoebe JONES, 0 0 0 – C 0 0 – 0 1 0 – 0 0 0
        Mary JONES, 0 0 0 – 0 0 0 – 0 1 0 – 0 0 0
        Jessy JONES, 0 0 0 – 0 0 0 – 0 1 0 – 0 0 0
        Sarah LONGSWORTH, 0 0 0 – 0 1 0 – 0 0 0 – 0 0 0
        Maria LONGSWORTH, 0 0 0 – 0 1 0 – 0 0 0 – 0 0 0
        Catherine LONGSWORTH, 0 0 0 – 0 0 1 – 0 0 0 – 0 0 0
        Betsey CATO, 0 0 0 – 0 0 1 – 0 0 0 – 0 0 0
        Charles COOKE, 0 0 0 – 0 0 1 – 0 0 0 – 0 0 0
        Mary Ann GRIFFITH, 0 C 0 – 0 0 1 – 0 0 0 – 0 0 0

Note: Cecilia CHINCILLA descends from Mary Ann JONES GRIFFITH and William
PAGE MORGAN, who married on the island of Roatan in 1862. The marriage cert.
names Mary Ann's father as John GRIFFITH of Belize.

#311:   Daniel McAULAY, 0 0 0 – 0 0 0 – 1 0 0 – 0 0 0
        Nancy McAULAY, 0 0 0 – 0 0 0 – 0 1 0 – 0 0 0
        Joseph GOODLAND, 0 0 0 – 0 0 0 – 1 0 0 – 0 0 0

p. 92:
#312:   Catherine WHITE, 0 0 0 – 0 1 0 – 0 0 0 – 10 3 5:
            Cuffy, 80; George, 45; John, 45; Willy, 46; Billy, 40; Scotland, 42; Adam,
            41; Simon, 25; Flora, 50; Phoebe, 40; Mary, 22; Henry, 19; Anthony, 18;
            Phyllis, 14; Emily, 10; Sophia, 7; Edmond, 5; Silvia, 2.

#313:   Robert F. ALEXANDER, 0 0 0 – 1 0 0 – 0 0 0 – 0 0 0
        Lydia S. ALEXANDER, 0 C 0 – 0 0 1 – 0 0 0 – 0 0 0
        Elizabeth E. ALEXANDER, 0 0 0 – 0 0 1 – 0 0 0 – 0 0 0
        Helen ALEXANDER, 0 0 0 – 0 0 1 – 0 0 0 – 0 0 0
        Marcia ALEXANDER, 0 0 C – 0 0 1 – 0 0 0 – 0 0 0

147

Amy FULLER, 0 0 0 – 0 0 0 – 0 1 0 – 0 0 0
Infant (not named,) 0 0 0 – 0 0 1 – 0 0 0 – 0 0 0

#314: Juan BATISTE, 0 0 0 – 1 0 0 – 0 0 0 – 0 0 0
Maria ALEXANDRE [*sic*], 0 0 0 – 0 1 0 – 0 0 0 – 0 0 0

p. 93:
#315: John HOARE, 0 0 0 – 0 0 0 – 1 0 0 – 0 0 0
Juana HOARE, 0 0 0 – 0 0 0 – 0 1 0 – 0 0 0
Manuel RUBIO, 0 0 0 – 0 0 0 – 1 0 0 – 0 0 0
Maria LAVATER, 0 0 0 – 0 1 0 – 0 0 0 – 0 0 0
Regala PATRONA, 0 0 0 – 0 0 0 – 0 1 0 – 0 0 0
Gregorio, 0 0 0 – 0 0 0 – 1 0 0 – 0 0 0   *(Surname not given.)*
Samuel LUKEFAST, 0 0 0 – 0 0 0 – 1 0 0 – 0 0 0
John HOARE, 0 0 0 – 0 0 1 – 0 0 0 – 0 0 0

#316: Thomas MILES, 0 0 0 – 0 0 0 – 1 0 0 – 0 0 0

#317: William TUXEY, 0 0 0 – 1 0 0 – 0 0 0 – 0 0 0
William TUXEY Jr., 0 0 0 – 0 0 1 – 0 0 0 – 0 0 0
Maria WILLIAMS, 0 0 0 – 0 1 0 – 0 0 0 – 0 0 0
Eve TUXEY, 0 0 0 – 0 0 1 – 0 0 0 – 0 0 0
Eve WILLIAMS, 0 0 0 – 0 1 0 – 0 0 0 – 0 0 0

#318: Jose M. AROYIO, 0 0 0 – 0 0 0 – 1 0 0 – 0 0 0
Maria M. BELA, 0 0 0 – 0 0 0 – 0 1 0 – 0 0 0
Juana FACUNDA, 0 0 0 – 0 0 0 – 0 1 0 – 0 0 0
Juan F. MOLINA, 0 0 0 – 0 0 0 – 1 0 0 – 0 0 0
Juan AROYIO, 0 0 0 – 0 0 0 – 1 0 0 – 0 0 0

#319: William CHARTER, 0 0 0 – 0 0 0 – 1 0 0 – 0 0 0
Joseph DRAKESIN, 0 0 0 – 0 0 0 – 1 0 0 – 0 0 0
James DEMSHAW, 0 0 0 – 0 0 0 – 1 0 0 – 0 0 0
Nancy FLOWERS, 0 0 0 – 0 0 0 – 0 1 0 – 0 0 0

p. 94:
#320: Stephen PANTING, 0 0 0 – 1 0 0 – 0 0 0 – 0 0 1:
George Wm PANTING, 0 0 0 – 0 0 1 – 0 0 0 – 0 0 0
Caroline PANTING, 0 0 0 – 0 0 1 – 0 0 0 – 0 0 0
Elizabeth PANTING, 0 0 0 – 0 0 1 – 0 0 0 – 0 0 0
John PANTING, 0 0 0 – 0 0 1 – 0 0 0 – 0 0 0
Margaret PANTING, 0 0 0 – 0 0 1 – 0 0 0 – 0 0 0
James, 12.

#321: James FREEMAN, 0 0 0 – 0 0 0 – 1 0 0 – 0 0 0
Maria Ann JAMES, 0 0 0 – 0 0 0 – 0 1 0 – 0 0 0

Harriet JAMES, 0 0 0 – 0 0 0 – 0 1 0 – 0 0 0
Rose JAMES, 0 0 0 – 0 0 0 – 0 1 0 – 0 0 0
Jimboe JAMES, 0 0 0 – 0 0 0 – 0 0 1 – 0 0 0
Elizabeth JAMES, 0 0 0 – 0 0 0 – 0 0 1 – 0 0 0
Catherine JAMES, 0 0 0 – 0 0 0 – 0 0 1 – 0 0 0

#322: Isadore DUMAS, 0 0 0 – 0 0 0 – 1 0 0 – 0 0 0
Maria DUMAS, 0 0 0 – 0 1 0 – 0 0 0 – 0 0 0
John LEMOINE, 0 0 0 – 1 0 0 – 0 0 0 – 0 0 0
Amelia LEMOINE, 0 0 0 – 0 1 0 – 0 0 0 – 0 0 0
Pierre LEMOINE, 0 0 0 – 0 0 1 – 0 0 0 – 0 0 0
S. BELISLE, 0 0 0 – 0 0 0 – 0 0 1 – 0 0 0 *(Male.)*
George BELISLE, 0 0 0 – 0 0 0 – 0 0 1 – 0 0 0
Sarah BELISLE, 0 0 0 – 0 0 0 – 0 0 1 – 0 0 0
Margaret ISIDORE, 0 0 0 – 0 0 0 – 0 0 1 – 0 0 0

#323: William COKER, 1 0 0 – 0 0 0 – 0 0 0 – 0 0 0
Mary COKER, 0 0 0 – 0 1 0 – 0 0 0 – 0 0 0
Susan COKER, 0 0 0 – 0 0 1 – 0 0 0 – 0 0 0

p. 95:
#324: Mary ROBINSON, 0 0 0 – 0 0 0 – 0 1 0 – 0 0 0
Isabella HEMSLEY, 0 0 0 – 0 0 0 – 0 0 1 – 0 0 0
John HEMSLEY, 0 0 0 – 0 0 0 – 0 0 1 – 0 0 0
Edward HEMSLEY, 0 0 0 – 0 0 0 – 0 0 1 – 0 0 0
George HEMSLEY, 0 0 0 – 0 0 0 – 0 0 1 – 0 0 0

#325: Cecilia ROBINSON, 0 0 0 – 0 0 0 – 0 1 0 – 0 0 0
Joseph BROASTER, 0 0 0 – 0 0 0 – 0 0 1 – 0 0 0
William BROASTER, 0 0 0 – 0 0 0 – 0 0 1 – 0 0 0
Francis ARTHUR, 0 0 0 – 0 0 0 – 0 0 1 – 0 0 0
Margaret ARTHUR, 0 0 0 – 0 0 0 – 0 0 1 – 0 0 0

#326: Nancy ROBINSON, 0 0 0 – 0 0 0 – 0 1 0 – 0 0 0
Charlotte ROBINSON, 0 0 0 – 0 0 0 – 0 0 1 – 0 0 0
Johnson ROBINSON, 0 0 0 – 0 0 0 – 0 0 1 – 0 0 0
Robert ROBINSON, 0 0 0 – 0 0 0 – 0 0 1 – 0 0 0
Ellen ROBINSON, 0 0 0 – 0 0 0 – 0 0 1 – 0 0 0
Charles ROBINSON, 0 0 0 – 0 0 0 – 0 0 1 – 0 0 0
Lizzy ROBINSON, 0 0 0 – 0 0 0 – 0 0 1 – 0 0 0

#327: John CELESTINE, 0 0 0 – 0 0 0 – 1 0 0 – 0 0 0
Mary LaROSE, 0 0 0 – 0 0 0 – 0 1 0 – 0 0 0
John CELESTINE, 0 0 0 – 0 0 0 – 0 0 1 – 0 0 0

149

#328: John KNOX, 0 0 0 – 0 0 0 – 1 0 0 – 0 0 0
       Elizabeth THOMPSON, 0 0 0 – 0 0 0 – 0 1 0 – 0 0 0

p. 96:
#329: Robert LOWRIE, 0 0 0 – 0 0 0 – 1 0 0 – 0 0 0
       Mary EMERY, 0 0 0 – 0 0 0 – 0 1 0 – 0 0 0
       James LOWRIE, 0 0 0 – 0 0 0 – 1 0 0 – 0 0 0
       William LOWRIE, 0 0 0 – 0 0 0 – 1 0 0 – 0 0 0
       V. LOWRIE, 0 0 0 – 0 0 0 – 0 1 0 – 0 0 0
       Benjamin LOWRIE, 0 0 0 – 0 0 0 – 1 0 0 – 0 0 0

#330: Family of MacDonald MACDONALD, 0 0 0 – 0 0 0 – 1 0 0 – 0 0 0
       Maria MACDONALD, 0 0 0 – 0 0 0 – 0 1 0 – 0 0 0
       Hannah MACDONALD, 0 0 0 – 0 0 0 – 0 0 1 – 0 0 0
       Janet MACDONALD, 0 0 0 – 0 0 0 – 0 0 1 – 0 0 0

#331: John AUGUSTINE, 0 0 0 – 0 0 0 – 1 0 0 – 0 0 0
       Mary Ann LAPOT, 0 0 0 – 0 0 0 – 0 1 0 – 0 0 0
       Alexander AUGUSTINE, 0 0 0 – 0 0 0 – 0 0 1 – 0 0 0
       Mary Ann S. DALA, 0 0 0 – 0 0 0 – 0 0 1 – 0 0 0
       Jane AUGUSTINE, 0 0 0 – 0 0 0 – 0 0 1 – 0 0 0
       John P. AUGUSTINE, 0 0 0 – 0 0 0 – 0 0 1 – 0 0 0

#332: Manuel PETER, 0 0 0 – 0 0 0 – 1 0 0 – 0 0 0
       Sarah LOWRY, 0 0 0 – 0 0 0 – 0 1 0 – 0 0 0
       Adam LOWRY, 0 0 0 – 0 0 0 – 0 0 1 – 0 0 0

#333: Francisco PABLO, 0 0 0 – 0 0 0 – 1 0 0 – 0 0 0
       Juana PACUALLA, 0 0 0 – 0 0 0 – 0 1 0 – 0 0 0
       Maria MANUEL, 0 0 0 – 0 0 0 – 0 1 0 – 0 0 0
       Jose NETARIO, 0 0 0 – 0 0 0 – 0 0 1 – 0 0 0

p. 97:
#334: John COLLINS, 1 0 0 – 0 0 0 – 0 0 0 – 3 1 0:
       Sarah COLLINS, 0 1 0 – 0 0 0 – 0 0 0 – 0 0 0
       Sarah A. COLLINS, 0 0 1 – 0 0 0 – 0 0 0 – 0 0 0
       John COLLINS, 0 0 1 – 0 0 0 – 0 0 0 – 0 0 0
       Henrietta COLLINS, 0 0 1 – 0 0 0 – 0 0 0 – 0 0 0
       Fanny COLLINS, 0 0 0 – 0 1 0 – 0 0 0 – 0 0 0
            William PITT, 41; Robert, 38; Harriet, 71.
            Runaway: Ben, 61.

#335: William GILL, 0 0 0 – 1 0 0 – 0 0 0 – 0 0 0
       Catherine GLADDEN, 0 0 0 – 0 1 0 – 0 0 0 – 0 0 0
       James GILL, 0 0 0 – 1 0 0 – 0 0 0 – 0 0 0
       Sarah Ann GILL, 0 0 0 – 0 1 0 – 0 0 0 – 0 0 0

Philip GILL, 0 0 0 – 1 C 0 – 0 0 0 – 0 0 0
Alexander GILL, 0 0 0 – 1 0 0 – 0 0 0 – 0 0 0

#336: Philip FALL, 1 0 0 – 0 C 0 – 0 0 0 – 0 0 0
Richard FALL, 0 0 0 – C 0 1 – 0 0 0 – 0 0 0
Margaret FALL, 0 0 0 – 0 0 1 – 0 0 0 – 0 0 0

#337: William CARD, 0 0 0 – 1 0 0 – 0 0 0 – 1 0 1:
Sarah McKENZIE, 0 0 0 – 0 1 0 – 0 0 0 – 0 0 0
Maria A. CARD, 0 0 0 – 0 0 1 – 0 0 0 – 0 0 0
John T. CARD, 0 0 0 – 0 0 1 – 0 0 0 – 0 0 0
Catherine CARD, 0 0 0 – 0 0 1 – 0 0 0 – 0 0 0
Susan CARD, 0 0 0 – 0 0 ⁚ – 0 0 0 – 0 0 0
Bristow, 39; Mary, ⁚2.

#338: John JOHNSTON, 1 0 0 – 0 0 0 – 0 0 0 – 0 0 0

p. 98:
#339: Joseph JONES, 0 0 0 – 1 0 0 – 0 0 0 – 0 0 0
Mary GILLETT, 0 0 0 – 0 1 0 – 0 0 0 – 0 0 0
Janet JONES, 0 0 0 – 0 0 1 – 0 0 0 – 0 0 0
Margaret JONES, 0 0 0 – C 0 1 – 0 0 0 – 0 0 0
Sarah JONES, 0 0 0 – 0 0 1 – 0 0 0 – 0 0 0
Ann JONES, 0 0 0 – 0 0 1 – 0 0 0 – 0 0 0

#340: John MEHAIR, 0 0 0 – 1 0 0 – 0 0 0 – 0 0 0
Sarah LEE, 0 0 0 – 0 1 0 – 0 0 0 – 0 0 0
Priscilla MEHAIR, 0 0 0 – 0 0 1 – 0 0 0 – 0 0 0
Joseph MEHAIR, 0 0 0 – 0 0 1 – 0 0 0 – 0 0 0
Benjamin MEHAIR, 0 0 0 – 0 0 1 – 0 0 0 – 0 0 0
Maria MEHAIR, 0 0 0 – 0 0 1 – 0 0 0 – 0 0 0

#341: Maria ANTONIO, 0 0 0 – 0 1 0 – 0 0 0 – 0 0 0

#342: Catherine JEFFRIES, 0 0 0 – 1 0 0 – 0 0 0 – 0 0 0 *(Enumerator's error: female.)*
Ann COLE, 0 0 0 – 0 1 0 – 0 0 0 – 0 0 0
David EVANS, 0 0 0 – 0 0 1 – 0 0 0 – 0 0 0
Mary H. EVANS, 0 0 0 – 0 0 1 – 0 0 0 – 0 0 0
Sarah G. EVANS, 0 0 0 – 0 0 1 – 0 0 0 – 0 0 0
Elizabeth C. EVANS, 0 0 0 – 0 0 1 – 0 0 0 – 0 0 0
John E. EVANS, 0 0 0 – 0 0 1 – 0 0 0 – 0 0 0
Charles J. EVANS, 0 0 0 – 0 0 1 – 0 0 0 – 0 0 0

#343: Margaret HARE, 0 0 0 – 0 1 0 – 0 0 0 – 0 0 0
Rosetta TIMMONS, 0 0 0 – 0 0 1 – 0 0 0 – 0 0 0

151

#344: Cato GRANT, 0 0 0 – 0 0 0 – 1 0 0 – 0 0 0
Acinta, 0 0 0 – 0 0 0 – 0 1 0 – 0 0 0 *(Surname not given.)*
Thomas GRANT, 0 0 0 – 0 0 0 – 0 0 1 – 0 0 0
James GRANT, 0 0 0 – 0 0 0 – 0 0 1 – 0 0 0
Charlotte GRANT, 0 0 0 – 0 0 0 – 0 1 0 – 0 0 0
Ellen GRANT, 0 0 0 – 0 0 0 – 0 1 0 – 0 0 0
Sarah GRANT, 0 0 0 – 0 0 0 – 0 0 1 – 0 0 0

#345: William WALSH, 1 0 0 – 0 0 0 – 0 0 0 – 7 5 4:
Mary J. WALSH, 0 1 0 – 0 0 0 – 0 0 0 – 0 0 0
Mary COLQUHOUN, 0 1 0 – 0 0 0 – 0 0 0 – 0 0 0 *(Archibald's widow.)*
R. W. CORVAN, 1 0 0 – 0 0 0 – 0 0 0 – 0 0 0
    Henry PASLOW, 37; John WALSH, 31; London, 47; Cuffee, 57;
    Thomas WALSH, 17; Daniel COLQUHOUN, 21; Pierce LAMB *(age not given;)* Nancy, 22; Fanny, 14; Kate, 27; Tinah, 44; Mary DIXON, 25.
Property of M. J. WALSH:
    Edmond, 5; Peter, 5½; Judith, 10; Emma, 7½.

#346: Thomas R. ARIS, 1 0 0 – 0 0 0 – 0 0 0 – 0 2 0:
Margaret ARIS, 0 1 0 – 0 0 0 – 0 0 0 – 0 0 0
Thomas HICKEY, 0 0 0 – 0 0 0 – 1 0 0 – 0 0 0
    Nelly YOUNG, 35; Fanny, 35.

#347: John GLOUD, 0 0 0 – 1 0 0 – 0 0 0 – 0 0 0
Margaret TUN, 0 0 0 – 0 1 0 – 0 0 0 – 0 0 0
Rose GLOUD, 0 0 0 – 0 0 1 – 0 0 0 – 0 0 0

#348: Susannah BURKE, 0 0 0 – 0 1 0 – 0 0 0 – 0 0 0
Sabina BURKE, 0 0 0 – 0 1 0 – 0 0 0 – 0 0 0
Elizabeth BURKE, 0 0 0 – 0 1 0 – 0 0 0 – 0 0 0
Emma BURKE, 0 0 0 – 0 1 0 – 0 0 0 – 0 0 0
Louisa HUNT, 0 0 0 – 0 1 0 – 0 0 0 – 0 0 0
James HENRY, 0 0 0 – 1 0 0 – 0 0 0 – 0 0 0
Mary A. MUCKLEHANY, 0 0 0 – 0 0 1 – 0 0 0 – 0 0 0
Elizabeth MUCKLEHANY, 0 0 0 – 0 0 1 – 0 0 0 – 0 0 0

#349: Robert WAGNER, 0 0 0 – 1 0 0 – 0 0 0 – 4 0 0:
    Friday, 43; Hazard, 45; Robert, 41; Peter, 46.

#350: Frederick COFFIN, 1 0 0 – 0 0 0 – 0 0 0 – 0 0 0
Phoebe TUCKER, 0 0 0 – 0 1 0 – 0 0 0 – 0 0 0
William C. COFFIN, 0 0 0 – 0 0 1 – 0 0 0 – 0 0 0
Eliza Ann COFFIN, 0 0 0 – 0 0 1 – 0 0 0 – 0 0 0

Susan COFFIN, 0 0 0 – 0 0 1 – 0 0 0 – 0 0 0
blank   0 0 0 – 0 0 1 – 0 0 0 – 0 0 0 *(Female. An infant not yet named?)*

#351: William RATHOMAN, 0 0 0 – 1 0 0 – 0 0 0 – 0 0 0
Amy SMITH, 0 0 0 – 0 1 0 – 0 0 0 – 0 0 0
William RATHOMAN Jr., 0 0 0 – 0 0 1 – 0 0 0 – 0 0 0

p. 101:
#352: Jane HUME, 0 0 0 – 0 1 0 – 0 0 0 – 20 7 9:
James HUME BLAKE, 0 0 0 – 1 0 0 – 0 0 0 – 0 0 0
Jane MEIGHAN, 0 0 0 – 0 0 1 – 0 0 0 – 0 0 0
Richard HUME, 0 0 0 – 0 0 1 – 0 0 0 – 0 0 0
Henry; Peter; Samson; Chance; Anthony; Thomas; William; Younghal;
Jas. FREDERICK. Benjamin; Collins; Peter WILSON; John; Frank;
Chance; George; James; England; Will; James; Francis; Joseph; Charles;
Britain; Amelia; Agnes; Statira; Sophia; Sarah; Kate; Mary; Elizabeth;
Betsy;

p. 102:   Kate; Elizabeth; Henrietta. *(Ages not given.)*

#353: Isaiah SIMMONS, 0 0 0 – 0 0 0 – 1 0 0 – 0 0 0
Eve SIMMONS, 0 0 0 – 0 0 0 – 0 1 0 – 0 0 0
Mary Ann SIMMONS, 0 0 0 – 0 0 0 – 0 1 0 – 0 0 0
Phoebe SIMMONS, 0 0 0 – 0 0 0 – 0 1 0 – 0 0 0
Daniel SIMMONS, 0 0 0 – 0 0 0 – 1 0 0 – 0 0 0
Adam SIMMONS, 0 0 0 – 0 0 0 – 1 0 0 – 0 0 0
Primus SIMMONS, 0 0 0 – 0 0 0 – 0 0 1 – 0 0 0
Eve SIMMONS, 0 0 0 – 0 0 0 – 0 0 1 – 0 0 0
Thomas SIMMONS, 0 0 0 – 0 0 0 – 0 0 1 – 0 0 0
Elizabeth SIMMONS, 0 0 0 – 0 0 0 – 0 0 1 – 0 0 0
Benjamin SIMMONS, 0 0 0 – 0 0 0 – 0 0 1 – 0 0 0
Maria SIMMONS, 0 0 0 – 0 1 0 – 0 0 0 – 0 0 0
William CLARKE, 0 0 0 – 0 0 0 – 0 0 1 – 0 0 0
Rebecca BURNS, 0 0 0 – 0 1 0 – 0 0 0 – 0 0 0

#354: James GUNN, 1 0 0 – 0 0 0 – 0 0 0 – 0 0 0
Mary GLADDEN, 0 0 0 – 0 1 0 – 0 0 0 – 0 0 0
James CARTY, 0 0 0 – 0 0 1 – 0 0 0 – 0 0 0

#355: Samuel HOWARD, 1 0 0 – 0 0 0 – 0 0 0 – 1 0 0:
Mary HOWARD, 0 1 0 – 0 0 0 – 0 0 0 – 0 0 0
Eliza HOWARD, 0 1 0 – 0 0 0 – 0 0 0 – 0 0 0
Margaret HOWARD, 0 1 0 – 0 0 0 – 0 0 0 – 0 0 0
George MENZIES, 1 0 0 – 0 0 0 – 0 0 0 – 0 0 0
Samuel COOPER, 0 0 1 – 0 0 0 – 0 0 0 – 0 0 0
Thomas, 50.

153

p. 103:

#356: Sarah BURGESS, 0 0 0 – 0 0 0 – 0 1 0 – 0 0 0
Abba BURGESS, 0 0 0 – 0 0 0 – 0 1 0 – 0 0 0
Hannah BURGESS, 0 0 0 – 0 0 0 – 0 1 0 – 0 0 0
Jane BURGESS, 0 0 0 – 0 0 0 – 0 1 0 – 0 0 0
John BURGESS, 0 0 0 – 0 0 0 – 0 0 1 – 0 0 0
Phyllis BURGESS, 0 0 0 – 0 0 0 – 0 0 1 – 0 0 0
James BURGESS, 0 0 0 – 0 0 0 – 0 0 1 – 0 0 0
Joseph BURGESS, 0 0 0 – 0 0 0 – 0 0 1 – 0 0 0
James YOUNG, 0 0 0 – 0 0 1 – 0 0 0 – 0 0 0

#357: William SMITH, 0 0 0 – 1 0 0 – 0 0 0 – 0 0 0
Levi SMITH, 0 0 0 – 1 0 0 – 0 0 0 – 0 0 0
Nancy ROBINSON, 0 0 0 – 0 0 0 – 0 1 0 – 0 0 0
Robert SMITH, 0 0 0 – 0 0 1 – 0 0 0 – 0 0 0
Elizabeth SMITH, 0 0 0 – 0 0 1 – 0 0 0 – 0 0 0
David SMITH, 0 0 0 – 0 0 1 – 0 0 0 – 0 0 0
James SMITH, 0 0 0 – 0 0 1 – 0 0 0 – 0 0 0
Patty SMITH, 0 0 0 – 0 0 1 – 0 0 0 – 0 0 0
Drury SMITH, 0 0 0 – 0 0 1 – 0 0 0 – 0 0 0
Elizabeth MEIGHAN, 0 0 0 – 0 0 0 – 0 1 0 – 0 0 0
Edward DAVIS, 0 0 0 – 0 0 0 – 0 0 1 – 0 0 0

#358: Simon SLUSHER, 0 0 0 – 0 0 0 – 1 0 0 – 0 0 0
Robert SLUSHER, 0 0 0 – 0 0 0 – 0 0 1 – 0 0 0
George SLUSHER, 0 0 0 – 0 0 0 – 0 0 1 – 0 0 0
Louisa SLUSHER, 0 0 0 – 0 0 0 – 0 0 1 – 0 0 0
Thomas SLUSHER, 0 0 0 – 0 0 0 – 0 0 1 – 0 0 0
James SLUSHER, 0 0 0 – 0 0 0 – 0 0 1 – 0 0 0
Eleanor SLUSHER, 0 0 0 – 0 0 0 – 0 0 1 – 0 0 0

p. 104:

#359: Joseph BURNEAU, 0 0 0 – 1 0 0 – 0 0 0 – 0 0 0
Margaret BURNEAU, 0 0 0 – 0 0 0 – 0 1 0 – 0 0 0
Mary Ann BURNEAU, 0 0 0 – 0 0 1 – 0 0 0 – 0 0 0
Henry BURNEAU, 0 0 0 – 0 0 1 – 0 0 0 – 0 0 0
William FERRELL, 0 0 0 – 0 0 1 – 0 0 0 – 0 0 0
Mary GINIS? 0 0 0 – 0 0 0 – 0 1 0 – 0 0 0   *(Note: G is uncertain.)*
John SIMMONS, 0 0 0 – 0 0 0 – 1 0 0 – 0 0 0

#360: Maria FRANCISCA, 0 0 0 – 0 0 0 – 0 1 0 – 0 0 0
Louis GABRIEL, 0 0 0 – 0 0 0 – 0 0 1 – 0 0 0
Juana MARIA, 0 0 0 – 0 0 0 – 0 1 0 – 0 0 0
Maria MERCEDES, 0 0 0 – 0 0 0 – 0 1 0 – 0 0 0
Catherine TAYLOR, 0 0 0 – 0 0 0 – 0 0 1 – 0 0 0
Henry THOMAS, 0 0 0 – 0 0 0 – 0 0 1 – 0 0 0

154

Pedro CANDARA, 0 0 0 – 0 0 0 – 1 0 0 – 0 0 0
Sarah CADLE, 0 0 0 – 0 0 0 – 0 0 1 – 0 0 0

#361: Robert WAGNER, 0 0 0 – 1 0 0 – 0 0 0 – 0 0 0
Ann HEMMON, 0 0 0 – 0 1 0 – 0 0 0 – 0 0 0
John WAGNER, 0 0 0 – 0 0 1 – 0 0 0 – 0 0 0
Peggy CARD, 0 0 0 – 0 1 0 – 0 0 0 – 0 0 0
Phyllis, 0 0 0 – 0 0 1 – 0 0 0 – 0 0 0
James, 0 0 0 – 0 0 1 – 0 0 0 – 0 0 0 *(Surnames not given.)*

#362: John BREWYER, 0 0 0 – 0 0 0 – 1 0 0 – 0 0 0
Mary BREWYER, 0 0 0 – 0 0 0 – 0 1 0 – 0 0 0

p. 105:
#363: Louis AUDINETT, 0 0 0 – 0 0 0 – 1 0 0 – 0 0 0
Maria AUDINETT, 0 0 0 – 0 0 0 – 0 1 0 – 0 0 0
Peter L. AUDINETT, 0 0 0 – 0 0 0 – 1 0 0 – 0 0 0
Catherine LOUIS, 0 0 0 – 0 0 0 – 0 0 1 – 0 0 0
Anthony LOUIS, 0 0 0 – 0 0 0 – 0 0 1 – 0 0 0
Victoria LOUIS, 0 0 0 – 0 0 0 – 0 0 1 – 0 0 0
Maria LOUIS, 0 0 0 – 0 0 0 – 0 0 1 – 0 0 0
Timothy LOUIS, 0 0 0 – 0 0 0 – 0 0 1 – 0 0 0

#364: Maria TAYLOR, 0 0 0 – 0 1 0 – 0 0 0 – 0 0 0
Catherine TAYLOR, 0 0 0 – 0 0 1 – 0 0 0 – 0 0 0
Anna MARIA, 0 0 0 – 0 0 1 – 0 0 0 – 0 0 0
Pedro, 0 0 0 – 1 0 0 – 0 0 0 – 0 0 0
Juanita, 0 0 0 – 0 1 0 – 0 0 0 – 0 0 0 *(Surnames not given.)*
Maria FRANCESCA, 0 0 0 – 0 1 0 – 0 0 0 – 0 0 0
Mary CADDLE, 0 0 0 – 0 0 1 – 0 0 0 – 0 0 0
Louis GEORGE, 0 0 0 – 0 0 1 – 0 0 0 – 0 0 0
Maria, 0 0 0 – 0 0 0 – 0 1 0 – 0 0 0 *(Surname not given.)*

#365: John ANTOINE, 0 0 0 – 0 0 0 – 1 0 0 – 0 0 0
Nancy WILSON, 0 0 0 – 0 0 0 – 0 1 0 – 0 0 0

#366: Charles ARMSTRONG, 0 0 0 – 0 0 0 – 1 0 0 – 0 0 0
Margaret ARMSTRONG, 0 0 0 – 0 0 0 – 0 1 0 – 0 0 0

#367: William GORDON, 0 0 0 – 0 0 0 – 1 0 0 – 0 0 0
Monday GORDON, 0 0 0 – 0 0 0 – 1 0 0 – 0 0 0

p. 106:
#368: Charles ANDREWS, 0 0 0 – 1 0 0 – 0 0 0 – 0 0 0
Elizabeth HUGHES, 0 0 0 – 0 1 0 – 0 0 0 – 0 0 0
Grace STEWART, 0 0 0 – 0 0 0 – 0 1 0 – 0 0 0

155

John STEWART, 0 0 0 – 0 0 0 – 0 0 1 – 0 0 0
Rose, 0 0 0 – 0 0 0 – 0 0 1 – 0 0 0
Jane, 0 0 0 – 0 0 0 – 0 0 1 – 0 0 0 *(Surnames not given.)*

#369: Joseph KEENE, 0 0 0 – 0 0 0 – 1 0 0 – 0 0 0
Janet KEENE, 0 0 0 – 0 0 0 – 0 1 0 – 0 0 0
Joseph KEENE, Jr., 0 0 0 – 0 0 0 – 0 0 1 – 0 0 0
Louisa KEENE, 0 0 0 – 0 0 0 – 0 0 1 – 0 0 0
Janet KEENE, 0 0 0 – 0 0 0 – 0 0 1 – 0 0 0
Samuel KEENE, 0 0 0 – 0 0 0 – 0 0 1 – 0 0 0
Andrew KEENE, 0 0 0 – 0 0 0 – 0 0 1 – 0 0 0
Priscilla KEENE, 0 0 0 – 0 0 0 – 0 0 1 – 0 0 0
Cyrus KEENE, 0 0 0 – 0 0 0 – 0 0 1 – 0 0 0
Perrine KEENE, 0 0 0 – 0 0 0 – 0 1 0 – 0 0 0
Mary KEENE, 0 0 0 – 0 0 0 – 0 0 1 – 0 0 0

#370: Joseph BENNETT, 0 0 0 – 0 0 0 – 1 0 0 – 0 0 0
Petrona GAMBOA, 0 0 0 – 0 0 0 – 0 1 0 – 0 0 0
Maria CREMENCIA, 0 0 0 – 0 0 0 – 0 0 1 – 0 0 0

#371: Emily BELISLE, 0 0 0 – 0 0 0 – 0 1 0 – 0 0 0
Mary BELISLE, 0 0 0 – 0 0 0 – 0 0 1 – 0 0 0
Joseph BELISLE, 0 0 0 – 0 0 0 – 0 0 1 – 0 0 0

p. 107:
#372: Francisco BULL, 0 0 0 – 0 0 0 – 1 0 0 – 0 0 0
Charles BULL, 0 0 0 – 0 0 0 – 1 0 0 – 0 0 0
Philip BULL, 0 0 0 – 0 0 0 – 0 0 1 – 0 0 0

#373: Charles BLADON, 1 0 0 – 0 0 0 – 0 0 0 – 1 0 0:
Sarah YOUNG, 0 0 0 – 0 1 0 – 0 0 0 – 0 0 0
Nancy YOUNG, 0 0 0 – 0 0 1 – 0 0 0 – 0 0 0
Robert YOUNG, 0 0 0 – 0 0 1 – 0 0 0 – 0 0 0
Agnes YOUNG, 0 0 0 – 0 0 1 – 0 0 0 – 0 0 0
James YOUNG. *(Age not given.)*

#374: William BURN, 1 0 0 – 0 0 0 – 0 0 0 – 5 3 6:
Lydia CADLE, 0 0 0 – 0 1 0 – 0 0 0 – 0 0 0
Margaret BURN, 0 0 0 – 0 0 1 – 0 0 0 – 0 0 0
George BURN, 0 0 0 – 0 0 1 – 0 0 0 – 0 0 0
James BURN, 0 0 0 – 0 0 1 – 0 0 0 – 0 0 0
Samuel BURN, 43; Charley, 29; Wm BURN, 23; John BURN, 21;
Joseph LAMB, 28; Wm BURN, 4; James BURN, 3;
Property of Wm BURN:
Jane BURN, 48; Betsy BURN, 26; Anney, 19; Rachael, 9; Sarah, 5;
Rabian, 21; Clemeni, 20.

156

#375: Family of Geo. CARD omitted in his return (#114:) *Margin note:* Error,
William BERNARD, 0 0 0 – 0 0 0 – 0 0 0 – 0 0 0 returned by Wm Bernard,
John BERNARD, 0 0 0 – 0 0 0 – 0 0 0 – 0 0 0 Fo. 35 #280. *(= folio, page.)*
Daniel BERNARD, 0 0 0 – 0 0 0 – 0 0 0 – 0 0 0
Mary Ann BERNARD, 0 0 0 – 0 0 0 – 0 0 0 – 0 0 0

#376: Robert BURKITT, 1 0 0 – 0 0 0 – 0 0 0 – 0 0 0

#377: Richard CADLE, 0 0 0 – 0 0 0 – 1 0 0 – 0 0 0

p. 108:
#378: Lewis BERNARD, 0 0 0 – 1 0 0 – 0 0 0 – 0 0 0
Mary La CASE, 0 0 0 – 0 1 0 – 0 0 0 – 0 0 0
John J. La CASE, 0 0 0 – 1 0 0 – 0 0 0 – 0 0 0
John L. La CASE, 0 0 0 – 1 0 0 – 0 0 0 – 0 0 0
Susan La CASE, 0 0 0 – 0 1 0 – 0 0 0 – 0 0 0
Janet La CASE, 0 0 0 – 0 1 0 – 0 0 0 – 0 0 0
Mary BENTON, 0 0 0 – 0 1 0 – 0 0 0 – 0 0 0
Rose BERNARD, 0 0 0 – 0 0 1 – 0 0 0 – 0 0 0
Renard NEALY, 0 0 0 – 0 0 1 – 0 0 0 – 0 0 0
William COPLEY, 0 0 0 – 0 0 1 – 0 0 0 – 0 0 0
Maria, 0 0 0 – 0 0 1 – 0 0 0 – 0 0 0 *(Surname not given.)*

#379: George BURN, 1 0 0 – 0 0 0 – 0 0 0 – 3 2 2:
George BURN, 41; Coffee BURN, 16; Thomas BURN, 16; Joseph BURN, 6; Richard BURN, 3; Sylvia BURN, 18; Fanny BURN, 17.

#380: Fame BELISLE, 0 0 0 – 0 0 0 – 1 0 0 – 0 0 0
Anne PREO, 0 0 0 – 0 0 0 – 0 1 0 – 0 0 0 *(Bapt. #120 spells the name PRIO.)*
Richard PREO, 0 0 0 – 0 0 0 – 0 0 1 – 0 0 0
Eve BELISLE, 0 0 0 – 0 0 0 – 0 0 1 – 0 0 0
Thomas BELISLE, 0 0 0 – 0 0 0 – 0 0 1 – 0 0 0
Benjamin BELISLE, 0 0 0 – 0 0 0 – 0 0 1 – 0 0 0

#381: Charles CRUTCHLEY, 0 0 0 – 0 0 0 – 1 0 0 – 0 0 0
Francis GADDIS, 0 0 0 – 0 0 0 – 1 0 0 – 0 0 0

p. 109:
#382: Joseph BEVINS, 0 0 0 – 1 0 0 – 0 0 0 – 0 0 0
William BEVINS, 0 0 0 – 1 0 0 – 0 0 0 – 0 0 0
Mary BEVINS, 0 0 0 – 0 1 0 – 0 0 0 – 0 0 0
Joseph BEVINS, 0 0 0 – 0 0 1 – 0 0 0 – 0 0 0
Margaret CLEMENT, 0 0 0 – 0 0 1 – 0 0 0 – 0 0 0

#383: Frances BARR, 0 0 0 – 0 0 0 – 0 1 0 – 0 0 0
John OSMAN, 1 0 0 – 0 0 0 – 0 0 0 – 0 0 0

157

Mary Ann OSMAN, 0 0 0 – 0 0 1 – 0 0 0 – 0 0 0
Elizabeth OSMAN, 0 0 0 – 0 0 1 – 0 0 0 – 0 0 0
John OSMAN, 0 0 0 – 0 0 1 – 0 0 0 – 0 0 0

#384: James A. CARMICHAEL, 1 0 0 – 0 0 0 – 0 0 0 – 0 0 0
Mary NEAL, 0 0 0 – 0 1 0 – 0 0 0 – 0 0 0
Francoise GORDON, 0 0 0 – 0 0 0 – 0 0 1 – 0 0 0

#385: Ann CRAPPER, 0 0 0 – 0 1 0 – 0 0 0 – 1 0 0:
Catherine ASKEW, 0 0 0 – 0 1 0 – 0 0 0 – 0 0 0
Fanny BETSON, 0 0 0 – 0 0 1 – 0 0 0 – 0 0 0
John A. CROFT, 0 0 0 – 0 0 1 – 0 0 0 – 0 0 0
James CROFT, 0 0 0 – 0 0 1 – 0 0 0 – 0 0 0
Betsey CROFT, 0 0 0 – 0 0 1 – 0 0 0 – 0 0 0
Eleanor CROFT, 0 0 0 – 0 0 1 – 0 0 0 – 0 0 0
George CAMPBELL, 40.

#386: Lewis CAIN, 0 0 0 – 0 0 0 – 1 0 0 – 0 0 0
Joseph NOWELL, 0 0 0 – 0 0 0 – 0 0 1 – 0 0 0
Elizabeth CAIN, 0 0 0 – 0 0 0 – 0 0 1 – 0 0 0

p. 110:
#387: Maria CHARLES, 0 0 0 – 0 0 0 – 0 1 0 – 0 0 0
Maria BAPTISTE, 0 0 0 – 0 0 1 – 0 0 0 – 0 0 0
Mary Ann THOMPSON, 0 0 0 – 0 0 0 – 0 0 1 – 0 0 0
John THOMPSON, 0 0 0 – 0 0 0 – 0 0 1 – 0 0 0
James THOMPSON, 0 0 0 – 0 0 0 – 0 0 1 – 0 0 0
Strephon THOMPSON, 0 0 0 – 0 0 0 – 0 0 1 – 0 0 0
Peter THOMPSON, 0 0 0 – 0 0 0 – 0 0 1 – 0 0 0
Louis THOMPSON, 0 0 0 – 0 0 0 – 0 0 1 – 0 0 0
Catherine THOMPSON, 0 0 0 – 0 0 0 – 0 0 1 – 0 0 0
Maria FELICIA, 0 0 0 – 0 0 0 – 0 1 0 – 0 0 0

#388: Manuel de Jesus CAFÉ, 0 0 0 – 0 0 0 – 1 0 0 – 0 0 0
Maria OFION, 0 0 0 – 0 0 0 – 0 1 0 – 0 0 0
Maria OFION Jr., 0 0 0 – 0 0 0 – 0 1 0 – 0 0 0

#389: Jose Maria CHAPARRO, 0 0 0 – 0 0 0 – 1 0 0 – 0 0 0
Rosa Maria MONTE, 0 0 0 – 0 0 0 – 0 1 0 – 0 0 0
Maria Josefa CHAPARRO, 0 0 0 – 0 0 0 – 0 1 0 – 0 0 0
Maria Tomase CHAPARRO, 0 0 0 – 0 0 0 – 0 1 0 – 0 0 0
Pablo Jose CHAPARRO, 0 0 0 – 0 0 0 – 0 0 1 – 0 0 0
Jose Cesario CHAPARRO, 0 0 0 – 0 0 0 – 0 0 1 – 0 0 0

#390: Benjamin CROFT, 0 0 0 – 1 0 0 – 0 0 0 – 0 0 1:
Fanny WALL, 0 0 0 – 0 1 0 – 0 0 0 – 0 0 0

158

Sarah J. CROFT, 0 0 0 – 0 0 1 – 0 0 0 – 0 0 0
Peter CROFT, 0 0 0 – 0 0 1 – 0 0 0 – 0 0 0
Louisa CROFT, 0 0 0 – 0 0 1 – 0 0 0 – 0 0 0
William CROFT, 0 0 0 – 0 0 1 – 0 0 0 – 0 0 0
Rose, 12.

p. 111:
#391: William COURTNEY, 0 0 0 – 1 0 0 – 0 0 0 – 0 1 4:
Eve COURTNEY, 0 0 0 – 0 1 0 – 0 0 0 – 0 0 0
Edward COURTNEY, 0 0 0 – 0 0 1 – 0 0 0 – 0 0 0
Elizabeth COURTNEY, 0 0 0 – 0 0 1 – 0 0 0 – 0 0 0
Amelia COURTNEY; Allen COURTNEY; Harriet COURTNEY; George
COURTNEY; Infant. *(Ages not given.)*

#392: Harriet CHASE, 0 0 0 – 0 1 0 – 0 0 0 – 0 1 0: *(= SCHAISE, CHAISE.)*
Fanny GODFREY, 0 0 0 – 0 0 1 – 0 0 0 – 0 0 0
Eliza GODFREY, 0 0 0 – 0 0 1 – 0 0 0 – 0 0 0
Elizabeth GODFREY, 0 0 0 – 0 0 1 – 0 0 0 – 0 0 0
George GODFREY, 0 0 0 – 0 0 1 – 0 0 0 – 0 0 0
Henrietta. *(Age not given.)*

#393: William CRABBE, 0 0 0 – 1 0 0 – 0 0 0 – 0 0 0
John CRABBE, 0 0 0 – 1 0 0 – 0 0 0 – 0 0 0
Silvia FOX, 0 0 0 – 0 1 0 – 0 0 0 – 0 0 0
Elizabeth CRABBE, 0 0 0 – 0 1 0 – 0 0 0 – 0 0 0
Eleanor CRABBE, 0 0 0 – 0 1 0 – 0 0 0 – 0 0 0

#394: James CARROLL, 0 0 0 – 1 0 0 – 0 0 0 – 0 0 0
Polly JAMES, 0 0 0 – 0 1 0 – 0 0 0 – 0 0 0
John CARROLL, 0 0 0 – 0 0 1 – 0 0 0 – 0 0 0
Sarah CARROLL, 0 0 0 – 0 0 1 – 0 0 0 – 0 0 0
Rose CARROLL, 0 0 0 – 0 0 1 – 0 0 0 – 0 0 0

#395: Rose DUPUI, 0 0 0 – 0 1 0 – 0 0 0 – 0 0 0
Jesse DUPUI, 0 0 0 – 0 1 0 – 0 0 0 – 0 0 0
------- [sic] TROSINA, 0 0 0 – 0 1 0 – 0 0 0 – 0 0 0
Richard DOMINGO, 0 0 0 – 0 0 1 – 0 0 0 – 0 0 0

p. 112:
#396: Eleanor DUNN, 0 0 0 – 0 0 0 – 0 1 0 – 0 0 0
Sarah DARBY, 0 0 0 – 0 0 0 – 0 0 1 – 0 0 0
Edward TUTTY, 0 0 0 – 0 0 0 – 0 0 1 – 0 0 0
Rachael TUTTY, 0 0 0 – 0 0 0 – 0 0 1 – 0 0 0
Louisa TUTTY, 0 0 0 – 0 0 0 – 0 0 1 – 0 0 0

#397: John DIXON, 0 0 0 – 0 0 0 – 1 0 0 – 0 0 0

159

#398: Pedro Jose EBO, 0 0 0 – 0 0 0 – 1 0 0 – 0 0 0
Maria V. PANDI, 0 0 0 – 0 0 0 – 0 1 0 – 0 0 0
Juana M. PANDI, 0 0 0 – 0 0 0 – 0 1 0 – 0 0 0
Felipe N. PANDI, 0 0 0 – 0 0 0 – 0 0 1 – 0 0 0
Calorino PANDI, 0 0 0 – 0 0 0 – 0 0 1 – 0 0 0   *(Male.)*
Pantino PANDI, 0 0 0 – 0 0 0 – 0 0 1 – 0 0 0   *(Male.)*

#399: Quamina EDWARDS, 0 0 0 – 0 0 0 – 1 0 0 – 0 1 0:
Sarah EDWARDS, 0 0 0 – 0 0 0 – 0 1 0 – 0 0 0
Jenny, 20.

#400: Daniel EWING, 0 0 0 – 1 0 0 – 0 0 0 – 0 0 0
Rosetta GREGORIA, 0 0 0 – 0 1 0 – 0 0 0 – 0 0 0
Maria DOMINGO, 0 0 0 – 0 1 0 – 0 0 0 – 0 0 0
Daniel HAMILTON, 0 0 0 – 0 0 1 – 0 0 0 – 0 0 0
Benjamin HAMILTON, 0 0 0 – 0 0 1 – 0 0 0 – 0 0 0
Elizabeth HAMILTON, 0 0 0 – 0 0 1 – 0 0 0 – 0 0 0

#401: Charles EVANS, 1 0 0 – 0 0 0 – 0 0 0 – 1 1 0:
Billy PEPPER, 42; Margaret, 26.

p. 113:
#402: Joseph ERNEST, 0 0 0 – 1 0 0 – 0 0 0 – 0 0 0
Matthew ERNEST, 0 0 0 – 1 0 0 – 0 0 0 – 0 0 0
Amelia ROBINSON, 0 0 0 – 0 1 0 – 0 0 0 – 0 0 0

#403: Louisa FOURMEAUX, 0 1 0 – 0 0 0 – 0 0 0 – 0 0 0
Maria FOURMEAUX, 0 1 0 – 0 0 0 – 0 0 0 – 0 0 0

#404: Thomas FLOWERS, 0 0 0 – 0 0 0 – 1 0 0 – 0 1 1:
Maria FLOWERS, 0 0 0 – 0 0 0 – 0 1 0 – 0 0 0
Peter FLOWERS, 0 0 0 – 0 0 0 – 0 0 1 – 0 0 0
Toney FLOWERS, 0 0 0 – 0 0 0 – 0 0 1 – 0 0 0
Anna FLOWERS, 0 0 0 – 0 0 0 – 0 1 0 – 0 0 0
Isabella FLOWERS, 22; Francis FLOWERS, 6.

#405: Jacob FLOWERS, 0 0 0 – 0 0 0 – 1 0 0 – 0 0 0

#406: William C. FLOWERS, 0 0 0 – 0 0 0 – 1 0 0 – 0 0 0
Margaret BELISLE, 0 0 0 – 0 0 0 – 0 1 0 – 0 0 0
Caesar FLOWERS, 0 0 0 – 0 0 0 – 0 0 1 – 0 0 0
Joanna FLOWERS, 0 0 0 – 0 0 0 – 0 0 1 – 0 0 0
Rosanna FLOWERS, 0 0 0 – 0 0 0 – 0 0 1 – 0 0 0
Elizabeth FLOWERS, 0 0 0 – 0 0 0 – 0 0 1 – 0 0 0
Maria FLOWERS, 0 0 0 – 0 0 0 – 0 0 1 – 0 0 0

#407: James FERGUSON, 0 0 0 – 0 0 0 – 1 0 0 – 0 0 0
Patty McAULAY, 0 0 0 – 0 0 0 – 0 1 0 – 0 0 0
Jane FERGUSON, 0 0 0 – 0 0 0 – 0 1 0 – 0 0 0

p. 114:
#408: Quamina FLOWERS, 0 0 0 – 0 0 0 – 1 0 0 – 0 0 0
Alexander FLOWERS, 0 0 0 – 0 0 0 – 0 0 1 – 0 0 0
John FLOWERS, 0 0 0 – 0 0 0 – 0 0 1 – 0 0 0
Sarah FLOWERS, 0 0 0 – 0 0 0 – 0 0 1 – 0 0 0
Catherine FLOWERS, 0 0 0 – 0 0 0 – 0 0 1 – 0 0 0
Maria FLOWERS, 0 0 0 – 0 0 0 – 0 1 0 – 0 0 0

#409: Juana FRANCISCA, 0 0 0 – 0 0 0 – 0 1 0 – 0 0 0
Maria LEONA, 0 0 0 – 0 0 0 – 0 1 0 – 0 0 0
Segundo, 0 0 0 – 0 0 0 – 1 0 0 – 0 0 0
Martina, 0 0 0 – 0 0 0 – 0 0 1 – 0 0 0
Camilla, 0 0 0 – 0 0 0 – 0 0 1 – 0 0 0 *(Surnames not given.)*
Jose ABENA, 0 0 0 – 0 0 0 – 1 0 0 – 0 0 0

#410: Robert FORMAN, 1 0 0 – 0 0 0 – 0 0 0 – 0 0 0
Jane FORMAN, 0 1 0 – 0 0 0 – 0 0 0 – 0 0 0
Clarissa GLADDEN, 0 0 0 – 0 1 0 – 0 0 0 – 0 0 0
Elizabeth FORMAN, 0 0 0 – 0 0 1 – 0 0 0 – 0 0 0
Catherine FORMAN, 0 0 0 – 0 0 1 – 0 0 0 – 0 0 0

#411: John GAMBOA, 0 0 0 – 0 0 0 – 1 0 0 – 0 0 0
Mary BAILEY, 0 0 0 – 0 0 0 – 0 1 0 – 0 0 0
Antonio GAMBOA, 0 0 0 – 0 0 0 – 0 0 1 – 0 0 0
Silviera GAMBOA, 0 0 0 – 0 0 0 – 0 0 1 – 0 0 0
Arabella GAMBOA, 0 0 0 – 0 0 0 – 0 0 1 – 0 0 0

#412: Joseph GAMBOA, 0 0 0 – 0 0 0 – 1 0 0 – 0 0 0

p. 115:
#413: Anne GABOUREL, 0 0 0 – 0 1 0 – 0 0 0 – 7 4 8:
Robert SMITH, 0 0 0 – 0 0 1 – 0 0 0 – 0 0 0
David BETSON Jun'r, 0 0 0 – 0 0 1 – 0 0 0 – 0 0 0
Frances Anne BETSON, 0 0 0 – 0 0 1 – 0 0 0 – 0 0 0
Mary Anne MOODY, 0 0 0 – 0 1 0 – 0 0 0 – 0 0 0
Angelina STANFORD, 0 0 0 – 0 0 0 – 0 1 0 – 0 0 0
Lucretia GABOUREL, 0 0 0 – 0 0 1 – 0 0 0 – 0 0 0
        James, 51; Joseph, 41; Tom, 31; Sampson, 24; Michael, 41; Jem, 38;
        Janette, 31; Jenny 26; Kate, 23; Tommy, 12; Johnny, 9; Eleanor, 4; Sam, 4;
        Alick, 2; Martha, 1.
Property of D. BETSON Jr.:
        Richard, 26.

161

Property of F. A. BETSON:
Margaret, 20; Rosanna, 2; Mary, 1.

#414: William GABOUREL, 0 0 0 – 1 0 0 – 0 0 0 – 6 1 0:
Diana USHER, 0 0 0 – 0 1 0 – 0 0 0 – 0 0 0
Mary GABOUREL, 0 0 0 – 0 1 0 – 0 0 0 – 0 0 0
George GABOUREL, 0 0 0 – 1 0 0 – 0 0 0 – 0 0 0
Joshua GABOUREL, 0 0 0 – 1 0 0 – 0 0 0 – 0 0 0
William GABOUREL, 0 0 0 – 0 0 1 – 0 0 0 – 0 0 0
James GABOUREL, 0 0 0 – 0 0 1 – 0 0 0 – 0 0 0
Elizabeth GABOUREL, 0 0 0 – 0 0 1 – 0 0 0 – 0 0 0
John GABOUREL, 0 0 0 – 0 0 1 – 0 0 0 – 0 0 0
Charles GABOUREL, 0 0 0 – 0 0 1 – 0 0 0 – 0 0 0
    Alick, 32; Toney, 50; America, 40; Harry MEIGHAN, 40; Charles, 42.
Property of D. USHER:
Bacchus, 55; Venus, 40.

p. 116:
#415: George L. GRISTOCK, 1 0 0 – 0 0 0 – 0 0 0 – 3 1 1:
Eliza GIBSON, 0 0 0 – 0 1 0 – 0 0 0 – 0 0 0
Richard GRISTOCK, 1 0 0 – 0 0 0 – 0 0 0 – 0 0 0
Caroline GRISTOCK, 0 0 0 – 0 0 1 – 0 0 0 – 0 0 0
Infant, 0 0 0 – 0 0 1 – 0 0 0 – 0 0 0
    Margaret, 18; Mary Anne, 9; Alick, 60; Hare, 63; Anthony, 54.

#416: Eleanor GIBSON, 0 0 0 – 0 0 0 – 0 1 0 – 0 0 0
Joanna GIBSON, 0 0 0 – 0 0 0 – 0 1 0 – 0 0 0
Peter C. GIBSON, 0 0 0 – 0 0 0 – 1 0 0 – 0 0 0

#417: William H. GIBSON, 0 0 0 – 1 0 0 – 0 0 0 – 0 0 0
Margaret CASTLE, 0 0 0 – 0 1 0 – 0 0 0 – 0 0 0
John Wm GIBSON, 0 0 0 – 0 0 1 – 0 0 0 – 0 0 0
Jane Elizth TALBOT, 0 0 0 – 0 0 1 – 0 0 0 – 0 0 0
Sarah W. GIBSON, 0 0 0 – 0 0 1 – 0 0 0 – 0 0 0
Catherine E. GIBSON, 0 0 0 – 0 0 1 – 0 0 0 – 0 0 0

#418: Joseph GRANT, 0 0 0 – 0 0 0 – 1 0 0 – 0 0 0
Henrietta MILES, 0 0 0 – 0 0 0 – 0 1 0 – 0 0 0
Harriet GRANT, 0 0 0 – 0 0 0 – 0 0 1 – 0 0 0
Margaret GRANT, 0 0 0 – 0 0 0 – 0 0 1 – 0 0 0

#419: George GRANT, 0 0 0 – 0 0 0 – 1 0 0 – 0 0 0
Jose LINO, 0 0 0 – 0 0 0 – 0 0 1 – 0 0 0
William GRANT, 0 0 0 – 0 0 0 – 1 0 0 – 0 0 0

p. 117:

#420: Hopewell GRANT, 0 0 0 – 0 0 0 – 1 0 0 – 0 0 0

#421: William GAMBLE, 0 0 0 – 1 0 0 – 0 0 0 – 1 1 0:
　　　　Letitia BROUGHTON, ꞓ 0 0 – 0 1 0 – 0 0 0 – 0 0 0
　　　　Patience GAMBLE, 0 0 0 – 0 1 0 – 0 0 0 – 0 0 0
　　　　Letitia GAMBLE, 0 0 0 – 0 0 1 – 0 0 0 – 0 0 0
　　　　　　Lizzy GAMBLE, 45; George FANTASSY, 17.

#422: John GRANT, 0 0 0 – 0 0 0 – 1 0 0 – 0 0 0
　　　　Thisbe SMITH, 0 0 0 – 0 0 0 – 0 1 0 – 0 0 0

#423: John GARBUTT, 1 0 0 – 0 0 0 – 0 0 0 – 0 0 0
　　　　John GARBUTT Junʳ, 0 ꞓ 0 – 0 0 1 – 0 0 0 – 0 0 0
　　　　Lucretia GARBUTT, 0 0 0 – 0 0 1 – 0 0 0 – 0 0 0
　　　　Aaron GARBUTT, 0 0 0 – 0 0 1 – 0 0 0 – 0 0 0
　　　　Margaret GARBUTT, 0 0 0 – 0 0 1 – 0 0 0 – 0 0 0
　　　　Jane PITT, 0 0 0 – 0 0 0 – ꞓ 1 0 – 0 0 0

#424: Samuel HUGHES, 0 0 0 – ꞓ 0 0 – 1 0 0 – 0 0 0
　　　　Elizabeth DUNCAN, 0 0 0 – 0 0 0 – 0 1 0 – 0 0 0

#425: Peter HARRIS, 0 0 0 – 0 0 ꝃ – 1 0 0 – 0 0 0
　　　　Mary JONES, 0 0 0 – 0 0 0 – 0 1 0 – 0 0 0
　　　　Peter BODE, 0 0 0 – 0 0 0 – 1 0 0 – 0 0 0

#426: John HARVEY, 0 0 0 – 0 0 ꞓ – 1 0 0 – 0 0 0

p. 118:

#427: Susan HYDE, 0 0 0 – 0 0 0 – 0 1 0 – 0 0 0
　　　　Thomas HYDE, 0 0 0 – 0 0 ꞓ – 0 0 1 – 0 0 0
　　　　Sarah HYDE, 0 0 0 – 0 0 0 – 0 0 1 – 0 0 0
　　　　Hannah HYDE, 0 0 0 – 0 0 0 – 0 0 1 – 0 0 0

#428: Henry HILL, 0 0 0 – 0 0 0 – 1 0 0 – 0 0 0
　　　　Mary THOMAS, 0 0 0 – 0 0 ꞓ – 0 1 0 – 0 0 0
　　　　Henry T. CADDLE, 0 0 0 – 0 0 0 – 0 0 1 – 0 0 0

#429: Gerald HILL, 0 0 0 – 0 0 0 – 1 ꝃ 0 – 0 0 0
　　　　John LOUIS, 0 0 0 – 0 0 0 – 1 0 0 – 0 0 0
　　　　Joseph HILL, 0 0 0 – 0 0 0 – 0 0 1 – 0 0 0
　　　　Josefa HILL, 0 0 0 – 0 0 0 – 0 1 0 – 0 0 0

#430: Jane JEFFRIES, 0 0 0 – 0 1 0 – 0 0 0 – 3 3 1:
　　　　Thomas M. SMITH, 0 0 0 – 0 0 1 – 0 0 0 – 0 0 0
　　　　　　Phillis; Peter, 10; Willberry. *(Ages of Phillis and Willberry are not given.)*

163

Property of Thomas M. SMITH:
Bristow, 35; Simon, 36; Maria, 21; Letitia, 18.

#431: Elizabeth JEFFRIES, 0 0 0 – 0 1 0 – 0 0 0 – 1 1 0:
Mary Jane GRAHAM, 0 0 0 – 0 0 1 – 0 0 0 – 0 0 0
David GRAHAM, 0 0 0 – 0 0 1 – 0 0 0 – 0 0 0
Sarah GRAHAM, 0 0 0 – 0 0 1 – 0 0 0 – 0 0 0
Samuel BAKER; Letitia JEFFRIES. *(Ages not given.)*

p. 119:
#432: William JONES, 0 0 0 – 0 0 0 – 1 0 0 – 0 0 0
Olive CRAWFORD, 0 0 0 – 0 1 0 – 0 0 0 – 0 0 0
Jane WILLIAMS, 0 0 0 – 0 1 0 – 0 0 0 – 0 0 0
Elizabeth WILLIAMS, 0 0 0 – 0 1 0 – 0 0 0 – 0 0 0
Mary WILLIAMS, 0 0 0 – 0 1 0 – 0 0 0 – 0 0 0
Anne NEAL, 0 0 0 – 0 1 0 – 0 0 0 – 0 0 0
James WILLIAMS, 0 0 0 – 0 0 0 – 1 0 0 – 0 0 0
Lavinia WILLIAMS, 0 0 0 – 0 1 0 – 0 0 0 – 0 0 0
William NEAL, 0 0 0 – 0 0 0 – 0 0 1 – 0 0 0
George NEAL, 0 0 0 – 0 0 0 – 0 0 1 – 0 0 0
Ann GOFF, 0 0 0 – 0 0 0 – 0 0 1 – 0 0 0
John NEAL, 0 0 0 – 0 0 0 – 0 0 1 – 0 0 0
Francis NEAL, 0 0 0 – 0 0 0 – 0 0 1 – 0 0 0
Olive NEAL, 0 0 0 – 0 0 0 – 0 0 1 – 0 0 0
Joseph MORRIS, 0 0 0 – 0 0 0 – 0 0 1 – 0 0 0

#433: Colin JONES, 0 0 0 – 1 0 0 – 0 0 0 – 0 0 0
Eliza DAVIS, 0 0 0 – 0 1 0 – 0 0 0 – 0 0 0
Esther JONES, 0 0 0 – 0 0 1 – 0 0 0 – 0 0 0
Samuel JONES, 0 0 0 – 0 0 1 – 0 0 0 – 0 0 0
Margaret JONES, 0 0 0 – 0 0 1 – 0 0 0 – 0 0 0

#434: James JONES, 0 0 0 – 1 0 0 – 0 0 0 – 0 0 0

#435: Rees JACOB, 0 0 0 – 0 0 0 – 1 0 0 – 0 0 0

#436: Nelson MEIGHAN, 0 0 0 – 0 0 0 – 1 0 0 – 0 0 0

p. 120:
#437: Louisa LAWRIE, 0 0 0 – 0 1 0 – 0 0 0 – 0 0 0
Kitty LAWRIE, 0 0 0 – 0 0 0 – 0 1 0 – 0 0 0
Grace SMITH, 0 0 0 – 0 1 0 – 0 0 0 – 0 0 0
Eve HINKS, 0 0 0 – 0 1 0 – 0 0 0 – 0 0 0
Frances FLOWERS, 0 0 0 – 0 0 1 – 0 0 0 – 0 0 0
Francis GRANT, 0 0 0 – 0 0 0 – 0 0 1 – 0 0 0
Adam GRANT, 0 0 0 – 0 0 0 – 0 0 1 – 0 0 0

164

Edward ADOLPHUS, C 0 0 – 0 0 1 – 0 0 0 – 0 0 0
Sarah ADOLPHUS, 0 0 0 – 0 0 1 – 0 0 0 – 0 0 0
William BELISLE, 0 0 0 – 0 0 0 – 0 0 1 – 0 0 0
Eliza Ann BELISLE, 0 0 0 – 0 0 0 – 0 0 1 – 0 0 0

Note: Were Edward and Sarah children of George D. Adolphus? Were they related to Capt. Peter Adolphus Wade of Bristol and Belize?

#438: Mary LOWRIE, 0 0 0 – 0 1 0 – 0 0 0 – 0 0 0
Patrick GRANT, 0 0 0 – 1 0 0 – 0 0 0 – 0 0 0
Charles CATO, 0 0 0 – 0 0 1 – 0 0 0 – 0 0 0
Jervis CATO, 0 0 0 – 0 0 1 – 0 0 0 – 0 0 0
Ann DAVIS, 0 0 0 – 0 0 1 – 0 0 0 – 0 0 0
Joseph DAVIS, 1 0 0 – C 0 0 – 0 0 0 – 0 0 0

#439: Benjamin LONGSWORTH, 0 0 0 – 1 0 0 – 0 0 0 – 0 0 0
Sarah KEENE, 0 0 0 – 0 1 0 – 0 0 0 – 0 0 0
Margaret LONGSWORTH, 0 0 0 – 0 1 0 – 0 0 0 – 0 0 0
Mary LOVELL, 0 0 0 – C 1 0 – 0 0 0 – 0 0 0

#440: Ann LONGSWORTH, 0 0 0 – 0 1 0 – 0 0 0 – 0 1 0
William LOWE, 0 0 0 – C 0 1 – 0 0 0 – 0 0 0
    Betty, 50.

p. 121:
#441: Manuel MABIALE, C 0 0 – 0 0 0 – 1 0 0 – 0 0 0
Tibarcio MABIALE, 0 0 C – 0 0 0 – 0 1 0 – 0 0 0 *(Marked and totaled as female.)*
Josefa MABIALE, 0 0 0 – 0 0 0 – 0 1 0 – 0 0 0

#442: John MOORE, 0 0 0 – 0 0 0 – 1 0 0 – 0 0 0
Peggy MOORE, 0 0 0 – 0 0 0 – 0 1 0 – 0 0 0
Nancy MOORE, 0 0 0 – 0 0 0 – 0 0 1 – 0 0 0
Sylvia MOORE, 0 0 0 – 0 0 0 – 0 0 1 – 0 0 0
Catherine MOORE, 0 0 0 – 0 0 0 – 0 0 1 – 0 0 0
Mary MOORE, 0 0 0 – 0 0 0 – 0 0 1 – 0 0 0
William MOORE, 0 0 0 – C 0 0 – 0 0 1 – 0 0 0

#443: Edward MOODY, 0 0 0 – 1 0 0 – 0 0 0 – 0 0 0
Prudence MOODY, 0 C 0 – 0 0 0 – 0 1 0 – 0 0 0
Edward MOODY, 0 0 0 – 0 0 1 – 0 0 0 – 0 0 0
Jane MOODY, 0 0 0 – 0 0 1 – 0 0 0 – 0 0 0
Catherine MOODY, 0 C 0 – 0 0 1 – 0 0 0 – 0 0 0
Lucretia MOODY, 0 0 0 – 0 0 1 – 0 0 0 – 0 0 0
Adriana MOODY, 0 0 C – 0 0 1 – 0 0 0 – 0 0 0
Maria MOODY, 0 0 0 – 0 0 1 – 0 0 0 – 0 0 0
Isabella MOODY, 0 0 0 – 0 0 1 – 0 0 0 – 0 0 0

165

#444: Thomas MYVETT, 0 0 0 – 0 0 0 – 1 0 0 – 0 0 0
Eleanor HUME, 0 0 0 – 0 0 0 – 0 1 0 – 0 0 0

#445: Margaret NEAL, 0 0 0 – 0 1 0 – 0 0 0 – 1 1 0:
Robert, 21.
Runaway: Catherine, 22.

p. 122:
#446: Joseph NEAL, 0 0 0 – 0 0 0 – 1 0 0 – 0 0 0
Eleanor NEAL, 0 0 0 – 0 0 0 – 0 0 1 – 0 0 0
Elizabeth NEAL, 0 0 0 – 0 0 0 – 0 0 1 – 0 0 0
Cecelia FLOWERS, 0 0 0 – 0 0 0 – 0 1 0 – 0 0 0

#447: Duncan NEAL, 0 0 0 – 1 0 0 – 0 0 0 – 0 0 0
Margaret NEAL, 0 0 0 – 0 0 0 – 0 1 0 – 0 0 0
Clarinda NEAL, 0 0 0 – 0 0 1 – 0 0 0 – 0 0 0
Sarah NEAL, 0 0 0 – 0 0 1 – 0 0 0 – 0 0 0

#448: Jacob NEAL, 0 0 0 – 0 0 0 – 1 0 0 – 0 0 0
Caroline NEAL, 0 0 0 – 0 0 0 – 0 1 0 – 0 0 0
Renard NEAL, 0 0 0 – 0 0 0 – 0 0 1 – 0 0 0

#449: Middleton O'CONNOR, 0 0 0 – 0 0 0 – 1 0 0 – 0 0 0
Venus MIDDLETON, 0 0 0 – 0 0 0 – 0 1 0 – 0 0 0
Cathline MIDDLETON, 0 0 0 – 0 0 0 – 0 0 1 – 0 0 0
Maurice MIDDLETON, 0 0 0 – 0 0 0 – 0 0 1 – 0 0 0
John MIDDLETON, 0 0 0 – 0 0 0 – 0 0 1 – 0 0 0
Mary Ann MIDDLETON, 0 0 0 – 0 0 0 – 0 0 1 – 0 0 0
Robert MIDDLETON, 0 0 0 – 0 0 0 – 0 0 1 – 0 0 0
Nancy FLOWERS, 0 0 0 – 0 0 0 – 0 0 1 – 0 0 0
James MIDDLETON, 0 0 0 – 0 0 0 – 0 0 1 – 0 0 0
Mimba MIDDLETON, 0 0 0 – 0 0 0 – 0 0 1 – 0 0 0
Samuel FLOWERS, 0 0 0 – 0 0 0 – 0 0 1 – 0 0 0
Abigail FLOWERS, 0 0 0 – 0 0 0 – 0 0 1 – 0 0 0

p. 123:
#450: Juan Miguel ORTEZ, 0 0 0 – 0 0 0 – 1 0 0 – 0 0 0
Juana Louisa CONAQUI, 0 0 0 – 0 0 0 – 0 1 0 – 0 0 0
Juana Louisa GANGA, 0 0 0 – 0 0 0 – 0 1 0 – 0 0 0
Irina Batista ORTEZ, 0 0 0 – 0 0 0 – 0 1 0 – 0 0 0
Helena Josefa ORTEZ, 0 0 0 – 0 0 0 – 0 1 0 – 0 0 0

#451: Property of F[k] PICKSTOCK under charge of G. L. GRISTOCK, 0 2 5:
Mary, 25; Rachael, 4 ½; Nancy, 2 ½; Maria, 24; Robert, 3; Sylvia,
3 months; Christiana, 5 months.

166

#452: John PATRICIO, 0 0 0 – 1 0 0 – 0 0 0 – 0 0 0
Maria OSAFO, 0 0 0 – 0 1 0 – 0 0 0 – 0 0 0
Fabiana SEBASTIANA, 0 0 0 – 0 0 1 – 0 0 0 – 0 0 0
Maria CLEMENTA, 0 0 0 – 0 1 0 – 0 0 0 – 0 0 0
Cayetano ALBERTO, 0 0 0 – 0 0 0 – 1 0 0 – 0 0 0

#453: Andrew PIPERSBURG, 0 0 0 – 0 0 0 – 1 0 0 – 0 0 0
Mary Ann PIPERSBURG, 0 0 0 – 0 0 0 – 0 1 0 – 0 0 0
Henry PIPERSBURG, 0 0 0 – 0 0 0 – 0 0 1 – 0 0 0
Fidelia PIPERSBURG, 0 0 0 – 0 0 0 – 0 0 1 – 0 0 0
David PIPERSBURG, 0 0 0 – 0 0 0 – 0 0 1 – 0 0 0
Joseph PIPERSBURG, 0 0 0 – 0 0 0 – 0 0 1 – 0 0 0
Nancy PIPERSBURG, 0 0 0 – 0 0 0 – 0 0 1 – 0 0 0

p. 124:
#454: Andrew POTTS, 0 0 0 – 0 0 0 – 1 0 0 – 0 0 0
Lucy POTTS, 0 0 0 – 0 0 0 – 0 1 0 – 0 0 0

#455: Peter PEREZ, 0 0 0 – 1 0 0 – 0 0 0 – 0 0 0
Caroline PEREZ, 0 0 0 – 0 1 0 – 0 0 0 – 0 0 0
Maria PEREZ, 0 0 0 – 0 1 0 – 0 0 0 – 0 0 0
Joseph HARDY, 0 0 0 – 1 0 0 – 0 0 0 – 0 0 0

#456: Clarissa PASLOW, 0 0 0 – 0 1 0 – 0 0 0 – 11 13 8:
Thomas PASLOW, 40; Isaac PASLOW, 39; John HARE, 35; Dibdin
PASLOW, 45; Vincent, 50; Thomas LAMB, 38; Thomas ENGLISH, 25;
Providence, 34; Samuel LAMB, 24; Tom LAMB, 24; James COOTE, 45;
Andrew PASLOW, 10; Thomas PASLOW Jr., 7; James PASLOW, 7;
Samuel PASLOW, 1 ½; Peggy PASLOW, 2; Venus PASLOW, 60;
Nancy WALDRON, 40; Margaret PASLOW, 44; Elizabeth PASLOW, 45;
Cecilia ENGLISH, 35; Cecilia HICKEY, 30;

p. 125:
#457: Family of Clarissa PASLOW. Continued:
Bessy LAME, 25; Diana LAMB, 26; Dorinda LAMB, 20; Kate LAMB, 25;
Agnes LAMB, 17; Judy LAMB, 16; Sally LAMB, 28; Sarah PASLOW, 1;
Mary Jane PASLOW, 2; Martha PASLOW, 3.

#458: John PANDY, 0 0 0 – 0 0 0 – 1 0 0 – 0 0 0
Maria de LA LUZ, 0 0 0 – 0 0 0 – 0 1 0 – 0 0 0
Francisca MILIANA, 0 0 0 – 0 0 0 – 0 0 1 – 0 0 0
Teodora JOSEFA, 0 0 0 – 0 0 0 – 0 0 1 – 0 0 0
Juan de LA CRUZ, 0 0 0 – 0 0 0 – 0 0 1 – 0 0 0
Pablo Jose PANDY, 0 0 0 – 0 0 0 – 1 0 0 – 0 0 0

167

#459: Duncan ROBINSON, 0 0 0 – 0 0 0 – 1 0 0 – 0 0 0
Leonard ROBINSON, 0 0 0 – 0 0 0 – 1 0 0 – 0 0 0
Susan PRICE, 0 0 0 – 0 0 0 – 0 1 0 – 0 0 0

#460: Sarah RAYBON, 0 1 0 – 0 0 0 – 0 0 0 – 1 0 0:
James WADDIE, 1 0 0 – 0 0 0 – 0 0 0 – 0 0 0
Mary Ann POTTAGE, 0 0 1 – 0 0 0 – 0 0 0 – 0 0 0 *(Dau. of Henry POTTAGE*
Dick, 45.   *and Sarah RAYBON.)*

#461: Thomas SLUSHER, 0 0 0 – 0 0 0 – 1 0 0 – 0 0 0
Sarah WILSON, 0 0 0 – 0 1 0 – 0 0 0 – 0 0 0
George SUTHERLAND, 0 0 0 – 0 0 1 – 0 0 0 – 0 0 0

p. 126:
#462: Robert SMITH, 0 0 0 – 0 0 0 – 1 0 0 – 0 0 0
Isabella SMITH, 0 0 0 – 0 0 1 – 0 0 0 – 0 0 0
Sarah SMITH, 0 0 0 – 0 0 1 – 0 0 0 – 0 0 0
Elizabeth SMITH, 0 0 0 – 0 0 1 – 0 0 0 – 0 0 0
Louisa BILLERY, 0 0 0 – 0 1 0 – 0 0 0 – 0 0 0

#463: William SUTHERLAND, 0 0 0 – 0 0 0 – 1 0 0 – 0 0 0
Nancy SUTHERLAND, 0 0 0 – 0 0 0 – 0 1 0 – 0 0 0

#464: Jose Miguel SUNGA, 0 0 0 – 0 0 0 – 1 0 0 – 0 0 0
Maria LAYA, 0 0 0 – 0 0 0 – 0 1 0 – 0 0 0
Jose VINCENTE, 0 0 0 – 0 0 0 – 1 0 0 – 0 0 0
Jose MARCO, 0 0 0 – 0 0 0 – 0 0 1 – 0 0 0
Lorenzo MARIAL, 0 0 0 – 0 0 0 – 1 0 0 – 0 0 0
Juana UNARIA, 0 0 0 – 0 0 0 – 0 1 0 – 0 0 0

#465: Nannette SWAN, 0 0 0 – 0 0 0 – 0 1 0 – 1 0 0:
John SWAN, 0 0 0 – 0 0 0 – 1 0 0 – 0 0 0
A. SWAN, 0 0 0 – 0 0 0 – 1 0 0 – 0 0 0
Pope SWAN, 40.

#466: Lydia BELISLE, 0 0 0 – 0 0 0 – 0 1 0 – 0 0 0
Catherine GOFF, 0 0 0 – 0 0 0 – 0 0 1 – 0 0 0
John SAVORY, 0 0 0 – 0 0 0 – 0 0 1 – 0 0 0
Eliza SAVORY, 0 0 0 – 0 0 0 – 0 0 1 – 0 0 0
Mary SAVORY, 0 0 0 – 0 0 0 – 0 0 1 – 0 0 0
Charles SAVORY, 0 0 0 – 0 0 0 – 0 0 1 – 0 0 0
Pamela SAVORY, 0 0 0 – 0 0 0 – 0 0 1 – 0 0 0
John SAVORY, 0 0 0 – 0 0 0 – 1 0 0 – 0 0 0

p. 127:
#467: William SUTHERLAND, 0 0 0 – 1 0 0 – 0 0 0 – 0 0 0

168

Mary WOOD, 0 0 0 – 0 1 0 – 0 0 0 – 0 0 0
Margaret M. PIERRE, 0 0 0 – 0 1 0 – 0 0 0 – 0 0 0
George SUTHERLAND, 0 0 0 – 1 0 0 – 0 0 0 – 0 0 0
Francis SUTHERLAND, 0 0 0 – 1 0 0 – 0 0 0 – 0 0 0
Tina SUTHERLAND, 0 0 0 – 0 1 0 – 0 0 0 – 0 0 0

#468: Orlando SUTTLE, 1 0 0 – 0 0 0 – 0 0 0 – 0 0 0 *(= SUTTIL)*
Mary SUTTLE, 0 0 1 – 0 0 0 – 0 0 0 – 0 0 0
Phoebe THOMPSON, 0 0 0 – 0 0 0 – 0 1 0 – 0 0 0
John M. CLARK, 1 0 0 – 0 0 0 – 0 0 0 – 0 0 0
Alexander HAY, 1 0 0 – 0 0 0 – 0 0 0 – 0 0 0

#469: Mary TATE, 0 1 0 – 0 0 0 – 0 0 0 – 0 6 3:
Matilda TATE, 0 1 0 – 0 5 0 – 0 0 0 – 0 0 0
    Catherine, 55; Jenny, 40; Molly, 36; Phyllis, 42; Margaret, 19; Henrietta, 17;
    Harriet, 9; Adele, 3; Robert, 8.

#470: Henry TUCKER, 0 0 0 – 0 0 0 – 1 0 0 – 0 0 0
Margarita ANTONIA, 0 0 0 – 0 0 0 – 0 1 0 – 0 0 0
Phillipio BARSO, 0 0 0 – 0 0 0 – 1 0 0 – 0 0 0
Francisco BARSO, 0 0 0 – 0 0 0 – 0 0 1 – 0 0 0
Cornelio [*sic*] BARSO, 0 0 0 – 0 0 0 – 0 0 1 – 0 0 0 *(Male.)*
Juan BARSO, 0 0 0 – 0 0 0 – 0 0 1 – 0 0 0

p. 128:
#471: Estate of JANE TRAPP, 4 3 6:
    Cynthia, 37; Bess, 35; Rose, 29; Thomas, 33; Richmond, 35; John
    LAMBERT, 36; Leith, 26; Daniel, 7; James, 6; Ephraim, 2; Selina, 5;
    Eliza, 4; Sarah, 1.

#472: Elizabeth THURSTON, 0 1 0 – 0 0 0 – 0 0 0 - 5 5 2:
Eleanor LEVEN, 0 1 0 – 0 0 0 – 0 0 0 – 0 0 0
Nancy CRANE, 0 0 0 – 0 1 0 – 0 0 0 – 0 0 0
Jonathan ROWLAND, 1 0 0 – 0 0 0 – 0 0 0 – 0 0 0
William BURNS, 1 0 0 – 0 0 0 – 0 0 0 – 0 0 0
Hannah STEVENS, 0 1 0 – 0 0 0 – 0 0 0 – 0 0 0
John LONGSWORTH, 1 0 0 – 0 0 0 – 0 0 0 – 0 0 0
Bella RAYNE, 0 0 1 – 0 0 0 – 0 0 0 – 0 0 0
    George; Harry; March; Adriana; Phyllis; Sarah; Mary; Diana; Thomas;
    Catherine.
    Runaway: Billy; Boatswain. *(Ages not given.)*

#473: Thomas TUCKER, 0 0 0 – 1 0 0 – 0 0 0 – 0 0 0
Joseph TUCKER, 0 0 0 – 0 0 0 – 1 0 0 – 0 0 0
John TUCKER, 0 0 0 – 0 0 0 – 1 0 0 – 0 0 0
Judith TUCKER, 0 0 0 – 0 0 0 – 0 1 0 – 0 0 0

169

p. 129:
#474: William TRAPP, 0 0 0 – 0 0 0 – 1 0 0 – 0 0 0
Elizabeth TRAPP, 0 0 0 – 0 0 0 – 0 1 0 – 0 0 0
James TRAPP, 0 0 0 – 0 0 0 – 0 0 1 – 0 0 0
David TRAPP, 0 0 0 – 0 0 0 – 0 0 1 – 0 0 0
William TRAPP, 0 0 0 – 0 0 0 – 0 0 1 – 0 0 0

#475: Uriah TRAPP, 0 0 0 – 1 0 0 – 0 0 0 – 1 0 0:
Elizabeth TRAPP, 0 0 0 – 0 1 0 – 0 0 0 – 0 0 0
James Ephraim TRAPP, 0 0 0 – 0 0 1- 0 0 0 – 0 0 0
Richard TRAPP, 0 0 0 – 0 0 1- 0 0 0 – 0 0 0
Uriah McDILLAM TRAPP, 0 0 0 – 0 0 1 - 0 0 0 – 0 0 0
George F^k HOARE, 0 0 0 – 0 0 1 – 0 0 0 – 0 0 0
George M. GRANT, 0 0 0 – 0 0 1 – 0 0 0 – 0 0 0
Harriet GRANT, 0 0 0 – 0 0 1 – 0 0 0 – 0 0 0
Property of ditto:
    King, 40.

#476: Catherine THOMPSON, 0 0 0 – 0 1 0 – 0 0 0 – 0 1 0:
Eliza MASSEY, 0 0 0 – 0 1 0 – 0 0 0 – 0 0 0
Mary Ann PICKSTOCK, 0 0 0 – 0 0 1 – 0 0 0 – 0 0 0
George RADFORD, 0 0 0 – 0 0 1 – 0 0 0 – 0 0 0
Catherine RADFORD, 0 0 0 – 0 0 1 – 0 0 0 – 0 0 0
Emma McPHERSON, 0 0 0 – 0 0 1 – 0 0 0 – 0 0 0
Jane BURNS, 0 0 0 – 0 0 1 – 0 0 0 – 0 0 0
    Maria, 14.

#477: Sarah WINTER, 0 0 0 – 0 1 0 – 0 0 0 – 1 1 1:
J. G. HUNT, 0 0 0 – 0 0 1 – 0 0 0 – 0 0 0 *(Male.)*
George A. BRADDOCK, 0 0 0 – 0 0 1 – 0 0 0 – 0 0 0
    Tony WINTER, 45; Fanny, 50; Nancy, 11.

p. 130:
#478: Samuel WARRIOR, 0 0 0 – 1 0 0 – 0 0 0 – 0 0 0
Phyllis WARRIOR, 0 0 0 – 0 1 0 – 0 0 0 – 0 0 0

#479: Cumberland WINTER, 0 0 0 – 0 0 0 – 1 0 0 – 0 0 0
Ann WINTER, 0 0 0 – 0 0 0 – 0 1 0 – 0 0 0

#480: Lewis WILLIAMS, 0 0 0 – 1 0 0 – 0 0 0 – 0 0 0
J. E. WILLIAMS, 0 0 0 – 0 1 0 – 0 0 0 – 0 0 0
Lewis WILLIAMS Jun'r, 0 0 0 – 0 0 1 – 0 0 0 – 0 0 0
J. Thomas WILLIAMS, 0 0 0 – 0 0 1 – 0 0 0 – 0 0 0
Emily WILLIAMS, 0 0 0 – 0 0 1 – 0 0 0 – 0 0 0

170

#481: Agnes WALL, 0 0 0 – 0 1 0 – 0 0 0 – 0 0 0
      John McWHIRTER, 0 0 0 – 0 0 1 – 0 0 0 – 0 0 0
      William McKAY, 0 0 0 – 0 0 1 – 0 0 0 – 0 0 0
      George CARMICHAEL, 0 0 0 – 0 0 1 – 0 0 0 – 0 0 0

#482: Michael WINTER, 0 0 0 – 1 0 0 – 0 0 0 – 0 0 0

#483: Francis YOUNG, 0 0 0 – 1 0 0 – 0 0 0 – 2 1 0:
      Amelia LONGSWORTH, 0 0 0 – 0 1 0 – 0 0 0 – 0 0 0
      William F. YOUNG, 0 0 0 – 0 0 1 – 0 0 0 – 0 0 0
      Mary F. YOUNG, 0 0 0 – 0 0 1 – 0 0 0 – 0 0 0
      Samanty YOUNG, 0 0 0 – 0 0 0 – 0 1 0 – 0 0 0
          Elizabeth F. YOUNG, 20; James LONGSWORTH, 30; Peter CADDLE, 22.

p. 131:
#484: William YOUNG, 0 0 0 – 1 0 0 – 0 0 0 – 1 0 0:
      George YOUNG, 0 0 0 – 1 0 0 – 0 0 0 – 0 0 0
      William YOUNG Jr., 0 0 0 – 1 0 0 – 0 0 0 – 0 0 0
      Robert YOUNG, 0 0 0 – 1 0 0 – 0 0 0 – 0 0 0
      Elizabeth SNOWDON, 0 0 0 – 0 1 0 – 0 0 0 – 0 0 0
      Nancy YOUNG, 0 0 0 – 0 1 0 – 0 0 0 – 0 0 0
      Jannette YOUNG, 0 0 0 – 0 1 0 – 0 0 0 – 0 0 0
      Catherine YOUNG, 0 0 0 – 0 1 0 – 0 0 0 – 0 0 0
      Maria YOUNG, 0 0 0 – 0 1 0 – 0 0 0 – 0 0 0
      Elizabeth YOUNG, 0 0 0 – 0 1 0 – 0 0 0 – 0 0 0
      Amelia YOUNG, 0 0 0 – 0 1 0 – 0 0 0 – 0 0 0
      Margaret YOUNG, 0 0 0 – 0 1 0 – 0 0 0 – 0 0 0
          Robert WILSON, 26.

#485: Family of Py CRAWFORD, 0 0 0 – 0 0 0 – 0 0 0 – 0 0 0 *(= Patty? No mark.)*
      Joanna J. GAMBOA, 0 0 0 – 0 0 0 – 0 1 0 – 0 0 0
      Francisca GAMBOA, 0 0 0 – 0 0 0 – 0 1 0 – 0 0 0
      Catalina GAMBOA, 0 0 0 – 0 0 0 – 0 0 1 – 0 0 0
      Martha RUNNALS, 0 0 0 – 0 0 0 – 0 0 1 – 0 0 0
      Clara GAMBOA, 0 0 0 – 0 0 0 – 0 0 1 – 0 0 0
      Francisco GAMBOA, 0 0 0 – 0 0 0 – 0 0 1 – 0 0 0

#486: Thomas TOWNSHEND, 0 0 0 – 1 0 0 – 0 0 0 – 1 0 0
      Rose CRAWFORD, 0 0 0 – 0 0 0 – 0 1 0 – 0 0 0
      John PETZOLD, 0 0 0 – 0 0 1 – 0 0 0 – 0 0 0
      Judith TOWNSHEND, 0 0 0 – 0 0 0 – 0 1 0 – 0 0 0
      Amy CARR, 0 0 0 – 0 0 1 – 0 0 0 – 0 0 0
          Derry, 75.

#487: Francis BALFOUR, 1 0 0 – 0 0 0 – 0 0 0 – 0 0 0

171

RECAPITULATION OF CENSUS

Whites: Males 143, Females 80; total number of Whites 223; deduct children 44; Total number of Adults 179.

Coloured: Males 420, Females 549, total number of Coloured 969, deduct children 483; Total number of Adults 486.

Free Blacks: Males 412, Females 407, total of number Free Blacks 819, deduct children 320; Total number of Adults 499.

Slaves: Males 1128, Females 649, total number of Slaves 1777, deduct children 447; add children omitted (No. 40) 6, Total number of Slaves 1783; Total number of Adults 1330.

	Males			Females	
Whites:	Children 24			Children 20	
	Adults 119			Adults 60	
Total number of White males		143	Total number of white Females		80
Coloured:	Children 230			Children 254	
	Adults 190			Adults 295	
Total number of Coloured Males		420	Total number of coloured Females		549
Free Blacks:	Children 172			Children 148	
	Adults 240			Adults 259	
Total number of Free Black Males 412			Total number of Free Black Females 407		
Slaves:	Children 233			Children 214	
	Adults 895			Adults 435	
Total number of Male Slaves		1128	Total number of Female Slaves		649
Add omitted (No. 40) children		4	Add omitted (No. 40) children		2
		1132			651

172

Final page, unnumbered:

Total number of White Males	143		Total number of White Females	80
" " Coloured Males	420		" " Coloured Females	549
" " Free Black Males	412		" " Free Black Females	407
" " Slave Males	<u>_132</u>		" " Slave Females	<u>651</u>
Total number of Males	2107		Total number of Females	1687

Total number of souls, settlers of Honduras: 3794
Return of His Majesty's Troops Stationed at
    Honduras to December 31st 1832,   251
Return of Military Pensioners on the 31st Dec.
1832 not included in the foregoing Census, <u>492</u>
    Grand Total of the Population: <u>4537</u>

Belize, Honduras, December 31st 1832.   *(signed)* Francis L. BALFOUR,
                                           Keeper of Records.

----oOo---

THE 1835 CENSUS OF BELIZE

This census, the first after emancipation, differed from earlier censuses by listing the freed slaves in their transitional legal status as Apprentice Labourers, and in failing to give their ages: a column headed "Supposed Ages of Apprentice Labourers" was not filled in. Total numbers were given in the customary order, men, then women, then children, and in many households the labourers were listed in this way; but in other households, adult and child labourers were intermixed. To clarify these mixed groups, the writer has prefixed the names with an M for man or men, W for woman or women, or C for child or children. For example, in Household #1 there are three men, no women, and two child Apprentice Labourers. In Household #2 the names make gender obvious. In #7, 2 2 0, the men and women are mixed, but there are no children and names make gender obvious, so prefixes are unnecessary. In #10, however, a woman is followed by a child, then another woman, then two men; they are shown as W: Sarah. C: Andrew. W: Sabina. M: Dick; Francis.

p.1:
#1:   John RAYBUN, 1 0 0 – 0 0 0 – 0 0 0 – 3 0 2:
      Susannah NEAL, 0 0 0 – 0 1 0 – 0 0 0 – 0 0 0
      John RAYBUN, 0 0 0 – 0 0 1 – 0 0 0 – 0 0 0
      Margaret RAYBUN, 0 0 0 – 0 0 1 – 0 0 0 – 0 0 0
      Agnes RAYBUN, 0 0 0 – 0 0 1 – 0 0 0 – 0 0 0
      Thomas RAYBUN, 0 0 0 – 0 0 1 – 0 0 0 – 0 0 0
         M: Robert; Frank; Limus. C: Beatrice; Edward.

#2:   Abigail DAWSON, 0 1 0 – 0 0 0 – 0 0 0 – 1 1 0:
      Mary DAWSON, 0 1 0 – 0 0 0 – 0 0 0
         Aberdeen; Rachel.

#3:   Margaret NEAL, 0 0 0 – 0 0 0 – 0 0 0 – 0 0 1   *(Head of household, erroneously*
      Monimia JONES, 0 0 0 – 0 1 0 – 0 0 0 – 0 0 0   *marked as a black child. Totals*
      Eliza WOOD, 0 0 0 – 0 0 1 – 0 0 0 – 0 0 0   *show 7 colored females and 1 black*
      Margaret, 0 0 0 – 0 0 1 – 0 0 0 – 0 0 0   *female.)*
      Susan, 0 0 0 – 0 0 1 – 0 0 0 – 0 0 0
      Henrietta, 0 0 0 – 0 0 1 – 0 0 0 – 0 0 0
      Mary Ann, 0 0 0 – 0 0 1 – 0 0 0 – 0 0 0
      Rebecca, 0 0 0 – 0 0 1 – 0 0 0 – 0 0 0 *(Surnames not given.)*

#4:   John USHER, 0 0 0 – 1 0 0 – 0 0 0 – 7 1 1:
      Sarah USHER, 0 0 0 – 0 1 0 – 0 0 0 – 0 0 0
      James H. USHER, 0 0 0 – 0 0 1 – 0 0 0 – 0 0 0
      Jane E. USHER, 0 0 0 – 0 0 1 – 0 0 0 – 0 0 0
      John H. USHER, 0 0 0 – 0 0 1 – 0 0 0 – 0 0 0

174

Robert USHER, 0 0 0 – 0 0 1 – 0 0 0 – 0 0 0
Charles B. USHER, 0 0 0 – 0 0 1 – 0 0 0 – 0 0 0 (= Charles Beach Usher, d. 1838.)
      M: Joseph USHER; Edward USHER; Ned USHER; Prince USHER; Jacob
      USHER; Lord USHER; Cuffee USHER. W: Jenny USHER. C: Francis
      USHER.

p. 2:
#5: William COURTNEY, 0 0 0 – 1 0 0 – 0 0 0 – 0 0 0
     Edward COURTNAY, 0 0 0 – 0 0 1 – 0 0 0 – 0 0 0
     Amelia COURTNEY, 0 0 0 – 0 0 1 – 0 0 0 – 0 0 0
     Elizabeth COURTNEY, 0 0 0 – 0 0 1 – 0 0 0 – 0 0 0
     Harriett COURTNEY, 0 0 0 – 0 0 1 – 0 0 0 – 0 0 0
     George COURTNEY, 0 0 0 – 0 0 1 – 0 0 0 – 0 0 0
     Allen COURTNEY, 0 0 0 – 0 0 1 – 0 0 0 – 0 0 0
     Eve COURTNEY, 0 0 0 – 0 1 0 – 0 0 0 – 0 0 0
     Ellen COURTNEY, 0 0 0 – 0 0 1 – 0 0 0 – 0 0 0

#6: Alexander FRANCE, 1 0 0 – 0 0 0 – 0 0 0 – 26 17 2:
     Ariadne FRANCE, 0 0 0 – 0 1 0 – 0 0 0 – 0 0 0

*Three of the labourers below are not marked either as men, women, or children, and are
not included in the totals. The 1832 census shows them as Robert, 24, George, 22, and
Evelina, 7. Were they incapacitated in some way?*

      M: Joe FRANCE; John FRANCE; Derry FRANCE; Charles FRANCE;
      Bachus [*sic*] FRANCE; Andrew FRANCE; Bill FRANCE; Adam FRANCE;
      Jackey FRANCE; Thomas FRANCE; Morgan FRANCE; James CADDLE;
      Glasgow FRANCE; James FRANCE; Robert FRANCE *(no mark;)* Richard
      FRANCE; George FRANCE *(no mark;)* Morrison FRANCE; Brown
      FRANCE; Richmond FRANCE; Harry FRANCE; Hamlet FRANCE.

p. 3:   Joe FRANCE; Otway FRANCE; Samuel FRANCE. C: Edward FRANCE;
      Marcus FRANCE; Thomas FRANCE; Johnston FRANCE; Nelson FRANCE;
      Jerry FRANCE; Caesar FRANCE; Hercules FRANCE; Robert FRANCE;
      Alexander FRANCE; Devonshire FRANCE; Prince FRANCE. W: Mary
      FRANCE; Sylvia FRANCE; Hetty FRANCE; Arabella FRANCE;
      Betsy FRANCE; Nelly FRANCE; Louisa FRANCE; Emma FRANCE; Molly
      FRANCE; Patience FRANCE; Jenny FRANCE; Nancy FRANCE; Prudence
      FRANCE; Evilina FRANCE *(no mark;)* Emily FRANCE; Elizabeth FRANCE;
      Phillis FRANCE; Jessie FRANCE;

p. 4:   C: Deanna FRANCE; Mary Frances FRANCE.

#7: James WAGNER, 0 0 0 – 1 0 0 – 0 0 0 – 2 2 0:
     Elizabeth SMITH, 0 0 0 – 0 0 0 – 0 1 0 – 0 0 0
     Catherine JOSEPH, 0 0 0 – 0 0 0 – 0 1 0 – 0 0 0

George WAGNER, 0 0 0 – 0 0 1 – 0 0 0 – 0 0 0
James WAGNER, 0 0 0 – 0 0 1 – 0 0 0 – 0 0 0
William NEAL, 0 0 0 – 0 0 1 – 0 0 0 – 0 0 0
    Diana; Simon; Jack; Eve.

#8:   Edward BOWMAN, 0 0 0 – 0 0 0 – 1 0 0 – 0 0 0
John BOWMAN, 0 0 0 – 0 0 0 – 1 0 0 – 0 0 0
Edward BOWMAN, 0 0 0 – 0 0 0 – 0 0 1 – 0 0 0
William H. BOWMAN, 0 0 0 – 0 0 0 – 0 0 1 – 0 0 0
George BOWMAN, 0 0 0 – 0 0 0 – 0 0 1 – 0 0 0
Maria BOWMAN, 0 0 0 – 0 0 0 – 0 0 1 – 0 0 0
Jane BOWMAN, 0 0 0 – 0 0 0 – 0 0 1 – 0 0 0
Emily BOWMAN, 0 0 0 – 0 0 0 – 0 0 1 – 0 0 0
Thomas D. BOWMAN, 0 0 0 – 0 0 0 – 0 0 1 – 0 0 0
Daniel T. BOWMAN, 0 0 0 – 0 0 0 – 0 0 1 – 0 0 0
William FANTESSAY, 0 0 0 – 0 0 0 – 0 0 1 – 0 0 0
Matilda GARRETT, 0 0 0 – 0 0 0 – 0 1 0 – 0 0 0
Molly HORN, 0 0 0 – 0 0 0 – 0 1 0 – 0 0 0

#9:   Patience GORDON, 0 0 0 – 0 1 0 – 0 0 0 – 0 2 4:
William CADLE, 0 0 0 – 0 0 1 – 0 0 0 – 0 0 0
    W: Amelia; Milly. C: James; William; Elizabeth; John.

p. 5:
#10: Ann ELRINGTON, 0 1 0 – 0 0 0 – 0 0 0 – 2 2 1:
Ann Eliza ELRINGTON, 0 1 0 – 0 0 0 – 0 0 0 – 0 0 0
George E. WARREN, 1 0 0 – 0 0 0 – 0 0 0 – 0 0 0
William PEEBLES, 1 0 0 – 0 0 0 – 0 0 0 – 0 0 0
    The property of G. E. WARREN & William PEEBLES:
    W: Sarah. C: Andrew. W: Sabina. M: Dick; Francis.
    (From the order given, one would think Sarah was Andrew's mother.)

#11: Francis FORD, 1 0 0 – 0 0 0 – 0 0 0 – 2 3 4:
Betheney FORD, 0 1 0 – 0 0 0 – 0 0 0 – 0 0 0
Sarah DAWSON, 0 1 0 – 0 0 0 – 0 0 0 – 0 0 0
    W: Betty; Maria; Nancy. M: George; James. C: Daniel; Harry; Richard;
    Francis.

#12: James HENRY, 0 0 0 – 0 0 0 – 1 0 0 – 0 0 0
Fidelia TUCKER, 0 0 0 – 0 0 0 – 0 1 0 – 0 0 0
Robert TUCKER, 0 0 0 – 0 0 0 – 1 0 0 – 0 0 0
William TUCKER, 0 0 0 – 0 0 0 – 0 1 0 – 0 0 0 *(Error - marked as female.)*
Lucy TUCKER, 0 0 0 – 0 0 0 – 0 1 0 – 0 0 0.
Sophia TUCKER, 0 0 0 – 0 0 1 – 0 0 0 – 0 0 0.

#13: James LEMOTE, [sic] 0 0 0 – 0 0 0 – 1 0 0 – 0 0 0
James LAMOTE Jr., [sic] 0 0 0 – 0 0 0 – 0 0 1 – 0 0 0
Phillip LAMOTE, 0 0 0 – 0 0 0 – 0 0 1 – 0 0 0

p. 6:
#14: Mary COKER, 0 0 0 – 0 1 0 – 0 0 0 – 0 1 0:
Harriet GODFREY.

#15: The Estate of Jane HINKS, 1 2 0:
Nancy HINKS; Matembe HINKS; Fatima HINKS.

#16: Anna MEIGHAN, 0 1 0 – 0 0 0 – 0 0 0 – 4 1 0:   *(Nee GAPPER; widow of*
Anna Maria ESTRADA, 0 0 0 – 0 0 1 – 0 0 0 – 0 0 0   *Edward MEIGHAN.)*
Joe; Philip; Prince; Henry; Maria.   *(Joe GAPPER.)*

#17: William CARR, 0 0 0 – 0 0 0 – 1 0 0 – 0 0 0
James CARR, 0 0 0 – 0 0 0 – 0 0 1 – 0 0 0

#18: William WALSH, 1 0 0 – 0 0 0 – 0 0 0 – 6 6 0:
Mary J. WALSH, 0 1 0 – 0 0 0 – 0 0 0 – 0 0 0
R. W. CORVAN, 1 0 0 – 0 0 0 – 0 0 0 – 0 0 0
Henry PASLOW; John WALSH; London; Thomas WALSH; Daniel
COLQUHOUN; Nancy; Kate; Tenah; Mary DIXON; Edmund;
Judith; Emma.

p. 7:
#19: Margaret PERRY, 0 1 0 – 0 0 0 – 0 0 0 – 1 4 1:
Catherine WEELER, [sic] 0 1 0 – 0 0 0 – 0 0 0 – 0 0 0
James BERTIE, 1 0 0 – 0 0 0 – 0 0 0 – 0 0 0
George PEDDIE, 1 0 0 – 0 0 0 – 0 0 0 – 0 0 0
Margaret PERRY, 0 1 0 – 0 0 0 – 0 0 0 – 0 0 0
M: Samuel. C: George NICHOLSON. W: Nancy; Sylvia HARRIS; Diana;
Nancy.

#20: Elizabeth TILLETT, 0 0 0 – 0 1 0 – 0 0 0 – 14 10 5:
Daniel TILLETT, 0 0 0 – 1 0 0 – 0 0 0 – 0 0 0
Catherine TILLETT, 0 0 0 – 0 0 1 – 0 0 0 – 0 0 0
Susan Elizabeth REYNOLDS, 0 0 0 – 0 0 1 – 0 0 0 – 0 0 0
M: Benjamin HEMMING; Joe COOLIN; Joe WILSON; Roderick; Joe
PURCELL; Hunter HUNT; Marriott; Felix; Ratcliff; Peter ANDERSON;
Harry BURNHAM; Peter CABBAGE RIDGE; Charles MUCKLEHANEY;
Dick. W: Present; Cladia [sic]; Hannah; Dorcas; Margaret; Louisa; Patty;
Nancy; Caroline; Franky. C: Jose;

p. 8:   C: Henry; Phoebe; Eleanor; Amelia.

177

#21: John POTTS, 0 0 0 – 1 0 0 – 0 0 0 – 14 0 0: *(Jr., son of J. Potts Sr.)*
Mary Ann POTTS, 0 0 0 – 0 0 1 – 0 0 0 – 0 0 0 *(Dau. J. P. Jr. & Eliz^(th) Tillett.)*
Chance WRIGHT; Eboe James; Charley WALL; James FLOWERS;
Richmond; Tom REDUGIN; John DESMO; Bat YOUNG; Hercules; John
PUPPO; Ben POPHAM; Jack SNOWDEN; John HERCULES;
Frederick.

#22: Ann CHAMPAGNE, 0 0 0 – 0 1 0 – 0 0 0 – 0 1 0:
Joshua APPLEBY, 0 0 0 – 1 0 0 – 0 0 0 – 0 0 0
Daniel McFOY, 0 0 0 – 0 0 1 – 0 0 0 – 0 0 0
Emma GENTLE, 0 0 0 – 0 0 1 – 0 0 0 – 0 0 0
Venus HEWLETT, 0 0 0 – 0 0 0 – 0 1 0 – 0 0 0
Benjamin HEWLETT, 0 0 0 – 0 0 0 – 0 0 1 – 0 0 0
William HEWLETT, 0 0 0 – 0 0 0 – 1 0 0 – 0 0 0
Sarah DeBRIEN, 0 0 0 – 0 0 0 – 0 0 1 – 0 0 0
Louisa.

p. 9:
#23: Samantee YOUNG, 0 0 0 – 0 1 0 – 0 0 0 – 0 0 0
William Francis YOUNG, 0 0 0 – 0 0 1 – 0 0 0 – 0 0 0
Mary Frances YOUNG, 0 0 0 – 0 0 1 – 0 0 0 – 0 0 0

#24: Catherine HUME, 0 0 0 – 0 1 0 – 0 0 0 – 1 1 0:
Frances H. WALDRON, 0 0 0 – 0 1 0 – 0 0 0 – 0 0 0
Jane R. WALDRON, 0 0 0 – 0 1 0 – 0 0 0 – 0 0 0
Brasilla, William.

#25: Isidore DUMAS, 0 0 0 – 0 0 0 – 1 0 0 – 0 0 0
Maria ISIDORE, 0 0 0 – 0 0 0 – 0 1 0 – 0 0 0
Amelia LEMOINE, 0 0 0 – 0 1 0 – 0 0 0 – 0 0 0
John LEMOINE, 0 0 0 – 1 0 0 – 0 0 0 – 0 0 0
Pear [sic] LEMOINE, 0 0 0 – 1 0 0 – 0 0 0 – 0 0 0 *(= Pierre.)*
Eleanor ISIDORE, 0 0 0 – 0 0 0 – 0 0 1 – 0 0 0
Sarah BELISLE, 0 0 0 – 0 1 0 – 0 0 0 – 0 0 0
Louisa BELISLE, 0 0 0 – 0 1 0 – 0 0 0 – 0 0 0
George BELISLE, 0 0 0 – 1 0 0 – 0 0 0 – 0 0 0
Margaret ISIDORE, 0 0 0 – 0 0 0 – 0 0 1 – 0 0 0

#26: George L. GRISTOCK, 1 0 0 – 0 0 0 – 0 0 0 – 2 1 4:
John VALPY, 1 0 0 – 0 0 0 – 0 0 0 – 0 0 0
Eliza GIBSON, 0 0 0 – 0 1 0 – 0 0 0 – 0 0 0
Carolina GRISTOCK, 0 0 0 – 0 0 1 – 0 0 0 – 0 0 0
Georgeanna GRISTOCK, 0 0 0 – 0 0 1 – 0 0 0 – 0 0 0
Sarah GRISTOCK, 0 0 0 – 0 0 1 – 0 0 0 – 0 0 0
George H. GRISTOCK, 0 0 0 – 0 0 1 – 0 0 0 – 0 0 0

W: Mintas LAMB. C: Sam LAMB; Amelia LAMB; Sophia JEAMES; William JEAMES. M: Alick; Doctor Hare.

p. 10:
#27: Nannett SWAN, 0 0 0 – 3 0 0 – 0 1 0 – 0 0 0
John SWAN, 0 0 0 – 0 0 C – 1 0 0 – 0 0 0
A. SWAN, 0 0 0 – 0 0 0 – 1 0 0 – 0 0 0
Margaret PERRUE, 0 0 0 – 0 0 0 – 0 1 0 – 0 0 0
The property of Nannett SWAN & Margaret PERRUE: 1 1 0:
Pope; Prudence.

#28: John CADDLE, 0 0 0 – 1 0 0 – 0 0 0 – 5 2 0:
Patty ENDIN, 0 0 0 – 0 1 0 – 0 0 0 – 0 0 0
William CADDLE, 0 0 0 – 0 0 1 – 0 0 0 – 0 0 0
Eleanor CADDLE, 0 0 0 – 0 1 0 – 0 0 0 – 0 0 0
Edward CODD, 0 0 0 – 0 0 1 – 0 0 0 – 0 0 0
The Property of John & Eleanor CADDLE:
George; Peggy; Billy; Joe; George; Prince; Olive.

#29: Robert PRICE, 0 0 0 – 0 0 C – 1 0 0 – 0 0 0
Thomas PRICE, 0 0 0 – 0 0 0 – 0 0 1 – 0 0 0
Richard PRICE, 0 0 0 – 0 C 0 – 0 0 1 – 0 0 0
Robert PRICE, 0 0 0 – 0 0 0 – 0 0 1 – 0 0 0

#30: Mary WINTER, 0 0 0 – 0 1 0 – 0 0 0 – 0 0 0
Nancy GADDIS, 0 0 0 – 0 0 0 – 0 1 0 – 0 0 0
Nancy MEIGHAN, 0 0 0 – 0 0 1 – 0 0 0 – 0 0 0
Codd BALDWIN, 0 0 0 – 0 0 1 – 0 0 0 – 0 0 0
The property of Codd BALDWIN: 1 3 2:
W: Evelina; Betsy; Cloe. M: Benjamin.
C: Ann Grace; George H. GRISTOCK.

p. 11:
#31: Francis YOUNG, 0 0 0 – 1 0 0 – 0 0 0 – 1 1 0
Amelia LONGSWORTH, 0 0 0 – 0 1 0 – 0 0 0 – 0 0 0
Elizabeth; Peter.

#32: Henry WHYER [*sic*], 0 0 0 – 0 0 0 – 1 0 0 – 0 0 0
Henrietta HOWE, 0 0 0 – 0 0 0 – 0 1 0 – 0 0 0
Peter HENRY, 0 0 0 – 0 0 0 – 0 0 1 – 0 0 0

#33: Jervis HARRISON, 1 0 0 – 0 0 0 – 0 0 0 – 0 1 0:
Nancy USHER.

#34: George TILLETT, 1 0 0 – 0 0 0 – 0 0 0 – 7 3 5:
Sarah TILLETT, 0 1 0 – 0 0 0 – 0 0 0 – 0 0 0

179

M: Nelson; Joseph; Teslar; Rum & Water; George WILSON; Jemmy; Moco Jem. C: James. W: Sue; Jane; Jenny. C: Daniel; Martha; Amelia; Charles.

p. 12:

#35: Joseph GOFF, 0 0 0 – 1 0 0 – 0 0 0 – 2 4 3:
Celia GOFF, 0 0 0 – 0 1 0 – 0 0 0 – 0 0 0
Joan WHITEHEAD, 0 0 0 – 0 1 0 – 0 0 0 – 0 0 0
W: Eleanor GOFF; Behaviour GOFF; Polly GOFF; Betsy GOFF.
C: John GOFF; Joan GOFF; Sarah GOFF. M: William GOFF;
Cuffee GOFF.

#36: Charles BLADON, 1 0 0 – 0 0 0 – 0 0 0 – 1 0 0:
Sarah YOUNG, 0 0 0 – 0 1 0 – 0 0 0 – 0 0 0
Ann E. GILL, 0 0 0 – 0 1 0 – 0 0 0 – 0 0 0
Robert H. GILL, 0 0 0 – 0 0 1 – 0 0 0 – 0 0 0
Agness GILL, 0 0 0 – 0 0 1 – 0 0 0 – 0 0 0
James YOUNG.

#37: The Property of George HYDE, 61 4 11:
M: Adam ANDERSON; Aaron ANDERSON; Adam YOUNG; Hamlet
ANDERSON; Sam BELISLE; Breechie HYDE; George BULL; Bogle;
Cato HYDE; William CADLE; Caesar HYDE; Daniel COURTNEY;

p. 13: Davy HYDE; Daniel HYDE; Edmund BURNS; Frank HYDE; Frederick
HYDE; Phillip GARNETT; George HYDE; Bob GAPPER; George
THOMAS; George HYDE; George WALDRON; George HOME;
Harry HYDE; Hercules HYDE; Hazard HYDE; William HUNT; Tom
HOME; Harry WALDRON; James HYDE; Jack HYDE; Louis WALDRON;
Tom LAURIE; Monday HYDE; McLACHLAN; Nelson HYDE; Ned
HYDE; Nicholas HYDE; Rodney PASLOW; Prince HYDE; Charles
PARKER; James POTTS; Quashie BONNY;*
*In earlier censuses, Bonny QUASHIE.

p. 14: Quashie Papa; Robert WALDRON; Rodney HYDE; Tom ROVER; Peter
RUMFORD; Jeffry SHAW; Tom HYDE; Thomas HYDE; Tom Eboe; Philip
TAIT; Tommy FERGUSON; John WOOD; Edward WALL; William
HYDE; Charles HARRIS; Harry HARRIS. W: Jeanette SHAW.
C: Lucretia HYDE, Charlotte HYDE; Mary LAMB; Fanny LAMB; Rachel
LAMB; John LAMB. M: Toby USHER. W: Phoebe USHER; Sabina
USHER; Rose USHER. C: William USHER; Betsy USHER; Daniel
USHER; Charles USHER; Ellick HYDE.

p. 15: W: Rose HYDE; Peggy HYDE.

180

#38: Thomas TONSEND [*sic*], 0 0 0 – 1 0 0 – 0 0 0 – 0 0 0
Judy TOWNSEND, 0 0 0 – 0 0 0 – 0 1 0 – 0 0 0
Derry POTTS, 0 0 0 – 0 0 0 – 1 0 0 – 0 0 0
Ann TOWNSEND, 0 0 0 – 0 1 0 – 0 0 0 – 0 0 0

#39: Isaiah SIMMONS, 0 0 0 – 0 0 0 – 1 0 0 – 1 0 1:
Thomas SIMMONS, 0 0 0 – 0 0 0 – 0 0 1 – 0 0 0
Isaiah SIMMONS, 0 0 0 – 0 0 0 – 0 0 1 – 0 0 0
        M: Adam SIMMONS. C: Cudjoe SIMMONS.

#40: John STAIN, 0 0 0 – 1 0 0 – 0 0 0 – 1 1 6 0:
Elizabeth STAIN, 0 0 0 – 0 1 0 – 0 0 0 – 0 0 0
John STAIN, 0 0 0 – 0 0 1 – 0 0 0 – 0 0 0
Francis STAIN, 0 0 0 – 0 0 1 – 0 0 0 – 0 0 0
        Toney; Alick; Scotland; Quamina; Harry; John; Thomas; William
        ALLICK; William WAIR [*sic*]; Edward; Henry.
        Lucretia; Mary; Eliza; Elizabeth; Lucretia [*sic*]; Harriott.

p. 16:
#41: John CROFT, 1 0 0 – 0 0 0 – 0 0 0 – 0 0 0
Jane PARKER, 0 1 0 – 0 0 0 – 0 0 0 – 0 0 0
Ann STAIN, 0 0 0 – 0 1 0 – 0 0 0 – 0 0 0
Maria CROFT, 0 0 0 – 0 1 0 – 0 0 0 – 0 0 0
Caroline A. CROFT, 0 0 0 – 0 0 1 – 0 0 0 – 0 0 0

#42: Alexander FORBES, 1 0 0 – 0 0 0 – 0 0 0 – 0 1 0:
James ROBERTS, 1 0 0 – 0 0 0 – 0 0 0 – 0 0 0
David HYDE, 0 0 0 – 0 0 1 – 0 0 0 – 0 0 0
        Christian BROSTER.

#43: William LEWIS, 1 0 0 – 0 0 0 – 0 0 0 – 0 0 0
Margaret LEWIS, 0 0 0 – 0 1 0 – 0 0 0 – 0 0 0
William T. LEWIS, 0 0 0 – 0 0 1 – 0 0 0 – 0 0 0
Mary E. LEWIS, 0 0 0 – 0 0 1 – 0 0 0 – 0 0 0
Julia A. LEWIS, 0 0 0 – 0 0 1 – 0 0 0 – 0 0 0
John A. LEWIS, 0 0 0 – 0 0 1 – 0 0 0 – 0 0 0
Mary BLYTH, 0 0 0 – 0 1 0 – 0 0 0 – 0 0 0

#44: George GARNETT, 0 0 0 – 1 0 0 – 0 0 0 – 5 3 0:
Ann Maria GARNETT, 0 0 0 – 0 1 0 – 0 0 0 – 0 0 0
John GARNETT, 0 0 0 – 0 0 1 – 0 0 0 – 0 0 0
William QUILTER, 0 0 0 – 0 0 1 – 0 0 0 – 0 0 0
Cloe SMALL, 0 0 0 – 0 1 0 – 0 0 0 – 0 0 0
Eliza HENRY, 0 0 0 – 0 0 0 – 0 1 0 – 0 0 0
George PETATLEY, 0 0 0 – 0 0 1 – 0 0 0 – 0 0 0 *(= PITKETHLY.)*
Martin LE CRUIT, 0 0 0 – 1 0 0 – 0 0 0 – 0 0 0

181

Joseph FORTUNE, 0 0 0 – 0 0 0 – 1 0 0 – 0 0 0
Jose ALBERTO, 0 0 0 – 1 0 0 – 0 0 0 – 0 0 0
Jose KELMUCO, 0 0 0 – 0 0 0 – 1 0 0 – 0 0 0
Quamina JACKSON, 0 0 0 – 0 0 0 – 0 0 1 – 0 0 0
     James DUNN; Samuel MEIGHAN; Jonathan MEIGHAN; Jespa [*sic*]
     WALDRON; Scotland WALDRON. Eliza GRAY; Eleanor YOUNG;
     Fanny MOODY.

p. 17:
#45:   Ann SWASEY, 0 0 0 – 0 1 0 – 0 0 0 – 6 2 4:
     M: Robert SWASEY; William SWASEY; Maligo SWASEY; Henry
     SWASEY; George SWASEY. C: Benjamin SWASEY. W: Nancy
     SWASEY; Eve SWASEY. C: Maria SWASEY; Daphne SWASEY; Cuba
     SWASEY. M: Francis SWASEY.

#46:   Maria EDWARDS, 0 0 0 – 0 0 0 – 0 1 0 – 0 0 0
     Henry RAND, 0 0 0 – 0 0 0 – 1 0 0 – 0 0 0

#47:   Andrew PIPERSBURG, 0 0 0 – 0 0 0 – 1 0 0 – 0 0 0
     Sarah PIPERSBURG, 0 0 0 – 0 0 0 – 0 1 0 – 0 0 0
     Mary Ann PIPERSBURG, 0 0 0 – 0 0 0 – 0 1 0 – 0 0 0
     Henry PIPERSBURG, 0 0 0 – 0 0 0 – 1 0 0 – 0 0 0
     Fidelia PIPERSBURG, 0 0 0 – 0 0 0 – 1 0 0 – 0 0 0
     David PIPERSBURG, 0 0 0 – 0 0 0 – 1 0 0 – 0 0 0
     George CATOOSE, 0 0 0 – 0 0 0 – 1 0 0 – 0 0 0 *(in 1832, CATOUCHE)*
     James CATOOSE, 0 0 0 – 0 0 0 – 1 0 0 – 0 0 0   "   "   "
     Maria FLOWERS, 0 0 0 – 0 0 0 – 0 1 0 – 0 0 0
     Nancy PIPERSBURG, 0 0 0 – 0 0 0 – 0 1 0 – 0 0 0
     Nancy PIPERSBURG, 0 0 0 – 0 0 0 – 0 0 1 – 0 0 0
     James H. PIPERSBURG, 0 0 0 – 0 0 0 – 0 0 1 – 0 0 0

p. 18:
#48:   Elizabeth JONES, 0 0 0 – 0 0 0 – 0 1 0 – 0 0 0
     Grace JONES, 0 0 0 – 0 0 0 – 0 1 0 – 0 0 0
     Silvia JONES, 0 0 0 – 0 0 0 – 0 1 0 – 0 0 0
     Margaret STANFORD, 0 0 0 – 0 0 0 – 0 1 0 – 0 0 0
     Ann STANFORD, 0 0 0 – 0 0 0 – 0 1 0 – 0 0 0
     Elizabeth STANFORD, 0 0 0 – 0 0 0 – 0 0 1 – 0 0 0
     Mary STANFORD, 0 0 0 – 0 0 0 – 0 0 1 – 0 0 0
     Bella STANFORD, 0 0 0 – 0 0 0 – 0 0 1 – 0 0 0
     Maria GORDON, 0 0 0 – 0 0 0 – 0 0 1 – 0 0 0
     Damon GORDON, 0 0 0 – 0 0 0 – 0 0 1 – 0 0 0
     James GIBSON, 0 0 0 – 0 0 0 – 0 0 1 – 0 0 0
     Mary WILLIAMS, 0 0 0 – 0 0 0 – 0 0 1 – 0 0 0
     John AUGUST, 0 0 0 – 0 0 0 – 0 0 1 – 0 0 0
     Anna EARNEST, 0 0 0 – 0 0 0 – 0 0 1 – 0 0 0

Rosanna EARNEST, 0 0 0 – 0 0 0 – 0 0 1 – 0 0 0
Adam EARNEST, 0 0 0 – 0 0 0 – 0 0 1 – 0 0 0
Flora JONES, 0 0 0 – 0 0 0 – 0 0 1 – 0 0 0
John BAKER, 0 0 0 – 0 0 0 – 0 0 1 – 0 0 0

#49:   Charles FLOWERS, 0 0 0 – 0 0 0 – 1 0 0 – 1 0 0:
       Margaret FLOWERS, 0 0 0 – 0 0 0 – 0 1 0 – 0 0 0
       Caesar FLOWERS, 0 0 0 – 0 0 0 – 1 0 0 – 0 0 0
       Richard FLOWERS, 0 0 0 – 0 0 0 – 1 0 0 – 0 0 0
       Fanny FLOWERS, 0 0 0 – 0 0 0 – 0 1 0 – 0 0 0
       Joseph FLOWERS, 0 0 0 – 0 0 0 – 0 0 1 – 0 0 0
       Prue FLOWERS, 0 0 0 – 0 0 0 – 0 0 1 – 0 0 0
       Stevenson FLOWERS, 0 0 0 – 0 0 0 – 0 0 1 – 0 0 0
          Prince.

p. 19:
#50:   William HAMILTON, 0 0 0 – 1 0 0 – 0 0 0 – 0 0 0
       Richard HAMILTON, 0 0 0 – 0 0 1 – 0 0 0 – 0 0 0
       William HAMILTON, 0 0 0 – 0 0 1 – 0 0 0 – 0 0 0
       John HAMILTON, 0 0 0 – 0 0 1 – 0 0 0 – 0 0 0
       Alexander M. HAMILTON, 0 0 0 – 0 0 1 – 0 0 0 – 0 0 0
       Sarah HAMILTON, 0 0 0 – 0 0 1 – 0 0 0 – 0 0 0
       Eliza HAMILTON, 0 0 0 – 0 0 1 – 0 0 0 – 0 0 0
       Sophia HAMILTON, 0 0 0 – 0 0 1 – 0 0 0 – 0 0 0
       Dorinda HUME, 0 0 0 – 0 0 0 – 0 1 0 – 0 0 0

#51:   Eliza BELISLE, 0 0 0 – 0 0 0 – 0 1 0 – 0 0 0
       Catherine BELISLE, 0 0 0 – 0 0 0 – 0 1 0 – 0 0 0

#52:   George BURN, 1 0 0 – 0 0 0 – 0 0 0 – 3 2 4:
       Elizabeth GILLETT, 0 0 0 – 0 1 0 – 0 0 0 – 0 0 0
       Mary BURN, 0 0 0 – 0 0 1 – 0 0 0 – 0 0 0
       (Not Christened) BURN, 0 0 0 – 0 0 1 – 0 0 0 – 0 0 0
          M: George; Cuffee; Thomas. C: John. W: Silvy; Fanny. C: Joseph;
          Richard; Nancy.

#53:   Joseph JONES, 0 0 0 – 0 0 0 – 1 0 0 – 2 0 0:
       Fanny JONES, 0 0 0 – 0 1 0 – 0 0 0 – 0 0 0
          Jemmy; Caesar.

p. 20:
#54:   John SAVORY, 0 0 0 – 1 0 0 – 0 0 0 – 0 0 0
       Celia BELISLE, 0 0 0 – 0 1 0 – 0 0 0 – 0 0 0
       John SAVORY, 0 0 0 – 0 0 1 – 0 0 0 – 0 0 0
       Eliza SAVORY, 0 0 0 – 0 0 1 – 0 0 0 – 0 0 0
       Mary SAVORY, 0 0 0 – 0 0 1 – 0 0 0 – 0 0 0
       Charles SAVORY, 0 0 0 – 0 0 1 – 0 0 0 – 0 0 0

183

Amelia SAVORY, 0 0 0 – 0 0 1 – 0 0 0 – 0 0 0
Lawrence SAVORY, 0 0 0 – 0 0 1 – 0 0 0 – 0 0 0

#55:   Charles ANDREWS, 0 0 0 – 1 0 0 – 0 0 0 – 0 0 0
       Elizabeth HUMES, 0 0 0 – 0 1 0 – 0 0 0 – 0 0 0

#56:   Mary ELRINGTON, 0 1 0 – 0 0 0 – 0 0 0 – 1 0 0:
       Robert ELRINGTON.

#57:   Richard ANDERSON, 0 0 0 – 1 0 0 – 0 0 0 – 25 11 0:
       Scipio; Murphy; Scotland; Quashie; November; Charlie; Charlie
       (Mandingo); Warwick; Cato; Bobby; Cuffee; Peter; Robert; Daniel;
       Duncan;

p. 21:   John; Toby; Blaknell; Jacob; Caesar; Nelson; Davy; Rodney; Henry; Cato;
         Sophia; Mary Ann; Maria; Hannah; Charlotte; Peggy; Sarah; Patience;
         Peggy; Grace; Friendship.

#58:   James TUCKER, 0 0 0 – 0 0 0 – 1 0 0 – 2 0 0:
       Maria TUCKER, 0 0 0 – 0 0 0 – 0 1 0 – 0 0 0
       Memba HEWLETT, 0 0 0 – 0 0 0 – 0 1 0 – 0 0 0
       Tamias; Francis.

#59:   Samuel FORBES, 1 0 0 – 0 0 0 – 0 0 0 – 0 0 0
       Jane AUGUST, 0 0 0 – 0 1 0 – 0 0 0 – 0 0 0
       Elizabeth FORBES, 0 0 0 – 0 0 1 – 0 0 0 – 0 0 0

p. 22:
#60:   Benjn ROBINSON, 0 0 0 – 0 0 0 – 1 0 0 – 0 0 0
       Adam ROBINSON, 0 0 0 – 0 0 0 – 0 0 1 – 0 0 0
       Mary ROBINSON, 0 0 0 – 0 0 0 – 0 0 1 – 0 0 0

#61:   Richd S. ALLEN, 1 0 0 – 0 0 0 – 0 0 0 – 0 0 0
       Eliza ALLEN, 0 1 0 – 0 0 0 – 0 0 0 – 0 0 0
       Jane ALLEN, 0 0 1 – 0 0 0 – 0 0 0 – 0 0 0

#62:   Jane PANTING, 0 0 0 – 0 1 0 – 0 0 0 – 0 2 0:
       Peter YOUNG, 0 0 0 – 0 0 1 – 0 0 0 – 0 0 0
       Alice C. HAMPSHIRE, 0 0 0 – 0 0 1 – 0 0 0 – 0 0 0
       Sally JACKSON; Eleanor PANTING.

#63:   Philip RICHARDSON, 0 0 0 – 0 0 0 – 1 0 0 – 0 0 0
       Mary RICHARDSON, 0 0 0 – 0 0 0 – 0 1 0 – 0 0 0

#64:   William SMITH, 1 0 0 – 0 0 0 – 0 0 0 – 6 3 0:
       Rebecca SMITH, 0 0 1 – 0 0 0 – 0 0 0 – 0 0 0

184

Francis SMITH, 0 0 1 – 0 0 0 – 0 0 0 – 0 0 0
Stephen SMITH, 0 0 1 – 0 0 0 – 0 0 0 – 0 0 0
     Sarah CLARK, Mary SMITH; Nanny SMITH; John SMITH;
     Sampson SMITH; William SMITH; Benjamin SMITH; Harry SMITH;
     Abel SMITH.

p. 23:
#65: James BELISLE, C 0 0 – 1 0 0 – 0 0 0 – 0 0 0
       C. BELISLE, 0 0 C – 0 1 0 – 0 0 0 – 0 0 0
       Joseph BELISLE, 0 0 C - 1 0 0 - 0 0 0 – 0 0 0
       Margaret BELISLE, 0 0 0 – 0 0 1 – 0 0 0 – 0 0 0
       Hannah BELISLE, 0 0 C – 0 0 1 – 0 0 0 – 0 0 0
       Jane BELISLE, 0 0 0 – 0 0 1 – 0 0 0 – 0 0 0
       John BELISLE, 0 0 0 – 0 0 1 – 0 0 0 – 0 0 0

#66: William GODFRY, 0 0 0 – 1 0 0 – 0 0 0 – 0 0 0
       Elsa GODFRY, 0 0 0 – 0 0 1 – 0 0 0 – 0 0 0
       William STAMFORD [sic], 0 0 0 – 0 0 0 – 0 0 1 – 0 0 0
       Henry WARIOR [sic], C 0 0 – 0 0 0 – 0 0 1 – 0 0 0
       Margaret Frances BARTHOLOMEW, 0 0 0 – 0 1 0 – 0 1 0 – 0 0 0
          (Enumerator's error: marked both as coloured and as black.)

#67: John WAGNOR, 0 0 0 – 1 0 0 – 0 0 0 – 0 0 0
       Elizabeth WAGNOR, C 0 0 – 0 1 0 – 0 0 0 – 0 0 0
       Sarah WAGNOR, 0 0 C – 0 0 1 – 0 0 0 – 0 0 0
       Robert WAGNOR. 0 0 0 – 0 0 1 – 0 0 0 – 0 0 0
       Luisa WAGNOR, 0 0 0 – 0 0 1 – 0 0 0 – 0 0 0
       Catherine WAGNOR, 0 0 0 – 0 0 1 – 0 0 0 – 0 0 0
       Mary WAGNOR, 0 0 0 – 0 0 1 – 0 0 0 – 0 0 0

p. 24:
#68: Jane JEFFRIES, 0 0 0 – 0 1 0 – 0 0 0 – 0 0 0
       Thomas M. SMITH, 0 0 0 – 0 0 1 – 0 0 0 – 0 0 0
       Elizabeth Ann DICKENSON, 0 0 0 – 0 0 1 – 0 0 0 – 0 0 0
       Latecia JEFFREYS, 0 0 0 – 0 0 0 – 0 1 0 – 0 0 0
       Maria JEFFREYS, 0 0 0 – 0 0 0 – 0 1 0 – 0 0 0
       Felis JEFFREYS, 0 0 0 – 0 0 1 – 0 0 0 – 0 0 0
       Wm BETTY, 0 0 0 – 0 0 0 – 1 0 0 – 0 0 0
       Simon JEFFREYS. 0 0 0 – 0 0 0 – 1 0 0 – 0 0 0
       Bresto JEFFRIES, [sic] 0 0 0 – 0 0 0 – 1 0 0 – 0 0 0
       Peter JEFFRIES, 0 0 0 – 0 0 0 – 0 0 1 – 0 0 0

#69: Elizabeth JEFFRIES, 0 0 0 – 0 1 0 – 0 0 0 – 0 0 0
       Mary Ann GRAEM, 0 0 0 – 0 0 1 – 0 0 0
       David GRAEM, 0 0 0 – 0 0 1 – 0 0 0 – 0 0 0
       Latitia JEFFRIES, 0 0 0 – 0 0 0 – 0 1 0 – 0 0 0

185

Samuel BAKER, 0 0 0 – 0 0 0 – 1 0 0 – 0 0 0
Frank JEFFRIES, 0 0 0 – 0 0 0 – 1 0 0 – 0 0 0

#70: Steven METCALF, 0 0 0 – 0 0 0 – 1 0 0 – 0 0 0
Maria TAXAR, 0 0 0 – 0 0 0 – 0 1 0 – 0 0 0

#71: Thomas MORICE, 1 0 0 – 0 0 0 – 0 0 0 – 0 0 0
Ann MORICE, 0 1 0 – 0 0 0 – 0 0 0 – 0 0 0
Mary WALLACE, 0 1 0 – 0 0 0 – 0 0 0 – 0 0 0

p. 25:
#72: Patrick C. DeBRIEN, 0 0 0 – 1 0 0 – 0 0 0 – 1 0 0 0:
Jane DeBRIEN, 0 1 0 – 0 0 0 – 0 0 0 – 0 0 0
Jane BARNES, 0 1 0 – 0 0 0 – 0 0 0 – 0 0 0
Pamella BARNES, 0 1 0 – 0 0 0 – 0 0 0 – 0 0 0
Jane DeBRIEN, 0 0 1 – 0 0 0 – 0 0 0 – 0 0 0
Maria Mc`KAY, 0 0 0 – 0 1 0 – 0 0 0 – 0 0 0
Jane COATES, 0 1 0 – 0 0 0 – 0 0 0 – 0 0 0
Lucretia ANDERSON, 0 0 0 – 0 0 0 – 0 1 0 – 0 0 0
Anne VERNON, 0 0 0 – 0 1 0 – 0 0 0 – 0 0 0
    Joe MASKALL; David DAVIES [*sic*]; Tom DAVIS [*sic*]; William LAMB;
    Harry DeBRIEN; Jem DeBRIEN; Dick LAMB; Samson DeBRIEN; Jack
    BARNES; Daniel COATES.

#73: Daniel EWING, 0 0 0 – 1 0 0 – 0 0 0 – 1 0 0:
Rosetta GREGORIA, 0 0 0 – 0 1 0 – 0 0 0 – 0 0 0
Daniel HAMILTON, 0 0 0 – 0 0 1 – 0 0 0 – 0 0 0
Benjamin HAMILTON, 0 0 0 – 0 0 1 – 0 0 0 – 0 0 0
Elizabeth HAMILTON, 0 0 0 – 0 0 1 – 0 0 0 – 0 0 0
Maria DOMINGO; 0 0 0 – 0 0 0 – 0 1 0 – 0 0 0
Francis ANTONIO, 0 0 0 – 0 0 0 – 1 0 0 – 0 0 0
    Billy.

#74: Louisa BAILEY, 0 0 0 – 0 0 0 – 0 1 0 – 1 0 0:
Mary BAILEY, 0 0 0 – 0 0 0 – 0 1 0 – 0 0 0
Phillis BAILEY, 0 0 0 – 0 0 0 – 0 1 0 – 0 0 0
Bryon BAILEY, 0 0 0 – 0 0 0 – 1 0 0 – 0 0 0
Jacob FLOWERS, 0 0 0 – 0 0 0 – 1 0 0 – 0 0 0
Abram BAILEY, 0 0 0 – 0 0 0 – 0 0 1 – 0 0 0
Isabella BAILEY, 0 0 0 – 0 0 0 – 0 0 1 – 0 0 0
Silvia BAILEY, 0 0 0 – 0 0 0 – 0 0 1 – 0 0 0
Anthony BAILEY, 0 0 0 – 0 0 0 – 0 0 1 – 0 0 0
Phillide [*sic*] BAILEY, 0 0 0 – 0 0 0 – 0 0 1 – 0 0 0
Agusta [*sic*] BAILEY, 0 0 0 – 0 0 0 – 0 0 1 – 0 0 0
Molly BAILEY, 0 0 0 – 0 0 0 – 0 0 1 – 0 0 0
    John BAILEY.

p. 26:
#75: Frederick COFFIN, 1 0 0 – 0 0 0 – 0 0 0 – 0 0 0
      Phoebe TUCKER, 0 0 3 – 0 1 0 – 0 0 0 – 0 0 0
      William C. COFFIN, 0 0 0 – 0 0 1 – 0 0 0 – 0 0 0
      Eliza M. COFFIN, 0 0 0 – 0 0 1 – 0 0 0 – 0 0 0
      Susan COFFIN, 0 0 0 – 0 0 1 – 0 0 0 – 0 0 0

#76: James R. CUNNINGHAM, 0 0 0 – 1 0 0 – 0 0 0 – 3 1 1:
      Catherine SMITH, 0 0 0 – 0 1 0 – 0 0 0 – 0 0 0
      John Nicholas CROFT. 0 0 0 – 1 0 0 – 0 0 0 – 0 0 0
      Edward CROFT, 0 0 0 – 0 0 1 – 0 0 0 – 0 0 0
      Juliana CUNNINGHAM, 0 0 0 – 0 0 1 – 0 0 0 – 0 0 0
            M: Marcus; Billy; Llewellyn. W: Sally. C: Nancy.

#77: Catherine JEFFRIES, 0 0 0 – 0 1 0 – 0 0 0 – 0 0 0
      Ann COLE, 0 0 0 – 0 1 0 – 0 0 0 – 0 0 0
      Infant (no name,) 0 0 0 – 0 0 1 – 0 0 0 – 0 0 0
      David EVANS, 0 0 0 – 1 0 0 – 0 0 0 – 0 0 0
      Sarah GOFF EVANS, 3 0 0 – 0 0 1 – 0 0 0 – 0 0 0
      Elizabeth C. EVANS, 0 0 0 – 0 0 1 – 0 0 0 – 0 0 0
      John E. EVANS, 0 0 0 – 0 0 1 – 0 0 0 – 0 0 0
      Charles JEFFRIES EVANS, 0 0 0 – 0 0 1 – 0 0 0 = 0 0 0
      John EVANS, 0 0 0 – 1 0 0 – 0 0 0 – 0 0 0

p. 27:
#78: Estate of Sarah GOFF under the charge of James McDONALD: 5 6 14:
            M: Sammy; Somerset; Harry; Jem; William. W: Clara; Elizabeth; Peggy;
            Hannah; Fanny; Agnes. C: John; Sambo; Adolphus; William; Derry;
            Robert; Richard; Joseph; Valentine; Hannah; Catherine; Nelly; Rhode [sic];
            Rose.

#79: John HOLME, 1 0 0 – 0 0 0 – 0 0 0 – 0 0 0
      Charles, 1 0 0 – 0 0 0 – 0 0 0 – 0 0 0 *(Surname not given.)*

p. 28:
#80: Memba BODE, 0 0 0 – 0 0 0 – 0 1 0 – 0 0 0
      Maria BODE, 0 0 0 – 0 0 0 – 0 0 1 – 0 0 0

*Note: An entry in a book of Private Records at the Archives shows that on 1 Feb 1830,
George Runnels purchased Memba Boade [sic] from Eliza Broaster and Anne Boade, and
manumitted her. Was Maria Bode his daughter?*

#81: James NEAL, 0 0 0 – 1 0 0 – 0 0 0 – 0 0 0
      Elizabeth NEAL, 0 0 0 – 0 1 0 – 0 0 0 – 0 0 0
      John NEAL, 0 0 0 – 0 0 1 – 0 0 0 – 0 0 0

187

Francis NEAL, 0 0 0 – 0 0 1 – 0 0 0 – 0 0 0
Olivia NEAL, 0 0 0 – 0 0 1 – 0 0 0 – 0 0 0

#82: William McKAY, 0 0 0 – 1 0 0 – 0 0 0 – 0 1 0:
Mary MORGAN, 0 0 0 – 0 1 0 – 0 0 0 – 0 0 0
Margaret E. McKAY, 0 0 0 – 0 0 1 – 0 0 0 – 0 0 0
Edward McKAY, 0 0 0 – 0 0 1 – 0 0 0 – 0 0 0
Anna.

#83: Estate of Mary HICKEY, Dec'd, under the charge of Messrs. WILLIAMSON &
BANKS, 23 10 0:
Shakespeare; London; Peter; Venture or Benture [*sic*]; Charley;
Joe; Mangola [*sic*] Adam; Anthony; Moca Jack; Henry; Hazard; Qualm;
Sandy; Stepney; Mandingo Harry;

p. 29: Moco Scotland; James; Bar; Alexander or Aleck; Ned WILSON; William;
John; Monday; Louiza; Patience; Mary; Nancy; Araminta; Grace;
Jenny; Memba; Esther; Nora.

#84: Catherine MEIGHAN, 0 0 0 – 0 1 0 – 0 0 0 – 0 0 0
Marcas [*sic*] BENNETT, 0 0 0 – 0 0 1 – 0 0 0 – 0 0 0 (=*Marcus Charles Bennett*)
Eliza MAIN [*sic*], 0 0 0 – 0 0 0 – 0 1 0 – 0 0 0
Margaret A. MEIGHAN, 0 0 0 – 0 0 0 – 0 0 1 – 0 0 0
John MEIGHAN, 0 0 0 – 0 0 0 – 0 0 1 – 0 0 0
Catherine MEIGHAN [*sic*], 0 0 0 – 0 0 1 – 0 0 0 – 0 0 0
Elizabeth BENNETT, 0 0 0 – 0 0 1 – 0 0 0 – 0 0 0

p. 30:
#85: Phoebe TRAPP, 0 0 0 – 0 1 0 – 0 0 0 – 0 0 0
Maria GODFRY, 0 0 0 – 0 0 1 – 0 0 0 – 0 0 0
Catherine WINTER, 0 0 0 – 0 0 0 – 0 1 0 – 0 0 0
Margaret POTTS, 0 0 0 – 0 0 1 – 0 0 0 – 0 0 0
Sarah REMIE, 0 0 0 – 0 0 1 – 0 0 0 – 0 0 0

#86: Margaret JONES, 0 0 0 – 0 1 0 – 0 0 0 – 0 0 0
Mary A. EVE, 0 0 0 – 0 0 1 – 0 0 0 – 0 0 0
Jane, 0 0 0 – 0 0 1 – 0 0 0 – 0 0 0   *(In 1839, VALPY)*
James, 0 0 0 – 0 0 1 – 0 0 0 – 0 0 0   "   "
Richard, 00 0 – 0 0 1 – 0 0 0 – 0 0 0   "   "
Penelope, 0 0 0 – 0 0 0 – 0 1 0 – 0 0 0 *(In 1839, JONES)*
Romeo, 0 0 0 – 0 0 0 – 0 0 1 – 0 0 0
Harry, 0 0 0 – 0 0 0 – 0 0 1 – 0 0 0 *(Surnames not given.)*

#87: William HENRY, 0 0 0 – 0 0 0 – 1 0 0 – 0 0 0
John HENRY, 0 0 0 – 0 0 0 – 0 0 1 – 0 0 0

188

#88: George GIBSON, 0 0 [– 1 0 0 – 0 0 0 – 3 1 0:
     John JOHN; Nelson; George; Violet.

#89: Ann GOFF, 0 0 0 – 0 1 0 – 0 0 0 – 0 1 0:
     Thomas Y. LIDDELL, 0 0 0 – 0 0 1 – 0 0 0 – 0 0 0
     Monimia GOFF.

p. 31:
#90: William HEMSLEY, 0 0 0 – 1 0 0 – 0 0 0 – 0 0 0
     Catherine HEMSLEY, 0 0 0 – 0 0 0 – 0 1 0 – 0 0 0

#91: William E. HAMPSHIRE, 1 0 0 – 0 0 0 – 0 0 0 – 0 0 1:
     Sarah TURNBULL.

#92: Simon T. ANDERSON, 1 0 0 – 0 0 0 – 0 0 0 – 0 0 0
     Matea S. ANDERSON, 0 0 0 – 0 0 0 – 0 1 0 – 0 0 0
     Silveria GAMBOA, 0 0 0 - 0 0 0 – 0 0 1 – 0 0 0
     Sarah PETERSGILL, 0 0 0 – 0 0 1 – 0 0 0 – 0 0 0
     Maria Rosaria KECHA, 0 0 0 – 0 0 0 – 0 1 0 – 0 0 0

#93: Clashmore LAWLESS, 0 0 0 – 0 0 0 – 1 0 0 – 0 1 0:
     Penelope LAWLESS, 0 0 0 – 0 0 0 – 0 1 0 – 0 0 0
     Judey GORDON, 0 0 [– 0 0 0 – 0 1 0 – 0 0 0
     George NICHOLSON, 0 0 0 – 0 0 1 – 0 0 0 – 0 0 0
     Joseph MASKALL, 0 0 0 – 0 0 0 – 0 0 1 – 0 0 0
     Nancy LAWLESS, 0 0 0 – 0 0 0 – 0 0 1 – 0 0 0
     James HUGHMAN, 0 0 0 – 0 0 0 – 0 0 1 – 0 0 0
     Charlotte.

#94: James PRICE, 1 0 0 – 0 0 0 – 0 0 0 – 1 1 0:
     Jane ROSS, 0 0 0 – 0 1 0 – 0 0 0 – 0 0 0
     Richard QUILTER, 0 0 0 – 0 0 1 – 0 0 0 – 0 0 0
     Alfred C. PRICE, 0 0 [– 0 0 1 – 0 0 0 – 0 0 0
     George LAMB; Lizzy.

p. 32:
#95: Charles RABAN, 0 0 (– 1 0 0 – 0 0 0 – 0 0 0
     Elizabeth WILLIAMS. 0 0 0 – 0 1 0 – 0 0 0 – 0 0 0
     David RABAN, 0 0 0 – 0 0 1 – 0 0 0 – 0 0 0

#96: James LAMB, 0 0 0 – 0 0 0 – 1 0 0 – 0 0 0
     Abigail LAMB, 0 0 0 – 0 0 0 – 0 1 0 – 0 0 0
     Quamina BOGES, 0 0 0 – 0 0 0 – 0 0 1 – 0 0 0
     Phillis BOGES, 0 0 0 – 0 0 0 – 0 0 1 – 0 0 0
     Rachael SLUSHER, 0 0 0 – 0 0 0 – 0 0 1 – 0 0 0

#97:   John H. SMITH, 0 0 0 – 1 0 0 – 0 0 0 – 0 0 0
          Jane SUTHERLAND, 0 0 0 – 0 1 0 – 0 0 0 – 0 0 0
          Hannah BENNETT, 0 0 0 – 0 1 0 – 0 0 0 – 0 0 0
          Edward SMITH, 0 0 0 – 0 0 1 – 0 0 0 – 0 0 0

#98:   Elizabeth CARD, 0 0 0 – 0 0 0 – 0 1 0 – 0 0 0
          Peter MEIGHAN, 0 0 0 – 0 0 0 – 0 0 1 – 0 0 0

#99:   Richard GRANT, 0 0 0 – 0 0 0 – 1 0 0 – 0 0 0
          Izabella GRANT, 0 0 0 – 0 0 0 – 0 0 1 – 0 0 0
          Mary GRANT, 0 0 0 – 0 0 0 – 0 0 1 – 0 0 0

#100: James BANKS, 1 0 0 – 0 0 0 – 0 0 0 – 0 0 0

p. 33:
#101: William M. SMITH, 1 0 0 – 0 0 0 – 0 0 0 – 0 0 0
          Fanny BURRELL, 0 1 0 – 0 0 0 – 0 0 0 – 0 0 0
          Thomas SMITH, 0 0 1 – 0 0 0 – 0 0 0 – 0 0 0
          James SMITH, 0 0 1 – 0 0 0 – 0 0 0 – 0 0 0
          Robert SMITH, 0 0 1 – 0 0 0 – 0 0 0 – 0 0 0
          William SMITH, 0 0 1 – 0 0 0 – 0 0 0 – 0 0 0

#102: Elizabeth STAIN, 0 0 0 – 0 1 0 – 0 0 0 – 1 0 0 0:
          Amelia YOUNG, 0 0 0 – 0 1 0 – 0 0 0 – 0 0 0
          Elenor YOUNG, 0 0 0 – 0 1 0 – 0 0 0 – 0 0 0
          Elizabeth YOUNG, 0 0 0 – 0 1 0 – 0 0 0 – 0 0 0
          Rebecca YOUNG, 0 0 0 – 0 1 0 – 0 0 0 – 0 0 0
          William EVERETT, 0 0 0 – 0 0 1 – 0 0 0 – 0 0 0
          James M. EVERITT, [sic], 0 0 0 – 0 0 1 – 0 0 0 – 0 0 0
          Margaret EVERITT, 0 0 0 – 0 0 1 – 0 0 0 – 0 0 0
          Richard MEIGHAN, 0 0 0 – 0 0 1 – 0 0 0 – 0 0 0
          Elizabeth MEIGHAN, 0 0 0 – 0 0 1 – 0 0 0 – 0 0 0
          Susanna NICHOLSON, 0 0 0 – 0 0 1 – 0 0 0 – 0 0 0
               Monday; March; Joe; Quashie; William; Friday; Lenan; Johnny; Billy;
               Tommy.

#103: George NICHOLSON, 1 0 0 – 0 0 0 – 0 0 0 – 0 0 0

p. 34:
#104: Simon THOMPSON, 0 0 0 – 0 0 0 – 1 0 0 – 1 0 7:
          Edward SPROAT, 0 0 0 – 0 0 0 – 1 0 0 – 0 0 0
          Elizabeth THOMPSON, 0 0 0 – 0 0 0 – 0 1 0 – 0 0 0
               M. Adam SPROAT. C. Richard SPROAT; Jeremiah SPROAT; James
               SPROAT; Grace SPROAT; Rose; Catherine; Elizabeth.
               (Surnames not given.)

#105: John Joseph LECUSE, 0 0 0 – 0 0 0 – 1 0 0 – 0 0 0
Lewis LECUSE, 0 0 0 – 0 0 0 – 1 0 0 – 0 0 0
Memie LECUSE, 0 0 0 – 0 0 0 – 0 1 0 – 0 0 0
Susanna LECUSE, 0 0 0 – 0 0 0 – 0 1 0 – 0 0 0
Jennett LECUSE, 0 0 0 – 0 0 0 – 0 1 0 – 0 0 0
Rose BERNARD, 0 0 0 – 0 0 0 – 0 0 1 – 0 0 0
William LECUSE, 0 0 0 – 0 0 1 – 0 0 0 – 0 0 0
Francis TIMOTHY, 0 0 0 – 0 0 0 – 0 0 1 – 0 0 0
Rennett [*sic*] NELLY, 0 0 0 – 0 0 0 – 0 0 1 – 0 0 0 *(Female.)*
Maria WAGNER, 0 0 0 – 0 0 0 – 0 0 1 – 0 0 0

#106: Thomas MYVETT, 0 0 0 – 0 0 0 – 1 0 0 – 0 0 0
Eleanor HUME, 0 0 0 – 0 0 0 – 0 1 0 – 0 0 0

p. 35:
#107: Thomas GIDDY, 0 0 0 – 0 0 0 – 1 0 0 – 0 0 0
Luiza HUGHES, 0 0 0 – 0 0 0 – 0 1 0 – 0 0 0
Patient [*sic*] HUGHES, 0 0 0 – 0 0 0 – 0 1 0 – 0 0 0
Ann PIPERSBURG, 0 0 0 – 0 0 0 – 0 1 0 – 0 0 0
Susannah HUGHES, 0 0 0 – 0 0 0 – 0 1 0 – 0 0 0
Jane GIDDY, 0 0 0 – 0 0 0 – 0 0 1 – 0 0 0
John GIDDY, 0 0 0 – 0 0 0 – 0 0 1 – 0 0 0
William HUGHES, 0 0 0 – 0 0 0 – 0 0 1 – 0 0 0
Elizabeth THOMPSON, 0 0 0 – 0 0 0 – 0 0 1 – 0 0 0
Thomas GIDDY, 0 0 0 – 0 0 0 – 0 0 1 – 0 0 0

#108: Harriet SMITH, 0 0 0 – 0 0 0 – 0 1 0 – 0 0 0
Richard SMITH, 0 0 0 – 0 0 0 – 1 0 0 – 0 0 0
Caesar FULLER, 0 0 0 – 0 0 0 – 1 0 0 – 0 0 0
Stephen SMITH, 0 0 0 – 0 0 0 – 0 0 1 – 0 0 0
Damon SMITH, 0 0 0 – 0 0 0 – 1 0 0 – 0 0 0

#109: William WILLIAMSON, 1 0 0 – 0 0 0 – 0 0 0 – 0 0 0

#110: Elizabeth JOSEPH, 0 0 0 – 0 1 0 – 0 0 0 – 0 0 0
Maria GUEST, 0 0 0 – 0 1 0 – 0 0 0 – 0 0 0
Eleanor DAW, 0 0 0 – 0 1 0 – 0 0 0 – 0 0 0

#111: Charles H. SMITH, 0 0 0 – 1 0 0 – 0 0 0 – 1 0 0:
John G. SMITH, 0 0 0 – 1 0 0 – 0 0 0 – 0 0 0
John SMITH, 0 0 0 – 0 0 1 – 0 0 0 – 0 0 0
Maria BATES, 0 0 0 – 0 0 0 – 0 1 0 – 0 0 0
Limas SMITH

p. 36:
#112: George GILLET, 0 0 0 – 1 0 0 – 0 0 0 – 0 0 0

191

Henrietta GILLET, 0 0 0 – 0 1 0 – 0 0 0 – 0 0 0
Mary FLOWERS, 0 0 0 – 0 1 0 – 0 0 0 – 0 0 0

#113: Henrietta GODFRY, 0 0 0 – 0 1 0 – 0 0 0 – 3 0 1:
Henrietta JOHNSTONE, 0 0 0 – 0 0 1 – 0 0 0 – 0 0 0
Mary JOHNSTONE, 0 0 0 – 0 0 1 – 0 0 0 – 0 0 0
Isabella JOHNSTONE, 0 0 0 – 0 0 1 – 0 0 0 – 0 0 0
Agnes JOHNSTONE, 0 0 0 – 0 0 1 – 0 0 0 – 0 0 0
Jane JOHNSTONE, 0 0 0 – 0 0 1 – 0 0 0 – 0 0 0
   M: Dick GODFRY; Peter GODFRY; Cyrus GODFRY. C: Ada GODFRY.

#114: Robert F. WADE, 0 0 0 – 1 0 0 – 0 0 0 – 0 0 4:
Belford; Thomas; Joseph; Betsy.

#115: Thomas JENNINGS, 0 0 0 – 1 0 0 – 0 0 0 – 1 2 0:
Catherine P. JENNINGS, 0 0 0 – 0 1 0 – 0 0 0 – 0 0 0
Levinia E. JENNINGS, 0 0 0 – 0 0 1 – 0 0 0 – 0 0 0
Angelina P. JENNINGS, 0 0 0 – 0 0 1 – 0 0 0 – 0 0 0
Catherine P. JENNINGS, 0 0 0 – 0 0 1 – 0 0 0 – 0 0 0
Thomas W. JENNINGS, 0 0 0 – 0 0 1 – 0 0 0 – 0 0 0
Eliza PEARSON, 0 0 0 – 0 1 0 – 0 0 0 – 0 0 0
Rebecca JAYS, 0 0 0 – 0 0 0 – 0 0 1 – 0 0 0
Rebecca LINDO, 0 0 0 – 0 1 0 – 0 0 0 – 0 0 0
   Judith JONES; Alexander CALLERMAN; Rosanna THOMAS.

p. 37:
#116: John Samuel SAMPSON, 0 0 0 – 1 0 0 – 0 0 0 – 0 0 0
Elizabeth SAMPSON, 0 0 0 – 0 1 0 – 0 0 0 – 0 0 0
William SAMPSON, 0 0 0 – 0 0 1 – 0 0 0 – 0 0 0
Elizabeth SAMPSON, 0 0 0 – 0 0 1 – 0 0 0 – 0 0 0

#117: Catherine SLUSHER, 0 0 0 – 0 1 0 – 0 0 0 – 1 1 0:
Nora SLUSHER; Ricais? EDWARDS.

#118; Jane GORDON, 0 0 0 – 0 1 0 – 0 0 0 – 0 2 1:
Ann Eliz[th] CODD, 0 0 0 – 0 0 1 – 0 0 0 – 0 0 0
Tenah GORDON, 0 0 0 – 0 0 0 – 0 1 0 – 0 0 0
Henry GORDON, 0 0 0 – 0 0 0 – 0 0 1 – 0 0 0
James USHER, 0 0 0 – 0 0 0 – 1 0 0 – 0 0 0
   W: Betsy GORDON; Margaret FRAZIER; C: James CLERHAM.

#119: Elizabeth GRANT, 0 0 0 – 0 1 0 – 0 0 0 – 0 1 0:
William G. ADOLPHUS, 0 0 0 – 0 0 1 – 0 0 0 – 0 0 0
John Henry HYDE, 0 0 0 – 0 0 1 – 0 0 0 – 0 0 0
Margaret.

#120: John BARROW, 0 0 0 – 1 0 0 – 0 0 0 – 2 0 0:
Mimba BARROW, 0 0 0 – 0 0 0 – 0 1 0 – 0 0 0
William BARROW, 0 0 0 – 0 0 1 – 0 0 0 – 0 0 0
Elizabeth BARROW, 0 0 0 – 0 0 1 – 0 0 0 – 0 0 0
Mary BARROW, 0 0 0 – 0 0 1 – 0 0 0 – 0 0 0
George BARROW, 0 0 0 – 0 0 1 – 0 0 0 – 0 0 0
Edward BARROW, 0 0 0 – 0 0 1 – 0 0 0 – 0 0 0
James MILLERBROOK; Henry GORDON.

p. 38:
#121: John McKINNON, 0 0 0 – 1 0 0 – 0 0 0 – 0 0 0
Margaret McKINNON, 0 0 0 – 0 1 0 – 0 0 0 – 0 0 0
Alexander McKINNON, 0 0 0 – 0 0 1 – 0 0 0 – 0 0 0

#122: William CARD, 0 0 0 – 1 0 0 – 0 0 0 – 0 2 0:
Sarah Mc`KINZEY, 0 0 0 – 0 1 0 – 0 0 0 – 0 0 0
Maria CARD, 0 0 0 – 0 0 1 – 0 0 0 – 0 0 0
John CARD, 0 0 0 – 0 0 1 – 0 0 0 – 0 0 0
Catherine CARD, 0 0 0 – 0 0 1 – 0 0 0 – 0 0 0
Lucretia CARD, 0 0 0 – 0 0 1 – 0 0 0 – 0 0 0
Jane CARD; Rose CARD.

#123: G. D. ADOLPHUS, 0 0 0 – 1 0 0 – 0 0 0 – 4 2 0:
Mary Ann ADOLPHUS, 0 0 0 – 0 1 0 – 0 0 0 – 0 0 0
Edward ADOLPHUS, 0 0 0 – 0 0 1 – 0 0 0 – 0 0 0
Batt LAWRIE; Samuel ROBERTSON; William JEYS; Billy PITT; Helen
DAVIS; Sarah HULSE.

#124: James FLOWERS, 0 0 0 – 0 0 0 – 1 0 0 – 0 0 0
Enwell FLOWERS, 0 0 0 – 0 0 0 – 0 0 1 – 0 0 0
Abigail FLOWERS, 0 0 0 – 0 0 0 – 0 0 1 – 0 0 0
John HEMSLEY, 0 0 0 – 0 0 0 – 0 0 1 – 0 0 0
David HEMSLEY, 0 0 0 – 0 0 0 – 0 0 1 – 0 0 0

p. 39:
#125: Lewis WILLIAMS, 0 0 0 – 1 0 0 – 0 0 0 – 0 0 0
Joannah WILLIAMS, 0 0 0 – 0 1 0 – 0 0 0 – 0 0 0
Lewis WILLIAMS, 0 0 0 – 0 0 1 – 0 0 0 – 0 0 0
John Thomas WILLIAMS, 0 0 0 – 0 0 1 – 0 0 0 – 0 0 0
Joseph James WILLIAMS, 0 0 0 – 0 0 1 – 0 0 0 – 0 0 0

#126: Francis GRAY, 0 0 0 – 1 0 0 – 0 0 0 – 0 0 0
Charlotte PORTER, 0 0 0 – 0 1 0 – 0 0 0 – 0 0 0
Sally, 0 0 0 – 0 1 0 – 0 0 0 – 0 0 0 *(Surname not given.)*
Charlotte GRAY, 0 0 0 – 0 0 0 – 0 1 0 – 0 0 0

193

#127: William MUCKLEHANEY, 0 0 0 – 1 0 0 – 0 0 0 – 0 1 0:
Elizabeth GOFF, 0 0 0 – 0 1 0 – 0 0 0 – 0 0 0
Elizabeth ARTHURS, 0 0 0 – 0 1 0 – 0 0 0 – 0 0 0
Thomas TOOTH, 0 0 0 – 0 0 1 – 0 0 0 – 0 0 0
Sarah KARR, 0 0 0 – 0 0 1 – 0 0 0 – 0 0 0
Elizabeth MUCKLEHANEY, 0 0 0 – 0 0 1 – 0 0 0 – 0 0 0
Patience GOFF.

#128: John TWEENY, 0 0 0 – 0 0 0 – 1 0 0 – 0 0 0
Rose TWEENY, 0 0 0 – 0 0 0 – 0 1 0 – 0 0 0
Polina TWEENY, 0 0 0 – 0 0 0 – 0 0 1 – 0 0 0
Samuel TWEENY, 0 0 0 – 0 0 0 – 0 0 1 – 0 0 0
Henry TWEENY, 0 0 0 – 0 0 0 – 0 0 1 – 0 0 0
Joseph TWEENY, 0 0 0 – 0 0 0 – 0 0 1 – 0 0 0
Elizabeth FANTESSAY, 0 0 0 – 0 0 0 – 0 0 1 – 0 0 0
Alexander DESURSE, 0 0 0 – 0 0 0 – 0 0 1 – 0 0 0
Lavinia TWEENY, 0 0 0 – 0 0 0 – 0 0 1 – 0 0 0
Mary Ann TWEENY, 0 0 0 – 0 0 0 – 0 0 1 – 0 0 0
Louisa TWEENY, 0 0 0 – 0 0 0 – 0 0 1 – 0 0 0

p. 40:
#129: Benjamin PATTERSON, 0 0 0 – 1 0 0 – 0 0 0 – 0 0 0
Elizabeth PATTERSON, 0 0 0 – 0 1 0 – 0 0 0 – 0 0 0
William PATTERSON, 0 0 0 – 0 0 1 – 0 0 0 – 0 0 0
Anne GLADDING, 0 0 0 – 0 1 0 – 0 0 0 – 0 0 0

#130: John H. PETZOLD, 1 0 0 – 0 0 0 – 0 0 0 – 4 1 0:
Margaret PETZOLD, 0 0 0 – 0 1 0 – 0 0 0 – 0 0 0
Francis PETZOLD, 0 0 0 – 1 0 0 – 0 0 0 – 0 0 0
Elizabeth PETZOLD, 0 0 0 – 0 0 1 – 0 0 0 – 0 0 0
Patrick; Jack NEAL; Henry; Charles; Mary.

#131: Ann WILSON, 0 0 0 – 0 1 0 – 0 0 0 – 0 0 0
Margaret ORGLES, 0 0 0 – 0 0 0 – 0 1 0 – 0 0 0 *(= ORGILL?)*
William LAMBERT, 0 0 0 – 0 0 1 – 0 0 0 – 0 0 0

#132: William TUXEY, 0 0 0 – 1 0 0 – 0 0 0 – 0 0 0
Polly WILLIAMS, 0 0 0 – 0 0 1 – 0 0 0 – 0 0 0
Eve WILLIAMS, 0 0 0 – 0 0 1 – 0 0 0 – 0 0 0
William TUXEY, 0 0 0 – 0 0 1 – 0 0 0 – 0 0 0
Eve TUXEY, 0 0 0 – 0 0 0 – 0 1 0 – 0 0 0

#133: James WHITE, 0 0 0 – 1 0 0 – 0 0 0 – 0 1 0:
Catherine WHITE.
p. 41:
#134: John CLARK [*sic*], 0 0 0 – 0 0 0 – 1 0 0 – 0 0 0

Sabina CLARK, 0 0 0 – 0 0 0 – 0 1 0 – 0 0 0
William CLARKE [*sic*], 0 0 0 – 0 0 0 – 0 0 1 – 0 0 0
Lucretia CLARKE, 0 0 0 – 0 0 0 – 0 0 1 – 0 0 0
Lucy CLARKE, 0 0 0 – 0 0 0 – 0 0 1 – 0 0 0
Joseph CLARKE, 0 0 0 – 0 0 0 – 0 0 1 – 0 0 0

#135: Thomas MILES, 0 0 0 – 0 0 0 – 1 0 0 – 0 0 0
Sarah MILES, 0 0 0 – 0 0 0 – 0 1 0 – 0 0 0
Lucretia MILES, 0 0 0 – 0 0 0 – 0 1 0 – 0 0 0
Julian SUTHERLAND, 0 0 0 – 0 0 0 – 0 0 1 – 0 0 0
Sarah HUMES, 0 0 0 – 0 0 0 – 0 0 1 – 0 0 0
Patitune [*sic*] HICKEY, 0 0 0 – 0 0 0 – 0 0 1 – 0 0 0
Thisby HICKEY, 0 0 0 – 0 0 0 – 0 1 0 – 0 0 0
Thomas CARD, 0 0 0 – 0 0 1 – 0 0 0 – 0 0 0
Kinsale HOAR, 0 0 0 – 0 0 0 – 1 0 0 – 0 0 0
Nancy MILES, 0 0 0 – 0 0 0 – 0 1 0 – 0 0 0

#136: Bella MEANY, 0 0 0 – 0 0 0 – 0 1 0 – 0 0 0
William JEFFREYS, 0 0 0 – 0 0 0 – 0 0 1 – 0 0 0
Mary MEANY, 0 0 0 – 0 0 0 – 0 0 1 – 0 0 0

#137: Lewis McLENAN, 1 0 0 – 0 0 0 – 0 0 0 – 1 0 0:
Fame

#138: John PARKS, 0 0 0 – 1 0 0 – 0 0 0 – 0 0 0
Abby FLOWERS, 0 0 0 – 0 0 0 – 0 1 0 – 0 0 0
Charley PARKS, 0 0 0 – 0 0 1 – 0 0 0 – 0 0 0

p. 42:
#139: George MASKALL, 0 0 0 – 1 0 0 – 0 0 0 – 1 0 0:
Elizabeth MASKALL, 0 0 0 – 0 1 0 – 0 0 0 – 0 0 0
Francis MASKALL.

#140: Margaret LeROY, 0 0 0 – 0 1 0 – 0 0 0 – 0 0 0
John FERGUSON, 0 0 0 – 0 0 1 – 0 0 0 – 0 0 0
Christian FERGUSON, 0 0 0 – 0 0 1 – 0 0 0 – 0 0 0

#141: Henry BAILEY, 0 0 0 – 0 0 0 – 1 0 0 – 1 0 0:
Jane BAILEY, 0 0 0 – 0 0 0 – 0 1 0 – 0 0 0
William ANDERSON, 0 0 0 – 0 0 0 – 0 0 1 – 0 0 0
Rodney KENNEDY.

#142: Robert WAGNER, 0 0 0 – 1 0 0 – 0 0 0 – 3 0 0:
Robert WAGNER; Friday; Hazard.

#143: Joseph BURNO, 0 0 0 – 1 0 0 – 0 0 0 – 0 0 0   *(= BURNEAU.)*
William FERREL, 0 0 0 – 0 0 1 – 0 0 0 – 0 0 0
Henry BURNO, 0 0 0 – 0 0 1 – 0 0 0 – 0 0 0
Mary A. BURNO, 0 0 0 – 0 0 1 – 0 0 0 – 0 0 0
Margaret BURNO, 0 0 0 – 0 0 0 – 0 1 0 – 0 0 0

#144: Joseph GRANT, 0 0 0 – 0 0 0 – 1 0 0 – 0 0 0
Henrietta MILES, 0 0 0 – 0 0 0 – 0 1 0 – 0 0 0
Noel CANE, 0 0 0 – 0 0 0 – 0 0 1 – 0 0 0
Elizabeth CANE, 0 0 0 – 0 0 0 – 0 0 1 – 0 0 0
Harriet GRANT, 0 0 0 – 0 0 0 – 0 0 1 – 0 0 0
Margaret GRANT, 0 0 0 – 0 0 0 – 0 0 1 – 0 0 0

p. 43:
#145: John NORO, 1 0 0 – 0 0 0 – 0 0 0 – 1 1 1:
M. A. UTOR, 0 0 0 – 0 1 0 – 0 0 0 – 0 0 0   *(= UTER.)*
C. A. NORO, 0 0 0 – 0 0 1 – 0 0 0 – 0 0 0
John UTOR, 0 0 0 – 1 0 0 – 0 0 0 – 0 0 0
Joseph UTOR, 0 0 0 – 1 0 0 – 0 0 0 – 0 0 0
Cerano ANBATO, 0 0 1 – 0 0 0 – 0 0 0 – 0 0 0
        George FOGHERTY; Margaret UTOR; Jane GOFF.

#146: George BELISLE, 0 0 0 – 1 0 0 – 0 0 0 – 0 0 0
Rosetta SAVIGNE, 0 0 0 – 0 1 0 – 0 0 0 – 0 0 0
Joseph EDWARDS, 0 0 0 – 0 0 1 – 0 0 0 – 0 0 0
James BELISLE, 0 0 0 – 0 0 1 – 0 0 0 – 0 0 0
John BELISLE, 0 0 0 – 0 0 1 – 0 0 0 – 0 0 0
Jane BELISLE, 0 0 0 – 0 0 1 – 0 0 0 – 0 0 0

#147: Ramy DESOUS, 0 0 0 – 1 0 0 – 0 0 0 – 0 1 0:   *(= DeSOURCE, De SOURCE,*
Joseph NOEL, 0 0 0 – 1 0 0 – 0 0 0 – 0 0 0   *DeSSOUS, DESOUS.)*
Maria SUPRIAN, 0 0 0 – 0 1 0 – 0 0 0 – 0 0 0
Muslen [*sic*] SUPRIAN, 0 0 0 – 0 0 1 – 0 0 0 – 0 0 0 (female.)
Frederick DESOUS, 0 0 0 – 0 0 1 – 0 0 0 – 0 0 0
Sera [*sic*] DESOUS, 0 0 0 – 0 0 1 – 0 0 0 – 0 0 0 *(Sarah, bapt. May 3 1828)*
Hariet [*sic*] DESOUS, 0 0 0 – 0 0 1 – 0 0 0 – 0 0 0
Elizabeth DESOUS, 0 0 0 – 0 0 1 – 0 0 0 – 0 0 0
Sera [*sic*] DESOUS, 0 0 0 – 0 0 0 – 0 1 0 – 0 0 0
Joseph CAZIE, 0 0 0 – 0 0 1 – 0 0 0 – 0 0 0
Catherine DESOUS, 0 0 0 – 0 0 1 – 0 0 0 – 0 0 0
        Joannah SANCHO. *(The name* Holland LAWES *has been struck out.)*

p. 44:
#148: Clarissa PASLOW, 0 0 0 – 0 1 0 – 0 0 0 – 11 9 0:
        Thomas PASLOW; Isaac; Dibden; Vincent; Thomas LAMB; Thomas
        ENGLISH; Providence; Sam LAMB; Tom LAMB; James COOTE; Tom

PASLOW; Venus PASLOW; Nanny WALDRONE; Elizabeth PASLOW; Cecilia HICKEY. Cecilia ENGLISH; Judy LAMB; Katie LAMB; Agnes; Sally LAMB.

#149:   Francis FITZGIBBON, 0 0 0 – 0 0 0 – 1 0 0 – 0 0 0
        Mary CURRANTS, 0 0 0 – 0 0 0 – 0 1 0 – 0 0 0
        Robert FITZGIBBON, 0 0 0 – 0 0 0 – 0 0 1 – 0 0 0

p. 45:
#150:   William B. TOOTH, 1 0 0 – 0 0 0 – 0 0 0 – 1 2 3:
        Ann B. TOOTH, 0 0 1 – 0 0 0 – 0 0 0 – 0 0 0
        Eliza TOOTH, 0 0 1 – 0 0 0 – 0 0 0 – 0 0 0
        Susan TOOTH, 0 0 1 – 0 0 0 – 0 0 0 – 0 0 0
        Elizabeth TOOTH, 0 0 1 – 0 0 0 – 0 0 0 – 0 0 0
        Caroline TOOTH, 0 0 1 – 0 0 0 – 0 0 0 – 0 0 0
        Clarissa TOOTH, 0 0 1 – 0 0 0 – 0 0 0 – 0 0 0
            Nelson TOOTH; Molly GOFF; Fanny EVANS; Daniel;
            Thomas; Pamelia.

#151:   Joseph GOFF, 0 0 0 – 1 0 0 – 0 0 0 – 0 0 0
        Catherine BENNETT, 0 0 0 – 0 1 0 – 0 0 0 – 0 0 0
        Elizabeth GOFF, 0 0 0 – 0 0 1 – 0 0 0 – 0 0 0
        John GOFF, 0 0 0 – 0 0 1 – 0 0 0 – 0 0 0
        Edward GOFF, 0 0 0 – 0 0 1 – 0 0 0 – 0 0 0
        Mary Ann GOFF, 0 0 0 – 0 0 1 – 0 0 0 – 0 0 0

#152:   Sarah BATES, 0 0 0 – 0 1 0 – 0 0 0 – 0 1 0:
        Eliza S. EVE, 0 0 0 – 0 1 0 – 0 0 0 – 0 0 0
        Mary PRICE, 0 0 0 – 0 1 0 – 0 0 0 – 0 0 0
        Edward ROSS, 0 0 0 – 0 0 1 – 0 0 0 – 0 0 0
            Bathsheba GRACE.

#153:   Joseph JONES, 1 0 0 – 0 0 0 – 0 0 0 – 0 0 0
        Mary GILLET, 0 1 0 – 0 0 0 – 0 0 0 – 0 0 0
        Janet JONES, 0 0 0 – 0 0 1 – 0 0 0 – 0 0 0
        Margaret JONES, 0 0 0 – 0 0 1 – 0 0 0 – 0 0 0
        Sarah JONES, 0 0 0 – 0 0 1 – 0 0 0 – 0 0 0
        Ann JONES, 0 0 0 – 0 0 1 – 0 0 0 – 0 0 0

p. 46:
#154:   William TRAPP, 0 0 0 – 1 0 0 – 0 0 0 – 0 0 0
        Mary LAMB, 0 0 0 – 0 0 0 – 0 1 0 – 0 0 0
        James TRAPP, 0 0 0 – 0 0 0 – 0 0 1 – 0 0 0
        David TRAPP, 0 0 0 – 0 0 0 – 0 0 1 – 0 0 0
        William TRAPP, 0 0 0 – 0 0 0 – 0 0 1 – 0 0 0
        Sarah TRAPP, 0 0 0 – 0 0 0 – 0 0 1 – 0 0 0

197

Fanny S. TRAPP, 0 0 0 – 0 0 0 – 0 0 1 – 0 0 0
Rachael TRAPP, 0 0 0 – 0 0 0 – 0 0 1 – 0 0 0

#155: Ceaser [*sic*] FULLER, 0 0 0 – 0 0 0 – 1 0 0 – 0 0 0
Stephen FULLER, 0 0 0 – 0 0 0 – 0 0 1 – 0 0 0
Harriot SMITH, 0 0 0 – 0 0 0 – 0 1 0 – 0 0 0

#156: James TRAPP, 0 0 0 – 0 0 0 – 1 0 0 – 1 0 0:
Clarinda TRAPP, 0 0 0 – 0 0 0 – 0 1 0 – 0 0 0
Edward TRAPP, 0 0 0 – 0 0 0 – 0 0 1 – 0 0 0
Edward TRAPP.

#157: Philip MEIGHAN, 0 0 0 – 1 0 0 – 0 0 0 – 1 0 0:
Jeanette SWASEY, 0 0 0 – 0 1 0 – 0 0 0 – 0 0 0
Lawrence MEIGHAN, 0 0 0 – 0 0 1 – 0 0 0 – 0 0 0
Ann R. MEIGHAN, 0 0 0 – 0 0 1 – 0 0 0 – 0 00
Edward MEIGHAN.

#158: John COURTNEY, 0 0 0 – 1 0 0 – 0 0 0 – 0 0 0
Jane WILLIAMS, 0 0 0 – 0 1 0 – 0 0 0 – 0 0 0
Catherine COURTNEY, 0 0 0 – 0 0 1 – 0 0 0 – 0 0 0

p. 47:
#159: Elizabeth SWASEY, 0 0 0 – 0 1 0 – 0 0 0 – 0 1 0:
John WRIGHT, 0 0 0 – 0 0 1 – 0 0 0 – 0 0 0
Selina ORGLES, 0 0 0 – 0 0 1 – 0 0 0 – 0 0 0   *(= ORGILL.)*
Mary Jane GAVIN, 0 0 0 – 0 0 1 – 0 0 0 – 0 0 0
Susana SWASEY.

#160: William GARRETT, 0 0 0 – 1 0 0 – 0 0 0 – 0 0 0
Mary A. HURST, 0 0 0 – 0 1 0 – 0 0 0 – 0 0 0
Matilda GARRETT, 0 0 0 – 0 1 0 – 0 0 0 – 0 0 0
Thomas BEAUMONT, 0 0 0 – 0 0 1 – 0 0 0 – 0 0 0
Daniel BEAUMONT, 0 0 0 – 0 0 1 – 0 0 0 – 0 0 0
Susan GARRETT, 0 0 0 – 0 0 1 – 0 0 0 – 0 0 0

#161: James FERGUSON, 0 0 0 – 0 0 0 – 1 0 0 – 0 0 0
Patty McAULEY, 0 0 0 -0 0 0 – 0 1 0 – 0 0 0
Patty FERGUSON, 0 0 0 – 0 0 0 – 0 1 0 – 0 0 0
Henry FERGUSON, 0 0 0 – 0 0 0 – 1 0 0 – 0 0 0

#162: Samuel F. AUGUST, 0 0 0 – 1 0 0 – 0 0 0 – 8 6 7: *(Son of John Samuel August.)*
Ann R. AUGUST, 0 0 0 – 0 1 0 – 0 0 0 – 0 0 0
Elizabeth AUGUST, 0 0 0 – 0 0 1 – 0 0 0 – 0 0 0
Ann R. AUGUST, 0 0 0 – 0 0 1 – 0 0 0 – 0 0 0
Samuel F. AUGUST, 0 0 0 – 0 0 1 – 0 0 0 – 0 0 0

Simon M. K. AUGUST, 0 0 0 – 0 0 1 – 0 0 0 – 0 0 0
Richard AUGUST, 0 0 0 – 0 0 1 – 0 0 0 – 0 0 0
Edgar AUGUST, 0 0 0 – 0 0 1 – 0 0 0 – 0 0 0
Elizabeth AUGUST, 0 0 0 – 0 0 0 – 0 1 0 – 0 0 0
 Andy; Charley; Jackey; Port Royal; Richard; Scotland; Toby; Middleton.
 W: Fanny; Fanny [sic]; Penelope; Eleanor;

p. 48: W: Cloe; Amelia. C: Sarah; Betheny; Robert; William; Thomas; Edwin;
 Simon.

#163: Edward SHIEL, 1 0 0 – 0 0 0 – 0 0 0 – 0 0 0
 David CUMMING, 1 0 0 – 0 0 0 – 0 0 0 – 0 0 0
 Samuel TUCKER, 0 0 0 – 0 0 0 – 1 0 0 – 0 0 0
 Manuel, 0 0 0 – 0 0 0 – 0 0 1 – 0 0 0 *(Surname not given.)*

#164: Rachael JEFFREYS, 0 0 0 – 0 1 0 – 0 0 0 – 0 0 0
 John JEFFREYS, 0 0 0 – 0 0 0 – 1 0 0 – 0 0 0
 Charles JEFFREYS, 0 0 0 – 0 0 0 – 0 0 1 – 0 0 0
 George JEFFREYS, 0 0 0 – 0 0 0 – 0 0 1 – 0 0 0

#165: John BROHIER, 0 0 0 – 0 0 0 – 1 0 0 – 0 0 0
 Mary BROHIER, 0 0 0 – 0 0 0 – 0 1 0 – 0 0 0
 George FLOWERS, 0 0 0 – 0 0 0 – 0 0 1 – 0 0 0

p. 49:
#166: Joseph VERNON, 0 0 0 – 1 0 0 – 0 0 0 – 4 1 0:
 Margaret NEAL, 0 0 0 – 0 1 0 – 0 0 0 – 0 0 0
 Janett VERNON, 0 0 0 – 0 1 0 – 0 0 0 – 0 0 0
 John VERNON, 0 0 0 – 1 0 0 – 0 0 0 – 0 0 0
 William VERNON, 0 0 0 – 0 0 1 – 0 0 0 – 0 0 0
 Michael VERNON, 0 0 0 – 0 0 1 – 0 0 0 – 0 0 0
 Benjamin VERNON, 0 0 0 – 0 0 1 – 0 0 0 – 0 0 0
 Alexander VERNON, 0 0 0 – 0 0 1 – 0 0 0 – 0 0 0
 Henry VERNON, 0 0 0 – 0 0 1 – 0 0 0 – 0 0 0
 Joseph VERNON, 0 0 0 – 0 0 1 – 0 0 0 – 0 0 0
  Moses JENKIN; Punch VERNON; Daniel VERNON; Joe VERNON;
  Catherine VERNON.

#167: William WAGNER, 0 0 0 – 1 0 0 – 0 0 0 – 1 0 0:
 Joannah BANNER, 0 0 0 – 0 1 0 – 0 0 0 – 0 0 0
 Charlotte WAGNER, 0 0 0 – 0 0 1 – 0 0 0 – 0 0 0
 Fedelia WAGNER, 0 0 0 – 0 0 1 – 0 0 0 – 0 0 0
  Congo John.

#168: Robert FLOWERS, 0 0 0 – 0 0 0 – 1 0 0 – 0 0 0
 Margaret FLOWERS, 0 0 0 – 0 1 0 – 0 0 0 – 0 0 0

199

#169: Susannah GORDON, 0 0 0 – 0 0 0 – 0 1 0 – 0 0 0
Maria ELCHABEREA, 0 0 0 – 0 0 1 – 0 0 0 – 0 0 0

#170: James WOODS, 1 0 0 – 0 0 0 – 0 0 0 – 3 1 0:
Elizabeth WOODS, 0 1 0 – 0 0 0 – 0 0 0 – 0 0 0
William WOODS, 1 0 0 – 0 0 0 – 0 0 0 – 0 0 0
Richard WOODS, 1 0 0 – 0 0 0 – 0 0 0 – 0 0 0
Mahitabel WOODS, 0 1 0 – 0 0 0 – 0 0 0 – 0 0 0
William H. WOODS, 0 0 1 – 0 0 0 – 0 0 0 – 0 0 0
S. M. WOODS, 0 0 1 – 0 0 0 – 0 0 0 – 0 0 0 *(Male.)*
N. K. WOODS, 0 0 1 – 0 0 0 – 0 0 0 – 0 0 0 *(Female.)*
W: Fanny. M: Quaco; Frederick; Sam.

p. 50:
#171: Richard GRISTOCK, 1 0 0 – 0 0 0 – 0 0 0 – 1 0 0:
Mary BURRELL, 0 0 0 – 0 1 0 – 0 0 0 – 0 0 0
George R. GRISTOCK, 0 0 0 – 0 0 1 – 0 0 0 – 0 0 0
Antonio.

#172: James GRANT, 1 0 0 – 0 0 0 0 – 0 0 0 – 0 1 0:
Hannah GRANT, 0 1 0 – 0 0 0 – 0 0 0 – 0 0 0
Robert FOREMAN, 1 0 0 – 0 0 0 – 0 0 0 – 0 0 0
John GODFREY, 0 0 0 – 0 0 1 – 0 0 0 – 0 0 0
John WOLDNAM [*sic*]; 0 0 1 – 0 0 0 – 0 0 0 – 0 0 0
Member BENNETT.

#173: Peter L. AUDINETT, 0 0 0 – 0 0 0 – 1 0 0 – 0 0 0
Marie LOUIS, 0 0 0 – 0 0 0 – 0 1 0 – 0 0 0
Catherine LOUIS, 0 0 0 – 0 0 0 – 0 1 0 – 0 0 0
Antony LOUIS, 0 0 0 – 0 0 0 – 0 0 1 – 0 0 0
Victoria LOUIS, 0 0 0 – 0 0 0 – 0 0 1 – 0 0 0
Maria LOUIS, 0 0 0 – 0 0 0 – 0 0 1 – 0 0 0
Timothy LOUIS, 0 0 0 – 0 0 0 – 0 0 1 – 0 0 0
Maria AUDINETT, 0 0 0 – 0 0 0 – 0 0 1 – 0 0 0
Caroline AUDINETT, 0 0 0 – 0 0 0 – 0 0 1 – 0 0 0
Francis AUDINETT, 0 0 0 – 0 0 0 – 0 0 1 – 0 0 0

#174: Charles GRANT, 0 0 0 – 0 0 0 – 1 0 0 – 0 0 0
Nancy TUCKER, 0 0 0 – 0 0 0 – 0 1 0 – 0 0 0
Molly GRANT, 0 0 0 – 0 0 0 – 0 1 0 – 0 0 0
Jenneh TUCKER, 0 0 0 – 0 0 0 – 0 0 1 – 0 0 0

p. 51:
#175: William BURN, 1 0 0 – 0 0 0 – 0 0 0 – 6 5 0:
Liddie CADDLE [*sic*]; 0 0 0 – 0 1 0 – 0 0 0 – 0 0 0

James BURN, 0 0 1 – 0 0 0 – 0 0 0 – 0 0 0
George BURN, 0 0 1 – 0 0 0 – 0 0 0 – 0 0 0
Robert BURN, 0 0 1 – 0 0 0 – 0 0 0 – 0 0 0
Margaret BURN, 0 0 1 – 0 0 0 – 0 0 0 – 0 0 0
 Samuel BURN; Charles BURN; William BURN; John BURN; James
 BURN; William BURN; Jane BURN; Betsey BURN; Ann BURN; Rachael
 BURN; Clemens PADLE [*sic*].

#176: Francis WILSON, 0 0 0 – 1 0 0 – 0 0 0 – 0 0 0
   Sarah MANUEL, 0 0 0 – 0 1 0 – 0 0 0 – 0 0 0
   Francis A. WILSON, 0 0 0 – 0 0 1 – 0 0 0 – 0 0 0
   William J. WILSON, 0 0 0 – 0 0 1 – 0 0 0 – 0 0 0
   Elizabeth A. WILSON, 0 0 0 – 0 0 1 – 0 0 0 – 0 0 0
   Margaret J. WILSON, 0 0 0 – 0 0 1 – 0 0 0 – 0 0 0
   Mary A. WILSON, 0 0 0 – 0 0 1 – 0 0 0 – 0 0 0
   Sarah J. WILSON, 0 0 0 – 0 0 1 – 0 0 0 – 0 0 0

#177: John HARVIE, 0 0 0 – 0 0 0 – 1 0 0 – 0 0 0

#178: Quamina EDWARDS, 0 0 0 – 0 0 0 – 1 0 0 – 1 1 0:
   Sally EDWARDS, 0 0 0 – 0 0 0 – 0 1 0 – 0 0 0
   John; Ginny.

#179: George KEENE, 1 0 0 – 0 0 0 – 0 0 0 – 0 0 0
   Mary A. KEENE, 0 1 0 – 0 0 0 – 0 0 0 – 0 0 0
   Elizabeth KEENE, 0 1 0 – 0 0 0 – 0 0 0 – 0 0 0

#180: Henry WHITNEY, 1 0 0 – 0 0 0 – 0 0 0 – 0 0 0
   Caroline M. WHITNEY, 0 0 0 – 0 0 1 – 0 0 0 – 0 0 0
   Eliza GRANT, 0 0 0 – 0 1 0 – 0 0 0 – 0 0 0

p. 52:
#181: Robert TURNBULL, 1 0 0 – 0 0 0 – 0 0 0 – 0 0 3:
   Frances TURNBULL, 0 1 0 – 0 0 0 – 0 0 0 – 0 0 0 *(Nee Frances GIBSON)*
   No name (infant), 0 0 1 – 0 0 0 – 0 0 0 – 0 0 0 *(Helen HYDE TURNBULL,*
   David TURNBULL, 0 0 0 – 0 0 1 – 0 0 0 – 0 0 0 *b. 23 Oct 1835)*
   Maria TURNBULL, 0 0 0 – 0 0 1 – 0 0 0 – 0 0 0
   Julia; Marina; Jane.

#182: John CONNOR, 1 0 0 – 0 0 0 – 0 0 0 – 0 0 0
   Elizabeth CONNOR, 0 0 0 – 0 1 0 – 0 0 0 – 0 0 0
   Charles ROGERS, 0 0 0 – 0 0 1 – 0 0 0 – 0 0 0
   Susan ROGERS, 0 0 0 – 0 0 1 – 0 0 0 – 0 0 0

#183: Catherine SAVORY, 0 0 0 – 0 1 0 – 0 0 0 – 0 0 0
   Susanah W. WOOD, 0 0 0 – 0 1 0 – 0 0 0 – 0 0 0

201

#184: George LeGEYT, 1 0 0 – 0 0 0 – 0 0 0 – 1 1 0:
Elizabeth LeGEYT, 0 1 0 – 0 0 0 – 0 0 0 – 0 0 0
Mary A. LeGEYT, 0 0 1 – 0 0 0 – 0 0 0 – 0 0 0
Elizabeth LeGEYT, 0 0 1 – 0 0 0 – 0 0 0 – 0 0 0
Eliza LeGEYT, 0 0 1 – 0 0 1 – 0 0 0 – 0 0 0
George H. LeGEYT, 0 0 1 – 0 0 0 – 0 0 0 – 0 0 0
John LeGEYT; Jeanette LeGEYT.

#185: Joseph FLOWERS, 0 0 0 – 0 0 0 – 1 0 0 – 0 0 0
Lucretia FLOWERS, 0 0 0 – 0 0 0 – 0 1 0 – 0 0 0
Joseph FLOWERS, 0 0 0 – 0 0 0 – 0 0 1 – 0 0 0
Peter FLOWERS, 0 0 0 – 0 0 0 – 0 0 1 – 0 0 0
Joshua FLOWERS, 0 0 0 – 0 0 0 – 0 0 1 – 0 0 0
Cyrus FLOWERS, 0 0 0 – 0 0 0 – 0 0 1 – 0 0 0
John FLOWERS, 0 0 0 – 0 0 0 – 0 0 1 – 0 0 0

p.53:
#186: James FLOWERS, 0 0 0 – 0 0 0 – 1 0 0 – 0 0 0

#187: William McCULLOCH, 0 0 0 – 1 0 0 – 0 0 0 – 0 0 0
Dorothy BURREY, 0 0 0 – 0 1 0 – 0 0 0 – 0 0 0
Thomas McCULLOCH, 0 0 0 – 0 0 1 – 0 0 0 – 0 0 0
William McCULLOCH, 0 0 0 – 0 0 1 – 0 0 0 – 0 0 0
John McCULLOCH, 0 0 0 – 0 0 1 – 0 0 0 – 0 0 0

#188: Mary BATES, 0 0 0 – 0 1 0 – 0 0 0 – 0 1 2:
Joseph RABOTEAU, 0 0 0 – 1 0 0 – 0 0 0 – 0 0 0
Margaret RABOTEAU, 0 0 0 – 0 1 0 – 0 0 0 – 0 0 0
Isaac RABATEAU, 0 0 0 – 1 0 0 – 0 0 0 – 0 0 0
Alfred RABOTEAU, 0 0 0 – 0 0 1 – 0 0 0 – 0 0 0
Caroline PANTING, 0 0 0 – 0 0 1 – 0 0 0 – 0 0 0
Adriana BATES; Cecilia BATES; Catherine BATES.

#189: George HEMSLEY, 0 0 0 – 1 0 0 – 0 0 0 – 0 0 0
Mary ROBINSON, 0 0 0 – 0 0 0 – 0 1 0 – 0 0 0
Isabella HEMSLEY, 0 0 0 – 0 0 1 – 0 0 0 – 0 0 0
John HEMSLEY, 0 0 0 – 0 0 1 – 0 0 0 – 0 0 0
Edward HEMSLEY, 0 0 0 – 0 0 1 – 0 0 0 – 0 0 0
George HEMSLEY, 0 0 0 – 0 0 1 – 0 0 0 – 0 0 0
Thomas HEMSLEY, 0 0 0 – 0 0 1 – 0 0 0 – 0 0 0
William HEMSLEY, 0 0 0 – 0 0 1 – 0 0 0 – 0 0 0

#190: Charles ARMSTRONG, 0 0 0 – 1 0 0 – 0 0 0 – 0 0 0
Margaret ARMSTRONG, 0 0 0 – 0 1 0 – 0 0 0 – 0 0 0
Mary ARMSTRONG, 0 0 0 – 0 0 1 – 0 0 0 – 0 0 0

p. 54:

#191: Reuben RABON [*sic*]; 1 0 0 – 0 0 0 – 0 0 0 – 3 1 0:
Ann FLOWERS, 0 0 0 – 0 1 0 – 0 0 0 – 0 0 0
William RAYBON [*sic*]; 0 0 0 – 1 0 0 – 0 0 0 – 0 0 0
Mary RAYBON, 0 0 0 – 0 1 0 – 0 0 0 – 0 0 0
Ann GLADDON, 0 0 0 – 0 0 1 – 0 0 0 – 0 0 0
Sarah MIVETT, 0 0 0 – 0 1 0 – 0 0 0 – 0 0 0
     Thomas RAYBON; Chelsea RAYBON; Charlotte JEFFREYS; Henry
     PADDLE [*sic*].

#192: Margaret FERRELL, C 0 0 – 0 1 0 – 0 0 0 – 0 0 0
Flora GOFF, 0 0 0 – 0 0 0 – 0 1 0 – 0 0 0
Mary A. FERRELL, 0 0 0 – 0 1 0 – 0 0 0 – 0 0 0
John Thomas WARREN, 0 0 0 – 0 0 1 – 0 0 0 – 0 0 0
Margaret FERRELL, C 0 0 – 0 0 0 – 0 1 0 – 0 0 0
Susanna FERRELL, 0 0 0 – 0 0 0 – 0 1 0 – 0 0 0

#193: Duncanett CAMPBELL, 0 0 0 – 0 1 0 – 0 0 0 – 2 5 1:
John A. LINDSAY, 0 0 0 – 0 0 1 – 0 0 0 – 0 0 0
     Kitty; Susannah; Molly; Amelia; Mary; Eleanor; William; Major.

p. 55:

#194: Ann BODE, 0 0 0 – 0 1 0 – 0 0 0 – 9 5 0: *(See will of Ann BOADE, 3 Oct 1835.)*
Martha MEIGHAN, 0 0 0 – 0 1 0 – 0 0 0 – 0 0 0
Peter STAIN, 0 0 0 – 1 0 0 – 0 0 0 – 0 0 0
Edmund MEIGHAN, 0 0 0 – 0 0 1 – 0 0 0 – 0 0 0
     Joe BODE; James BODE; John; Hamlett; Tenius; Blandford; Berry; Jeoffry;
     Elizabeth; Lucy; Catherine; Fanny; Dianna; Harry.

#195: Stephen JARRETT, 0 0 0 – 0 0 0 – 1 0 0 – 0 0 2:
Margaret A. JARRETT. 0 0 0 – 0 1 0 – 0 0 0 – 0 0 0
Ann THOMPSON, 0 0 0 – 0 1 0 – 0 0 0 – 0 0 0
     Andrew FLOWERS; Emma WALSH.

#196: Flora MILLER, 0 0 0 – 0 0 0 – 0 1 0 – 0 0 0
Margaret BRADLEY, C 0 0 – 0 0 1 – 0 0 0 – 0 0 0
Caroline McQUAY, 0 C 0 – 0 0 1 – 0 0 0 – 0 0 0
Julia EAKINS, 0 0 0 – 0 0 1 – 0 0 0 – 0 0 0

#197: John LaCROIX, 0 0 0 – 1 0 0 – 0 0 0 – 0 0 0
D. M. MILLER, 0 0 0 – 0 1 0 – 0 0 0 – 0 0 0
James LaCROIX, 0 0 0 – 1 0 0 – 0 0 0 – 0 0 0
Ann M. LaCROIX, 0 C 0 – 0 1 0 – 0 0 0 – 0 0 0
Isabella LaCROIX, 0 C 0 – 0 0 1 – 0 0 0 – 0 0 0
Margaret R. LaCROIX, 0 0 0 – 0 0 1 – 0 0 0 – 0 0 0

203

p. 56:
#198: James McDONALD, 1 0 0 – 0 0 0 – 0 0 0 – 4 3 4:
Valencourt McDONALD, 0 0 1 – 0 0 0 – 0 0 0 – 0 0 0
Elmira McDONALD, 0 0 1 – 0 0 0 – 0 0 0 – 0 0 0
Isabella SUTHERLAND, 0 1 0 – 0 0 0 – 0 0 0 – 0 0 0
    M: John HENDY. W: Amelia COURTNEY. M: George NICHOLSON.
    C: Ellen CATO. M: Quamina TAYLOR; Lord HOWE. W: Betty.
    C: Walter; John the Baptist; Henry WALTERS. W: Betsey MASKALL.

#199: Amelia GORDON, 0 1 0 – 0 0 0 – 0 0 0 – 5 2 0:
    Katy; William; Warwick; Bill; Richard; Davie; Mary.

#200: The Property of John YOUNG & Co., 2 1 0:
    Horatio YOUNG; Dickey YOUNG; Amelia YOUNG.

p. 57:
#201: Francis YOUNG, 0 0 0 – 1 0 0 – 0 0 0 – 5 3 2:
Ann C. YOUNG, 0 0 0 – 0 1 0 – 0 0 0 – 0 0 0
Albert YOUNG, 0 0 0 – 0 0 1 – 0 0 0 – 0 0 0
John YOUNG, 0 0 0 – 0 0 1 – 0 0 0 – 0 0 0
Christian YOUNG, 0 0 0 – 0 0 1 – 0 0 0 – 0 0 0
Francis YOUNG, 0 0 0 – 0 0 1 – 0 0 0 – 0 0 0
    W: Sophia USHER; Susannah USHER. C: George USHER; Hercules
    USHER. M: Daniel WINTER; Larry USHER; Alexander USHER;
    Nicholas USHER; Cyrus USHER. W: Hagar USHER.

#202: Archibald W. FLOWERS, 0 0 0 – 0 0 0 – 1 0 0 – 2 0 0:
Mary A. FLOWERS, 0 0 0 – 0 0 0 – 0 1 0 – 0 0 0
Margaret FLOWERS, 0 0 0 – 0 0 0 – 0 0 1 – 0 0 0
Nora FLOWERS, 0 0 0 – 0 0 0 – 0 0 1 – 0 0 0
William FLOWERS, 0 0 0 – 0 0 0 – 0 0 1 – 0 0 0
Fanny FLOWERS, 0 0 0 – 0 0 0 – 0 0 1 – 0 0 0
Satyra FLOWERS, 0 0 0 – 0 0 0 – 0 0 1 – 0 0 0
    London; Joseph.

#203: John BAILEY, 0 0 0 – 0 0 0 – 1 0 0 – 0 0 0
Memba BAILEY, 0 0 0 – 0 0 0 – 0 1 0 – 0 0 0
Joseph BAILEY, 0 0 0 – 0 0 0 – 0 0 1 – 0 0 0
Abram BAILEY, 0 0 0 – 0 0 0 – 0 0 1 – 0 0 0

#204: Agnes WALL, 0 0 0 – 0 1 0 – 0 0 0 – 0 0 0
William MACKAY, 0 0 0 – 0 0 1 – 0 0 0 – 0 0 0
George CARMICHAEL, 0 0 0 – 0 0 1 – 0 0 0 – 0 0 0
James QUILTER, 0 0 0 – 0 0 1 – 0 0 0 – 0 0 0

#205: Family of Charles EVANS, 0 1 0: *(No mark for him, i.e. he was elsewhere.)*
Morris EVANS, 0 0 1 – 0 0 0 – 0 0 0 – 0 0 0
Thomas RHYSE, 1 0 0 – 0 0 0 – 0 0 0 – 0 0 0
    Margaret EVANS.

#206: Anthony BAILEY, 0 0 0 – 0 0 0 – 1 0 0 – 2 0 0:
Damon BAILEY, 0 0 0 – 0 0 0 – 1 0 0 – 0 0 0
James BAILEY, 0 0 0 – 0 0 0 – 1 0 0 – 0 0 0
William BAILEY, 0 0 0 – 0 0 0 – 1 0 0 – 0 0 0
Sarah BAILEY, 0 0 0 – 0 0 0 – 0 1 0 – 0 0 0
Sabinah BAILEY, 0 0 0 – 0 0 0 – 0 1 0 – 0 0 0
    Success; Charley.

#207: Elsey GENTLE, 0 0 0 – 0 0 0 – 0 1 0 – 0 0 0

#208: James HAMILTON, 0 0 0 – 1 0 0 – 0 0 0 – 0 0 0
Sarah HAMILTON, 0 0 0 – 0 1 0 – 0 0 0 – 0 0 0

#209: James RUMBALL, 0 0 0 – 1 0 0 – 0 0 0 – 0 0 0
Maria TAYLOR, 0 0 0 – 0 1 0 – 0 0 0 – 0 0 0
Catherine TAYLOR, 0 0 0 – 0 0 1 – 0 0 0 – 0 0 0
Henry TAYLOR, 0 0 0 – 0 0 1 – 0 0 0 – 0 0 0

#210: Catherine THOMPSON, 0 1 0 – 0 0 0 – 0 0 0 – 0 1 0:
Eliza MASSEY, 0 1 0 – 0 0 0 – 0 0 0 – 0 0 0
George RADFORD, 0 0 1 – 0 0 0 – 0 0 0 – 0 0 0
Catherine L. RADFORD, 0 0 1 – 0 0 0 – 0 0 0 – 0 0 0
Emma McPHERSON. 0 0 1 – 0 0 0 – 0 0 0 – 0 0 0
Jane BURN, 0 0 1 – 0 0 0 – 0 0 0 – 0 0 0
    Maria THOMPSON.

#211: Thomas MOODY, 0 0 0 – 1 0 0 – 0 0 0 – 1 0 0:
Rebecca SMITH, 0 0 0 – 0 1 0 – 0 0 0 – 0 0 0
Margaret, 0 0 0 – 0 0 1 – 0 0 0 – 0 0 0
James, 0 0 0 – 0 0 1 – 0 0 0 – 0 0 0
Charles, 0 0 0 – 0 0 1 – 0 0 0 – 0 0 0
Frederick, 0 0 0 – 0 0 1 – 0 0 0 – 0 0 0 *(Surnames not given.)*
    William.

#212: Charles BENNETT, 0 0 0 – 0 0 0 – 1 0 0 – 0 0 0
Judy BENNETT, 0 0 0 – 0 0 0 – 0 0 1 – 0 0 0

#213: Jane E. LONGSWORTH, 0 0 0 – 0 1 0 – 0 0 0 – 2 0 0:
Mrs. James USHER, 0 0 0 – 0 1 0 – 0 0 0 – 0 0 0

William H. LOW, 0 0 0 – 0 0 1 – 0 0 0 – 0 0 0
Benjamin MEIGHAN; Quamina.

Note: Mrs. James Usher was Abigail Ewing. Jane E. Longsworth, Abigail Ewing Usher, and Sarah Purcell Usher, the wife of James Usher's brother John, were half sisters.

#214: Ann HOME, 0 0 0 – 0 1 0 – 0 0 0 – 11 2 0:
Mary A. CLEMENT, 0 0 0 – 0 1 0 – 0 0 0 – 0 0 0
Margaret CLEMENT, 0 0 0 – 0 0 1 – 0 0 0 – 0 0 0
William STANDFORD; Dick GUTHRIE; Anthony DAWKINS; Prince CAMPBELL; Sandy STANDFORD; Henry STANDFORD; William STANDFORD; Blucher; John DAWKINS; Billy RODGERS; John STANDFORD; Maria STANDFORD; Rose.

p. 60:
#215: Harriet CHAISE, 0 0 0 – 0 1 0 – 0 0 0 – 0 0 0
Fanny GODFREY, 0 0 0 – 0 1 0 – 0 0 0 – 0 0 0
Eliza GODFREY, 0 0 0 – 0 1 0 – 0 0 0 – 0 0 0
Elizabeth GODFREY, 0 0 0 – 0 1 0 – 0 0 0 – 0 0 0
George GODFREY, 0 0 0 – 0 0 1 – 0 0 0 – 0 0 0
Fanny GODFREY, 0 0 0 – 0 0 1 – 0 0 0 – 0 00
Harriet CHAISE, 0 0 0 – 0 0 1 – 0 0 0 – 0 0 0
Mary MORE, 0 0 0 – 0 0 0 – 0 0 1 – 0 0 0
James LeMONT, 0 0 0 – 0 0 0 – 0 0 1 – 0 0 0

#216: Hopewell GRANT, 0 0 0 – 0 0 0 – 1 0 0 – 0 0 0

#217: John LINDORE [*sic*]; 0 0 0 – 0 0 0 – 1 0 0 – 0 0 0
Mary LINDO [*sic*]; 0 0 0 – 0 0 0 – 0 1 0 – 0 0 0
Molly LINDO, 0 0 0 – 0 0 0 – 0 1 0 – 0 0 0
John CHARLEY, 0 0 0 – 0 0 0 – 0 0 1 – 0 0 0

#218: Elizabeth GODFREY, 0 0 0 – 0 1 0 – 0 0 0 – 0 0 0
Eliza BENNETT, 0 0 0 – 0 1 0 – 0 0 0 – 0 0 0
George MONK, 0 0 0 – 1 0 0 – 0 0 0 – 0 0 0
John NEAL, 0 0 0 – 1 0 0 – 0 0 0 – 0 0 0
Lucretia NEAL, 0 0 0 – 0 0 1 – 0 0 0 – 0 0 0
Alice NEAL, 0 0 0 – 0 0 1 – 0 0 0 – 0 0 0

#219: James JAMIESON, 1 0 0 – 0 0 0 – 0 0 0 – 0 0 0

p. 61:
#220: Elizabeth THURSTON, 0 0 0 – 0 1 0 – 0 0 0 – 2 4 2:
Eleanor LEAVOR, 0 0 0 – 0 1 0 – 0 0 0 – 0 0 0
Nancy FRAIN, 0 0 0 – 0 1 0 – 0 0 0 – 0 0 0
Jonathan ROWLEY, 0 0 0 – 1 0 0 – 0 0 0 – 0 0 0

William BURNS, 0 0 0 – 1 0 0 – 0 0 0 – 0 0 0
Hannah STEPHENS, 0 0 0 – 0 1 0 – 0 0 0 – 0 0 0
   M: George; March. W: Sarah; Phillis; Andria. C: Thomas; Sarah.
   W: Mary.

#221: Charles FELIX, 0 0 0 – 0 0 0 – 1 0 0 – 0 0 0
   Elizabeth FELIX, 0 0 0 – 0 0 0 – 0 1 0 – 0 0 0
   Elizabeth FELIX, 0 0 0 – 0 0 0 – 0 0 1 – 0 0 0
   Charles Henry FELIX, 0 0 0 – 0 0 0 – 0 0 1 – 0 0 0
   Charles Lewis FELIX, 0 0 0 – 0 0 0 – 0 0 1 – 0 0 0
   Charles Dash FELIX, 0 0 0 – 0 0 0 – 0 0 1 – 0 0 0
   Eliza FELIX, 0 0 0 – 0 0 0 – 0 0 1 – 0 0 0

#222: Elizabeth POTTS, 0 0 0 – 0 1 0 – 0 0 0 – 1 2 0:
   Robert COLQUHOUGNE [sic]; 0 0 0 – 0 0 1 – 0 0 0 – 0 0 0
   William M. HARRISON, 1 0 0 – 0 0 0 – 0 0 0 – 0 0 0
   William HARRISON, 0 0 0 – 0 0 1 – 0 0 0 – 0 0 0
      Jevis [sic] HARRISON; Angelina POTTS; Nancy USHER.

#223: James H. CROZIER, 1 0 0 – 0 0 0 – 0 0 0 – 0 0 0
   James R. CROZIER, 0 0 1 – 0 0 0 – 0 0 0 – 0 0 0
   Jacob H. CROZIER, 2 0 0 – 0 0 1 – 0 0 0 – 0 0 0
   Ann S. CROZIER, 0 1 0 – 0 0 1 – 0 0 0 – 0 0 0

p. 62:
#224: Behavior TUCKER, 0 0 0 – 0 0 0 – 0 1 0 – 0 0 0
   Anney TUCKER, 0 0 0 – 0 0 0 – 0 1 0 – 0 0 0
   William TUCKER, 0 0 0 – 0 0 0 – 1 0 0 – 0 0 0
   Francis TUCKER, 0 0 0 – 0 0 0 – 1 0 0 – 0 0 0
   Rebecca TUCKER, 0 0 0 – 0 0 0 – 0 0 1 – 0 0 0
   Molly TUCKER, 0 0 0 – 0 0 0 – 0 0 1 – 0 0 0
   James TUCKER, 0 0 0 – 0 0 0 – 0 0 1 – 0 0 0

#225: Peter STAIN, 0 0 0 – 1 0 0 – 0 0 0 – 0 3 6:
   Betsy CARD, 0 0 0 – 0 0 0 – 1 0 0 – 0 0 0 *(Enumerator's error: marked as male.)*
   Richard STAIN, 0 0 0 – 0 0 0 – 1 0 0 – 0 0 0
   Catherine STAIN, 0 0 0 – 0 1 0 – 0 0 0 – 0 0 0
   Maria STAIN, 0 0 0 – 0 1 0 – 0 0 0 – 0 0 0
   Dorothy STAIN, 0 0 0 – 0 1 0 – 0 0 0 – 0 0 0
   Amelia STAIN, 0 0 0 – 0 1 0 – 0 0 0 – 0 0 0
   Sophia STAIN, 0 0 0 – 0 1 0 – 0 0 0 – 0 0 0
   Susannah STAIN, 0 0 0 – 0 0 1 – 0 0 0 – 0 0 0
   John STAIN, 0 0 0 – 0 0 1 – 0 0 0 – 0 0 0
   Henry STAIN, 0 0 0 – 0 0 1 – 0 0 0 – 0 0 0
   Mary A. STAIN, 0 0 0 – 0 0 1 – 0 0 0 – 0 0 0
   Elizabeth ALEXANDER, 0 0 0 – 0 0 1 – 0 0 0 – 0 0 0

George GILBERT, 0 0 0 – 0 0 1 – 0 0 0 – 0 0 0
W: Joanna STAIN; Rose; Jane. C: Stephen; Amelia; Mary; John; George; Sarah.

#226: Catherine ASKEW, 0 0 0 – 0 1 0 – 0 0 0 – 1 0 0:
John A. CROFT, 0 0 0 – 0 0 1 – 0 0 0 – 0 0 0
James T. CROFT, 0 0 0 – 0 0 1 – 0 0 0 – 0 0 0
Elizabeth A. CROFT, 0 0 0 – 0 0 1 – 0 0 0 – 0 0 0
George CAMPBELL.

p. 63:
#227: Lucy PATTENETT, 0 1 0 – 0 0 0 – 0 0 0 – 3 0 0:
John HUNT, 1 0 0 – 0 0 0 – 0 0 0 – 0 0 0
Catherine MARTIN, 0 1 0 – 0 0 0 – 0 0 0 – 0 0 0
Ann TINKAM, 0 1 0 – 0 0 0 – 0 0 0 – 0 0 0
George TINKAM, 1 0 0 – 0 0 0 – 0 0 0 – 0 0 0
Lucy PATTENETT, 0 0 1 – 0 0 0 – 0 0 0 – 0 0 0
Elizabeth CASTLE, 0 1 0 – 0 0 0 – 0 0 0 – 0 0 0
Thomas HUNT, 0 0 1 – 0 0 0 – 0 0 0 – 0 0 0
John HUNT, 0 0 1 – 0 0 0 – 0 0 0 – 0 0 0
George H. HUNT, 0 0 1 – 0 0 0 – 0 0 0 – 0 0 0
George PATTENETT, 0 0 0 – 1 0 0 – 0 0 0 – 0 0 0
John PATTENETT; Peter VENTURE; Joe PATTENETT.

#228: Eleanor ROBINSON, 0 0 0 – 0 0 0 – 0 1 0 – 0 0 0
Thomas ROBINSON, 0 0 0 – 0 0 0 – 1 0 0 – 0 0 0
John ROBINSON, 0 0 0 – 0 0 0 – 1 0 0 – 0 0 0
Louisa ROBINSON, 0 0 0 – 0 0 0 – 0 1 0 – 0 0 0

#229: Frances HUGHES, 0 0 0 – 0 0 0 – 0 1 0 – 0 0 0
Memba HUGHES, 0 0 0 – 0 0 0 – 0 1 0 – 0 0 0
Fibby HUGHES, 0 0 0 – 0 0 0 – 0 1 0 – 0 0 0
William HUGHES, 0 0 0 – 0 0 0 – 0 0 1 – 0 0 0
Augusta HUGHES, 0 0 0 – 0 0 0 – 0 1 0 – 0 0 0
Benjamin HUGHES, 0 0 0 – 0 0 0 – 0 0 1 – 0 0 0
Joseph HUGHES, 0 0 0 – 0 0 0 – 0 0 1 – 0 0 0
Abraham HUGHES, 0 0 0 – 0 0 0 – 0 0 1 – 0 0 0

#230: John COLLINS, 0 0 0 – 1 0 0 – 0 0 0 – 0 0 0
Dianna SMITH, 0 0 0 – 0 0 0 – 0 1 0 – 0 0 0

p. 64:
#231: John MILES, 0 0 0 – 0 0 0 –1 0 0 – 0 0 0
Ann MILES, 0 0 0 – 0 0 0 – 0 1 0 – 0 0 0
Hannah MILES, 0 0 0 – 0 0 0 – 0 0 1 – 0 0 0

Rachael GRANT, 0 0 0 – 0 0 0 – 0 0 1 – 0 0 0
Simon GRANT, 0 0 0 – 0 0 0 – 0 0 1 – 0 0 0

#232: Joseph SWASEY, 0 0 0 – 1 0 0 – 0 0 0 – 6 2 2:
Nisida SWASEY, 0 0 0 – 0 1 0 – 0 0 0 – 0 0 0
Maria SWASEY, 0 0 0 – 0 1 0 – 0 0 0 – 0 0 0
Frances SWASEY, 0 0 0 – 0 0 1 – 0 0 0 – 0 0 0
Jane SWASEY, 0 0 0 – 0 0 1 – 0 0 0 – 0 0 0
James M. SWASEY, 0 0 0 – 0 0 1 – 0 0 0 – 0 0 0
Alexander SWASEY, 0 0 0 – 0 0 1 – 0 0 0 – 0 0 0
    M: Henry SWASEY; Joe BULL; Ireland; Davey; March GRANT; Joe YOUNG; W: Nancy; Sukey. C: Amelia; Bella.

#233: Violet CARD, 0 0 0 – 0 0 0 – 0 1 0 – 0 0 0
George CARD, 0 0 0 – 0 0 0 – 1 0 0 – 0 0 0
Richard CARD, 0 0 0 – 0 0 0 – 1 0 0 – 0 0 0
Rachael CARD, 0 0 0 – 0 0 0 – 0 1 0 – 0 0 0
Matilda CARD, 0 0 0 – 0 0 0 – 0 1 0 – 0 0 0
Mary A. CARD, 0 0 0 – 0 0 0 – 0 0 1 – 0 0 0
Hague [sic] CARD, 0 0 0 – 0 0 0 – 0 0 1 – 0 0 0
John CARD, 0 0 0 – 0 0 0 – 0 0 1 – 0 0 0
Robert CARD, 0 0 0 – 0 0 0 – 0 0 1 – 0 0 0
Lenon CARD, 0 0 0 – 0 0 0 – 0 0 1 – 0 0 0

p. 65:
#234: Peter HARRIS, 0 0 0 – 0 0 0 – 1 0 0 – 1 0 0:
Mary HARRIS, 0 0 0 – 0 0 0 – 0 1 0 – 0 0 0
    Peter BODE.

#235: Adam SMITH, 0 0 0 – 0 0 0 – 1 0 0 – 0 0 0
Thomas SMITH, 0 0 0 – 0 0 0 – 0 1 0 – 0 0 0 *(Error, marked as female.)*
Molly SESTEN [sic]; 0 0 0 – 0 0 0 – 0 1 0 – 0 0 0 *(= Sally LESTER?)*
Jodetta BURKE, 0 0 0 – 0 0 0 – 0 0 1 – 0 0 0
Marcus DeBRIEN 0 0 0 – 0 0 0 – 0 0 1 – 0 0 0

#236: Serjeant JOSEPH, 0 0 0 – 1 0 0 – 0 0 0 – 0 0 0
Susannah JOSEPH, 0 0 0 – 0 1 0 – 0 0 0 – 0 0 0

#237: Joseph RENNOW, 0 0 0 – 1 0 0 – 0 0 0 – 0 0 0
Mary KENNEDY, 0 0 0 – 0 0 0 – 0 1 0 – 0 0 0
Harriot RENNOW, 0 0 0 – 0 0 1 – 0 0 0 – 0 0 0
Benjamine RENNOW, 0 0 0 – 0 0 1 – 0 0 0 – 0 0 0
Alexander RENNOW, 0 0 0 – 0 0 1 – 0 0 0 – 0 0 0
Lucy RENNOW, 0 0 0 – 0 0 1 – 0 0 0 – 0 0 0
James RENNOW, 0 0 0 – 0 0 1 – 0 0 0 – 0 0 0
Jane RENNOW, 0 0 0 – 0 0 1 – 0 0 0 – 0 0 0

#238: Richard C. WARDLAW, 1 0 0 – 0 0 0 – 0 0 0 – 3 3 2:
     Georgiana WARDLAW, 0 0 0 – 0 1 0 – 0 0 0 – 0 0 0
     Anne C. WARDLAW, 0 0 0 – 0 0 1 – 0 0 0 – 0 0 0
        M: John HUME; Daniel HUME; George FREDERICK. W: Emma;
        Betsy McAULAY; Mary P. JONES. C: James; Thomas.

p. 66
#239: James WELSH, 1 0 0 – 0 0 0 – 0 0 0 – 2 0 0
     Angelina M. WELSH, 0 1 0 – 0 0 0 – 0 0 0 – 0 0 0
     Richard HAWKINS, 1 0 0 – 0 0 0 – 0 0 0 – 0 0 0
     Edward CONEL, 1 0 0 – 0 0 0 – 0 0 0 – 0 0 0
     Frederick LINDO, 1 0 0 – 0 0 0 – 0 0 0 – 0 0 0
     Margaret FALL, 0 0 1 – 0 0 0 – 0 0 0 – 0 0 0
        Philip DAVIS (apprentice;) Billy MASKALL.

#240: Margaret HARE, 0 0 0 – 0 1 0 – 0 0 0 – 0 0 0
     Rosannah SYMMONDS, 0 0 0 – 0 0 1 – 0 0 0 – 0 0 0

#241: John S. AUGUST, 1 0 0 – 0 0 0 – 0 0 0 – 27 8 0:   *(John Samuel August)*
     Sarah AUGUST, 0 1 0 – 0 0 0 – 0 0 0 – 0 0 0
     Leonard M. BYRON, 1 0 0 – 0 0 0 – 0 0 0 – 0 0 0
     Mary BYRON, 0 1 0 – 0 0 0 – 0 0 0 – 0 0 0
     George AUGUST, 0 0 1 – 0 0 0 – 0 0 0 – 0 0 0
     James AUGUST, 0 0 1 – 0 0 0 – 0 0 0 – 0 0 0
        Andy; Bristow; Charles; John; Primus; Polydore; Taylor; Simon; George;
        Ned WALDRON; Daniel; Abel; Middleton; William; Nelson; Harry; Rose;
        Sally PEACHEY; Hannah; Sarah EVE;

p. 67:   Margaret; Sophia; Mary Ann; *(her name and mark lined through)* Frank;
        Peter BAKER; Edward; Cherry; Ned; Duncan; Francis; John; Edward;
        Nicholas; James; Mary Ann.

#242: John M. DALY, 0 0 0 – 1 0 0 – 0 0 0 – 0 0 0=

#243: John COLLINS, 1 0 0 – 0 0 0 – 0 0 0 – 2 1 0:
     Sarah COLLINS, 0 1 0 – 0 0 0 – 0 0 0 – 0 0 0
     Sarah A. COLLINS, 0 0 1 – 0 0 0 – 0 0 0 – 0 0 0
     John H. COLLINS, 0 0 1 – 0 0 0 – 0 0 0 – 0 0 0
     Henrietta COLLINS, 0 0 1 – 0 0 0 – 0 0 0 – 0 0 0
     Ellen COLLINS, 0 0 1 – 0 0 0 – 0 0 0 – 0 0 0
     Eliza M COLLINS, 0 0 1 – 0 0 0 – 0 0 0 – 0 0 0
        Robert COLLINS; William PITT; Harriett.

p. 68:
#244: William MASKALL, 1 0 0 – 0 0 0 – 0 0 0 – 5 0 0:

Rebeca [*sic*] MASKALL, 0 1 0 – 0 0 0 – 0 0 0 – 0 0 0
Ann MASKALL, 0 1 0 – 0 0 0 – 0 0 0 – 0 0 0
Henry A. GRAY, 1 0 0 – 0 0 0 – 0 0 0 – 0 0 0
Margaret M. MASKALL, 0 0 1 – 0 0 0 – 0 0 0 – 0 0 0
Frederick N. MASKALL, 0 0 1 – 0 0 0 – 0 0 0 – 0 0 0
    John DRACKSON; Boney Peter [*sic*]; Fortune; Joe; Jem GRAY.

#245: John ARMSTRONG, 0 0 0 – 1 0 0 – 0 0 0 – 17 3 0:
    Martha ARMSTRONG, 0 0 0 – 0 1 0 – 0 0 0 – 0 0 0
    Walter B. ARMSTRONG, 0 0 0 – 0 0 1 – 0 0 0 – 0 0 0
    Martha S. ARMSTRONG, 0 0 0 – 0 0 1 – 0 0 0 – 0 0 0
    Mary A. ARMSTRONG, 0 0 0 – 0 0 1 – 0 0 0 – 0 0 0
    Agnes ARMSTRONG, 0 0 0 – 0 0 1 – 0 0 0 – 0 0 0
        George ARMSTRONG; Tom ARMSTRONG; Richard WEDLOCK;
        London ARMSTRONG; Nelson AMSTRONG; Austice [*sic*]
        ARMSTRONG; William ARMSTRONG; Ben ARMSTRONG;
        Harry ARMSTRONG; Adam ARMSTRONG; Peter ARMSTRONG; Joseph
        ARMSTRONG; Thomas ARMSTRONG; Cupid ARMSTRONG; Titus
        ARMSTRONG; Charles SLUSHER; Jenny; Lucretia; Clarissa; Edward
        ARMSTRONG.

p. 69:
#246: John B. ERSKINE, 0 0 0 – 1 0 0 – 0 0 0 – 1 0 0:
    Lydia M. ERSKINE, 0 0 0 – 0 1 0 – 0 0 0 – 0 0 0
    Sarah M. ERSKINE, 0 0 0 – 0 0 1 – 0 0 0 – 0 0 0
    George K. McAULAY, 0 0 0 – 0 0 0 – 0 0 0 – 0 0 0 *(no mark)*
        George Keith McAULAY *(listed with the family, then as an Appr. Lab'r.)*

#247: Estate of Jane TRAPP. dec'd: 5 5 2: *(should read 5 3 2)*
        W: Cynthya; Bess; Rose. M: Thomas; Richard; John LAMBERT; Leith.
        W: [*sic*] Daniel; James. M: John. C: Selina; Sarah.
    (Numbers are incorrect because Daniel and James are marked as women.)

#248: Estate of Margaret GRANT, Robert WAGNER, Trustee, 2 0 0:
        Peter; Harry.

#249: Coolen JONES, 0 0 0 – 1 0 0 – 0 0 0 – 0 0 0
    Eliza DAVIS, 0 0 0 – 0 1 0 – 0 0 0 – 0 0 0
    Esther JONES, 0 0 0 – 0 0 1 – 0 0 0 – 0 0 0
    Margaret JONES, 0 0 0 – 0 0 1 – 0 0 0 – 0 0 0
    Samuel JONES, 0 0 0 – 0 0 1 – 0 0 0 – 0 0 0

p. 70:
#250: Benjamin TUCKER, 0 0 0 – 0 0 0 – 1 0 0 – 0 0 0
    Arabella LOWRIE, 0 0 0 – 0 0 0 – 0 1 0 – 0 0 0
    John TUCKER, 0 0 0 – 0 0 0 – 0 0 1 – 0 0 0

Joseph TUCKER, 0 0 0 – 0 0 0 – 0 0 1 – 0 0 0
Eleanor TUCKER, 0 0 0 – 0 0 0 – 0 0 1 – 0 0 0

#251: George BRADDICK, 1 0 0 – 0 0 0 – 0 0 0 – 1 1 1:
Sarah WINTER, 0 0 0 – 0 1 0 – 0 0 0 – 0 0 0
John G. HUNT, 0 0 0 – 0 0 1 – 0 0 0 – 0 0 0
George BRADDICK, 0 0 0 – 0 0 1 – 0 0 0 – 0 0 0
Ann E. BRADDICK, 0 0 0 – 0 0 1 – 0 0 0 – 0 0 0
William H. BRADDICK, 0 0 0 – 0 0 1 – 0 0 0 – 0 0 0
    Toney WINTER; Fanny WINTER; Nancy WINTER.

#252: William USHER, 1 0 0 – 0 0 0 – 0 0 0 – 6 2 2:
Sarah F. USHER, 0 0 0 – 0 1 0 – 0 0 0 – 0 0 0
Frederick W. USHER, 0 0 0 – 0 0 1 – 0 0 0 – 0 0 0
Maria BAYNTUN, 0 0 0 – 0 1 0 – 0 0 0 – 0 0 0
    M: Jack JACKSON; Joe McKAW; Lawrence; Tom PASLOW; Tom
    LONGSWORTH; Ellick. W: Leah, Calista. C: James; Nancy.

#253: William HARDY, 0 0 0 – 1 0 0 – 0 0 0 – 0 0 0
Rosanna HARDY, 0 0 0 – 0 1 0 – 0 0 0 – 0 0 0

p. 70: *(Enumerator's error - two pages with the same number.)*
#254: Francis JOHNSON, 0 0 0 – 0 0 0 – 1 0 0 – 0 0 0
Integrity MEIGHAN, 0 0 0 – 0 0 0 – 0 1 0 – 0 0 0
Margaret MEIGHAN, 0 0 0 – 0 0 0 – 0 1 0 – 0 0 0
Robert MEIGHAN, 0 0 0 – 0 0 0 – 0 0 1 – 0 0 0
Eliza MEIGHAN, 0 0 0 – 0 0 0 – 0 0 1 – 0 0 0
William JOHNSON, 0 0 0 – 0 0 0 – 0 0 1 – 0 0 0

#255: William GAMBLE, 0 0 0 – 0 0 0 – 1 0 0 – 0 0 0
Patina GAMBLE, 0 0 0 – 0 0 0 – 0 1 0 – 0 0 0
Lettie GAMBLE, 0 0 0 – 0 0 0 – 0 1 0 – 0 0 0
Robert HAYLOP, 0 0 0 – 0 0 0 – 1 0 0 – 0 0 0 *(variant of HAYLOCK.)*
Lettie BROUGHTON, 0 0 0 – 0 0 0 – 0 1 0 – 0 0 0

#256: Francis W. COLLINS, 1 0 0 – 0 0 0 – 0 0 0 – 0 1 0:
Caroline ABRAHAM, 0 0 0 – 0 1 0 – 0 0 0 – 0 0 0
    Eliza BURNS.

#257: Henry GARDINER, 0 0 0 – 1 0 0 – 0 0 0 – 0 0 0
Eliza A. HEWLETT, 0 0 0 – 0 1 0 – 0 0 0 – 0 0 0
William W. GARDINER, 0 0 0 – 0 0 1 – 0 0 0 – 0 0 0

#258: Mary WALL, 0 1 0 – 0 0 0 – 0 0 0 – 0 0 0
Mary A. RICHARDSON, 0 1 0 – 0 0 0 – 0 0 0 – 0 0 0

212

#259: George R. SAVERY, 0 0 0 – 1 0 0 – 0 0 0 – 1 3 1:
Amelia JACKSON, 0 0 0 – 0 1 0 – 0 0 0 – 0 0 0
George S. SAVERY, C 0 0 – 0 0 1 – 0 0 0 – 0 0 0
Eliza A. SAVERY, 0 C 0 – 0 0 1 – 0 0 0 – 0 0 0
James DeBRIEN SAVERY, 0 0 0 – 0 0 1 – 0 0 0 – 0 0 0
        W: Cecilia. M: Dublin; James; Morris. C: Richard.

p. 71:
#260: Elizabeth KINGSTONE, 0 0 0 – 0 1 0 – 0 0 0 – 0 0 1:
Richard DeBRIEN, 0 0 0 – 0 0 1 – 0 0 0 – 0 0 0
Hannah WOOD, 0 0 0 – 0 0 1 – 0 0 0 – 0 0 0
William FORRESTER 0 0 0 – 0 0 1 – 0 0 0 – 0 0 0
        Catherine KINGSTONE.

#261: John HUGHES 1 0 0 – 0 0 0 – 0 0 0 – 0 0 0
Ann E. HUGHES, 0 1 0 – 0 0 0 – 0 0 0 – 0 0 0
Edward H. HUGHES, 0 0 1 – 0 0 0 – 0 0 0 – 0 0 0

#262: Corroden [*sic*] TIMMERMAN, 0 0 0 – 0 0 0 – 1 0 0 – 0 0 0 *(= Corydon)*
Isabell STAFFORD, 0 0 0 – 0 0 0 – 0 1 0 – 0 0 0
Susannah CRABBER, 0 0 0 – 0 0 0 – 0 1 0 – 0 0 0
Sampson HOME, 0 0 0 – 0 0 0 – 1 0 0 – 0 0 0
William STANFORD, 0 0 0 – 0 0 0 – 1 0 0 – 0 0 0
Richard WILLIAMS, 0 0 0 – 0 0 0 – 0 0 1 – 0 0 0

#263: Ann SUTHERLAND, 0 0 0 – 0 0 0 – 0 1 0 – 0 0 0

#264: Charles CRAIG, 1 0 0 – 0 0 0 – 0 0 0 – 0 0 0

#265: George WESTBY, 0 0 0 – 1 0 0 – 0 0 0 – 0 0 0
Ariadne WESTBY, 0 0 0 – 0 1 0 – 0 0 0 – 0 0 0
Catherine WESTBY, 0 0 0 – 0 0 1 – 0 0 0 – 0 0 0
Nathaniel WESTBY, 0 0 0 – 0 0 1 – 0 0 0 – 0 0

p. 72:
#266: Peter FRANKLIN, 0 0 0 – 0 0 0 – 1 0 0 – 0 0 0
Elizabeth CURRENT, 0 0 0 – 0 0 0 – 0 1 0 – 0 0 0
Sarah FRANKLIN, 0 0 0 – 0 0 0 – 0 1 0 – 0 0 0
Cloe FRANKLIN, 0 0 0 – 0 0 0 – 0 1 0 – 0 0 0
Peter FRANKLIN, 0 0 0 – 0 0 0 – 0 0 1 – 0 0 0
William FRANKLIN, 0 0 0 – 0 0 0 – 0 0 1 – 0 0 0
Fanny FRANKLIN, 0 0 0 – 0 0 0 – 0 0 1 – 0 0 0
Susan FRANKLIN, 0 0 0 – 0 0 0 – 0 0 1 – 0 0 0
Elizabeth FRANKLIN, 0 0 0 – 0 0 0 – 0 0 1 – 0 0 0
Sarah FRANKLIN, 0 0 0 – 0 0 0 – 0 0 1 – 0 0 0

#267: Charles MIDDLETON, 1 0 0 – 0 0 0 – 0 0 0 – 0 0 0
David MIDDLETON, 0 0 0 – 0 0 1 – 0 0 0 – 0 0 0

#268: Thomas PHILLIPS, 1 0 0 – 0 0 0 – 0 0 0 – 0 0 0
Sarah BURNS, 0 0 0 – 0 1 0 – 0 0 0 – 0 0 0
Ann G. GRAY, 0 0 0 – 0 1 0 – 0 0 0 – 0 0 0
Caroline PHILLIPS, 0 0 0 – 0 0 1 – 0 0 0 – 0 0 0
James PHILLIPS, 0 0 0 – 0 0 1 – 0 0 0 – 0 0 0
Martha TUCKY, 0 0 0 – 0 0 0 – 0 1 0 – 0 0 0
Mary SAVORY, 0 0 0 – 0 0 0 – 0 0 1 – 0 0 0
Rosett BROSTER, 0 0 0 – 0 0 0 – 0 0 1 – 0 0 0
James F. BOOTH, 1 0 0 – 0 0 0 – 0 0 0 – 0 0 0

p. 73:
#269: Rodger GOFF, 0 0 0 – 1 0 0 – 0 0 0 – 0 0 0
Eliza GORDON, 0 0 0 – 0 1 0 – 0 0 0 – 0 0 0
John GORDON, 0 0 0 – 1 0 0 – 0 0 0 – 0 0 0
Elizabeth GOFF, 0 0 0 – 0 1 0 – 0 0 0 – 0 0 0
Elizabeth FOREMAN, 0 0 0 – 0 0 1 – 0 0 0 – 0 0 0
Catherine FOREMAN, 0 0 0 – 0 0 1 – 0 0 0 – 0 0 0
Marina GILLETT, 0 0 0 – 0 1 0 – 0 0 0 – 0 0 0
Thomas BALLAD, 0 0 0 – 0 0 1 – 0 0 0 – 0 0 0

#270: Benjamin LONGSWORTH, 0 0 0 – 1 0 0 – 0 0 0 – 0 0 0
Sarah KEENE, 0 0 0 – 0 1 0 – 0 0 0 – 0 0 0
Margaret LONGSWORTH, 0 0 0 – 0 0 1 – 0 0 0 – 0 0 0
Mary KEENE 0 0 0 – 0 0 1 – 0 0 0 – 0 0 0

#271: Percilla HICKEY, 0 0 0 – 0 1 0 – 0 0 0 – 0 0 0
William HAMILTON, 0 0 0 – 0 0 0 – 1 0 0 – 0 0 0
Mary Ann WAGNER, 0 0 0 – 0 0 0 – 0 0 1 – 0 0 0
Elizabeth WAGNER, 0 0 0 – 0 0 0 – 0 0 1 – 0 0 0
Caesar HICKEY, 0 0 0 – 0 0 0 – 1 0 0 – 0 0 0

p. 74:
#272: Phoebe FLOWERS, 0 0 0 – 0 1 0 – 0 0 0 – 0 1 1:
Eleanor CHERRINGTON, 0 0 0 – 0 1 0 – 0 0 0 – 0 0 0
William CHERRINGTON, 0 0 0 – 0 0 1 – 0 0 0 – 0 0 0
Sarah A. CHERRINGTON, 0 0 0 – 0 1 0 – 0 0 0 – 0 0 0
Elizabeth CHERRINGTON, 0 0 0 – 0 0 1 – 0 0 0 – 0 0 0
Emma CHERRINGTON, 0 0 0 – 0 0 1 – 0 0 0 – 0 0 0
Henry U. CHERRINGTON, 0 0 0 – 0 0 1 – 0 0 0 – 0 0 0
John S. CHERRINGTON, 0 0 0 – 0 0 1 – 0 0 0 – 0 0 0
James CHERRINGTON, 0 0 0 – 0 0 1 – 0 0 0 – 0 0 0
Clarissa WILLIAMS, 0 0 0 – 0 0 0 – 0 0 1 – 0 0 0

Jane FLOWERS, 0 0 0 – 0 0 0 – 0 0 1 – 0 0 0
Bella FLOWERS. Francis FLOWERS.

#273: Henry GRANT, 0 0 0 – 1 0 0 – 0 0 0 – 0 0 0
Caroline GRANT, 0 0 0 – 0 1 0 – 0 0 0 – 0 0 0

#274: John E. HENDERSON, 0 0 0 - 1 0 0 – 0 0 0 – 3 0 0:
Eliza A. BROSTER, 0 0 0 – 0 1 0 – 0 0 0 – 0 0 0
John E. HENDERSON. 0 0 0 – 0 0 1 – 0 0 0 – 0 0 0
George H. HENDERSON, 0 0 0 – 0 0 1 – 0 0 0 – 0 0 0
Eliza A. HENDERSON, 0 0 0 – 0 0 1 – 0 0 0 – 0 0 0
Charles A. HENDERSON, 0 0 0 – 0 0 1 – 0 0 0 – 0 0 0
George HENDERSON, 0 0 0 – 0 0 0 – 1 0 0 – 0 0 0
Moland; Thomas; Kelly.

#275: Francis HAYLOCK, 0 0 0 – 1 0 0 – 0 0 0 – 0 0 0
Catherine COFFELL, 0 0 0 – 0 1 0 – 0 0 0 – 0 0 0
Francis HAYLOCK, 0 0 0 – 1 0 0 – 0 0 0 – 0 0 0
James HAYLOCK, 0 0 0 – 0 0 1 – 0 0 0 – 0 0 0
Maria HAYLOCK, 0 0 0 – 0 0 1 – 0 0 0 – 0 0 0
Robert HAYLOCK, 0 0 0 – 0 0 1 – 0 0 0 – 0 0 0
Joseph HAYLOCK, 0 0 0 – 0 0 1 – 0 0 0 – 0 0 0

p. 75:
#276: Leonard P. COX, 1 0 0 – 0 0 0 – 0 0 0 – 0 0 0

#277: James KELLY, 0 0 0 – 0 0 0 – 1 0 0 – 0 0 0
Mary KELLY, 0 0 0 – 0 1 0 – 0 0 0 – 0 0 0
Frederick WALL, 0 0 0 – 0 0 0 – 1 0 0 – 0 0 0
Mary SMITH, 0 0 0 – 0 0 0 – 0 0 1 – 0 0 0
Eleanor HUME, 0 0 0 – 0 0 0 – 0 1 0 – 0 0 0

#278: Clarissa DeBRIEN, 0 0 0 – 0 0 0 – 0 1 0 – 0 0 0
Julius DeBRIEN, 0 0 0 – 1 0 0 – 0 0 0 – 0 0 0
Aloria DeBRIEN, 0 0 0 – 0 0 0 – 0 1 0 – 0 0 0
Sarah DeBRIEN, 0 0 0 – 0 0 0 – 0 1 0 – 0 0 0
Maria DeBRIEN, 0 0 0 – 0 0 0 – 0 0 1 – 0 0 0
Cleo DeBRIEN, 0 0 0 – 0 0 0 – 0 0 1 – 0 0 0
Angelina DeBRIEN, 0 0 0 – 0 0 0 – 0 0 1 – 0 0 0
Elizabeth FLOWERS, 0 0 0 – 0 0 0 – 0 1 0 – 0 0 0

#279: William CHARTER, 0 0 0 – 0 0 0 – 1 0 0 – 0 0 0
Joseph DRAKSON, 0 0 0 – 0 0 0 – 1 0 0 – 0 0 0
James DERNSHAW, 0 0 0 – 0 0 0 – 1 0 0 – 0 0 0
Nancy TUCKER, 0 0 0 – 0 0 0 – 0 1 0 – 0 0 0
Jane TUCKER, 0 0 0 – 0 0 0 – 0 0 1 – 0 0 0

215

#280: William GUILD, 1 0 0 – 0 0 0 – 0 0 0 – 0 0 0
      Charles ROBERTSON, 1 0 0 – 0 0 0 – 0 0 0 – 0 0 0
      Robert BOWDEN, 1 0 0 – 0 0 0 – 0 0 0 – 0 0 0
      William G. ROBERTSON, 1 0 0 – 0 0 0 – 0 0 0 – 0 0 0
      Rochfort, 0 0 0 – 0 0 0 – 1 0 0 – 0 0 0 *(Surname not given.)*
      Pedro J. SABIO, 0 0 0 – 0 0 0 – 1 0 0 – 0 0 0
      Florentin, 0 0 0 – 0 0 0 – 1 0 0 – 0 0 0
      Peter, 0 0 0 – 0 0 0 – 1 0 0 – 0 0 0 *(Surnames not given.)*

#281: John GORDON, 0 0 0 – 0 0 0 – 1 0 0 – 0 1 0:
      Julian [*sic*] GORDON, 0 0 0 – 0 0 0 – 0 1 0 – 0 0 0   *[= Juliana)*
      Charlotte JOHNSTON, 0 0 0 – 0 0 0 – 0 1 0 – 0 0 0
      George DUNBAR, 0 0 0 – 0 0 0 – 0 0 1 – 0 0 0
          Jemima GORDON.

#282: William BLOND, 1 0 0 – 0 0 0 – 0 0 0 – 0 0 0
      Hannah, 0 0 0 – 0 1 0 – 0 0 0 – 0 0 0 *(Surname not given.)*
      A. McKENZIE, 0 0 0 – 1 0 0 – 0 0 0 – 0 0 0
      Mary A. CORD, 0 0 0 – 0 0 1 – 0 0 0 – 0 0 0
      Rebecca CORD, 0 0 0 – 0 0 1 – 0 0 0 – 0 0 0
      Isabella CORD, 0 0 0 – 0 0 1 – 0 0 0 – 0 0 0

#283: Robert HOPE, 0 0 0 – 0 0 0 – 1 0 0 – 1 0 0:
      Caesar ANDREWS, 0 0 0 – 0 0 0 – 1 0 0 – 0 0 0
      Phillis DORSETT, 0 0 0 – 0 0 0 – 0 1 0 – 0 0 0
      Clarissa HOPE, 0 0 0 – 0 0 0 – 0 1 0 – 0 0 0
      James HOPE, 0 0 0 – 0 0 0 – 0 0 1 – 0 0 0
      Phillis ROBERT, 0 0 0 – 0 0 0 – 0 0 1 – 0 0 0
      Eliza ROBERT, 0 0 0 – 0 0 0 – 0 0 1 – 0 0 0
          Ned PORTER.
#284: Robert LOWRIE, 0 0 0 – 1 0 0 – 0 0 0 – 0 0 0
      Mary EMERY, 0 0 0 – 0 1 0 – 0 0 0 – 0 0 0
      James LAWRIE, 0 0 0 – 1 0 0 – 0 0 0 – 0 0 0
      William LAWRIE, 0 0 0 – 1 0 0 – 0 0 0 – 0 0 0
      Venus LAWRIE, 0 0 0 – 0 1 0 – 0 0 0 – 0 0 0
      Benjamin LAWRIE, 0 0 0 – 1 0 0 – 0 0 0 – 0 0 0
      William B. CRAFT, 0 0 0- 1 0 0 – 0 0 0 – 0 0 0

#285: William H. GIBSON, 0 0 0 – 1 0 0 – 0 0 0 – 0 0 0
      Sarah A. CASTLE, 0 0 0 – 0 1 0 – 0 0 0 – 0 0 0
      Elizabeth J. TALBOT, 0 0 0 – 0 0 1 – 0 0 0 – 0 0 0
      John W. GIBSON, 0 0 0 – 0 0 1 – 0 0 0 – 0 0 0
      Catherine E. GIBSON, 0 0 0 – 0 0 1 – 0 0 0 – 0 0 0
      Ann A. GIBSON, 0 0 0 – 0 0 1 – 0 0 0 – 0 0 0

#286: Catherine ROBINSON, 0 1 0 – 0 0 0 – 0 0 0 – 10 5 0:
Isabella STEWART, 0 1 0 – 0 0 0 – 0 0 0 – 0 0 0
     Henry, alias Chance; Joseph ERNEST; Cloe ERNEST; Henry
     ROBINSON; Mary A. ROBINSON; Ernest; John ROBINSON; Jane P.
     FLOWERS; Phœbe ROBINSON; Elizabeth ROBINSON; James ERNEST;
     Meligo ERNEST; Peter ROBINSON; Edmund ROBINSON; George
     ROBINSON.

p. 78:
#287: Ann WAIGHT, 0 1 0 – 0 0 0 – 0 0 0 – 1 0 0: *(widow of James, who d. 3 Oct 1831.)*
Mary A. WAIGHT, 0 0 1 – 0 0 0 – 0 0 0 – 0 0 0
William WAIGHT, 0 0 1 – 0 0 0 – 0 0 0 – 0 0 0
Eliza WAIGHT, 0 0 1 – 0 0 0 – 0 0 0 – 0 0 0
     George WHITE *[sic]*.

#288: William POWEL, 0 0 0 – 0 0 0 – 1 0 0 – 0 0 0
Fanny POWEL, 0 0 0 – 0 0 0 – 0 1 0 – 0 0 0

#289: Ado FLOWERS, 0 0 0 – 0 0 0 – 1 0 0 – 0 0 0
Harriot TENA, 0 0 0 – 0 0 0 – 0 1 0 – 0 0 0
John FLOWERS, 0 0 0 – 0 0 0 – 0 0 1 – 0 0 0
James FLOWERS, 0 0 0 – 0 0 0 – 1 0 0 – 0 0 0

#290: Frances WALL, 0 0 0 – 0 1 0 – 0 0 0 – 0 0 1:
Sarah J. CROFT, 0 0 0 – 0 0 1 – 0 0 0 – 0 0 0
Louiza R. CROFT, 0 0 0 – 0 0 1 – 0 0 0 – 0 0 0
     Rose.

#291: Robert PRICE, 0 0 0 – 0 0 0 – 1 0 0 – 0 0 0
Elizabeth GOFF, 0 0 0 – 0 0 0 – 0 1 0 – 0 0 0
Thomas PRICE, 0 0 0 – 0 0 0 – 0 0 1 – 0 0 0
Richard PRICE, 0 0 0 – 0 0 0 – 0 0 1 – 0 0 0
Robert PRICE, 0 0 0 – 0 0 0 – 0 0 1 – 0 0 0

#292: John D. BETSON, 1 0 0 – 0 0 0 – 0 0 0 – 0 0 0
Nancy CRAPPER, 0 0 0 – 0 1 0 – 0 0 0 – 0 0 0
Fanny DAY BETSON, 0 0 0 – 0 0 1 – 0 0 0 – 0 0 0

p. 79: *The Keeper of the Records mistakenly wrote the household numbers on this page
as #193-195; the writer has corrected the error.*

#293: James A. WILLS, 1 0 0 – 0 0 0 – 0 0 0 – 3 0 0
Catherine F. WILLS, 0 1 0 – 0 0 0 – 0 0 0 – 0 0 0
     Ned; Robert WEATHERBY; Robert LAMB.

217

Note: Dr. James Alexander Wills' wife, Catherine Ferrill Potts (the writer's GGG-aunt) was a daughter of John Potts Jr. and Elizabeth Tillett.

#294: Rev'd M. NEWPORT, 1 0 0 – 0 0 0 – 0 0 0 – 0 0 0
Matthew NEWPORT Jr., 1 0 0 – 0 0 0 – 0 0 0 – 0 0 0

#295: Property of R. J. ANDREW & Co, 24 8 0:
Jenny ARMSTRONG; Archibald ARMSTRONG*; Lucretia ARMSTRONG; Mary ARMSTRONG; Clarissa ARMSTRONG. Thomas ARMSTRONG; Francis ARMSTRONG; Nelson; Cupid; Sarah Ann; George ARMSTRONG; Harry; William ARMSTRONG; Nelson T; Tom; London; Scotland; Ben BLOCK; Adam ARMSTRONG; Peter ARMSTRONG; Charles SLUSHER; Edward; Ned; *incorrectly marked as a woman.*

p. 80: Robert; Richard; Knight; Charles; Lawrence; Edward; Sampson; Grace; Sophia.

#296: Mary HUME, 0 0 0 – 0 1 0 – 0 0 0 – 2 1 0:
Louisa ALTEREITH, 0 0 0 – 0 1 0 – 0 0 0 – 0 0 0
Mary J. ALTEREITH, 0 0 0 – 0 0 1 – 0 0 0 – 0 0 0
Rebecca ALTEREITH, 0 0 0 – 0 0 1 – 0 0 0 – 0 0 0
Margaret ALTEREITH, 0 0 0 – 0 0 1 – 0 0 0 – 0 0 0
George ALTEREITH, 0 0 0 – 0 0 1 – 0 0 0 – 0 0 0
Robert HUME, 0 0 0 – 1 0 0 – 0 0 0 – 0 0 0
William HUME; Adam HUME; Clara HUME.

#297: Susannah BURREL, 0 0 0 – 0 1 0 – 0 0 0 – 0 3 1:
Janett DUNWELL, 0 0 0 – 0 1 0 – 0 0 0 – 0 0 0
W: Ann POTTS; Patience POTTS; Jenny POTTS. C: Mimba POTTS.

#298: Margaret HULSE, 0 0 0 – 0 1 0 – 0 0 0 – 2 3 5:
Thomas ORD, 0 0 0 – 0 0 1 – 0 0 0 – 0 0 0
George HULSE, 0 0 0 – 0 0 1 – 0 0 0 – 0 0 0
Hannah HULSE, 0 0 0 – 0 0 1 – 0 0 0 – 0 0 0
W: Tabitha; Jula. M: Robert EVE; Robert WILLIS. C: Sarah LOCK, Josep [*sic*]; Thomas;

p. 81: C: Emily; Thomas.

#299: J. A. CRAIG, 1 0 0 – 0 0 0 – 0 0 0 – 5 4 0:
Louisa HILL, 0 0 0 – 0 1 0 – 0 0 0 – 0 0 0
Jane A. CRAIG, 0 0 0 – 0 0 1 – 0 0 0 – 0 0 0
Elizabeth CRAIG, 0 0 0 – 0 0 1 – 0 0 0 – 0 0 0
Charles; Lewis; Jem, John; Lucy; Stella; Saraha [*sic*]; George; Eliza.

218

#300: Joseph LORD, 0 0 0 – 1 0 0 – 0 0 0 – 1 0 0
Margaret NEAL, 0 0 0 – 0 1 0 – 0 0 0 – 0 0 0
Robert.

p. 82:
#301: Sarah KEEF [sic]; 0 1 0 – 0 0 0 – 0 0 0 – 11 14 0:
Charles CUNNINGHAM, 1 0 0 – 0 0 0 – 0 0 0 – 0 0 0
Mary A. SPROAT, 0 1 0 – 0 0 0 – 0 0 0 – 0 0 0
Sarah BENNETT, 0 0 1 – 0 0 0 – 0 0 0 – 0 0 0
Harry BENNETT, 0 0 1 – 0 0 0 – 0 0 0 – 0 0 0
Andrew CUNNINGHAM, 1 0 0 – 0 0 0 – 0 0 0 – 0 0 0
    Peter; Quashie; Brittain; Bennett; November; William; Peter [sic]; Adam;
    Middleton; John; Henry; Sylvia; Cythia [sic]; Venus; Harriot; Ariadne;
    Diana; Rebecca; Bella; Eve; Phillis; Sabina; Cuba; Eliza; Mary.

*Note: Sarah and Harry, Henry Cunningham Bennett, were children of Marshal Bennett
Jr. and Catherine Cunningham, who died in November 1833. Their older brother, John,
was probably at school in England. Henry C. married Catherine "Katie" Brennan and
had children Henry Marshall and Georgiana McKay Bennett, who went to the Bay
Islands. What became of Sarah? Was George Sproat the father of Mary A. Sproat?*

#302: Susanna USHER, 0 1 0 – 0 0 0 – 0 0 0 – 1 2 0:
Elizabeth S. USHER, 0 0 1 – 0 0 0 – 0 0 0 – 0 0 0
Eliza USHER, 0 0 1 – 0 0 0 – 0 0 0 – 0 0 0
George C. USHER, 0 0 1 – 0 0 0 – 0 0 0 – 0 0 0
    W: Lucretia; Elizabeth; M: Joseph.

p. 83:
#303: William TILLETT, 1 0 0 – 0 0 0 – 0 0 0 – 7 6 0:
Sarah JONES, 0 1 0 – 0 0 0 – 0 0 0 – 0 0 0
Solomon TILLETT, 0 0 1 – 0 0 0 – 0 0 0 – 0 0 0
John TILLETT, 0 0 1 – 0 0 0 – 0 0 0 – 0 0 0
George TILLETT, 0 0 1 – 0 0 0 – 0 0 0 – 0 0 0
Robert TILLETT, 0 0 1 – 0 0 0 – 0 0 0 – 0 0 0
David TILLETT, 0 0 1 – 0 0 0 – 0 0 0 – 0 0 0
William TILLETT, 0 0 1 – 0 0 0 – 0 0 0 – 0 0 0
Mary W. TILLETT, 0 0 1 – 0 0 0 – 0 0 0 – 0 0 0 *(Mary White Tillett)*
Thomas TILLETT, 0 0 1 – 0 0 0 – 0 0 0 – 0 0 0
Mary A. TILLETT, 0 0 1 – 0 0 0 – 0 0 0 – 0 0 0
    Dan; Boston; William; Prince LOWRIE; Robert CURLIER; Jessy; James;
    Richard; Present; Jane; Kitty DUNCAN; Betsy; Elizabeth.

*Note: This census identifies ten of the twelve children mentioned in William Tillett's will,
which is available at the Belize National Archives. William was a son of Capt. William
Tillett and Mary White, and a grandson of Capt. William White and Elizabeth --?--. Does
anyone know Elizabeth's maiden name and parentage?*

219

p. 84:

#304: Marshal BENNETT, 1 0 0 – 0 0 0 – 0 0 0 – 32 0 0 + 28 4 0 + 25 7 0 + 15 17 0 +
George COLLINS, 1 0 0 – 0 0 0 – 0 0 0 – 0 0 0 children 18 + 18 and 11 women
Frederick KNOTH, 1 0 0 – 0 0 0 – 0 0 0 – 0 0 0
Tabia, 1 0 0 – 0 0 0 – 0 0 0 – 0 0 0 *(Error: in previous censuses, a black woman.)*
Phillip BENNETT, 1 0 0 – 0 0 0 – 0 0 0 – 0 0 0
William R. COOKE, 1 0 0 – 0 0 0 – 0 0 0 – 0 0 0 *(Wm R^t SMITH COOKE.)*
Thomas BENNETT; William BODEN; Wiliam MARTIN; Prince POTTS;
Moco FRANK; Phillip BRENNAN; John MOODY; George MORAVIA;
Sampson POTTS; Robin POTTS; Duke BENNETT; Cudjoe POTTS;
Michael MARTIN; John BENNETT; Titus BENNETT; Benjamin BULL;
Joseph BENNETT; London DOUGLAS; Joseph POTTS; Smart BENNETT;
Thomas DOUGLAS; Johnson BENNETT; Julius; Mark; Thomas COOKE;
David BENNETT; Alexander MARTIN; Alexander MIDDLETON; George
SLATER; J----- *(illegible, lined out;)* Joseph GOFF; William J. CRABB;
James BENNETT; *(32 men.)*

*Note: W. R. S and Mary Byron Cooke went to Adelaide in 1839. The name and mark for
Duke Bennett were interlined, in a different hand from that of the enumerator.*

p. 85: Robert GALLIMORE; John SMITH; William SMITH; Francis SMITH;
James BENNETT; George BENNETT; Bristol; Thomas HEWLETT;
Scotland BENNETT; Adam BENNETT; Joseph TRAPP; James MEIGHAN;
Bath. ARTHURS; Peter ARTHURS; Memory ARTHURS; Kinsale; Francis
BENNETT; Richard WALKER; Kato; Thomas MARTIN; George POTTS;
William POTTS; John YOUNG; Richard POTTS; Archibald POTTS;
Robert POTTS; Adam POTTS; Richard BARRET; Diana STAIN; Anne
STAIN; Abba STAIN; Mary MUDIAN; *(28 men, 4 women.)*

p. 86: Chatham; Betsy LAMB; Dorinda LAMB; Rachel JACKSON; William
BENNETT; Thomas BRENNAN; Catherine GOFFE; Maria GOFFE;
Patience BENNETT; Princess BENNETT; George CRAWFORD; Delort
TOWNSEND; Thomas AUGUST; Guildford BENNETT; Robert
BENNETT; Rodney; Middleton; Fortune BENNETT; Giddy BENNETT;
Otway BENNETT; Stafford BENNETT; Bob HIBBERT; Cudjoe YOUNG;
Batty HOMES; David BETSON; David FUNDY; Dick ALEXANDER;
Peter WALDRON; Rift HARE; Adam JACKSON; Chelsea STAIN; Sammy
HENDERSON. *(25 men, 7 women.)*

p. 87: Hamilton; Richmond; Pollydore; George ELRINGTON; John; James WHITE;
James JAMAICA; Robert BENNETT; Abel BENNETT; Quawrm; Duncan;
John RAMSAY; Charles BENNETT; George GRAHAM; Tom JONES;
Thomas JOHNSON; John BAPTISTE; Devonshire MEIGHAN; Richard
YATE; Limerick PASLOW; Harry GIBSON; William MARTIN; Duckworth;
Murphy COURTAY [*sic*]; Andrew KEENE; Settle JACK; Marcus;

Johnson; Quashie; Moco Simon; London Moco; Kingstone. *(32 men.)*

p. 88:   Caesar; Bill BENNETT; Devonshire; Joe KEENE; Hector; Vick; Philime;
            Tom Mandingo; Bob; Ned; Cork; Murphy; Mary ELLICE; Sue DeBRIEN;
            Margaret GOFFE; Diana LAMB; Damon BENNETT; Moco Peter; George
            ELLICE; Susannah; Juba; Catherine GOFF; Judy; Patience; Sarah CRABB;
            Hannah; Jane SMITH; Elizabeth SMITH; Susannah; Tabia BENNETT;
            Mary CHARLES; Betsy BENNETT. *(15 men, 17 women.)*

p. 89:   Children:
            Henrietta; Eve BENNETT; Estella HOARE; Eleanor HOARE; Maria
            BENNETT; Elizabeth EVE; Aurelia BENNETT; Elizabeth BENNETT;
            Catherine ARTHURS; Sarah ARTHURS; Maria; Bella ARTHURS; Diana
            BENNETT; Margaret MOODY; Catherine BENNETT; Flora BENNETT;
            Anne MOORE; Mary A. FRAZIER; Sabina; Mary BENNETT; Amelia;
            Theresa; Prudence; Clara; Mary MARTIN; Jessy BENNETT; Patty
            CRAWFORD; Maria BENNETT; Polly POTTS; Diana POTTS; Sarah
            POTTS; Mary J. POTTS; *(18 boys, 18 girls.)*

p. 90:   Women:
            Jenny POTTS; Amelia POTTS; Betsy POTTS; Mary BURNETT; Polly
            POTTS; Diana POTTS; Sarah POTTS; Mary J. POTTS; Jenny POTTS;
            Amelia POTTS; Betty POTTS. *(11 women.)*

*Students of history will note that far fewer people were enumerated in this census than in
the 1832, and far less than in the 1839. We know that no part of the 1835 census is
missing; the page numbers continue from the 1835 to the 1839 in the same book.
The 1832 shows a total population of 4537, of whom 1783 were slaves, the 1835 a total
population of 2534, of whom only 1084 were apprenticed labourers. There were 487
households in 1832, only 304 in 1835, and 552 in 1839. One possible explanation is that
many of the men who gained their freedom in 1834 avoided servitude as apprentice
labourers by leaving town, taking their families up the river to settle in the interior. But
subsistence farming is very hard work, and wives accustomed to going to market and
shopping for the wide variety of household goods arrayed in Back Street stores would
have been found life in the bush unpleasant, so families would have drifted back to town.*

221

p. 91:   RECAPITULATION OF CENSUS

Whites:

				Males		Females	
	Males	134		Males		Females	
	Females	88		Children	36	Children	33
Total Number of Whites		222		Adults	98	Adults	55
Deduct Children		69		Total Males	134	Females	88
Total number of Adults		153	153				

Coloured:

				Males		Females	
	Males	298		Males		Females	
	Females	372		Children	179	Children	172
Total Number of Coloured		670		Adults	110	Adults	200
Deduct Children		351		Total Males	298*	Females	372
Total number of Adults		319	319				

Free Blacks:

				Males:		Females:	
	Males	222		Males:		Females:	
	Females	245		Children	99	Children	93
Total Number of Free Blacks		467		Adults	123	Adults	152
Deduct Children		192		Total Males	222	Females	245
Total Number of Adults		275	275				

Slaves:

				Males:		Females	
	Males	768		Males:		Females	
	Females	416		Children	82	Children	98
Total Number of Slaves		1084		Adults	686	Adults	318
Deduct Children		180		Total Males	768	Females	416
Total Number of Adults		1004	1004				

Total Males:
   White, 134; Coloured, 298;* Free Black, 222; Slaves, 768, total Males - 1422.*

Total Females:
   White, 88; Coloured, 372; Free Black, 245; Slaves, 416; total Females - 1121

Total Number of Settlers according to Returns received in Record Office   - 2543.*

Belize, Honduras, December 31st 1835.

Errors – colored males should read 289, total males 1413, and total settlers 2534.

----o0o----

222

THE 1839 CENSUS OF BELIZE

The 1839 census follows the 1835 in the same book, with the first entry on page 93. The Keeper of the Records filled out the book with household #407 but had many more families to enumerate, so he started a new book. He entered households #408 - #552 on pages he numbered 1 – 34, but for some reason did not continue to give totals at the bottom of the pages. Later in time, somebody assumed the new book was a separate census, and wrote at the top of the first sheet "1840." Pages 1-34 were placed in a separate folder and photographed by the LDS as "the 1840 census." There is no such thing! Families enumerated on pages 93 – 177 of the old book do not appear on pages 1 - 34 of the new, and vice versa. The next census after 1839 was not taken until 1861.

As in previous censuses, three sets of columns show white, colored, and black men, women, and children - but the fourth set is blank, because the apprenticed labourers of 1835 had no further obligation to their masters. Most will be found in their own households; a few were listed as domestics. Many had chosen surnames, or variants of surnames: Carroll - Carel, Courtnay – Coatney, Hewlett –Ewlett, etc.

To find a family in the original record, search by page number, not by household number. Why? Because the 1839 census has multiple numbering errors. The enumerator doubled back: household #154 is followed by 146; numbers then run consecutively until 159 is followed by 157, continue until 199 is followed by 101, 102, etc. So there are two households 101-199, three 146-54, 158-159... and the numbering mistakes go on and on.

Another peculiarity of the 1839 census is that some surnames are indicated by dashes instead of ditto marks. At the end of a list in which dashes represent surnames there may be a child of the same color without dashes or with a solid line instead of dashes. Lacking further evidence, we cannot tell whether this child shared the surname of those above, or lacked a surname.

p. 93:
#1: Richard ANDERSON, 0 0 0 – 1 0 0 – 0 0 0
      William ANDERSON, 0 0 0 – 0 0 1 – 0 0 0
      James, 0 0 0 – 0 0 1 – 0 0 0
      John, 0 0 0 – 0 0 1 – 0 0 0
      Eliza, 0 0 0 – 0 0 1 – 0 0 0 *(Surnames not given.)*
      Diana ANDERSON, 0 0 0 – 0 0 0 – 0 1 0
      Sally ANDERSON, 0 0 0 – 0 0 0 – 0 1 0
      Mary, 0 0 0 – 0 0 0 – 0 1 0

Jane, 0 0 0 – 0 0 0 – 0 1 0
Thomas, 0 0 0 – 0 0 0 – 0 0 1
Alick, 0 0 0 – 0 0 0 – 0 0 1
Ben, 0 0 0 – 0 0 0 – 1 0 0
Jose, 0 0 0 – 0 0 0 – 1 0 0
William, 0 0 0 – 0 0 0 – 1 0 0
Quashie, 0 0 0 – 0 0 0 – 1 0 0
Scipio, 0 0 0 – 0 0 0 – 1 0 0
August, 0 0 0 – 0 0 0 – 1 0 0
Bull, 0 0 0 – 0 0 0 – 1 0 0 *(Surnames not given.)*

#2:   J. C. ALTEREITH, 1 0 0 – 0 0 0 – 0 0 0 *(James Christopher Altereith.)*
C. J. ALTEREITH, 1 0 0 – 0 0 0 – 0 0 0 *(Not in previous censuses.)*
Mrs. ALTEREITH, 0 0 0 – 0 1 0 – 0 0 0 *(Probably Louisa, James' wife in 1826.)*
G. McAULAY ALTEREITH, 0 0 0 – 0 0 1 – 0 0 0
Mary Jane ALTEREITH, 0 0 0 – 0 0 1 – 0 0 0
Rebecca ALTEREITH, 0 0 0 – 0 0 1 – 0 0 0
Mary GRAHAM ALTEREITH, 0 0 0 – 0 0 1 – 0 0 0
Jem, 0 0 0 – 0 0 0 – 0 0 1
George, 0 0 0 – 0 0 0 – 0 0 1 *(Surnames not given.)*

#3:   Robert ANDERSON, 0 0 0 – 0 0 0 – 1 0 0
Tenah O'BRIEN, 0 0 0 – 0 0 0 – 0 1 0

p. 94:
#4:   G. D. ADOLPHUS, 0 0 0 – 1 0 0 – 0 0 0
Mary Ann ADOLPHUS, 0 0 0 – 0 1 0 – 0 0 0
Susan E. DALY, 0 0 0 – 0 1 0 – 0 0 0
Edwin ADOLPHUS, 0 0 0 – 0 0 1 – 0 0 0
   Domestics:
Ann JARRATT, 0 0 0 – 0 0 0 – 0 1 0
John FRANCISCO, 0 0 0 – 0 0 0 – 0 0 1

#5:   Peter AUDINETT, 0 0 0 – 0 0 0 – 1 0 0
Antonio LEWIS, 0 0 0 – 0 0 0 – 1 0 0
Rosannah STAIN, 0 0 0 – 0 0 0 – 0 1 0
Francis AUDINETT, 0 0 0 – 0 0 0 – 1 0 0
Timothy LEWIS, 0 0 0 – 0 0 0 – 0 0 1

#6:   Ann R. AUGUST, 0 0 0 – 0 1 0 – 0 0 0
John S. AUGUST, 0 0 0 – 1 0 0 – 0 0 0
Ann AUGUST, 0 0 0 – 0 0 1 – 0 0 0
Richard AUGUST, 0 0 0 – 0 0 1 – 0 0 0
Edgar AUGUST, 0 0 0 – 0 0 1 – 0 0 0
Hannah AUGUST, 0 0 0 – 0 0 0 – 0 1 0

#7:   David ANDERSON, 0 0 0 – 0 0 0 – 1 0 0
        Phillis LAWRIE, 0 0 0 – 0 0 0 – 0 1 0

#8:   Edward ADOLPHUS, 0 0 0 – 1 0 0 – 0 0 0
        Abigail ADOLPHUS, 0 0 0 – 0 1 0 – 0 0 0
        Martha Jane ADOLPHUS, 0 0 0 – 0 0 1 – 0 0 0
        Francis John ADOLPHUS, 0 0 0 – 0 0 1 – 0 0 0
           A domestic:
        Rachael WINTER, 0 0 0 – 0 1 0 – 0 0 0

p. 95:
#9:   John AUGUSTA, 0 0 0 – 1 0 0 – 0 0 0
        Leonard MITCHEL, 0 0 0 – 0 0 0 – 1 0 0
        Francis AUGUSTA, 0 0 0 – 0 0 1 – 0 0 0
        Matilda AUGUSTA, 0 0 0 – 0 0 1 – 0 0 0
        Mary Ann AUGUSTA, 0 0 0 – 0 0 1 – 0 0 0

#10: Alexander, 0 0 0 – 0 0 0 – 1 0 0 *(Surname not given.)*
        Paul BENNIE, 0 0 0 – 0 0 0 – 1 0 0

#11: Charles ANDERSON, 0 0 0 – 0 0 0 – 1 0 0
        Sally Jane, 0 0 0 – 0 0 0 – 0 1 0 *(Surname not given.)*

#12: William ARMSTRONG, 0 0 0 – 0 0 0 – 1 0 0

#13: Toby AUGUST, 0 0 0 – 0 0 0 – 1 0 0
        Jane BROASTER, 0 0 0 – 0 0 0 – 0 1 0
        Simon AUGUST, 0 0 0 – 0 0 0 – 1 0 0

#14: Catherine ASKIE, 0 0 0 – 0 1 0 – 0 0 0   *(= ASKEW)*
        Betsy CROFT, 0 0 0 – 0 0 1 – 0 0 0
        Joseph MILLAR, 0 0 0 – 1 0 0 – 0 0 0
        John A. CROFT, 0 0 0 – 0 0 1 – 0 0 0
        Joseph MILLAR Junr, 0 0 0 – 0 0 1 – 0 0 0
        James F.? CROFT, 0 0 0 – 0 0 1 – 0 0 0

#15: Jane AUGUST, 0 0 0 – 0 1 0 – 0 0 0
        Frederick FORBES, 0 0 0 – 0 0 1 – 0 0 0
        Samuel FORBES 0 0 0 – 0 0 1 – 0 0 0

p. 96:
#16: Handy AUGUST, 0 0 0 – 0 0 0 – 1 0 0
        Arelia BENNETT, 0 0 0 – 0 0 0 – 0 1 0
        Elizabeth COOKE, 0 0 0 – 0 0 0 – 0 0 1

#17: Charles ANDREWS, 0 0 0 – 0 0 0 – 1 0 0

#18: Caesar ANDREWS, 0 0 0 – 0 0 0 – 1 0 0
Lydia LOWRIE, 0 0 0 – 0 0 0 – 0 1 0
Charles COLQUHOUN, 0 0 0 – 0 0 0 – 1 0 0

#19: James ARTHURS, 0 0 0 – 1 0 0 – 0 0 0
Lavinia JONES, 0 0 0 – 0 1 0 – 0 0 0
Robert ARTHURS, 0 0 0 – 0 0 1 – 0 0 0
James ARTHURS, 0 0 0 – 0 0 1 – 0 0 0
Amelia ARTHURS, 0 0 0 – 0 0 1 – 0 0 0
Mary ARTHURS, 0 0 0 – 0 0 1 – 0 0 0
Jane ARTHURS, 0 0 0 – 0 0 1 – 0 0 0

#20: R. S. ALLEN, 1 0 0 – 0 0 0 – 0 0 0
Eliza ALLEN, 0 1 0 – 0 0 0 – 0 0 0
Jane ALLEN, 0 1 0 – 0 0 0 – 0 0 0

#21: Dick ALLEN, 0 0 0 – 0 0 0 – 0 0 1
John ALLEN, 0 0 0 – 0 0 0 – 0 0 1
Sylvia, 0 0 0 – 0 0 0 – 0 1 0 *(Surname not given.)*

p. 97:
#22: Henry ARNOLD, 0 0 0 – 1 0 0 – 0 0 0
Maria ARNOLD, 0 0 0 – 0 1 0 – 0 0 0
Mary PETSOLD, 0 0 0 – 0 0 1 – 0 0 0   *(= PETZOLD.)*
Emma PANTON, 0 0 0 – 0 0 1 – 0 0 0
Henry ARNOLD Junr, 0 0 0 – 0 0 1 – 0 0 0
Benjamin ARNOLD, 0 0 0 – 0 0 1 – 0 0 0
William ARNOLD, 0 0 0 – 0 0 1 – 0 0 0
Maddock ARNOLD, 0 0 0 – 0 0 1 – 0 0 0
Janett ARNOLD, 0 0 0 – 0 0 1 – 0 0 0

#23: Frederick AUGUST, 0 0 0 – 0 0 0 – 1 0 0
Elizabeth MEIGHAN, 0 0 0 – 0 0 0 – 0 1 0

#24: Joseph ARMSTRONG, 0 0 0 – 0 0 0 – 1 0 0

#25: Charles AUGUST, 0 0 0 – 0 0 0 – 1 0 0
Rosette AUGUST, 0 0 0 – 0 0 0 – 0 1 0
Nelson AUGUST, 0 0 0 – 0 0 0 – 0 0 1
John STANFORD, 0 0 0 – 0 0 0 – 0 0 1

#26: John AUGUSTINE, 0 0 0 – 0 0 0 – 1 0 0
Selina AUGUSTINE, 0 0 0 – 0 0 0 – 0 1 0

#27: Richard AUGUST, 0 0 0 – 0 0 0 – 1 0 0
Chloe AUGUST, 0 0 0 – 0 0 0 – 0 1 0
George AUGUST, 0 0 0 – 0 0 0 – 1 0 0

p.98:
#28: John ALEXIS, 0 0 0 – 0 0 0 – 1 0 0
Betsy GRANT, 0 0 0 – 0 0 0 – 0 1 0
Patience GABOUREL, 0 0 0 – 0 0 0 – 0 1 0

#29: Francis AUTHER, 0 0 0 – 0 0 0 – 1 0 0
Celia AUTHER, 0 0 0 – 0 0 0 – 0 1 0
Joseph BROASTER, 0 0 0 – 0 0 0 – 1 0 0
William BROASTER, 0 0 0 – 0 0 0 – 0 0 1
Francis AUTHER Junr, 0 0 0 – 0 0 0 – 0 0 1
Margaret AUTHER, 0 0 0 – 0 0 0 – 0 0 1
James AUTHER, 0 0 0 – 0 0 0 – 0 0 1
George AUTHER, 0 0 0 – 0 0 0 – 0 0 1
David AUTHER, 0 0 0 – 0 0 0 – 0 0 1
Samuel AUTHER, 0 0 0 – 0 0 0 – 0 0 1

#30: Venture ADNEY, 0 0 0 – 0 0 0 – 1 0 0
Clarisa De BRIEN, 0 0 0 – 0 0 0 – 0 1 0
Sarah De BRIEN, 0 0 0 – 0 0 0 – 0 1 0
Maria De BRIEN, 0 0 0 – 0 0 0 – 0 0 1
Chloe De BRIEN, 0 0 0 – 0 0 0 – 0 0 1
Angelina De BRIEN, 0 0 0 – 0 0 0 – 0 0 1

#31: John ARCHER, 0 0 0 – 0 0 0 – 1 0 0

#32: Cesaria ARBISA, 0 1 0 – 0 0 0 – 0 0 0
Juana FORTUNA, 0 0 0 – 0 0 0 – 0 1 0

#33: Andy AUGUST, 0 0 0 – 1 0 0 – 0 0 0
Amelia AUGUST, 0 0 0 – 0 1 0 – 0 0 0
Elizabeth AUGUST, 0 0 0 – 0 0 1 – 0 0 0

p. 99:
#33: Adam ANDERSON, 0 0 0 – 0 0 0 – 1 0 0
Nancy WALDON, 0 0 0 – 0 0 0 – 0 1 0   *(= WALDRON)*
Thomas JOHNSON, 0 0 0 – 0 0 0 – 0 0 1
Henry JOHNSON, 0 0 0 – 0 0 0 – 0 0 1
Henry WALDON, 0 0 0 – 0 0 0 – 0 0 1

#35: Hamlet ANDERSON, 0 0 0 – 0 0 0 – 1 0 0
Francis TILLETT, 0 0 0 – 0 0 0 – 1 0 0

227

Dan TILLETT, 0 0 0 – 0 0 0 – 1 0 0
Thomas TILLETT, 0 0 0 – 0 0 0 – 1 0 0

#36: Ralph ABERCROMBY, 0 0 0 – 0 0 0 – 1 0 0
Mary Ann WILLIAMS, 0 0 0 – 0 0 0 – 0 1 0
Margaret ABERCROMBY, 0 0 0 – 0 1 0 – 0 0 0

#37: Eleanor ANDERSON, 0 0 0 – 0 1 0 – 0 0 0
Lucretia ANDERSON, 0 0 0 – 0 1 0 – 0 0 0
Emily WILY, 0 0 0 – 0 1 0 – 0 0 0
Eleanor WALTON, 0 0 0 – 0 1 0 – 0 0 0
James REED, 0 0 0 – 0 0 1 – 0 0 0
Amelia ANDERSON, 0 0 0 – 0 0 0 – 0 1 0
Friendship ANDERSON, 0 0 0 – 0 0 0 – 0 1 0
Sarah AUGUST, 0 0 0 – 0 0 0 – 0 0 1
Thomas BANNA, 0 0 0 – 0 0 0 – 0 0 1

#38: Philip ANDREWIN, 0 0 0 – 1 0 0 – 0 0 0
Sarah ANDREWIN, 0 0 0 – 0 1 0 – 0 0 0
Catherine SALLY, 0 0 0 – 0 1 0 – 0 0 0

#39: John AUGUST, 0 0 0 – 0 0 0 – 1 0 0

p. 100:
#40: Maria ANCHAWA, 0 0 0 – 0 0 0 – 0 1 0
Peter FLOWERS, 0 0 0 – 0 0 0 – 1 0 0
Joseph DOMINGO, 0 0 0 – 0 0 0 – 1 0 0
Tony FLOWERS, 0 0 0 – 0 0 0 – 0 0 1
Joselyn GAMBOUR, 0 0 0 – 0 0 0 – 1 0 0
Pablo Jose GAMBOUR, 0 0 0 – 0 0 0 – 1 0 0
Marcus JUAN, 0 0 0 – 0 0 0 – 1 0 0
Juana GAMBOUR, 0 0 0 – 0 0 0 – 0 1 0
D. Maria DOMINGO, 0 0 0 – 0 0 0 – 0 1 0
Sophia GAMBOUR, 0 0 0 – 0 0 0 – 0 1 0
Duncan NEAL, 0 0 0 – 0 0 0 – 0 0 1
Atanana, 0 0 0 – 0 0 0 – 0 0 1 *(Surname not given.)*
Maria GREGORIA, 0 0 0 – 0 0 0 – 0 0 1

#41: Jno. ARMSTRONG, 0 0 0 – 1 0 0 – 0 0 0
Walter B. ARMSTRONG, 0 0 0 – 0 0 1 – 0 0 0
Martha S. ARMSTRONG, 0 0 0 – 0 0 1 – 0 0 0
Mary Ann ARMSTRONG, 0 0 0 – 0 0 1 – 0 0 0
Jenny ARMSTRONG, 0 0 0 – 0 0 0 – 0 1 0
Andrew ARMSTRONG, 0 0 0 – 0 0 0 – 0 0 1
Charlotte DOUGLAS, 0 0 0 – 0 1 0 – 0 0 0

228

Adney, 0 0 0 – 0 0 1 – C 0 0
Calista, 0 0 0 – 0 0 0 – C 0 1 *(Surnames not given.)*

#42: Lucie ARMSTRONG, 0 0 0 – 0 0 0 – 0 1 0
Henry RAIN, 0 0 0 – 0 C 0 – 0 0 1

#43: Grace MILLER, 0 0 0 – 0 1 0 – 0 0 0
Amelia EVANS, 0 0 0 – 0 0 1 – 0 0 0
Robert Charles CUNNINGHAM, 0 0 0 – 0 0 1 – 0 0 0
George WATERS, 0 0 0 – 0 0 1 – 0 0 0

p. 101:
#44: Margaret AUGUST, 0 0 0 – 0 0 0 – 0 1 0
Daniel AUGUST, 0 0 0 – 0 0 0 – 1 0 0
Abel AUGUST, 0 0 0 – 0 0 0 – 1 0 0
Thomas HOMES, 0 0 0 – 0 0 0 – 1 0 0
Middleton AUGUST, 0 0 0 – 0 0 0 – 1 0 0
Sophia AUGUST, 0 0 0 – 0 0 0 – 0 0 1
John YOUNG, 0 0 0 – 0 0 0 – 0 0 1
William AUGUST, 0 C 0 – 0 0 0 – 1 0 0
Nelson AUGUST, 0 0 0 – 0 0 0 – 0 0 1
Taylor AUGUST, 0 0 C – 0 0 0 – 1 0 0

#45: Murphy ANDERSON, 1 0 C – 0 0 0 – 0 0 0
Mary Ann ANDERSON, 0 1 0 – 0 0 0 – 0 0 0
Frederick ANDERSON, 1 0 0 – 0 0 0 – 0 0 0
Charlotte ANDERSON, 0 1 0 – 0 0 0 – 0 0 0
Elizabeth ANDERSON, 0 1 0 – 0 0 0 – 0 0 0
Grace ANDERSON, 0 1 0 – 0 0 0 – 0 0 0
John MURPHY, 1 0 0 – 0 0 C – 0 0 0

#46: William ADRED [*sic*], 0 0 0 – 0 0 0 – 1 0 0
Dianah THOMAS, 0 0 0 – 0 0 0 – 0 1 0

#47: Martha ABRAHAMS, 0 0 0 – 0 1 0 – 0 0 0
Hannah STEPHENS, 0 0 0 – 0 0 1 – 0 0 0
Rebecca STEPHENS, 0 0 0 – 0 0 1 – 0 0 0
Mary Jane DEANS, 0 0 0 – 0 C 1 – 0 0 0

#48: George AUGUST, 0 0 0 – 0 0 0 – 1 0 0

#49: Charles ARMSTRONG, 0 0 0 – 0 0 0 – 1 0 0
Margaret ARMSTRONG, 0 0 0 – 0 0 0 – 0 1 0
Mary ARMSTRONG, 0 0 C – 0 0 0 – 0 0 1

229

p. 102:

#50: James ARTHUR, 0 0 0 – 1 0 0 – 0 0 0
      Patience HUGHES, 0 0 0 – 0 1 0 – 0 0 0
      John ARTHUR, 0 0 0 – 0 0 1 – 0 0 0
      Edward ARTHUR, 0 0 0 – 0 0 1 – 0 0 0
      William HUGHES, 0 0 0 – 0 0 1 – 0 0 0
      Elizabeth HUGHES, 0 0 0 – 0 0 1 – 0 0 0
      Louisa CATOUCHE, 0 0 0 – 0 0 1 – 0 0 0

#51: Elizabeth ARTHURS, 0 0 0 – 0 0 0 – 0 1 0
      Catherine ARTHURS, 0 0 0 – 0 0 0 – 0 1 0
      Sarah ARTHURS, 0 0 0 – 0 0 0 – 0 01
      Peter ARTHURS, 0 0 0 – 0 0 0 – 0 0 1
      Amelia ARTHURS, 0 0 0 – 0 0 0 – 0 0 1
      Joseph ARTHURS, 0 0 0 – 0 0 0 – 0 0 1
      Maria ARTHURS, 0 0 0 – 0 0 0 – 0 0 1
      Jane ARTHURS, 0 0 0 – 0 0 0 – 0 0 1

#52: Phillis ARTHURS, 0 0 0 – 0 0 0 – 0 1 0
      Emily GIBSON, 0 0 0 – 0 1 0 – 0 0 0
      Simon BRASTER, 0 0 0 – 0 0 0 – 0 0 1   *(= BROASTER)*
      David BRASTER, 0 0 0 – 0 0 0 – 0 0 1
      Louisa LAWRIE, 0 0 0 – 0 0 0 – 0 0 1
      Margaret LAWRIE, 0 0 0 – 0 0 0 – 0 0 1
      Catherine BRASTER, 0 0 0 – 0 0 1 – 0 0 0
      Joseph FRANCIS, 0 0 0 – 0 0 1 – 0 0 0

#53: Frederick ANDERSON, 0 0 0 – 0 0 0 – 1 0 0
      Rose SMITH, 0 0 0 – 0 0 0 – 0 1 0
      Eliza ANDERSON, 0 0 0 – 0 0 0 – 0 0 1

#54: Scotland ANDERSON, 0 0 0 – 0 0 0 – 1 0 0

p. 103:

#55: Edward ADAMS, 1 0 0 – 0 0 0 – 0 0 0
      Sarah ADAMS, 0 1 0 – 0 0 0 – 0 0 0
      Louisa ADAMS, 0 0 1 – 0 0 0 – 0 0 0
      Mary Ann ADAMS, 0 0 1 – 0 0 0 – 0 0 0
      Infant ADAMS, 0 0 1 – 0 0 0 – 0 0 0
      Sarah, 0 0 0 – 0 0 0 – 0 1 0 *(Surname not given.)*
      Elisha COLBOURN, 1 0 0 – 0 0 0 – 0 0 0

#56: Edward ARMSTRONG, 0 0 0 – 1 0 0 – 0 0 0

#57: Charles AUGUSTIAN, 0 0 0 – 0 0 0 – 1 0 0
      Maria BENIAN, 0 0 0 – 0 0 0 – 0 1 0

230

Joseph AUGUSTIAN, 0 0 0 – 0 0 0 – 0 0 1
Joseph Charles AUGUSTIAN, 0 0 0 – 0 0 0 – 0 0 1
Catherine AUGUSTIAN, 0 0 0 – 0 0 0 – 0 0 1
Jennett AUGUSTIAN, 0 0 0 – 0 0 0 – 0 0 1

#58: Johnson BENNETT, 0 C 0 – 0 0 0 – 1 0 0
Nancy BENNETT, 0 0 0 – 0 0 0 – 0 1 0
Robert ROBINSON, 0 0 0 – 0 0 0 – 0 0 1
Ellen ROBERTSON [*sic*], 0 0 0 – 0 0 0 – 0 0 1
Charles ROBINSON, 0 0 0 – 0 0 0 – 0 0 1
Jno. ROBINSON, 0 0 0 – 0 0 0 – 0 0 1
Jane ROBINSON, 0 0 0 – 0 0 0 – 0 0 1
Joseph ROBINSON, 0 0 0 – 0 0 0 – 0 0 1

#59: Adam BROASTER, 0 0 0 – 0 0 0 – 1 0 0
Sophia BROASTER, 0 0 0 – 0 0 0 – 0 1 0
Daniel ALLEN, 0 0 0 – C 0 0 – 0 0 1
John GENTLE, 0 0 0 – 0 0 0 – 0 0 1

p. 104:
#60: Hamlet BROASTER, 0 0 0 – 0 0 0 – 1 0 0
Belvil TAIT, 0 0 0 – 0 0 0 – 0 1 0
Mary Ann BROASTER, 0 0 0 – 0 0 0 – 0 0 1

#61: Marcus BELISLE, C 0 0 – 1 0 0 – 0 0 0

#62: Thomas BENNER, 0 0 0 – 1 0 0 – 0 0 0
Clement CADLE, 0 0 0 – 0 0 0 – 0 1 0

#63: Duke BENNETT, 0 0 0 – 0 0 0 – 1 0 0

#64: James R. BAIN, 0 0 0 – 0 0 0 – 1 0 0
Mary FRANCIS, 0 0 0 – C 1 0 – 0 0 0
Benjamin HODSON, 0 0 0 – 0 0 0 – 0 0 1

#65: Alick BENNETT, 0 0 0 – 0 0 0 – 1 0 0

#66: William BANNER, C 0 0 – 1 0 0 – 0 0 0
Maria BAPTISTE, 0 0 0 – 0 1 0 – 0 0 0
John PATTERSON, 0 0 0 – 0 0 1 – 0 0 0
Catharine THOMPSON, 0 0 0 – 0 0 1 – 0 0 0
William BANNER, 0 0 0 – 0 0 1 – 0 0 0

#67: William BOWDEN, 0 0 0 – 0 0 0 – 1 0 0
Elinor BOWDEN, 0 C 0 – 0 0 0 – 0 1 0
William POTTS, 0 0 0 – 0 0 0 – 0 0 1

#68: Eliza BAYLY alias MONRO, 0 0 0 – 0 0 0 – 0 1 0
Elizabeth BAYLY, 0 0 0 – 0 0 0 – 0 1 0

#69: James BULL, 0 0 0 – 1 0 0 – 0 0 0

p. 105:
#70: Samuel BLAKE, 0 0 0 – 1 0 0 – 0 0 0
Simon THOMPSON, 0 0 0 – 0 0 0 – 1 0 0
Mary WHITE, 0 0 0 – 0 0 0 – 0 1 0
Leah DOUGLASS, 0 0 0 – 0 0 0 – 0 1 0
James DRAXON, 0 0 0 – 0 0 0 – 0 0 1   *(= DRACKSON, DERIXON.)*
Mary GABOUREL, 0 0 0 – 0 0 0 – 0 1 0
Calista DOUGLASS, 0 0 0 – 0 0 0 – 0 0 1
Phillis GABOUREL, 0 0 0 – 0 0 0 – 0 0 1

#71: Mary BATES, 0 0 0 – 0 1 0 – 0 0 0
Joseph RABOTEAU, 0 0 0 – 1 0 0 – 0 0 0
Margaret RABOTEAU, 0 0 0 – 0 1 0 – 0 0 0
Isaac RABOTEAU, 0 0 0 – 1 0 0 – 0 0 0
Caroline PANTING, 0 0 0 – 0 1 0 – 0 0 0
Alphonse RABOTEAU, 0 0 0 – 0 0 1 – 0 0 0

#72: James F. BOOTH, 1 0 0 – 0 0 0 – 0 0 0

#73: George BRADDICK Senr, 0 0 0 – 1 0 0 – 0 0 0
George BRADDICK Junr, 0 0 0 – 0 0 1 – 0 0 0
Mrs. Sarah BRADDICK, 0 0 0 – 0 1 0 – 0 0 0
John HUNT, 1 0 0 – 0 0 0 – 0 0 0
Stephen WINTER, 0 0 0 – 1 0 0 – 0 0 0
Thomas WINTER, 0 0 0 – 1 0 0 – 0 0 0
Francis WINTER, 0 0 0 – 0 0 1 – 0 0 0
Isaiah BRADDICK, 0 0 0 – 0 0 1 – 0 0 0
Lucretia BRADDICK, 0 0 0 – 0 0 1 – 0 0 0
Anne BRADDICK, 0 0 0 – 0 0 1 – 0 0 0
Elizabeth JANNETTE, 0 1 0 – 0 0 0 – 0 0 0
Hagar SWASEY, 0 0 0 – 0 0 0 – 0 1 0

#74: Charles BURNS, 0 0 0 – 0 0 0 – 1 0 0

p. 106:
#75: James BANKS, 1 0 0 – 0 0 0 – 0 0 0
Kate HUME, 0 0 0 – 0 0 0 – 0 1 0

#76: James BELL, 0 0 0 – 0 0 0 – 1 0 0

#77: Julius BENNETT, 0 0 0 – 0 0 0 – 1 0 0
Fanny BENNETT, 0 0 0 – 0 0 0 – 0 1 0
Familla BENNETT, 0 0 0 – 0 0 0 – 0 0 1
Nancy BENNETT, 0 0 0 – 0 0 0 – 0 0 1

#78: George BELISLE, 0 0 0 – 0 0 0 – 1 0 0
Rosette LAVIGNE, 0 0 0 – 0 0 0 – 0 1 0
James BELISLE, 0 0 0 – 0 0 0 – 0 0 1
Jane BELISLE, 0 0 0 – 0 0 0 – 0 0 1
John BELISLE, 0 0 0 – 0 0 0 – 0 0 1

#79: Louis LA BRUCE, 0 0 0 – 0 0 0 – 1 0 0

#80: Harry BATIAS, 1 0 0 – 0 0 0 – 0 0 0
Alexander DELANDRE, 1 0 0 – 0 0 0 – 0 0 0
Robert MAIN, 0 0 0 – 0 0 0 – 0 0 1   *(= MEIGHAN.)*
Antonio FLOWERS, 0 0 0 – 0 0 0 – 0 0 1
Francisco GARCIA, 0 0 0 – 0 0 0 – 0 0 1
Lewis, 0 0 0 – 0 0 0 – 0 0 1 *(Surname not given.)*

#81: Daniel BELISLE, 0 0 0 – 0 0 0 – 1 0 0
Mary BROSTER, 0 0 0 – 0 0 0 – 0 1 0
Nelly BROSTER, 0 0 0 – 0 0 0 – 0 1 0
Nancy BROSTER, 0 0 0 – 0 0 0 – 0 1 0

p. 107:
#82: William BURN, 0 0 0 – 0 0 0 – 1 0 0
Nancy BURN, 0 0 0 – 0 0 0 – 0 1 0
Amelia BURN, 0 0 0 – 0 0 1 – 0 0 0

#83: Thomas BRADFORD, 0 0 0 – 0 0 0 – 1 0 0

#84: John BROWN, 0 0 0 – 0 0 0 – 1 0 0
Susannah SHORT, 0 0 0 – 0 0 0 – 0 1 0

#85: Ann BODE, 0 0 0 – 0 1 0 – 0 0 0
Eliza BROASTER, 0 0 0 – 0 1 0 – 0 0 0
John HENDERSON, 0 0 0 – 0 0 1 – 0 0 0
George HENDERSON, 0 0 0 – 0 0 1 – 0 0 0
Ann HENDERSON, 0 0 0 – 0 0 1 – 0 0 0
Charles HENDERSON, 0 0 0 – 0 0 1 – 0 0 0
Edmund MEIGHAN, 0 0 0 – 0 0 1 – 0 0 0
Henrietta WAGNER, 0 0 0 – 0 0 1 – 0 0 0
Mary HUNTER, 0 0 0 – 0 0 1 – 0 0 0
Betty HENDERSON, 0 0 0 – 0 0 0 – 0 1 0
Mary HENDERSON, 0 0 0 – 0 0 0 – 0 1 0

233

Sarah HENDERSON, 0 0 0 – 0 0 0 – 0 0 1
Rebecca HENDERSON, 0 0 0 – 0 0 0 – 0 0 1
Nancy HENDERSON, 0 0 0 – 0 0 0 – 0 0 1
Clarinda HENDERSON, 0 0 0 – 0 0 0 – 0 0 1
Thomas HENDERSON, 0 0 0 – 0 0 0 – 0 0 1

#86:   Joseph BANKS, 0 0 0 – 0 0 0 – 1 0 0
        Antonia FORES, 0 0 0 – 0 0 0 – 0 1 0
        John BANKS, 0 0 0 – 0 0 0 – 0 0 1
        Condelario BANKS, 0 0 0 – 0 0 0 – 0 0 1

p. 108:
#87:   Andrew BELL, 1 0 0 – 0 0 0 – 0 0 0
        Fanny GODFREY, 0 0 0 – 0 1 0 – 0 0 0

#88:   Edward BOWMAN, 0 0 0 – 0 0 0 – 1 0 0
        Susana [sic] BOWMAN, 0 0 0 – 0 0 0 – 0 1 0
        John BOWMAN, 0 0 0 – 0 0 0 – 0 0 1
        George BOWMAN, 0 0 0 – 0 0 0 – 0 0 1
        Maria BOWMAN, 0 0 0 – 0 0 0 – 0 0 1
        Emillia [sic] BOWMAN, 0 0 0 – 0 0 0 – 0 0 1
        Jane BOWMAN, 0 0 0 – 0 0 0 – 0 0 1
        Thomas BOWMAN, 0 0 0 – 0 0 0 – 0 0 1
        Daniel BOWMAN, 0 0 0 – 0 0 0 – 0 0 1
        Moses BOWMAN, 0 0 0 – 0 0 0 – 0 0 1
        Isaac BOWMAN, 0 0 0 – 0 0 0 – 0 0 1
        Harry GORDON, 0 0 0 – 0 0 0 – 0 0 1
        Eliza BOWMAN, 0 0 0 – 0 0 0 – 0 0 1
        William, 0 0 0 – 0 0 0 – 0 0 1 *(Surname not given.)*

#89:   Henry HICKEY, 0 0 0 – 0 0 0 – 1 0 0
        Mimba BODE, 0 0 0 – 0 0 0 – 0 1 0
        Fanny BODE, 0 0 0 – 0 0 0 – 0 0 1
        Diana BODE, 0 0 0 – 0 0 0 – 0 0 1
        Maria BODE, 0 0 0 – 0 0 0 – 0 0 1
        Olivera BODE, 0 0 0 – 0 0 0 – 0 0 1

#90:   Simon BURNHAM, 0 0 0 – 0 0 0 – 1 0 0
        Hannah JACKSON, 0 0 0 – 0 0 0 – 0 1 0
        Sally JACKSON, 0 0 0 – 0 0 0 – 0 1 0
        Adam JACKSON, 0 0 0 – 0 0 0 – 1 0 0
        Chance JACKSON, 0 0 0 – 0 0 0 – 1 0 0
        Jack JACKSON, 0 0 0 – 0 0 0 – 1 0 0

p. 109:
#91:   Joseph BELISLE, 0 0 0 – 1 0 0 – 0 0 0

234

Elizabeth PANTING, 0 0 0 – 0 1 0 – 0 0 0
John BELISLE, 0 0 0 – 0 0 1 – 0 0 0

#92: Elizabeth BOWEN, 0 1 0 – 0 0 0 – 0 0 0
Sophia BOWEN, 0 0 0 – 0 1 0 – 0 0 0
Matilda BOWEN, 0 0 0 – 0 1 0 – 0 0 0
Three   0 0 0 – 0 0 0 – 0 0 1
African 0 0 0 – 0 0 0 – 0 0 1
Girls [sic] 0 0 0 – 0 0 0 – 0 0 1   (Names not given.)

#93: Andrew BROUGHTON, 0 0 0 – 0 0 0 – 1 0 0
John BROUGHTON, 0 0 0 – 0 0 0 – 1 0 0

#94: John BRUCE, 0 0 0 – 0 0 0 – 1 0 0
Sue BRUCE, 0 0 0 – 0 0 0 – 0 1 0

#95: Joseph BURNAL, 0 0 0 – 1 0 0 – 0 0 0
Margaret BURNAL, 0 0 0 – 0 0 0 – 0 1 0
Mary Ann BURNAL, 0 0 0 – 0 0 1 – 0 0 0
William FENAL, 0 0 0 – 1 0 0 – 0 0 0
Joseph BERNAL FLOWERS, 0 0 0 – 0 0 0 – 0 0 1

#96: William BURN, 0 0 0 – 0 0 0 – 0 0 0

#97: Simon BENNETT, 0 0 0 – 0 0 0 – 1 0 0
Arabella BENNETT, 0 0 0 – 0 0 0 – 0 1 0
Francis FLOWERS, 0 0 0 – 0 0 0 – 0 0 1

#98 Thomas BLAND, 0 0 0 – 0 0 0 – 1 0 0
Jesse BENNETT, 0 0 0 – 0 0 0 – 0 1 0

p. 110:
#99: James BERTIE, 1 0 0 – 0 0 0 – 0 0 0
George PEDDIE, 1 0 0 – 0 0 0 – 0 0 0
Flora JONES, 0 0 0 – 0 1 0 – 0 0 0
James E. BERTIE, 0 0 0 – 0 0 1 – 0 0 0
Margaret MOODY, 0 0 0 – 0 1 0 – 0 0 0

#100: Daniel BOWMAN, 0 0 0 – 0 0 0 – 1 0 0

#101: Ned BURK, 0 0 0 – 0 0 0 – 1 0 0
Amelia BURK, 0 0 0 – 0 0 0 – 0 1 0
Jane BURK, 0 0 0 – 0 0 0 – 0 1 0

#102: Luis BOSTICK, 0 0 0 – 0 0 0 – 1 0 0

235

#103: William GUILD, 1 0 0 – 0 0 0 – 0 0 0
Robert BOWDEN, 1 0 0 – 0 0 0 – 0 0 0
John KIDD, 1 0 0 – 0 0 0 – 0 0 0
Alex^r KIDD, 1 0 0 – 0 0 0 – 0 0 0
Robert WALKER, 1 0 0 – 0 0 0 – 0 0 0
William JEX, 1 0 0 – 0 0 0 – 0 0 0 *(Believed to have m. Ada or Agnes FOWLER)*
John JEX, 1 0 0 – 0 0 0 – 0 0 0
Daniel JEX, 1 0 0 – 0 0 0 – 0 0 0 *(Said to have died in 1879.)*
Jeremiah CARROL, 1 0 0 – 0 0 0 – 0 0 0
Joseph TENCH, 0 0 0 – 0 0 0 – 1 0 0

#104: Hamlet BODE, 0 0 0 – 0 0 0 – 1 0 0
Betty ROBINSON, 0 0 0 – 0 0 0 – 0 1 0
Margaret WILLIAMS, 0 0 0 – 0 0 0 – 0 0 1
W. Charles PICKETT, 0 0 0 – 0 0 0 – 0 0 1

p. 111:
#105: Philip C. BRENNAN, 0 0 0 – 0 0 0 – 1 0 0
Mary HEWLETT, 0 0 0 – 0 0 0 – 0 1 0
John P. BRENNAN, 0 0 0 – 0 0 0 – 0 0 1
Charles J. BRENNAN, 0 0 0 – 0 0 0 – 0 0 1
Charlotte BRENNAN, 0 0 0 – 0 0 0 – 0 0 1
Caroline BRENNAN, 0 0 0 – 0 0 0 – 0 0 1

#106: Rodney BENNETT, 0 0 0 – 0 0 0 – 1 0 0

#107: William BOWDEN, 0 0 0 – 0 0 0 – 1 0 0
Frances BOWDEN, 0 0 0 – 0 0 0 – 0 1 0

#108: Sarah BURREL, 0 0 0 – 0 1 0 – 0 0 0
Mary KENNEDY, 0 0 0 – 0 1 0 – 0 0 0
Sarah KENNEDY, 0 0 0 – 0 1 0 – 0 0 0
Katrine KENNEDY, 0 0 0 – 0 1 0 – 0 0 0

#109: Francis BRADLEY, 1 0 0 – 0 0 0 – 0 0 0 *(Francis Alexander BRADLEY)*
Mary Frances GABOUREL, 0 0 0 – 0 1 0 – 0 0 0
Richard BRADLEY, 0 0 0 – 0 0 1 – 0 0 0

#110: John BREWER, 0 0 0 – 0 0 0 – 1 0 0
Mary BREWER, 0 0 0 – 0 0 0 – 0 1 0

#111: Johnson BENNETT, 0 0 0 – 0 0 0 – 1 0 0

#112: Richard BENNETT, 0 0 0 – 0 0 0 – 1 0 0

p. 112:
#113:   Joseph BURLEY, 0 0 0 – 0 0 0 – 1 0 0

#114:   George BETTIE, 0 0 0 – 0 0 0 – 1 0 0

#115:   William BLACKWIRE, 0 0 0 – 0 0 0 – 1 0 0

#116:   Lewis BEATRIX, 0 0 0 – 0 0 0 – 1 0 0
        Maria BEATRIX, 0 0 0 – 0 0 0 – 0 1 0
        Rose TEAKER, 0 0 0 – 0 0 0 – 0 1 0
        James BEATRIX, 0 0 0 – 0 0 0 – 0 0 1

#117:   Joseph BEARD, 0 0 0 – 0 0 0 – 1 0 0

#118:   Danail *[sic]* BROASTER, 0 0 0 – 0 0 0 – 1 0 0
        Elizabeth GOFF, 0 0 0 – 0 0 0 – 0 1 0
        Eleanor TILLETT, 0 0 0 – 0 0 0 – 0 0 1
        Henry TILLETT, 0 0 0 – 0 0 0 – 0 0 1
        Thomas TILLETT, 0 0 0 – 0 0 0 – 0 0 1
        Richard TILLETT, 0 0 0 – 0 0 0 – 0 0 1
        Robert TILLETT, 0 0 0 – 0 0 0 – 0 0 1
        John TILLETT, 0 0 0 – 0 0 0 – 0 0 1

#119:   Thomas BERNARD, 0 0 0 – 0 0 0 – 1 0 0
        Catherine BENNETT, 0 0 0 – 0 0 0 – 0 1 0
        William BERNARD, 0 0 0 – 0 0 0 – 0 0 1
        John BERNARD, 0 0 0 – 0 0 0 – 0 0 1
        Henry B. BERNARD, 0 0 0 – 0 0 0 – 0 0 1
        Nancy BERNARD, 0 0 0 – 0 0 0 – 0 0 1
        Joannah BERNARD, 0 0 0 – 0 0 0 – 0 0 1

#120:   John BOWMAN, 0 0 0 – 0 0 0 – 1 0 0
        Eliza BOWMAN, 0 0 0 – 0 0 0 – 0 0 1

p. 113:
#121:   Joseph BOURN, 1 0 0 – 0 0 0 – 0 0 0 *(Did Mehetiable die or return to New York?)*
        Catharine HEMSLEY, 0 0 0 – 0 0 0 – 0 1 0

#122:   Simon BROASTER, 0 0 0 – 0 0 0 – 1 0 0
        Agnes DOREL, 0 0 0 – 0 0 0 – 0 1 0
        Robt BROASTER, 0 0 0 – 0 0 0 – 1 0 0
        Simon JAMES, 0 0 0 – 0 0 0 – 1 0 0
        Daniel BROASTER, 0 0 0 – 0 0 0 – 1 0 0

#123:   Elizabeth BODE, 0 0 0 – 0 0 0 – 0 1 0

237

Lucy BODE, 0 0 0 – 0 0 0 – 0 1 0
John YOUNG, 0 0 0 – 0 0 0 – 1 0 0

#124: James BELL, 0 0 0 – 0 0 0 – 1 0 0
Eliza BARNES, 0 0 0 – 0 0 0 – 0 1 0

#125: James BENNETT, 0 0 0 – 0 0 0 – 1 0 0
Margaret TENAH, 0 0 0 – 0 0 0 – 0 1 0
James FLOWERS, 0 0 0 – 0 0 0 – 0 0 1
Clarissa FLOWERS, 0 0 0 – 0 0 0 – 0 0 1
Thomas FLOWERS, 0 0 0 – 0 0 0 – 1 0 0

#126: Richard H. BOWEN, 0 0 0 – 1 0 0 – 0 0 0
Dick BOWEN, 0 0 0 – 0 0 0 – 0 0 1

#127: Robert BRUYER, 0 0 0 – 1 0 0 – 0 0 0
Venus BRUYER, 0 0 0 – 0 1 0 – 0 0 0
Frederick De SOURSE, 0 0 0 – 0 0 1 – 0 0 0
Sarah DE SOURSE, 0 0 0 – 0 0 1 – 0 0 0
Elizth DE SOURSE, 0 0 0 – 0 0 1 – 0 0 0
Henry CUNNINGHAM, 0 0 0 – 0 0 1 – 0 0 0
Charles BRUYER, 0 0 0 – 0 0 1 – 0 0 0

p. 114:
#128: Johannah BREWYER [sic], 0 0 0 – 0 0 0 – 0 1 0
Nancy BREWER [sic], 0 0 0 – 0 0 0 – 0 0 1
Eleanor BREWER, 0 0 0 – 0 0 0 – 0 0 1
Rosannah WILLIAMS, 0 0 0 – 0 0 0 – 0 0 1
Elizabeth WILLIAMS, 0 0 0 – 0 0 0 – 0 0 1
Agar [sic] WILLIAMS, 0 0 0 – 0 0 0 – 0 0 1 (= Hagar.)
James WILLIAMS, 0 0 0 – 0 0 0 – 0 0 1
John WILLIAMS, 0 0 0 – 0 0 0 – 0 0 1
Joseph WILLIAMS, 0 0 0 – 0 0 0 – 0 0 1
Robert WILLIAMS, 0 0 0 – 0 0 0 – 0 0 1
Henry WILLIAMS, 0 0 0 – 0 0 0 – 0 0 1
Thomas WILLIAMS, 0 0 0 – 0 0 0 – 0 0 1

#129: Charles BENNETT, 0 0 0 – 0 0 1 – 0 0 0
Ester BENNETT, 0 0 0 – 0 0 1 – 0 0 0
Judy BENNETT, 0 0 0 – 0 0 0 – 0 1 0

#130: Florah BUND, 0 0 0 – 0 0 0 – 0 1 0

#131: John BEAKS, 1 0 0 – 0 0 0 – 0 0 0
Maria LONGSWORTH, 0 0 0 – 0 1 0 – 0 0 0
Emma Jane BEAKS, 0 0 0 – 0 0 1 – 0 0 0

238

#132: James T? BAYNTON, 0 0 0 – 0 0 0 – 1 0 0
Mary BAYNTON, 0 0 0 – 0 0 0 – 0 1 0
George BAYNTON, 0 0 0 – 0 0 0 – 0 0 1
Gabriel BAYNTON, 0 0 0 – 0 0 0 – 0 0 1
Rebecca BAYNTON, 0 0 0 – 0 0 0 – 0 0 1

#133: James BERNARD, 0 0 0 – 0 0 0 – 1 0 0
Aloiza De BRIEN, 0 0 0 – 0 0 0 – 0 1 0
Clarissa BERNARD, 0 0 0 – 0 0 0 – 0 0 1

p. 115:
#134: Louisa BAILY, 0 0 0 – 0 0 0 – 0 1 0
Mary BAILY, 0 0 0 – 0 0 0 – 0 1 0
Philis BAILY, 0 0 0 – 0 0 0 – 0 1 0
Bella BAILY, 0 0 0 – 0 0 0 – 0 1 0
Selony BAILY, 0 0 0 – 0 0 0 – 0 1 0
Molly BAILY, 0 0 0 – 0 0 0 – 0 1 0
Philidy BAILY, 0 0 0 – 0 0 0 – 0 1 0
Augusta BAILY, 0 0 0 – 0 0 0 – 0 1 0
Jacob BAILY, 0 0 0 – 0 0 0 – 1 0 0
Byron BAILY, 0 0 0 – C 0 0 – 1 0 0
Abraham BAILY, 0 0 0 – 0 0 0 – 1 0 0
Toney BAILY, 0 0 0 – C 0 0 – 1 0 0
James WARRIOR, 0 0 0 – 0 0 0 – 1 0 0

#135: Staford [sic] BENNETT, 0 0 0 – 0 0 0 – 1 0 0

#136: Ann BRUYER, 0 0 0 – 0 1 0 – 0 0 0
Robert GLADDEN, 0 0 0 – 0 0 1 – 0 0 0

#137: Cuffie BRYAN, 0 0 0 – 0 0 0 – 1 0 0

#138: Richard BULL, 0 0 0 – 1 0 0 – 0 0 0

#139: Catherine BUTLER, 0 0 0 – 0 1 0 – 0 0 0
Jane BUTLER, 0 0 0 – 0 1 0 – 0 0 0

#140: Duckworth BENNETT, 0 0 0 – 0 0 0 – 1 0 0
Elizabeth BENNETT, 0 0 0 – 0 0 0 – 0 1 0
James YOUNG, 0 0 0 – 0 0 0 – 0 0 1
Susannah GALLOWAY, 0 0 0 – 0 0 0 – 0 1 0

p. 116:
#141: Samuel BURN, 0 0 0 – 0 0 0 – 1 0 0
Jane BURN, 0 0 0 – 0 0 0 – 0 1 0

239

Anne BURN, 0 0 0 – 0 0 0 – 0 1 0
Catharine BURN, 0 0 0 – 0 0 0 – 0 1 0
Rachael BURN, 0 0 0 – 0 0 0 – 0 1 0
James BURN, 0 0 0 – 0 0 0 – 1 0 0

#142: Clear [sic] BURKE, 0 0 0 – 0 1 0 – 0 0 0
Joannah HEMMONDS, 0 0 0 – 0 1 0 – 0 0 0
William HEMMONDS, 0 0 0 – 1 0 0 – 0 0 0
John HEMMONDS, 0 0 0 – 0 0 1 – 0 0 0
Thomas HEMMONDS, 0 0 0 – 0 0 1 – 0 0 0
Amelia HEMMONDS, 0 0 0 – 0 0 1 – 0 0 0
Sophia HEMMONDS, 0 0 0 – 0 0 1 – 0 0 0

#143: John D. BETSON, 1 0 0 – 0 0 0 – 0 0 0
Ann CRAPPER, 0 0 0 – 0 1 0 – 0 0 0
Fanny D. BETSON, 0 0 0 – 0 0 1 – 0 0 0

#144: William BURN, 1 0 0 – 0 0 0 – 0 0 0
Lydia CADLE, 0 0 0 – 0 1 0 – 0 0 0
Margaret BURN, 0 0 0 – 0 0 1 – 0 0 0
James BURN, 0 0 0 – 0 0 1 – 0 0 0
George BURN, 0 0 0 – 0 0 1 – 0 0 0
Robert BURN, 0 0 0 – 0 0 1 – 0 0 0
Sarah BURN, 0 0 0 – 0 0 1 – 0 0 0
Mary Ann BURN, 0 0 0 – 0 0 1 – 0 0 0
Cuffy BURN, 0 0 0 – 0 0 0 – 1 0 0

#145: (Blank) 0 0 0 – 0 0 0 – 1 0 0

p. 117:
#146: Joannah BENTLACE, 0 0 0 – 0 0 0 – 0 1 0

#147: Guildford BENNETT, 0 0 0 – 0 0 0 – 1 0 0
Mary BENNETT, 0 0 0 – 0 0 0 – 0 1 0
Olive BENNETT, 0 0 0 – 0 0 0 – 0 0 1

#148: Henry BAILEY, 0 0 0 – 0 0 0 – 1 0 0

#149: January BAYNBRIDGE, 0 0 0 – 0 0 0 – 1 0 0
Hosana [sic] BAYNBRIDGE, 0 0 0 – 0 0 0 – 0 1 0

#150: James BELISLE, 0 0 0 – 1 0 0 – 0 0 0
Charlotte BELISLE, 0 0 0 – 0 1 0 – 0 0 0
Margaret BELISLE, 0 0 0 – 0 0 1 – 0 0 0
Hannah BELISLE, 0 0 0 – 0 0 1 – 0 0 0
Jane BELISLE, 0 0 0 – 0 0 1 – 0 0 0

Ester BELISLE, 0 0 0 – 0 0 1 – 0 0 0
Benjamin BELISLE, C 0 0 – 0 0 1 – 0 0 0

#151: Jane BARNES, 0 1 0 – 0 0 0 – 0 0 0
Jane De BRIEN, 0 1 0 – 0 0 0 – 0 0 0
Pamela R. BARNES, C 1 0 – 0 0 0 – 0 0 0
Jane Adelaide De BRIEN, 0 0 1 – 0 0 0 – 0 0 0
Jane P. S. COATES, 0 1 0 – 0 0 0 – 0 0 0
Maria McKAY, 0 0 0 – 0 1 0 – 0 0 0
Mary Ann HUGHES, 0 0 0 – 0 1 0 – 0 0 0
Anne HUGHES, 0 0 0 – 0 1 0 – 0 0 0
Anne VERNON, 0 0 0 – 0 1 0 – 0 0 0
Mary Ann ANDERSON, 0 0 0 – 0 0 1 – 0 0 0
Elizabeth PITZOLD, 0 0 0 – 0 0 1 – 0 0 0
Edward HUGHES, 0 0 0 – 0 0 1 – 0 0 0

p. 118:
#152: Sam BAKER, 0 0 0 – 0 0 0 – 1 0 0
Nancy FORTH, 0 0 0 – 0 0 0 – 0 1 0
Jean GOFF, 0 0 0 – 0 0 0 – 0 0 1
Elizabeth GOFF, 0 0 0 – 0 0 0 – 0 0 1

#153: Charles BELISLE, 1 0 0 – 0 0 0 – 0 0 0

#154: Thomas BENNETT, 0 0 0 – 0 0 0 – 1 0 0
Jane BRENAN, 0 0 0 – 0 0 0 – 0 1 0
Maria BENNETT, 0 0 0 – 0 0 0 – 0 0 1

Note: Enumerator's errors. The next number is #146 instead of #155, and two households are numbered #148.

#146: John BENNETT, 0 0 0 – 0 0 0 – 1 0 0
Ellenor HUMES, 0 0 0 – C 0 0 – 0 1 0

#147: Bill BENNETT, 0 0 0 – 0 0 0 – 1 0 0
Sabina BAILY, 0 0 0 – 0 0 0 – 0 1 0

#148: Thomas BELISLE, 0 0 0 – 0 0 0 – 1 0 0
Abberdean [sic] BELISLE, 0 0 0 – 0 0 0 – 1 0 0
Dolly BIRD, 0 0 0 – 0 0 0 – 0 1 0

#148: Andria [sic] BORDER, 0 0 0 – 0 0 0 – 1 0 0
Nancy BELISLE, 0 0 0 – 0 0 0 – 0 1 0

#149: Henry BAGNEL, 0 0 0 – 0 0 0 – 1 0 0
Joanna BAGNEL, 0 0 0 – 0 0 0 – 0 1 0

241

Hannah KENEDY, 0 0 0 – 0 0 1 – 0 0 0
Sarah BAGNEL, 0 0 0 – 0 0 0 – 0 0 1
Henry BAGNEL, 0 0 0 – 0 0 0 – 0 0 1
Richard BAGNEL, 0 0 0 – 0 0 0 – 0 0 1

p. 119:
#150:   James BAILEY, 0 0 0 – 0 0 0 – 1 0 0
        Elizabeth USHER, 0 0 0 – 0 0 0 – 0 1 0

#151:   Jane BELISLE, 0 0 0 – 0 0 0 – 0 1 0
        John LEWIS, 0 0 0 – 0 0 0 – 1 0 0

#152:   Amelia BENNETT, 0 0 0 – 0 0 0 – 1 0 0 [sic]   *(marked as male)*
        John LAWNEYS, 0 0 0 – 0 0 0 – 0 1 0 [sic]   *(marked as female)*
        Mary Ann BHANS [sic], 0 0 0 – 0 0 0 – 0 1 0

#153:   Mary BELYTHE, 0 0 0 – 0 1 0 – 0 0 0   *(= BELISLE.)*
        Margaret LEWIS, 0 0 0 – 0 1 0 – 0 0 0
        Julia LEWIS, 0 0 0 – 0 0 1 – 0 0 0
        John LEWIS, 0 0 0 – 0 0 1 – 0 0 0
        Jane CARMICHAEL, 0 0 0 – 0 0 1 – 0 0 0
        Sarah CARMICHAEL, 0 0 0 – 0 0 1 – 0 0 0
        Phoebe LEWIS, 0 0 0 – 0 0 0 – 0 1 0
        Rosannah FLOWERS, 0 0 0 – 0 0 0 – 0 1 0

#154:   John BAILEY, 0 0 0 – 0 0 0 – 1 0 0
        Membra BAILEY, 0 0 0 – 0 0 0 – 0 1 0
        Joseph BAILEY, 0 0 0 – 0 0 0 – 1 0 0
        Abraham BAILEY, 0 0 0 – 0 0 0 – 1 0 0
        Mathew [sic] BAILEY, 0 0 0 – 0 0 0 – 1 0 0

#155:   Joe BENNETT, 0 0 0 – 0 0 0 – 1 0 0
        Emilia HUMES, 0 0 0 – 0 0 0 – 0 1 0
        Cetira HUMES, 0 0 0 – 0 0 0 – 0 0 1

#156:   Titus BENNETT, 0 0 0 – 0 0 0 – 1 0 0
        Prudence, 0 0 0 – 0 0 0 – 0 1 0   *(Surname not given.)*

p. 120:
#157:   Peter BAKER, 0 0 0 – 0 0 0 – 1 0 0
        Molly JONES, 0 0 0 – 0 0 0 – 0 1 0
        Henry BAKER, 0 0 0 – 0 0 0 – 0 0 1

#158:   George BURN, 1 0 0 – 0 0 0 – 0 0 0   *(married Ann M. Wade on 23 Aug 1827.)*
        Elizabeth TILLETT, 0 0 0 – 0 1 0 – 0 0 0
        Mary BURN, 0 0 0 – 0 0 1 – 0 0 0

Betsy BURN, 0 0 0 – 0 0 1 – 0 0 0
Anne BURN, 0 0 0 – 0 0 1 – 0 0 0
George BURN, 0 0 0 – 0 0 1 – 0 0 0

Note: Were George and Ann the parents of all the children? Ann Wade Burns was not in the household; she appears on p. 121 below, with Mary Cunningham, probably her cousin, and a child, Elizabeth Wade, probably the child who died aged 9 in December 1840. In 1835 George Burns - presumably her husband - had a daughter by Eliza Williams. Ann Wade Burns died before 1849, when other heirs of her mother, Elizabeth Tillett, sold their interest in Ferrill's Landing to her sister Elizabeth Wade Runnals Bennett; in 1866 Ann's heirs (not named) are mentioned in a Deed of Lease and Release concerning this property.

#159:   M. BARROW, 0 0 0 – 0 0 0 – 0 1 0
John BRIEN, 0 0 0 – 0 0 0 – 1 0 0
Toby FRAZELLE 0 0 0 – 0 0 0 – 1 0 0
William T. BARROW, 0 0 0 – 0 0 1 – 0 0 0
E. A. BARROW, 0 0 0 – 0 0 1 – 0 0 0
M. T. BARROW, 0 0 0 – 0 0 1 – 0 0 0
George H. BARROW, 0 0 0 – 0 0 1 – 0 0 0
James E. BARROW, 0 0 0 – 0 0 1 – 0 0 0

Note: This household number should be #160; instead, it is #157.
#157:   David BETSON, 1 0 0 – 0 0 0 – 0 0 0
Ann GABOUREL, 0 1 0 – 0 0 0 – 0 0 0
Robert SMITH, 1 0 0 – 0 0 0 – 0 0 0
David BETSON Junr, 1 0 0 – 0 0 0 – 0 0 0
Amanda JONES, 0 0 0 – 0 0 0 – 0 1 0
Rosannah BETSON, 0 0 0 – 0 0 0 – 0 1 0
Mary BETSON, 0 0 0 – 0 0 0 – 0 1 0
James BETSON, 0 0 0 – 0 0 0 – 1 0 0

#158:   Hannibal BILLERY, 0 0 0 – 0 0 0 – 1 0 0

p. 121:
#159:   Ann BURNS, 0 1 0 – 0 1 0 – 0 0 0   *(Two marks on the same line.)*
Mary CUNNINGHAM 0 0 0 – 0 0 0 – 0 0 0   *(No mark for her.)*
Elizabeth WADE, 0 0 0 – 0 0 1 – 0 0 0

#160:   Jean BAPTISTE, 0 0 0 – 0 0 0 – 1 0 0
Rebecca THOMPSON, 0 0 0 – 0 0 0 – 0 1 0

#161:   Peter BILLERY, 0 0 0 – 0 0 0 – 1 0 0
Catherine MEIGHAN, 0 0 0 – 0 0 0 – 0 1 0
Frances MEIGHAN, 0 0 0 – 0 0 0 – 0 1 0
Andrew BILLERY, 0 0 0 – 0 0 0 – 1 0 0

243

#162: Francis BROADBELT, 0 0 0 – 0 0 0 – 1 0 0 *(Lined and totaled with #163.)*

#163: John LORAN BARNARD, 0 0 0 – 0 0 0 – 1 0 0
John Peter BARNARD, 0 0 0 – 0 0 0 – 0 0 1
Rohe [sic] BARNARD, 0 0 0 – 0 0 0 – 0 0 1

#164: George BULL, 0 0 0 – 0 0 0 – 1 0 0
Maria BENTURA [sic], 0 0 0 – 0 0 0 – 0 1 0

#165: Richard BROSTER, 0 0 0 – 0 0 0 – 1 0 0
Susan UTHER [sic], 0 0 0 – 0 0 0 – 0 1 0
Amelia RICHARDS, 0 0 0 – 0 0 0 – 0 0 1
Charles UTHER, 0 0 0 – 0 0 0 – 0 0 1
Molly RICHARDS, 0 0 0 – 0 0 0 – 0 0 1

#166: Tinah BEATTIE, 0 0 0 – 0 1 0 – 0 0 0

#167: Raswell [sic] BENNETT, 0 0 0 – 0 0 0 – 1 0 0

p. 122:
#168: John D. CONNOR, 0 0 0 – 1 0 0 – 0 0 0

#169: John CARD, 0 0 0 – 0 0 0 – 1 0 0

#170: Peter CRAIG, 0 0 0 – 0 0 0 – 1 0 0

#171: John CROFT, 0 0 0 – 1 0 0 – 0 0 0
Sylvia HARRIS, 0 0 0 – 0 1 0 – 0 0 0
Robert CROFT, 0 0 0 – 0 0 1 – 0 0 0

p. 123:
#172: Lewellin CUNNINGHAM, 0 0 0 – 0 0 0 – 1 0 0
Ann GADDESS, 0 0 0 – 0 0 0 – 0 1 0
Frances CUNNINGHAM, 0 0 0 – 0 0 0 – 0 0 1
Molly CUNNINGHAM, 0 0 0 – 0 0 0 – 0 0 1
Rebecca CUNNINGHAM, 0 0 0 – 0 0 0 – 0 0 1

#173: Prince CADLE, 0 0 0 – 0 0 0 – 1 0 0

#174: Richard CADLE, 0 0 0 – 0 0 0 – 1 0 0
Catharine BURKE, 0 0 0 – 0 0 0 – 0 1 0

#175: John McCLOUD, 0 0 0 – 1 0 0 – 0 0 0
Wm. CROWELL, 0 0 0 – 1 0 0 – 0 0 0
Thos. GREY, 0 0 0 – 0 0 1 – 0 0 0
Rebecca HUME, 0 0 0 – 0 1 0 – 0 0 0

244

#176: Eliza COURTENAY, 0 0 0 – 0 1 0 – 0 0 0

#177: Ann CHAMPAGNE, 0 0 0 – 0 1 0 – 0 0 0
        Joshua APPLEBY, 0 0 0 – 1 0 0 – 0 0 0
        Daniel McFOY, 0 0 0 – 1 0 0 – 0 0 0
        Venus HEWLETT, 0 0 0 – 0 0 0 – 0 1 0
        John TUCKER, 0 0 0 – 0 0 0 – 1 0 0
        Ellen, 0 0 0 – 0 0 0 – 0 1 0
        Juliana, 0 0 0 – 0 0 0 – 0 1 0
        Evelina, 0 0 0 – 0 0 0 – 0 1 0 *(Surnames not given.)*

#178: Adam CARD, 0 0 0 – 0 0 0 – 1 0 0

p. 124:
#179: Peter CADLE, 0 0 0 – 0 0 0 – 1 0 0
        Maria CADLE, 0 0 0 – 0 0 0 – 0 1 0
        Sarah CADLE, 0 0 0 – 0 0 0 – 0 1 0
        Mary CADLE, 0 0 0 – 0 0 0 – 0 0 1
        Eliza CADLE, 0 0 0 – 0 0 0 – 0 0 1
        William CADLE, 0 0 0 – 0 0 0 – 0 0 1
        Clemine CADLE, 0 0 0 – 0 0 0 – 0 0 1

#180: John COLLINGS [*sic*], 0 0 0 – 0 0 0 – 1 0 0
        Diana SMITH, 0 0 0 – 0 0 0 – 0 1 0

#181: John A. CROFT, 0 0 0 – 1 0 0 – 0 0 0
        Diana STAIN, 0 0 0 – 0 1 0 – 0 0 0

#182: Nelson COLLINS, 0 0 0 – 0 0 0 – 1 0 0
        Juliana BUNGEM, 0 0 0 – 0 0 0 – 0 0 1

#183: George CLARKE, 0 0 0 – 1 0 0 – 0 0 0
        Catharine STEPHENS, 0 0 0 – 0 1 0 – 0 0 0
        George M. CLARKE, 0 0 0 – 0 0 1 – 0 0 0

#184: James CARD, 0 0 0 – 0 0 0 – 1 0 0
        Jane CARD, 0 0 0 – 0 0 0 – 0 1 0

#185: John CELISTINE, 0 0 0 – 0 0 0 – 1 0 0
        Rose CELISTINE, 0 0 0 – 0 0 0 – 0 1 0

#186: Robert CARD, 0 0 0 – 0 0 0 – 1 0 0
        Phoebe CARD, 0 0 0 – 0 0 0 – 0 1 0
        Benjamin SPROAT, 0 0 0 – 0 0 0 – 0 0 1

245

p. 125:

#187: W. H. COFFIN, 1 0 0 – 0 0 0 – 0 0 0
Eliza COFFIN, 0 0 0 – 0 1 0 – 0 0 0
Sophia BENNETT, 0 0 0 – 0 1 0 – 0 0 0
John BENNETT, 1 0 0 – 0 0 0 – 0 0 0
Harry FISHER, 0 0 0 – 0 0 0 – 1 0 0
Kitty FISHER, 0 0 0 – 0 0 0 – 0 1 0
Jenny or Jerry [sic], 0 0 0 – 0 0 0 – 1 0 0
Ben, 0 0 0 – 0 0 0 – 1 0 0
Peter, 0 0 0 – 0 0 0 – 1 0 0
Evans, 0 0 0 – 0 0 0 – 1 0 0 *(Surnames not given.)*
Alick TILLOTE [sic], 0 0 0 – 0 0 0 – 1 0 0
Hero ANDERSON, 0 0 0 – 0 0 0 – 1 0 0
Molly, 0 0 0 – 0 0 0 – 0 1 0
Nancy, 0 0 0 – 0 0 0 – 0 1 0
Mary, 0 0 0 – 0 0 0 – 0 1 0
Ben, 0 0 0 – 0 0 0 – 1 0 0
John, 0 0 0 – 0 0 0 – 1 0 0
Alfred, 0 0 0 – 0 0 0 – 1 0 0 *(Surnames not given.)*

#188: Corpl [sic] J. CORK, 0 0 0 – 0 0 0 – 1 0 0
Maria HILARIA, 0 0 0 – 0 0 0 – 0 1 0
Margaret NUGENT, 0 0 0 – 0 0 0 – 0 1 0
Paulina, 0 0 0 – 0 0 0 – 0 1 0
Teenah, 0 0 0 – 0 0 0 – 0 1 0 *(Surnames not given.)*

#189: Phillis CATOUCHE, 0 0 0 – 0 1 0 – 0 0 0
Thomas FAIRFAX, 0 0 0 – 1 0 0 – 0 0 0
Osanna BENBRIDGE, 0 0 0 – 0 1 0 – 0 0 0

p. 126:

#190: William CROSBIE, 0 0 0 – 1 0 0 – 0 0 0
Maria DOMINGO, 0 0 0 – 0 1 0 – 0 0 0
Daniel HAMILTON, 0 0 0 – 0 0 1 – 0 0 0
Benjamin PETZOLD, 0 0 0 – 0 0 1 – 0 0 0
Frank, 0 0 0 – 0 0 0 – 0 0 1 *(Surname not given.)*

#191: George CARD, 0 0 0 – 1 0 0 – 0 0 0
Elizabeth TUKS, 0 0 0 – 0 1 0 – 0 0 0

#192: Joseph CAIN Senr, 0 0 0 – 0 0 0 – 1 0 0
Joseph CAIN Junr, 0 0 0 – 0 0 0 – 1 0 0
Sampson CAIN, 0 0 0 – 0 0 0 – 0 0 1
Andrew CAIN, 0 0 0 – 0 0 0 – 0 0 1
Samuel CAIN, 0 0 0 – 0 0 0 – 0 0 1
Jannette CAIN Senr, 0 0 0 – 0 0 0 – 0 1 0

Jannette CAIN Junr, 0 0 0 – 0 0 0 – 0 1 0
Matilda CAIN, 0 0 0 – 0 0 0 – 0 0 1
Mary CAIN, 0 0 0 – 0 0 0 – 0 0 1
Adelaide CAIN, 0 0 0 – 0 0 1 – 0 0 0

#193: Bristow COATQUELVIN, 0 0 0 – 0 0 0 – 1 0 0

#194: Christopher CHARLES, 0 0 0 – 0 0 0 – 1 0 0

#195: Austin W. COX, 1 0 0 – 0 0 0 – 0 0 0
Mary COX, 0 1 0 – 0 0 0 – 0 0 0
Georgiana COX, 0 0 1 – 0 0 0 – 0 0 0
Henrietta COX, 0 0 1 – 0 0 0 – 0 0 0
Sophia WALLIS GABOUREL, 0 0 0 – 0 0 0 – 0 1 0

p. 127:
#196: Thomas McCANTY, 0 0 0 – 0 0 0 – 1 0 0
Fanny McCANTY, 0 0 0 – 0 0 0 – 0 1 0
Margaret McCANTY, 0 0 0 – 0 0 0 – 0 0 1
Robert McCANTY, 0 0 0 – 0 0 0 – 0 0 1
William McCANTY, 0 0 0 – 0 0 0 – 0 0 1
Mary Ann McCANTY, 0 0 0 – 0 0 0 – 0 0 1

#197: William CAMPBELL, 1 0 0 – 0 0 0 – 0 0 0
John VERNON, 0 0 0 – 0 0 1 – 0 0 0 – 0 0 0
Sarah CALDWELL, 0 0 0 – 0 1 0 – 0 0 0
Margaret CAMPBELL, 0 0 0 – 0 0 1 – 0 0 0
Jessie CAMPBELL, 0 0 0 – 0 0 1 – 0 0 0

#198: Edward COOTE, 0 0 0 – 0 0 0 – 1 0 0
Rebecca COOTE, 0 0 0 – 0 0 0 – 0 1 0

#199: William CUNNINGHAM, 0 0 0 – 0 0 0 – 1 0 0
Mary THOMPSON, 0 0 0 – 0 0 0 – 0 1 0
Sarah A. CUNNINGHAM, 0 0 0 – 0 0 0 – 0 0 1

Note: The Keeper of the Records made another numbering error at this point. The next household should be #201: instead, it is #101.

#101: William CRAMMOND, 1 0 0 – 0 0 0 – 0 0 0
Edward CRAMMOND, 1 0 0 – 0 0 0 – 0 0 0
Charlotte SIMSON [*sic*], 0 0 0 – 0 1 0 – 0 0 0

#102: Ralph CUNNINGHAM, 0 0 0 – 1 0 0 – 0 0 0
Isabella MEANEY, 0 0 0 – 0 0 1 – 0 0 0 [*sic*]
Andrew CUNNINGHAM, 0 0 0 – 0 0 0 – 0 1 0 [*sic*]

247

Note: Was Isabella the black woman and Andrew the coloured child?

#103: Jean Pierre CARLE, 0 0 0 – 0 0 0 – 1 0 0

p. 128:
#104: William COURTNAY, 0 0 0 – 1 0 0 – 0 0 0
       Eve COURTNAY, 0 0 0 – 0 1 0 – 0 0 0
       Amelia COURTNAY, 0 0 0 – 0 1 0 – 0 0 0
       Elizabeth COURTNAY, 0 0 0 – 0 1 0 – 0 0 0
       Harriett COURTNAY, 0 0 0 – 0 1 0 – 0 0 0
       Allen COURTNAY, 0 0 0 – 0 0 1 – 0 0 0
       George NICHOLSON, 0 0 0 – 0 0 1 – 0 0 0
       Edward COURTNAY, 0 0 0 – 0 0 1 – 0 0 0

#105: Robert COLQUHOUN, 0 0 0 – 0 0 0 – 1 0 0
       Franc [*sic*] SUTHERLAND, 0 0 0 – 0 0 0 – 1 0 0

#106: Jane CADLE, 0 0 0 – 0 0 0 – 0 1 0

#107: Quashba CUNNINGHAM, 0 0 0 – 0 0 0 – 0 1 0
       James La MONT, 0 0 0 – 0 0 0 – 0 0 1

#108: James CADLE, 0 0 0 – 0 0 0 – 1 0 0
       Maria Teresa VALLROS, 0 0 0 – 0 0 0 – 0 1 0
       Joseph CADLE, 0 0 0 – 0 0 0 – 0 0 1
       William CADLE, 0 0 0 – 0 0 0 – 0 0 1

#109: Benjamin CARTER, 0 0 0 – 1 0 0 – 0 0 0
       Mary BELISLE, 0 0 0 – 0 1 0 – 0 0 0

#110: John COLOSSUS, 0 0 0 – 0 0 0 – 1 0 0
       Violet GIBSON, 0 0 0 – 0 0 0 – 0 1 0
       Nelson GIBSON, 0 0 0 – 0 0 0 – 1 0 0
       Qushima DIXON, 0 0 0 – 0 0 0 – 0 1 0
       Roseal NUGENT, 0 0 0 – 0 0 0 – 0 0 1

p. 129:
#111: William COX, 1 0 0 – 0 0 0 – 0 0 0
       Leonard P. COX, 1 0 0 – 0 0 0 – 0 0 0
       Talbot COX, 1 0 0 – 0 0 0 – 0 0 0
       Mary COX, 0 1 0 – 0 0 0 – 0 0 0
       Venus, 0 0 0 – 0 0 0 – 0 1 0
       Adriana, 0 0 0 – 0 0 0 – 0 1 0
       George, 0 0 0 – 0 0 0 – 0 0 1
       William 0 0 0 – 0 0 0 – 0 0 1 *(Surnames not given.)*

248

#112: Charles CRAIG, 1 0 0 – 0 0 0 – 0 0 0
Jenny CRAIG, 0 0 0 – 0 0 0 – 0 1 0
Betsy CRAIG, 0 0 0 – 0 0 0 – 0 0 1
Charles CRAIG Junr, 0 0 0 – 0 0 0 – 0 0 1

#113: John COLUMBUS, 0 0 0 – 0 0 0 – 1 0 0

#114: John COLLINS, 1 0 0 – 0 0 0 – 0 0 0
Sarah COLLINS, 0 1 0 – 0 0 0 – 0 0 0
Saran Ann COLLINS. 0 0 1 – 0 0 0 – 0 0 0
John H. COLLINS, 0 0 1 – 0 0 0 – 0 0 0
Henrietta COLLINS, 0 0 1 – 0 0 0 – 0 0 0
Ellen COLLINS, 0 0 1 – 0 0 0 – 0 0 0
Eliza Mary, 0 0 1 – 0 0 0 – 0 0 0 *(Surname not given: in 1835, COLLINS.)*
Mary COLLINS, 0 0 0 – 0 0 0 – 0 0 1
Nancy COLLINS, 0 0 0 – 0 0 0 – 0 0 1
Charles COLLINS, 0 0 0 – 0 0 0 – 1 0 0
John COLLINS, 0 0 0 – 0 0 0 – 0 0 1

#115: Britain CUNNINGHAM, 0 0 0 – 0 0 0 – 1 0 0

p. 130:
#116: William CORTQUELVIN [*sic*], 0 0 0 – 0 0 0 – 1 0 0
Diana TURNBULL, 0 0 0 – 0 0 0 – 0 1 0
Mary TURNBULL, 0 0 0 – 0 0 0 – 0 0 1
Fortune, 0 0 0 – 0 0 0 – 0 0 1 *(Surname not given.)*

#117: John CHURREN Sr, 0 0 0 – 0 0 0 – 1 0 0
John CHURREN Jr, 0 0 0 – 0 0 0 – 0 0 1
Ann Maria CHURREN, 0 0 0 – 0 0 0 – 0 1 0
Rose CHURREN, 0 0 0 – 0 0 0 – 0 0 1
Elizabeth CHURREN, 0 0 0 – 0 0 0 – 0 0 1

#118: Peter AVILLER, 0 0 0 – 1 0 0 – 0 0 0
David AVILLER, 0 0 0 – 0 0 1 – 0 0 0
Silby MOOR, 0 0 0 – 0 0 0 – 0 1 0

#119: Francisco CAMOYANO, 1 0 0 – 0 0 0 – 0 0 0
Jose SOTO, 1 0 0 – 0 0 0 – 0 0 0
Paulino GONZALES, 0 0 0 – 1 0 0 – 0 0 0

#120: Margaret CUNNINGHAM, 0 0 0 – 0 1 0 – 0 0 0
Mary CUNNINGHAM, 0 0 0 – 0 0 1 – 0 0 0
John CUNNINGHAM, 0 0 0 – 0 0 1 – 0 0 0
William CUNNINGHAM, 0 0 0 – 0 0 1 – 0 0 0
James CUNNINGHAM. 0 0 0 – 0 0 1 – 0 0 0

#121: Wm C. CARD, 0 0 0 – 1 0 0 – 0 0 0
        Sarah CARD, 0 0 0 – 0 1 0 – 0 0 0
        Ann CARD, 0 0 0 – 0 0 1 – 0 0 0

Note: From this point on (in many but not all instances) the enumerator made a line of dashes in place of a surname. This was his equivalent of ditto marks.

p. 131:
#122: Thomas CUNNINGHAM
        Celia - - - - - ,   *(There are no marks for Thomas or Celia.)*

#123: Daniel COLQUHOUN 0 0 0 – 0 0 0 – 1 0 0
        Margaret YOUNG, 0 0 0 – 0 0 0 – 0 1 0
        Margaret GRANT, 0 0 0 – 0 0 0 – 0 0 1
        James USHER, 0 0 0 – 0 0 0 – 1 0 0
        Margaret Jane COLQUHOUN, 0 0 0 – 0 0 0 – 0 0 1
        Alvarez CADO, 0 0 0 – 0 0 0 – 1 0 0

#124: Dick COLQUHOUN, 0 0 0 – 0 0 0 – 1 0 0

#125: Isaac CLARKE, 0 0 0 – 0 0 0 – 1 0 0
        Teresa FARLEY, 0 0 0 – 0 1 0 – 0 0 0
        Rebecca CLARKE, 0 0 0 – 0 0 1 – 0 0 0

#126: Marcus CUNNINGHAM, 0 0 0 – 0 0 0 – 1 0 0

#127: James CARD, 0 0 0 – 0 0 0 – 1 0 0
        Rose Ana - - - - - , 0 0 0 – 0 0 0 – 0 1 0
        Arabella - - - - - , 0 0 0 – 0 0 0 – 0 1 0

#128: Abraham CRAIG, 0 0 0 – 0 0 0 – 1 0 0
        Maria CRAIG, 0 0 0 – 0 0 0 – 0 1 0
        Eliza CRAIG, 0 0 0 – 0 0 0 – 0 0 1
        Celby CRAIG, 0 0 0 – 0 0 0 – 0 0 1

#129: J. A. CRAIG, 0 0 0 – 0 0 0 – 1 0 0
        Selina R. HEWLETT, 0 0 0 – 0 0 0 – 0 1 0
        Jno. B. CRAIG, 0 0 0 – 0 0 0 – 0 0 1
        Frances - - - - -, 0 0 0 – 0 0 0 – 0 0 1

p. 132:
#130: James CANTOUSE, 0 0 0 – 0 0 0 – 1 0 0
        Emma HUMES, 0 0 0 – 0 0 0 – 0 1 0

#131: Nancy CRANE, 0 0 0 – 0 1 0 – 0 0 0
        Emma CRANE, 0 0 0 – 0 0 1 – 0 0 0

#132: Eleanor CADLE, 0 0 0 – 0 1 0 – 0 0 0
Catharine MUCKLEHANY, 0 0 0 – 0 0 1 – 0 0 0
Philip CODD, 0 0 0 – 0 0 1 – 0 0 0
William AUGUST, 0 0 0 – 0 0 1 – 0 0 0

#133: Frederick CROWE, 1 0 0 – 0 0 0 – 0 0 0
Louise - - - - -, 0 1 0 – 0 0 0 – 0 0 0

#134: John CLARK, 0 0 0 – 0 0 0 – 1 0 0
Sabina - - - - -, 0 0 0 – 0 0 0 – 0 1 0
W^m - - - - -, 0 0 0 – 0 0 0 – 1 0 0
Lucretia - - - - -, 0 0 0 – 0 0 0 – 0 1 0
Lucy - - - - -, 0 0 0 – 0 0 0 – 0 1 0
Joseph - - - - -, 0 0 0 – 0 0 0 – 1 0 0
Daniel - - - - -, 0 0 0 – 0 0 0 – 1 0 0
Frances - - - - -, 0 0 0 – 0 0 0 – 0 1 0

#135: Matilda CARD, 0 0 0 – 0 0 0 – 0 1 0
Nancy - - - - -, 0 0 0 – 0 0 0 – 0 0 1

#136: John CONNER, 1 0 0 – 0 0 0 – 0 0 0
Catharine - - - - -, 0 0 0 – 0 1 0 – 0 0 0
Mary - - - - -, 0 0 0 – 0 0 1 – 0 0 0

p. 133:
#137: Hugh CARMICHAEL, 0 0 0 – 0 0 0 – 1 0 0
Fillis - - - - -, 0 0 0 – 0 0 0 – 0 1 0
Susannah - - - - -, 0 0 0 – 0 0 0 – 0 1 0
Venas [sic] TUCKER, 0 0 0 – 0 0 0 – 0 1 0
John Thomas POTTS, 0 0 0 – 0 0 0 – 0 0 1
Henry CAMP, 0 0 0 – 0 0 0 – 1 0 0

#138: John CANY COOTE, 0 0 0 – 0 0 0 – 1 0 0
James - - - - - , 0 0 0 – 0 0 0 – 0 0 1
John - - - - - , 0 0 0 – 0 0 0 – 0 0 1

#139: John COURTNAY, 0 0 0 – 1 0 0 – 0 0 0
Maria GUMBOWERS, 0 0 0 – 0 1 0 – 0 0 0 *(= GAMBOA.)*
Catharine COURTNAY, 0 0 0 – 0 0 0 – 0 1 0

#140: Robert CARROTT, 0 0 0 – 0 0 0 – 1 0 0
Callyan, 0 0 0 – 0 0 0 – 1 0 0 *(Surname not given.)*

#141: Fernando CABRERA, 0 0 0 – 1 0 0 – 0 0 0
Salome GARCIA, 0 0 0 – 0 0 0 – 0 1 0

251

Juana KERINA, 0 0 0 – 0 0 0 – 0 1 0
Juan MANUEL, 0 0 0 – 0 0 0 – 0 0 1
Estevan CABRERA, 0 0 0 – 0 0 0 – 0 0 1
Magdeleno - - - - -, 0 0 0 – 0 0 0 – 0 0 1
Maria Olya - - - - -, 0 0 0 – 0 0 0 – 0 0 1
Maria Eustachia - - - - -, 0 0 0 – 0 0 0 – 0 0 1
Candelaria COLOMA, 0 0 0 – 0 0 0 – 0 0 1

#142: John COURAN, 0 0 0 – 0 0 0 – 1 0 0
Susanna SWEASEY, 0 0 0 – 0 0 0 – 0 1 0

p. 134:
#143: William CHARTER, 0 0 0 – 0 0 0 – 1 0 0
Ann TUCKER, 0 0 0 – 0 0 0 – 0 1 0
Joseph - - - - -, 0 0 0 – 0 0 0 – 0 0 1
Jannett - - - - -, 0 0 0 – 0 0 0 – 0 0 1

#144: Edward COWELL, 1 0 0 – 0 0 0 – 0 0 0
Frederick W. COWELL, 1 0 0 – 0 0 0 – 0 0 0
George Edwd - - - - -, 1 0 0 – 0 0 0 – 0 0 0
Curly LYNCH, 0 0 0 – 0 0 1 – 0 0 0
Smart WELSH, 0 0 0 – 0 0 0 – 0 0 1

#145: Andrew COX, 0 0 0 – 0 0 0 – 1 0 0
Mary COXE, [sic], 0 0 0 – 0 0 0 – 0 1 0
Eleanor CUNNINGHAM, 0 0 0 – 0 0 0 – 0 1 0
Rachel - - - - -, 0 0 0 – 0 0 0 – 0 1 0
Amelia - - - - -, 0 0 0 – 0 0 0 – 0 1 0
John GLADDON, 0 0 0 – 0 0 0 – 0 0 1
Mary Jane HYDE, 0 0 0 – 0 0 0 – 0 0 1
Juliana NICHOLSON, 0 0 0 – 0 0 0 – 0 0 1
Thomas PATTIESON, 0 0 0 – 0 0 0 – 0 0 1

#146: Elizabeth CARD, 0 0 0 – 0 0 0 – 0 1 0
Peter COATNEY, 0 0 0 – 0 0 0 – 1 0 0
Amela - - - - -, 0 0 0 – 0 0 0 – 0 0 1
Alexander - - - - - , 0 0 0 – 0 0 0 – 0 0 1
Danael [sic] - - - - -, 0 0 0 – 0 0 0 – 0 0 1

#147: Maria GOFF, 0 0 0 – 0 0 0 – 0 1 0
Thomas CAMEL, 0 0 0 – 0 0 0 – 1 0 0
John GOFF, 0 0 0 – 0 0 0 – 0 0 1
Joseph PITT, 0 0 0 – 0 0 0 – 0 0 1

p. 135:
#148: Charles CASTLE, 0 0 0 – 0 0 0 – 1 0 0

#149: Charles CROSSLEY, 0 0 0 – 0 0 0 – 1 0 0

#150: Robert COOTE, 0 0 0 – 0 0 0 – 1 0 0
George DAVIS, 0 0 0 – 0 0 0 – 0 0 1

#151: Rachael CLARE, 0 0 0 – 0 0 0 – 0 1 0
Joseph McDONALD, 1 0 0 – 0 0 0 – 0 0 0
Wm DAVID, 0 0 0 – 0 0 0 – 1 0 0
Ismael CLARE, 0 0 0 – 0 0 0 – 0 0 1
Juddy [sic] HUDSON, 0 0 0 – 0 0 0 – 0 1 0
Matilda COPLEY, 0 0 0 – 0 0 0 – 0 1 0

#152: James CANNOW, 0 0 0 – 0 0 0 – 1 0 0
Hannah - - - - -, 0 0 0 – 0 0 0 – 0 1 0
Mary Ann - - - - -, 0 0 0 – 0 0 0 – 0 0 1
James - - - - -, 0 0 0 – 0 0 0 – 0 0 1

#153: Phoebe CHERRINGTON, 0 0 0 – 0 1 0 – 0 0 0
Clarinda WILLIAMS, 0 0 0 – 0 1 0 – 0 0 0
Eleanor CHERRINGTON, 0 0 0 – 0 1 0 – 0 0 0
William - - - - -, 0 0 0 – 1 0 0 – 0 0 0
Sarah Anne - - - - -, 0 0 0 – 0 1 0 – 0 0 0
Elizabeth - - - - -, 0 0 0 – 0 1 0 – 0 0 0
Emma - - - - -, 0 0 0 – 0 1 0 – 0 0 0
Henry U. - - - - -, 0 0 0 – 0 0 1 – 0 0 0
John S. - - - - -, 0 0 0 – 0 0 1 – 0 0 0
James - - - - -, 0 0 0 – 0 0 1 – 0 0 0

p. 136:
#154: Lewis CAIN, 0 0 0 – 0 0 0 – 1 0 0
Noel CAIN, 0 0 0 – 0 0 0 – 0 0 1
Elizabeth - - - - -, 0 0 0 – 0 0 0 – 0 0 1

#155: John CONGHOUN [sic], 0 0 0 – 0 0 0 – 1 0 0 *(= COLQUHOUN.)*

#156: Thomas CARD, 0 0 0 – 1 0 0 – 0 0 0
Margaret - - - - -, 0 0 0 – 0 0 0 – 0 1 0
Rosannah REVEY, 0 0 0 – 0 0 0 – 0 1 0

#157: George COOKE, 0 0 0 – 0 0 0 – 1 0 0
John HOLME, 0 0 0 – 0 0 0 – 1 0 0
Agnes COLQUHOUN, 0 0 0 – 0 0 0 – 0 1 0
Jane SEMPLES, 0 0 0 – 0 0 0 – 0 0 1
Jenny ANDERSON, 0 0 0 – 0 0 0 – 0 1 0
George HOLME, 0 0 0 – 0 0 0 – 1 0 0

#158: Eyre COOTE, 0 0 0 – 0 0 0 – 1 0 0
Mary HIGGIN, 0 0 0 – 0 0 0 – 0 1 0
Jane COOTE, 0 0 0 – 0 0 0 – 0 0 1

#159: James CHANCEL, 0 0 0 – 0 0 0 – 1 0 0
Emelia - - - - -, 0 0 0 – 0 1 0 – 0 0 0
Agnes - - - - -, 0 0 0 – 0 0 1 – 0 0 0
Betsy - - - - -, 0 0 0 – 0 0 1 – 0 0 0
Henry - - - - -, 0 0 0 – 0 0 1 – 0 0 0
James - - - - -, 0 0 0 – 0 0 1 – 0 0 0 *(Marked as both a male and a female child.)*
Anne - - - - -, 0 0 0 – 0 0 0 – 0 0 0 *(No mark; totaled as a coloured female child.)*

#160: John COOTE, 0 0 0 – 0 0 0 – 1 0 0

p. 137:
#161: William CLARK, 0 0 0 – 0 0 0 – 1 0 0
Lucretia JEFFERS, 0 0 0 – 0 0 0 – 0 1 0

#162: James CATTO, 0 0 0 – 1 0 0 – 0 0 0
Jane NEAL, 0 0 0 – 0 0 1 – 0 0 0
Elizabeth CATTO, 0 0 0 – 0 0 0 – 0 1 0

#163: George COATQUELVIN, 0 0 0 – 0 0 0 – 1 0 0
Maria - - - - -, 0 0 0 – 0 0 0 – 0 1 0

#164: James CUNNINGHAM, 0 0 0 – 1 0 0 – 0 0 0
Catherine SMITH, 0 0 0 – 0 0 0 – 0 1 0
Edward CROFT, 0 0 0 – 0 0 1 – 0 0 0
James CLENAN, 0 0 0 – 0 0 1 – 0 0 0
Rebecca, 0 0 0 – 0 0 0 – 0 1 0
Sarah, 0 0 0 – 0 0 0 – 0 0 1
Juda Ann, 0 0 0 – 0 0 1 – 0 0 0 *(Surnames not given.)*
Sarah FAIRWEATHER, 0 0 0 – 0 0 1 – 0 0 0
Eleanor LOCK, 0 0 0 – 0 0 1 – 0 0 0
Maria LOCK, 0 0 0 – 0 0 1 – 0 0 0
Barclet *(or Bardet?)* 0 0 0 – 0 0 0 – 0 1 0 *(Surname not given.)*
Sarah Anne, 0 0 0 – 0 0 0 – 0 1 0
Sarah CUNNINGHAM, 0 0 0 – 0 0 0 – 0 1 0
Mary CUNNINGHAM, 0 0 0 – 0 0 0 – 0 0 1
Benjamin - - - - -, 0 0 0 – 0 0 0 – 0 0 1

#165: Mary COKER, 0 0 0 – 0 1 0 – 0 0 0
Elssy [*sic*] GODFREY, 0 0 0 – 0 0 1 – 0 0 0
Maria DICKSON, 0 0 0 – 0 0 0 – 0 1 0

p. 138:

#166: R. DeBAPTISTE, 0 0 0 – 1 0 0 – 0 0 0
      John - - - - -, 0 0 0 – 1 0 0 – 0 0 0
      James - - - - -, 0 0 0 – 1 0 C – 0 0 0
      Elizabeth - - - - -, 0 0 0 – 0 1 0 – 0 0 0
      Frances - - - - -, 0 0 0 – 0 1 0 – 0 0 0
      Esther - - - - -, 0 0 0 – 0 1 C – 0 0 0
      Isabella - - - - -, 0 0 0 – 0 0 1 – 0 0 0
      Sophia MARTIN, 0 0 0 – 0 1 0 – 0 0 0

#167: Richard DEYE, 0 0 0 – 0 0 0 – 0 0 1
      Janette - - - - -, 0 0 0 – 0 0 0 – 0 0 1 *(No adult shown in this household.)*

#168: Chas. M. DANCE, 0 0 0 – 0 0 – 0 0 0
      Catherine McLENEN? *(or McLEUEN?)* 0 0 0 – 0 0 1 – 0 0 0
      Mary BEVANS, 0 0 0 – 0 1 0 – 0 0 0
      Jane DANCE, 0 0 0 – 0 0 1 – 0 0 0
      Abygail - - - - -, 0 0 0 – 0 0 1 – 0 0 0

#169: Horatio DAVID, 0 0 0 – 0 0 0 – 1 0 0
      Elizabeth CARD, 0 0 0 – 0 0 0 – 0 1 0

#170: Jose DOLORES, 0 0 0 – 1 0 0 – 0 0 0
      Maria FORD, 0 0 0 – 0 1 0 – 0 0 0

#171: Joseph DIAMOND, 0 0 0 – 0 0 0 – 1 0 0

#172: Richard DAVIS, 0 0 0 – 0 0 0 – 1 0 0
      Catherine GRANT, 0 0 0 – 0 0 0 – 0 1 0
      William DAVIS, 0 0 0 – 0 0 0 – 0 0 1

#173: Philip DeBRIEN, 0 0 0 – 0 0 0 – 1 0 0

p. 139:

#174: James DRUMMOND, 0 0 0 – 0 0 0 – 1 0 0
      Mary FANCY, 0 0 0 – 0 0 0 – 0 1 0
      Sarah FORTUNE, 0 0 0 – 0 C 0 – 0 1 0

#175: Henry DICKSON, 0 0 0 – 0 C 0 – 1 0 0

#176: James DACRES, 0 0 0 – 0 0 0 – 1 0 0

#177: John McDALY, 0 0 0 – 1 0 0 – 0 0 0

#178: Isidore DUMAS, 0 0 0 – 1 0 0 – 0 0 0
      Maria - - - - -, 0 0 0 – 0 1 0 – 0 0 0

255

John LAMOIN, 0 0 0 – 1 0 0 – 0 0 0
Peter LAMOIN, 0 0 0 – 1 0 0 – 0 0 0
George BELISLE, 0 0 0 – 1 0 0 – 0 0 0
Amelia LEMOIN, 0 0 0 – 0 1 0 – 0 0 0
Celia BELISLE, 0 0 0 – 0 0 1 – 0 0 0
Sarah - - - - -, 0 0 0 – 0 0 1 – 0 0 0
Elizabeth DUMAS, 0 0 0 – 0 0 1 – 0 0 0
Margaret - - - - -, 0 0 0 – 0 0 1 – 0 0 0

#179:   John DIGBY, 0 0 0 – 0 0 0 – 1 0 0
Jem HOGG, 0 0 0 – 0 0 0 – 1 0 0

#180:   Joseph DARLEY, 0 0 0 – 0 0 0 – 1 0 0

#181:   Nancy [*sic*] DICK, 0 0 0 – 0 0 0 – 1 0 0   *(Marked and totaled as male.)*

#182:   Richard DUGARD, 0 0 0 – 0 0 0 – 1 0 0
Rebecca DUGARD, 0 0 0 – 0 0 0 – 0 0 1
Richard - - - - -, 0 0 0 – 0 0 0 – 0 0 1

p. 140:
#183:   Batty DELORIOUS, 0 0 0 – 0 0 0 – 1 0 0
Flora JONES, 0 0 0 – 0 0 0 – 0 1 0
Adam - - - - -, 0 0 0 – 0 0 0 – 1 0 0
Joseph DOMINGUES, 0 0 0 – 0 0 0 – 1 0 0
Rosannah JONES, 0 0 0 – 0 0 0 – 0 1 0
Isaac DOMINGUES, 0 0 0 – 0 0 0 – 1 0 0
Marteo [*sic*] JONES, 0 0 0 – 0 0 0 – 1 0 0

#184:   Thomas DENT, 0 0 0 – 0 0 0 – 1 0 0

#185:   Edward DRUMMOND, 0 0 0 – 0 0 0 – 1 0 0

#186:   David, 0 0 0 – 0 0 0 – 1 0 0   *(Surname not given.)*
Lucy DANCE, 0 0 0 – 0 0 0 – 0 1 0
Thomas, 0 0 0 – 0 0 0 – 0 0 1   *(Surname not given.)*

#187:   Sarah DAVIE, 0 1 0 – 0 0 0 – 0 0 0
Michael McCAMBLY, 1 0 0 – 0 0 0 – 0 0 0

#188:   Emelia DOUGLASS, 0 0 0 – 0 0 0 – 0 0 0 *(No mark; totaled as a coloured female.)*
Thomas HEWLETT, 0 0 0 – 0 0 0 – 0 1 0   *(Marked as female)*

#189:   John DREYSON, 0 0 0 – 1 0 0 – 0 0 0
Note: Households #188 and 189 are lined and totaled together as one colored male, one black male, and one black female.

256

#190: Edwd DeBRIEN, 0 0 0 – 1 0 0 – 0 0 0
Sarah HOAR, 0 0 0 – 0 0 0 – 0 1 0
Elizabeth EVE, 0 0 0 – 0 1 0 – 0 0 0
Sarah TURNBULL, 0 0 0 – 0 0 1 – 0 0 0
Danael [sic] EVE, 0 0 0 – 0 0 1 – 0 0 0
Thomas - - - - -, 0 0 0 – 0 0 1 – 0 0 0
Philip SMITH, 0 0 0 – 1 0 0 – 0 0 0

p. 141:
#191: John DAVIS, 0 0 0 – 0 0 0 – 1 0 0
Elener - - - - -, 0 0 0 – 0 0 0 – 0 1 0

#192: Betsy DAVIS, 0 0 0 – 0 1 0 – 0 0
- - - - - - - - - -, 0 0 0 – 0 1 0 – 0 0 0
- - - - - - - - - -, 0 0 0 – 0 0 1 – 0 0 0   *(Male)*
Note: *This and the next household are lined and totaled together. An extended family?*

#193: Joseph DYER, 0 0 0 – 1 0 0 – 0 0 0
Mary - - - - -, 0 0 0 – 0 1 0 – 0 0 0
James - - - - -, 0 0 0 – 0 0 1 – 0 0 0
Ann - - - - -, 0 0 0 – 0 0 1 – 0 0 0
Nehamon - - - - -, 0 0 0 – 0 0 1 – 0 0 0
George - - - - -, 0 0 0 – 0 0 1 – 0 0 0

#194: John DeCOSTA, 0 0 0 – 0 0 0 – 1 0 0

#195: Peter DOBSON, 0 0 0 – 0 0 0 – 1 0 0
Mary - - - - -, 0 0 0 – 0 0 0 – 0 1 0

#196: John DUNDAS, 0 0 0 – 0 0 0 – 1 0 0

#197: Joseph DAVIS, 0 0 0 – 1 0 0 – 0 0 0
Eleanor - - - - -, 0 0 0 – 0 1 0 – 0 0 0
Maria - - - - -, 0 0 0 – 0 1 0 – 0 0 0
Joseph - - - - - Jr, 0 0 0 – 1 0 0 – 0 0 0
Rebecca - - - - -, 0 0 0 – 0 1 0 – 0 0 0

#198: William DY, 0 0 0 – 0 0 0 – 1 0 0
Mary MALBRUCK, 0 0 0 – 0 0 0 – 0 1 0
James - - - - -, 0 0 0 – 0 0 0 – 1 0 0

#199: Edward DOUGHTY, 0 0 0 – 0 0 0 – 1 0 0

p. 142:
#200: Julius DeBRIEN, 0 0 0 – 1 0 0 – 0 0 0

257

Eliza, 0 0 0 – 0 0 0 – 0 1 0
Ralph, 0 0 0 – 0 0 1 – 0 0 0

#201: Joseph JONES, 0 0 0 – 0 0 0 – 1 0 0
Fanny - - - - -, 0 0 0 – 0 1 0 – 0 0 0
James DAVIS, 0 0 0 – 0 0 1 – 0 0 0
Thomas - - - - -, 0 0 0 – 0 0 1 – 0 0 0

#202: John DOUGLASS, 0 0 0 – 0 0 0 – 1 0 0
Jane GIPSON, 0 0 0 – 0 0 0 – 0 1 0
Amelia CONNOR, 0 0 0 – 0 0 0 – 0 0 1
Jas. DOUGLASS, 0 0 0 – 0 0 0 – 0 0 1

#203: Ann DAVIS, 0 0 0 – 0 0 0 – 0 1 0
Joseph - - - - -, 0 0 0 – 0 0 0 – 1 0 0
Horastro [*sic*] MEIGHAN, 0 0 0 – 0 0 0 – 1 0 0
Mary THOMAS, 0 0 0 – 0 0 0 – 0 0 1

#204: Harriot DUNCAN, 0 0 0 – 0 0 0 – 0 1 0
Phillis - - - - -, 0 0 0 – 0 0 0 – 0 0 1

#205: James DAVIS, 0 0 0 – 0 0 0 – 1 0 0

#206: Helen DAVIS, 0 0 0 – 0 1 0 – 0 0 0
- - - - -   - - - - -, 0 0 0 – 0 0 1 – 0 0 0 *(Female. An infant not yet named?)*
Note: #206 and #207 are lined and totaled together. An extended family?

#207: Patrick C. DeBRIEN, 0 0 0 – 1 0 0 – 0 0 0
Jane A. DeBRIEN, 0 1 0 – 0 0 0 – 0 0 0
Sampson KEENE, 0 0 0 – 0 0 0 – 1 0 0
George GRAHAM, 0 0 0 – 0 0 0 – 1 0 0
Quaw BENNETT, 0 0 0 – 0 0 0 – 1 0 0

p. 143:
#208: David DEENE, 0 0 0 – 1 0 0 – 0 0 0
Judy TUCKSY, 0 0 0 – 0 0 1 – 0 0 0
Mary Jane DEENE, 0 0 0 – 0 0 0 – 0 1 0

#209: Margaret DeBERION, 0 0 0 – 0 0 0 – 0 1 0 *(= DeBRIEN.)*
Jane WINTER, 0 0 0 – 0 0 0 – 0 1 0
Louisa DeBERION, 0 0 0 – 0 0 0 – 0 1 0

#210: Elizabeth DELORE, 0 0 0 – 0 0 0 – 0 1 0

#211: George DECENCY, 0 0 0 – 1 0 0 – 0 0 0
Rose DIPPLE, 0 0 0 – 0 1 0 – 0 0 0

Catharine DECENCY, 0 0 0 – 0 0 1 – 0 0 0
Ann HEWLETT, 0 0 0 – 0 1 0 – 0 0 0
Joseph DOMINGO, 0 0 0 – 0 0 1 – 0 0 0
Joseph HEWLETT, 0 0 0 – 0 0 1 – 0 0 0

#212: Henry DUNBAR, 0 0 0 – 0 0 0 – 1 0 0
     Catharine - - - - -, 0 0 0 – 0 0 0 – 0 1 0
     George - - - - -, 0 0 0 – 0 0 0 – 1 0 0

#213: Jose DEBRELL, 0 0 0 – 0 0 0 – 1 0 0

#214: William DAWSON, 1 0 0 – 0 0 0 – 0 0 0
     Elizabeth RAYBAN, 0 1 0 – 0 0 0 – 0 0 0
     Daniel DAWSON, 0 0 1 – 0 0 0 – 0 0 0
     Sarah - - - - -, 0 0 1 – 0 0 0 – 0 0 0
     Peter - - - - -, 0 0 1 – 0 0 0 – 0 0 0
     Frances - - - - -, 0 0 1 – 0 0 0 – 0 0 0

p. 144:
#215: Anthony DAWKIN, 0 0 0 – 0 0 0 – 1 0 0
     Phillis WHITE, 0 0 0 – 0 0 0 – 0 1 0
     Mary Ann DAWKIN, 0 0 0 – 0 0 0 – 0 1 0
     Frances - - - - -, 0 0 0 – 0 0 0 – 0 1 0
     John - - - - -, 0 0 0 – 0 0 0 – 1 0 0
     Edwd - - - - -, 0 0 0 – 0 0 0 – 1 0 0
     James - - - - -, 0 0 0 – 1 0 0 – 0 0 0

#216: John DAWKIN, 0 0 0 – 1 0 0 – 0 0 0
     Quasheba - - - - -, 0 0 0 – 0 1 0 – 0 0 0

#217: Augusteen DIVERGE, 0 0 0 – 0 0 0 – 1 0 0
     Harriett LOUIS, 0 0 0 – 0 0 0 – 0 1 0

#218: James DUNFORD, 0 0 0 – 0 0 0 – 1 0 0
     Philedia PIPERSBURG, 0 0 0 – 0 0 0 – 0 1 0

#219: James DANIEL, 0 0 0 – 0 0 0 – 1 0 0
     Frances TUCKER, 0 0 0 – 0 0 0 – 0 1 0

#220: Robert DALE, 0 0 0 – 0 0 0 – 1 0 0

#221: Peter DOUGLASS, 0 0 0 – 0 0 0 – 1 0 0

#222: Joseph EARNEST, 0 0 0 – 1 0 0 – 0 0 0
     Amelia ROBINSON, 0 0 0 – 0 0 0 – 0 1 0

#223: Richard ELRINGTON, 0 0 0 – 0 0 0 – 1 0 0
Esther TRAPP, 0 0 0 – 0 0 0 – 0 1 0
James ELRINGTON, 0 0 0 – 0 0 0 – 1 0 0

p. 145:
#224: William EMERY, 0 0 0 – 1 0 0 – 0 0 0
Joanna SANCHO, 0 0 0 – 0 1 0 – 0 0 0

#225: Chas. EVE, 0 0 0 – 0 0 0 – 1 0 0
Catherine - - - - -, 0 0 0 – 0 0 0 – 0 1 0
Letitia SAVERY, 0 0 0 – 0 0 1 – 0 0 0
Catherine DEMARS, 0 0 0 – 0 0 1 – 0 0 0

#226: Glasgow EDWARDS, 0 0 0 – 0 0 0 – 1 0 0
Wm CLIVE, 0 0 0 – 0 0 0 – 1 0 0

#227: David EVANS, 0 0 0 – 1 0 0 – 0 0 0
Eliza BURRELL, 0 0 0 – 0 1 0 – 0 0 0
Morgan EVANS, 0 0 0 – 0 0 1 – 0 0 0
Richard WINTER, 0 0 0 – 0 0 1 – 0 0 0
Margaret GILLETT, 0 0 0 – 0 1 0 – 0 0 0

#228: Frances ELRINGTON, 0 0 0 – 0 0 0 – 1 0 0
Jane MORRIS, 0 0 0 – 0 0 0 – 0 1 0
John FRANCIS, 0 0 0 – 0 0 0 – 0 0 1
George - - - - -, 0 0 0 – 0 0 0 – 0 0 1
Matteo - - - - -, 0 0 0 – 0 0 0 – 0 0 1

#229: John ELLIOTT, 0 0 0 – 0 0 0 – 1 0 0

#230: Robt EILY, 1 0 0 – 0 0 0 – 0 0 0
Ann GARBUTT, 0 1 0 – 0 0 0 – 0 0 0
Alick CARTER, 0 0 1 – 0 0 0 – 0 0 0
Jane, 0 0 0 – 0 0 1 – 0 0 0 *(Surname not given.)*

p. 146:
#231: Ann ELRINGTON, 0 1 0 – 0 0 0 – 0 0 0
Ann E. ELRINGTON, 0 1 0 – 0 0 0 – 0 0 0
Wm. J. PEEBLES, 1 0 0 – 0 0 0 – 0 0 0
Fanny, 0 0 0 – 0 0 0 – 0 0 1
Jane, 0 0 0 – 0 0 0 – 0 0 1
Emma, 0 0 0 – 0 0 0 – 0 0 1
Nelson, 0 0 0 – 0 0 0 – 0 0 1
Harry, 0 0 0 – 0 0 0 – 0 0 1
Sophia, 0 0 0 – 0 0 0 – 0 1 0 *(Surnames not given.)*

#232: Maria EVERITT, 0 0 0 – 0 1 0 – 0 0 0
Louisa SMITH, 0 0 0 – 0 1 0 – 0 0 0
Ann EVERITT, 0 0 0 – 0 1 0 – 0 0 0
Catherine HINKS, 0 0 0 – 0 1 0 – 0 0 0
George EVERITT, 0 0 0 – 1 0 0 – 0 0 0
Jacob EVERITT, 0 0 0 – 1 0 0 – 0 0 0
John BLADON, 0 0 0 – 1 0 0 – 0 0 0
Richard HINKS, 0 0 0 – 0 0 1 – 0 0 0
Richard WATKINS, 0 0 0 – 0 0 0 – 1 0 0

#233: Harriott EVERETT [sic], 0 0 0 – 0 1 0 – 0 0 0
James C. CROZER, 0 0 0 – 0 0 1 – 0 0 0 *(= CROZIER.)*
Jacob H. - - - - -, 0 0 0 – 0 0 1 – 0 0 0
Anne B. - - - - -, 0 0 0 – 0 0 1 – 0 0 0

#234: Eliza EDWARDS, 0 0 0 – 0 0 0 – 0 1 0
Silvia EDWARDS, 0 0 0 – 0 0 0 – 0 0 1

#235: Philip EDWARD, [sic], 0 0 0 – 0 0 0 – 1 0 0

p. 147:
#236: Sarah EVE, 0 0 0 – 0 1 0 – 0 0 0
Eliza EVE, 0 0 0 – 0 1 0 – 0 0 0
Mary PRICE, 0 0 0 – 0 1 0 – 0 0 0
Edward ROSS, 0 0 0 – 0 0 1 – 0 0 0
Eliza TILLETT, 0 0 0 – 0 0 1 – 0 0 0 *(Marked as a male child.)*
Sarah NOEL, 0 0 0 – 0 0 1 – 0 0 0

#237: Samuel EDWARDS, 0 0 0 – 0 0 0 – 1 0 0

#238: Henry ENDHAM, 0 0 0 – 0 0 0 – 1 0 0
Thomas - - - - -, 0 0 0 – 0 0 0 – 0 0 1

#239: Richard EDWARDS, 0 0 0 – 0 0 0 – 1 0 0

#240: James EARNEST, 0 0 0 – 0 0 0 – 1 0 0
Samuel L. - - - - -, 0 0 0 – 0 0 0 – 1 0 0
Wm. S. - - - - -, 0 0 0 – 0 0 0 – 0 0 1
Robert T. - - - - -, 0 0 0 – 0 0 0 – 0 0 1
Arminta LAMB, 0 0 0 – 0 0 0 – 0 1 0
Anne A. ERNEST, 0 0 0 – 0 0 0 – 0 0 1
Sophia 0 0 0 – 0 0 0 – 0 0 1
George, 0 0 0 – 0 0 0 – 0 0 1 *(Surnames not given.)*

#241: Gankey EDWARDS, 0 0 0 – 0 0 0 – 1 0 0
Susannah ANDERSON, 0 0 0 – 0 0 0 – 0 1 0

Daniel EDWARDS, 0 0 0 – 0 0 0 – 0 0 1
Peter GORDON, 0 0 0 – 0 0 0 – 0 0 1
Abigail GALLON, 0 0 0 – 0 0 0 – 0 1 0

p. 148:
#242: John B. ERSKINE, 0 0 0 – 1 0 0 – 0 0 0
Agnes - - - - -, 0 0 0 – 0 1 0 – 0 0 0
John B. - - - - - Jr., 0 0 0 – 0 0 1 – 0 0 0
Manuel ARSO? *(or CERSO?)* 0 0 0 – 0 0 0 – 0 0 1

#243: James EARNEST, 0 0 0 – 0 0 0 – 1 0 0
Huesafar [*sic*] MAYER, 0 0 0 – 0 0 0 – 0 1 0
Thomas SMITH, 0 0 0 – 0 0 0 – 1 0 0
John AVILLAR, 0 0 0 – 0 0 0 – 0 0 1
Frances De BRIEN, 0 0 0 – 0 0 0 – 0 0 1

#244: Elwin ELWIN, 1 0 0 – 0 0 0 – 0 0 0   *(born England; a magistate in Roatan.)*
Maryann WARD, 0 0 0 – 0 1 0 – 0 0 0   *(Mary Ann Chappel 5/3/1819-26/9/1888.)*
Elizabeth ELWIN, 0 0 0 – 0 1 0 – 0 0 0   *(Elizabeth born 3 Feb 1838 Belize.*
Helen - - - - -, 0 0 0 – 0 0 1 – 0 0 0   *(Helen Priscilla Elwin b. 26 Oct 1841 and*
(Robert Henry Elwin b. 26 Oct 1841, twins.
#245: Maria EMERY, 0 0 0 – 0 1 0 – 0 0 0   *(Emma Elwin b. Apr 8 1842; to Roatan.*
Maria CARD, 0 0 0 – 0 1 0 – 0 0 0   *(8 more children, all born Roatan.*
Mary, 0 0 0 – 0 0 0 – 0 1 0
Betty, 0 0 0 – 0 0 0 – 0 1 0
Fanny, 0 0 0 – 0 0 0 – 0 1 0
Grace, 0 0 0 – 0 0 0 – 0 0 1
Sarah, 0 0 0 – 0 0 0 – 0 0 1
Louis, 0 0 0 – 0 0 0 – 0 0 1
Peter, 0 0 0 – 0 0 0 – 0 0 1
Oscar, 0 0 0 – 0 0 0 – 0 0 1
Alfred, 0 0 0 – 0 0 0 – 0 0 1   *(Surnames not given.)*

#246: Chas. EVANS, 1 0 0 – 0 0 0 – 0 0 0
Gregorio, 0 0 0 – 0 0 0 – 1 0 0   *(Surname not given.)*
Sarah MASKALL, 0 0 0 – 0 0 0 – 0 1 0

p. 149:
#247: Marcus EWING, 0 0 0 – 1 0 0 – 0 0 0
Elizabeth CRABB, 0 0 0 – 0 1 0 – 0 0 0
John EWING, 0 0 0 – 0 0 1 – 0 0 0
Jane - - - - -, 0 0 0 – 0 0 1 – 0 0 0

#248: Daniel EWING, 0 0 0 – 1 0 0 – 0 0 0   *(Marks for a white man and woman erased.)*
Rosetta GREGARIO, 0 0 0 – 0 1 0 – 0 0 0   *(= GREGORIO.)*
Maria BENNETT, 0 0 0 – 0 0 1 – 0 0 0

262

Francis ANTHONY, 0 0 0 – 0 0 0 – 1 0 0
Elizabeth E. HAMILTON, 0 0 0 – 0 0 1 – 0 0 0
Robert, 0 0 0 – 0 0 0 – 0 0 1
George, 0 0 0 – 0 0 0 – 0 0 1
Juana, 0 0 0 – 0 0 0 – 0 1 0 *(Surnames not given.)*

#249: Thomas EVE, 0 0 0 – 1 0 0 – 0 0 0
Eliza FELIX, 0 0 0 – 0 1 0 – 0 0 0
Thomas EVE, 0 0 0 – 0 0 0 – 0 0 1
Daniel - - - - -, 0 0 0 – 0 0 1 – 0 0 0

#250: Benjamin ENGLAND, 0 0 0 – 0 0 0 – 1 0 0
Brown BROASTER, 0 0 0 – 0 0 0 – 1 0 0
Silvey ENGLAND, 0 0 0 – 0 0 0 – 0 1 0

#251: Robert ELRINGTON, 0 0 0 – 0 0 0 – 1 0 0
Susannah WAGNER, 0 0 0 – 0 0 0 – 0 1 0
John, 0 0 0 – 0 0 0 – 0 0 1
Maria, 0 0 0 – 0 0 0 – 0 0 1 *(Surnames not given.)*

p. 150:
#252: Sarah EDWARDS, 0 0 0 – 0 0 0 – 0 1 0
Fanny- - - - -, 0 0 0 – 0 0 0 – 0 1 0
Elizabeth - - - - -, 0 0 0 – 0 0 0 – 0 1 0
John - - - - -, 0 0 0 – 0 0 0 – 0 0 1
Jane, 0 0 0 – 0 0 0 – 0 0 1 *(Surname not given.)*
Elizabeth THOMSON, 0 0 0 – 0 0 0 – 0 0 1

#253: Daniel FLOWERS, 0 0 0 – 0 0 0 – 1 0 0
Lucretia - - - - -, 0 0 0 – 0 0 0 – 0 1 0
Inwell - - - - -, 0 0 0 – 0 0 0 – 0 0 1
Abigail, 0 0 0 – 0 0 0 – 0 0 1 *(Surname not given.)*
Julian SUTHERLAND, 0 0 0 – 0 0 0 – 0 0 1
Sarah HUMES, 0 0 0 – 0 0 0 – 0 0 1
Ann FLOWERS, 0 0 0 – 0 0 0 – 0 0 1
Francis HUMES, 0 0 0 – 0 0 0 – 0 0 1

#254: George FORD, 0 0 0 – 0 0 0 – 1 0 0
Presence PASLOW, 0 0 0 – 0 0 0 – 0 1 0

#255: Susan FLOWERS, 0 0 0 – 0 0 0 – 0 1 0
Thomas HYDE, 0 0 0 – 0 0 1 – 0 0 0
Hannah GOFF, 0 0 0 – 0 0 1 – 0 0 0
Sarah HARRIS, 0 0 0 – 0 0 0 – 0 0 1
Charles - - - - -, 0 0 0 – 0 0 0 – 0 0 1

263

Francis GARRETT, 0 0 0 – 0 0 0 – 0 0 1
Matilda - - - - -, 0 0 0 – 0 0 0 – 0 0 1

#256: Andrew FOY, 0 0 0 – 0 0 0 – 1 0 0

#257: Matthias FELIX, 0 0 0 – 0 0 0 – 1 0 0
Maria DIONISIA, 0 0 0 – 0 1 0 – 0 0 0

p. 151:
#258: Robert FLOWERS, 0 0 0 – 0 0 1 – 0 0 0 [sic] *(Both marked as children, but lined*
Margaret - - - - -, 0 0 0 – 0 0 1 – 0 0 0 [sic]   *off as a separate household.)*

#259: Archibald FLOWERS, 0 0 0 – 1 0 0 – 0 0 0
Sophia FLOWERS, 0 0 0 – 0 1 0 – 0 0 0
Margaret - - - - -, 0 0 0 – 0 0 1 - 0 0 0
Nora - - - - -, 0 0 0 – 0 0 1 - 0 0 0
William - - - - -, 0 0 0 – 0 0 1 - 0 0 0
Fanny - - - - -, 0 0 0 – 0 0 1 - 0 0 0
Satira - - - - -, 0 0 0 – 0 0 1 - 0 0 0
Mary - - - - -, 0 0 0 – 0 0 1 - 0 0 0

#260: Thos. FERGUSSON, 0 0 0 – 0 0 0 – 1 0 0
Catherine - - - - -, 0 0 0 – 0 0 0 – 0 1 0
Nancy PITTS, 0 0 0 – 0 0 0 – 0 1 0
Mary O'CONNOR, 0 0 0 – 0 0 0 – 0 0 1
Tessy FERGUSSON, 0 0 0 – 0 0 0 – 0 0 1
William BLACK, 0 0 0 – 0 0 0 – 0 0 1
Peter O'CONNOR, 0 0 0 – 0 0 0 – 0 0 1

#261: James FLOWERS, 0 0 0 – 0 0 0 – 1 0 0
Nora BOWERS [sic], 0 0 0 – 0 0 0 – 0 1 0

#262: Joseph FORTUNE, 0 0 0 – 0 0 0 – 1 0 0
Martha FORTUNE, 0 0 0 – 0 0 0 – 0 1 0
Suffe [sic] - - - - -, 0 0 0 – 0 0 0 – 0 1 0
Jacob BRIEN, 0 0 0 – 0 0 0 – 0 0 1
Rose BEGFORD, 0 0 0 – 0 0 0 – 0 0 1
Trasa [sic] FARLIN, 0 0 0 – 0 0 0 – 0 0 1
Daniel AUGUST, 0 0 0 – 0 0 0 – 1 0 0
Chas. BEGFORD, 0 0 0 – 0 0 0 – 1 0 0

p. 152:
#263: Flora GOFF, 0 0 0 – 0 0 0 – 0 1 0
Margaret FERRELL, 0 0 0 – 0 1 0 – 0 0 0
Mary Ann - - - - -, 0 0 0 – 0 1 0 – 0 0 0
John S. WARREN, 0 0 0 – 0 0 1 – 0 0 0

Note: The households above and below are both numbered #263.

#263: Mary FLOWERS, 0 0 0 – 0 0 0 – 0 1 0
       Angela - - - - -, 0 0 0 – 0 0 0 – 0 1 0
       Annita GRACIANO, 0 0 0 – 0 0 1 – 0 0 0
       Matilda - - - - -, 0 0 0 – 0 0 1 – 0 0 0
       Christino - - - - -, 0 0 0 – 0 0 1 – 0 0 0
       Jose EUSTACIO, 0 0 0 – 0 0 1 – 0 0 0
       Grandina VERGES, 0 0 0 – 0 0 1 – 0 0 0
       Joseph FLOWERS, 0 0 0 – 0 0 0 – 1 0 0
       Maria ---------, 0 0 0 – 0 0 1 – 0 0 0 *(Line is solid, not dashed. Surname?)*
       Juana, 0 0 0 – 0 0 0 – 0 0 1 *(Surname not given.)*

#264: Samuel FERRIER, 0 0 0 – 1 0 0 – 0 0 0
       Polly CRAWFORD, 0 0 0 – 0 0 0 – 0 1 0
       John CLOUDY, 0 0 0 – 0 0 0 – 0 0 1

#265: Catherine FLOWERS, 0 0 0 – 0 0 0 – 0 1 0
       Antoine AUDINET, 0 0 0 – 0 0 0 – 1 0 0

#266: Chas. FLOWERS, 0 0 0 – 0 0 0 – 1 0 0
       Caeser - - - - -, 0 0 0 – 0 0 0 – 1 0 0
       Richard - - - - -, 0 0 0 – 0 0 0 – 1 0 0 *(His parents were Charles and Cloe.)*
       Joseph - - - - -, 0 0 0 – 0 0 0 – 1 0 0   "   "   "   "   "   "
       Steaphin [*sic*] - - - - -, 0 0 0 – 0 0 0 – 0 0 1 *(1835 census: Stevenson Flowers.)*
       Margaret - - - - -, 0 0 0 – 0 0 0 – 0 1 0
       Funy [*sic*] - - - - -, 0 0 0 – 0 0 0 – 0 1 0
       Prin [*sic*] - - - - -, 0 0 0 – 0 0 0 – 0 1 0
       William - - - - -, 0 0 0 – 0 0 0 – 0 0 1

p. 153:
#267: Peter FISHER, 0 0 0 – 0 0 0 – 1 0 0
       Mary - - - - -, 0 0 0 – 0 0 0 – 0 1 0 *(Surname not given.)*
       Louisa ELRINGTON, 0 0 0 – 0 0 0 – 0 1 0

#268: Joseph FERRELL, 0 0 0 – 1 0 0 – 0 0 0

#269: Patty FERGUSON, 0 0 0 – 0 0 0 – 0 1 0
       Tabia BENNETT, 0 0 0 – 0 0 0 – 0 1 0
       Maria PABLO, 0 0 0 – 0 0 0 – 0 0 1

#270: John FORREST, 0 0 0 – 0 0 0 – 1 0 0

#271: James FERGUSON, 0 0 0 – 0 0 0 – 1 0 0
       Patty McAULAY, 0 0 0 – 0 0 0 – 0 1 0
       Susannah BENNETT, 0 0 0 – 0 0 0 – 0 1 0

Tabia BENNETT, 0 0 0 – 0 0 0 – 0 1 0
John ROBINSON, 0 0 0 – 0 0 0 – 0 0 1
Thomas - - - - -, 0 0 0 – 0 0 0 – 0 0 1
Delia FERGUSON, 0 0 0 – 0 0 0 – 0 0 1
Mary - - - - -, 0 0 0 – 0 0 0 – 0 0 1
Samuel - - - - -, 0 0 0 – 0 0 0 – 0 0 1
Johnson BENNETT, 0 0 0 – 0 0 0 – 0 0 1

#272: John D. FINSEY, 0 0 0 – 1 0 0 – 0 0 0

#273: James FORBES, 0 0 0 – 0 0 0 – 1 0 0
William BURN, 0 0 0 – 0 0 0 – 0 0 1

#274: Edward FENCER, 0 0 0 – 0 0 0 – 1 0 0

p. 154:
#275: John FRISBY, 0 0 0 – 0 0 0 – 1 0 0
Behaviour, 0 0 0 – 0 0 0 – 0 1 0 *(Surname not given.)*
Wm GADDES, 0 0 0 – 0 0 0 – 1 0 0

#276: John FOREMAN, 0 0 0 – 0 0 0 – 1 0 0

#277: Alexander FRANCE, 1 0 0 – 0 0 0 – 0 0 0
Ariadne - - - - -, 0 0 0 – 0 1 0 – 0 0 0
John STRANGE, 0 0 0 – 1 0 0 – 0 0 0
Alexander, 0 0 0 – 0 0 0 – 0 0 1
William, 0 0 0 – 0 0 0 – 0 0 1
John, 0 0 0 – 0 0 0 – 0 0 1
Thomas 0 0 0 – 0 0 0 – 0 0 1
Peter, 0 0 0 – 0 0 0 – 0 0 1
Sally, 0 0 0 – 0 0 0 – 0 0 1
Sarah, 0 0 0 – 0 0 0 – 0 0 1
Margaret, 0 0 0 – 0 0 0 – 0 0 1 *(Surnames not given.)*
Phillis FRANCE, 0 0 0 – 0 0 0 – 0 1 0

#278: John A. FLORENCE, 0 0 0 – 1 0 0 – 0 0 0
John JOSEPH, 0 0 0 – 1 0 0 – 0 0 0

#279: Elizabeth FERRELL, 0 0 0 – 0 0 0 – 0 1 0
Jeanette VERNON, 0 0 0 – 0 0 0 – 0 1 0
Margaret FERRELL, 0 0 0 – 0 0 0 – 0 1 0

#280: Lowry [*sic*] FERRELL, 0 0 0 – 0 1 0 – 0 0 0 *(Marked as female.)*
Robert HUGHES, 0 0 0 – 1 0 0 – 0 0 0
Dublin TINKER, 0 0 0 – 0 0 1 – 0 0 0
Margaret CRUMMELL, 0 0 0 – 0 1 0 – 0 0 0

p. 155:
#281: John FLOWERS, 0 0 0 – 0 0 0 – 1 0 0
Maria VENSEN, 0 0 0 – 0 0 0 – 0 1 0
Mathias FLOWERS, 0 0 0 – 0 0 0 – 0 0 1
George - - - - -, 0 0 0 – 0 0 0 – 0 0 1
Maria - - - - -, 0 0 0 – 0 0 0 – 0 0 1

#282: Margaret FRAZER, 0 0 0 – 0 0 0 – 0 1 0
Charlotte GRAY, 0 0 0 – 0 0 0 – 0 0 1
Jane GORDON, 0 0 0 – 0 0 0 – 0 0 1
Clannan LOUIST [sic], 0 0 0 – 0 0 0 – 0 0 1
John GRAY, 0 0 0 – 0 0 0 – 0 0 1

#283: Caesar FULLAR [sic], 0 0 0 – 0 0 0 – 1 0 0
Sarah UTER, 0 0 0 – 0 0 0 – 0 1 0
Stephen FULLER, 0 0 0 – 0 0 0 – 1 0 0
John LAWRIE, 0 0 0 – 0 0 0 – 1 0 0

#284: Francis FORD, 0 0 0 – 1 0 0 – 0 0 0
Mathena - - - - -, 0 0 0 – 0 1 0 – 0 0 0
Sarah DAWSON, 0 0 0 – 0 1 0 – 0 0 0
John - - - - -, 0 0 0 – 1 0 0 – 0 0 0

#285: Chas. FELIX, 0 0 0 – 0 0 0 – 1 0 0
Elizabeth - - - - -, 0 0 0 – 0 0 0 – 0 1 0
Chas. HENRY - - - - -, 0 0 0 – 0 0 0 – 1 0 0
Chas. LEWIS - - - - -, 0 0 0 – 0 0 0 – 1 0 0
Eliza - - - - -, 0 0 0 – 0 0 0 – 0 1 0
Chas. DASH - - - - -, 0 0 0 – 0 0 0 – 1 0 0

#286: Bacchus FRANCE, 0 0 0 – 0 0 0 – 1 0 0

p. 156:
#287: James FLOWERS, 0 0 0 – 0 0 0 – 1 0 0
Lucretia - - - - -, 0 0 0 – 0 0 0 – 0 1 0
Sarah - - - - -, 0 0 0 – 0 0 0 – 0 0 1
Ann - - - - -, 0 0 0 – 0 0 0 – 0 0 1
Julian SUTHERLAND, 0 0 0 – 0 0 0 – 0 0 1

#288: Alex^r FORBES, 1 0 0 – 0 0 0 – 0 0 0
Johnston BROASTER, 0 0 0 – 0 0 0 – 1 0 0
Jose PALACIO, 0 0 0 – 0 0 0 – 1 0 0
John FORBES, 0 0 0 – 0 0 0 – 0 0 1
Manuel CENTRA, 0 0 0 – 0 0 0 – 1 0 0
Leandro BATISTE, 0 0 0 – 0 0 0 – 1 0 0
Chas. HYDE, 0 0 0 – 0 0 0 – 1 0 0

267

#289: Providence FLOWERS, 0 0 0 – 0 0 0 – 1 0 0
Maria VICTORIA, 0 0 0 – 0 1 0 – 0 0 0
Tina FLOWERS, 0 0 0 – 0 0 0 – 0 0 1
Francis - - - - -, 0 0 0 – 0 0 0 – 0 0 1
Jose - - - - -, 0 0 0 – 0 0 0 – 0 0 1
Madelin - - - - -, 0 0 0 – 0 0 0 – 0 0 1
Antony - - - - -, 0 0 0 – 0 0 0 – 0 0 1

#290: Joseph FRANCES [sic], 0 0 0 – 1 0 0 – 0 0 0
Susan CUNNINGHAM, 0 0 0 – 0 0 0 – 0 1 0
Philip LAMONT, 0 0 0 – 0 0 1 – 0 0 0
William FRANCES, 0 0 0 – 0 0 0 – 0 0 1 *(Marked as colored but mark erased.)*
Elinor - - - - -, 0 0 0 – 0 1 0 – 0 0 0

#291: Paddy FINGALL, 0 0 0 – 0 0 0 – 1 0 0
Mary Ann, 0 0 0 – 0 0 0 – 0 1 0
Jeannette, 0 0 0 – 0 0 0 – 0 0 1 *(Surnames not given.)*

p. 157:
#292: Robert FRANCE, 0 0 0 – 0 0 0 – 1 0 0
George BURN, 0 0 0 – 0 0 0 – 1 0 0
Marcy? FRANCE, 0 0 0 – 0 0 0 – 0 1 0
John JUNE? 0 0 0 – 0 0 0 – 0 0 1
Elizabeth BURN, 0 0 0 – 0 0 0 – 0 0 1
Elinor - - - - -, 0 0 0 – 0 0 0 – 0 0 1
Cate CATSON, 0 0 0 – 0 0 0 – 0 0 1 *(Female.)*

#293: James FLOWERS, 0 0 0 – 0 0 0 – 1 0 0
Susannah - - - - -, 0 0 0 – 0 0 0 – 0 1 0

#294: Gerald FITZGIBBON, 0 0 0 – 0 0 0 – 1 0 0
Agnes GRANT, 0 0 0 – 0 0 0 – 0 1 0
James FITZGIBBON, 0 0 0 – 0 0 0 – 0 0 1
Gerald - - - - -, 0 0 0 – 0 0 0 – 0 0 1
Frances - - - - -, 0 0 0 – 0 0 0 - 0 0 1
Tenah - - - - -, 0 0 0 – 0 0 0 – 0 0 1

#295: Clarissa FORES, 0 0 0 – 0 0 0 – 0 1 0
Charlotte WILLIAMS, 0 0 0 – 0 0 0 – 0 1 0

#296: George FERGUSON, 0 0 0 – 0 0 0 – 1 0 0
Rebecca BARNES, 0 0 0 – 0 1 0 – 0 0 0
Catharine GENTLE, 0 0 0 – 0 0 1 - 0 0 0

#297: Chas. FORMAN, 0 0 0 – 1 0 0 – 0 0 0
W^m - - - - -, 0 0 0 – 1 0 0 – 0 0 0

Mary USHER, 0 0 0 – 0 1 0 – 0 0 0
Susan - - - - - FORMAN, 0 0 0 – 0 1 0 – 0 0 0

p. 158:
#298: Joseph FLOWERS, 0 0 0 – 0 0 0 – 1 0 0
Lucretia - - - - -, 0 0 0 – 0 0 0 – 0 1 0
Joseph - - - - - Jr., 0 0 0 – 0 0 0 – 0 0 1
Peter - - - - -, 0 0 0 – 0 0 0 – 0 0 1
Joshua - - - - -, 0 0 0 – 0 0 0 – 0 0 1

#299: James FREEMAN, 1 0 0 – 0 0 0 – 0 0 0
Thomas - - - - -, 1 0 0 – 0 0 0 – 0 0 0
Maryann, 0 0 0 – 0 0 0 – 0 1 0
Harriet, 0 0 0 – 0 0 0 – 0 1 0
Rose, 0 0 0 – 0 0 0 – 0 1 0
Leza [sic], 0 0 0 – 0 0 0 – 0 1 0
Tenibo, 0 0 0 – 0 0 0 – 1 0 0
Catherine, 0 0 0 – 0 0 0 – 0 0 1
George, 0 0 0 – 0 0 0 – 0 0 1
Charley, 0 0 0 – 0 0 0 – 0 0 1
Dolly, 0 0 0 – 0 0 0 – 0 0 1
Robert, 0 0 0 – 0 0 0 – 0 0 1
Thomas, 0 0 0 – 0 0 0 – 0 0 1 *(Surnames not given.)*

#300: John FRANCE, 0 0 0 – 0 0 0 – 1 0 0
Evelina THOMSON, 0 0 0 – 0 0 0 – 0 1 0
Ann Grace, 0 0 0 – 0 0 0 – 0 0 1

#301: Michael FLOWERS, 0 0 0 – 0 0 0 – 1 0 0
Mary - - - - -, 0 0 0 – 0 0 0 – 0 1 0
Sophia - - - - -, 0 0 0 – 0 0 0 – 0 1 0
Aby [sic] - - - - -, 0 0 0 – 0 0 0 – 0 0 1 *(Female.)*
John - - - - -, 0 0 0 – 0 0 0 – 0 0 1

p. 159:
#302: Philip FALL, 1 0 0 – 0 0 0 – 0 0 0
Richard - - - - -, 1 0 0 – 0 0 0 – 0 0 0
Margaret - - - - -, 0 1 0 – 0 0 0 – 0 0 0
Frances Ann - - - - -, 0 1 0 – 0 0 0 – 0 0 0

#303: Thomas FISHER, 0 0 0 – 0 0 0 – 1 0 0
Maria - - - - -, 0 0 0 – 0 0 0 – 0 0 1
Victoria LOUIS, 0 0 0 – 0 0 0 – 0 1 0

#304: John GORDON, 0 0 0 – 0 0 0 – 1 0 0
Judy - - - - -, 0 0 0 – 0 0 0 – 0 1 0

Charlotte JOHNSON, 0 0 0 – 0 0 0 – 0 1 0
Peter FRENKLING [*sic*], 0 0 0 – 0 0 0 – 0 0 1
George DUNBAR, 0 0 0 – 0 0 0 – 0 0 1
John BRANNAN, 0 0 0 – 0 0 0 – 0 0 1

#305: C^a GLADDIN, 0 0 0 – 0 1 0 – 0 0 0 *(In other censuses, Catherine.)*
Susan GLADDIN, 0 0 0 – 0 0 1 – 0 0 0
Catherine FOREMAN, 0 0 0 – 0 0 1 – 0 0 0
John GOFF, 0 0 0 – 0 0 1 – 0 0 0
Marie GOFF, 0 0 0 – 0 0 1 – 0 0 0

#306: James GABOUREL, 0 0 0 – 0 0 0 – 1 0 0
Phoebe - - - - -, 0 0 0 – 0 0 0 – 0 1 0
Emily - - - - -, 0 0 0 – 0 0 0 – 0 0 1
Phillis - - - - -, 0 0 0 – 0 0 0 – 0 0 1
Sophia - - - - -, 0 0 0 – 0 0 0 – 0 0 1
Henry - - - - -, 0 0 0 – 0 0 0 – 0 0 1
Duncan - - - - -, 0 0 0 – 0 0 0 – 0 0 1
Edmond - - - - -, 0 0 0 – 0 0 0 – 0 0 1

p. 160:
#307: Joseph F. GRANT, 0 0 0 – 0 0 0 – 1 0 0
George MACDELO [*sic*], 0 0 0 – 0 0 0 – 1 0 0
Henry - - - - -, 0 0 0 – 0 0 0 – 1 0 0
Harriet - - - - -, 0 0 0 – 0 0 0 – 0 1 0
Harriet MILES, 0 0 0 – 0 0 0 – 0 1 0
Harriet - - - - -, 0 0 0 – 0 0 0 – 0 0 1
Margaret - - - - -, 0 0 0 – 0 0 0 – 0 0 1
Elizabeth - - - - -, 0 0 0 – 0 0 0 – 0 0 1
Noel - - - - -, 0 0 0 – 0 0 0 – 0 0 1

#308: Wm GABOUREL, 0 0 0 – 0 0 0 – 1 0 0
Phoebe - - - - -, 0 0 0 – 0 0 0 – 0 1 0

#309: Alexander GENTLE, 0 0 0 – 0 0 0 – 1 0 0

#310: Bedford GENTLE, 0 0 0 – 0 0 0 – 1 0 0
Clara GOFF, 0 0 0 – 0 0 0 – 0 1 0
Mary Ann GENTLE, 0 0 0 – 0 0 0 – 0 0 1
Joseph GOFF, 0 0 0 – 0 0 0 – 0 0 1
Thomas - - - - -, 0 0 0 – 0 0 0 – 0 0 1
Betty SPROAT, 0 0 0 – 0 0 0 – 0 0 1
Andrew GENTLE, 0 0 0 – 0 0 0 – 0 0 1
Frederick GENTLE, 0 0 0 – 0 0 0 – 1 0 0
Betty - - - - -, 0 0 0 – 0 0 0 – 0 0 1

270

#311: James GRANT, 0 0 0 – 0 0 0 – 1 0 0
Petronia FLOWERS, 0 0 0 – 0 0 0 – 0 1 0
William GRANT, 0 0 0 – 0 0 0 – 1 0 0

#312: London GENTLE, 0 0 0 – 0 0 0 – 1 0 0
Sarah Ann MIDCALF, 0 0 0 – 0 0 0 – 0 1 0
Maria GENTLE, 0 0 0 – 0 0 0 – 0 1 0

p. 161:
#313: William GILL, 0 0 0 – : 0 0 – 0 0 0
- - - - - - - - - -. 0 0 0 – 0 0 1 – 0 0 0 *(Female. An infant not yet named?)*
Elizabeth KETTO, 0 0 0 – 0 0 0 – 0 1 0   *(= CATO?)*
John CRAFT, 0 0 0 – 0 0 0 – 1 0 0

#314: John GOUGH, 1 0 0 – 0 0 0 – 0 0 0
Emily B. - - - - -, 0 1 0 – 0 0 0 – 0 0 0
Jane WELSH, 0 1 0 – 0 0 0 – 0 0 0
Emily F. GOUGH, 0 0 1 – 0 0 0 – 0 0 0
WILSON WELSH - - - - -, 0 0 1 – 0 0 0 – 0 0 0
James - - - - -, 0 0 1 – 0 0 0 – 0 0 0
Edward GOUGH, 0 0 0 – 0 0 0 – 1 0 0

#315: Clark GRAHAM, 0 0 0 – 0 0 0 – 1 0 0
Eve GENTLE, 0 0 0 – 0 0 0 – 0 1 0
Robert - - - - -, 0 0 0 – 0 0 0 – 0 0 1
David - - - - -, 0 0 0 – 0 0 0 – 0 0 1
James - - - - -, 0 0 0 – 0 0 0 – 0 0 1

#316: John GENTLE, 0 0 0 – 0 0 0 – 1 0 0

#317: Samuel GOFF, 0 0 0 – 0 0 0 – 1 0 0
Esther FLOWERS, 0 0 0 – 0 0 0 – 0 1 0

#318: James GUNN, 1 0 0 – 0 0 0 – 0 0 0
Mary - - - - -, 0 0 0 – 0 1 0 – 0 0 0 *(In the 1832 census, Mary GLADDEN.)*
E. S. - - - - -, 0 0 0 – 0 0 1 – 0 0 0 *(Male.)*
F. - - - - -, 0 0 0 – 0 0 1 – 0 0 0   *(Female.)*
S. - - - - -, 0 0 0 – 0 0 1 – 0 0 0   *(Female.)*

p. 162:
#319: Thomas GRIFFITHS, 0 0 0 – 0 0 0 – 1 0 0
Martha MENGAN, 0 0 0 – 0 0 0 – 0 1 0   *(= MEIGHAN?)*
Jannett SMITH, 0 0 0 – 0 0 0 – 0 1 0
Joseph BROSTER, 0 0 0 – 0 0 0 – 1 0 0

271

#320: Elizabeth GODFREY, 0 0 0 – 0 1 0 – 0 0 0 *(Mother of Selina=Eliza=Celina.)*
      Celina BENNETT, 0 0 0 – 0 1 0 – 0 0 0 *(Dau. of Marshal Bennett- Sr. or Jr.?)*
      Isabella ERSKINE, 0 0 0 – 0 0 1 – 0 0 0
      Lucretia NEAL, 0 0 0 – 0 0 1 – 0 0 0
      John - - - - -, 0 0 0 – 0 0 1 – 0 0 0
      Alice - - - - -, 0 0 0 – 0 0 1 – 0 0 0
      Bird, 0 0 0 – 0 0 0 – 0 1 0 *(Surname not given.)*

#321: George GRANT, 0 0 0 – 0 0 0 – 1 0 0
      Elizabeth FLOWERS, 0 0 0 – 0 0 0 – 0 1 0
      Benjamin GRANT, 0 0 0 – 0 0 0 – 0 0 1

#322: Margaret GREEN, 0 0 0 – 0 1 0 – 0 0 0
      Emma Le GEYT, 0 0 0 – 0 0 1 – 0 0 0
      Robert, 0 0 0 – 0 0 0 – 0 0 1 *(Surname not given.)*

#323: Ann GLADDIN, 0 0 0 – 0 1 0 – 0 0 0
      John UNDERWOOD, 0 0 0 – 0 0 1 – 0 0 0
      Eliza MENZIES, 0 0 0 – 0 0 1 – 0 0 0
      Margaret YOUNG, 0 0 0 – 0 0 1 – 0 0 0

#324: James GOFF, 0 0 0 – 0 0 0 – 1 0 0
      Sarah - - - - -, 0 0 0 – 0 0 0 – 0 1 0

#325: Robert GLADDING, 0 0 0 – 1 0 0 – 0 0 0
      Ann - - - - -, 0 0 0 – 0 0 0 – 0 1 0

p. 163:
#326: Somerset GOUGH, 0 0 0 – 0 0 0 – 1 0 0
      Maria KETRUE, 0 0 0 – 0 0 0 – 0 1 0
      Juana, 0 0 0 – 0 0 0 – 0 1 0 *(Surname not given.)*

#327: Henry GARDINER, 0 0 0 – 1 0 0 – 0 0 0
      Eliza Ann - - - - -, 0 0 0 – 0 1 0 – 0 0 0
      William WALLACE - - - - -, 0 0 0 – 0 0 1 – 0 0 0
      Henry - - - - -, 0 0 0 – 0 0 1 – 0 0 0
      Jane Jesse - - - - , 0 0 0 – 0 0 1 – 0 0 0

#328: Sisee La GRENADE, 0 0 0 – 0 0 0 – 1 0 0

#329: William GRANT, 0 0 0 – 0 0 0 – 1 0 0

#330: Joseph GABOUREL, 0 0 0 – 0 0 0 – 1 0 0

#331: Leah GRANT, 0 0 0 – 0 0 0 – 1 0 0 [sic] *(The marks for gender are reversed.)*
      John O'CONNOR, 0 0 0 – 0 0 0 – 0 1 0 [sic]

272

#332: George GRAHAM, 0 0 0 – 0 0 0 – 1 0 0

#333: John GOMIAH, 0 0 0 – 0 0 0 – 1 0 0
     Ann - - - - -, 0 0 0 – C 0 0 – 0 1 0
     Maria - - - - -, 0 0 0 – 0 0 0 – 0 1 0
     Daphne - - - - -, 0 0 0 – 0 0 0 – 0 1 0
     Cuba - - - - -, 0 0 0 – 0 0 0 – 0 1 0
     Benjamin - - - - -, 0 0 0 – 0 0 0 – 0 0 1
     Henry - - - - -, 0 0 0 – 0 0 0 – 1 0 0

p. 164:

#334: William GENTLE Jn: 0 0 0 – 1 0 0 – 0 0 0
     Leonard - - - - -, 0 0 0 – 0 0 0 – 0 0 1
     Albert - - - - -, 0 0 0 – 0 0 0 – 0 0 1
     Walter - - - - -, 0 0 0 – 0 0 0 – 1 0 0
     Patrick - - - - -, 0 0 0 – 0 0 0 – 1 0 0
     Duncan - - - - -, 0 0 0 – 0 0 0 – 1 0 0
     Adam - - - - -, 0 0 0 – 0 0 0 – 1 0 0
     Danuel [sic] - - - - -, 0 0 0 – 0 0 0 – 1 0 0
     Peter - - - - -, 0 0 0 – 0 0 0 – 1 0 0

#335: Cato GRANT, 0 0 0 – 0 0 0 – 1 0 0
     Acinta, 0 0 0 – 0 0 0 – 0 1 0 *(Surname not given.)*

#336: Toby GOFF, 0 0 0 – 0 0 0 – 1 0 0
     Jenny BOWEN, 0 0 0 – 0 0 0 – 0 1 0

#337: William GENEROUS. 0 0 0 – 0 0 0 – 1 0 0
     Maria - - - - -, 0 0 0 – 0 0 0 – 0 1 0
     Israel - - - - -, 0 0 0 – C 0 0 – 0 0 1
     William - - - - -, 0 0 0 – 0 0 0 – 0 0 1
     Bet - - - - -, 0 0 0 – 0 0 0 – 0 0 1
     Jane - - - - -, 0 0 0 – 0 0 0 – 0 01
     Lymia [sic] - - - - -, 0 0 0 – 0 0 0 – 0 0 1

#338: Andrew GOOD, 0 0 0 – 0 0 0 – 1 0 0

#339: Chas. GRAHAM, 0 0 0 – 0 0 0 – 1 0 0

#340: Philip GEAR, 0 0 0 – 0 0 0 – 1 0 0
     Harriet BAKER, 0 0 0 – 0 0 0 – 0 1 0

p. 165:

#341: William GABOUREL, 1 0 0 – 0 0 0 – 0 0 0
     Diana USHER, 0 1 0 – 0 0 0 – 0 0 0

273

George - - - - -, 1 0 0 – 0 0 0 – 0 0 0
William Jr. - - - - - , 1 0 0 – 0 0 0 – 0 0 0
John - - - - -, 0 0 1 – 0 0 0 – 0 0 0
Charles - - - - -, 0 0 1 – 0 0 0 – 0 0 0
Henry GABOUREL, 0 0 1 – 0 0 0 – 0 0 0
Dublin, 0 0 0 – 0 0 0 – 1 0 0
John, 0 0 0 – 0 0 0 – 1 0 0
George, 0 0 0 – 0 0 0 – 1 0 0
Sampson, 0 0 0 – 0 0 0 – 1 0 0
Peter, 0 0 0 – 0 0 0 – 0 0 1
James, 0 0 0 – 0 0 0 – 0 0 1
Edmund, 0 0 0 – 0 0 0 – 0 0 1
Flora, 0 0 0 – 0 0 0 – 0 1 0
Dorcus [*sic*], 0 0 0 – 0 0 0 – 0 1 0
Rosella [*sic*], 0 0 0 – 0 0 0 – 0 0 1   *(Rosetta with uncrossed t's?)*
Betsy, 0 0 0 – 0 0 0 – 0 0 1

#342:   Alex^r GRANT, 0 0 0 – 0 0 0 – 1 0 0

#343:   Thomas GILBERT, 0 0 0 – 0 0 0 – 1 0 0
Eliza - - - - -, 0 0 0 – 0 0 0 – 0 1 0

#344:   William GAMBLE, 0 0 0 – 0 0 0 – 1 0 0
Patience - - - - -, 0 0 0 – 0 0 0 – 0 1 0
Letty BROUGHTON, 0 0 0 – 0 0 0 – 0 1 0
- - - - - GAMBLE, 0 0 0 – 0 0 0 – 0 1 0
Rebecca - - - - -, 0 0 0 – 0 0 0 – 0 1 0

p. 166:
#345:   Mary GRAHAM, 0 0 0 – 0 0 0 – 0 1 0
Thomas GENTLE, 0 0 0 – 0 0 0 – 1 0 0
Judy - - - - -, 0 0 0 – 0 0 0 – 0 1 0
Rebecca - - - - -, 0 0 0 – 0 0 0 – 0 1 0
Francis SLUSHER, 0 0 0 – 0 0 0 – 0 0 1
Mary - - - - -, 0 0 0 – 0 0 0 – 0 0 1
John ROBINSON, 0 0 0 – 0 0 0 – 0 0 1
Chloe FANTASIE, 0 0 0 – 0 0 0 – 0 0 1

#346:   George GILLETT Sr., 0 0 0 – 1 0 0 – 0 0 0
Mary BURRELL, 0 0 0 – 0 1 0 – 0 0 0
Maria GILLETT, 0 0 0 – 0 1 0 – 0 0 0
James - - - - -, 0 0 0 – 1 0 0 – 0 0 0
George - - - - - Jr, 0 0 0 – 1 0 0 – 0 0 0
Hannah - - - - -, 0 0 0 – 0 1 0 – 0 0 0
Mary - - - - -, 0 0 0 – 0 1 0 – 0 0 0
Jane BURN, 0 0 0 – 0 1 0 – 0 0 0

274

James - - - - -, 0 0 0 – 0 0 1 – 0 0 0
Eliza - - - - -, 0 0 0 – 0 0 1 – 0 0 0
Richard - - - - -, 0 0 0 – 0 0 1 – 0 0 0
Betsey SMITH, 0 0 0 – 0 1 0 – 0 0 0

#347: Elizabeth GRANT, 0 0 0 – 0 1 0 – 0 0 0
William ADOLPHUS, 0 0 0 – 0 0 1 – 0 0 0
John Henry HYDE, 0 0 0 – 0 0 1 – 0 0 0
George HYDE, 0 0 0 – 0 0 1 – 0 0 0
Fanny LAWRIE, 0 0 0 – 0 0 0 – 0 1 0
Georgiana WHITE, 0 0 0 – 0 0 0 – 0 0 1

#348: Peter GORDON, 0 0 0 – 0 0 0 – 1 0 0
Susan HYDE, 0 0 0 – 0 0 0 – 0 1 0
George KEITH, 0 0 0 – 0 0 0 – 1 0 0

p. 167:
#349: Daniel GORDON, 0 0 0 – 0 0 0 – 1 0 0
Diana KIEF [sic], 0 0 0 – 0 1 0 – 0 0 0 *(= KEEFE)*
Julian - - - - -, 0 0 0 – 0 0 0 – 0 0 1

#350: Catherine GRANT   *(There are no marks for this family. The totals*
Mary DOUGLAS   *at the bottom of the page show 12 colored males,*
Chloe - - - - -   *6 colored females, 2 black males, and 6 black*
Ancilla - - - - -   *females.)*
Margaret PETZOLD
Francis - - - - -
Joseph GENTLE
Eliza - - - - -
George - - - - -
Sarah - - - - -
James TOOLE
Hannah - - - - -
Richard STAIN
Jane MOYER
Nelly - - - - -
Clarissa - - - - -
Betty - - - - -
Peter - - - - -
Robert ARNOLD
Thomas - - - - -
James - - - - -
Henry - - - - -
Benjamin
William
Morton *(No dashed lines, i.e., no surnames shown for these three.)*

p. 168:

#351: Josient *(or Josunt?)* GIDEON, 0 0 0 – 0 0 0 – 1 0 0
       Flora CAMPBELL, 0 0 0 – 0 0 0 – 0 1 0
       Elizabeth GIDEON, 0 0 0 – 0 0 0 – 0 1 0
       James CAMPBELL, 0 0 0 – 0 0 0 – 0 0 1
       Duncan - - - - -, 0 0 0 – 0 0 0 – 0 0 1

#352: Francois GALLAY, 1 0 0 – 0 0 0 – 0 0 0
       Jean CLAUDIN, 0 1 0 – 0 0 0 – 0 0 0
       Ambrose AGNANT, 1 0 0 – 0 0 0 – 0 0 0
       Guatecla [*sic*], 0 0 0 – 0 1 0 – 0 0 0 *(Surname not given.)*

#353: John JOHNSTON, 0 0 0 – 1 0 0 – 0 0 0
       Henrietta GODFREY, 0 0 0 – 0 1 0 – 0 0 0
       Mary JOHNSTON, 0 0 0 – 0 1 0 – 0 0 0
       Henrietta - - - - -, 0 0 0 – 0 1 0 – 0 0 0
       Isabella - - - - -, 0 0 0 – 0 1 0 – 0 0 0
       Agnes - - - - -, 0 0 0 – 0 1 0 – 0 0 0
       Jane - - - - -, 0 0 0 – 0 1 0 – 0 0 0
       - - - - - - - - -, 0 0 0 – 0 0 0 – 0 0 0 *(Name erased; no mark.)*
       Ellen, 0 0 0 – 0 0 0 – 0 1 0
       Sarah, 0 0 0 – 0 0 0 – 0 0 1
       Alfred, 0 0 0 – 0 0 0 – 0 0 1
       Matthew, 0 0 0 – 0 0 0 – 0 0 1 *(Surnames not given.)*

#354: William GODFREY, 0 0 0 – 0 1 0 – 0 0 0
       Maria - - - - -, 0 0 0 – 0 0 1 – 0 0 0
       Fanny - - - - -. 0 0 0 – 0 0 1 – 0 0 0
       Rach^l JONES, 0 0 0 – 0 1 0 – 0 0 0

#355: Eustace GRAFTON, 0 0 0 – 0 0 0 – 1 0 0

p. 169:

#356: Patty GORDON, 0 0 0 – 0 1 0 – 0 0 0
       William CADLE, 0 0 0 – 0 0 1 – 0 0 0
       James RODGERS, 0 0 0 – 0 0 1 – 0 0 0
       - - - - - - HAYLOCK, 0 0 0 – 0 0 1 – 0 0 0 *(An infant not yet named?)*
       John - - - - -, 0 0 0 – 0 0 1 – 0 0 0

#357: Bella GOFF   *(There are no marks for this family. However, the totals*
       Sue NEAL   *show 2 colored males, 1 black male,*
       John RECRUIT   *and 3 black females.)*
       John LECRUIT
       John GEORGE

276

#358: Sophia GARRETT, 0 0 0 – 0 1 0 – 0 0 0
Nancy HENRY, C 0 0 – 0 1 0 – 0 0 0
Olive FLOWERS. 0 0 0 – 0 0 0 – 0 1 0
Mary WILLIAMS, 0 0 0 – 0 0 1 – 0 0 0
John KELLY, 0 0 0 – : 0 0 – 0 0 0
Anthony MYRES, 0 0 0 – 1 0 0 – 0 0 0

#359: John GREEN, 0 0 0 – 0 0 0 – 1 0 0
Henry COATQULVIN. 0 0 0 – 0 0 0 – 1 0 0

#360: Robart [sic] GARBET, *(= GARBUTT.)*
Patience - - - - -,
Member - - - - -,
Sophia - - - - -,   *(There are no marks and no totals*
John - - - - -,   *for this family.)*

#361: Thomas GILL, 0 0 0 – 0 0 0 – 1 0 0

p. 170:
#362: Michael GLADDEN, 0 0 0 – 0 0 0 – 1 0 0
James - - - - -, 0 0 0 – 0 0 0 – 0 0 1
John - - - - -, 0 0 0 – 0 0 0 – 0 0 1
Phoebe - - - - -, 0 0 0 – 0 0 0 – 0 0 1

#363: Catalina GORDON, 0 0 0 – 0 0 0 – 0 1 0
Francisca - - - - -, 0 0 0 – 0 0 0 – 0 0 1
Ann BLACK, 0 0 0 – 0 0 0 – 0 0 1
Matteo WHITE, 0 0 0 – 0 0 0 – 0 0 1
Joseph SHACLINE, 0 0 0 – 0 0 0 – 0 0 1
- - - - - TUXEY, 0 0 0 – 0 0 0 – 0 0 1

#364: Edward GRINNOCK, 0 0 0 – 0 0 0 – 1 0 0
Mary - - - - -, 0 0 0 – 0 0 0 – 0 1 0

#365: Ann GEDDIS, 0 0 0 – 0 1 0 – 0 0 0
Mary WINTER, 0 0 0 – 0 1 0 – 0 0 0
Nancy MEIGHAN, 0 0 0 – 0 1 0 – 0 0 0
James PEEBLES, 0 0 0 – 0 0 0 – 1 0 0
Sarah LAMB, 0 0 0 – 0 0 0 – 0 0 1

#366: John GIDEON, 0 0 0 – 0 0 0 – 1 0 0
Sarah FLOWERS, 0 0 0 – 0 0 0 – 0 1 0
Daniel GIDEON, 0 0 0 – 0 0 0 – 0 0 1
Sarah - - - - -, 0 0 0 – 0 0 0 – 0 0 1
Elizabeth - - - - -, 0 0 0 – 0 0 0 – 0 0 1

277

#367: James GRANT, 1 0 0 – 0 0 0 – 0 0 0
Hannah - - - - -, 0 1 0 – 0 0 0 – 0 0 0
John GODFREY, 0 0 0 – 0 0 1 – 0 0 0
Catherine BARNES, 0 0 0 – 0 0 0 – 0 0 1

p. 171:
#368: William GAPPER, 0 0 0 – 0 0 0 – 1 0 0
Maria - - - - -, 0 0 0 – 0 0 0 – 0 1 0
Edie JOHNSTONE, 0 0 0 – 0 0 0 – 0 0 1

#369: Randal GOSSOP, 0 0 0 – 0 0 0 – 1 0 0
Jane WATERS, 0 0 0 – 0 0 0 – 0 1 0
Rennett [sic] NELLY, 0 0 0 – 0 0 0 – 1 0 0

#370: Susan GORDON, 0 0 0 – 0 0 0 – 0 1 0
Maria CHAVARECIA, 0 0 0 – 0 1 0 – 0 0 0
Maria, 0 0 0 – 0 0 0 – 0 1 0
Hannah, 0 0 0 – 0 0 0 – 0 1 0
Sam, 0 0 0 – 0 0 0 – 1 0 0 (Surnames not given.)

#371: Catherine GLADDEN, 0 0 0 – 0 1 0 – 0 0 0
Philip GILL, 0 0 0 – 1 0 0 – 0 0 0
Alexʳ - - - - -, 0 0 0 – 0 0 1 – 0 0 0
John - - - - -, 0 0 0 – 0 0 1 – 0 0 0
Elizabeth SMITH, 0 0 0 – 0 0 1 – 0 0 0
Norah PRATT, 0 0 0 – 0 0 1 – 0 0 0
Elizabeth FOREMAN, 0 0 0 – 0 0 1 – 0 0 0
Catherine J. PARKER, 0 0 0 – 0 0 1 – 0 0 0

#372: John GIDNEY, 0 0 0 – 0 0 0 – 1 0 0

#373: Richard GUTHERY, 0 0 0 – 0 0 0 – 1 0 0
Dianna - - - - -, 0 0 0 – 0 0 0 – 0 1* 0

#374: Thomas GRANT, 0 0 0 – 0 0 0 – 1 0 0
Frances BRYAN, 0 0 0 – 0 0 0 – 0 1* 0
Sarah BURNS, 0 0 0 – 0 0 0 – 0 1* 0

*Inferred. There are no other marks for Dianna Guthery, Frances Bryan, and Sarah
Burns, and at this point on the page the column for black women is missing, torn away.

p. 172:
#375: Catherine GENTLE, 0 0 0 – 0 0 0 – 0 1 0
Benjamin GENTLE, 0 0 0 – 0 0 0 – 1 0 0
Sutherland - - - - -, 0 0 0 – 0 0 0 – 1 0 0
Able - - - - -, 0 0 0 – 0 0 0 – 0 0 1

278

Charles - - - - -, 0 0 0 – 0 0 0 – 0 0 1
Chloe - - - - -, 0 0 0 – 0 0 0 – 0 1 0
Johannah - - - - -, 0 0 0 – 0 0 0 – 0 1 0
Caronine [*sic*] - - - - -, 0 0 0 – 0 0 0 – 0 0 1
James - - - - -, 0 0 0 – 0 0 1 – 0 0 0
Catherine - - - - -, 0 0 0 – 0 0 1 – 0 0 0
Joseph, 0 0 0 – 0 0 0 – 0 0 1
George, 0 0 0 – 0 0 0 – 0 0 1
Eliza, 0 0 0 – 0 0 0 – 0 0 1
Lucretia, 0 0 0 – 0 0 0 – 0 0 1 *(Surnames not given.)*

#376: Catto GRAHAM, 0 0 0 – 0 0 0 – 1 0 0
Maria ANDERSON, 0 0 0 – 0 0 0 – 0 1 0
Rodney GRAHAM, 0 0 0 – 0 0 0 – 1 0 0
David - - - - -, 0 0 0 – 0 0 0 – 0 0 1
Henry - - - - -, 0 0 0 – 0 0 0 – 0 0 1
Catto - - - - -, 0 0 0 – 0 0 0 – 0 0 1
Patience - - - - -, 0 0 0 – 0 0 0 – 0 0 1

#377: Amelia GORDON, 0 1 0 – 0 0 0 – 0 0 0
Kitty - - - - -, 0 0 0 – 0 0 0 – 0 1 0
Flora, 0 0 0 – 0 0 0 – 0 1 1 *(Did the enumerator forget to make dashes?)*
Amelia - - - - -, 0 0 0 – 0 0 0 – 0 0 1

#378: Robert GALLIMORE, 0 0 0 – 0 0 0 – 1 0 0
Kitty GORDON, 0 0 0 – 0 0 0 – 0 1 0
Emily GALLIMORE, 0 0 0 – 0 0 0 – 0 0 1

p. 173:
#379: Mary GILLETT, 0 0 0 – 0 1 0 – 0 0 0
Josep [*sic*] JONES, 0 0 0 – 1 0 0 – 0 0 0 *(Head of household in earlier censuses.)*
Janet - - - - -, 0 0 0 – 0 0 1 – 0 0 0   *(Janet JONES.)*
M. - - - - -, 0 0 0 – 0 0 1 – 0 0 0   *(Margaret JONES.)*
S. - - - - -, 0 0 0 – 0 0 1 – 0 0 0   *(Sarah JONES.)*
C. - - - - -, 0 0 0 – 0 0 1 - 0 0 0   *(Male.)*
P. *(or D?)* - - - - -, 0 0 0 – 0 0 1 – 0 0 0   *(Male.)*

#380: Leman GENTLE, 0 0 0 – 0 0 0 – 1 0 0
Clarissa MENDES, 0 0 0 – 0 0 0 – 0 1 0
Mary - - - - -, 0 0 0 – 0 0 0 – 0 0 1
Betsy - - - - -, 0 0 0 – 0 0 0 – 0 0 1
Eliza - - - - -, 0 0 0 – 0 0 0 – 0 0 1
Philip - - - - -, 0 0 0 – 0 0 0 – 0 0 1
Ebene - - - - -, 0 0 0 – 0 0 0 – 0 0 1 *(Male.)*

279

#381: George GILLETT, 0 0 0 – 0 0 0 – 1 0 0
Henrietta GILLETT, 0 0 0 – 0 0 0 – 0 1 0
Thomas GILLETT, 0 0 0 – 0 0 0 – 0 0 1
Maly [sic] FLOWERS, 0 0 0 – 0 0 0 – 0 0 1 *(Female.)*

#382: Peter GORDON, 0 0 0 – 0 0 0 – 1 0 0
Maria MATTEA [sic], 0 0 0 – 0 0 0 – 0 1 0
Martha GORDON, 0 0 0 – 0 0 0 – 0 1 0
Catherine - - - - -, 0 0 0 – 0 0 0 – 0 1 0
Charles - - - - -, 0 0 0 – 0 0 0 – 1 0 0
Daniel - - - - -, 0 0 0 – 0 0 0 – 1 0 0

#383: James GRANT, 0 0 0 – 0 0 0 – 1 0 0

#384: William GARRICK, 0 0 0 – 0 0 0 – 1 0 0

p. 174:
#385: Thomas GREEN, 0 0 0 – 0 0 0 – 1 0 0
Margaret MAYBERRY, 0 0 0 – 0 0 0 – 0 1 0
James GREEN, 0 0 0 – 0 0 0 – 0 0 1
Peggy - - - - -, 0 0 0 – 0 0 0 – 0 0 1

#386: John GARBUTT, 1 0 0 – 0 0 0 – 0 0 0
Jane E. PITTS, 0 0 0 – 0 0 0 – 0 1 0
J. GARBUTT Jr, 0 0 0 – 0 0 1 – 0 0 0
Aaron - - - - -, 0 0 0 – 0 0 1 – 0 0 0
Thomas - -- - -, 0 0 0 – 0 0 1 – 0 0 0
Joseph - - - - -, 0 0 0 – 0 0 1 – 0 0 0
Lucretia - - - - -, 0 0 0 – 0 0 1 – 0 0 0
Margaret - - - - -, 0 0 0 – 0 0 1 – 0 0 0

#387: Wm. GORDON, 0 0 0 – 0 0 0 – 1 0 0
Margaret HEWLETT, 0 0 0 – 0 0 0 – 0 1 0
Eliza WILLIAMS, 0 0 0 – 0 0 0 – 0 0 1
James STAIN Jr, 0 0 0 – 0 0 0 – 0 0 1

#388: George GALLIARD, 1 0 0 – 0 0 0 – 0 0 0
Mary LYNCH, 0 0 1 – 0 0 0 – 0 0 0
Mary ANDREWS, 0 0 0 – 0 0 0 – 0 1 0
Lucy POTTS, 0 0 0 – 0 0 0 – 0 0 1

#389: A. GUBAIN, 0 0 0 – 0 0 0 – 1 0 0

#390: Elizabeth GREGORIO, 0 0 0 – 0 1 0 – 0 0 0
Sophia BULL, 0 0 0 – 0 1 0 – 0 0 0
Eliza - - - - -, 0 0 0 – 0 1 0 – 0 0 0

Chas. R. PRICE, 0 0 0 – 0 0 1 – 0 0 0
Wm H. PRICE, 0 0 0 – 0 0 1 – 0 0 0
James, 0 0 0 – 0 0 0 – 0 0 1 *(Surname not given.)*

p. 175:
#391: Ann GOFF, 0 0 0 – 0 1 0 – 0 0 0
Robert GIBSON, 0 0 0 – 1 0 0 – 0 0 0
Thomas LIDDLE, 0 0 0 – 0 0 1 – 0 0 0
Mary Ann, 0 0 0 – 0 0 0 – 0 1 0
Jack, 0 0 0 – 0 0 0 – 0 0 1
Henry, 0 0 0 – 0 0 0 – 0 0 1 *(Surnames not given.)*

#392: Francis GRAY, 0 0 0 – 1 0 0 – 0 0 0
Charlotte - - - - -, 0 0 0 – 0 1 0 – 0 0 0
James C. - - - - -, 0 0 0 – 0 0 1 – 0 0 0
Ann ANDERSON, 0 0 0 – 0 0 0 – 0 1 0

#393: Jacob GENTLE, 0 0 0 – 1 0 0 – 0 0 0
Marie ARBETTE, 0 0 0 – 0 1 0 – 0 0 0
Juan FECUNDA, 0 0 0 – 1 0 0 – 0 0 0
Elicio, 0 0 0 – 0 0 1 – 0 0 0
Julie, 0 0 0 – 0 0 0 – 0 0 1 *(Surnames not given.)*

#394: John GEORGE, 0 0 0 – 0 0 0 – 1 0 0
Mary GEORGE, 0 0 0 – 0 0 0 – 0 1 0
Mary MAGDALEN, 0 0 0 – 0 0 0 – 0 1 0
Jno. GEORGE, 0 0 0 – 0 0 0 – 1 0 0
Gabourel - - - - -, 0 0 0 – 0 0 0 – 1 0 0

#395: Malcolm GLASSFORD, 1 0 0 – 0 0 0 – 0 0 0
Jose FRANCISCO, 0 0 0 – 0 0 0 – 0 0 1

#396: Joseph GRANT, 0 0 0 – 0 0 0 – 1 0 0
Jane SHEDDIN, 0 0 0 – 0 0 0 – 0 1 0

#397: John GLADDIN, 0 0 0 – 0 0 0 – 1 0 0

p. 176:
#398: Jane GORDON, 0 0 0 – 0 1 0 – 0 0 0
Ann E. CODD, 0 0 0 – 0 1 0 – 0 0 0
Tenah GORDON, 0 0 0 – 0 0 0 – 0 1 0
Henry - - - - -, 0 0 0 – 0 0 0 – 1 0 0
Mary - - - - -, 0 0 0 – 0 0 0 – 0 0 1
Margaret PETZOLD, 0 0 0 – 0 0 0 – 0 0 1
Sophia, 0 0 0 – 0 0 0 – 0 0 1
James, 0 0 0 – 0 0 0 – 0 0 1 *(Surnames not given.)*

281

#399: George GIBSON, 0 0 0 – 1 0 0 – 0 0 0
Elizabeth POTTS, 00 0 – 0 1 0 – 0 0 0
William GIBSON, 0 0 0 – 0 0 1 – 0 0 0
Eve - - - - -, 0 0 0 – 0 0 1 – 0 0 0
Sarah GASSAY, 0 0 0 – 0 0 1 – 0 0 0
Catharine - - - - -, 0 0 0 – 0 0 1 – 0 0 0

#400: Joseph GIDEON, 0 0 0 – 1 0 0 – 0 0 0
James H. BELIZAIRE, 0 0 0 – 0 0 0 – 1 0 0

#401: Richd GRISTOCK, 1 0 0 – 0 0 0 – 0 0 0
Mary BURRELL, 0 0 0 – 0 1 0 – 0 0 0
George H. GRISTOCK, 0 0 0 – 0 0 1 – 0 0 0
Alick, 0 0 0 – 0 0 0 – 1 0 0 *(Surname not given.)*

#402: George GRANT, 0 0 0 – 0 0 0 – 1 0 0
Sarah HILL, 0 0 0 – 0 0 0 – 0 1 0
G. GRANT Jr., 0 0 0 – 0 0 0 – 0 0 1
Eliza - - - - -, 0 0 0 – 0 0 0 – 0 0 1
Jane - - - - -, 0 0 0 – 0 0 0 – 0 0 1
Archibald - - - - -, 0 0 0 – 0 0 0 – 0 0 1

p. 177:
#403: Wm GILL, 0 0 0 – 1 0 0 – 0 0 0
Catherine DAVIES, 0 0 0 – 0 1 0 – 0 0 0
Elizabeth HINKS, 0 0 0 – 0 0 1 – 0 0 0
Hannah SELOSTINA, 0 0 0 – 0 0 1 – 0 0 0

#404: James GENTLE, 0 0 0 – 0 0 0 – 1 0 0

#405: George B. GARNETT, 0 0 0 – 1 0 0 – 0 0 0
Ann M. - - - - -, 0 0 0 – 0 1 0 – 0 0 0
John B. - - - - -, 0 0 0 – 0 0 1 – 0 0 0
Jane A. - - - - -, 0 0 0 – 0 0 1 – 0 0 0
Ann M. - - - - - Jr, 0 0 0 – 0 0 1 – 0 0 0
Eliza HENRY, 0 0 0 – 0 0 0 – 0 1 0
Chloe SMALL, 0 0 0 – 0 0 0 – 0 1 0
Joseph FORTUNE, 0 0 0 – 0 0 0 – 1 0 0
Jose La MARCO, 0 0 0 – 0 0 0 – 1 0 0
David PRATT, 0 0 0 – 0 0 0 – 1 0 0
Francis SHACKLING, 0 0 0 – 0 0 0 – 1 0 0
Jem BATISTE, 0 0 0 – 0 0 0 – 1 0 0
Wm HARRISON, 0 0 0 – 0 0 0 – 1 0 0
Alberto, 0 0 0 – 0 0 0 – 1 0 0 *(Surname not given.)*
Wm CRAWFORD, 0 0 0 – 0 0 0 – 1 0 0

John CURRANT, 0 0 0 – 0 0 0 – 1 0 0
Joseph GARNETT, 0 0 0 – 0 0 0 – 1 0 0
Charles GARNETT, 0 0 0 – 0 0 0 – 1 0 0

#406: Bathsheba GINGER, 0 0 0 – 0 0 0 – 0 1 0
       - - - - - - - - -, 0 0 0 – 0 0 1 – 0 0 0 *(Female. An infant not yet named?)*
       Thomas PAYNE, 0 0 0 – 0 00 – 0 0 1
       William - - - - -, 0 0 0 – 0 0 0 – 0 0 1

Note: This entry filled out the last page in the record book. The Keeper of the Records continued his enumeration in a new book, entering households #407- #552 on pages he numbered 1 – 34, but no longer giving totals at the bottom of each page.

p. 1
#407: Joseph GOFF, 0 0 0 – 1 0 0 – 0 0 0
       Juda BENNETT, 0 0 0 – 0 0 0 – 0 1 0
       Catherine - - - - -, 0 0 0 – 0 0 0 – 0 1 0
       Joseph GOFF, 0 0 0 – 1 0 0 – 0 0 0
       Catherine - - - - -, 0 0 0 – 0 1 0 – 0 0 0
       Elizabeth - - - - -, 0 0 0 – 0 1 0 – 0 0 0
       John - - - - -, 0 0 0 – 1 0 0 – 0 0 0
       Edward - - - - -, 0 0 0 – 1 0 0 – 0 0 0
       Thomas - - - - -, 0 0 0 – 1 0 0 – 0 0 0
       Mary Ann, 0 0 0 – 0 1 0 – 0 0 0 *(Surname not given.)*
       William MEIGHAN, 0 0 0 – 1 0 0 – 0 0 0
       Matia HUSTA, 0 0 0 – 1 0 0 – 0 0 0

#408: Harry GOFF, 0 0 0 – 1 0 0 – 0 0 0
       Caroline - - - - -, 0 0 0 – 0 0 0 – 0 1 0

#409: John GRANT, 0 0 0 – 0 0 0 – 1 0 0
       Isabella - - - - -, 0 0 0 – 0 0 0 – 0 1 0

#410: Thomas GLADDEN, 0 0 0 – 0 0 1 – 0 0 0
       Sarah PITTS, 0 0 0 – 0 0 0 – 0 1 0
       Margaret GLADDEN, 0 0 0 – 0 0 0 – 0 0 1
       Thomas GRAYSTOCK, 0 0 0 – 0 0 0 – 1 0 0

#411: George HUNT, 0 0 0 – 0 0 0 – 1 0 0
       Martha - - - - -, 0 0 0 – 0 0 0 – 0 1 0

p. 2:
#412: John E. HENDERSON, 0 0 0 – 1 0 0 – 0 0 0
       Martha USHER, 0 0 0 – 0 1 0 – 0 0 0
       Janet S. VERNON, 0 0 0 – 0 1 0 – 0 0 0
       Louisa HENDERSON, 0 0 0 – 0 1 0 – 0 0 0

John E. - - - - - Jr, 0 0 0 – 1 0 0 – 0 0 0
George - - - - -, 0 0 0 – 1 0 0 – 0 0 0
Ann - - - - -, 0 0 0 – 0 1 0 – 0 0 0
Charles - - - - -, 0 0 0 – 1 0 0 – 0 0 0
Caroline - - - - -, 0 0 0 – 0 1 0 – 0 0 0

#413: James HEMSLEY, 0 0 0 – 1 0 0 – 0 0 0
James E. - - - - -, 0 0 0 – 0 0 1 – 0 0 0
Joseph - - - - -, 0 0 0 – 0 0 1 – 0 0 0
Abigail - - - - -, 0 0 0 – 0 1 0 – 0 0 0
Seraphine - - - - -, 0 0 0 – 0 1 0 – 0 0 0
Elizabeth DAW, 0 0 0 – 0 0 0 – 0 1 0
Catherine HEMSLEY, 0 0 0 – 0 1 0 – 0 0 0

Note: There is no #414. This number was skipped.

#415: John HARRISON, 0 0 0 – 0 0 0 –1 0 0
Mary PARRY, 0 0 0 – 0 0 0 – 0 1 0
Robt MARTIN, 0 0 0 – 0 0 1 – 0 0 0
Diana BENNETT, 0 0 0 – 0 0 0 – 0 0 1
David GENTLE, 0 0 0 – 0 0 0 – 0 0 1

#416: Patience HICKEY, 0 0 0 – 0 0 0 – 0 1 0
Cadjon [*sic*] HUGHES, 0 0 0 – 0 0 0 – 1 0 0
John BOWEN, 0 0 0 – 0 0 0 – 1 0 0
Leonora HICKEY, 0 0 0 – 0 0 0 – 0 1 0

#417: Louisa HICKEY, 0 0 0 – 0 0 0 – 0 1 0
Grace - - - - -, 0 0 0 – 0 0 0 – 0 1 0
Providence - - - - -, 0 0 0 – 0 0 0 – 1 0 0

p. 3:
#418: George HUME, 0 0 0 – 1 0 0 – 0 0 0
Louisa - - - - -, 0 0 0 – 0 1 0 – 0 0 0
Jane - - - - -, 0 0 0 – 0 0 1 – 0 0 0
Sarah - - - - -, 0 0 0 – 0 0 1 – 0 0 0
Jane CRAIG, 0 0 0 – 0 0 1 – 0 0 0
Elizabeth - - - - -, 0 0 0 – 0 0 1 – 0 0 0
Rachael, 0 0 0 – 0 0 0 – 0 1 0
Frances, 0 0 0 – 0 0 0 – 0 1 0
Joseph, 0 0 0 – 0 0 0 – 0 0 1 *(Surnames not given.)*

#419: George HUME, 0 0 0 – 0 0 0 – 1 0 0
Peter FRANCIS, 0 0 0 – 0 0 0 – 1 0 0
Martha GORDON, 0 0 0 – 0 0 0 – 0 1 0
Mary NOEL, 0 0 0 – 0 0 0 – 0 1 0

284

Thomas PHILIP, 0 0 0 – 0 0 0 – 0 0 1
Theresa GEORGE, 0 0 0 – 0 0 0 – 0 0 1
George FRANCIS, 0 0 0 – 0 0 0 – 0 0 1
Leah GEORGE, 0 0 0 – 0 0 0 – 0 0 1
Lucretia - - - - -, 0 0 0 – 0 0 0 – 0 0 1
Prissy - - - - -, 0 0 0 – 0 0 0 – 0 0 1

#420: Chas. HUME, 0 0 0 – 0 0 0 – 1 0 0
Wil^m [sic] - - - - -, 0 0 0 – 0 0 0 – 1 0 0
Richard BENNET, 0 0 0 – 0 0 0 – 1 0 0
Henrietta - - - - -, 0 0 0 – 0 0 0 – 0 1 0

#421: Frances HOARE, 0 0 0 – 0 0 0 – 0 1 0
James - - - - -, 0 0 0 – 0 0 0 – 1 0 0
Elizabeth THURSTON, 0 0 0 – 0 0 0 – 0 1 0
James COOKE, 0 0 0 – 0 0 1 – 0 0 0

p. 4:
#422: Catherine HUME, 0 0 0 – 0 0 1 – 0 0 0
Frances WALDRON, 0 0 0 – 0 1 0 – 0 0 0
Jane - - - - -, 0 0 0 – 0 1 0 – 0 0 0
Sally, 0 0 0 – 0 00 – 0 1 0
David, 0 0 0 – 0 0 0 – 0 0 1 *(Surnames not given.)*

#423: Jack HYDE, 0 0 0 – 0 0 0 – 1 0 0
Maria MYCATA, 0 0 0 – 0 1 0 – 0 0 0

#424: John HARTYN, 0 0 0 – 0 0 0 – 1 0 0

#425: Peter HARRIS, 0 0 0 – 0 0 0 – 1 0 0
Elizabeth GLASS, 0 0 0 – 0 0 0 – 0 1 0

#426: Peter HICKEY, 0 0 0 – 0 0 0 – 1 0 0
Wm STANFORD, 0 0 0 – 0 0 0 – 1 0 0
Sampson HERLINE, 0 0 0 – 0 0 0 – 1 0 0
Richard STANFORD, 0 0 0 – 0 0 0 – 0 0 1
Isabella - - - - -, 0 0 0 – 0 0 0 – 0 1 0

#427: Amelia HINKS, 0 0 0 – 0 1 0 – 0 0 0
Isabella HINKS, 0 0 0 – 0 1 0 – 0 0 0
Wm JOHNSTON, 0 0 0 – 1 0 0 – 0 0 0
Susan - - - - -, 0 0 0 – 0 0 0 – 0 0 0
Frederick RUNNALS, 0 0 0 – 1 0 0 – 0 0 0
Richard MILES, 0 0 0 – 1 0 0 – 0 0 0

#428: John HENRY, 0 0 0 – 1 0 0 – 0 0 0

#429: Clark HYE [*sic*], 0 0 0 – 0 0 0 – 1 0 0
Mary HOARE, 0 0 0 – 0 0 0 – 0 1 0

p. 5:
#430: Thomas HUME, 0 0 0 – 0 0 0 – 1 0 0
Margaret BETSON, 0 0 0 – 0 0 0 – 0 1 0
Maria HUME, 0 0 0 – 0 0 0 – 0 0 1
Edward - - - - -, 0 0 0 – 0 0 0 – 0 0 1

#431: Achylles [*sic*] HYDE, 0 0 0 – 0 0 0 – 1 0 0

#432: Margaret HULSE, 0 0 0 – 0 1 0 – 0 0 0
Hannah - - - - -, 0 0 0 – 0 0 1 – 0 0 0
Henry - - - - -, 0 0 0 – 0 0 1 – 0 0 0
Henry - - - - -, 0 0 0 – 0 0 0 – 1 0 0
Ellen - - - - -, 0 0 0 – 0 0 0 – 0 1 0
Rosannah McLEOD, 0 0 0 – 0 0 0 – 0 0 1
Maria HULSE, 0 0 0 – 0 0 0 – 0 0 1

#433: Chance HUME, 0 0 0 – 0 0 0 – 1 0 0
Henrietta, 0 0 0 – 0 0 0 – 0 1 0
Jose, 0 0 0 – 0 0 0 – 0 0 1
Marcella, 0 0 0 – 0 0 0 – 0 1 0 *(Surnames not given.)*

#434: Peter HEWLETT, 0 0 0 – 0 0 0 – 1 0 0
Elizabeth TRAP, 0 0 0 – 0 0 0 – 0 1 0
Catherine HEWLETT, 0 0 0 – 0 0 0 – 0 0 1
Jane - - - - -, 0 0 0 – 0 0 0 – 0 0 1
Celina TRAP, 0 0 0 – 0 0 0 – 0 0 1
Sarah - - - - -, 0 0 0 – 0 0 0 – 0 0 1

#435: James HAWK, 0 0 0 – 0 0 0 – 1 0 0

#436: James HAMILTON, 0 0 0 – 1 0 0 – 0 0 0
Priscilla - - - - -, 0 0 0 – 0 1 0 – 0 0 0

p. 6:
#437: Benjamin HEMMONDS, 0 0 0 – 0 0 0 – 1 0 0
Maria CHARLES, 0 0 0 – 0 0 0 – 0 1 0
Benjamin HEMMONDS Jr., 0 0 0 – 0 0 0 – 0 0 1
Charles - - - - -, 0 0 0 – 0 0 0 – 0 0 1
Phillis - - - - -, 0 0 0 – 0 0 0 – 0 0 1
James THOMPSON, 0 0 0 – 0 0 0 – 0 0 1
S. - - - - -, 0 0 0 – 0 0 0 – 0 0 1 *(Male.)*

#438: Samuel HUME, 0 0 0 – 0 0 0 – 1 0 0

286

#439: Ann HOME, 0 0 0 – 0 1 0 – 0 0 0
Mary Ann CLEMENTS, 0 0 0 – 0 1 0 – 0 0 0
Margaret - - - - -, 0 0 0 – 0 1 0 – 0 0 0
George HOME, 0 0 0 – 0 0 0 – 0 0 1
Chas. - - - - -, 0 0 0 – 0 0 0 – 1 0 0
Molly - - - - -, 0 0 0 – 0 0 0 – 0 1 0
Rosannah - - - - -, 0 0 0 – 0 0 0 – 0 1 0
William STANFORD, 0 0 0 – 0 0 0 – 1 0 0
John TRAIL, 0 0 0 – 0 0 0 – 1 0 0
Rosannah HOME, 0 0 0 – 0 0 0 – 0 1 0

#440: Anthony HICKEY, 0 0 0 – 0 0 0 – 1 0 0
Judith BRITTAN, 0 0 0 – 0 0 0 – 0 1 0
Alex' KELLERMAN, 0 0 0 – 0 0 0 – 1 0 0

#441: William HICKEY, 0 0 0 – 0 0 0 – 1 0 0

#442: James HILL, 0 0 0 – 0 0 0 – 1 0 0

#443: Francis HUME, 0 0 0 – 0 0 0 – 0 1 0

p. 7:
#444: Sophia HUME, 0 0 0 – 0 0 0 – 0 1 0
Catherine - - - - -, 0 0 0 – 0 0 0 – 0 0 1
Elizabeth - - - - -, 0 0 0 – 0 0 0 – 0 0 1
Richard - - - - -, 0 0 0 – 0 0 0 – 1 0 0

#445: William HARDY, 0 0 0 – 0 0 0 – 1 0 0
Rosannah - - - - -, 0 0 0 – 0 0 0 – 0 1 0
Edward - - - - -, 0 0 0 – 0 0 0 – 1 0 0
William - - - - - Jr, 0 0 0 – 0 0 0 – 1 0 0
Anthony BURKE, 0 0 0 – 0 0 0 – 1 0 0
Thomas DONALL, 0 0 0 – 0 0 0 – 0 0 1
Phillis LOWRY, 0 0 0 – 0 0 0 – 0 1 0

#446: Robert HEWLETT, 0 0 0 – 0 0 0 – 1 0 0
Patty CUNNINGHAM, 0 0 0 – 0 0 0 – 0 1 0
Sarah HEWLETT, 0 0 0 – 0 0 0 – 0 0 1
Robert - - - - -, 0 0 0 – 0 0 0 – 0 1 0 *(Marked as a woman.)*
Maria - - - - -, 0 0 0 – 0 0 0 – 0 0 1
Jane - - - - -, 0 0 0 – 0 0 0 – 0 0 1
Margaret EARNEST, 0 0 0 – 0 0 0 – 0 0 1
Maria HEWLETT, 0 0 0 – 0 0 0 – 0 1 0
Anthony - - - - -, 0 0 0 – 0 0 0 – 1 0 0
Richard - - - - -, 0 0 0 – 0 0 0 – 0 0 1
Nora - - - - -, 0 0 0 – 0 0 0 – 0 0 1

287

#447: John HAIR [*sic*], 0 0 0 – 0 0 0 – 1 0 0

#448: David HYDE, 0 0 0 – 0 0 0 – 1 0 0

#449: Francis HARE [*sic*], 0 0 0 – 0 0 0 – 1 0 0
Jenny LORD, 0 0 0 – 0 0 0 – 0 1 0

p. 8:
#450: John HOAR, 0 0 0 – 0 0 0 – 1 0 0
Huana [*sic*] MARIA, 0 0 0 – 0 0 0 – 0 1 0
Manuel DECIDORA, 0 0 0 – 0 0 0 – 0 0 1
Patrona REGALAER, 0 0 0 – 0 0 0 – 0 0 1
Gragorio [*sic*] ANTOLIAN, 0 0 0 – 0 0 0 – 0 0 1
Maria ROBERTA, 0 0 0 – 0 0 0 – 0 0 1
John BAPTISTE, 0 0 0 – 0 0 0 – 0 0 1

#451: Temple HEWLETT, 0 0 0 – 1 0 0 – 0 0 0
Sukey JEFFRIES, 0 0 0 – 0 1 0 – 0 0 0
Bella SWASEY, 0 0 0 – 0 1 0 – 0 0 0
Maria GONZALES, 0 0 0 – 0 1 0 – 0 0 0
Caroline SWASEY, 0 0 0 – 0 1 0 – 0 0 0

#452: James HENRY, 0 0 0 – 0 0 0 – 1 0 0
Philedia TUCKER, 0 0 0 – 0 0 0 – 0 1 0
Amelia - - - - -, 0 0 0 – 0 0 0 – 0 1 0
Lucia - - - - -, 0 0 0 – 0 0 0 – 0 1 0
Sophia - - - - -, 0 0 0 – 0 0 0 – 0 1 0
Robert - - - - -, 0 0 0 – 0 0 0 – 1 0 0
Benjamin CARTER, 0 0 0 – 0 0 0 – 1 0 0
Mary HENRY, 0 0 0 – 0 0 0 – 0 0 1
Thomas DEFRIST [*sic*], 0 0 0 – 0 0 0 – 0 0 1

#453: Margaret HEWLETT, 0 0 0 – 1 0 0 – 0 0 0 [*sic*]
George D. - - - - -, 0 0 0 – 0 1 0 – 0 0 0   "
Daniel - - - - -, 0 0 0 – 0 1 0 – 0 0 0   "
Wm H. MITCHELL, 0 0 0 – 0 1 0 – 0 0 0   "

Note: This family is marked and totaled as a man and three women. It seems probable that the marks were misplaced one column to the left, and that Margaret was a woman and George, Daniel, and William H. were children.

#454: William HOARE, 0 0 0 – 0 0 0 – 1 0 0
Davinda - - - - -, 0 0 0 – 0 0 0 – 0 1 0
Martha WESTBY, 0 0 0 – 0 0 0 – 0 0 1

288

p. 9:
#455: George HEMSLEY, 0 0 0 – 1 0 0 – 0 0 0
     Mary ROBINSON, 0 0 0 – 0 0 0 – 0 1 0
     Isabella HEMSLEY, 0 0 0 – 0 0 1 – 0 0 0
     John - - - - -, 0 0 0 – 0 0 1 – 0 0 0
     Edward - - - - -, 0 0 0 – 0 0 1 – 0 0 0
     George - - - - -, 0 0 0 – 0 0 1 – 0 0 0
     Thomas - - - - -, 0 0 0 – 0 0 1 – 0 0 0
     William - - - - -, 0 0 0 – 0 0 1 – 0 0 0
     Wilson - - - - -, 0 0 0 – 0 0 1 – 0 0 0
     Elizabeth - - - - -, 0 0 0 – 0 0 1 – 0 0 0

#456: Laurence HUME, 0 0 0 – 0 0 0 – 1 0 0
     Eve - - - - -, 0 0 0 – 0 0 0 – 0 1 0
     Jane - - - - -, 0 0 0 – 0 0 0 – 0 1 0

#457: John EWLETT [sic], 0 0 0 – 0 0 0- 1 0 0   *(= HEWLETT.)*
     Clara - - - - -, 0 0 0 – 0 0 0 – 0 1 0
     Jane - - - - -, 0 0 0 – 0 0 0 – 0 1 0

#458: Richard HARRIS, 0 0 0 – 0 0 0 – 1 0 0
     Jane POTTS, 0 0 0 – 0 0 0 – 0 1 0
     Francis BENNETT, 0 0 0 – 0 0 1 – 0 0 0
     Robert - - - - -, 0 0 0 – 0 0 0 – 1 0 0
     Elinor - - - - -, 0 0 0 – 0 0 1 – 0 0 0
     Jo^s POTTS, 0 0 0 – 0 0 1 – 0 0 0
     Emelia - - - - -, 0 0 0 – 0 0 1 – 0 0 0
     Richard HAYWOOD, 0 0 0 – 0 0 0 – 0 0 1
     Archy BENNETT, 0 0 0 – 0 0 0 – 0 0 1
     John POTTS, 0 0 0 – 0 0 0 – 0 0 1

#459: James HUME, 0 0 0 – 0 0 0 – 1 0 0
     Patience BROASTER, 0 0 0 – 0 0 0 – 0 1 0

p. 10:
#460: Thomas HOARE, 0 0 0 – 0 0 0 – 1 0 0
     Simon HOARE, 0 0 0 – 0 0 0 – 1 0 0
     Eliza - - - - -, 0 0 0 – 0 0 0 – 0 1 0
     Emeline - - - - -, 0 0 0 – 0 0 0 – 0 0 1
     Prince - - - - -, 0 0 0 – 0 0 0 – 0 0 1
     Catherine - - - - -, 0 0 0 – 0 0 0 – 0 0 1
     Joseph BROASTER, 0 0 0 – 0 0 0 – 1 0 0
     Patience - - - - -, 0 0 0 – 0 0 0 – 0 1 0
     William - - - - -, 0 0 0 – 0 0 0 – 1 0 0

#461: Billy HARE, 0 0 0 – 0 0 0 – 1 0 0
Adeline, 0 0 0 – 0 0 0 – 0 1 0 *(Surname not given.)*

#462: Wm. HOARE, 0 0 0 – 0 0 0 – 1 0 0
- - - - - - - -, 0 0 0 – 0 0 0 – 0 1 0 *(Davinda?)*
- - - - - - - -, 0 0 0 – 0 0 0 – 0 0 1 *(Martha WESTBY?)*
- - - - - - - -, 0 0 0 – 0 0 0 – 0 0 1
- - - - - - - -, 0 0 0 – 0 0 0 – 0 0 1
- - - - - - - -, 0 0 0 – 0 0 0 – 0 0 1
- - - - - - - -, 0 0 0 – 0 0 0 – 0 0 1 *(names not given.)*

#463: Luke HORN, 0 0 0 – 0 0 0 – 1 0 0
Robert - - - - -, 0 0 0 – 0 0 0 – 1 0 0
Molly - - - - -, 0 0 0 – 0 0 0 – 0 1 0
Charles - - - - -, 0 0 0 – 0 0 0 – 0 0 1
Elizabeth - - - - -, 0 0 0 – 0 0 0 – 0 0 1
Anny, 0 0 0 – 0 0 0 – 0 0 1
Catherine, 0 0 0 – 0 0 0 – 0 0 1
Benjamin, 0 0 0 – 0 0 0 – 0 0 1
Henry, 0 0 0 – 0 0 0 – 0 0 1 *(Surnames not given.)*

p. 11:
#464: George E. HAYLOCK, 0 0 0 – 1 0 0 – 0 0 0
Jane E. -- - - -, 0 0 0 – 0 1 0 – 0 0 0
George J. - - - - -, 0 0 0 – 0 0 1 – 0 0 0
Eliza, 0 0 0 – 0 0 0 – 0 1 0
Susan, 0 0 0 – 0 0 0 – 0 1 0
Susannah, 0 0 0 – 0 0 0 – 0 1 0
Margaret, 0 0 0 – 0 0 0 – 0 1 0
Catherine, 0 0 0 – 0 0 0 – 0 1 0
James, 0 0 0 – 0 0 0 – 1 0 0
William, 0 0 0 – 0 0 0 – 1 0 0
John, 0 0 0 – 0 0 0 – 0 0 1
Thomas, 0 0 0 – 0 0 0 – 0 0 1
Lawrence, 0 0 0 – 0 0 0 – 1 0 0 *(Surnames not given.)*

#465: Ann TUKS, 0 0 0 – 0 0 0 – 0 1 0
Elizabeth - - - - -, 0 0 0 – 0 0 0 – 0 1 0
Ann - - - - -, 0 0 0 – 0 0 0 – 0 1 0
Susan - - - - -, 0 0 0 – 0 0 0 – 0 1 0
John - - - - -, 0 0 0 – 0 0 0 – 1 0 0
Robert - - - - -, 0 0 0 – 0 0 0 – 1 0 0
John JICKSON [*sic*], 0 0 0 – 0 0 0 – 1 0 0
Richard TUKS, 0 0 0 – 0 0 0 – 0 0 1

290

#466: Dennis HAYES, 1 0 0 – 0 0 0 – 0 0 0
Mary - - - - -, 0 1 0 – 0 0 0 – 0 0 0
Dennis - - - - -, 0 0 1 – 0 0 0 – 0 0 0
Ellen - - - - -, 0 0 1 – 0 0 0 – 0 0 0
Sarah - - - - -, 0 0 1 – 0 0 0 – 0 0 0

#467: Alex^r HUME, 0 0 0 – 0 0 0 – 1 0 0
Henry ANDERSON, 0 0 0 – 0 0 0 – 1 0 0
Sophia - - - - -, 0 0 0 – 0 0 0 – 0 1 0

p. 12:
#468: Peter HARRIS, 0 0 0 – 0 0 0 – 1 0 0
Mary - - - - -, 0 0 0 – 0 0 0 – 0 1 0
Joseph BENNETT, 0 0 0 – 0 0 0 – 0 0 1

#469: Sergeant HAMILTON, 0 0 0 – 0 0 0 – 1 0 0
Sarah - - - - -, 0 0 0 – 0 0 0 – 0 1 0

#470: James HILL, 0 0 0 – 0 0 0 – 1 0 0
Eliza TENNER, 0 0 0 – 0 0 0 – 0 1 0

#471: Polydore HAMER, 0 0 0 – 0 0 0 – 1 0 0
Sally PRICE, 0 0 0 – 0 0 0 – 0 1 0

#472: Charles HOARE, 0 0 0 – 1 0 0 – 0 0 0
Werna [*sic*] HOARE, 0 0 0 – 0 0 0 – 0 1 0
Lucy - - - - -, 0 0 0 – 0 0 1 – 0 0 0
Sabia- - - - -, 0 0 0 – 0 0 1 – 0 0 0
Lotaria - - - - -, 0 0 0 – 0 0 1 – 0 0 0
Joseph - - - - -, 0 0 0 – 0 0 1 – 0 0 0
Diana - - - - -, 0 0 0 – 0 0 1 – 0 0 0
Sam - - - - -, 0 0 0 – 0 0 0 – 1 0 0

#473: Thomas HULSE, 0 0 0 – 0 0 0 – 1 0 0
Peggy WILLIAMS, 0 0 0 – 0 0 0 – 0 1 0

#474: Chas. HARRIS, 0 0 0 – 0 0 0 – 1 0 0
Chas. - - - - - Jr, 0 0 0 – 0 0 0 – 1 0 0
Henry MARTIN, 0 0 0 – 0 0 0 – 1 0 0
Ann JENNISON, 0 0 0 – 0 0 0 – 0 1 0
Maria LEONA, 0 0 0 – 0 0 0 – 0 1 0
Sarah HARRIS, 0 0 0 – 0 0 0 – 0 1 0

p. 13:
#475: Mary HUME, 0 0 0 – 0 1 0 – 0 0 0
Ann L. MEIGHAN, 0 0 0 – 0 1 0 – 0 0 0

King,
William,
Frank,
Isaac,
Richard,
Moses,
Henry,
Laurence,
Harry   *(from totals, the nine black men.)*
Aaron,
Nelson   *(from totals, the two black male children.)*
Joanna,
Mary   *(from totals, the two black women.)*
Shela,
Maria,
Matilda *(from totals, the three black female children. Surnames not given.)*

Totals: 2 colored women, 9 black men, 2 black women, 2 black male children, and 3 black female children.

#476: Wm HARLEY, 1 0 0 – 0 0 0 – 0 0 0
Lydia HARLEY, 0 1 0 – 0 0 0 – 0 0 0
Susannah - - - - -, 0 0 1 – 0 0 0 – 0 0 0
Diana - - - - -. 0 0 1 – 0 0 0 – 0 0 0

#477: Joseph HEMSLEY, 0 0 0 – 0 0 0 – 1 0 0
John - - - - -, 0 0 0 – 0 0 0 – 1 0 0

#478: Henry HUME, 0 0 0 – 0 0 0 – 1 0 0
Sabina HINKS, 0 0 0 – 0 0 0 – 0 1 0
Richard - - - - -, 0 0 0 – 0 0 0 – 1 0 0

p. 14:
#479: Peter HECTOR, 0 0 0 – 0 0 0 – 1 0 0
Mary ELRINGTON, 0 0 0 – 0 0 0 – 0 1 0
Joseph NEAL, 0 0 0 – 0 0 0 – 1 0 0

#480: Richard HARE, 0 0 0 – 0 0 0 – 1 0 0
Margaret - - - - -, 0 0 0 – 0 1 0 – 0 0 0
Susan FRANKLIN, 0 0 0 – 0 0 0 – 0 0 1
George BANTUN, 0 0 0 – 0 0 0 – 0 0 1
Rose FLOWERS, 0 0 0 – 0 1 0 – 0 0 0

#481: William HENRY, 0 0 0 – 1 0 0 – 0 0 0
John - - - - -, 0 0 0 – 0 0 0 – 1 0 0

#482: Prince HENRY, 0 0 0 – 0 0 0 – 1 0 0
Catarine [*sic*] STAIN, 0 0 0 – 0 0 0 – 0 1 0
Maryann HENRY, 0 0 0 – 0 0 0 – 0 0 1
William - - - - -, C 0 0 – 0 0 0 – 0 0 1

#483: Joseph HILL, 0 0 0 – 1 0 0 – 0 0 0
Catherine COLQUHOUN, 0 0 0 – 0 0 0 – 0 1 0
Sophia O'BRIEN, 0 0 0 – 0 0 0 – 0 1 0
Judy COLQUHOUN, C 0 0 – 0 0 1 – 0 0 0
Emma - - - - -, 0 0 0 – 0 0 1 – 0 0 0
Philip HILL, 0 0 0 – 0 C 1 – 0 0 0
Charlotte - - - - -, 0 0 0 – 0 0 1 – 0 0 0
Elizabeth - - - - -, 0 0 0 – 0 0 1 – 0 0 0

#484: John HEWLETT, 0 0 0 – 1 0 0 – 0 0 0
Elizabeth SMITH, 0 0 0 – 0 1 0 – 0 0 0
John HEWLETT, 0 0 0 – 0 0 1 – 0 0 0

Note: Another numbering error. household #484 is followed by #445.

#445: Hooksbill HOOK, 0 C 0 – 0 0 0 – 1 0 0

p. 15:
#446: William E. HAMPSHIRE, ‍ 0 0 – 0 0 0 – 0 0 0
Sarah E. - - - - -, 0 1 0 – 0 C 0 – 0 0 0
Susan WARD, 0 1 0 – 0 0 0 – 0 0 0
Stanley FORBES HAMPSHIRE, 0 0 1 – 0 0 0 – 0 0 0

Edward, 0 0 0 – 0 0 0 – 0 0 1
William, 0 0 0 – 0 0 0 – 0 0 1
Mary, 0 0 0 – 0 0 0 – 0 C 1

Note: The line between the families is centered on the list of names, and solid, not dashed to indicate the name above. Perhaps the mother of the children died after the return was handed in, and her name was deleted before the list was copied into the book.

#447: George HILL, 0 0 0 – 0 0 0 – 1 0 0
Susan FRANCIS, 0 0 0 – 0 0 C – 0 1 0

#448: Wm HUMBLE, 0 0 0 – 0 C 0 – 1 0 0
Hannah GRAHAM, 0 0 0 – 0 0 0 – 0 1 0
Thomas - - - - -, 0 0 0 – 0 C 0 – 1 0 0
Sarah - - - - -, 0 0 0 – 0 0 0 – 0 1 0
Ellen - - - - -, 0 0 0 – 0 0 0 – 0 1 0
Wm HUMBLE Jr, 0 0 0 – 0 0 0 – 1 0 0

#449: Louisa HUGHES, 0 1 0 – 0 0 0 – 0 0 0
Present - - - - -,   0 1 0 – 0 0 0 – 0 0 0 *(These marks are very faint.)*
- - - - - - - - - -
- - - - - - - - - -
- - - - - - - - - -,
Susannah - - - - -,
- - - - - - - - - -,
Jane - - - - -,
John GIDEY.

Totals: 4 white women, 1 white male child, 4 white female children, total whites, 9.

Note: The marks for totals were entered in the wrong columns. This was a black family: see the 1832 census p. 83, household #271, and the 1835 census p. 35, household #107.

#450:   James Jos^h HUME, 0 0 0 – 0 0 0 – 1 0 0
Elizabeth - - - - -, 0 0 0 – 0 0 0 – 0 0 1

p. 16:
#451:   John HENDY, 0 0 0 – 1 0 0 – 0 0 0
Ann - - - - -, 0 1 0 – 0 0 0 – 0 0 0
John - - - - -. 0 0 0 – 0 0 1 – 0 0 0
Margaret SMITH, 0 0 0 – 0 0 1 – 0 0 0
- - - - - MEANING, 0 0 0 – 0 0 0 – 0 1 0
Amelia BRESTOW, 0 0 0 – 0 0 0 – 0 1 0
Eve - - - - -, 0 0 0 – 0 0 0 – 0 1 0
Jos. RENNALS, 0 0 0 – 0 0 1 – 0 0 0
William, 0 0 0 – 0 0 0 – 0 0 1 *(Surname not given.)*

#452:   Archibald HANDYSIDE, 1 0 0 – 0 0 0 – 0 0 0
Kitty MEIGHAN, 0 0 0 – 0 1 0 – 0 0 0
Edranna BENNETT, 0 0 0 – 0 1 0 – 0 0 0
Kitty MEIGHAN, 0 0 0 – 0 1 0 – 0 0 0
Betsy PERRY, 0 0 0 – 0 1 0 – 0 0 0
John SAVORY, 0 0 0 – 0 0 1 – 0 0 0
Commilla - - - - -, 0 0 0 – 0 0 1 – 0 0 0
W^m - - - - -, 0 0 0 – 0 0 1 – 0 0 0

Note: Archibald Handyside was the shipbuilder for whom Handyside Street in Belize City was named. He died in 1866, leaving property to his widow, Catherine Meighan. When did she die? Was Edranna her daughter by Marshal Bennett Jr.? Who were the parents of Kitty Meighan Jr.? Did Edranna and Kitty marry and have children?

#453:   John HUNT, 1 0 0 – 0 0 0 – 0 0 0
Elizabeth CASTLE, 0 0 0 – 0 1 0 – 0 0 0
Thomas HUNT, 0 0 0 – 0 0 1 – 0 0 0

John - - - - -, 0 0 0 – C 0 1 – 0 0 0
George - - - - -, 0 0 0 – 0 0 1 – 0 0 0
Alexander - - - - -, 0 0 0 – 0 0 1 – 0 0 0
Samuel - - - - -, 0 0 0 – 0 0 1 – 0 0 0
Elizabeth - - - - -, 0 0 0 – 0 0 1 – 0 0 0

#454:   James HOARE, 0 0 0 – 0 0 0 – 1 0 0
Daniel - - - - -, 0 0 0 – 0 0 0 – 0 0 1
Margaret CRABBY, 0 C 0 – 0 0 0 – 0 1 0

p. 17:
#455:   Joseph HINKS, 0 0 0 – 0 0 0 – 1 0 0
Malsey GRANT, 0 0 0 – 0 0 0 – 0 1 0
Robert HINKS, 0 0 0 – 0 0 0 – 0 0 1
Philip - - - - -, 0 0 0 – 0 0 0 – 0 0 1
Rebecca - - - - -, 0 0 0 – C 0 0 – 0 0 1
Martha - - - - -, 0 0 0 – 0 0 0 – 0 0 1
Clarinda, 0 0 0 – 0 0 0 – C 0 1
Clary, 0 0 0 – 0 0 0 – 0 1 0 *(Surnames not given.)*

Note: The Keeper of the Records skipped #456.

#457:   John HALL, 0 0 0 – 0 0 0 – 1 0 0
Cylby - - - - -, 0 0 0 – 0 0 C – 0 1 0
Biddy - - - - -, 0 0 0 – 0 0 0 – 0 0 1
Sarah - - - - -, 0 0 0 – 0 0 C – 0 0 1
Edward La BOY, 0 0 0 – 0 0 0 – 0 0 1

#458:   Jervis HARRISON, 1 0 0 – 0 0 0 – 0 0 0
Elizabeth POTTS, 0 0 0 – 0 1 0 – 0 0 0
George A. HARRISON, 0 0 0 – 0 0 1 – 0 0 0
Charlotte, 0 0 0 – 0 0 0 – 0 1 0 *(Surname not given.)*
Rob[t] SHORT, 0 0 0 – 0 0 0 – 0 0 1
Simon, 0 0 0 – 0 0 0 – 0 0 1
Sam, 0 0 0 – 0 0 0 – 0 0 1
Cato, 0 0 0 – 0 0 0 – 0 0 1 *(Surnames not given.)*

Note: Was Elizabeth the daughter of Thomas Potts and Susannah Burrell?

#459:   Thomas HUME, 0 0 0 – 0 0 0 – 1 0 0
Sampson - - - - -, 0 0 0 – 0 0 0 – 1 0 0
Phoebe O'BRIEN, 0 0 0 – 0 0 0 – 0 1 0

#460:   Henry HUME, 0 0 0 – 0 0 0 – 1 0 0
E. - - - - -, 0 0 0 – 0 0 0 – 0 1 0
Hannah LAMB, 0 0 0 – 0 0 0 – 0 1 0

p. 18:
#461: Jane HUME, 0 0 0 – 0 1 0 – 0 0 0
Jane C. MEIGHAN, 0 0 0 – 0 1 0 – 0 0 0
J. W. BLAKE, 0 0 0 – 1 0 0 – 0 0 0
William, 0 0 0 – 0 0 0 – 1 0 0
Chance, 0 0 0 – 0 0 0 – 1 0 0
Henry, 0 0 0 – 0 0 0 – 1 0 0
Harry, 0 0 0 – 0 0 0 – 0 0 1
Thomas, 0 0 0 – 0 0 0 – 0 0 1
Betsy, 0 0 0 – 0 0 0 – 0 1 0
Nancy, 0 0 0 – 0 0 0 – 0 1 0
Eve, 0 0 0 – 0 0 0 – 0 1 0
Jannette, 0 0 0 – 0 0 0 – 0 0 1 *(Surnames not given.)*

#462: George HINKS, 0 0 0 – 0 0 0 – 1 0 0

#463: Wm HYDE, 0 0 0 – 0 0 0 – 1 0 0

#464: USHER HULSE, 0 0 0 – 0 0 0 – 1 0 0
Mary MURRAY, 0 0 0 – 0 0 0 – 0 1 0
Thomas GARNET, 0 0 0 – 0 0 0 – 1 0 0
Matilda - - - - -, 0 0 0 – 0 0 0 – 0 1 0
Thomas BOWMAN, 0 0 0 – 0 0 0 – 0 0 1
Banyan - - - - -, 0 0 0 – 0 0 0 – 0 0 1
Isaac - - - - -, 0 0 0 – 0 0 0 – 0 0 1
Mary MEIGHAN, 0 0 0 – 0 0 0 – 0 1 0

#465: Wm HAMMOND, 0 0 0 – 0 0 0 – 1 0 0
Jn° BASIL, 0 0 0 – 0 0 0 – 1 0 0

#466: John HOLMES, 0 0 0 – 0 0 0 – 1 0 0
Mary McPHERSON, 0 0 0 – 0 0 0 – 0 1 0

p. 19:
#467: George HEWLETT, 0 0 0 – 0 0 0 – 1 0 0
Nancy NELLING, 0 0 0 – 0 0 0 – 0 1 0 *(= SNELLING?)*

#468: Robert HAMILTON, 0 0 0 – 0 0 0 – 1 0 0

#469: Adam HUME, 0 0 0 – 0 0 0 – 1 0 0

#470: Nicholas HUME, 0 0 0 – 0 0 0 – 1 0 0

#471: John L. HUME, 0 0 0 – 0 0 0 – 1 0 0

#472: Robert HUME, 0 0 0 – 0 0 0 - 1 0 0
Charlotte - - - - -, 0 0 0 – 0 0 0 – 0 1 0

#473: Lewey HEFTING, 0 0 0 – 0 0 0 – 1 0 0

#474: James JONES, 0 0 0 – 1 0 0 – 0 0 0
Patty CRAWFORD, 0 0 0 – 0 1 0 – 0 0 0
Maria PATTNETT, 0 0 0 – 0 0 1 – 0 0 0
Annie - - - - -, 0 0 0 – 0 0 1 – 0 0 0
Rose - - - - -, 0 0 0 – 0 0 1 – 0 0 0

#475: Monimia JONES, 0 0 0 – 0 0 0 – 0 1 0
Jane DEMART, 0 0 0 – 0 0 0 – 0 1 0
Rebecca GOFF, 0 0 0 – 0 0 0 – 0 1 0
Eve HOSARIO, [sic], 0 0 0 – 0 0 0 – 0 1 0

#476: Thomas JEX, 0 0 0 – 0 0 0 – 1 0 0

Note: The numbers regress again. The last household on page 19 is #476, and the first on page 20 is #468.

p. 20:
#468: Samuel JOYNER, 1 0 0 – 0 0 0 – 0 0 0
John H. - - - - -, 0 0 1 – 0 0 0 – 0 0 0
W^m - - - - -, 0 0 1 – 0 0 0 – 0 0 0
Mary Ann - - - - -, 0 0 1 – 0 0 0 – 0 0 0
Samuel - - - - -, 0 0 1 – 0 0 0 – 0 0 0

#469: Danael [sic] JAMES, 0 0 0 – 0 0 0 – 1 0 0
Nancy GRANT, 0 0 0 – 0 0 0 – 0 1 0
Elizabeth - - - - -, 0 0 0 – 0 0 0 – 0 0 1

#470: Thomas JOHNSON, 0 0 0 – 0 0 0 – 1 0 0
Clarissa PROVIDENCE, 0 0 0 – 0 0 0 – 0 1 0

#471: William JONES, 0 0 0 – 0 0 0 – 1 0 0
Olive CRAWFORD, 0 0 0 – 0 0 0 – 0 1 0
Joseph Morris O'CONNOR, 0 0 0 – 0 0 0 – 1 0 0

#472: James JONES, 0 0 0 – 0 0 0 – 1 0 0
Margaret MYVETT. 0 0 0 – 0 0 0 – 0 1 0
Sophia JONES, 0 0 0 – 0 0 0 – 0 0 1

#473: Isaac JENKINS, 0 0 0 – 0 0 0 – 1 0 0
Catherine LOUIS, 0 0 0 – 0 0 0 – 0 1 0
Louis JENKINS, 0 0 0 – 0 0 0 – 0 0 1

297

#474: Francis JOHNSON, 0 0 0 – 0 0 0 – 1 0 0
Integrity MEIGHAN, 0 0 0 – 0 0 0 – 0 1 0
Susan - - - - -, 0 0 0 – 0 0 0 – 0 1 0
Robert - - - - -, 0 0 0 – 0 0 0 – 0 0 1
Eliza JOHNSON, 0 0 0 – 0 0 0 – 0 0 1
W^m - - - - -, 0 0 0 – 0 0 0 – 0 0 1

p. 21:
#475: Thomas JENNINGS, 0 0 0 – 1 0 0 – 0 0 0
James - - - - -, 0 0 0 – 1 0 0 – 0 0 0
Catherine P. - - - - -, 0 0 0 – 0 1 0 – 0 0 0
Rebecca LINDO, 0 0 0 – 0 1 0 – 0 0 0
Angeline JENNINGS, 0 0 0 – 0 0 1 – 0 0 0
Lavinia - - - - -, 0 0 0 – 0 0 1 – 0 0 0
Catherine - - - - -, 0 0 0 – 0 0 1 – 0 0 0
Rebecca L. - - - - -, 0 0 0 – 0 0 1 – 0 0 0
Mary Ann ROBINSON, 0 0 0 – 0 0 0 – 0 1 0
Nathanael [*sic*], 0 0 0 – 0 0 1 – 0 0 0
Thomas, 0 0 0 – 0 0 1 – 0 0 0 *(Surnames not given.)*
Royalford WEBSTER, 0 0 0 – 0 0 0 – 1 0 0
Chas. SEBASTIAN, 0 0 0 – 0 0 0 – 1 0 0

#476: Simon JEFFREYS, 0 0 0 – 0 0 0 – 1 0 0

#477: James JONES, 0 0 0 – 0 0 0 – 1 0 0
Elizabeth - - - - -, 0 0 0 – 0 0 0 – 0 1 0
E. - - - - -, 0 0 0 – 0 0 0 – 0 0 1 *(Marked as female.)*
Bella - - - - -, 0 0 0 – 0 0 0 – 0 0 1
Manda - - - - -, 0 0 0 – 0 0 0 – 0 0 1
Nancy, 0 0 0 – 0 0 0 – 0 0 1 *(Surname not given.)*
Clara BAPTIST, 0 0 0 – 0 0 0 – 0 0 1
Diamond JONES, 0 0 0 – 0 0 0 – 0 0 1 *(Marked as male.)*
Maria - - - - -, 0 0 0 – 0 0 0 – 0 0 1
Mary - - - - -, 0 0 0 – 0 0 0 – 0 0 1

#478: Sarah JONES, 0 0 0 – 0 0 0 – 0 1 0
Polly - - - - -, 0 0 0 – 0 0 0 – 0 1 0
Adam SMITH, 0 0 0 – 0 0 0 – 1 0 0
Thomas - - - - -, 0 0 0 – 0 0 0 – 1 0 0
Perdita - - - - -, 0 0 0 – 0 0 0 – 0 1 0

p. 22:
#479: M. JONES, 0 0 0 – 0 1 0 – 0 0 0
Margaret - - - - -, 0 0 0 – 0 1 0 – 0 0 0
Susannah - - - - -, 0 0 0 – 0 1 0 – 0 0 0

298

Henrietta MARIETTA, 0 0 0 – 0 0 1 – 0 0 0
Mary Ann JONES, 0 0 0 – 0 0 1 – 0 0 0
Rebecca - - - - -, 0 0 0 – 0 0 1 – 0 0 0
Joseph LAMB, 0 0 0 – 0 0 0 – 1 0 0

#480: - - - - - JOSEPH, 0 0 0 – 1 0 0 – 0 0 0
- - - - - - - - - -, 0 0 0 – 0 1 0 – 0 0 0

#481: James JEFFERSON, 0 0 0 – 0 0 0 – 1 0 0
Nancy - - - - -, 0 0 0 – 0 0 0 – 0 1 0
Thomas - - - - -, 0 0 0 – 0 0 0 – 0 0 1

#482: Richard JEFFRIES, 0 0 0 – 0 0 0 – 1 0 0
Jane CARD, 0 0 0 – 0 0 0 – 0 1 0
Bess HUMES, 0 0 0 – 0 0 0 – 0 0 1
George HYDE, 0 0 0 – 0 0 0 – 1 0 0

#483: Betsy JEFFREYS [sic], 0 0 0 – 0 1 0 – 0 0 0
Sarah GRAHAM, 0 0 0 – 0 0 1 – 0 0 0
Victoria JAMIESON, 0 0 0 – 0 0 1 – 0 0 0
David GRAHAM, 0 0 0 – 0 0 1 – 0 0 0
Mary JEFFRIES [sic], 0 0 0 – 0 0 0 – 0 1 0

#484: Jane JEFFREYS [sic], 0 0 0 – 0 1 0 – 0 0 0
Thomas SMITH, 0 0 0 – 0 0 1 – 0 0 0
Eliza Ann DICKENSON, 0 0 0 – 0 0 1 – 0 0 0
Rachael JANE, 0 0 0 – 0 0 1 – 0 0 0
Jose MARIA, 0 0 0 – 0 0 0 – 0 0 1

Note: Since many people in this time period lacked surnames, the name of a parent was often added to the name of a child as a second name or surname, and passed down as a surname. In the family above, Rachel's mother may have been Jane, and Jose's mother, Maria. The writer has indexed second names such as Jane and Maria as surnames because they may have come down to descendants as surnames.

p. 23:
#485: Jane JONES, 0 0 0 – 0 0 0 – 0 1 0
Marina - - - - -, 0 0 0 – 0 0 0 – 0 1 0
Anne SLUSHER, 0 0 0 – 0 0 0 – 0 0 1
James - - - - -, 0 0 0 – 0 0 0 – 0 0 1
Jos. WAGNER, 0 0 0 – 0 0 0 – 0 0 1
Mary REMMINGTON, 0 0 0 – 0 1 0 – 0 0 0
Harriet RENNIE, 0 0 0 – 0 0 1 – 0 0 0
John GUYTON, 0 0 0 – 0 0 1 – 0 0 0
Fran^s GOUTROUT, 0 0 0 – 0 0 1 – 0 0 0
Cath^n JONES, 0 0 0 – 0 0 0 – 0 0 1

John MOODY, 0 0 0 – 1 0 0 – 0 0 0
Francis BENNETT, 0 0 0 – 0 0 0 – 1 0 0
Edward AVINO, 0 0 0 – 0 0 1 – 0 0 0
John ANDERSON, 0 0 0 – 0 0 0 – 0 0 1
Ann BENNETT, 0 0 0 – 0 1 0 – 0 0 0
Cath^n WESTBY, 0 0 0 – 0 0 1 – 0 0 0
Jas. PATNETT, 0 0 0 – 0 0 1 – 0 0 0

#486: John EVANS, 0 0 0 – 1 0 0 – 0 0 0
Catherine JEFFREYS, 0 0 0 – 0 1 0 – 0 0 0
Ann COLE, 0 0 0 – 0 1 0 – 0 0 0
Sarah EVANS, 0 0 0 – 0 1 0 – 0 0 0
Elizabeth - - - - -, 0 0 0 – 0 1 0 – 0 0 0
John E. - - - - -, 0 0 0 – 0 0 1 – 0 0 0
Charles - - - - -, 0 0 0 – 0 0 1 – 0 0 0
Alex^r ROBINSON, 0 0 0 – 0 0 1 – 0 0 0

#487: Rees JACOB, 0 0 0 – 0 0 0 – 1 0 0
Jesse GOOD, 0 0 0 – 0 0 0 – 0 1 0
Emily Frances COCKBURN, 0 0 0 – 0 0 0 – 0 1 0
Rushby, 0 0 0 – 0 0 0 – 1 0 0

p. 24:
#488: Margaret JONES, 0 0 0 – 0 1 0 – 0 0 0
Penelope - - - - -, 0 0 0 – 0 0 0 – 0 1 0
Mary A. EVE, 0 0 0 – 0 1 0 – 0 0 0
Jane VALPY, 0 0 0 – 0 0 1 – 0 0 0
James - - - - -, 0 0 0 – 0 0 1 – 0 0 0
Richard - - - - -, 0 0 0 – 0 0 1 – 0 0 0
Thomas, 0 0 0 – 0 0 0 – 1 0 0
George, 0 0 0 – 0 0 0 – 0 0 1 *(Surnames not given.)*
Lucy GLASS, 0 0 0 – 0 0 0 – 0 0 1

#489: Polly JONES, 0 0 0 – 0 0 0 – 0 1 0
Thomas - - - - -, 0 0 0 – 0 0 0 – 0 0 1
Quashie - - - - -, 0 0 0 – 0 0 0 – 0 0 1
Elizabeth - - - - -, 0 0 0 – 0 0 0 – 0 0 1
Matilda - - - - -, 0 0 0 – 0 0 0 – 0 0 1

#490: Joseph JONES, 0 0 0 – 0 0 0 – 1 0 0
Bethsheba - - - - -, 0 0 0 – 0 0 0 – 0 1 0
Adam - - - - -, 0 0 0 – 0 0 0 – 1 0 0
Amelia - - - - -, 0 0 0 – 0 0 0 – 0 0 1
Richard - - - - -, 0 0 0 – 0 0 0 – 0 0 1
Monimia - - - - -, 0 0 0 – 0 0 0 – 0 1 0
Eve - - - - -, 0 0 0 – 0 0 0 – 0 0 1

Jane D. - - - - -, 0 0 0 – 0 0 0 – 0 0 1
Rebecca GOFF, 0 0 0 – 0 0 0 –0 0 1

#491: Genevah JORDON, 0 0 0 – 0 0 0 – 1 0 0
       Francis - - - - -, 0 0 0 – 0 0 0 – 0 0 1

#492: Alex^r JONES, 0 0 0 – 0 0 0 – 1 0 0

p. 25:
#493: Rachel JEFFREYS,   *(The black woman.)*
       Manuel ANTONIO,   *(Manuel and Richard are the two white men.)*
       Richd HANDYSIDE,   *(How was Richard related to Archibald Handyside?)*
       George JEFFREYS,
       Charles - - - - -,
       W^m - - - - -,   *(The three colored male children.)*
       Hannah,   *(The colored female child.)*
       John DAVIS,
       Robert GILLERMO,
       Andreid, [*sic*]
       Edward,
       Abraham,   *(The five black men.)*
       Hope,
       Connor,
       Billy,
       Tony,   *(The four black male children.)*
       Mary.   *(The black female child.)*
       (Surnames not given.)
No marks. Totals: 2 0 0 – 0 0 4 (3 male, 1 female,) 5 1 5 (3 male, 1 female.)

Note: Several people in this household can be identified in previous censuses. Other designations are drawn from the totals and the customary order of listing: head of household regardless of color or gender, then white men, women, and children, colored men, women, and children, and black men, women, and children. In some families the children were named in birth order, but in others, males were listed first, so further evidence is needed to determine the order of birth.

#494: Richard JONES, 0 0 0 – 0 0 0 – 1 0 0
       Sarah HUMES, 0 0 0 – 0 0 0 – 0 1 0
       James - - - - -, 0 0 0 – 0 0 0 – 1 0 0
       Amelia - - - - -, 0 0 0 – 0 0 0 – 0 1 0
       Elizabeth - - - - -, 0 0 0 – 0 0 0 – 0 1 0
       Satira - - - - -, 0 0 0 – 0 0 0 – 0 0 1

#495: Jonathan JENKINS, 0 0 0 – 0 0 0 – 1 0 0
       Lydia JENKINS, 0 0 0 – 0 0 0 – 0 1 0
       Isaac - - - - -, 0 0 0 – 0 0 0 – 1 0 0

Chas. - - - - -, 0 0 0 – 0 0 0 – 0 0 1
George - - - - -, 0 0 0 – 0 0 0 – 0 0 1
Silvia - - - - -, 0 0 0 – 0 0 0 – 0 0 1

p. 26:
#496: John G. JONES, 1 0 0 – 0 0 0 – 0 0 0
Sarah - - - - -, 0 0 0 – 0 1 0 – 0 0 0
Mary Ann - - - - -, 0 0 0 – 0 0 1 – 0 0 0
John - - - - -, 0 0 0 – 0 0 1 – 0 0 0
Phoebe - - - - -, 0 0 0 – 0 0 1 – 0 0 0

#497: Robt JACKSON, 0 0 0 – 0 0 0 – 1 0 0
Ann BURGESS, 0 0 0 – 0 0 0 – 0 1 0
Joseph - - - - -, 0 0 0 – 0 0 0 – 0 0 1
Frederick - - - - -, 0 0 0 – 0 0 0 – 0 0 1
Peter - - - - -, 0 0 0 – 0 0 0 – 0 0 1
John - - - - -, 0 0 0 – 0 0 0 – 0 0 1
Stephen - - - - -, 0 0 0 – 0 0 0 – 0 0 1
Lucia - - - - -, 0 0 0 – 0 0 0 – 0 0 1
Anntotenna *(or Auntotenna?)* 0 0 0 – 0 0 0 – 0 1 0

#498: Cooling JONES, 0 0 0 – 1 0 0 – 0 0 0
Eliza - - - - -, 0 0 0 – 0 1 0 – 0 0 0
Hester - - - - -, 0 0 0 – 0 1 0 – 0 0 0
Saml - - - - -, 0 0 0 – 0 0 1 – 0 0 0
Marg^t - - - - -, 0 0 0 – 0 0 1 – 0 0 0
Anne BENNETT, 0 0 0 – 0 1 0 – 0 0 0

#499: Cudjoe ISLES, 0 0 0 – 0 0 0 – 1 0 0
Jose F. DOMINGO, 0 0 0 – 0 0 0 – 0 0 1
Maria S. - - - - -, 0 0 0 – 0 0 0 – 0 1 0

#500: John TUCK, 0 0 0 – 0 0 0 – 1 0 0

#501: Samuel JESSOP, 0 0 0 – 1 0 0 – 0 0 0
Sarah Anne - - - - -, 0 0 0 – 0 1 0 – 0 0 0

p. 27:
#502: Sarah KEEFFE, 0 1 0 – 0 0 0 – 0 0 0
Mary Ann SPROAT, 0 1 0 – 0 0 0 – 0 0 0
Sarah BENNETT, 0 0 1 – 0 0 0 – 0 0 0
Harry - - - - -, 0 0 1 – 0 0 0 – 0 0 0
Mary Ann JOINER, 0 0 1 – 0 0 0 – 0 0 0
Chas. CUNNINGHAM, 1 0 0 – 0 0 0 – 0 0 0
Andrew - - - - -, 1 0 0 – 0 0 0 – 0 0 0
Agnes, 0 0 0 – 0 0 0 – 0 1 0

Annette, 0 0 0 – 0 0 C – 0 0 1
Alice, 0 0 0 – 0 0 0 – 0 0 1
Frederick, 0 0 0 – 0 0 0 – 0 0 1
Francis, 0 0 0 – 0 0 0 – 0 0 1 *(Surnames not given.)*
Wm CUNNINGHAM, 1 0 0 – 0 0 0 – 0 0 0

#503: Synthia KEITH, 0 0 0 – 0 0 0 – 0 1 0 *(= KEEFE?)*
Rose - - - - -, 0 0 0 – 0 0 0 – 0 1 0
Bella - - - - -, 0 0 0 – 0 0 0 – 0 1 0
Mary - - - - -, 0 0 0 – 0 0 0 – 0 0 1
Nicholas USHER, 0 0 0 – 0 0 0 – 1 0 0

#504: James C. KENT, 1 0 C – 0 0 0 – 0 0 0
Eleanor YOUNG, 0 1 C – 0 0 0 – 0 0 0

#505: George KEENE, 1 0 0 – 0 0 0 – 0 0 0
John - - - - -, 0 0 0 – 0 C 1 – 0 0 0
Catherine MATHIESON, 0 0 0 – 0 1 0 – 0 0 0

#506: John KELLY, 0 0 0 – 0 0 0 – 1 0 0
Mary - - - - -, 0 0 0 – 0 0 0 – 0 1 0
John - - - - -, 0 0 0 – 0 0 0 – 1 0 0
James - - - - -, 0 0 0 – C 0 0 – 1 0 0

p. 28:
#507: John KELLY, 0 0 0 – C 0 0 – 1 0 0
Hannah - - - - -, 0 0 0 – 0 0 0 – 0 1 0
Thomas - - - - -, 0 0 0 – 0 0 0 – 1 0 0
John - - - - -, 0 0 0 – 0 C 0 – 1 0 0
Julian [sic] - - - - -, 0 0 0 – 0 0 0 – 0 1 0 *(Marked as a woman.)*
Joseph - - - - -, 0 0 0 – C 0 0 – 0 0 1
George - - - - -, 0 0 0 – 0 0 0 – 0 0 1
Jane - - - - -, 0 0 0 – 0 0 0 – 0 0 1
Edward - - - - -, 0 0 0 – 0 0 0 – 0 0 1
Elizabeth - - - - -, 0 0 0 – 0 0 0 – 0 0 1

#508: John KNOX, 0 0 0 – 0 C 0 – 1 0 0
Betsy - - - - -, 0 0 0 – 0 0 0 – 0 1 0

#509: Archibald KEITH, 0 0 0 – 0 0 0 – 1 0 0
Marynette - - - - -, 0 0 0 – 0 0 0 – 0 1 0
Peggy - - - - -, 0 0 0 – 0 0 0 – 0 1 0
Margaret McLEAN, 0 0 0 – 0 0 0 – 0 0 1
Sarah NOTT, 0 0 0 – 0 0 0 – 0 0 1 *(= KNOTH?)*
Helena COOK, 0 0 0 – 0 0 0 – 0 0 1

#510: Wm KENYON, 1 0 0 – 0 0 0 – 0 0 0
Elizabeth - - - - -, 0 1 0 – 0 0 0 – 0 0 0
Mary Ann FITZGERALD, 0 1 0 – 0 0 0 – 0 0 0
Ann CASSITEY, [sic], 0 0 1 – 0 0 0 – 0 0 0
Wm KENYON, 0 0 0 – 0 0 0 – 1 0 0

#511: John KEIF [sic], 0 0 0 – 0 0 0 – 1 0 0   (= KEEFE.)
Angelica WARRIOR, 0 0 0 – 0 0 0 – 0 1 0
John KEIF, 0 0 0 – 0 0 0 – 0 0 1
Warrior - - - - -, 0 0 0 – 0 0 0 – 0 0 1 (Marked as female.)

p.29:
#512: James KELLY, 0 0 0 – 0 0 0 – 1 0 0
Maria KELLY, 0 0 0 – 0 1 0 – 0 0 0
Mary SMITH, 0 0 0 – 0 0 0 – 0 0 1
Frederick KELLY, 0 0 0 – 0 0 0 – 1 0 0
Robert - - - - -, 0 0 0 – 0 0 0 – 1 0 0

#513: Adrianna KIEF, 0 0 0 – 1 1 5 (4 male, 1 female children) – 0 0 0. (= KEEFE.)

Note: Who were the unnamed members of Adrianna's household?

#514: Andrew KEENE,
Maria - - - - -,
Asintha - - - - -,
Andew - - - - -,
Maria ANTONIO,
Namoon LOPEZ, 0 0 0 – 1 0 2 (female children) – 1 0 2 (male children.)

#515: John McKENNY, 0 0 0 – 1 0 0 – 0 0 0
Ann Margaret - - - - -, 0 0 0 – 0 1 0 – 0 0 0
Alexander - - - - -, 0 0 0 – 0 0 1 – 0 0 0

#516: John KELLEY, 0 0 0 – 0 0 0 – 1 0 0

#517: Corodon CROWL, 0 0 0 – 0 0 0 – 1 0 0

#518: Thomas KING, 0 0 0 – 0 0 0 – 1 0 0

#519: William KEATH, 0 0 0 – 0 0 0 – 1 0 0

#520: Catherine LAMB, 0 0 0 – 0 0 0 – 0 1 0
Mary Jane - - - - -, 0 0 0 – 0 0 0 – 0 0 1
Sarah - - - - -, 0 0 0 – 0 0 0 – 0 0 1
James - - - - -, 0 0 0 – 0 0 0 – 0 0 1

304

Note: Another numbering error: the households above and below are both #520.

p. 30:
#520:   Aines? LINE, 0 0 0 – 0 0 0 – 1 0 0

#521:   Edward LUCKIE, 0 0 0 – 0 0 0 – 1 0 0

#522:   Joseph LOWRY, 0 0 0 – 0 0 0 – 1 0 0
        Eliza JENNINGS, 0 0 0 – 0 0 0 – 0 1 0

#523:   Margaret LEWIS, 0 0 0 – 0 0 0 – 0 1 0

#524:   John LOCK, 0 0 0 – 1 0 0 – 0 0 0
        Maria PENCER [*sic*], 0 0 0 – 0 1 0 – 0 0 0   *(= SPENCER?)*
        C. LOCK, 0 0 0 – 0 1 0 – 0 0 0

Note: The enumerator skipped #525.

#526:   John LOCK, 0 0 0 – 0 0 1 – 0 0 0
        Frances YOUNG, 0 0 0 – 0 0 1 – 0 0 0
        - - - - - E. LOCK, 0 0 0 – 0 0 1 – 0 0 0 *(= Frances Jr.)*
        Maria - - - - -, 0 0 0 – 0 0 1 – 0 0 0
        James H. - - - - -, 0 0 0 – 0 0 1 – 0 0 0
        Addelette O. - - - - -, 0 0 0 – 0 0 1 – 0 0 0

Note: The enumerator made his marks in the wrong columns. John and Frances were adults, not children: baptism #789 shows John Lock, pilot, of Half Moon Key, and Frances Young as the parents of Ann Maria Lock.

#527:   Arabella LOWRIE,   *(From totals, the black woman.)*
        Henry TUCKER,
        March - - - - -,   *(From totals, the two black men.)*
        Dempshire - - - - -,
        John - - - - -,
        Thomas - - - - -,
        Rose - - - - -,
        Sarah SMALL, 0 0 0 –0 0 0 – 2 1 5 *(3 male and 2 female children.)*

p. 31:
#528:   Lucretia LAWRIE,
        Henry - - - - -,
        Eliza YOUNG, 0 0 0 – 0 0 0 – 1 2 0

#529:   Wm LYNCH, 0 0 0 – 0 0 0 – 1 0 0
        Sarah - - - - -, 0 0 0 – 0 0 0 – 0 0 1
        Charlotte YOUNG, 0 0 0 – 0 0 0 – 0 1 0

305

#530: Michael La FLEUR, 0 0 0 – 0 0 0 – 1 0 0
Mrs. - - - - -, 0 0 0 – 0 0 0 – 0 1 0
John Pier [*sic*] - - - - -, 0 0 0 – 0 0 0 – 1 0 0

#531: Francis LIND, 0 0 0 – 0 0 0 – 1 0 0
Mary - - - - -, 0 0 0 – 0 0 0 – 0 1 0
Robert - - - - -, 0 0 0 – 0 0 0 – 0 0 1

#532: Thos. LONGSWORTH,
Lucretia - - - - -,
Judy YARBOROUGH,
Jenny LONGSWORTH,
Susan USHER HARRIS,
Thos. GRIFFITHS, 0 0 0 – 0 0 1 – 1 4 0

#533: Benjamin LONGSWORTH,
Sarah - - - - -,
Isabella MOODY,
Amelia HEMMONDS,
Alvino SUART [*sic*], 0 0 0 – 2 1 2 *(female children)* – 0 0 0

p. 32:
#534: Wᵐ LAMB, 0 0 0 – 0 0 0 – 1 0 0
Grace PEAR, 0 0 0 – 0 0 0 – 0 1 0 *(= PIERRE?)*
Emelia - - - - -, 0 0 0 – 0 0 0 – 0 1 0

#535: James LAWRIE, 0 0 0 – 0 0 0 – 1 0 0
S –. JEFFRIES, 0 0 0 – 0 0 0 – 0 1 0

#536: Edmund LOVELL, 0 0 0 – 1 0 0 – 0 0 0
Amelia GABOURELL, 0 0 0 – 0 0 0 – 0 1 0

#537: Benjamin LONGSWORTH, 0 0 0 – 0 0 0 – 1 0 0
Petrona - - - - -, 0 0 0 – 0 0 0 – 0 1 0
Betty - - - - -, 0 0 0 – 0 0 0 – 0 0 1
Henry - - - - -, 0 0 0 – 0 0 0 – 0 0 1

#538: Betty LONGSWORTH, 0 0 0 – 0 1 0 – 0 0 0

#539: Edward M. LEWIS, 0 0 0 – 1 0 0 – 0 0 0
Dolly STAIN, 0 0 0 – 0 1 0 – 0 0 0
Caroline KEENE, 0 0 0 – 0 0 1 – 0 0 0

#540: James LAWRIE, 0 0 0 – 1 0 0 – 0 0 0
Ann - - - - -, 0 0 0 – 0 0 0 – 0 1 0

Thomas PARKES, 0 0 0 – 1 0 0 – 0 0 0
Peter - - - - -, 0 0 0 – 1 0 0 – 0 0 0
Lucy - - - - -, 0 0 0 – 0 1 0 – 0 0 0
Richard De BAPTISTE, 0 0 0 – 0 0 1 – 0 0 0
John - - - - -, 0 0 0 – 0 1 1 – 0 0 0
William PARKES, 0 0 0 – 1 0 0 – 0 0 0

p. 33:
#541: Thomas LAWLER, 0 0 0 – 0 0 0 – 1 0 0
Mary - - - - -, 0 0 0 – 0 0 0 – 0 1 0

#542: Penelope LAWLESS, 0 0 0 – 0 0 0 – 0 1 0
Clashmore - - - - -, 0 0 0 – 0 0 0 – 1 0 0
Esther - - - - -, 0 0 0 – 0 0 0 – 0 1 0
Diana GORDON, 0 0 0 – 0 0 0 – 0 1 0
William LAWLESS, 0 0 0 – 0 0 0 – 1 0 0
Charles - - - - -, 0 0 0 – 0 0 0 – 1 0 0
Susan - - - - -, 0 0 0 – 0 0 0 – 0 1 0
Penny - - - - -, 0 0 0 – 0 0 0 – 0 1 0
George NICHOLSON, 0 0 0 – 0 0 0 – 1 0 0
Nancy CADLE, 0 0 0 – 0 0 0 – 0 1 0
Philip MYVETT, 0 0 0 – 0 0 0 – 1 0 0
Joseph LAWLESS, 0 0 0 – 0 0 0 – 1 0 0
Elizabeth GORDON, 0 0 0 – 0 0 0 – 0 1 0

#543: John LINDO, 0 0 0 – 0 0 0 – 1 0 0

#544: Robert LAMB, 0 0 0 – 0 0 0 – 1 0 0
Maria LONGSWORTH, 0 0 0 – 0 0 0 – 0 1 0
Jane FLOWERS, 0 0 0 – 0 0 0 – 0 1 0
Joe JACKSON, 0 0 0 – 0 0 0 – 1 0 0

#545: Hamlet LAMB, 0 0 0 – 0 0 0 – 1 0 0
Maria LAMB, 0 0 0 – 0 0 0 – 0 1 0
Abby LAMB, 0 0 0 – 0 0 0 – 0 1 0

#546: Samuel LAMB, 0 0 0 – 0 0 0 – 1 0 0
Rose CARD, 0 0 0 – 0 0 0 – 0 1 0

p. 34:
#547: Robert LOWRIE, 0 0 0 – 0 0 0 – 1 0 0
Mary AMMERY, 0 0 0 – 0 0 0 – 0 1 0 (= *EMERY*.)

#548: Eleanor LOWRIE, 0 0 0 – 0 0 0 – 0 1 0

#549: Elizabeth LOWRIE, 0 0 0 – 0 0 0 – 0 1 0
Edward FOOT, 0 0 0 – 0 0 0 – 1 0 0
Phoebe JACKSON, 0 0 0 – 0 0 0 – 0 1 0

#550: John LINDO, 0 0 0 – 0 0 0 – 1 0 0
Molly LINDO, 0 0 0 – 0 0 0 – 0 1 0
Victoria LINDO, 0 0 0 – 0 0 0 – 0 1 0

#551: Robert LAMB, 0 0 0 – 0 0 0 – 1 0 0

#552: Diana LEWIS,
Sarah BELISLE,
Nancy - - - - -,
Elizabeth - - - - -,
Henry - - - - -,
Helena NEAL.   *There are no marks for this family.*

Note: It appears that this was the final entry of the 1839 census, as the remainder of the page and the whole of the next are blank. The recapitulation, if it was every made, has not survived.

---o0o---

Births, Marriages, and Deaths in Family Records
and British Newspapers

Amelia Patience ANTRAM, second daughter of Joshua ANTRAM and his wife Elizabeth POTTS, a daughter of John POTTS Jr. of Belize, was born in 1829 "in the West Indies." Mark RIGHTON, who contributed this information, descends from Joshua and Elizabeth; port records (see the *Second Parish Register)* show Joshua was master of the Petrel, and the couple were in Belize in 1826. Was Amelia born in Belize? She was baptized in 1835 at St. Dunstan's, Stepney, London. Was she named for Amelia and Patience GORDON? The names Amelia and Patience do not appear in Joshua's family.

Marshal BENNETT Sr. bought Appley House in the Isle of Wight in 1826. His wife, Elizabeth COOKE Bennett of Bristol, lived there with her niece, John Bennett's daughter Elizabeth Bennett, who married Henry Benjamin WYATT, a Captain in the Royal Navy, in 1836. The Wyatts lived at Ryde, on the Isle of Wight. Marshal died in 1839, and his widow went to Bristol to live with a sister; his brother Charles sold the property to James HYDE, a merchant enumerated in the 1816 census of Belize as a very rich man. George Hyde, James' son by Ariadne BROASTER, born in 1795, took charge of his father's affairs in Belize, and was also a wealthy man. After James Hyde married Susan CAMPBELL, Ariadne Broaster became the companion of Alexander FRANCE. James retired to live at Appley House with his wife and their children; the 1841 census shows them there. He died at Appley House on 23 Dec 1859; Susan died there in December 1865. Their son James BARTLETT HYDE sold the property in 1871.

Marcus Charles BENNETT was born to Marshal Bennett Jr. and Catherine MEIGHAN in 1820; the family appears in the 1823 census. Marshal had children by Catherine CUNNINGHAM: John in 1825, Sarah, Henry "Harry," and Marshal (born July 1827, d. Oct 1831) but censuses do not show them as a family: in 1826 he, Catherine Meighan, and Catherine Cunningham with baby John were in three separate households. In 1829 and 1832 he was living with Catherine Meighan. Was the child Catherine Meighan living with them in 1829 Catherine's, or the daughter born to John Meighan and Esther Grant in 1827? Catherine Cunningham died in 1832. Marshal died in 1835; his will has not survived. Catherine Meighan remarried to Archibald HANDYSIDE, and was living in 1866 when Archibald made his will. Sarah and Harry Bennett were living with Sarah Keefe in 1835. The will of John Bennett of Sheffield, proved in 1847, bequeathed £100 each to his deceased son Marshal's three sons, Marcus Charles, John, and Henry, but did not mention the child Catherine Meighan, or Selina, daughter of Elizabeth Godfrey, or Sarah, who appears in censuses as white. Was she Sarah Bennett who died in October 1840, aged 10, listed in the register as coloured? Generations of unions between Europeans and Creoles of white/Amerindian or black/white ancestry bred children described as white in one record and coloured in another.

Meredith BERNARD, who descends from John Samuel AUGUST and his wife, Sarah, nee MASKALL formerly BYRON, has researched the COOKE, Maskall, and August families and solved the mystery of the two Sarah Maskalls. The Sarah who married Dr

309

Thomas MURRAY in 1808 was the daughter of Henry Maskall and Mary Maskall (nee Cooke formerly August), and a half sister to John Samuel August. John Samuel August's wife, Sarah Maskall, was the widow of Joseph Byron and the niece of Henry Maskall: a Leeds newspaper reported that John Samuel August, Esq., Lt-Col. in the Royal Honduras Militia, married Mrs. Byron, widow of Mr. J. Byron, late of the York Grand Stand, on 1 March 1821. See the TURNBULL-GIBSON link below.

Byron BODDEN's GGG-grandmother, Mary Ann CHAPPEL, born 5 Mar 1819 in Belize, married 1) WARD and 2) Elwin ELWIN, and died 26 Sep 1888 in Roatan. His GG-grandfather, Henry C. BENNETT, born ca. 1828 to Marshal Bennett Jr. and Catherine CUNNINGHAM, married Catherine "Katie" BRENNAN; they had children Henry Marshall Bennett and Georgina McKAY, who both went to Roatan.

Mike VASQUEZ` is researching Charles METZGEN, Denmark to Belize ca. 1825, Francis A. BRADLEY (from England) and wife Mary Frances GABOUREL, ROSADO, and VASQUEZ, from Spain via Mexico (Yucatan.)

Who were the parents of John PANTING and Isabella NEAL (Isabella was from Mullins River) who had a daughter Alice Amelia Panting, 1886-1973? Isabella died when Alice was young, and John moved the family and remarried. John Panting was married three times. Alice m. Robert Ernest BELISLE, 1883 - 1976, son of --- BELISLE and Sheran.

Robert BEACH USHER, son of John and Sarah Purcell Usher (household #4 in the 1835 census) married Mary Ann COCHRANE, daughter of Archbishop Richard COCHRANE WARDLOW and Georgiana McAULAY. In 1829 Georgiana McAulay was living with her mother Mary HUME and child Louisa MEIGHAN (p. 364, #332.) John Purcell Usher, whose book of gravestone inscriptions was published in 1907, was a son of R. B. Usher and Mary Ann Cochrane. Leah McAulay was interred on 26 Jan 1827 aged 81; she left property to Georgina and Louisa as natural children of Mary Hume, suggesting that Georgina and Louisa were Leah's grand or great-grandchildren. Censuses show Mary Hume as a child in the household of George Hume and Mary COLQUHOUN; a later census shows Rebecca J. Usher, and Louisa as Louisa ALTEREITH, in her household.

Jill WAIGHT-GOLDING descends from James and Ann WAIGHT, from England by 1826, and from Joseph RABOTEAU, from France via Jamaica and Haiti ca. 1810.

The following links to British roots are given in chronological order. When a place of origin is not shown, look for it, and for relatives who provided the information, in the area the newspaper served: the death of a man from Aberdeen would not be reported in Kent.

Lt. GOULD, whose burial appears in the *First Parish Register* on 13 May 1801, was identified in the *Aberdeen Journal* as Lieut. William Gould of the 5th West India Reg't, late of Glasgow.

On 13 Oct 1804 the *Caledonian Mercury* reported the death of Lt. Alexander ROBERTSON in Belize, in his 25th year.

In August 1806 the *Aberdeen Journal* reported the death of William GIBSON, Esq., son of Mr. William GIBSON of the Customs, Glasgow.

Same source: At Hutchisontown on 4 Oct 1813, Robert DOUGLAS Esq. of Honduras married Margaret, daughter of the late Mr. William WATSON, at Abbotsinch.

Same source: Hugh MOODY, Esq. died on 11 Oct 1813 at Honduras, and William LECKIE Esq. died on 19 Oct 1813.

On 24 Jun 1806, the *Aberdeen Journal* reported the death in the Bay of Honduras of Mr. John McLEAN, eldest son of the late Mr. John McLean, merchant of Glasgow.

In May 1813 Henry MARTIN, originally from Glasgow, was murdered by a slave; the *Caledonian Mercury* of April 1814 reported he had emancipated the man in his will. *Magistates Minutes give the date as July 25; the quarrel was over a woman and the killing self defence, but the unfortunate slave, John, was executed for murder.*

Same source: Miss PRINGLE HOME, daughter of the late Alexander Home, Esq, formerly of Bassendean in Berwickshire, died on 15 Apr 1820 at Belize..

In August 1822 the *Worcester and the Hereford Journal* reported the death of Mr. Richard EDWARDS, in the 24th year of his age, describing him as the eldest surviving son of the late Mr. William Edwards of Ludlow; and in March 1825 the death of Charles Edwards, youngest son of the same man, linen draper. St. John's burial register is complete for 1821 and 1822, but does not mention Richard; Charles was buried on 1 Dec 1824.

St. John's register shows the burial of the Rev. John FLEMING and his wife, Amelia, on 13 and 17 Sep 1824. The *Bath Chronicle* describes him as a native of Heytesbury, Wilts, sent out by the Baptist Missionary Scciety in May 1824, and Amelia as the eldest daughter of Charles TALMADGE, mercer, of Oxford; an infant daughter survived them.

St. John's register does not show the burial of Mr. Richard BRIDGE, died 9 Oct 1826, aged 25, son of Captain Thomas BRIDGE of Liverpool. The death was reported in the *Liverpool Mercury*.

Elizabeth Ann Blake was baptized in March 1815 to Geo. H. BLAKE & Jane HUME, Assistant Clerk of Court. The *London Standard* reported that she died on 28 Nov 1827, aged 16, while living with her uncle at 7 Albion Terrace, Canonbury, London. *Was her uncle a Blake or a Hume?*

St. John's register does not show the burial of James HARVIE, son of Mr. Alexander Harvie, merchant of Glasgow, whose death was reported in the *Aberdeen Journal* in October 1826. However, James HARVEY, Poyaisian immigrant, was buried on 25 August 1824. *The same man? Would news have been so slow in reaching Scotland?*

A census return shows Henry POTTAGE as a blacksmith, but the *Leeds Mercury*, reporting his death on 21 May 1828, described him as a whitesmith aged 35, second son of the late Mr. John Pottage, whitesmith, of Wakefield. His wife was Sarah RAEBON or RAYBON. *(Blacksmiths work iron; whitesmiths work tin or pewter.)*

The *Caledonian Mercury* shows the birth on 29 Nov 1829 of a son to Mrs. R. J. ANDREW; St. John's register for 1829-1830, which should have shown the baptism, has not survived.

St. John's register shows Augustus Henry ELSTER, W, London, was buried 5 Dec, 36 years. The *Morning Chronicle* gives the same day of death, but the name as ELITER, aged 37.

St. John's register shows the burial of Mary GAVIN on 28 July 1830. The *Freeman's Journal of Dublin* reported that she died on the 27th, and was the wife of Michael Gavin Esq., Provost Marshal General, and the sister of Mrs. Captain KANE of Whitehall, near Limerick.

Robert and Frances TURNBULL, who appear in baptismal and census records in Belize, were married on 21 Nov 1831 at St. John's; Yorkshire papers described Robert as Esq., and Frances as Fanny GIBSON, granddaughter of Mr. MASKALL of York. *How did Mr. Maskall connect to the Maskalls of Belize?*

George HOME Esq. died in Honduras on 9 Jan 1832; the *Caledonian Mercury* describes him as the only son of the late Alexander HOME, Esq. of Bassendean.

In reporting that Mrs. Elizabeth SCOTS, mother of William, Edwin, and Frederick COFFIN Esqrs, of Honduras, died on 23 Aug 1834 at Belize, aged 68 years, the *Liverpool Mercury* gives us a long sought maiden name. *Sadly, her tomb has not survived.*

In October 1834 at St. Pancras, James WELSH Esq. of Honduras married Angelina TILSTON of New York.

The *Aberdeen Journal* reported the marriage of Margaret DOUGLAS, only daughter of Mr. William BURN of Honduras, to John WILSON, Esq., of Berwick, on 11 Nov 1834 at Edinburgh.

On 25 March 1838, Francis YOUNG Esq., M.D. of Belize, Honduras, died at Morningside. This information is given in the *Caledonian Mercury*.

St. John's register does not show the burial of Mr. Henry PHILPOTT, youngest son of Mr. S. Philpott of Sturry, whose death on 7 Sep 1838 in Belize in his 22nd year was reported in the *Kentish Gazette*.

On 22 Jul 1838, the Rev. W. WEATHERALL, Baptist missionary to Belize, married Selina, youngest daughter of Mr. SPARKES, merchant of Ballingdon, at All Saints

Sudbury, Essex. He left for Belize shortly after the marriage, and died of fever on 10 September 1839, aged 23. *What became of his wife?*

On 4 Nov 1839 at Howden, Mr. Richard WEDDALL, who had trained at the Wesleyan Theological Institution in London and was going out to Honduras as a missionary, married Miss Mildred WEST of Howden. *Did this couple live to have children? So many people did not survive what people called the year of seasoning, but fell victim to tropical diseases and succumbed within weeks or months of their arrival in the colony.*

The *Hampshire Telegraph* reported that John T. LOWER, Esq., Acting Ordnance Stores Keeper, died of fever on 17 Sep 1841. *Active duty men did not appear in censuses; those who died were buried in the military cemetery at the fort or at the barracks..*

In June 1843, Edward SHIEL, Esq. died at Madeira on his passage to Honduras; he was a brother of the Rt. Hon R. L. SHIEL, M.P. Reported in the *Exeter & Plymouth Gazette.*

Patrick WALKER, Esq., the Colonial Secretary of Belize, married Elizabeth CADOGAN, eldest daughter of William Cadogan, Esq, Albion Street, Hyde Park, on 18 Jan 1844 at St. John's Paddington.

The *Yorkshire Gazette* reported that Mr. H. CAMPION, of London, married Marian, second daughter of Mr. ANDREWS of Clarence Street, York, in July 1844 at Belize. *How was Marian related to the merchant R. J. Andrew?*

The birth of a daughter on 15 July 1844 to the lady of Thomas STUART, Esq. *(Isabella BALFOUR STUART)* was reported in the *Glasgow Herald.*

John NEWELL, Esq. son of the late D. Newell, Esq. and grandson of the late William ANDERSON Esq. of Whiteside, Kirk-gunzeon, Galloway, married Fanny DAY BETSON, daughter of D. *(=David)* Betson, Esq. of Belize, at St. John's on 14 Jan 1846. This was reported in the *Dumfries & Galloway Standard. Did William Anderson connect to the Andersons of Belize?*

The *Freeman's Gazette* reported that in London on 1 Jul 1846, John HODGE Esq of Great St. Helens married Maria, relict of Capt. DICKSON of the 86th Regiment, and daughter to the late John GREY, Esq., Treasurer of Honduras. The marriage entry (St Pancras 1 315) gives Maria's surname as DICKINSON.

Archibald MONTGOMERY, Esq., of Belize, married Eliza Anne SAUNDERS at St. James Westminster on 11 May 1847. The *London Standard* gives her address as Golden Square, Regent Street. *Who was her father?*

---o0o---

The *BELIZE ADVERTISER*
June 9th 1839 – January 11th 1840
Henry WHITNEY, Proprietor.

All items of historical and genealogical value in this newspaper are given below in extracts, abstracts, and summaries. There was never enough local news to report, and so, as in the Honduras Gazette of 1826-27, the publisher fleshed out his pages with news from elsewhere in the British Empire, the Caribbean, the U.S., and Central and South America and other parts of the world, focusing on anything concerning trade, the lifeblood of the colony. The Subscriber is the person who wrote the article or placed the advertisement. The printed page numbers, which commence at 180 and jump to the 200's and 300's, are probably not original. Notes and explanations are given in italics. Some advertisements were repeated in later issues; repeats were not copied.

Issue No. 40. Saturday, June 29th 1839, Vol. 1:

Motto at the head of this and each succeeding issue: "Tis not in mortals to command success, but we'll do more, Sempronius. We'll deserve it."

World News: The yellow fever is said in a recent letter from Guadalupe to be making dreadful havoc in that colony, where the first Regiment of Marines is stated to have lost 5 captains, 2 lieutenants, 3 sub-lieutenants, an adjutant and 3 sergeant majors. In the artillery, of a total of 80 men, 53 including 3 captains and a lieutenant had fallen victims to the malady.

p. 180:

Supreme Court, Monday, 24[th:] On Monday last the Court was opened by His Excellency Col. MacDONALD, Her Majesty's Superintendent, President, and their Honors, W[m] MASKALL, James McDONALD, W[m] USHER, John YOUNG, M.D., W[m] GUILD, and Patrick WALKER, Acting Clerk of Courts and Keeper of Government Records, Judges. The New Commission was read... by H. A. GRAY, Esq., Asst. Clerk of Court. Afterwards a respectable Jury was empanelled. No criminal cases... His Excellency commented on the orderly and well behaved conduct of the emancipated apprenticeship... Now upwards of 18 months since any criminal case. Visit of inspection of the Gaol... highly pleased with the cleanliness and improved state in which it is kept.

Grand Court, Tuesday, 25[th:] James McDONALD, William USHER, John YOUNG, M.D., Esqs. The first case was a Replevin issued by Mr. Daniel TILDESLEY, upon the house in possession of Mr. Chas. CRAIG. On Mr. T.'s leaving the country in 1833 he was not indebted to any one. He left a Power of Attorney with Mr. George HYDE for the purpose of receiving monies from him in this place. He left a house and lot hired to Mr. Hyde at

314

Hyde had repeatedly requested Mr. T. to sell him the house and lot that he had hired – this, however, Mr. T. had refused to do, asserting that he would not sell it for any consideration. During Mr. T's absence in England Mr. Hyde gave a Bill of Sale to Mr. Craig with a receipt that £350 had been paid for it, notwithstanding that he well knew, according to the statement of Mr. T., that he, Mr. T., would not have sold it for treble that sum, and that not being indebted to any person here, there was not the slightest occasion for the disposal of any portion of his property. Mr. C. Craig in his defence produced a Bill of Sale given him by Mr. George Hyde, and Hyde showed a Power of Attorney from Tildesley. The jurors had some doubts as to the validity of the Power of Attorney as it was not on the Records of the Court, but a majority of the magistrates observed that it was valid to all intents and purposes, the jurors could not do otherwise than return a verdict unfavorable to the grossly injured party Mr. Tildesley. A Gentleman present in the Court upon the occasion, who has filled the Magistrates Chair for many years with the greatest credit to himself and benefit to the public, was much surprised at the decision as to the validity of the Power of Attorney; he however, like ourselves, is too accustomed to the world's hackneyed ways to be surprised at anything.

It is not unworthy of remark that Mr. T. went to the expense of several pounds, a short time before he sailed for England, to have his property formally recorded by the Clerk of Court & Keeper of Records.

The next case that occupied the attention of the Court was Thomas WAKEFIELD -v- Steamer *Vera Paz* & Owners, for arrears of wages due. Plaintiff produced an agreement by a Company with a very magnificent title, viz., "The Eastern Coast of Central America Commercial and Agricultural Company," showing he was hired for 3 years at £10 per month, as Engineer of the steamer. The agreement was a most illegal document on the part of the Company. The wages of every alternate month were to remain in the Company's hands as security for his good behavior; upon the slightest fault against him the Agent of the Company or Commander of the Vessel had it in their power to turn him adrift in a foreign country without providing him a passage back to his own – and in short, every care was taken by this liberal Company to protect its own interests and totally disregard those of its servants. The Plaintiff after doing duty on board the steamer for about 14 months became anxious for a settlement for the first 12 months of service past, particularly as the pittance of 10/- a week that he had stipulated should be allowed his wife during his absence had been stopped since April or May 1838, leaving her destitute. He was told by Mr. KENNEDY, the Agent for the Company, that he should be paid as soon as he (Mr. K.) was in possession of funds, as his claim was undoubtedly just. Unfortunately, however, shortly after this Mr. K. resigned and retired to England.

Mr. YOUNG ANDERSON, Superintendent of the Company's noble town of "New Liverpool," assumed the direction of the Company's affairs; he, of course, defended the action against the company, and most unwarrantably used his utmost endeavors to vilify the character of the plaintiff, accusing him of desertion. His efforts, however, were most completely abortive, and he admitted the skill and diligence of the engineer. The Jury found for the Plaintiff for the balance of wages due him in this country, but referred settlement of the amount arising from the accumulation of the alternate months to a Court of Justice in England.

p. 181:

Last case, Thursday 27th, HYDE, George & HYDE & PETZOLD –v– HYDE, FORBES & Co.; countersuit, each for £10,000. Patrick WALKER, Esq. took oath as Magistrate.

Belize Amateur Theatre. On the arrival of Col. McDONALD the national anthem was played by the Orchestra. Mr. George M. USHER recited a prologue. "Peter Punctillio or the Gentleman in Black" was dramatised, and an old farce, "Bombastes Furioso," performed by Messrs. G. M. USHER, Fred. LINDO, T. COX, J. McDONALD and A. McLENAN.

To the Editor of the Belize Advertiser:
Sir: In your paper of late Saturday you have grossly misrepresented the testimony that I gave on oath, on the examination of Captain CAREY of the barque *La Bonne Mere,* at the Court House. My evidence was as follows:

I stated that on going alongside and speaking the vessel, I asked the Captain the following questions: Where he was from? he answered, Demerara; If there was any sickness on board, answer, No. I then questioned the Pilot, and asked him what was wrong with the Mate? He made the same reply as Capt. Carey did, that he was struck by one of the spars of the Studding Sail Boom, and partly occasioned by drinking. I then left the vessel.

I expect, Sir, that you will do me the justice to insert this. I am Sir, your obed't serv't. *(signed)* Philip MEIGHAN.

We cheerfully give insertion to the above… we shall be always willing to make the amende honorable, by acknowledging our error.

p. 181:

Saturday evening, 7 p.m.
Special Jury engaged since 9 a.m. on Thursday on HYDE's case, deciding on the merits of the cases… for a settlement of accounts. Verdicts:

HYDE, and HYDE & PETZOLD … for plaintiffs, £2024.16.10 with costs.

Judgement against HYDE & PETZOLD   £9095. 11. 11
  Ditto in favor of HYDE, George, £8288.10.10
Ditto against HYDE PETZOLD & BETSON,   <u>2806. 16. 05</u>
             £<u>11901. 08. 04</u>

Certificate of Dr. WILLS exonerates Capt. CAREY of charge of bringing contagion to our shores.

Shipping Information: *(Date, kind and name of ship, name of master, city the ship come from and any port en route, and the company to which the cargo was consigned.)*

Arrived:
29th: Brig *Friendship*, LAWSON, London, last Jamaica, 5 days, to Alex BRYMNER, Esq; Schooner *Rolls* - New Orleans, 12 days to R. J. ANDREWS & CO.

Sailed:
27th: Barque *McInroy*, SINCLAIR - Monkey River to load.
29th: " *La Bonne Mere*, CAREY - Ulloa, ditto.

The drogher *Reform* arrived at the Bogue on Thursday last from Rio Hondo – her second trip with mahogany for the barque *Fair Arcadian*, now loading there.

Passengers arrived:
In the *Friendship*, Alexander BRYMNER Esq. and lady.

Gazette, Secretary's Office, 27th June 1839: His Excellency has been pleased to appoint the Undersigned to be one of the Magistrates of Honduras. By Command, Patrick WALKER, Secretary.

Belize Agricultural Company- Meeting of Shareholders. L. P. COX, Sec., James WOODS.

For Public and Positive Sale: The Ship *Minerva*, as also the Yards, Standing and Running Rigging, Anchors, Chain Cables, Sails, Rope, and a quantity of Iron Ballast. Also the Stores of the said Vessel - Barrels of Beef, Pork, and Flour, bags of Bread, Coffee, and Cocoa. The main and fore Masts of the Vessel will be allowed to remain, and she will be placed in a situation convenient for being hove down and stripped of her copper. James McDONALD, Agent appointed by the Captain.

Boarding House. Miss Margaret JONES respectfully acquaints her Friends and the Public, that she has taken the spacious Premises belonging to Mme. J. J. RABOTEAU, on the South side of the Town, to establish a Table for the reception of regular Boarders of Respectability... the strictest attention will be paid in supplying every thing of the best which the Markets of Belize will afford. Belize, June 20th 1839.

Notice: The Subscriber begs to inform persons who have Tanks to repair or build up, that he has just procured a quantity of Roman Cement and will engage to perform either on the most reasonable terms.... Thomas WILLIAMS.

All persons having claims against the Estate of the late Charles MIDDLETON and indebted to the same... Stuart M. THOMSON, Agent for the Executors. 8th June 1839.

For Sale by the Subscriber: Imported by the *McInroy* and *Fair Arcadian* from London, Ale and Porter in Casks. 3 dozen each Wine, Champagne, Cognac. Butter in Firkins. Hams. Pork and Flour in barrels. Preserved Meats in canisters, preserved fruits in stone bottles. Paint... Pomatum, Macassar Oil and other Perfumery. Mould, Sperm, and Wax Candles. Gents Wellingtons, Cloth, Cossack Boots. Ladies Kid and Prunella Shoes. Shawls, handkerchiefs. Full dress Tortoiseshell Hair Combs. Ladies and Gent's Silk Hose and fine Cotton ditto. Jaconet, mull, cross bar, striped, and satin spot Muslins. Assorted Pearl and other Buttons for Shirts, and Cambric for do. Gingham Dresses, in 6 and 12 yard pieces. Fancy Prints and Handkerchiefs. Green Baize, Duck and Oznaburgs... Patent Leads for Mordens ever pointed Pencils; Stationery. Soaps, in 28 and 56 lb. boxes. Blacking...

And by the *Historian* from New York, Almonds, Prunes, and Raisins in small boxes. Currants for Pastry. Pilot and Navy Bread, and Water Crackers... Hams... Lard... Kentucky and Cavendish Tobacco, Linseed and Whale Oil, Tar, Pitch... Black Pepper... Pails and Brooms... Garden Seeds...

By the *Othello* from Jersey, liquers in cases...
For Sale: Imported from St. Croix for sale, Jamaica Rum, Proof 18, Jamaican Sugar, Cases Bitters... R. J. ANDREWS & Co.

Notice: To be sold immediately after the Venditional Sales,* on Sat. 29th June 1839, on behalf of the Public Funds by order of the Superintendent: Allotments of Land in vicinity of Town of Belize, forfeited for non-compliance with the Terms upon which the Grants were issued. Provost Marshal General's Office, 18th June. 1839 *Public auctions.*

p. 182:

The British Constitution Produced... *(a sketch of British political history since 1649.)*

Imported per the *Historian* and for sale by the Subscribers: Flour, coffee, barrels and half barrels Mackeral, boxes Codfsh, bales 6-4 India Matting, Cases Axes and Hatchets, etc. etc. R. J. ANDREWS & CO.

For Sale, Cordage of all sizes, hawsers, etc., Hogsheads of Superior Brandy, Geneva, Cases of Hollands... At a liberal credit, the Schooner Boat *Crusader* and extensive premises at Supa Ridge cornering the property of Wm MASKELL Esq., per De ST. CROIX & CO, W. E. HAMPSHIRE, 20th June 1829.

To be sold immediately – Irish Prime Mess Pork, Double Rose Butter, and Smoked Bacon, all of the best quality, and moderate. Jno MacDONALD.

Note: Issue No. 41 is missing.

No. 42, Saturday, July 13th 1839, Vol. 1:

Sir: Mr. YOUNG ANDERSON deserves a better fate than to superintend such an unthankful undertaking as the Central American Agricultural, Commerical, and Colonization Company. The following lines are from *Blackwoods Magazine:*

Song of Migration:

"Away, away o'er the foaming main
This was the free and the joyous strain.
There are clearer skies than ours afar
We will shape our course by a brighter star.
There are plains whose verdure no foot has pressed
And whose wealth is all for the first brave guest.
But, alas! that we should go!
Sang the farewell voices then,
From the home-steads warm and low
By the brook and in the glen…

We will give the names of our fearless race
To each bright river whose course we trace…
Home, Home, and friends, farewell!"

I only wish, Mr. Editor, that these projectors would come out… would find mosquitoes, bay-sores, rheumatisms, a scorching sun and fevers, death… A Subscriber, 18th June 1839.

Summary Court. Magistrates Wm MASKALL, Wm USHER, John YOUNG M.D., Patrick WALKER Esqrs.

Complaint of Alexander FORBES Esq. attorney to John F. AUGUST Esq. -v- Henry BROWN, Sam BILLY, Paulina, Martin BROSTER, Joe GENTLE and Clementine. The prisoners, who were engaged in cutting logwood in the New River for Mr. J. BOWEN, had stolen two cattle the property of Mr. AUGUST. Mr. MASKALL, who had left the Bench, was sworn, and stated that he visited New River to look after his cattle, and heard some bearing his brand had been killed by the people. He went to Mr. Bowen's bank, found the track of the cattle that had been shot and slaughtered, and was able to identify them from marks on the horns as having been disposed by him to Mr. August. The prisoners were sentenced to 12 months imprisonment at hard labour.

Importance of planting Cotton – Belize now in a critical situation as Mahogany, its staple commodity, is getting scarce… Some shareholders of the Belize Agricultural Co. are so dissatisfied from the bad prospects, many have expressed an inclination to forfeit the first installment already paid up and withdraw themselves…

Mr. FLETCHER, who arrived from England in the Barque *Sarah,* is on his way to Guatemala charged from some London Merchants to the Government, to establish a Bank in that city. Should the former succeed… to have a Branch Bank in Belize…

Note: With civil war in the Central American States and dictators battling for power, readers of the Advertiser would have considered any Guatemalan bank as highly unsafe.

319

Rebellion at Tismin: a criminal named IMAN with deserters had gone to San Fernando. Central America: General MORAZON at head of the Federal Army… General FERRARA of the Allied People's Army… meditating the most sanguinary butchery… a people devoted to destruction.

p. 188:

Mahogany got out: River Montagua, June 24th: Mr. FOREMAN, 180 logs. River San Francisco, June 26^{th:} Mr. PITKEITHLY, 264 logs, Mr. ADOLPHUS, 130, Mr. BLAKE, 112.

It will appear by an advertisement in our present number that John MacDONALD, Esq. has again got himself into a "scrape." It is somewhat surprising that a man of his age and consequent knowledge of the world, and experience in business should be so often mistaken in making his bargains. We wish him "better luck next time."

We are informed that the Mate and one Seaman of the barque *Science*, loading at the Rio Tinto, were unfortunately drowned at that place a short time since.

Discourse by the Rev. Mr. GREENWOOD, Wesleyan Minister, in the Wesleyan Chapel on the 30th ultimo.

p. 189:

Shipping Information:
Arrived 11^{th:} Barque *Sarah,* ADOLPHUS, Omoa 2 days in ballast, to Messrs. HYDE, FORBES & Co.

H. M. Packet *Hope,* Lt. REES, Commander, from Falmouth, G.B., with the May mail on board, left Wednesday for Vera Cruz after taking on board Specie to a large amount, shipped by some of the merchants here. H. M. Brig *Pilot*, Commander RAMSAY, sailed Thursday for Jamaica with a detachment of Artillery, relieved by those who arrived on the same vessel. Brig *Favorite* to leave England for this port a few days after the sailing of the *Hope* Packet.

For Public Auction at the Store of the Subscriber, to be resold on account and risk of the original purchaser, Mr. John MacDONALD, he having failed to comply with the Terms of Sale as then declared, being articles landed and others on board the Ship *Minerva.* By order of James Mc'DONALD, Esq., Agent appointed by the Captain, July 12th 1839. James WOODS, Auctioneer.

Belize Amateur Theatre, on Wednesday evening 17th July – The Admired Comedy of the Mock Doctor or the Dumb Lady Cured. Characters: Gregory, Mr. SNODGRASS. Sir Jasper, Mr. FARREN. James, Mr. TWISS. Harry, Mr. WINCLE. Squire Robert, Mr. OXBERRY. Doctor Hellebore, Mr. Sam WELLER. Leander (a lover,) Mr. LOVEL. Charlotte, Miss C. BYRON. Dorcas, Mrs. NESBIT. To conclude with (by particular

320

desire,) Mr. Peter Punctillio, The Gentleman in Black. Mr. Peter Punctillio, Mr. FARREN. Mr. Solid, Mr. SNODGRASS. Frank Forage, Mr. TWISS. Snip, Mr. TOMLINS. Cecelia, Miss BOBSTER. Sally, Louisa BOBSTER.

Notice of Survey – Having been employed by Mr. Francis YOUNG to survey the Southern Boundary of his Grant at Silver Creek, I hereby give notice to each and all concerned that at or after the expiration of 22 days from Date, I shall proceed to run the said Line as by bearing and distance laid down by the Crown plan. ... H. GARDINER, Sworn Surveyor.

p. 190:

About 1st May 1837 several queries were drawn up by Mr. J. B. and submitted by Mr. George HYDE, relative to the Cotton and labourers in the Bahamas... which being transmitted through Major ANDERSON to his brother at Nassau... Replies received from Mr. Robert MILLAR there... Mr MILLAR, at the head of Bahama planters, says a planter from Demerara procured 101 liberated Africans to accompany him back under indentures for three years at $5 per month... cost $2000 to charter a vessel to convey them to Demerara. The temperature and latitude of Honduras and Belize is much the same. About 300-400 weight seed cotton to the acre, yielding 100 – 120 lbs clean cotton to the acre. One able bodied man can tend 5 acres, fifty hands including women and children aged 10-14 years can manage 300 acres of cotton and corn. Plant annually... recommend Georgia seed. *(One would think that Mr. J. B. was Mr. James W. Bowen.)*

Notice: Closing the affairs of the Estate of J. H. PETZOLD, Dec'd. Alexander FORBES, Attorney to the Heirs. 5th July 1839.

Note: Issues 43 and 44 are missing.

No. 45, Saturday, August 3rd 1839, Vol. 1:

Saturday, Aug 3: ...a Bill to provide certain laws for the Island of Jamaica... Several fires have taken place on different estates and some acts of violence have been committed, occasioning not only serious injuries to individuals but loss of life. Even those labourers who engage to work cannot be depended on, many instances having occurred where they have done the hardest labour, such as digging holes for planting cane, for which they receive extra wages, yet afterwards refuse to plant the canes in the holes they have been paid for digging, because the work being easier they do not get paid such high wages; and on Coffee properties they will not undertake the easy task of keeping the young coffee free from weeds, nor when the place gets too foul will they undertake to clear it, because the work being laborious they cannot get over it quickly... The situation of the Planters is as vexatious as it is precarious.

Her Majesty's schooner *Pickle* fell in with a slaver last month off the Isle of Pines, and after a chase of six hours drove her ashore, when the crew perceiving the schooner boats approaching to take them, after throwing several of the poor slaves overboard, swam ashore themselves. On taking possession of the slaver 180 poor negroes were found in her in a most emaciated state – 225 had been the original number. Lt. HOLLAND, of the *Pickle,* was obliged to remove them into his own vessel as the *Sierra Del Pilar,* the slaver, though got off, was in danger of foundering; but having such an addition to his complement was obliged to steer for the Havanna, the nearest port, where from the papers found on board the slaver, she was condemned.

Coronation - On Thursday the 25th, the double Ceremony of a Marriage and a Coronation took place in Belize, the latter rivaling in splendour that most elaborately splendid one of his lamented Majesty the late George the Fourth. The renowned Nelson SHAW, whose qualities of bravery and eloquence equal, if not exceed, those said to be possessed by the magnanimous Macedonian, who cried because there were no more worlds to conquer, was the King, and Lucy BODE, whose beauty and chastity have long been the theme of every tongue, was Queen – their dominions are in the hearts of their Subjects and their subjects in the heart of their dominions. The ceremony was most august... numerous toasts... On Sunday last their Majestys proceeded in State to Church... beautiful anthem... His Highness Prince Mingo STEWART and the majority of the most distinguished Nobles and their Ladies were present on the occasion... After the service, a dejeuner a la fourchette*...

Fork breakfast; a cold collation with meat and wine; lunch.

On Thursday last, 1st August, our Town was enlivened by a numerous procession of both sexes, carrying flags, and proceeded by our Militia Band playing "Twas In the Merry Month of May," went to church to attend divine service and give thanks for their complete emancipation, on the 1st anniversary of that great event. ... They then proceeded to Government House to pay their respects to Col. McDONALD. The Hon. John BOWEN, appointed poet laureate, delivered a suitable speech. King Nelson and his Queen, who of course were present, behaved in the most dignified manner. Parties, drinking, dancing....

Letter from London, 15th June last – Cargo of Mahogany sold on 11th did not fetch quite 5 3/4d per foot... Large stock of small wood in the market. In Liverpool, stock is now 651,000 feet, of which 111,000 are in the hands of importers. There will be a large sale of St. Domingo wood here (London) shortly. Logwood sales keep declining, present price is about £8 although I have not heard of any sales having been made at that rate. The stock is now 1703 tons with a heavy importation shortly expected.

Fire alarm on Thursday night, at 10 o'clock in South West suburbs of Belize. Fire engines sped to the spot and speedily extinguished the fire. Fire wardens met, and awarded No. 2 Engine £10 and No. 1 £5, and to Henry GARDNER, whose exertions to extinguish the fire were most arduous and who received a severe fall, £2. They also ordered two lanthorns to be attached to each engine and fresh suction pipes to be procured. A witness said that "notwithstanding all the exertions of Mr. GARDNER, had it not been for Mr. William PEEBLES, the poor old woman to whom the house belonged would not have saved a vestige of her property. He was the first on the spot and, perceiving the poor woman standing outside almost in a state of nudity and stupefied with terror and grief, he

322

immediately, on ascertaining there were no children in danger, proceeded to take out, unassisted by any one, her property, in which laudable attempt though with much exertion and some injury to himself, he succeeded."

Letters to the Editor: On religion, signed, A Methodist. Hints for Establishing a Circulating Library, signed, Amicus Redivivus.

p. 200:

Letters: Advocating formation of a Literary and Scientific Society, signed, H. & U. F. C. On celibacy: "I have and shall ever have the terror of Matrimony – would as soon be tied to the tail of a mad horse as to be tied to any woman..." signed, An Inveterate Bachelor.

Government Secretary's Office, Belize 31st July 1839. The Secretary respectfully begs to direct the attention of the public to the following in the Navigation Act 3 & 4 W. IV: - All Ships built in the British Settlements in Honduras and owned and navigated as British Ships shall be entitled to the privileges of British Registered Ships in all direct trade between the United Kingdom or the British possessions in America and the said Settlements, provided the Master shall produce a Certificate in the hand of the Superintendent of those Settlements that satisfactory proof has been received before him that said Ship was built in said Settlement and is wholly owned by British Subjects, and time of clearance of said ship from said settlement for every voyage shall be endorsed upon said certificate by said Superintendent. Patrick WALKER, Government Secretary.

Gazette HQ, 31st July 1839: 1st Lieut J. H. CADDY of the Royal Artillery to be Adjutant of the Honduras Artillery, vice J. W. PATTEN who has retired from the Service. By command, Jas. R. MACDONALD, Military Secretary.

Shipping Information:

Arrived:
July 30th: Brig *James Lyon*, SHEDDON, Liverpool, general cargo to Messrs R. J. ANDREWS & CO.
July 31st: Barque *William,* BLACK, Demerara, Ulloa, to George A. USHER, Esq.
" Barque *William Shana* POTTS, Jamaica, ballast to William VAUGHAN, Esq.
" Ship *Admiral Moorsom*, METCALFE, Jamaica, ballast to Messrs. R. J. ANDREW & Co.

Sailed:
July 28th: Barque *Fair Arcadian*, RODGERS, London, 219 logs (138,695 feet) mahogany, 40 tons logwood, 195 seroons cochineal, 89 ditto indigo, 500 cocoa-nuts, cleared by Messrs. YOUNG & TOLEDO.
Aug 1st: Barque *Science*, McLENAN, Liverpool, 124,587 feet mahogany 52 tons logwood, cleared by A. BRYMNER Esq.
" Brig Friendship, LAWSON, Cork, for orders, 85,294 feet making 24 ½ tons logwood, 1500 lbs sarsaparilla, cleared by same.

323

"   Brig *Lord Lampton,* PRATT, Cork, 102,802 feet mahogany, 40 tons logwood, cleared by W. VAUGHAN, Esq.

"   Brig *M'Inroy,* SINCLAIR, Glasgow, 70,726 feet mahogany, 57 tons logwood, cleared by same.

Aug 3rd:   Brig *Mary Ann,* HAMPTON, New-York, 28,819 feet mahogany, 34 ½ tons Logwood, cleared by Messrs. COFFIN & CO.

The following vessels are expected from England: The barque *Lavinia,* HILL, from London, in ballast, consigned to Messrs. R. J. ANDREW & Co., arrived at Omoa on the 23rd inst. *Elizabeth & Jane* via Jamaica; *Wandsbeck* via Demerara, sailed on May 30th; *Sutherland,* via Barbados, sailed June 12th; *Duncan; Norns; Trinidad; Perseverence; Ardent,* via Demerara, sailed May 30th; *Orynthia* via Demerara, sailed May 31st; *Ceylon; Mariner,* via Trinidad, sailed June 3rd; *Europa; Mary.*

Mr. LEE, Clerk to the Commissariat Department, came passenger in the *William Shand* from Jamaica; and Mr. & Mrs. HOLMES went passengers in the *McInroy,* for London, Edwin COFFIN and YOUNG ANDERSON Esq'rs in the *Mary Ann,* for New York – and Mr. James W. BOWEN in the *Science.*

The Brig *Alert* arrived from Nassau, N.P. this forenoon. *(N.P. = New Providence.)*

p. 201:

Public Notice: Notice is hereby given that from and after this day and date I will not become responsible for any debts contracted by my reputed wife Ann Maria MORRIS. Thomas MORRIS. Belize, 19th July 1839.

Survey - Having been employed to run a Division Line between Sancho COOKROM and Ants Nest Lagoon Works, in Spanish Creek, commencing at Sancho Cookrom and running a-back a course due West... Joseph SMITH, Sworn Surveyor. July 18th 1839.

Public Auction: In consequence of the death of Madame FOURMEAUX, the firm of FORMEAUX & ROUQUIE is hereby dissolved. Stock of goods belonging to the late establishment will be offered for Public Competition twice per week till cleared off. Ladies and Gentlemen may obtain articles by private purchase on other days... *(no signature.)* Belize, July 18th 1839.

For Sale: Barrels of Fresh Superfine Flour, and Prime Mess Pork. Patrick De BRIEN.

Estate of S. T. ANDERSON, Dec'd. The undersigned Trustees in the above Estate are now prepared to pay a first Dividend of 8/4d per 20/-. Persons to whom the above Estate is indebted are requested to call for payment. Geo. A. USHER, Leonard P. COX, Trustees. Belize, 25th July 1839.

Note: Issues 46 and 47 are missing.

324

No. 48, Saturday, August 24ᵗʰ 1839, Vol 1:

The Bank of England resolved that the rate of interest on bills and notes discounted at the Bank of England be 5½% from this day.

Editorial: The declining price of cotton...

Fourth Anniversary of the Belize Branch of the Wesleyan Missionary Society. Chair, William MASKALL, Esq. The meeting was addressed by William H. COFFIN and John ARMSTRONG, Esqrs... The Rev. S. STANTON and Captain SODEN (in his uniform), the Rev. John GREENWOOD, and James BANKS, and W. E. HAMPSHIRE, Esqrs... Collection totaled £37. Information was given about missionary work around the world.

p. 212:

The Amateur Theatre closed on Wednesday Evening for the season. Farewell address by Mr. SNODGRASS, followed by a "petit souper", with music and dancing.

In the harbour is a beautiful Baltimore clipper, late from Campeche. She is well armed and manned, no less than 13 men and possesses every requisite for carrying on a forced trade, and is suspected by the "knowing ones" of having come for the purpose of purchasing Goods to supply the provinces westward of Campeche and in the Mexican Gulf. A person who has been on board reports that he has seen a large quantity of specie in the possession of the Captain and Supercargo. We should like to hear from the Public Searcher a true account of this schooner, as we have no doubt he visited her immediately on her arrival. Since the arrival of Mr. BROWN (who left here lately) from the province of Tobasco, a complete mania exists among certain individuals who, as a last resort to gain a livelihood by force-trading in that province are endeavoring to get advances from merchants; the latter are of course not so simple as to lay out their property on adventures that are likely to turn out like so many other speculations – beautiful and imposing in idea, but the results ruinous to all concerns...

Note: The last lines should be mandatory reading for speculators everywhere!

Captain WILLIAMS and Captain HILL, both of the 2ⁿᵈ West India, are reported to have died, the former in England and the latter on his passage from Jamaica to Nassau.

Mr. COX of this place, who in conjunction with Mr. FRANCE has a gang in the River Roman cutting mahogany, on proceeding to join them met people coming down from the Bank, in course of having being warned by the Spaniard to leave it, upon pain of being expelled by force, the place being as they alleged, without the pale of the English limits. Mr. COX having in vain endeavored to prevail on them to return with him, went to Truxillo to remonstrate with the authorities there.

Shipping Information: Belize, Saturday August 24ᵗʰ 1839:

Arrived:

17th: H. M. Packet *Swift*, Commander WELCH, Falmouth, GB, last the Havana, with the June mails – she left the following morning for Vera Cruz.

" Brig *Victoria*, MAY, New York, 22 days, with an assorted cargo to J. E. SWASEY Esq.

21st: Schooner *Morning Star*, BARNET, Nassau (N. P.,) last from Jamaica, in 5 days to J. E. SWASEY Esq.

Sailed:

20th: Barque *Arab*, ROBINSON, Cork, with 302 logs (219843 feet) mahogany, 68 tons logwood and 8000 cocoa-nuts.

24th: Schooner *Alert*, WILSON, Nassau (N. P.) with 60 tons logwood and a box of tortoise shell.

The barque *Elizabeth & Jane*, HART, in 38 days from London, arrived at Kingston, Jamaica on the 9th instant, bound for this port. The barque *Ceylon* was to leave London on the 15th instant.

Notice: The Subscriber not being able to devote his personal attention to his Cotton Estate at Seven Hills, offers for sale on lease for 5 or 7 years, the whole of the Improvements on that Estate, consisting of Provisions – about 2,300 Plaintain Suckers in full bearing, 1000 planted in June last – Fields of Rice, Corn, Cocoa, Yams and Yampa* – 1 acre Sugar Cane. Cotton Fields, about 25 acres just planted off, and Land cleared and burned off, which may be filled with Cotton to the extent of 80 or 100 acres, before December next. For Terms, apply to W.USHER.

Yampa is a root crop, Perideridia gairdneri. Tasting like sweet parsnip, the root can eaten as a snack, cooked as a vegetable, or ground into flour for baking cakes.

For Sale, A New Cutter or Gig, 16 or 17 feet long, with 4 Oars, Rudder, &c. complete – May be seen at the Subscriber's Premises. W. USHER.

Notice: All persons having any Demands against the firm of FOURMAUX & ROUQUIE are requested to bring in their Accounts to be liquidated, and all those indebted to the Firm to come forward to settle their account immediately, as the Subscriber is about to leave the Settlement…if not paid, to be sued next Court. N. B. – 3 Notices as above mentioned have been put up in the Court House 3 days following and torn off as soon as they appeared. The Undersigned informs the Public that they shall make a Sale on Tuesday next 27th for Fourmaux & Rouquie. D. VIELAJUS.

p. 213:

Another Capture of an Hispano-American Slaver – More Developments – the Slave Trade – The Way it is Done. Arrival at Quarantine of another American slave vessel – getting to be an every day occurrence. The vessel was the brig *Wyoming*, formerly owned in New York, and brought here under the command of Lt. C. H. of the Royal Navy, attached to

H.M.S. *Harlequin,* Lord Francis RUSSELL, Commander, one of the English fleet off the coast of Africa.

It appears the *Wyoming* was sold to Capt. John EDWARDS of New London, Connecticut, who purchased her expressly for the slave trade, and who previously owned the brig *Texas* which runs between Havana and New Orleans. He shipped a Spanish crew and Spanish supercargo, 14 Spanish passengers who were well known on the coast as notorious slave factors. They then sailed from Havana for the River Gallinas with a cargo of blacks...

On the 18th Captain EDWARDS burst a blood vessel and died the same day. Immediately before his death he admitted he was on a slave cruise... When captured he had no slaves on board, and like the *Clara* and *Eagle* displayed the American flag. Capt. Edwards is of Connecticut, a State that pretends to great sanctity but will occasionally dip into slavery, though many of the inhabitants are such rank abolitionists. (*New York Herald*, July 6th.)

Upwards of 100 beautiful American clipper-built brigs are engaged in the trade at this moment... A ship master in Havana was offered $4000 to make a single trip. Nearly every slaver that has recently been captured has had an American ship master on board; he, of course, is immediately set at liberty, and so are the Spaniards, but their property confiscated... In the meantime, what will be done with the *Wyoming, Clara, and Eagle?* Can our Government do anything with them? Will an arrangement be effected between the American and British governments for the capture of all slavers with the American flag?

A sermon by an English parson, the Rev. Mr. STEPHENS, quoted at length. The Queen was conducted through the streets of London by her courtiers to the Royal Theatre to see wild animals, lions and tigers, fed rounds of beef and legs of mutton, while in the Strand Union Workhouse there was more bloodshed, more awful crimes committed, her people starve...

Mahogany trees for sale in the River Roman. Terms... on application at the store of Messrs. WELSH & GOUGH. Thomas JENNINGS, Belize, 14th August 1839.

For Sale: Of late importation, barrels or ½ barrels fine Navy Bread, suited for Droghers and Coasting Boats. Hogsheads and bales long leaf Tobacco, fine flavour. Boxes of Codfish, Kegs of Lard, and Prime Yorkshire Hams. W. M. VAUGHAN, 15th Aug 1839.

Notice: All persons to whom the Estate of the late George L. GRISTOCK is indebted are requested to send in their accounts duly attested to the Subscriber on or before Saturday the 14th proximate... All indebted... make immediate payment or they will be sued indiscriminately at the ensuing Courts. J. WOODS, Attorney to the Trustees of the Estate of G. L. Grimstock, Dec'd. Belize, 21st August 1839.

No. 49: Saturday, August 31st 1839, Vol. 1:

An article giving a very detailed comparison of wages in England and the West Indies. The totals show Jamaican negro labourers are better off by £48 sterling each year than English labourers.

p. 215:

An article about the treaty between Guatemala and other Central American states.

Police Office – On Tuesday last an examination took place before Wm MASKALL and Lewis McLENAN, Esqs - Julius De BRIEN on complaint of his wife. *(Tongue in cheek account of the quarrel, ending)* ...the lady saluted the mug of her lord and master with a mug of such a different description that the poor fellow's seriously injured by the collision... he is presently under the doctor's hands and in a very precarious state – defendant remanded for a further examination when the medical gentleman is prepared to make a report. *(The lady was Eliza De Brien – see issue 55.)*

p. 216:

Shareholders in the Belize Agricultural Company having been called in by the Directors to pay a further instalment do not respond to the call as they ought to do, but demur... To be regretted... Cultivating cotton is a very different thing from cutting mahogany.

About 9 o'clock on Thursday evening Serjeant KEAN's premises at Yarborough were entered by two incendiaries for the purpose of setting his house on fire. They were discovered and the mischief prevented, the scoundrels making their escape. A great number of the very worst description of American Spaniards at present residing amongst us requires an unusual degree of vigilance on the part of our Police...

An unfortunate Spaniard, sent to the plantation of the Belize Agricultural Company at Ambergris, arrived at a key and retired to rest, after partaking of which he found his dory adrift. Being in view, he attempted to regain her by embarking on a plank and using his hands for paddles, but in vain... after gaining a landing on the main land, he traveled for near nine days without arriving at any human habitation, and was without food during the whole of that period. His person is so dreadfully emaciated, that he might be exhibited to advantage as a living skeleton.

Some Spanish Performers, commonly known in Belize by name of "The Piaso," are erecting a building on the Premises adjoining those of Miss Mary HUME for the purpose of exhibiting their performances. It is most intolerable that these strollers should be permitted (if indeed they have permission from the Governor) to establish themselves in a populous part of our Town, to the excessive annoyance of the peaceable inhabitants. Their clamour...

A facetious Letter to the Editor, concerning productions such as "Cuddie Headriggs and his old chum Guse Gubbie..." signed, A Creole.

An article on Temperance, quoting Dr. PATTON as stating that on autopsy, the blood and liquid in the brains of alcoholics contain so much alcohol that these substances burn when put to a candle.

Shipping Information, Saturday, August 31st 1839:

Arrived:
24th: Schooner *Guatemala Packet,* LE BRUN, Havana, with sundries consigned to
            F. CAMOYANO, Esq.
25th: Steamer *Vera Paz,* LOPEZ, Yzabal.

Sailed:
27th: Schooner *Guatemala Packet,* LE BRUN, Havana, 107 seroons indigo, 43 ditto
            cochineal, 2000 Hides, 14 bales sarsaparilla, cleared by F. CAMOYANO,
            Esq.
         Schooner *Rosella,* WALKER, Truxillo.
         Schooner *Morning Star,* BARNET, ditto.
30th: Steamer *Vera Cruz,* LOPEZ, Yzabal.
         Schooner *San Pedro,* LOPEZ, [sic], ditto.

The barques *William Shand,* and *Sarah,* and brig *Joseph Hume* are now nearly loaded, and will sail shortly. The droghers *John Inglis* and *Eliza* are actively employed running the mahogany with which the above vessels are loading. The drogher *Alice* arrived on Thursday evening from Yzabal with a cargo of American Lumber for Marshal BENNETT, Esq. The brig *Lady Mary Fox* arrived late yesterday evening from Truxillo with 90 logs mahogany, to fill up here.

For Great Britain: The Brig *Carron,* J. POTTER, Master, will leave this Port on or about the 6th September and call at Cork, for orders. All demands against the above Vessel or Master must be rendered previous to the above date, otherwise they will not be paid. Geo. A. USHER, Belize, 29th Aug 1839.

The Subscriber offers for sale at Black Creek, 200 head of Prime Cattle in lots to suit Purchasers. Among them are many Heavy Working Steers and the whole are in the best condition – fit either for the Truck or Market. J. WALKER, 31st August 1839.

For Sale, A Negro Yard, with 5 lately erected Negro Rooms, in the rear of the premises of Mr. John COLLINS. Also a Negro Yard, with 5 Negro Rooms, built last year at the elbow of the Canal, opposite the Shop occupied by Captain Andrew BELL. J. WELSH, 31st August 1839.

To be Rented: The House and Premises lately occupied by the Rev. Mr. GREENWOOD. For particulars apply to Patrick C. De BRIEN.

For Sale: A fine tractable pony, late the property of a Person deceased. Apply at this Office.

Notice of Survey: Having been employed to survey the Upper Line of a Works granted to Dorlisca NOEL in Labouring Creek, I hereby give Notice that I intend to run the said line 21 days from the date hereof according to the Government plan. Joseph SMITH, Sworn Surveyor. Belize, 7th August 1839.

p. 217:

Notice: For the 3rd and last time, Estate of the late Geo. L. GRIMSTOCK... J. WOODS, Attorney to the Trustees...

Note: Issue No. 50 is missing.

No. 51, Saturday, September 14th 1839, Vol. 1:

The Responsibility of Britain for Slavery in the States: England's cotton mills and manufacturers are to blame for encouraging Georgia planters to continue slavery.

p. 223:

Editorial quotations: "War – The expense of a single campaign would be sufficient to endow a school in every parish in England and Ireland forever." DYMOND.

An article on the evils of slavery, citing the difference between the viewpoint of people in this and other colonies. In British Honduras the free man has long worked side by side with the former slave...

p. 224:

Shipping Information, Belize, Saturday Sep 14th 1839:

Arrived:

8th: Mary, ROSWELL, Liverpool, 65 days, with merchandise to Messrs. KENNEDY & MONTGOMERY.
11th: Barque Trinidad, CAIRNIE, Clyde, last St. Thomas, 9 days, general cargo merchandise, spirits &c, to William VAUGHAN, Esq.
12th: Barque Elizabeth & Jane, HART, Jamaica, 7 days, merchandise and government stores, consigned to Messrs. HYDE, FORBES & Co.
13th: H. M. Packet *Express*, Commander CROKE, Falmouth (G. B.,) whence she left on 17th July. She will leave this forenoon for Vera Cruz.

Sailed:
10th: Brig Carron, POTTER, Cork, for orders, with 99 logs, 56,351 feet mahogany and 39 tons logwood, cleared by Geo. A. USHER, Esq.
"   Brig *Margaret,* McKINLEY, Kinsale, for orders, with 135 logs, 117,881 feet mahogany and 33 tons logwood, cleared by Jervis HARRISON, Esq.,

Representative of A. BRYMNER, dec.

11th: Barque *William Shand* POTTS, Cork, for orders, with 216 logs, 107,739 feet mahogany and 130 tons logwood, cleared by William VAUGHAN Esq.

12th: " *William*, BLAKE, Omoa, 31 tons logwood.

14th: Brigt. *Victoria*, MAY, New York, with 87 logs, 23,413 feet mahogany, 33 bales sarsaparilla, 221 ox hides, 40 tons logwood, and box specie.

The brig *Ardent*, from Demerara to Messrs. R. J. ANDREW & Co., arrived at Omoa on the 5th inst. The barque *Le Borne Mere*, CARRY, sailed from Omoa on the 1st inst. for Falmouth, G.B., with 768 logs, 134,394 feet mahogany, and 40 tons logwood. The brig *Visiter*, Capt. MOPPETT, was advertised in Liverpool on the 29th July, for this port. The barque *Reliance*, Capt. HOWELL, had arrived in England previous to the sailing of the Packet. The barque *Ceylon*, Capt. COX, was loading at London for Jamaica and this port.

Edward SHIEL, Esq. of the Mercantile House of Messrs. SHIEL & CARMICHAEL, came passenger in the Packet. Messrs. George, Robert, and David TILLETT,* and Charles CUNNINGHAM, came passengers in the *Elizabeth & Jane*. MR. PIGG went passenger in the *Victoria*.

Sons of William and Sarah Jones Tillett, all under 14 in 1835. Were they educated in Jamaica, or had they returned from school in England or the U.S. by way of Jamaica?

Notice: For Public Sale on Wednesday next, the 17th inst., at the Store of Geo A. USHER Esq., the Brig *Shannon*, as she now lays off the Fort. The Purchaser will receive the Register belonging to the vessel.

For Sale: The House and Premises adjacent to the Bridge on the North side of Belize, belonging to John Samuel AUGUST Esquire – well adapted either for Business or for the Residence of a Family. Terms will be liberal and may be known on application to Alexander FORBES.

The Subscriber having disposed of his Settlement at the Haul Over, offers for sale the stock thereon – A fine lot of Cows, either singly or the lot. A superior Bull. 17 prime picked Steers. A small choice flock of Goats. J. WELSH, Sept 7th 1839.

The Subscriber offers for sale Mahogany Trees on the East bank of the River Papaloteca, situated directly south of the Hog Islands and about 20 miles west of Truxillo. Advantageous terms... WELSH & GOUGH. Sept 9th 1839.

For Public Sale on Monday 16th inst. at the Residence of the late Alexander BRYMNER Esq. The whole of his Household Furniture, &c, and the remaining property of the late Captain Mc'KINLEY. Jervis HARRISON, Rep. Belize, 12th Sept 1839.

The Subscriber requests that all persons indebted to the Estate of Alexander BRYMNER and John HUGHES will make immediate payment of their accounts so as to enable him to liquidate... and all persons indebted... Jervis HARRISON, Rep. 12th Sept 1839.

p. 225:

Letter to the Editor: Sir: It was talked of some time ago to cut a canal across the bar, in order to admit of Boats of a certain draught to come inside. The American vessels and boats in the coasting trade are obliged to employ lighters at $3 per day... inconvenience and risk in landing goods... SERVUS UTILITATUS.

Notice: Government Secretary's Office, September 6th 1839: From the above date no Powder will be issued from the Magazine at Freetown Barracks for the purpose of being carted through the streets of Belize. Vessels taking on board Gunpowder shall send their Boats to the Magazine for the same; and every Boat, Bungay, Dorey or other Craft taking on board Powder in the River in greater quantities than 25 lbs shall remove out of the River within 6 hours after having taken on board the Powder... Transgressors, in addition to confiscation will be severely punished. Patrick WALKER, Government Secretary. Aviso: *the same notice, translated into Spanish.*

Sir: The circumstances of Gunpower being brought into the Town on Carts in large quantities has repeatedly been brought before the notice of the Board of Fire Wardens, and the disastrous effect to which it may lead, impressed on their attention... Powder is placed from the Carts upon the Wharves, and often left there exposed without guard or care... shipped upon Spanish Bungays laying in the River and often remaining for days in the River with large quantities of Powder onboard. The Fire Wardens feel it their imperative duty to lay the circumstances before Your Excellency, and respectfully to suggest the following remedy. The Board respectfully offers the following Regulations for the consideration of Your Excellency... J. McDONALD, Chairman. To His Excellency Col. MACDONALD, H.M. Superintendent.

October Grand Court *(calendar set.)* Last dates given for Rendering Accounts, Issuing Summons, etc. H.A. GRAY, Asst. Clerk of Courts.

Notice: The Subscriber intending to abandon his Cotton Estate at Seven Hills, Offers for Sale the whole of the Produce of the Plantation for a limited time – but not the soil – 2400 suckers... Sugar Cane, Sweet Potatoes, a large crop Corn. For terms apply to W. USHER.

Proclamation by His Excellency Col. Alexander MACDONALD: Fire Wardens are empowered to impose fines of not less than £5 or more than £50 on occupiers when a fire has arisen from culpable neglect. A. MACDONALD, 3rd Sept 1839. By Command, Patrick WALKER.

Editorial: The Case of Gunpowder being brought into the Town on Carts in large quantities was repeatedly brought before the notice of the Board of Fire Wardens...

No. 52, Saturday, September 21st 1839, Vol. 1:

p. 227:

Melancholy Occurrence – On the 10th Inst. the Rev. Mr. WETHERALL, Baptist Missionary, passenger on board the *Favourite,* Capt. BLENKINSOP, flung himself through one of her cabin windows into the sea. Capt. B. instantly put the barque about, lowered a boat, and recovered the body of the unfortunate gentleman, but all efforts to restore life were unavailing. He had only been married the week previous to his leaving England, and was on his passage to this country to assist the Rev. Mr. HENDERSON in performing his duties as pastor and schoolmaster, which the declining state of his health has caused him to find too laborious It is supposed, and justly, that the late Mr. W.'s exertions while in Trinidad, where the *Favourite* touched during her passage out, has been the cause of that indisposition, the fatal effects of which deprived a young and amiable woman of a beloved husband. Capt. Blenkinsop's conduct to his passengers has been of the most kind and gentlemanly description, and we are happy to say that every consolation possible to be administered to the Reverend gentleman's unhappy widow is afforded by the Reverend Alexr. Henderson and Lady.

To the northward... The grant of a mahogany works in possession of a Spaniard having been given to Mr. William USHER by his Excellency, H. M.'s Superintendent, Mr. Usher on attempting to establish himself and gang on the property a few days ago was resisted, vi et armis, by the previous occupant. Returning to Belize, he informed his Excellency of the matter, who dispatched Capt. SODEN of the 2nd W. India with a detachment of that regiment to put Mr. Usher in possession of his Grant. How the affair will end we know not...

Police Report: A number of "Happy Jacks" who were amusing themselves in a most unfriendly manner at the "Friendship Tavern" were brought up in a very unhappy manner yesterday before William MASKALL, James McDONALD, Lewis McLENAN, and Patrick WALKER, Esqrs. The Jolly Tars had adopted the opinion that "Man being reasonable, must get drunk... the best of life is but intoxication." For "Happy Jack" to get drunk and not have a row would be depriving him of half the pleasure of intoxication. Sentence, 30 days hard labour on the Public Works. The tavern forfeited its license.

A Member of the Public Meeting is contemplating to propose at the next sitting of the Legislative Assembly (if his Excellency Col. MacDONALD's permission is not refused) that an Act should be made for the relief of Insolvent Debtors.

We are sorry to say that a benevolent, talented and respected Merchant, many years resident among us, is about to take his departure shortly, and that there is no hope of his return. We wish there were many more of his stamp left in Belize, and hope he may meet on his safe arrival at home, all whom he holds dear in good health, and that his voyage may be pleasant.

To the Editor: Do you, Mr. Editor, or your Readers know that the period appointed by our wise Legislators for legalizing the offspring of marriages contracted "Bay-fashion," without paper and without Parson is near to a close? - that the New Marriage Act of Parliament provides that in case of parties who have been living together in an unmarried state, shall, previous to the 1st day of December 1839 be lawfully married, the children

333

born anterior to that period shall... Trusting that all whom it may concern, will concern themselves about it, and not let so honorable and beneficial an amend to themselves and their families to slip. I am Sir, devotedly yours, B. M.

p. 228:

Shipping Information, September 21st 1839:

Arrived:
17th: Barque *Favourite*, BLENKINSOP, London, last Trinidad, Ballast, to Geo. A. USHER, Esq.
Sailed:
17th: Steamer *Vera Paz*, LOPEZ , Yzaval. [*sic*]

The *Norra*, WESTLAKE, which sailed from this port on the 2nd June, arrived at Liverpool on the 15th July. The *Belmont* and *Lilburn* had both arrived in England, the former on the 7th and the latter on the 8th June.

The barque *Mary*, PATTISON, arrived yesterday from Limas (Mosquito Shore) with a full cargo of mahogany and logwood.

Vessels loading in Harbour: Barques *Duncan* -----; *Trinidad*, CAIRNIE; barque *Elizabeth & Jane*, HART; and *Favourite*, BLENKINSOP; brig *Mary*, ROSWELL.
Loading at the Southward – Ship *Admiral Moorsome*, METCALF; barque *William*, BLAKE; brigs *Mariner*, CRAWFORD, and *Ardent*.

The barque *Lavinia*, HALL, sailed from Omoa, bound for London with 121 logs, 147,317 feet mahogany, 30 tons logwood and 6 tons fustic. (*Fustic is a wood used to make yellow dye, or with mordants, shades of gold or green.*)

A Mail to be forwarded by the barque *Mary*, will be made up at the Counting House of William VAUGHAN, Esq. on Tuesday 23rd inst.

Prices current – Guatemala Indigo, per lb in bond, Floras, 2/7d – 7/6d; Sobres, 5/6 – 7/9; Cortes, 4/6 – 5/4. Caracas 4/6 – 7/6d. Cochineal, per lb duty paid, Silver, ungarbled 5/4 – 5/9, Black ditto 5/9 – 6/6d... (*More prices given.*)

Notice: The Firm of SHEIL & CARMICHAEL is dissolved by mutual consent... Edward SHEIL, Jno. CARMICHAEL.

For Great Britain – the barque *Mary*, PATTISON master, will leave this port on the 24th inst. All demands must be rendered prior to that date. Room for Passage and Cabin Freight. William VAUGHAN.

For Sale: Ex Trinidad, – Casks, Bottled Porter, ditto ditto in quarts and pints. R. J. ANDREW & Co. September 15th 1839.

334

For Sale: About 30 head Prime Working Cattle at Red-Bank in Belize River, for terms apply to R. J. ANDREW & Co. N.B. The above Cattle being large sized and heavy are well suited for Market.

The Subscribers will receive orders to procure from Jamaica, Madeira and Teneriffe Wines, in Pipes, Hogsheads or Quarter Casks. The Madeira will be "Newton, Gordon & Murdoch's private order." WELSH & GOUGH. September 21st 1839.

Notice: The Magistrates today taking into consideration the irregularity and frequent disturbances arising from the Grog Shops in the Town being kept open to so late an hour, it is hereby Ordered, that from or after Monday next the 23rd inst., All such Shops shall be closed every night at Eight o'clock precisely. And in event of any Shop of this description being found open after this hour, the Proprietor of the same will subject himself to the immediate forfeiture of his License. By order of the Magistrates, H. A. GRAY, Asst. Clk. Ct., Court-House, September 20th 1839.

No. 53, Saturday, September 28th 1839, Vol. 1:

p. 229:

Grenada: Lt. WALKER of the 89th Regiment was attacked in the dead of night in the house of a fair and frail lady, by three persons who had, or imagined they had, an exclusive right to her favours. As might be expected, the police, being rather of the same caliber as the quondam charlies of Tom and Jerry… so, naturally, a row ensued…

A successful operation was performed by Richard TUTHILL, M.D., on Catherine BAILLIE, a 60-64 year old black woman in Jamaica, to remove a 9lb 2oz fatty tumor from her neck. The patient was given opium and calomel for several days before the operation, and brandy and water during the procedure, which took about 3 minutes. The wound was left exposed to the atmosphere for half an hour, then the integuments brought together with a few sutures and narrow strips of adhesive plaster. Calomel and opium pills were given… The patient is making a satisfactory recovery.

The Present number completes the term of the last half-years subscription…. The Editor solicits continuance.

p. 231:

A Coroners Inquest was held on Wednesday last on the body of a child named Betsy, about 18 months old, which was found drowned in a canal on the premises of Miss Sarah BATES. As no evidence was found as to how the child got into the canal, the Jury brought in the verdict, Accidentally drowned. That cases of a similar nature do not more frequently occur is almost a matter of astonishment, as the lower classes of women here are so utterly inattentive … that their young ones wander about like sucking pigs.

An inquest was held on the following afternoon on the body of a Government Pensioner, Pascal DEBLOIS, who died in his bed. The house was in a dilapidated state, the sticks on which it was supported bending outwards so ominously that the jurors were unanimously of the opinion, that if they proceeded en masse to enjoy the treat of looking at the deceased, some of them would be equally object of interest for another inquest very shortly, as the Provost Marshall most disinterestedly told them; they therefore marched in single file. The body was in a very emaciated state, without external marks of violence. Dr. YOUNG was of the opinion that the poor fellow was very old and had died of natural causes. The Jury verdict was "Died from the Visitation of God."

Another Coroners Jury yesterday: Inquest on the body of the late Mr. George Le BOIT. Evidence of Dr. YOUNG and Dr. WILLS was "termination of blood to the head," which verdict was accordingly returned by the Jury.

On Saturday last, the Wesleyan Methodist Chapel was discovered to be on fire. The Congregation fortunately was in at that time, and Messrs. FORBES, VAUGHAN and UTER, assisted by others, extinguished the fire. The cause was sparks from a light used by Arabella LOWRIE for lighting the Lamps in the Chapel. The Fire Wardens meeting next morning to investigate, Mr. WARREN, Officer of Police, laid before them a full account of every particular. Mrs. Arabella received a severe reprimand for her carelessness.

Considerable progress has been made in the New Road being cut in a direction about Southwesterly from Yarborough... COULSON's Pine Ridge... The Editor suggests a Poll Tax on cattle being driven to town on this road, to keep it in repair.

Lately seen in the shop of Mr. GRANT, a machine for compressing Corks, we believe the invention of Ensign NICHOLS of the 2nd West India Regiment. We compliment Ensign Nichols on the simplicity and ingenuity of his contrivance, and Mr. Grant on the beauty of the workmanship.

Police Report. Examination before William MASKALL and Lewis McLENAN, Esqs. Complaint by a gentleman residing "too near to be pleasant... in the vicinity of the frequent matrimonial duets of a loving couple on the North side of Belize..." The tender doves were brought up before the Magistrates. The cock dove was clamourous... the frequent quarrels with his partner arose from the "green eyed monster," who annoyed him shamefully when he was a little the worse for liquor, a circumstance of not infrequent occurrence. The Magistrates fined the husband $16 and recommended that "his worthy or unworthy partner avoid giving him cause for suspicion, by being less suspicious in her conduct."

A Warrant examined on Monday last before William MASKALL and P. WALKER, Esqrs – Queen, on complaint of Mr. Chas. CRAIG, Clerk of the Market, vs. William BURNS, a Butcher well known in the Market, and an African named J. WELSH. Defendants killed an ox and sent it to market for sale, when Mr. Craig on examining the hide and horns, a duty he performs very strictly, found the mark on the horns cut out, and the brand on the hide only a Spanish one… Defendants not being able to prove to the Magistrates their right to the property, they were remanded for trial at the next Summary Court.

Numerous complaints have been made to us of shopkeepers having fraudulent weights and measures. This might be remedied by having an Inspector of Weights and Measures. Another circumstance worthy of note: Spaniards from northward who bring logwood, cigars, sugar and corn are allowed to vend these and other articles themselves, without paying an agent, whereas a British or American Captain cannot, according to the Transient Act, be allowed to do so without paying commission on his account sales to whatever agent he may choose to appoint.

A Subscriber suggests a "Belize Matrimonial Enlistment Society" to urge people to get married.

JACINTO's turtle hunt on the Southern Spanish Main. Jacinto, a native, watched the beach night after night until, in the blackness, he saw a dark form moving at the water's edge. He crept up, gathered all his strength, and threw himself upon it - the astonished Tiger (Jaguar,) which was on a hunt of its own for Hawksbills and their eggs, gave poor Jacinto a blow on the shoulder that took away at least a pound of flesh before springing away into the night. What was the poor man's fright when he discerned that he had been catching a Tiger!

p. 232:

Shipping Information, Belize, Saturday, September 28th 1839:

Arrived:
23rd: Brig *Lord Glenelg,* SIMPSON, Barbados, in ballast to Messrs. HYDE,
    FORBES & Co.
25th: Barque *Wansbeck,* JOHNSON, Demerara, in ballast to ditto.

Sailed:
25th: Barque *Mary,* PATTISON, Cork, with 185 logs, 127,984 feet mahogany and 80
    tons logwood.
    Brig *Lady Mary,* FOX, Cork, 188 logs 110,000 feet mahogany and 32 tons
    logwood.

Vessels loading in Harbour: Barques *Duncan* -----; *Trinidad,* CAIRNIE; barque *Elizabeth & Jane,* HART; *Wansbeck,* JOHNSTON; & *Favourite,* BLENKINSOP; brigs *Mary,* ROSWELL, and *Lord Glenelg,* SIMPSON.

Loading at the Southward: Ship *Admiral Moorsome,* METCALF; barque *William,* BLAKE; brigs *Mariner,* CRAWFORD, and *Ardent.*

The droghers *Eliza* and *John Inglis* have both arrived during the week from Rio Hondo, with mahogany intended for vessels loading in the harbour.

337

A Bag is now open for the reception of Letters at the Counting House of Messrs. R. J. ANDREW & CO., to be forwarded by the ship *Admiral Moorsom* for London.

Died - on the 29th inst., Mr. John Henry WOOLMAN.

Notice: The Public is respectfully informed that from the increase of Goats and the Proprietors of the same allowing them to roam about the Town, a very considerable nuisance has been occasioned. Proprietors are earnestly recommended to keep these animals confined within their proper Premises, otherwise severe measures must be resorted to, to remedy the evil. By Order of the Magistrates, H. A. GRAY, Asst. Clrk Ct., Court House, Belize, 26th Sept 1839.

For London – The Ship *Admiral Moorsom,* METCALFE, Master will sail on the 1st prox. – Accounts… must be rendered… R. J. ANDREWS & CO.

Notice – The Firm hitherto known as FORMEAUX & ROUQUIEU has ceased to exist – The Public and his Friends are respectfully informed that the Business in future will be carried on by DOMINGO VIELAJOS… Sept 27th 1839.

p. 233:

World news: From the *Lincoln Mercury*: Present of a Kitten to Her Majesty.
Our readers will recall an account in the *Mercury*, a few months ago, of an old woman named BAKER, living at Scrodlington, near Sleaford, who dreamed that on the day of the Coronation her favourite tabby would give birth to three kittens, and she was commanded to send one to the Queen. The day arrived and, wondrous to behold, the cat did bring forth three kittens in accordance with her midnight vision. The old woman, not at all surprised, selected the finest of the feline trio and dispatched it by coach, in a basket with white cloths for it to lie on, and ample bread and butter for the journey, in a hamper addressed "To the Queen, in Lonnon or elsewhere; to be taken great care of." Many months later the old woman received a letter bearing the Royal Arms, which she could not read. When opened, it was found to contain a letter from the Queen, informing her that the kitten was now a very fine cat, and enclosing two Five Pound notes. She immediately laid in a stock of tea, purchased two pigs, and put the remainder of the money in the savings bank – enough to keep her in comfort for the rest of her days.

Note: Henry Whitney was strongly against religious intolerance. He welcomed the Wesleyan missionary and reprinted the following from an English paper:

Mary WOOLFRAY – How shall insidious attacks such as those of Mary Woolfrey, who, without consulting the authorities of the Church, dared to insert, on the tomb of her late husband, "Pray for the soul of Joseph Woolfrey," thereby indicating a most pernicious tendency to Papistry… How shall these diabolical designs be frustrated? By the Rev. W. DEATHLEY, citing the offender before the authorities at Doctor's Commons, and calling upon her to be interrogated… concerning the health of her soul…

p. 235:

No. 54, Saturday, October 5ᵗʰ 1839, Vol. 2:

The Bank of England increased the interest rate to 6%.

Article on the Portuguese slave trade, from the *Colonial Gazette*: Vessels to Rio de Janiero landed 13,300 slaves from October to December of 1838; in Havana, 5546 in January, February and March 1839.

The *Pandora* Packet, Commander INNIS, left the harbour on the 30ᵗʰ, on the night of which she encountered such severe weather and was so narrowly saved from being wrecked on the Reef, that she put back in on the 1ˢᵗ inst. The conduct of the Pilot, Francis LONGSWORTH, was highly praiseworthy, and the Captain does not scruple to say that the escape of the Packet was owing to his skill and good management.

Considerable alarm existed in the town as to the fate of Lawrence MEIGHAN, son of P. MEIGHAN,* the late Harbour Master, and two boys who were supposed to be lost, as the Boat on which they were to receive Mr. LONGSWORTH to land him after leaving the Packet, was discovered the following morning on the Reef, and no one visible on board; providentially, however, they escaped from the wreck of the Boat in a dorey, and found shelter on some Kay, and on Thursday returned to Belize to the sincere delight of every one. The Packet finally sailed on Thursday morning. *Son of Edmond Meighan.*

On Tuesday night, during the storm, the Store of the late Mr. Alexander BRYMNER was broken into and a small amount, $4 ½, taken, the contents of a drawer. The villains could do nothing with the Iron Chest.

Captain SODEN of the 2ⁿᵈ West India Reg't with detachment returned on Sunday Evening last from the Rio Hondo. On his arrival at his destination with Mr. William USHER, he met Victorio RODRIGUEZ, the party who disputed Mr. USHER's right of possession, and who after being assured by the Captain that the land was within the British limits, quietly acquiesced, and allowed the British Standard to remain, as planted by Captain SODEN's order.

Police Report: Thursday last, Examination by Wm. MASKALL, Jas McDONALD, L. McLENAN, and P. WALKER Esqs. Warrant... on complaint of Madame Cesaria ARVIESA -v- Mr. John MacDONALD. The Defendant liked a good cup of coffee; the Deponent being celebrated for the excellence of that beverage furnished by her to her customers, he called daily and partook of some. Now it so happened that the deponent affixed two prices, 5d without milk and 10d with. The defendant was bibbing with milk, and his pocket also rejoiced at paying only half price for it. This, however, was too felicitous a state to last forever. Madame, knowing the gentleman had hams and bacon, wished to become a customer on reasonable terms, with a reasonable credit. Oh ho! said the gentleman, No cash, no ham or bacon! Oh ho! thought the lady, no more coffee with milk for your scurvy 5d! She omitted the milk, which imparts at the same time an

339

agreeable flavour and a requisite degree of coolness. The omission inflamed the defendant to such a degree as to cause the commission of sundry extravagances during the ebulliation of his wrath, and designating the deponent by a variety of names, none of which could be called names of endearment. After patiently investigating the case, the Magistrates adjudged the defendant to pay cost of the warrant &c, £5/11/8d and to stand committed until the same be paid.

Mr. MacDonald must be worth a fortune to the Officers of Court.

p. 236:

Letter to the Editor: To Restore the Apparently Drowned... 1) Do not hold up by the feet. 2) Do not roll the body over casks. Method of Treatment: Rub dry, wrap in hot blankets, immerse in warm bath... persevere for 3 or 4 hours... Signed, A Frequent Traveller by Water.

Note: One wonders how many people who could have been resuscitated were killed by this advice! When a drowning victim was held up by the feet, gravity drained water from the lungs. Rolling over a barrel forced water from the lungs, and the release of pressure drew in air; repeated compression and release simulated modern CPR.

On Thursday the 3rd inst. about 3 p.m. Died, Marshall BENNETT, Esquire, the oldest Settler, and perhaps one of the oldest Inhabitants of Belize, after a tedious illness of some months. The late Mr. Bennett was a Brigadier General of the Militia, and it is upwards of 30 years since he first took his seat on the Magisterial Bench. At the time Mr. B. took leave of Belize, some years ago, to proceed to Central America, where he had purchased considerable property in Mines, Estates, &c., he was supposed to be richer, and possessed of more property in land, houses, and negroes, than any other person in Belize. It would have been well had he been contented to remain here, and, by the employment of his capital and great influence made improvements in and about the Town, where he had amassed so much of his wealth, instead of embarking almost, if not quite his all in a country where the safety of life has been so long most notoriously precarious. The prospect of a return for the investment of a portion of his capital in performing the former was not so inviting, it is true, as that afforded by prosecuting the latter scheme; but the return, though small and slow at first, would be sure; increase in value every year, and have been attended with the thanks and blessings of the Inhabitants, a great majority of whom, at that period, looked upon him as the Father of the Settlement. That he has not been repaid for the immense sums sunk in Mines and other property, and the difficulties and dangers he has had to contend with, we have all long seen, and we doubt whether his relatives will ever have occasion to rejoice at the use made of his Capital...

The remains of the late Mr. Bennett were attended to the grave last evening, by almost the whole of the most respectable Inhabitants that were in Town, and numbers of persons ranking among the lower classes, dressed scrupulously neat, followed the procession. Arrangements, we understand, having been entered into by some of the masters of vessels in harbour, to honor his memory by half-masting the Ensign, and discharge of minute guns, 11 were fired upon the occasion, and the time between each discharge accurately observed. What may be the precise age of the late Mr. Bennett we do not know, but suppose it to be about 80 years, as it is known that he had been 5 years in Jamaica, previously to his coming down here which is now at least 53 years ago. He was a man whom few in this country equaled in habits of temperance – none excelled.

Note: Marshal Bennett Esq. was baptized on 1 July 1763 at Sheffield, England to Thomas and Elizabeth Cooper Bennett. Apprenticed as a cutler, he was in Jamaica by 1784, where his older brother Thomas died, and moved on to Belize by 1789. His oldest brother, William, went first to the American colonies, evacuated to the Shore as a Loyalist at the end of the Revolution, went on to Belize, and died in London in 1804. Marshal married Elizabeth Cooke in England in 1803; their only known child, Marshal Cooper Bennett, born in 1810 in London, died there in 1814. His wife was in Belize in 1821, but returned to live at Appley House on the Isle of Wight. His brother John, who married Sarah Warburton at Sheffield in 1796, was in Belize only briefly, but had sons who spent their lives there: Thomas, who appears in censuses in Marshal Sr's household, and Marshal Jr, who worked for him and died in 1835. His brother Charles, who married Diana --?--, was with him in Belize in 1789 and for many years thereafter, but returned to England and died in 1844 at Clapham. His will, probated in London in August 1840, names legatees including nephews and nieces by his sisters.

Shipping Information:

Arrived
5th: Steamer *Vera Paz*, LOPEZ, Yzabel, with indigo and a number of Spanish
             gentlemen.
Sailed
2nd: Ship *Admiral Moorsome* METCALF, London, 208 logs, 192,452 feet
             mahogany, 45 tons logwood, 315 serons cochineal and 2 serons indigo,
             cleared by Messrs. R. J. ANDREWS & Co.

H.M. Packet *Pandora,* Commander INNIS, from Falmouth (GB) in 41 days, anchored in this harbour on Saturday evening last, 28th ult., with the August mails. She left for Vera Cruz on the 30th but was compelled to return to port owing to bad weather. She sailed again on the 3rd inst

The brig *Rose*, JACKSON, cleared from London for Cape Gracias a Dios on the 12th July last.

Vessels loading in Harbour and at the Southward: *(as in the previous edition.)*

Robert BOWDEN, Esq. came passenger in the Packet.
John CARMICHAEL, Esq. went passenger in the Packet.

FIVE HUNDRED DOLLARS REWARD - whereas some evil disposed Person or Persons entered my Low Store between the hours of 10 last night and 2 o'clock this morning, and

341

stole therefrom a large quantity of goods, amongst which the following are the most conspicuous: 18 pieces Gray Cottons, 5 ditto 28 yards Prints, 3 ditto 7 yards Prints, 2 pairs Cossack Boots, 40 ditto Rafters, 2 dozen Shawls, 3 pr Silk Bracers [sic],18 Panama Hats, White Headed Razors – I hereby offer the above Reward to any Person or Persons who shall give such Information as may cause the offenders to be brought to Conviction. W. VAUGHAN, Belize, October 5th 1839.

Editorial: Either the villains who were successful in accomplishing the above Robbery, or some others, made an attempt in the earlier part of the week on the Store of the late Mr. BRYMNER, as already reported. The utmost vigilance of the Police.... The number of idle and disorderly persons of both sexes who infest our streets, the back street in particular, without any visible means of livelihood, annoying industrious passengers by their offensive language... has long been complained of by numerous persons, shopkeepers and others of the community, and calls loudly for the Police. Caribs, Spaniards, and Vagabonds of all sizes, ages, and descriptions take possession of this street. Mr. VAUGHAN's loss is a somewhat serious one, and his engagements with mahogany cutters have not turned out so prosperously as to make him indifferent to such an operation.

p. 241:

October Supreme Court:

You are hereby required to give your attendance at the ensuing Supreme and Grand Court to be held in Belize on the 28th and 29th inst., then and there to serve as Jurors. H. A. GRAY, Court House, Belize October 5th 1839.

Richard ANDERSON	John COLLINS
James C. ALTEREITH	Leonard P. COX
James ALLISON	William CROSBIE
John ARMSTRONG	John CRAIG
George D. ADOLPHUS	Francis C. CHRISTIE
Edward ADOLPHUS	Patrick De BRIEN
Amado ARGUILLES	Charles M. DANCE
James BANKS	Charles EVANS
David BETSON	John B. ERSKINE
James H. BLAKE	Alexander FRANCE
James F. BOOTH	Alexander FORBES
Robert BOWDEN	Robert FOREMAN
William BURN	William GABOUREL
George BURN	Joshua GABOUREL.
William H. COFFIN	William GENTLE Jr
George CLARKE	Henry GARDINER
Andrew CUNNINGHAM	Richard GRISTOCK
Charles CUNNINGHAM	Michael GLASSFORD
Ralph CUNNINGHAM	John E. HENDERSON

342

George HAYLOCK
George HUME
Robert HUME
Jervis HARRISON
Thomas JENNINGS
George LE GEYT
Joseph LORD
James LAWRIE
John McDONALD
George MENZIES
Archibald MONTGOMERY
George NICHOLSON
Thomas PHILLIPS
Stephen PANTING
John POTTS
William PEEBLES
James J. RABOTEAU
James ROBERT
Joseph E. SWASEY
Thomas STUART

James SIMPSON
Stephen B. SAVAGE
Joseph SMITH
Robert SMITH
Robert TURNBULL
Stuart M. THOMSON
Philip TOLEDO
William VAUGHAN
John USHER
John UTER
George A. USHER
James WELSH
William WILLIAMSON
Henry WHITNEY
Richard C. WARDLAW
James WOODS
Robert WADE
William WADE
George WATTERS
Edward WILY

Can anyone add information about people on this list? If so, please contact the writer, happyman70@cableone.net, 407 Oaklawn Pl., Biloxi, MS USA 39530, 228-432-0856. We know that John Usher married Sarah Purcell, daughter of Elizabeth Tillett by her first husband, Capt. Purcell. What was Captain Purcell's given name? Sarah was a small child when her father died; her mother remarried to Capt. Peter Adolphus Wade, so Sarah grew up with her Wade sibs, and appears in some records as Sarah Wade.

Robert Ferrill Wade, who married Jane Braddick, and his brother William Wade, who married Agnes Craig, daughter of Charles Craig, are also on this list. They and their sister Elizabeth Ramsay Wade, who married 1) George Runnals or Runnels (records spell the name both ways), and 2) Marcus Charles Bennett, were children of Elizabeth Tillett by Capt. Peter Adolphus Wade, son of Capt. Peter and Susanna Forsyte Wade of Bristol. Were George and Edward Adolphus, listed above, related to the Wades?

John Potts on this list was the son of John Potts Sr., the nephew of Thomas Potts, the third husband of Elizabeth Tillett, and the father of Catherine Ferrill Potts, who married Dr. James Alexander Wills, and Mary Ann Potts who married James Robert, also on the list above. John Potts had sisters Sarah, who married Capt. Richard Ward, and Elizabeth, who married Capt. Joshua Antram. As a physician, Dr. Wills was exempt from jury duty.

Does anybody know what became of Thomas Potts' son John Potts Jr., who was described as a student in Germany when his father made his will in 1806?

p. 237:

An article opposing the death penalty, describing raucous crowds attending the public hanging of a little boy for killing, with malice aforethought... Shoplifting in London...

No. 55, Saturday, October 12th 1839, Vol. 2:

An article on the increase in the production of cotton in America, and the concomitant increase in the number of slaves there.

Revolt on a slave ship. The Spanish schooner *La Amistad* left Havana with a master and crew, two white passengers, and 59 slaves, bound for an estate in a different part of Cuba. The slaves rose, led by a man named CINQUE, murdered all but one of the crew, and kept the passengers alive to navigate the vessel. The slaves steered by the sun for Africa by day, the passengers North and West at night. They arrived at Long Island, anchored in a bay, and were captured by C.S. Brig *Worthington*. The blacks are now in prison at New Haven while the authorities decide what is to be done with them. In the meantime, anyone who wishes can see them for the price of a shilling.

p. 240:

The Brig of War *Buzzard* and the slavers *Wyoming, Clara,* and *Eagle* are still at anchor at the quarantine station. Their cause is now before the grand jury and will probably be tried by the United States District Court within the month. It is a new feature of our relations with Great Britain, and we shall carefully watch developments... respecting them. On the result of their trial will depend the employment of over 100 slave vessels which sail under the American Flag, and are now engaged in catching thousands of poor black wretches on the coast of Africa.

Texas is in a most flourishing and prosperous condition. Emigration thither is increasing daily, and their settlers are men of enterprise and wealth.

Shipping Information, Belize, Saturday, October 12th 1839.

Arrived:
> Schooner *William Wallace,* ALLEYN, New York, 23 days, assorted cargo consigned to Messrs. WELSH & GOUGH.
9th   *Guatemala Packet,* LEBRUN, Havana, produce consigned to F. COMAYANO, Esq.

Sailed:
10th Steamer *Vera Paz,* LOPEZ, Yzabal.
11th Brig *Mariner,* CRAWFORD, Liverpool, 136 logs 122357 feet mahogany, 35 tons logwood, and 30 bales sarsaparilla.

Vessels loading in Harbour: Barques *Duncan* -----; *Trinidad,* CAIRNIE; *Elizabeth & Jane,* HART; *Wansbec,* JOHNSTON; & *Favourite,* BLENKINSOP; brigs *Mary,* ROSWELL, and *Lord Glenelg,* SIMPSON.

Loading at the Southward: barque *William,* BLAKE; and brig *Ardent.*

The brig *Mary,* ROSWELL cleared this forenoon for Liverpool; her homeward cargo consists of 143 1/2 tons logwood, 50 serons cochineal.* The brig *Mary Ann,* HAMPTON, which sailed from this port on the 3rd August, arrived New York on the 24th.

Cochineal, red scale insects made carmine dye. A seron (or bale) weighed 140 lbs.

James HARRIS Esq. & Mrs. HARRIS came passengers in the *William Wallace.*

Prices Current, New York, September 11th: Mahogany, duty fee – Honduras 6 to 14 cents per foot, St. Domingo 14 to 55 cents. Logwood duty free, Honduras 25 to 26 $, Campeachy 32 to 50 $, St. Domingo 27 to 28 $ per ton weight. Sarsaparilla, duty free – Honduras 25-26 cents, Vera Cruz 12-13 cents per lb. Indigo 15% ad valorem. Guatemala $1.45 to $1.86 per lb. Caraccas $1.25 - $1.65. Hides, duty free, West Indies and Southern, 10-12 cents per lb. Horns, Ox and Cow, per 100, $3 to $9.

The American Schooner *William Wallace,* burthen 120 tons, ALLEYN, Master, will sail for New York on Saturday next For Freight or Passage, having good accommodations, apply to WELSH & GOUGH. 12th October 1839.

For Sale: That fast sailing Schooner Boat the *Water Witch,* Coppered and Copper fastened (nearly new,) Burthen 10 tons with all her Materials as she now lays in the Harbour. For particulars apply to Alex. FRANCE. 11th October 1839.

CAUTION: I hereby give notice that I will not be responsible for any Debts contracted by my reputed wife, Eliza DE BRIEN, from this date. Julius De BRIEN. Sept 28th 1839.

To be Sold: The House & Premises situate in Dean Street on the South side of the town, and adjoining those occupied by Miss Harriet CHAISE. The terms will be liberal and immediate possession given. Also, To be Rented: The House and Premises in Widow Lane, in which the Subscriber formerly resided. For further particulars apply to D. B. LOCKWARD. Belize, Oct 12th 1839.

Note: Issues 56 and 57 are missing.

No. 58, Saturday, November 2nd 1839, Vol. 2:

Articles reprinted from an English newspaper, the *Despatch*: On the English Magistracy. The Chartists. State of the Labouring Population in England. A harrowing picture... How long will it be before the millions obtain justice?

Note: The editor was a reformer. The Sanitary Condition of the Labouring Population, a government investigation, makes horrific reading. Overcrowded, damp, unsanitary housing drove workers to gin; starvation and disease were endemic. Two of three children born in the slums of Liverpool died before reaching their fifth birthday, and conditions for the poor in the countryside were little better. The investigation racked the conscience of the nation, and Parliamentary reformers fought for sanitation laws.

Supreme Court, Monday 28th Oct:

No criminal cases. Gentlemen of the Grand Jury to perambulate the Town and see if there was any occasion for their making any presentments to the Court, which on reassembly they did, as regarding the very improper condition of the back Street. His Excellency assured them that he was fully impressed of the justice of their statement, and would lose no means untried to remedy the grievance.

Grand Court, Tuesday 29th:

Cases rather numerous, but only one, Mrs. AUGUST, representative of the estate of her late husband, S. F. AUGUST, deceased, vs. Mr. W. VAUGHAN, exercised any particular interest.

The Plaintiff stated that she handed over sometime in 1837 to Mr. Vaughan a note of hand of the value of £600 and odd pounds that was due to her husband's estate, he being one of the principal creditors, but on the express condition that it was to be refunded when required. She also stated that Mr. FORBES had received some money from her, he also being a principal creditor, upon the same conditions, and had complied with them to refund the money when called upon, which Mr. Forbes corroborated on oath. Mr. Vaughan not doing so was the ground of the present action.

Mr. Vaughan in his defence stated that he had received the note of hand, but only as payment of his demand against the estate, and had given an equivalency for it by surrendering notes that were in his possession, bearing interest, which the late Mr. S. F. August had he lived would have had to pay. He admitted, however, that some considerable time back, when called upon to refund the proceeds of the estate, and in consequence of his refusal to do so, a meeting of the then Magistrates was called, which he was required to attend, he had said of his own free will that he would not give up his hold on the money, which he had received as a bona fide payment, yet he would, if the estate did not pay in full, pay over all that he had received, over and above what would be due to him, if he stood upon the same footing with other creditors.

The Case stood before the Court on Wednesday. The Jurors remained in the jury room all that night but being unable to agree, were dismissed next morning, A fresh jury decided for the Plaintiff, though each of the jurors considered Mr. Vaughan hardly treated, as a claim had been made upon the estate for upwards of £1300, twenty two months after the decease of Mr. S. F. AUGUST, which he nor any other person ever drempt of, and which also prevented the estate from paying in full and which claim Mrs. August, as representative to the estate, might have set aside by objecting to, which she had not.

A grossly libellous paragraph is published in the *Colonial Gazette* in London regarding this Settlement and its affairs… in our opinion, a certain gentleman who left here some six months since and who was most notorious for his overbearing ungentlemanly behavior to all who had the misfortune to need his assistance in the way of business... An assertion infamously false and scandalous is made respecting the Gentlemen of the Bench... also reflections on His Excellency...

p. 252:

On Monday about 5 p.m. a lad named George MARTINY, who was on board Mr. UTER's boat lying at the mouth of the River, fell overboard and drowned. Apathy of lookers on... the other man on board knew the poor fellow could swim. Mr. UTER used every effort in his power to save the lad's life and recover his body, but without success. On Wednesday last, during a salute fired from the fort in honor of the American Charge D'Affairs, Mr. STEVENS, who has embarked on board the *Vera Cruz* for Vera Cruz, the body was found about 20 yards from the place where the accident occurred. The Coroners Jury brought in a verdict of accidental death by drowning.

Insurrection in Jamaica (From the *New York Herald*.) Blood has been shed by the Baptist negroes in Jamaica... labourers on an estate called Silver Hill... the negroes were persuaded by the Baptists neither to pay rent nor abandon their houses... served with writs of ejectment... Constables... shower of stones... Detachment of black troops from Point Antonio to quell the disturbance. Accounts of the 14th September- The negroes demanded such exorbitant prices for their labour that the planters would not in many instances employ them. The negro government of Hayti have excited the Jamaica negroes to rise and kill the whites, and sent a ship with arms, which was seized by a British cruiser.

Shipping Information, Saturday, November 2nd 1839:

Arrived:
Oct 30th: Brig *Mary Ann*, HAMPTON, New York, 23 days, assorted cargo to Messrs. COFFIN & CO.

Cleared Nov 2nd: Barque *William*, BLAKE, Cork, with 182 logs 118,016 feet mahogany and 36 tons logwood.

The brig *Ann Mondel*, ROBERTS, sailed from Omoa for Falmouth or Cork for orders, with 130 logs, 117,498 feet mahogany, and 30 tons logwood on the 11th ult.

Loading in Harbour: *(as listed in a previous edition.)*
Loading at the Southward: Barque *Wansbeck*, JOHNSTON; and *Orynthia*.

Her Majesty's Packet *Pigeon*, Lt. JAMES, Commander, arrived yesterday from Falmouth, G.B. with the September mail. She will leave today for Vera Cruz.

The brig *Friendship*, which sailed from this port on the 8th August, arrived at Cork on the 13th September.

The barque *Reliance*, HOWELL, was to leave London on the 22nd September for this port.

347

The brig *James Lyon* arrived at New York from this port on the 6th ult.

John B. STEPHENS, Esq.,* American Charge D'Affairs for Central America, and Mr. CATHERWOOD, came passengers on the *Mary Ann.* William SIMMONS, Esq., Clerk of Courts & Keeper of Records of this Settlement, and Charles ROBERTSON, Esq. came passengers in the Packet. *Explorer; the author of *Travels in Yucatan.*

p. 253:

Commissariat, Honduras, 26th October 1839 – Army Contracts. Tenders... will be received for... American Superfine Flour, 370 barrels, Fresh Meat, Fuel Wood, Land Transport from Belize to Newtown Barracks, &c. Payment to be made in Doubloons at the rate of £3.4, in $ at the rate of 4s 2d sterling, or in Bills on the Lords Commissary of H. M. Treasury... Tenders to be accompanied by the written offer of two responsible persons as Securities.

For Sale by Auction. On the 5th inst., immediately after the Sale of the Property belonging to the estate of Marshal BENNETT Esq:
Houses, Mahogany Works, Etc. belonging to the estate of the late J. H. PETZOLD:
A House and Land with Buildings thereon, on the North side of Belize.
A Mahogany and Logwood works in North River Lagoon.
A Mahogany Works in the River Timash extending 3 miles on each bank of said River.
Belonging to the estate of the late J. ALEXANDER:
A lot of Land in Belize on the west side of HYDE's Lane.
A Mahogany Works in New River.
One half of the Breeding Stock of Cattle, &c.
Belonging to J. S. AUGUST Esq., deceased:
The House and premises on the North side of Belize adjacent to those occupied by Messrs. GRAY & THOMPSON & CO.
A Mahogany and Logwood Works in Rio Hondo
The Schooner Boat *Sylph.*
Terms will be made known at the time of sale, on application to Alex. FORBES.
Belize, 1st November 1839.

Advertisements for Tenders for Army Contracts for Flour, Fresh Beef, Fuel Wood, Washing Barracks Bedding, Land Transport.

For Sale by Auction, on or about 6th November 1839, a House and premises situated in the Back street lately occupied and owned by Chas. MIDDLETON, Dec'd. James WOODS, Auctioneer.

Notice: The following Property of the Estate of John HUGHES, Dec'd, will be put up for Public Sale immediately after the Venditional Sales at the Court House – consisting of – Household furniture; a lot of Glassware; Liquor Cases; a set of Silver Plate; a Ladies' splendid Gold Watch, with Chain and Seals; a Gentleman's ditto; a House and Lane adjoining the premises of Mr. VAUGHAN; a House and Lot in St. Georges Quay; 2

Plantations in Settee River; a Lot of land adjoining Dr. YOUNG; Mahogany establishments at Omoita, River Ulloa – with all the Mahogany, Trucks, and Truck Gear. Also - a large quantity of Property on the said Bank; 54 logs Mahogany at Rio Peto, in Ulloa, and a lot of other articles too numerous to be inserted. Signed, Jervis HARRISON, Representative.

Also 42 head of Prime Working Cattle at River Grande, the property of the estate of Samuel FORBES, Dec'd, and 11 head of Cattle and one Truck the property of FORBES & Mc'KINNON. Jervis HARRISON, Exor.

To be Sold: Immediately after the Venditional Sales, a House and Lot the property of Abigail HELMSLEY, Dec'd, situated in the front street. Lewis M'LENAN, Trustee.

The Subscriber offers for Sale a House and Lot in St. George's Quay, formerly the property of J. S. AUGUST Esq. For terms, apply to Wm VAUGHAN.

Estate of Marshal BENNETT Dec'd. For Public Sale on Tuesday the 5th November next, on the premises of the late Marshal BENNETT, Esq.
A variety of Stores, Provisions, and Tools suitable to Mahogany Cutters.
Carpenters and Blacksmiths Tools.
A Saw Mill and Machinery.
The Drogher *Alicia*.
The Schooner *Albion* and other Crafts.
Some Plate, Watches, Clocks, etc.
Dry Goods, Wines and Sugars, Paints & Oil.
Lumber and Shingles, Manilla and Hemp Rope.
Rock Salt, suitable for Cattle Pens – and
A Variety of other articles too numerous for advertisement –
all to be seen on the premises at any time between this and the day of Sale. Also –
A Tract of Pasturage Land, situated at the Haulover Point.
A valuable Plantation called FOWLER's Bank, near Convention Town, and
A Valuable House and Lot on St. George's Key
The Houses and Lots of Land in the Town of Belize; also
Mahogany and Logwood Works, the property of the Estate, will be disposed of about the end of the Year, of which time notice will be given. Terms will be made known at the time and place of Sale. Wm WALSH, Thos PHILLIPS, Executors on the Estate of M. BENNETT, Dec'd .

Just Imported per *William Henry Angas,* and by other recent arrivals, the following Articles, and for sale by Retail at the store of the Subscribers:
Brown and Green Silk Umbrellas and Parasols. Silks for Ladies Dresses of various colors. Wide or narrow Black Crape. Wide Black Bombazeen. Ladies white and black Silk Stockings, Lace Silk Gloves and Mittens, assorted colors. White Jaconets 6-4 12 yard, assorted qualities... Gentlemens Dress and Walking Shoes, Pumps, Morning Slippers... Cossack, Clarence and Cloth Boots. Planters' Shoes, single and double tie. Gentlemens Linen Shirts. Ditto Cotton Shirts with Linen Front. Merino Shirts (without

sleeves). Merino Drawers. Riding Boots, Whips, and Walking Sticks. Gents' plain white Silk Hose, white cotton half-hose and grey Vigonia. Gents' Woodstock, Norway, and Berlin Gloves. Ditto India Rubber Bracers. Blue Cloth Jacket & Trowsers (Sailors.) Flushing Pea Jackets. Red Caps. Blue and Red Shirts, plain and twilled. Duck Trowsers and Shirts. Sheeting duck. Check and stripe Shirts... Witney Blankets... Fowling pieces, assorted... Cutlass Blades... 16 and 18 sheet Copper and 3-4 and 7-8 Sheathing Nails. Canvas, 1-7 and Cordage of all sizes. Cases Hollands, Barrels Jamaica Sugar, Jars Tripe and Jugs Pease, Cases Champagne, Candles, Cider, Kegs Paint and Jugs Paint Oil, and various other articles... For De ST. CROIX & CO., W. E. HAMPSHIRE.

Note: Issue No. 59 is missing.

No. 60, Saturday, November 16th, Vol. 2:

p. 259:

Editorial, advocating Negro schools.

The Government now has a contract... Mails to be conveyed by steam twice a month.

p. 260:

Failure of American Banks – Philadelphia – disgrace and dishonor. Commercial system unstable. November 16th – The New York banks, to their immortal honor, have determined not to suspend specie payment. The gross and wicked mismanagement of the United States Bank...

Departure of Patrick WALKER Esq. and Lt. CADDY of the Royal Artillery on Wednesday last, to visit the ruins at Palanque.

Magistrates order: The Saturday market is not to open until 4 p.m. Many servants under pretence of going to the market, waste the whole afternoon to the great inconvenience and loss of time of their employers.

Summary Court, Monday last, 11th, before Wm MASKALL, James McDONALD & James YOUNG, M.D. Esqrs, Magistrates of this Settlement. Summons few, for sums under £10 currency, which created no interest whatsoever and were soon disposed of.

2 o'clock Saturday morning – Suspension of the Baltimore Banks. All the Banks have suspended specie payment...

Shipping Information, Saturday, Nov 16th:

Arrived:
12th: Brig *Papaneau,* ALLEN, Clyde, 60 days, with merchandise consigned to
            Messrs. JOHNSTON & CO.

350

13th: Brig *Visiter*, MOPPETT, Liverpool, 55 days, with merchandise consigned to Messrs. YOUNG & TOLEDO.

15th: American brig *Tallyrand*, COOPER, New York, 21 days, with assorted cargo, produce, consigned to Wm VAUGHAN, Esq.

Sailed:

14th: Brig *Mary Ann*, HAMPTON, New York, with 82 logs, 24666 feet mahogany, 40 tons logwood, 7 seroons cochineal, 650 lbs old copper, 6 bales sarsaparilla, and 9 boxes specie – cleared by Messrs. COFFIN & Co.

13th: *Rosella*, RHODES, Lucca, Jamaica, in ballast.

Vessels loading in Harbour: barques *Elizabeth & Jane*, HART; *Favourite*, BLANKENSOP; and brigs *Lord Glenarm*, SIMPSON; *Papaneau*, ALLAN, and *Visitor*, MOPPETT.

Vessels loading at the Southward: barque *William*, ------ ; *Trinidad*, CAIRNIE; and *Orynthia*.

Passengers sailed - In the *Mary Ann*, F. C. CHRISTIE, Esq., Mr. FLETCHER, and Mr. ROUQUIE. In the *Rosella*, James HARRIS Esq. and Lady.

The barque *Wansbeck*, John JOHNSTON, Master, was lost between the Rio Ulloa and Chimlico, during a severe gale from the northward, on the evening of Thurs. the 7th inst.

The drogher *Eliza* arrived yesterday evening from the Rio Hondo, with a cargo of mahogany for Messrs. HYDE, FORBES & Co., her owners.

The brig *Victory*, MARY, from this port, arrived at New York on the 17th ult. after a passage of 34 days.

Dreadful Shipwreck. The ship *Glasgow*, Capt. LITTLE, arrived at Baltimore on Saturday last from Liverpool, and brought three men who had been taken from a raft, the sole survivors of the crew of nineteen men of the ship *Arab*, of and for Hull, from Belize. The *Arab* was dismasted in the gale of the 13th September and finally went to pieces. Those saved were on the side of the poop, being four planks 20' long. They were picked up on the 18th, and during the five days they were on the raft they had no food except two cocoanuts. There were nine men on the raft originally, but six of them perished before the *Glasgow* fell in with them.... The above vessel sailed from Belize for Cork on the 26th August last, with 149,834 feet mahogany, 68 tons logwood, 8000 cocoanuts, shipped by Mr. VAUGHAN.

Died – In this Town on Thursday last, Mr. William SMITH, clerk in the employ of Messrs. YOUNG & TOLEDO.

Gazette - Appointments: George JESTY Esq., late of the Honorable East India Company's Service, to be acting Harbour Master in the absence of Lt. CADDY, R. A., on leave. R. M. NICHOLS Esq., 2nd West India Regt, to be Acting Captain at Fort George, and Acting Keeper of Militia Arms and Clothes during the absence of the undersigned on leave. Jervis HARRISON Esq. to be Acting Queens Advocate during the absence of the undersigned on leave. Patrick WALKER.

Notice: The Market House will be open in future for the sale of Butchers' Meat &c. every Saturday Afternoon at 4 o'clock. By order of the Magistrates, Chas. CRAIG, Clerk Market. Belize, 15th November 1835.

Notice: The Barque *Wansbeck* of London, John JOHNSTON late Master, having been wrecked on the Southern coast between the Rivers Ulloa and Chimlico during a heavy gale from the Northward on the 7th inst., Persons having Boats and Droghers are requested to send them for the purpose of saving the Cargo and Materials of said Vessel, for which they will be allowed such Salvage as the Honorable Board of Magistrates may award. James McDONALD, Agent Appointed by the Captain, for the Underwriters and all concerned.

p. 261:

Editorial on the Chartists: Uncommon punishment for Common People. *(Again, the editor is highly critical of the authorities in England.)*

The Subscriber has good reason to believe a misrepresentation exists in the Minutes of the Honduras Auxiliary Bible Society relative to the cause of his resignation, and he therefore calls upon the present Secretary to publish the said Minute in next weeks paper. Alexander HENDERSON, Baptist Missionery.

Notice: Gibraltar Side. To let, House lately occupied by F. C. CHRISTIE, Esq., 2 houses at M'KENZIEs Point, also Spare Rooms – and for Hire, Boats fit for landing either Dry Goods or Ballast (in good order) also a Sailing Boat. Mahogany Boards and Planks always on hand for sale. George LeGEYT.

The Subscriber offers For Sale, a House and Lot at St. George's Quay, formerly the property of J. S. AUGUST Esq. Wm VAUGHAN.

No. 61, Saturday, Nov 23rd 1839, Vol. 2:

p. 263:

Causes of the present state of the Banks in America: Paper currency. Martin Van Buren and Nicholas Biddle. Vast expansion.... Prices rose, extravagance flourished, debt was incurred... rescue by the House of Rothschild.

We are informed that the American gentlemen, Mr. CATHERWOOD and Mr. STEPHENS have gone to Guatemala and Palenque.

We urge heads of families to make their returns for the census... Indifference of inhabitants... A more favourable means of keeping alive our importance in the Colonial policy of Government does not exist, than stating the numbers of our large and increasing population...

School fete. On Friday last the children of the Schools of the Baptist Missions had their annual treat of Cake and Tea. The sermon given was more impressive as mention was made of one of their number, who was at that time waiting for interment. 126 smiling children... That evening, 100 accompanied the funeral procession of their deceased to the house appointed for all living.

p. 264:

Don Victorio RODRIGUES in Rio Hondo has made a representation to His Excellency Col. MacDONALD that he had at the time of Mr. USHER's taking possession, a quantity of trees felled and prepared for trucking. His Excellency has issued an order empowering Rodriguez to take possession of his wood felled... This is much to be regretted, as we believe Mr. Usher, with the expectation of trucking out the whole of the wood by which he would realize his great outlay, has abandoned his plantation at Seven Hills, at which he had been at enormous expense of establishing, and concentrated the whole of his gang and resources at the above mentioned Mahogany Works. It would have been better for all parties if a strict and more mature enquiry had been made before proceeding to such lengths, in securing to Mr. Usher a supposed right in which he is to suffer such disappointment.

The Barque *Ceylon*, Austin COX, owned by Geo. A. USHER Esq. is taking on cargo, and will sail about 12 January. Mr. Usher is obtaining Indigo and Cochineal for shipment... the homeward cargo will exceed in value the one cleared out from this port on 1st April last, which amounted to upwards of £100,000. The accommodations of the *Ceylon* are superior, and from the gentlemanly behavior and attention paid by Captain Cox to his passengers, he has always the full enjoyment of company, either on his out or homeward voyages. We have heard several persons named as having engaged passage...

Sudden death of two seamen of the *Elizabeth & Jane*, HART, supposed, of an infections disease. The Magistrates directed her to the Quarantine grounds. The order not being complied with, Mr. Hart was summoned to the Court House and fined £100 currency.

Died: On Saturday last, 16th inst., at the house of Mr. EVANS, Mr. Jose Maria GUIROLA, aged 17, only recently arrived, and on his way to Guatemala.

On Thursday the 21st after a short illness of fever, Mr. Charles KNOTH. This gentleman had been appointed in the Will of the late Mr. BENNETT, one of the Executors on his estate, for the purpose of adjusting his affairs in Central America; and from his knowledge of Mr. Bennett's connexions in that country, would no doubt have afforded great facility in conjunction with the other Executors in closing the estate.

353

Wanted, An Active Person as Store Porter - only persons with testimonials as to character may apply to ROBERTSON & URQUHART. Also - A Hand Cart. Any person having one to dispose of please apply at the store of the subscribers. Belize, 23rd Nov 1839.

For Sale, A Fast Sailing Creau,* complete, for parts. Apply to James GRANT. Nov 23rd 1839. *A sailing dorey.

Shipping Information, Belize, Saturday, Nov 23rd 1839:

Arrived:
16th: Ship *Ceres*, PALLOT, Liverpool, 54 days, with merchandise to Messrs. De ST. CROIX & Co.
21st: Barque *Addington*, WATSON, St Andrews, N. B. with 164,464' pitch pine lumber and 150,060 pine shingles, consigned to Messrs. HYDE, FORBES & Co.
"   American schooner *Guatemala Packet*, ETCHBURGER, Havannah and Omoa, consigned to F. CAMOYANO & CO.

Vessels loading in Harbour – Ship *Ceres; Favourite*, BLANKENSOP; *Addington*, WATSON; and brigs *Papaneau*, ALLAN, and *Visiter*, MOPPETT.

Vessels loading at the Southward – barque *William Henry Angus*, ------; *Trinidad*, CAIRNIE; and *Orynthia*.

The brig *Ardent*, HARTGRAVE, Master, for Cork, with 181 logs 118,107 feet mahogany and 30 tons logwood, sailed from Omoa the 5th inst. The barque *Calista*, Capt. BLAMPIED, from Jersey, sailed for this port, and may be hourly expected. The ship *Vanguard*, SABISTON, which sailed from Omoa on the 1st August last with 210,340 feet mahogany and 42 tons logwood, arrived in the Downs on the 22nd Sept. The brig *Inca*, HARRISON, was loading in Liverpool for this port when the *Ceres* left. *Hope* is also expected from the Clyde. The barque *Hebe* was chartered and was expected to sail on the 10th Oct. for this port. The *St. Croix* arrived at Liverpool on the 18th and the *Lord Lampton* reported at Cove on the 20th Sept., to proceed to Liverpool. The barque *Science* and the *Fair Arcadian* had both arrived home.

The ship Ceres, in her passage out, and in latitude 10 N, longitude 43 W, wind E.S.E., fell in with a cloud of locusts on the 26th Oct. which covered the decks of the vessel. The Captain has preserved many of them, which he now has on board.

The Guatemala Packet will sail for Havana tomorrow.
Charles SAVAGE, Esq. came passenger in the Guatemala Packet from Havana.

Just as we were going to press, the *James Lyon* arrived from New York.

Notice: The barque *Elizabeth & Jane*, William HART, Master, will sail for London direct on Saturday the 30th currant. All demands... per HYDE, FORBES & CO...

...M. GLASSFORD. The above vessel has room for Cabin Freight and superior accommodation for passengers. Belize, 22nd November 1839.

For Public & Positive Sale on Saturday, 30th November at the store of Mr. VAUGHAN, to close sales, Cases Raspberry Brandy, Cases Sparking Champagne, Cases Gerofle, Citron, Peppermint & Cinnamon. Do. Noyeau, Aniseed, and Cherry Brandies. Do. Perry, and Port Wine. Do. Vinegar. Hogsheads superior Cognac Brandy. Mahogany Secretaries, Dwarf Presses, Bedsteads. Hair Mattresses and Feather Bolsters. Night Commodes and Card Tables. Cases of Empty Vials. Cases Handkerchiefs and Ginghams, also A Lot Books – chiefly Novels.

p. 265:

For Sale, imported per brig *Tallyrand* from New York – Barrels and half-barrels Flour, Prime Pork, Pilot Bread. ½ barrels Family Mess Beef. Ditto #1, 2, and 3 Mackerel. Boxes Codfish and Herring. Tierces Rice. Bales and ½ bales Tobacco, bags Coffee. ½ boxes Raisins. Hams and Lard. Barrels Turpentine and Tar. Ships Buckets, Pails and Brooms. Boxes Mould Candles, 6's and 8's. Boxes Cast Steel Kentucky Axes, short bill. Bales of Hay and boxes Loaf Sugar. Boxes Muscat Wine. Boxes Seidlitz Preparations. Cases and Canisters Gunpowder Tea. Boat Oars, &c. William VAUGHAN.

Note: Issue No. 62 is missing.

No. 63, Saturday, 2 December 1839, Vol. 2:

Editorial: The failure of U.S. banks. Transfer of the Pennsylvania's stock, at $4,000,000, now held by the United States Bank, to bond holders in Europe. A curious passage occurs in a private letter, written on the other side of the American continent, at St. Louis, Mississippi on the 31st of August last, relative to the Bank of England, and which has since been verified to the letter. The writer says – "I hope, for the honor and credit of the country, she will not go a-borrowing abroad, as they do in this country, on stocks and securities almost unknown to the lender."

Note: Jean-Baptiste Karr's epigram comes to mind: " plus ça change, plus c'est la même chose!"

Summary Court, Mon Dec 2nd: Complaint of a black man, Charles WALL, that a gentleman of Belize had deprived him of a plantation. An informal agreement had been made before a Magistrate, and fully explained to the plaintiff at that time, and signed by him, with a clause added at the desire of the plaintiff, that if in future they could not agree, the agreement would no longer be binding. The plaintiff was to keep the plantation clean in exchange for the right to live there and cut plantains. He complained that he had been driven off. The defendant proved that he had neglected to clean all the plantation but the part allotted to him. Case dismissed.

p. 672 *(should be 372- 672 is a misprint.)* Published by request of W. H. COFFIN, Colonel Commandant of R. H. Militia, 4th Dec 1839: A Regulation for the Better Government of the Prince Regent's Royal Honduras Militia, passed 7th July 1823: Every male inhabitant of the Settlement... shall be obliged to serve in the Militia of the said Settlement... every person arriving or becoming resident shall be considered as one composing the said Militia, 6 weeks after arrival. Any failing to enroll... penalty £10 Jamaica currency. Militia shall muster and be on duty during the whole of the Christmas holidays, say from 23rd December to 3rd January inclusive, muster once each day during that time. Fines for absence: Captain £3, Ensign £2, Sergeant £1, or Corporal, Private, Drummer, Fifer, Musician 13/4d. General Return to be sent in at the close of the muster. 30 days in gaol for failure to pay fine, and pay expences of confinement.

Note: All wood cutting and manufacture stopped in the Bay for the Christmas and New Year holiday, allowing the distant work gangs of free men and slaves to come to town for a wild and roisterous celebration. With the managers and owners who lived up the rivers in town, the militia could muster at full strength. The sight of men in uniform and sound of marching feet was a deterrent to trouble, helping the police to keep order.

War Office, September 27th: 2nd West India Regt: Lt. R. ELLIOTT, Capt. without purchase, vice HILL, Dec'd. J. W. FRASER, gent. to be Ensign without purchase. Oct 4th: Lt. W. LARDNER to be Captain without purchase, vice WILLIAMS, Dec'd; Ensign R. M. NICHOLLS to be Lieut. vice LARNER; J. HILL, gent. to be Ensign, vice NICHOLLS. 18th: Assist. Surgeon J. SHERIFFS, from the Staff, to be Asst. Surgeon, vice WILSON, promoted in the 52nd Foot; W.A. HEISE. M.D. to be Assist. Surgeon to the Forces, vice SHERIFFS appt. to the 2nd West India Regt.

Shipping Information, Belize, Saturday, December 7th 1830:

Arrived:
2nd: Brigt. *Patsey Blunt,* PEDERSON, New York, 14 days, assorted cargo to F. CAMOYANO, Esq.
5th: Schooner *Hope,* GUTHRIE, Glasgow, 60 days, with merchandise to Messrs. JOHNSTON & CO.
6th: Ship *Calista,* BLAMPIED, Jersey, with merchandise &c. to Messrs. ST. CROIX & Co.

Vessels loading in Harbour: Ship *Ceres,* PALLOT; *Calista,* BLAMPIED; barques *Ceylon,* COX; *Addington,* WATSON; and brigs *Papaneau,* ALLAN, and *Visitor,* MOPPETT; brigt's *Victoria,* MAY; *James Lyon,* SEDDON; and schooner *November,* DAWES.
Loading at the Southward: barque *William Henry Angus,* ------; *Trinidad,* CAIRNIE; and *Orynthia.*
Loading at River Grande: American brig *Tallyrand,* COOPER.

The barque *Elizabeth & Jane* has finished loading and will sail tomorrow for London. A letter bag will be made up at the Counting House of Messrs. HYDE, FORBES & CO. to

356

be forwarded by her. The American brig *Carib*, NICKERSON, sailed from Truxillo for Boston on the 5th inst. with a cargo consisting of sarsaparilla, hides, horns, and a small quantity of braziletto wood. The steamer *Vera Paz* arrived on the 5th from Yzabal, with indigo. A number of Spanish gentlemen, passengers, came in her. The ship *Calista* spoke the barque *Hebe* from this port, off the Western Islands, bound for London.

Notice: The barque *Trinidad*, Neil CAIRNIE, Master, will leave this port on the 11th for Cork. All persons having Claims... William VAUGHAN. 5th December 1839.

Militia General Orders, H.Q. Belize, 3rd December 1839: The Annual Muster to take place on the 23rd inst. By order of His Excellency the Commander in Chief, R. M. NICHOLS, Acting. Fort Adj't.

R. M. Orders: Those who have not Enrolled themselves, do forthwith... Many young men, natives of this place, and others who are fit to serve in the Militia have hitherto skulked from that duty they owe the country... Requests all persons to report to him the names of such Individuals and their places of abode... G. E. WARREN, Acting Adjutant.

Notice: Letters of Trust on the Estate and Affairs generally of William WILLIAMSON, Dec'd will be granted by the Magistrates at the expiration of 21 days from this date to William GENTLE, William WALSH, and William E. HAMPSHIRE. By order of the Magistrates, H. A. GRAY, Asst. Clerk Courts, 3th December 1839.

Notice: Letters of Trust on the Estate of William PATTISON, Dec'd will be granted by the Magistrates at the expiration of 21 days from this date to William VAUGHAN, should no better claims appear... H. A. GRAY...

Tenders to be received for Barrels Prime Irish Pork, Rum per gallon, Sperm Candles per lb., Bread to weigh 16 ozs each in such quantities as may be required for the Militia and Flotilla during the Xmas [*sic*] muster. James McDONALD, Deputy Commissary General, 30th December 1839.

To be Sold: The House and Lot adjoining the premises of Mr. CRAIG near the Commissariat. For particulars apply to Mr. WOODS, auctioneer, or the owner, Tiburcio SALINE.

To be Sold: A fine fast sailing coppered and copper fastened Craft called the *Joseph*, belonging to the Subscriber, Robert EILEY.

For Public Auction, at the Mart on Monday the 23rd inst., all the remaining effects of the late Samuel F. AUGUST, Esq., consisting of Household Furniture, Plate, Glass, Watches, Wearing Apparel, &c., of which particulars will be furnished in the Bills of the day. By order of the Executrix, J. WOODS, Auctioneer & General Agent. Rock House, Belize December 4th 1839.

Notice: The Subscriber being about to leave the Settlement shortly, requests that all demands against him may be forthwith rendered for payment. Robert EILEY, December 6th 1839.

To be Sold or Broke Up Immediately: The Ship *Minerva* as she now lays, with her Materials consisting of Masts and Spars, value £200, 2 Anchors & Cable 90 fathoms each £200 outside – three tons of Copper Bolts, all pure Copper, at 1/8d per lb., £1333/6/8d; hanging Knees and Beams, £150, making a total of £1833/6/8. Large and small cabin furniture consisting of 8 apartments, with elegant Mahogany Beds, and many other articles not mentioned. The *Minerva* is a handsome vessel, and cost £13,000 – has been afloat here 5 months during which time she has not been pumped, and made no water – admeasuring 400 tons – only 9 years old – built of genuine oak. Approved Bills on London will be taken in payment. *(The owner or agent is not named.)*

p. 373:

Pilotage to the Southward: For all Vessels 12 feet Draught and upwards. For Vessels under 12 feet and more than 8, 1/3 less. For Vessels under 8' one half.
From Belize to Sibun and back, £5.0.0.
From Belize to Manatee and back, £6.0.0.
From Belize to Settee and back, taking all Rivers and Creeks between that River and Manatee, £10.0.0.
From Belize to Point Placentia and back, taking in all Rivers and Creeks between that point and Belize, £12.0.0.
From Belize to Point Icacos and back, taking in all Rivers and Creeks between Points Placentia and Point Icacos, £15.0.0.
To Rio Grande and back, taking in all Rivers and Creeks between that River and Point Icacos, £20.0.0.
To River Sarstoon and back, taking in all Rivers and Creeks between this River and Rio Grande, £25.0.0.
With an additional half $ per foot for removing vessels within the above stated limits. The usual allowance of 7/6d per day to be given to the Pilot when detained on service. Rates fixed by the Magistrates were approved in January 1836, and are again Published for general information. By order of the Magistrates, H. A. GRAY, Asst Clk Court, Court House Belize, Nov 25th 1839.

Census of 1839: Notice is hereby given that a Census of the Population of this Settlement will be taken for this year, according to Law. Persons are therefore requested to send into this Office corrected Returns of their Families, Domestics, and Labourers on or before the 31st December next, or they will be subject to such fines as the Law in such cases directs. Patrick WALKER, Acting Keeper of Records. Office of Records, Belize, May 10th 1839. Blank Forms or Returns to be had at the above Office.

No application having been made for the Forms, or attention paid to the above Order of the 10th May last, their Worships the Magistrates have directed that notice be given that the infliction of Fines will be taken into consideration on all parties not having made their

358

Returns on or before the last day of December next. H. SYMONS, Clerk of Court, Court House, Belize, November 23rd 1839.

Notice: Estate of John HUGHES, Dec'd. The Subscriber requests that persons having Disbursement Claims against the last Season's Cutting of the late John Hughes, not yet rendered, will furnish him with attested statement of the same, prior to 10th December next or they will forfeit their claim as Disbursement Creditors on that Estate. He has also to request that all other Demands be rendered as soon as possible, as on the 10th December next he will pay a Dividend to the Creditors out of the Cash funds in his possession. Jervis HARRISON, Rep. Belize, 25th November 1839.

Notice: All persons having Demands against the estate of Samuel FORBES, Dec'd are requested to do so immediately, as Creditors are informed that the same will be closed on 31st December next. JERVIS HARRISON, Exor. 25th November 1839.

No. 64, Saturday, December 14th Vol. 2:

Sunday trading, A Little Knot of Mawworms. *(Colloquialism for hypocrites, from a character depicted as a hypocritical worm, in a play by Isaac Bickerstaffe.)*

The following lines, taken from an English County paper, are highly expressive of the feelings universally experienced by the lower and middling classes towards the aristocracy:

National Hymn, from the *Sheffield Iris*, 5th September 1839:

How long shall idlers tax the bread
Which famish'd toil hath earned?
And toiling men, half clothed, half-fed
Like dogs be spurned? ....

p. 375:

The incendiary who furnished the Editor of the *Colonial Gazette* with the libelous matter published in that paper has again been at work. If the Editor were aware of the character of... *(this man, not named)* we think he would hesitate... *(to print such misinformation.)* With regard to Ruatan there is no doubt that Central America can have no claim to territory that Old Spain did not possess. The letter to the Commandant at Truxillo was absolutely required, and His Excellency Col. MacDONALD would have been negligent in his duty had he tamely looked on and suffered the English settlers in Ruatan to be aggressed with impunity. Mr. WALKER, who is absent from Belize, would doubtless be very glad if the estimate of his income were anything like correct.

A certain Town of New Liverpool gentleman who sang its praises here some months ago in such enchanting strains that he caused a perfect mania in some of our towns-folk, who were red-hot for going there, is, we suspect, an ally of the person who has been humbugging the Editor of the *Colonial Gazette*. The consistency of his information is highly amusing - in one paragraph he traduces and vilifies the Magistrates, in another he holds them up as victims of the caprice of His Excellency. He forgets the kindness of His Excellency and the inhabitants to the poor deluded emigrants of his splendid Town of New Liverpool, from whence they were brought to escape from perishing from utter want, when they arrived here; he also forgets that had it not been for the courage of a woman, Mrs McINNIS, who gallantly took charge of the ship in which she and many others had come out to that place, many more would have stood every chance of perishing from disease and destitution. It is notorious that of the first batch that went out, many of the white women submitted to the most degrading intercourse with black men of the lowest description to avoid starvation. So much for the prospects of the emigrants who leave their own country on the faith of the representative of a Grand Company, with "a long name on a h-ell of a long brass plate on the door of their office," as the poor Engineer whom they cheated said...

Note: The Enginer, Thomas Wakefield, obtained a judgment againt the owners of the steamer Vera Paz for his wages. One would like to know more of this story. The Colonial Gazette was published in England from 1838-1847, and has been filmed.

Examinations took place on Thursday morning last, of the Scholars of the Free School...

Mahogany cutters have suffered losses from labourers signing on with half a dozen different cutters, obtaining considerable advances from each, and disappearing from Belize with their booty. They get away to Stann Creek, Omoa, Truxillo and elsewhere...

p. 376:

On Monday last, a trio of "elegantes of the fair sex" that are to be seen every morning in the purlieus of the market were brought up before William MASKALL and Lewis Mc'LENAN on the charge of mal-treating a woman employed as a nurse by Mr. HAMPSHIRE. Some gallant gay Lothario, we believe, has been the cause of the fray, the consequence of which might have been serious to Mr. Hampshire's son and heir, who was in his nurse's arms at the time she was attacked by the interesting trio, her former acquaintants. Passersby were treated to the spectacle of three Furies shredding the clothing from her back... The trio were sentenced to six days in gaol, and brooms provided them to clean the public streets.

As our town will now soon be crowded with "the unwashed" of all sorts, sizes, ages, and descriptions, the Police will have ample opportunity of exercising vigilance. Now may the Back Street shopkeepers brush up and look bright, for crowds will congregate, whether customers or not, and they had better look sharp that some of their customers are not sharper than themselves... The numerous virgins in the Back slums will no longer have occasion to deplore, like nuns in a nunnery, their forlorn condition, as they will soon have at their feet an abundant harvest of captivating suitors... Now will Fowls, Ducks, Geese, or Turkey have to be on the qui vive, and their owners a vast deal more so or they may be sadly disappointed some bright or misty morning. Soon will the Back Street be redolent of every description of lovely and sweet perfumes, lovelier and sweeter enchanters in petticoats, military men proud of their spic and span new clothing (if it is arrived... having been shipped on the *Reliance,* Capt. HOWELL, who sailed 12 days before the *Hebe*)... Larks of all descriptions will be plentiful.

Shipping Information: Belize, December 14th 1839:

Arrived:
H. M. Packet *Lapwing,* John COGHLIN, Commander, on Wednesday last from Falmouth, G. B., 56 days, with the October mails... left the following day for Vera Cruz.

Sailed:
10th: Barque *Elizabeth & Jane,* HART, London, with 98½ logs or 153,905 feet mahogany and 45 ½ tons logwood, cleared by Messrs. HYDE & FORBES & Co.
11th: Schooner *November,* DAWES, Boston, with 19 logs or 31,913 feet mahogany, 28 tons logwood, and 10 tons old copper and iron, cleared by Stephen B. SAVAGE, Esq.
13th: Brig *Trinidad,* CAIRNIE, Cork, with 68 logs or 112,264 feet mahogany, 140 tons logwood, cleared by Wm. VAUGHAN, Esq.

The Barque *Orynthia,* BARKER, sailed from Ruatan on the 6th inst. for London. Her cargo consisted of 84 logs or 154,000 feet mahogany, 40 tons logwood, 11,000 cocoanuts.

Vessels loading in Harbour: Ship *Ceres,* PALLOT; *Calista,* BLAMPIED; barques *Ceylon,* COX; *Addingham,* WATSON; and brigs *Visiter,* MOPPETT and *James Lyon,* SHEDDEN.

Loading at the Southward: Brig *William Henry Angas.*
Loading at River Grande: American brig *Tallyrand,* COOPER.
Loading at Golden Stream Quay: Brigantine *Victoria*, MAY.

The brigantine *Patsey B. Blount,* Capt. PEDERSON, will sail for New York tomorrow. A bag will be forwarded from the store of F. CAMOYANO, Esq., which is now open for letters.

The Brig *Shannon,* which was laid up some time in consequence of the report of a board of survey that she was not seaworthy without repairs, is now completely repaired, and loading in harbor with mahogany from Alexander FORBES and William VAUGHAN Esqrs, the Owners, who purchased the brig at public auction a short time ago- she was being sold by order of the Underwriters.

Died: We omitted to mention in our last, the death of Mr. David SMITH, which took place on the 1st inst. at the house of Mr. G. MENZIES.   His funeral was numerously attended by his family and friends, who sincerely deplored his loss.

361

At Mannatee on Tuesday the 3rd inst., William, the son of Lt. PATTEN of the Royal Artillery, and in Belize on the 7th, Maria, sister of the deceased. Mrs. PATTEN's case is peculiarly distressing, as her husband is at Mannatee dangerously ill, and she was under the necessity of going thither immediately after the funeral of her daughter.

Notice to Foreigners and Others: Much inconvenience and expense has arisen from the sickness and vagrancy of Foreigners and others left in this Settlement by the Owners or Masters of Vessels trading to and from the neighbouring ports. Be it known that the leaving of Foreigners and others under the plea of sickness or desertion or under any plea... as paupers or unregistered Servants... which made them chargeable to the Public – is ILLEGAL – expenses will in future be charged on the Owner or Master of the Vessel so leaving the Person. And be it further known, That all persons harbouring such Foreigners or others shall... be held responsible for a willful misdemeanor and be chargeable with such portion of the expenses incurred by the sickness or death of such foreigner or other, as the discretion of the Magistrates may seem fit. By order of the Worshipful the Magistrates, H. SYMONS, Clk of Cts. Court House, Belize 11th December 1839.

New Dry Goods Store – A general assortment of Dry Goods... at low prices for Cash. Also per Brig *Hope,* a few Hogsheads superior Brandy, and a case of "Murrays" Tea Biscuits and Rusks, in 6lb Trammels at 15/- each. ROBERTSON & URQUHART, Belize, 14th December 1839.

Wines lately received for sale at the Store of the Subscribers – Choice Madeira, and Sherries... Champagne, Port and Claret. ROBERTSON & URQUHART, Belize, 14th December 1839.

Estate of William WILLIAMSON, Dec'd. For Public Sale, on Saturday the 21st Inst. at the late residence of the deceased: Household Furniture, Plate, Glass, China and Crockeryware, Military Appointments, Books, and sundry other articles. Terms to be made known at the time and place of sale. William WALLACE, Trustee.

Estate of Samuel F. AUGUST: The sale will take place on the 21st instead of the 23rd inst. as before informed, and for convenience, the goods will be removed to the residence of the late William WILLIAMSON, Esq. J. WOODS, Belize, 13th December 1839.

Notice: The Subscriber begs to inform his Friends and the Public that he has been appointed Agent for the sale of the *Spectator* Newspaper, also the *Court, Colonial, and Gardner's Gazette*, of each of which several numbers are on hand. A list of Subscribers for either is now open at the Mart – single papers for sale. In addition to his other avocations the Subscriber has resumed that of Gauging, with which he is practically acquainted, and will be thankful for any employment afforded him. J. WOODS, Auctioneer and General Agent, Rock House, December 13th 1839.

For Sale, 150 head of Prime Working Cattle. Can be delivered any time after Christmas, and in lots to suit Purchaser. Belize, 12th December 1836. W. H. COFFIN.

Notice – The Subscriber offers For Sale his House and premises in Widow Lane, eligibly suited for business. A Cash purchaser would be liberally treated with. A. REVEU, December 12th 1839.

Saturday, December 12th 1839:

p. 371 *(Misprint, should read 377.)*

World news: From a speech by BUXTON, on the Slave Trade: A slaver, the *Rodeur*, 200 tons burthen, took on board 160 negroes. Fifteen days out, the crew observed the slaves had contracted a considerable redness of the eyes, which spread with singular rapidity… At this time they were limited to 8 ozs of water a day, afterwards reduced to half a wine glass. By advice of the surgeon the slaves in the hold were brought on deck for fresh air, but many, affected with nostalgia, threw themselves into the sea locked in each others' arms. The opthalmia soon began to infect all on board. The danger of infection or perhaps the cause which produced the disease, increased by a violent dysentery, attributed to the use of rain water. The number of the blind augmented every day. The vessel reached Guadaloupe on June 21st 1839 with the crew in a most deplorable condition. Three days after her arrival the only man who, during the voyage, had withstood the contagion, and whom Providence appeared to have preserved as a guide to his unfortunately companions, was seized with the same malady. Of the negroes, 39 had become perfectly blind, 12 had lost one eye, and 14 were affected with blemishes more or less considerable.

This case excited much interest, and several additional circumstances connected with it were printed and given to the public. It was stated that the Captain had caused several of the negroes who were prevented from throwing themselves overboard to be shot and hung, in hope the example might deter the rest. It was further stated that 30 who had become blind were thrown into the sea and drowned, as if they had landed no one would have bought them, while by throwing them overboard the expense of maintaining them was avoided, while a claim was laid on the Underwriters by whom the cargo had been insured, and who are said to have allowed it, and made good the value of the slaves destroyed.

What more need be said to illustrate the extremity of suffering induced by the middle passage, as demonstrated by the case of the *Rodeur?* But the supplement must not be omitted. At the time when only one man could see to steer the vessel, a large ship appeared "which appeared to be totally at the mercy of the wind and wave." The crew of the vessel, hearing the voices of the crew of the *Rodeur,* cried out most vehemently for help. They told the melancholy tale as they passed along, that their ship was a Spanish one , and that a contagion had seized the eyes of all on board, so that there was not one individual, sailor or slave, who could see. But alas! This pitiable narrative was in vain; for no help could be given. The *St. Leon* sailed on, and was never seen again.

Note: What caused the opthalmia that blinded these men?

363

A Transatlantic Venus - Story of an Alderman who was called to marry a widower to a widow. On arriving at the house, he found the bride in a corner with the bridesmaids holding a blanket before her. Only her bare head and shoulders and two little unshod feet were visible. The widower explained that his bride's late husband owed $150, and that if he married her with no clothes on he, the new husband, would not be responsible for the debt. The Alderman laughed and said, no, if he married her without her skin it would not save him from his precurser's debt. The Venus then wrapped herself in the blanket, went upstairs, put on the costume of a goddess, and descended in attire more fully appropriate to a modern wedding, when the couple were joined for better or worse. (From the *Philadelphia World*.)

For Sale: Just Received per *Victoria*, Baskets Champagne, "Duc de Nemours" brand – Madeira, Sherry… and a few Dozen very rich Old Port. Wines in Cases of two dozen each. The very first quality… moderate prices… ROBERTSON & URQUHART.

No. 65: Saturday, December 21st 1839:

A lengthy article on the ruins at Palanque, continued from a previous issue.

p. 378:

Messrs. A. FRANCE, COX, BOOTH, and JENNINGS have all been cutting mahogany in the territory of the Mosquito Indians. The wood has been detained by some of CARRERA's party, commanded by Col. BUSTILLO (who demand payment or they will confiscate it.) That his Excellency Col. MACDONALD will protect the interest of the cutters concerned, no one can doubt.

A woman who was offered last week for sale in Rotherham marketplace, came forward with a halter around her waist under her gown, the end of which was passed through her pocket hole. The "lady" in this instance fetched 4s 10d, which in all probability was more than she was worth – a fact which proves that horns are looking up and husbands looking down.

Note: An ancient and illegal custom continued sub rosa in the countryside: a cuckolded husband put his wife up for sale, to be bought by her lover. At this time, there was no such thing as divorce for ordinary people in England or her colonies.

H.M.'s brig *Ringdove*, Commander STEWART, has started for Omoa to demand the property carried there for security by Mr. BLAKE, who assisted in saving the lives of the crew of the *Wansbeck*, which have been most improperly detained by Mr. FOLLIN on the plea that he has a lien against them, having forwarded the Captain and crew of the *Wansbeck* to Belize. The Agent for the vessel, James McDONALD, Esq., is very willing to entertain his claim, and has written him to that effect, but he very properly requires the articles to be delivered for sale in Belize, where they are most likely to bring quadruple the amount they would fetch if sold in Omoa.

On Monday last a Warrant was taken out by HILL-RAVEN against a man commonly called French JOHN (or John FRENCH – which name is correct we know not) for threatening the complainant with danger to his life, property, etc. It appears by evidence adduced before W. MASKALL and L. McLENAN, Esqs, that Hill-Raven had seduced the affections of French John's better half (whom he had not taken for better or worse in the legal manner.) French John saw the Raven of the Hill sitting in his chair, close to his table, drinking his brandy and water, and enjoying the smiles and caresses of his ci-devant mistress… while he, French John, could get nothing from her but Turnips. The Magistrates decided that as he had not been property tied, he had no occasion to lament himself, or his lady being loose, and ordered him to pay costs of the warrant, and keep the peace for six months; bond £25 and two securities £12.10 each.

Next case: Richard BALL, Steward of the *Addingham,* -v- Thomas WATSON, the Master, for giving him a first rate starting with a rope's end. Adjudged the complainant to pay 2/3 and the prisoner Thomas WATSON 1/3 of the expence, and the warrant was thereon dismissed.

Alexander MURRAY, Mate of the brig *Hope,* was next brought up, charged with attempting to shoot the master of the vessel, John GUTHRIE, with a pistol. Capt. GUTHRIE had gone on board in company with Capt. WATSON, was not received as usual by his mate on the deck, and on entering his cabin found the gentleman quaffing his tea… the mate paid no attention to the Captain's remonstrations, refused to leave the cabin, and when an effort was made to eject him, he tried to shoot Capt. GUTHRIE. The Captain interfering in his behalf, he was sentenced to pay expence of warrant and go on board and pay better attention to his duty.

John Le MOIN was also brought up, charged with chopping with a macheat Joseph GIDEON. A woman, as usual, was the cause of the quarrel – and a most worthless subject she proved to be. As the matter was serious, Le MOIN was ordered to stand trial at the next Summary Court.

Fisher WARRIOR was examined on a charge of assaulting a white boy in the employ of Mr. Frederick COWELL, a shop keeper in the Back Street. The charge was fully established in the evidence produced. The bold WARRIOR was mulcted the expenses of the warrant, and in default of payment thereof, to enjoy the pleasure of working 28 days for the benefit of the Public, of which pleasure he is now partaking.

As Belize is now filling up with the arrival of the various Mahogany Cutters and their dependents, it may not be amiss to notice the defective state of our Police force. The public now pays for a Police establishment which is so totally ineffective that the "force" might be well dispensed with. The men do their duty well, but are not numerous enough to be effective. Unless the Stipendary Magistrates obtain permission from His Excellency Col. MacDONALD to reinforce the Police, our streets will be almost impassable, even for men. The lower class of Spaniards seem to consider Belize a town belonging to them…

Clothing for the Militia has arrived. William GUILD Esq. and Colonel COFFIN have exhibited great activity in obtaining the clothing and distributing it as quickly as possible so as to give each and all an opportunity to get a good fit.

The scarcity of Mahogany in the market at the present time is so great that the *Ceres*, which sailed on the 19th inst., had nothing but logwood on board, and the *Calista* and *James Lyon* now loading in our harbour will have a similar cargo. What the vessels expected out will do... There are anticipated, the *Europa, Friendship, Redman, Crusader, Ann Mondell, Countess Durham, Science*, and *Inca*. We hope that those who already have their Mahogany houses in the West India Docks, and other places, may benefit by the scarcity, which ought surely be productive of a rise in the market.

Education: The schools of the Baptist Mission were vacated on Thursday last for the season, and will reassemble on Tuesday, 31st. The Public is respectfully informed that while Religion holds a prominent position in the method of instruction adopted in these schools, all that would render it of a sectarian nature is carefully avoided, there being neither catechism, creed, nor form of prayer of any kind admitted.

Our readers will find in our columns a very extensive list of very valuable property, belonging to the Estate of the late Marshal Bennett, Esq., which will be disposed of on the 6th prox. – and we hope that the various cutters and others in Belize will not neglect the opportunity offered of purchasing Mahogany Works indisputably situated in British territory, in preference to being humbugged when cutting out of the limits of Belize.

p. 379:

Shipping Information: Belize, Saturday, December 21st 1839:

Arrived:
H. M. brig *Ringdove,* Commander STEWART, came to anchor at Water Quay on Monday last from Jamaica. She sailed for Omoa, Truxillo, and Ruatan on Thursday.
17th: Barque *Reliance*, HOWELL, London, with cargo of merchandise amounting to upwards of $100,000, to various mercantile houses in Belize.

Sailed:
15th: Brigt. *Patsey Blunt*, PEDERSON, New York, with 9 serones indigo and 52½ tons logwood.
19th: Ship *Ceres,* PALLOT, Cork, 292 tons logwood and 3000 cocoanuts, cleared by Messrs. De ST. CROIX & Co.

Vessels Loading in Harbour: Barques *Ceylon,* COX; *Addingham,* WATSON; and brigs *Visitor,* MOPPETT, and *James Lyon,* SHEDDEN.
Loading at the Southward: Brig *William Henry Angas.*
Loading at Golden Stream Quay: Brigt. *Victoria,* MAY.

The American brig *Tallyrand*, COOPER, will sail this day for New York. Her cargo consists of 48,000 feet of mahogany and 35 tons logwood. The schooner *Rosella*, WALKER, arrived on Thursday last from Jamaica, last Truxillo. The ship *Calista*, BLAMPIED, is advertised on the window of the store of Messrs. KENNEDY & Co. to sail on Tuesday next for Cork.

Messrs. James GANN, and Frederick TEMPLES, came passengers in the *Reliance*.

H. Q., Government House, Belize, December 14th 1839: Military General Orders: The Commander in Chief has been pleased to make the following Promotions and Appointments in the Prince Regent's Royal Honduras Militia – Thomas STEWART to be Paymaster, commission dated 23rd Sepember. J. SHAW, gent. to be Ensign, commission dated 6th November. W. URQUHART, gent. to be Ensign, commission dated 6th December. By Command, R. M. NICHOLLS, Gov't Secretary.

Blank forms for Powers of Attorney, Bills of Lading, Commissions for Militia Officers (printed on parchment,) and Mahogany and Logwood Cutters' Books of Agreements are on Sale at the Office of this Paper.

Notice: For Sale, just received per *Hebe* and *Reliance* – Wesphalia and Yorkshire Hams. Baskets of Potatoes. White and Merino Striped Regatta Shirts. Hair Brooms. Spirit Bubbles. Boots & Shoes. Osnaburghs. Fancy Cotton Prints (fashionable patterns.) Cases of Geneva. Cases of Cheese. Ironmongery. Kegs of patent Shot. Barrels of bottled Porter, ditto Pale Ale. Cask of Wine Glasses. Ditto of Gun Flints. Cases Tobacco Pipes. Cutlery. Stationery. Wearing Apparel. Irish Linens. Duck Frocks and Trowsers. Brown Holland. Britannias. Dowlas. Bleached Canvas, &c, &c. William VAUGHAN, Belize, December 21st 1839.

Note: Spirit bubbles were used to test the alcohol content of rum, whisky, etc. Oznaburghs were coarse linen or cotton cloths. Britannias were domestic utensils made of a silvery metal alloy. Dowlas were coarse linen cloths.

Notice: Tuesday, 7th January at 11 o'clock in the morning, the Wesleyan Methodists will hold their Centenary Meeting in the Chapel... 20th December.

Just Imported and For Sale: Superior Scotch Ale, by the Cask or dozen. Also, To Let, very eligibly situated for either wholesale or retail business, the Stores and Wharf at present in the occupancy of Messrs. COX & SON. For particulars apply on the premises, or to J. WOODS. Rock House, Belize, December 16th 1839.

Dress Making &c.: Mrs. IRELAND begs leave to announce to the Ladies and Inhabitants of Belize, that she will undertake to make up Dresses and Plain Work on the most reasonable terms. Mrs. Ireland having served her time in one of the most fashionable Shops in Dublin, trusts that she will please those that may favor her with their work. All orders sent to the Fort will be immediately attended to. Fort George, December 18th 1839.

Shops in Dublin, trusts that she will please those that may favor her with their work. All orders sent to the Fort will be immediately attended to. Fort George, December 18th 1839.

Note: "Served her time" meant that Mrs. Ireland had completed a formal apprenticeship, normally of seven years. Since she was living at the fort it appears she was married to one of the military men there.

Estate of Marshal BENNETT, Esq., Dec'd.
For Public Sale, on Monday the 6th January next, at the residence of the late M. Bennett, Esq.:

The House and Premises recently occupied by the deceased,
The House and Premises called "POTTS" – these premises being very extensive will be disposed of in divisions.
A Lot adjoining the Artillery Parade Ground.
A Lot, over the Pond, adjoining Mr. William GODFREY's Lot.
A House and Lot over the pond called GUILDFORD's.
A House and Lot, South side of the Canal, late J. MUSLAR's.
A large Premises on north side of the Canal, which will be disposed of in Four Lots.

MAHOGANY WORKS:

1. Hermitage – Works –	River Belize
2. Mount Hope	" "
3. ROBINSONS	" "
4. More To-morrow	" "
5. Cockrico	" "
6. ½ of Monkey Falls	" "
7. Erindale or Big Falls	" "
8. Gaffers, or Double-headed Cabbage	" "
9. Black Rock, GARBUT's Creek,	" "
10. ALEXANDER's, Barton Creek,	" "
11. BENNETT's, " "	" "
12. LEWIS, Roaring Creek	" "
13. ANDERSONS, " "	" "
14. GRAHAM's No. 1 Beaver Dam Creek " "	
15. GRAHAM's No. 2, " " " " "	
16. BENNETTs, " " " " "	
17. GRAHAM's No. 3 " " " " "	
18. NELSON's " " " " "	
19. WALLS " " " " "	
20. HOBSON's Choice, COOKS Lagoon " "	

Two Logwood Works in Northern Lagoon
One ditto In New River
A Plantation at Convention Town, called FOWLER's bank
Also, Household Furniture, A Saw Mill, A variety of Tools suitable for Mahogany Cutters or others. Some Dry Goods, &c &c &c, all to be seen on the premises.

Terms will be made known at the time and place of sale.
Wm WALSH, Thomas PHILLIPS, Executors on the Estate of Marshal BENNETT, Dec'd, Belize, 20th December 1839.

p. 381:

Sir: At the examination of the Honduras Free School... I was not a little surprised on entering the airy and commodious School-room, to find that so few of the inhabitants were in attendance. Very few were aware of the event, as no public notification had been given. This was regrettable, as it was an opportunity for the children to display their learning. Mr. William MACKAY, the headmaster of the school... boys from the 1st, 2nd, 3rd, and 4th classes.... Silver honorary medals. The writer advises that a distinct prize should be given for English reading. I remain, yrs., SPECTATOR.

Gaol Supplies: Tenders will be received for provisions during the year 1840. To each prisoner per diem, for five days of the week, 2 Mackerel and 7 Horse Plantains or 14 Maiden Plantains. For two days of the week, 1lb of Fresh Beef or 1½ lbs of Turtle, with Plantains as above. Terms of Contract must be specify at what rate per diem each prisoner shall be supplied with the above Provisions, distinguishing the Mackerel from the other days. The Person contracting shall bind himself to provide good and wholesome Provisions, as they may be rejected, by order of the Local Inspector, if found unwholesome... personal bond £100, two securities of £50 each for fulfillment of Contract. The lowest Tender if approved will be accepted. By order of the Magistrates, H. A. GRAY, Asst Clk Ct, Clerk of Cts Office, Belize, 14th December 1839.

Public Medical Department: Sealed Tenders will be received until the 30th inst. from Persons desirous of undertaking the duties of the Public Medical Dept., and of Health Officer for the year 1840. The Individual who may be appointed will be required to attend the sick in the Gaol, to furnish all Medicine, and perform all Surgical Operations necessary at the Public Hospital – to attend all Inquests and to board and report on all vessels suspected of being in an unhealthy state. By order of the Magistrates, H. A. GRAY... 14th December 1839.

Naval Dept., Secretary's Office, Belize, 16th Deember – It is Hereby Notified that Officers, Petty Officers and Seamen of H. M.'s Flotilla will assemble at the quarters of the Admiral Commanding on Monday next, 23rd inst. at 7 a.m. Fines and Forfeitures on Absenteeism will be strictly enforced... for Nonattendance: Admiral Commanding £10, Captains £5, Commanders or Secretary £4, Lieutenants £3, Midshipmen, Inspectors, Armourers, Sailing or Quartermasters £2, Seamen and others of same rank 13/4d.

It is intended to establish a Rendesvous on Shore with a Lieutenant's Guard – 2 Midshipmen and 12 Seamen, for the purpose of picking up all skulkers and absentees.

There are vacancies for a few respectable young Gentlemen as Midshipmen, and Volunteers are invited to enroll to fill up the required complement of Men. By Command, J. WOODS, Secretary to the Admiral.

369

An article about the opening session of the House of Assembly in Jamaica. Difficulties and distresses. The losses which property owners, chiefly in the sugar plantations, are sustaining for the want of continuous or abundant labour...

p. 382:

Editorial: England has already been taught some severe lessons, what it is for a short sighted or selfish minister to invest Governors with authority, who instead of consulting the opinions and wishes of the community, blindly execute orders... Before closing our remarks, we cannot but allude to the peculiarly delicate situation of a Governor, directed by a minister to carry measures into effect that are disagreeable to the inhabitants, whom he is unwilling to displease on the one hand, and on the other by disobeying runs the risk of losing his situation, or incurring the displeasure of his government, on which perhaps their future welfare depends – If in this harassing sort of trial he should commit errors, by precipitation or ill temper, we ought to look on them with the leniency for human weakness to which the strongest and wisest are liable.

Note: Was the editor referring to Col. MacDonald's execution of his orders concerning Honduras' claim to Roatan? Some previous Superintendents had been highly unpopular; one conducted what settlers called "a reign of terror" while in office in Belize.

New Years' resolutions made for the Settlement: the folly of quarreling, etc.

We were in error as regards the mahogany cutters named - Messrs. FRANCE, BOOTH, and JENNINGS - having no intimation of any obstruction to their proceedings, Mr. L. P. COX alone having been written to by BUSTILLO.

On Thursday last a Soldier of the 2nd West India Regt. attempted to cut off the head of a lad, a servant of Capt. SOWDEN, and inflicted several severe wounds with a razor. Crimes of this nature ought not to go unpunished.

Notwithstanding the very unpropitious weather, the Militia and Flotilla have mustered pretty regularly... New clothing has given general satisfaction, and the caps now in use must be a vast deal more comfortable to the men than the abominably heavy shaco formerly in use... The Band, as we foretold, have proved successful competition with that of the Barracks, and their new clothing is very elegant.

World news: "Your Worship." A man having business with a Magistrate, who was an auctioneer, gave much offence by neglecting to call him Your Worship, on which he committed him to gaol for contempt. When the man obtained his discharge he constantly attended his worship's sales, bidding for almost every lot "Threepence, Your Worship," "Sixpence, Your Worship," which caused such gales of laughter at the auctioneer's expense, that he was glad to give the man ten guineas never to attend any more. *(Source not given.)*

p. 383:

World News: Sumptuous preparations for Her Majesty's approaching Nuptials.

A Labourer's Child Starved to Death. An inquest was held on Monday week at Stanton St Bernard, Wilts, on the body of Samuel COX, about ten years of age. It happened that early on the previous Friday morning the lad, accompanied by his father, left Broughton with a flock of lambs to go to Shaw Farm in Overton. They had no refreshment before starting... It rained for the greater part of the day so that they were completely drenched. They took shelter in a skilling on the down. After they had rested the father wanted to go on, but the boy said, A little longer, Father... A little longer... At dawn his father took him in his arms, and saw that he was dying. The body was emaciated, the bones of the poor lad almost protruding through the skin. Verdict, Died through inclemency of the weather and the want of the proper necessities of life.

Military General Orders – Every Officer in command of a company is responsible for the return into Store of the Clothing and Appointments he received out... every Non Commissioned Officer and Private is responsible for loss or injury of the same. Lists (to be turned in) of men to whom clothing and appointments have been given.

War Office: 2nd West Indies Reg't: Lt. J. GROGAN from the 33rd Foot to be Lt., vice GRIFFEN who exchanges; Ensign W. ANDERSON to be Lt. without purchase, vice BRUCE, appointed to the 18th foot; Ensign J. D. MENDS to be Lt. without purchase, vice MURRAY, appointed to the 94th Foot. To be Ensign without purchase, Sergeant Major J. HARGER; G. BENNETT, Gentleman, vice MacLEAN, appointed to the 94th foot.

Shipping Information, Saturday, December 28th 1839:

Arrived:
21st: Barque *Othello,* GRUCHY, Jersey, 54 days with merchandise &c. consigned to Wm VAUGHAN Esq.
28th: Schooner *Morning Star,* BARRETT, Truxillo.

Sailed:
24th: Ship *Calista,* BLAMPIER, Cork, with 215 tons Logwood, cleared by Messrs. ST. CROIX & Co.

Vessels loading in Harbour: Barques *Ceylon,* COX; *Addingham,* WATSON; and brigs *Visiter,* MOPPETT, and *James Lyon,* SHEDDEN.

Vessels loading at the Southward: Brig *William Henry Angas.*

The brigantine *Victory,* MAY, arrived in harbour Wednesday last from the Southward.

Notice: A Sermon will be preached tomorrow morning in St. John's Church by the Rev. M. NEWPORT, B.M., when a Collection will be made in aid of the Society for Promoting

371

Christian Knowledge, the Funds of which are chiefly employed in furnishing Books for the Honduras Free School. Subscriptions will be thankfully received by Charles EVANS, Esq., Treasurer. Wm MASKALL, Churchwarden. 28th December 1839.

A meeting of the Board of Fire Wardens will take place at the Court House on Monday next, 30th inst., for the purpose of auditing accounts. All persons having Demands against said Board must submit on or before that date or they will not be entertained. By order of the Chairman, J. WOODS, Clerk to the Board of Fire Wardens. Belize, 27th December 1839.

Estate of Marshall BENNETT, Dec'd:
For Sale on Monday the 6th proximo at the late Residence of Marshal Bennett Esq., deceased, along with the Property already addressed – Also, The Whole of the Property at the Sarse River, consisting of A Prime Gang of Working Cattle, Truck, Truck Gear, and a variety of Tools, &c., also Mahogany. For further particulars apply to William WALSH, Thomas PHILIPS, Esqrs. Belize, December 28th 1839.

p. 384:

Booby Justices: A lad was taken by his brutal master before the Bench of Squire Justices in Loughborough, Leicestershire, for "desecrating the Sabbath" by cleaning his lace-ups in an outhouse. The lad only wanted his boots to be clean to go to church. There was public outrage over the 40/- fine imposed, out of his wages of £7 a year. The Squire had his horses rubbed down by a groom and the lady perfumed her hair with the help of her maid before going to church... A public subscription paid the fine. If fanaticism is not checked the Sabbath, instead of being a blessing, will become a monstrous curse to the people.

Notice: Persons having demands against the Public are requested to render their account at this office previous to 12 o'clock on Monday next the 30th inst. By order of the Magistrates... H. A. GRAY...

Wanted Immediately – About 400 full grown Botans* of 8' length, suitable for staking in a Wharf, and for which a liberal price will be given. Apply to W. VAUGHAN – None need apply but those who understand the sort required. *A variety of palm.

No. 67: Saturday, January 4th 1840, Vol. 2.

p. 386:

Review of Militia, Sat. January 4th. A body of men who meet only a few days in each year, and many of whom (being raw recruits) had never handed a musket before... arrived at a degree of discipline that would be credible to even a regular troop... attributed to the judicious conduct of Colonel COFFIN.

The Flotilla – The seamen have done themselves credit...

The Regatta – Eighteen boats entered, each subscribing $10. Three other individuals made the sum total $210 by putting down $10 each. The race came off... The 8 first received sums as follows: 1. *Morning Star*, $50. 2. *Diamond*, $40. 3. *George*, $30. 4. *Clarendon*, $25. 5. *Seagull*, $22. 6. *Andrew Kennedy*, $18. 7. *Bryon*, $15. 8. *Vixen*, $10. On account of the *Morning Star* and *Diamond* being said to have reached the goal at the same time, they will either obtain equally or decide it by a fresh trial - they were first in.

His Excellency has been pleased to appoint the same Gentlemen to the Magistrate's office for the present year... the Magistrates took the usual Oath of Office, and took their seats on the 1st inst.

Two enterprising gentlemen in Pitpans visited Palenque, returned... *(The men were Patrick WALKER and Lt. CADDY, who had both taken leave in November.)*

Fire Wardens: Messrs. GUILD and WALSH retiring, Messrs. EVANS and SHIEL were chosen in their stead.

Editorial: The difficulties of an Editor who cannot step without treading on somebody's toes. Some want small print, some want large. One subscriber wants a more literary newspaper, while another complains that it is too literary... Each has a plan of his own for conducting a journal. The labour of Sisyphus was recreation when compared with that of an editor who tries to please them all.

p. 387:

Shipping Information:

Arrived:
Dec 30th: Schooner *William Wallace*, ALLYNE, New York, 25 days with assorted cargo to Messrs. WALSH & GOUGH.

H. M.'s brig *Serpent*, Commander GORE, arrived today from Jamaica with about $14,000 in specie for the Commissariat. She is expected to sail shortly for Vera Cruz.

Sailed:
Jan 2nd: Brigt *Victoria*, MAY, New York, with a cargo of mahogany, logwood, sarsaparilla, hides, and a few boxes specie– cleared by Joseph E. SWASEY, Esq.

Loading in the Harbour: Barques *Ceylon*, COX; *Addington*, WATSON; and brigs *Visiter*, MOPPETT and *James Lyon*, SHEDDEN.

Loading at the Southward: Brig *William Henry Angas*.

Messrs. B. C. WOOD, DRISSILDORFF, and BILLEGRAND came passengers in the *William Wallace*.

373

We have to apologize for the late issue of the Paper – but our kind Friends, doubtless, will excuse us on account of our Militia duty.

Marriage: In this Town on Wednesday the 1ˢᵗ Instant, by the Rev. Matthew NEWPORT, Mr. Richard WOODS, to Miss Susan B. TOOTH, of this place.

Secretary's Office, 1ˢᵗ January 1840: H. M's. Superintendent has been pleased to appoint the following Gentlemen Magistrates for the year 1840: William MASKALL, James McDONALD, William H. USHER, John YOUNG, M.D., and Patrick WALKER, for this Settlement; John Edward HENDERSON, Esq. a Magistrate for that part of the Settlement situated between the Rivers Sibun and Sarstoon; and Richard D. ANDERSON, Esq., Magistrate for the Belize River. By Command, R. M. NICHOLLS, Gov't Secretary.

Court House, Belize, January 3ʳᵈ 1840: The undersigned Gentlemen are appointed Fire Wardens of the Settlement for the year 1840: James McDONALD, William H. COFFIN, William WALSH, Charles EVANS, Edward SHIEL, Esqrs. James McDONALD to be Chairman of the Board. By order of the Magistrates, H. A. GRAY.

Honduras Bible Society – His Excellency Col. MacDONALD, H. M.'s Superintendent, Patron of the Bible Society, will preside…

For Public Sale immediately after the Summary Court Venditional Sale, the Schooner *Fifeshire,* better known as being formerly the property of the late John H. PETZOLD, Dec'd, now under levy on writ, Estate of John H. PETZOLD –v- James STAIN. By Order of the Magistrates, Lewis McLENAN, P. M. General*. A credit of six months will be given. Belize, 4ᵗʰ January 1840. *Provost Marshal General.*

For Sale at the store of the Subscriber, the following articles just received per *Reliance* and *Hebe:* Cases and Hogsheads of Geneva. Ironmongery. Paints. Kegs of patent Shot. Fish Hooks. Barrels of Pork. Haberdashery. Quills. Stationery. Pocket and Memorandum Books (assorted sizes,) with military pencils. Umbrellas – Light Silk and Gingham, Fine White Regatta and Stripe Shirts. Fine Irish Linen. Matches. Dowlas. Wine Glasses. Corks. Osnaburgh. Pipes. Linens. Shawls. London Bottled Port and Ale. Per *Othello:* Cases of Vinegar. Cheese. Eau de Cologne. Mahogany Four Post Bedsteads and Mattresses. Westphalia and Yorkshire Hams. Cases Pickles and Fish Sauces. William VAUGHAN, 4ᵗʰ January 1840.

No. 68, Saturday, January 11ᵗʰ 1840:

Jamaica – Fine furniture is now being made from native woods.

Barbadoes – Prison discipline. Nine labourers, taken in the act of robbing a potato-piece, were sentenced to ten days imprisonment with hard labour. On release they were returned to the property on which they committed the robbery, and appeared rather dissatisfied. Asked the reason, they unanimously declared their regret at being released from confinement in the town, and wished some one would be so kind as to put them back -

adding that they could want no more than what they got while in prison, for they had daily a belly full, and but little or nothing to do.

p. 390:

Summary Court, Monday, January 6th. Five warrants:

Complaint of Representative of the late Dr F. YOUNG'S estate, -v- Francisco DIEGO, a Carib. Mr. HAYLOCK , the attorney, stated the defendant had breached an agreement entered into in 1837, having absconded and not been seen until captured. Sentence, 12 months at hard labour. The second warrant concerned a similar offence, on the complaint of Wm. USHER Esq., who left the Bench to his brother Magistrates, against Manuel ANGLESIA. The prisoner in 1837 received a three months' advance on having signed an agreement, proceeded to the Works up the Old River, but shortly after acted as El Senor Don Francisco Diego by visiting the town of Petan... for what length of stay, or for what reason, he did not apprise his fellow labourers - a serious loss to the Complainant. The same Defendant had hired to Mr. L. COX, who also advanced him a large sum. These gentlemen are not the only bankers to the accomplished Senor, for we in our time have debited him by his receipt of £12/10 from us - then he treated us as he did Mr. USHER, by setting out on his travels, which must close now for twelve months. Jury's verdict, 12 months' hard labour.

Next case: Mr. Ralph CUNNINGHAM against Clashmore LAWLESS, for purloining Logwood. There were contradictions in the testimony, leading to a verdict of acquittal.

The next case was John USHER, Esq. –v- Francis BOWDEN, who having once been in his employ, had obtained a Pea Jacket in the name of another person employed by him... The Defendant said that a party to whom he lent a similar jacket never returned it, deeming the borrower could have no objection to pay for it when required. What an illusion of the brain! As he had not presented an order from the party (who perhaps was illiterate) the jury returned a verdict of Guilty, £10 fine or become an inmate of Mr. LOCKWARD's for thirty days.

The last warrant was the serious complaint of Joseph GIDEON against John LAMOINE, Bugler to the Light Infantry Company of H.M. Honduras Militia, who instead of applying the vocal instrument to awakening the martial spirit of the Corps, brought it into contact with Mr. Gideon's's nose, then inflicted a fresh wound with a macheat... Guilty. Enrolled in Capt. DIEMAS' Company for three months' drill. Jealousy was the cause, but we are not aware of what fair one it was .. but this, in fact, is immaterial, as it is an everyday occurrence among gentry of their class...

p. 391:
The attention of cutters and their disbursers has now turned to forming their respective gangs, to return to their work... Let them encourage their labourers by fair prices, not only to cut Mahogany, but other valuable woods for furniture, dyeing, etc. They may meet with a ready market.

Shipping Information, Belize, Saturday, January 11th 1840:

Arrived:
6th: Brig *Friendship,* LAWSON, London, with a cargo of merchandise consigned to
        the late Alexr. BRYMNER.

Sailed:
Her Majesty's brig *Serpent,* Commander GORE, sailed on Monday last from
        English Quay for Vera Paz.

Loading in the Harbour: Barques *Ceylon,* COX; *Addingham,* WATSON; brig *Visiter,*
MOPPETT, *James Lyon,* SHEDDEN, and *Friendship,* LAWRIE.

Married: In this Town on Thursday last, by the Rev. Matthew NEWPORT, B.M.,
Alexander FORBES, Esq, to Miss Emma LLEWELLYN RHYSE [*sic*] of this place.

*Note: Emma, born June 20th 1820, and Edward Llewellyn Rhys, born March 27th 1822,
were children of Thomas RHYS, Asst. Surgeon on half pay, and Eleanor POTTS.*

Died: On the 6th instant after a short illness, Mr. William A. CRAMMOND, aged 22
years, a native of Nassau, N.P., much lamented by his relatives and friends. On the same
day, Mr. Joseph TIDDESLEY.

For London, the barque *Ceylon,* Austin W. COX, Master, will leave this Port on or about
the 13th inst. All demands... The above Vessel has room for Cabin Freight. Geo. A.
USHER.

Just Imported per *Friendship,* and For Sale at the Store of the Subscriber – Bales Russia
Sheetings and Ravenducks.* Bales Sailcloth. Oznaburghs, in half and quarter pieces.
Bales 7-4 and 10-4 Witney Blankets. Superfine Beaver Hats. Trunks of different sizes.
Reindeer Tongues. Assorted Sauces. Bottles Curry, Assorted Pickles. Jars Butter. And
a variety of Perfumery, etc. Per De ST CROIX & Co., Wm. E. HAMPSHIRE. *A fine
quality of sailcloth.*

Notice: Having been employed by John E. HENDERSON Esq. to run the Division Line
between HEINDALE or Brig Falls, and Gaffers or Double Headed Cabbage Works in the
Biloxi River, I hereby give notice to all it may concern, that I shall proceed to run the said
line on a course of 49 degrees east, 21 days from the date hereof. Joseph SMITH, Land
Surveyor. Belize, 11th January 1840.

p. 392:

World news – from the *North American*: An Exchange – A carriage containing two ladies
who represented themselves as mother and daughter stopped at the outer gate of the Alms
House over the Schuylkill on Thursday last, when the youngest informed the keeper that
her mother was anxious to adopt a white child, an infant if possible, she having lost one.

She was shown several, made a selection, and requested permission to show it to her mother who was in the carriage; if suited, they would obtain an order from the Guardians of the Poor and call in a day or two for it. She wrapped up the child in its cradle clothes and carried it herself to the carriage, and after a few moments delay returned, placed the babe where it was found, and said they would call next day to take it away. The carriage drove off. When it became necessary to remove the child for some cause, it was discovered that the white child had been taken by the person in the carriage, and a colored one left in its place!

Note: This is a genealogical puzzle with very few clues: date, place, and proximity. To save her marriage and her family's reputation, the woman in the carriage abandoned her child to the alms house to grow up as a foundling. The baby could have been no more than a few days old or, no matter how it was concealed in swaddling clothes, her husband would have taken a close look and realized that he was not the father. The ladies must have lived near enough to Schuylkill to have learned that there would be infants at the alms house, but not so near that they or their carriage would be known to the staff. How far away they lived is uncertain. They could have left their home early in the morning and returned the same day, or left on a journey to visit relatives in another county, and detoured to Schuylkill on the way. The latter is the most likely scenario; relatives who had not seen the newborn could not compare it with the infant presented on arrival, and if the women returned home after several days or weeks, any change in its appearance would be passed off as due to growth.

As Sir Walter Scott so truly said: "Oh, what a tangled web we weave, when first we practice to deceive!" How utterly astonished descendants of both those infants would be if they could tear away the web of secrecy those two women wove!

---oOo---

INDEX

As readers will have noted, many people who appear in records in this book did not have surnames. Those who had no surname are indexed by given name; those who had a surname are indexed only by surname. At the start of the "A"s, for example, Aaron, Abba, and Abel do not have surnames; ABEL, ABENA, and ABERCROMBY are surnames. For differentiation, all surnames are in capitals. People recorded only as "an Indian woman," "a man found drowned," etc., are not indexed, as they cannot be identified. Information about Government military pensioners whose names were not given may be available in War Department records at the British National Archives. Please check the index carefully for every possible variant spelling of the name you seek: due to alphabetization, some variants may be very far apart. Can anyone fill in the missing letters in the first four, partially illegible names?

–ICH-----, 73
.....LER, 67
...WORTH, 24
A....., 44
Aaron, 292
Abba, 133
Abel, 104, 132, 210
ABEL, 68
ABENA, 161
ABERCROMBY, 228
Aberdeen, 103, 174
Abigail, 263
Abraham, 301
ABRAHAM, 212
ABRAHAMS, 229
ABRAMS, 72
ACHISON, 22
Acinta, 152, 273
ADAEAR, 67
Adam, 61, 102, 103, 108, 116, 121, 128, 132, 138, 147, 219
ADAM, 2, 6, 27, 30, 80, 138
Adam, an African, 65
ADAMS, 230
Adele, 169
Adeline, 290
Adney, 229
ADNEY, 227

Adolphus, 125, 187
ADOLPHUS, 37, 139, 165, 192, 193, 224, 225, 275, 320, 342
ADRED, 229
Adriana, 126, 169, 248
AGNANT, 276
AGNER, 63
Agnes, 125, 128, 153, 187, 197, 302
AGNEW, 54
AIKMAN, 80, 98
Alberto, 282
ALBERTO, 167, 182
ALBINA, 38
ALBINO, 10
ALCANTRA, 62
Aleck, 188
Alexander, 44, 121, 129, 188, 225, 266
ALEXANDER, 25, 45, 47, 55, 64, 73, 74, 105, 129, 132, 133, 142, 147, 207, 220, 348, 368
ALEXANDRE, 148
ALEXIS, 227
Alfred, 130, 246, 262, 276
Alice, 303
Alick, 104, 113, 161, 162, 179, 181, 224, 282
Allan, 146
ALLAN, 351, 356

378

ALLEN, 25, 26, 56, 134, 184, 226, 231, 350
ALLEYN, 344, 345
ALLICK, 181
ALLISON, 342
ALLYNE, 373
ALTEREITH, 116, 218, 224, 310, 342
Amanda, 124, 129
Amelia, 102, 107, 108, 117, 125, 128, 133, 134, 140, 153, 176, 177, 180, 199, 203, 208, 209, 221
America, 162
AMMERY, 307
ANBATO, 196
ANCHAWA, 228
ANDERSON, v, 5, 22, 32, 37, 60, 61, 62, 65, 66, 71, 80, 98, 110, 114, 117, 130, 135, 147, 177, 180, 184, 186, 189, 195, 223, 224, 225, 227, 228, 229, 230, 241, 246, 253, 261, 279, 281, 291, 300, 313, 315, 318, 321, 324, 342, 368, 371, 374
ANDRE, 80, 98
Andreid, 301
Andrew, 62, 107, 120, 121, 127, 176
ANDREW, 33, 35, 38, 80, 108, 116, 218
ANDREW & Co., 317, 323, 324, 331, 334, 335, 338
ANDREWIN, 228
ANDREWS, 64, 155, 184, 216, 226, 280, 312, 313, 323
ANDREWS & Co., 318, 338, 341
Andria, v, 207
Andy, 199, 210
ANESTECA, 71
Angelina, 117
ANGLESIA, 375
ANGO, 125
Ann, 132
Ann Grace, 179, 269
Anna, 116, 188
Anne, 111, 131, 133
Annette, 303
Anney, 156
Anntotenna, 302
Anny, 290

ANSELMO, 48
Anthony, 114, 121, 147, 153, 162, 188
ANTHONY, 263
ANTOINE, 155
ANTOLIAN, 288
Antonia, 40
ANTONIA, 17, 41, 169
Antonio, 200
ANTONIO, 44, 70, 73, 143, 151, 186, 301, 304
AOSNER, 46
APPLEBY, 178, 245
APRISE, 48
Arabella, 121
Arabian, v
ARAENGAS, 48
Araminta, 114, 188
ARBETTE, 281
ARBISA, 55, 227
ARCHER, 227
ARCHIBALD, 120
Archie, 108
ARCHY, 35
Ardent, 324
ARGUELLAS, 109
ARGUILLES, 342
Ariadne, 103, 219
ARIS, 152
ARMSTRONG, 58, 65, 75, 76, 79, 80, 106, 107, 155, 202, 211, 218, 225, 226, 228, 229, 230, 325, 342
ARNOLD, 11, 226, 275
ARNSTEL, 63
AROYIO, 148
Arran, 117
ARSO, 262
ARTHERS, 55
ARTHUR, 2, 6, 74, 79, 129, 145, 149, 230
ARTHURS, 15, 132, 136, 194, 220, 221, 226, 230
ARVIESA, 339
ASCAIYO, 48
ASKEW, 3, 158, 208, 225
ASKIE, 225
Atanana, 228

ATKIN, 80
ATKINSON, 31
AUDINET, 59, 265
AUDINETT, 13, 155, 200, 224
AUGISTE, 52
August, 224
AUGUST, 3, 4, 13, 52, 57, 75, 81, 90,
104, 107, 137, 140, 182, 184, 198,
199, 210, 220, 224, 225, 226, 227,
228, 229, 251, 264, 309, 319, 331,
346, 348, 349, 352, 357, 362
Augusta, 133
AUGUSTA, 12, 225
AUGUSTIAN, 230, 231
AUGUSTIN, 141
Augustine, 64
AUGUSTINE, 150, 226
AUTHER, 227
AVARIZA, 57
AVARRO, 81, 98
AVEMAN, 98
AVEMANN, 81
Averino, 50
AVILLA, 41, 64, 130
AVILLAR, 262
AVILLER, 249
AVINO, 300
J. B., Mr., 380
S. B., 98 *(Tombstone inscription.)*
Bacchus, 121, 162
BACCHUS, 32
BAGNEL, 241, 242
BAGSHAW, 41
BAILEY, 7, 28, 31, 64, 66, 110, 139,
161, 186, 195, 204, 205, 240, 242
BAILLIE, 335
BAILY, 11, 46, 55, 239, 241
BAIN, 118, 231
BAKER, 17, 33, 43, 44, 81, 98, 111, 135,
164, 183, 186, 210, 241, 242, 273, 338
BALDWIN, 108, 179
BALFOUR, 25, 44, 81, 93, 171, 173,
313
BALL, 365
BALLAD, 214
BALLARINE, 50

BANES, 98
BANKES, 123
BANKS, 81, 85, 98, 100, 188, 190, 232,
234, 325, 342
BANNA, 228
BANNER, 199, 231
BANTUN, 292
BAPTIST, 132, 298
BAPTISTE, 42, 67, 158, 220, 231, 243,
288, 307
Bar, 188
Barclet (or Bardet?), 254
BARKER, 361
BARNARD, 71, 119, 244
BARNES, v, 25, 81, 92, 98, 106, 135,
186, 238, 241, 268, 278
BARNET, 326, 329
Barney, 70
BARR, 157
BARRET, 220
BARRETT, 132, 133, 371
BARROW, 58, 138, 193, 243
BARSO, 169
BARTHOLOMEW, 185
BARTLET, 76
BARTLETT, 132, 309
BASIL, 296
BASQUEZ, 43
BATES, 11, 30, 75, 126, 128, 191, 197,
202, 232, 335
Bathsheba, 128
BATIAS, 233
BATISTE, 148, 267, 282
BATTISTA, 110
BAYFIELD, 81
BAYLEY, 67
BAYLY, 37, 232
BAYNBRIDGE, 240
BAYNTON, 41, 239
BAYNTUN, 58, 212
BEACH, 95, 107, 310
BEAKE, 144
BEAKS, 238
BEARD, 39, 237
Beatrice, 174
BEATRIX, 237

BEATTIE, 127, 244
BEATTY, 55
BEAUMONT, 198
BECK, 10, 50
BEDDOES, 326
BEDFORD, 40, 81, 97
BEDHILL, 61
BEGFORD, 264
Behavior, 146
Behaviour, 266
BELA, 148
Belford, 130, 192
BELILE, 35, 38, 48, 53
BELISARE, 35
BELISLE, 5, 8, 24, 31, 41, 75, 113, 117,
   123, 141, 149, 156, 157, 160, 165,
   168, 178, 180, 183, 185, 196, 231,
   233, 234, 235, 240, 241, 242, 248,
   256, 308, 310
BELIZAIRE, 282
Belize Agricultural Company, 317, 319,
   328
Belize Amateur Theatre, 316, 320
BELL, 74, 232, 234, 238, 329
----BELL, 40
Bella, 103, 108, 113, 133, 209, 219
Belle, 109
BELLNOE, v
BELYTHE, 242
Ben, 108, 113, 114, 117, 146, 150, 224,
   246
BENBRIDGE, 246
BENIAN, 230
Benjamin, 50, 72, 107, 115, 144, 153,
   179, 275, 290
Benjamin G, 9
Bennaba, 133
BENNER, 231
BENNET, 14, 17, 285
Bennett, 103, 219
BENNETT, v, 3, 10, 11, 16, 17, 20, 21,
   22, 29, 33, 37, 40, 49, 53, 54, 59, 61,
   62, 64, 65, 66, 68, 73, 79, 82, 98, 103,
   129, 130, 132, 133, 137, 143, 145,
   146, 156, 188, 190, 197, 200, 205,
   206, 219, 220, 221, 225, 231, 233,

235, 236, 237, 238, 239, 240, 241,
   242, 244, 246, 258, 262, 265, 266,
   272, 283, 284, 289, 291, 294, 300,
   302, 309, 310, 329, 340, 343, 348,
   349, 353, 368, 369, 371, 372
BENNIE, 225
BENOIT, 24
BENTLACE, 240
BENTON, 157
BENTURA, 244
Benture, 188
BERK, 101
BERN, 118
BERNARD, 1, 28, 43, 143, 157, 191,
   237, 239, 309
Berry, 122, 203
BERTIE, 44, 73, 106, 177, 235
BERTRAND, 27
BERTY, 27
BESCENTE', 39
Bess, 128, 169, 211
BESS, 6, 28
Bessey, 100
Bessy, 133
BETANCEN, 41
Betheny, 199
Betsey, 101, 102, 113, 116, 121, 122,
   124, 131, 143, 146
BETSON, 3, 70, 74, 79, 127, 158, 161,
   162, 217, 220, 240, 243, 286, 313,
   316, 342
Betsy, 9, 52, 153, 179, 192, 219, 274,
   296, 335
BETTIE, 237
Betty, 101, 106, 141, 165, 176, 204, 262
BETTY, 185
BEVANS, 76, 255
BEVINS, 15, 157
BHANS, 242
BIBBY, 56
BICKHAM, 93
BIDDLE, 82, 98
BIDDOCK, 68
BIGGIN, 26
Bill, 54, 105, 121, 132, 133, 204
BILLEGRAND, 373

BILLERY, 17, 62, 144, 168, 243
Billy, 101, 107, 110, 117, 132, 147, 179, 186, 187, 190, 301
BILLY, 319
Bird, 272
BIRD, 2, 14, 15, 56, 94, 103, 241
BIRKHARD, 46
BISENT, 36
BISHOP, 4, 26
BLACK, 22, 264, 277, 323
Black Adam, 117
BLACKBOURN, 27
Blackwick, 130
BLACKWIRE, 237
BLADEN, 11
BLADON, 156, 180, 261
BLAKE, 29, 50, 127, 153, 232, 296, 311, 320, 331, 334, 337, 342, 345, 347, 364
Blaknell, 184
BLAMPIED, 354, 356, 361, 367
BLANCHFORD, 66
BLANCO, 20
BLAND, 235
Blandford, 122, 203
BLANKENSOP, 354
BLENKINSOP, 333, 334, 337, 344
BLOCK, 218
BLOCKLEY, 27, 29, 82, 98, 113, 129
BLOND, 216
BLOOMFIELD, 46
Blucher, 206
BLYGH, 68
BLYTH, 8, 181
BLYTHE, 11
BOADE, 187, 203
Boatswain, 147, 169
Bob, 101, 104, 114, 132, 221
Bobby, 130, 184
BOBSTER, 321
BODDEN, 310
BODE, 106, 122, 163, 187, 203, 209, 233, 234, 236, 237, 238, 322
BODEN, 132, 220
BOGES, 189
Bogle, 117, 180
BOLT, 53

BONCHANCE, 45
BOND, 52
Boney Peter, 211
BONGARD, 33
BONHAM, 12
BONYEAR, 16
BOOTH, 214, 232, 342, 364, 370
BORDER, 241
BORGES, 51
BOSTICK, 235
BOSTOCK, 24
Boston, 104, 219
BOURKE, 141
BOURN, 139, 237
BOWDEN, 216, 231, 236, 341, 342, 375
BOWEN, 32, 74, 82, 87, 98, 235, 238, 273, 284, 319, 322, 324
BOWERS, 264
BOWMAN, 8, 51, 60, 105, 176, 234, 235, 237, 296
BOYLE, 101
BRADDICK, 16, 82, 96, 98, 212, 232, 343
BRADDOCK, 170
BRADFORD, 24, 233
BRADLEY, 69, 203, 236
BRAGELOW, 43
BRANNAN, 270
Brasilla, 136, 178
BRASTER, 121, 230
Breetchie, 117
BRENAN, 241
BRENNAN, 46, 73, 132, 219, 220, 236, 310
BRENNER, 48
BRESTOW, 294
BREWER, 118, 236, 238
BREWYER, 38, 155, 238
BRIDGE, 311
BRIEN, 7, 60, 128, 227, 239, 243, 262, 264
BRINTON, 82
Brister, 103
Bristol, 121, 132, 133, 220
Bristow, 104, 151, 164, 210
BRISTOW, 6

Britain, 103, 153
BRITON, 98
BRITT, 71
Brittain, 219
BRITTAN, 287
BRITTEN, 22, 75
BROADBELT, 244
BROASTER, 58, 76, 104, 105, 106, 117,
   121, 149, 187, 225, 227, 230, 231,
   233, 237, 263, 267, 289, 309
BROHAIR, 25
BROHIER, 199
BROSCHER, 26
BROSTER, 3, 8, 11, 14, 15, 53, 63, 64,
   122, 181, 214, 215, 233, 244, 271, 319
BROUGHTON, 163, 212, 235, 274
Brown, 113, 121
BROWN, 26, 50, 64, 66, 73, 98, 233,
   319, 325
BRUCE, 235, 371
BRUNO, 42
BRUYER, 238, 239
BRYAN, 6, 75, 80, 239, 278
BRYMNER, 317, 323, 331, 339, 342,
   376
BRYNNER, 67
BUCKNOR, 138
Bull, 224
BULL, 27, 31, 52, 71, 98, 102, 108, 112,
   114, 117, 135, 156, 180, 209, 220,
   232, 239, 244, 280
BUND, 238
BUNGEM, 245
Buonaparte?, 55
BURGESS, 2, 15, 19, 63, 71, 133, 154,
   302
BURK, 16, 39, 235
BURKE, 47, 50, 118, 152, 209, 240, 244,
   287
BURKITT, 157
BURLEY, 237
BURN, 21, 27, 32, 156, 157, 183, 200,
   201, 205, 233, 235, 239, 240, 242,
   243, 266, 268, 274, 312, 342
BURNAL, 235
BURNAN, 55

BURNEAU, 154, 196
BURNELL, 51
BURNHAM, 102, 177, 234
BURNO, 196
BURNS, 12, 13, 16, 50, 136, 143, 153,
   169, 170, 180, 207, 212, 214, 232,
   243, 278, 336
BURREL, 218, 236
BURRELL, 17, 83, 98, 102, 120, 121,
   123, 127, 190, 200, 260, 274, 282
BURREY, 202
BURTEY, 67
BURTING, 67
Busso, 102
BUSTILLO, 364, 370
BUTCHER, 133
BUTLER, 239
BUXTON, 363
BYAS, 70
Byron, 130
BYRON, 51, 54, 81, 83, 98, 104, 111,
   210, 309, 320
CABASAR, 72
CABBAGE RIDGE, 177
CABRERA, 251, 252
CADDLE, 101, 110, 117, 121, 134, 140,
   155, 163, 171, 175, 179, 200
CADDY, 323, 350, 351, 373
CADEL, 11, 12
CADELL, 5, 15, 16
CADET, 54
CADLE, 5, 155, 156, 157, 176, 180, 231,
   240, 244, 245, 248, 251, 276, 307
CADO, 250
CADOGAN, 313
Caesar, 38, 117, 121, 130, 133, 146, 183,
   184, 221
CAFÉ, 158
CAIN, 158, 246, 247, 253
CAIRNIE, 330, 334, 337, 344, 351, 354,
   356, 357, 361
CALDERONA, 147
CALDWELL, 25, 247
CALERMON, 128
Calista, 212, 229
CALLERMAN, 192

Callyan, 251
CALVO, 92
CAMAYANA, 12
CAME, 75
Camilla, 101, 161
CAMOYANO, 249, 329, 354, 356, 361
CAMP, 251
Campbell, 107
CAMPBELL, 3, 4, 5, 10, 13, 21, 25, 35,
    42, 50, 59, 83, 105, 126, 140, 158,
    203, 206, 208, 247, 276, 309
CANAUN, 6
CANDARA, 155
CANE, 196
CANNOR, 50
CANNOW, 253
CANTOUSE, 250
CANY, 251
CAPAH, 53
CARD, 2, 29, 49, 50, 55, 56, 65, 110,
    119, 121, 133, 137, 142, 144, 151,
    155, 157, 190, 193, 195, 207, 209,
    244, 245, 246, 250, 251, 252, 253,
    255, 262, 299, 307
Cardigan, 100
CAREL, 138
CAREY, 316, 317
Carib, 25, 375
CARLE, 248
CARMICHAEL, 10, 51, 63, 107, 109,
    158, 171, 204, 242, 251, 331, 334, 341
Caroline, 102, 108, 177
CARR, 27, 64, 171, 177
CARRERA, 364
CARROL, 236
CARROLL, 62, 63, 68, 159
CARROTT, 251
CARRY, 331
CARTER, 83, 98, 119, 128, 131, 133,
    248, 260, 288
CARTY, 59, 153
CASE, 129, 157
CASSELS, 27
CASSIDY, 12, 51, 59
CASSIMERE, 133
CASSITEY, 304

CASTELLAN, 12
CASTLE, 9, 19, 40, 131, 162, 208, 216,
    252, 294
CATALAN, 67
CATALINA, 47
CATES, 45
Catherine, 102, 114, 117, 119, 122, 125,
    133, 166, 169, 187, 190, 203, 269, 290
Catherine Elizabeth, 103
CATHERWOOD, 348, 352
Cato, 117, 130, 184, 295
CATO, 65, 147, 165, 204, 271
CATOOSE, 182
CATOUCHE, 141, 182, 230, 246
CATSON, 268
CATTO, 61, 254
CAZIE, 196
Cecilia, 126, 128, 213
CELESTINE, 149
CELISTINE, 245
CENTRA, 267
CERSO?, 262
CHAISE, 159, 206, 345
Chamba Jack, 133
CHAMPAGNE, 178, 245
Chance, 140, 153, 217, 296
Chance alias Henry, 121
CHANCEL, 254
CHANDLER, 6
CHANN, 52
CHAPARRO, 158
CHAPMAN, 13, 52, 69, 86, 91
CHAPPEL, 262, 310
CHAPPELL, 83, 98
CHAREL, 50
CHARLEMAN, 38
Charles, 104, 105, 111, 116, 117, 121,
    128, 132, 153, 162, 180, 187, 194,
    205, 210, 218
CHARLES, 27, 133, 141, 158, 221, 247,
    286
Charles E, 98
Charles, an African, 58
Charley, v, 107, 108, 114, 127, 156, 188,
    199, 205, 269
CHARLEY, 206

384

Charlie, 130, 184
Charlie Mandingo, 184
Charlotte, 66, 117, 130, 146, 147, 184,
189, 295
Charlotte Ida, 98
CHARTER, 148, 215, 252
CHARVIS, 52
CHASE, 159
Chatham, 132, 220
CHAVARECIA, 278
CHECK-PENNELL, 75, 76, 79, 88, 96
Chelsea, 140
CHERRINGTON, 1, 45, 124, 214, 253
Cherry, 111, 210
CHESTER, 96, 99
CHICHINACUS, 72
CHICO, 125
Child, 107, 112
CHILD, 50
CHINCILLA, 147
Chloe, 121, 131
Choucoo *(or Choncus,)* 61
CHRISTENSEN, 51
CHRISTIAN, 45
Christiana, 121, 166
CHRISTIE, 51, 342, 351, 352
Christopher, 45
CHURREN, 249
CINQUE, 344
CIORE, 118
Cladia, 177
CLAPPER, 22
Clara, 46, 100, 116, 125, 128, 133, 187,
221
CLARE, 253
Clarinda, 107, 295
Clarissa, 108, 127, 211
CLARK, 6, 83, 98, 137, 169, 185, 194,
195, 251, 254
CLARKE, 47, 74, 83, 111, 153, 195,
245, 250, 342
Clary, 295
CLAUD, 25
Claudia, 102
CLAUDIN, 276
Clemeni, 156

CLEMENT, 27, 33, 71, 126, 157, 206
CLEMENTA, 167
Clementine, 101, 319
CLEMENTS, 287
CLENAN, 254
CLERHAM, 192
CLIVE, 260
Cloe, 107, 179, 199
CLOUDY, 265
COATES, 81, 98, 112, 135, 186, 241
COATNEY, 252
COATQUELVIN, 30, 122, 247, 254
COATQULVIN, 277
COBBALD, 98
COBBOLD, 91
Cobus, 130
COCHRAN, 9
COCHRANE, 116, 310
COCKBURN, 300
COCKERILL, 130
CODD, 4, 5, 6, 79, 110, 138, 179, 192,
251, 281
COFFELL, 215
COFFILL, 13
COFFIN, 3, 12, 13, 25, 51, 55, 83, 98,
112, 113, 135, 152, 153, 187, 246,
312, 324, 325, 342, 356, 362, 366,
372, 374
COFFIN & Co., 324, 347, 351
COFFLE, 8
COGHLIN, 361
COHEN, 29
COKER, 42, 149, 177, 254
COLBOURN, 230
COLE, 22, 151, 187, 300
COLEMAN, 71
COLLIN, 98
COLLINGS, 51, 245
Collins, 153
COLLINS, 21, 83, 98, 126, 150, 208,
210, 212, 220, 245, 249, 329, 342
COLOMA, 252
COLOSSUS, 248
COLQUHOUN, 2, 18, 31, 46, 50, 65, 83,
98, 115, 117, 131, 139, 152, 177, 226,
248, 250, 253, 293, 310

COLUMBINE, 41
COLUMBUS, 249
COMAYANO, 344
Commodore, 100
CONALLY, 58
CONAQUI, 166
CONEL, 210
CONGHOUN, 253
Congo Edward, 100
Congo George, 117
Congo John, 199
Congo Thomas, 117
CONNER, 251
Connor, 130, 301
CONNOR, 11, 44, 50, 58, 72, 139, 201,
  244, 258
COOK, 44, 303, 368
Cooke, 68
COOKE, 39, 44, 46, 57, 104, 132, 147,
  220, 225, 253, 285, 309, 341
COOKROM, 324
COOLIN, 102, 177
Cooper, 68
COOPER, 25, 153, 341, 351, 356, 361,
  367
Cooper Ned, 116
COOTE, 138, 167, 196, 247, 251, 253,
  254
COPELEY, 6
COPLEY, 157, 253
CORD, 216
CORDERO, 58
Cork, 132, 221
CORK, 246
CORNI, 35
CORNITT, 24
Coromantee George, 117
CORTQUELVIN, 249
CORVAN, 152, 177
COULSON, 336
COURAN, 252
COURTAY, 220
COURTENAY, 245
COURTNAY, 175, 248, 251
COURTNEY, 15, 34, 59, 132, 144, 159,
  175, 180, 198, 204

COUSE, 130
COUTTEUSE, 14
COWELL, 252, 365
COX, 54, 55, 70, 71, 76, 84, 98, 215,
  247, 248, 252, 316, 317, 324, 325,
  331, 342, 353, 356, 361, 364, 366,
  367, 370, 371, 373, 375, 376
CRABB, 8, 36, 37, 70, 220, 221, 262
CRABBE, 116, 133, 159
CRABBER, 213
CRABBY, 295
CRAFT, 14, 18, 41, 44, 216, 271
CRAIG, 7, 20, 46, 59, 73, 79, 104, 213,
  218, 244, 249, 250, 284, 314, 336,
  342, 343, 352, 357
CRAMER, 17, 76, 84
CRAMMAND, 70
CRAMMOND, 247, 376
CRANE, 169, 250
CRAPPER, 158, 217, 240
CRAWFORD, 1, 7, 23, 37, 46, 110, 111,
  132, 133, 164, 171, 220, 221, 265,
  282, 297, 334, 337, 344
CREMENCIA, 156
CROFT, 3, 23, 40, 42, 52, 64, 109, 158,
  159, 181, 187, 208, 217, 225, 244,
  245, 254
CROKE, 330
CROMPTON, 34
CROOK, 84
CROPPER, 56
CROSBIE, 111, 246, 342
CROSKEY, 40
CROSSLEY, 253
CROWE, 251
CROWELL, 244
CROWL, 304
CROZER, 261
CROZIER, 53, 106, 207, 261
CRUIKSHANK, 26
CRUMMELL, 266
CRUMP, 51
CRUTCHLEY, 157
Cuba, 139, 219
CUBOE, 64
Cudjoe, 130

Cuffee, 146, 152, 183, 184
Cuffie, 130
Cuffy, 147
CUMMING, 55, 199
CUMMINGS, 60
CUMMINS, 6, 46
CUNLIFF, 84
CUNLIFFE, 84, 98
CUNNINGHAM, v, 2, 3, 8, 5, 16, 20,
    34, 44, 46, 49, 52, 55, 66, 52, 103,
    108, 109, 113, 140, 145, 146, 187,
    219, 229, 238, 243, 244, 247, 248,
    249, 250, 252, 254, 268, 287, 302,
    303, 309, 310, 331, 342, 375
Cupid, 108, 130, 218
CURLIER, 219
CURRAN, 70
CURRANT, 6, 36, 144, 145, 283
CURRANTS, 64, 197
CURRENT, 213
CUTHBERT, 76, 78
Cynthia, 19, 103, 169
Cynthya, 211
CYPIE, 46
Cyrus, 106, 120, 132
Cythia, 219
G. S. D., 84, 98 *(child's tombstone)*
L. M. D., 84, 98   "   "
D'ACUSTA, 33
DACIE, 21
DACRES, 255
DALA, 150
DALE, 45, 259
DALGETTY, 39, 84
DALGETY, 39
DALY, 49, 84, 98, 126, 210, 224
Damon, 133
Dan, 103, 114, 219
DAN, 44
DANCE, 141, 255, 256, 342
Daniel, 103, 104, 112, 116, 117, 128,
    130, 141, 169, 176, 180, 184, 197,
    210, 211
DANIEL, 259
Daphne, 139
DARBY, 159

DARLEY, 256
DARLING, 54, 114
DARNALL, 51
DARNEL, 27
DARYLEMENT, 69
DASH, 7, 267
Dasher, 107
Davey, 121, 209
David, 101, 119, 256, 285
DAVID, 253, 255
DAVIDSON, 24, 32, 33
Davie, 204
DAVIE, 30, 256
DAVIES, 186, 282
DAVIS, 3, 10, 17, 53, 59, 66, 109, 111,
    133, 135, 139, 154, 164, 165, 186,
    193, 210, 211, 253, 255, 257, 258, 301
Davy, 105, 108, 117, 130, 184
DAVY, 67
DAW, 112, 191, 284
DAWES, 356, 361
DAWKIN, 259
DAWKINS, 126, 206
DAWSON, 37, 103, 111, 136, 141, 174,
    176, 259, 267
DeBRIEN, De BRIEN, 10, 22, 31, 58,
    73, 134, 135,178, 186, 209, 213, 215,
    221, 241, 255, 257, 258, 324, 328,
    329, 342, 345
De JIMINEZ, 98
de LA CRUZ, 167
de LA LUZ, 167
DE LA RIOS, 39
De SOURSE, 238
De ST. CROIX, 131
De ST. CROIX & Co, 318, 350, 354,
    366. 376
DEANS, 229
DEATHLEY, 338
DeBAPTIST, 3, 37, 42
DeBAPTISTE, 13, 14, 48, 255
DeBECK, 41
DeBERION, 258
DEBLOIS, 336
DEBRELL, 259
DECENCY, 27, 258, 259

DECIDORA, 288
DECKNER, 92, 99
DeCOSTA, 257
DEENE, 258
DEERE, 60
DEFRIST, 288
DeLaHOUSIE, 48
DELANDRE, 233
Delia, 133, 142
DELORE, 258
DELORIOUS, 256
DELTORO, 131
Delvit, 132
DeMACK, 16
DEMARS, 260
DEMART, 297
DEMAS, 30
DEMSHAW, 148
DENT, 256
DeRIVEAU, 37
DERIXON, 232
DERNSHAW, 215
Derry, 125, 171, 187
DERRY, 26
Des NIEVES, 46
DESIRE', 31
DESMO, 101, 178
DeSOURCE, 44, 60, 196
DESOUS, 196
DESOYCE, 44
DESOYNER, 49
DESPIAGES, 25
DESSONS, 40
DeSSOUS, 4, 196
DESURSE, 194
Devonshire, 121, 220, 221
DEWAR, 49
DEYE, 255
DEYRUCHE', 62
Diamond, 121, 298
DIAMOND, 19, 255
Diana, 19, 103, 106, 114, 121, 122, 123, 133, 169, 176, 177, 219
Dianna, 203
Dibden, 196
DIBDIN, 41

Dick, 52, 120, 123, 132, 168, 176, 177
DICK, 52, 256
DICKENSON, 185, 299
DICKINSON, 313
DICKSON, 73, 116, 254, 255, 313
DIEGO, 375
DIEMAS, 375
DIGBY, 256
DIONISIA, 264
DIPPLE, 258
DITMAS, 4
DIVERGE, 259
DIXON, 3, 12, 37, 45, 54, 152, 159, 177, 248
DOBSON, 125, 257
DODSON, 27
Dolly, 113, 269
DOLORES, 255
DOMINGO, 8, 125, 159, 160, 186, 228, 246, 259, 302
DOMINGUES, 256
DOMINGUEZ, 17, 56, 66
DONALL, 287
Dorcas, 102, 177
Dorcus, 274
DOREL, 237
Dorset, 119
DORSET, 37, 116
DORSETT, 216
DOUGHTY, 257
DOUGLAS, 1, 11, 56, 68, 75, 101, 123, 132, 220, 228, 275, 311, 312
DOUGLASS, 232, 256, 258, 259
DOUGLE, 30
DOWSETT, 30
DOYLE, 27, 51, 100
DRACKSON, 111, 211, 232
DRAKESIN, 148
DRAKSON, 111, 215
DRAXON, 232
DREYSON, 256
DRISSILDORFF, 373
DRUMMOND, 32, 255, 256
DUAMI, 48
Dublin, 107, 128, 213, 274
DUBRAIL, 5

388

Duckworth, 132, 220
DUGARD, 47, 73, 256
Duke, 104, 132
DUMAS, 10, 149, 178, 255, 256
DUNBAR, 126, 216, 259, 270
Duncan, 104, 111, 130, 132, 184, 210, 220, 324
DUNCAN, 102, 163, 219, 258
DUNCANETTE, 59
DUNDAS, 257
DUNFORD, 259
DUNN, 67, 141, 159, 182
DUNSTAN, 68
DUNWELL, 131, 218
DUORMILL, 29
DUPUI, 159
DURHAM, 25, 50
DWYER, 52
DY, 257
DYER, 55, 71, 72, 128, 257
DYMOND, 330
Eabo Tom, 117
Eado [= Eabo] Rodney, 117
Eady, 130
Eager, v
EAGLETON, 60
EAKINS, 203
EARNEST, 16, 182, 183, 259, 261, 262, 287
EBO, 160
Ebo HERCULES, 101
Ebo James, 101
Ebo John, 101
Eboe James, 178
Edie, 121
Edinburgh, 133
Edith, 120
Edmond, 117, 147, 152
Edmund, 177, 274
Edward, 16, 71, 108, 111, 116, 121, 124, 129, 133, 144, 174, 181, 210, 218, 293, 301
EDWARD, 261
Edward, an African, 69

EDWARDS, v, 30, 37, 58, 65, 75, 110, 160, 182, 192, 196, 201, 260, 261, 262, 263, 311, 327
Edwin, 103, 121, 199
EGERTON, 49
EGLEBY, 66
EILEY, 357, 358
EILY, 260
ELCHABEREA, 200
Eleanor, 102, 107, 113, 117, 140, 161, 177, 199, 203
Elenor, 102
ELGAR, 57
ELIAS, 58
Elicio, 281
Elinor, 132
ELITER, 312
Eliza, 104, 110, 129, 144, 169, 181, 218, 219, 223, 258, 279, 290
Eliza Mary, 249
Elizabeth, 18, 57, 72, 98, 105, 113, 117, 121, 122, 125, 128, 129, 133, 134, 138, 153, 176, 179, 181, 187, 190, 203, 219
Elizann, 71
Ellen, 245, 276
Ellice, 117
ELLICE, 127, 132, 221
Ellick, 107, 212
ELLIOTT, 133, 260, 356
ELLIS, 64, 133, 145
ELRINGTON, 10, 11, 13, 62, 120, 133, 176, 184, 220, 260, 263, 265, 292
Elsey, 101
ELSTER, 31, 312
ELWIN, 262
Emanuel, 30
EMERY, 37, 77, 104, 134, 150, 216, 260, 262, 307
Emily, 119, 121, 131, 134, 147, 218
Emma, 116, 121, 152, 177, 210, 260
Emma Maria, 98
Emmaline, 121
EMMONS, 76
EMORY, 127
ENDHAM, 261

ENDIN, 101, 179
England, 153
ENGLAND, 263
ENGLISH, 167, 196, 197
ENNIS, 18, 47
Ephraim, 169
Ernest, 217
ERNEST, 70, 160, 217, 261
ERSKINE, 9, 55, 63, 65, 130, 143, 211, 262, 272, 342
ESCALAN, 12
ESCARFIT, 33
ESTAVEZ, 98
ESTEVEZ, 84
Esther, 42, 114, 188
ESTILL, 76
ESTRADA, 65, 177
ETCHBURGER, 354
EUSTACIO, 265
Eustatia, 131
Evans, 246
EVANS, 42, 45, 49, 71, 79, 84, 151, 160, 187, 197, 205, 229, 260, 262, 300, 342, 353, 372, 373, 374
Eve, 18, 101, 103, 114, 128, 133, 139, 146, 176, 219, 296
EVE, 36, 104, 105, 115, 128, 132, 133, 146, 188, 197, 210, 218, 221, 257, 260, 261, 263, 300
Evelina, 121, 131, 179, 245
EVERETT, 190, 261
EVERITT, 11, 106, 190, 261
EVINS, 43
EWING, 8, 49, 74, 115, 160, 186, 262
EWLETT, 289
FACEY, 66
FACUNDA, 148
FAIMO, 38
FAIRFAX, 125, 246
FAIRWEATHER, 8, 15, 49, 84, 254
FALL, 138, 151, 210, 269
FALLS, 43, 82, 98
Fame, 130, 195
FANCY, 255
Fanny, 46, 107, 122, 123, 125, 138, 152, 170, 183, 187, 199, 200, 203, 260, 262

FANTASIE, 274
FANTASSY, 105, 163
FANTESSAY, 176, 194
FANTISSY, 73
FARLEY, 250
FARLIN, 264
FARQUHARSON, 85, 98
FARRELL, 24
FARREN, 320
FARRO, 63
Fatima, 116, 117
FAXARDO, 34, 39
FAYARD, 72
FECUNDA, 281
FELICIA, 158
Felix, 54, 102, 177
FELIX, v, 7, 207, 263, 264, 267
FELLOWS, 10
FENAL, 235
FENCER, 266
FERGUSON, 12, 71, 132, 133, 161, 180, 195, 198, 265, 266, 268
FERGUSSON, 264
FERNIE, 115
FERRAL, 77
FERRALL, 13, 76
FERRARA, 320
FERREL, 196
FERRELL, 123, 154, 203, 264, 265, 266
FERRIER, 265
FERRILL, 102
FERRO, 85, 98
Fidelia, 124
FIFE, 32
Figaro, 38
FINDLING, 52
FINGALL, 268
FINSEY, 266
FIRBY, 37
FISHER, 30, 246, 265, 269
FITZGERALD, 26, 38, 57, 304
FITZGIBBON, 10, 61, 197, 268
FLEMING, 311
FLETCHER, 319, 351
Flora, 133, 147, 274, 279
FLORENCE, 126, 266

Florencio, 103
Florentin, 216
FLORENTINE, 35
FLORES, 47
FLOWERS, 1, 2, 4, 7, 8, 10, 12, 18, 19,
    22, 27, 28, 30, 31, 34, 38, 47, 49, 53,
    59, 101, 107, 118, 120, 121, 123, 124,
    125, 129, 133, 134, 138, 139, 141,
    142, 143, 148, 160, 161, 164, 166,
    178, 182, 183, 186, 192, 193, 195,
    199, 202, 203, 204, 214, 215, 217,
    228, 233, 235, 238, 242, 263, 264,
    265, 267, 268, 269, 271, 272, 277,
    280, 292, 307
FLUIDEO, 46
FOGARTY, 31
FOGHERTY, 196
FOLLIN, 364
FONCERA, 11
FONT, 35
FOOT, 35, 308
FORBES, 52, 55, 72, 105, 137, 181, 184,
    225, 266, 267, 293, 316, 319, 320,
    321, 330, 331, 336, 337, 342, 346,
    348, 349, 351, 354, 356, 359, 361, 376
FORBES & Mc'KINNON, 349
Force-trading, 325
FORD, 14, 15, 176, 255, 263, 267
FOREMAN, 7, 65, 200, 214, 266, 270,
    278, 320, 342
FORES, 234, 268
FORMAN, 7, 161, 268, 269
FORMEAUX & ROUQUIE, 324
FORMEAUX & ROUQUIEU, 338
FORREST, 82, 98, 265
FORRESTER, 85, 98, 105, 213
FORSYTH, 96, 99, 131
FORT, 14, 140
FORTH, 241
FORTUNA, 227
Fortune, 111, 132, 211, 249
FORTUNE, 182, 255, 264, 282
FOSTER, 33
FOURMAUX, 326
FOURMAUX & ROUQUIE, 326
FOURMEAUX, 160, 324

FOWLER, 236, 368
FOWLER's Bank, 349
FOX, 65, 93, 159, 337
FOY, 264
FRAIN, 24, 117, 206
FRANCE, 56, 79, 121, 175, 266, 267,
    268, 269, 309, 325, 342, 345, 364, 370
Frances, 102, 111, 133, 284
FRANCES, 115, 268
FRANCESCA, 155
Francis, 67, 103, 116, 117, 120, 128,
    132, 133, 153, 176, 184, 210, 303
FRANCIS, 18, 20, 36, 53, 61, 145, 230,
    231, 260, 284, 285, 293
Francisca, 67
FRANCISCA, 154, 161
Francisco, 48
FRANCISCO, 28, 31, 224, 281
Frank, 104, 117, 140, 153, 174, 210, 246,
    292
FRANKLIN, 144, 213, 292
Franky, 177
FRANOIS, 51
FRANON, 51
FRASER, 356
FRAZELLE, 243
FRAZER, 2, 36, 66, 131, 133, 267
FRAZIER, 192, 221
Frederick, 61, 100, 101, 103, 105, 117,
    121, 178, 200, 205, 303
FREDERICK, 116, 153, 210
FREEMAN, 25, 119, 148, 269
FRENCH, 365
FRENKLING, 270
Friday, 100, 152, 190, 195
Friendship, 130, 184
FRISBY, 266
FULLAR, 267
FULLER, 10, 119, 135, 148, 191, 198,
    267
FULLICK, 41
FUNDY, 220
FYLIY, 42
GABOUREL, 3, 18, 29, 51, 55, 69, 70,
    72, 124, 161, 162, 227, 232, 236, 243,
    247, 270, 272, 273, 274, 310, 342

GABOURELL, 306
GABRIEL, 32, 154
GADDES, 39, 45, 266
GADDESS, 244
GADDIS, 54, 157, 179
GALAGHER, 69
GALE, 76
GALES, 75
GALLAY, 276
GALLIARD, 280
GALLIMORE, 63, 132, 220, 279
GALLINO, 36
GALLON, 262
GALLOWAY, 239
GALT, 76, 79
GAMBER, 65
GAMBLE, 50, 163, 212, 274
Gamboa, 11
GAMBOA, v, 44, 45, 65, 156, 161, 171, 189, 251
GAMBOUR, 228
GANGA, 166
GANN, 71, 367
GANNON, 33
GAPPER, 117, 129. 177, 180, 278
GARBET, 277
GARBUT, 115, 368
GARBUTT, 12, 54, 66, 71, 163, 260, 277, 280
GARCIA, 24, 233, 251
GARDINER, 10, 104, 125, 212, 272, 321, 342
GARDNER, 48, 104, 322
GARIET, 38
GARNET, 296
GARNETT, 5, 32, 36, 60, 69, 117, 141, 180, 181, 282, 283
GAROCI, 75
GARRETT, 14, 70, 73, 176, 198, 264, 277
GARRICK, 280
GASSAY, 282
GAVIN, 2, 30, 33, 109, 198, 312
GEAR, 273
GEDDES, 108, 131
GEDDICE, 124

GEDDIS, 277
GENEROUS, 273
GENIOUS, 56
GENTLE, 8, 9, 16, 21, 29, 47, 51, 65, 72, 75, 79, 85, 98, 100, 101, 103, 178, 205, 231, 268, 270, 271, 273, 274, 275, 278, 279, 281, 282, 284, 319, 342, 357
George, 1, 11, 13, 20, 31, 54, 66, 100, 101, 103, 104, 107, 108, 110, 113, 117, 121, 123, 127, 129, 141, 147, 153, 169, 176, 179, 183, 189, 207, 208, 210, 218, 224, 248, 261, 263, 269, 274, 279, 300; Old George, 102; Papa George, 117
GEORGE, 71, 119, 155, 276, 281, 285
George Isaac, 11
Georgiana, 57, 121
GERETSON, 8
GERRARD, 122
GIBBES, 86, 98
GIBDON, 66
GIBSON, 5, 9, 12, 17, 18, 19, 39, 51, 52, 53, 61, 63, 67, 73, 101, 116, 121, 127, 132, 139, 162, 178, 182, 189, 201, 216, 220, 230, 248, 281, 282, 311, 312
GIBSTON, 66
Giddy, 132
GIDDY, 5, 57, 141, 142, 191
GIDEON, 12, 13, 35, 58, 62, 119, 123, 276, 277, 282, 365, 375
GIDEY, 294
GIDNEY, 278
GIFFORD, 85
Gift, 132
GILBERT, 208, 274
GILCHRIST, 47
GILL, 13, 28, 41, 51, 56, 75, 150, 151, 180, 271, 277, 278, 282
GILLERMO, 301
GILLET, 191, 192, 197
GILLETT, 16, 22, 72, 120, 123, 151, 183, 214, 260, 274, 279, 280
Ginger, 133
GINIS, 154
Ginny, 201

392

GIPSON, 258

GLADDEN, 7, 10, 13, 18, 25, 36, 122, 123, 141, 150, 153, 161, 239, 271, 277, 278, 283

GLADDIN, 270, 272, 281

GLADDING, 194, 272

GLADDON, 203, 252

Glasgow, 70, 121, 130

GLASS, 18, 61, 285, 300

GLASSFORD, 281, 342, 355

GLOUD, 152

GLOVER, 33

GODFREY, 6, 20, 120, 135, 137, 138, 159, 177, 200, 206, 234, 254, 272, 276, 278, 368

GODFRY, 185, 188, 192

GOFF, 13, 15, 17, 20, 22, 27, 49, 56, 66, 101, 105, 114, 116, 123, 125, 126, 129, 130, 133, 145, 146, 164, 168, 180, 187, 189, 194, 196, 197, 203, 214, 217, 220, 221, 237, 241, 252, 263, 264, 270, 271, 272, 273, 276, 281, 283, 297, 301

GOFFE, 220, 221

GOLT, 76

GOMEZ, 70, 122

GOMIAH, 273

GONDISCOURT, 60

GONZALES, 52, 249, 288

GOOD, 115, 273, 300

GOODLAND, 147

Goodluck, 114

GOODROW, 67

GOOLBURN, 61

GORDON, v, 5, 6, 22, 33, 79, 102, 105, 118, 127, 134, 138, 155, 158, 176, 182, 189, 192, 193, 200, 204, 214, 216, 234, 262, 267, 269, 275, 276, 277, 278, 279, 280, 281, 284, 307, 309

GORE, 373, 376

GOREY, 71

GOSSOP, 278

GOUDECOURT, 28

GOUGH, 56, 85, 271, 272, 327, 331, 335, 344, 345, 373

GOULD, 310

GOURDEN, 27

GOUTROUT, 299

GOW, 64

Grace, 107, 114, 116, 121, 128, 130, 184, 188, 218, 262

GRACE, 75, 78, 131, 197

GRACIA, 12

GRACIANO, 265

GRAEM, 185

GRAEME, 18

GRAFHEAD, 31

GRAFTON, 276

GRAHAM, v, 24, 27, 41, 45, 100, 101, 111, 132, 133, 164, 220, 224, 258, 271, 273, 274, 279, 293, 299, 368

GRAMIZES, 54

GRANT, 2, 3, 6, 15, 18, 24, 27, 29, 36, 39, 47, 54, 57, 61, 67, 68, 69, 71, 85, 87, 98, 110, 123, 125, 129, 137, 144, 146, 152, 162, 163, 164, 165, 170, 190, 192, 196, 200, 201, 206, 209, 211, 215, 227, 250, 255, 268, 270, 271, 272, 273, 274, 275, 278, 280, 281, 282, 283, 295, 297, 336, 354

GRAVES, 28, 48

GRAY, 83, 86, 98, 111, 136, 141, 182, 193, 211, 214, 267, 281, 314, 332, 335, 338, 342, 348, 357, 358, 369, 372, 374

GRAY & THOMPSON & Co., 348

GRAYSTOCK, 283

GREEN, 2, 14, 28, 39, 72, 126, 145, 272, 277, 280

GREENOCK, 41

Greenwich, 133

GREENWOOD, 320, 325, 329

GREGARIO, 262

GREGORIA, 160, 186, 228

Gregorio, 148, 262

GREGORIO, 118, 262, 280

GRENOUGH, 4

Gretta, 85

GRETTON, 27

GREY, 24, 43, 76, 244, 313

GREYSON, 23, 54

GRIFFEN, 371

GRIFFITH, 147
GRIFFITHS, 11, 13, 86, 271, 306
GRIGG, 51
GRIMSTOCK, 330
GRINNOCK, 277
GRISTOCK, 17, 21, 39, 122, 162, 166,
178, 179, 200, 282, 327, 342
GRIZZLE, 119
GROGAN, 371
GROVES, 52
GRUCHY, 371
Guatecla, 276
GUBAIN, 280
GUBREN, 25
GUEST, 112, 191
GUILD, 115, 216, 236, 314, 366, 373
Guildford, 131, 132
GUIROLA, 37, 68, 353
GUISSANT, 32
GUMBOWERS, 251
GUNN, 40, 153, 271
GUNN, Dr. Thomas,75
GUNNERY, 32
GUNNING, 32
GURNEY, 70
GUTHERY, 278
GUTHRIE, 126, 206, 356, 365
GUYTON, 299
HA......, 68
HADLEY, 86
HAGAN, 51
HAIR, 288
HALE, 46
HALES, 44
HALFHIDE, 39
HALL, 15, 16, 24, 25, 53, 84, 86, 98,
295, 334
HALLIDAY, 76, 86, 98
HAMER, 118, 291
Hamilton, 133, 220
HAMILTON, 1, 8, 33, 35, 63, 138, 160,
183, 186, 205, 214, 246, 263, 286,
291, 296
Hamlet, 107, 117, 121
Hamlett, 203
HAMLYN, 34

HAMMOND, 2, 46, 296
HAMPSHIRE, 52, 86, 102, 109, 184,
189, 293, 318, 325, 350, 357, 360, 376
HAMPTON, 324, 345, 347, 351
Handle, 102
Handy, 104
HANDY, 106
HANDYSIDE, 82, 115, 143, 294, 301,
309
Hannah, 102, 104, 117, 125, 133, 146,
177, 184, 187, 210, 216, 221, 278, 301
HANNAM, 33
HANSEN, 61
Hardwicke, 130
HARDY, 34, 143, 167, 212, 287
Hare, 162, 179
HARE, 151, 167, 210, 220, 288, 290,
292
HARGER, 371
HARLEY, 292
HARMAN, 90
HARPER, 49, 86, 98
HARRAL, 75
Harriet, 98, 103, 121, 130, 150, 169, 269
Harriett, 210
Harriot, 219
Harriott, 181
HARRIS, 8, 29, 53, 86, 106, 119, 124,
132, 163, 177, 180, 209, 244, 263,
285, 289, 291, 306, 345, 351
HARRISON, 24, 117, 179, 207, 282,
284, 295, 330, 331, 343, 349, 352,
354, 359
HARROLD, 75
Harry, 24, 101, 104, 108, 113, 117, 121,
125, 128, 141, 146, 169, 176, 181,
187, 188, 203, 210, 211, 218, 260,
292, 296
Harry Corromantee, 114
HART, 68, 326, 330, 334, 337, 344, 351,
353, 354, 361
HARTGRAVE, 354
HARTYN, 285
HARVEY, 45, 86, 98, 163, 311
HARVIE, 201, 311
HASTING, 43

HATTEN, 18
HAWES, 63
HAWK, 286
HAWKINS, 43, 115, 210
HAY, 34, 169
HAYES, 33, 66, 74, 291
HAYLOCK, 6, 8, 13, 26, 41, 56, 98, 109, 112, 212, 215, 276, 290, 343, 375
HAYLOP, 212
HAYWOOD, 289
Hazard, 114, 152, 188, 195
Hector, 131, 133, 221
HECTOR, 46, 292
HEFTING, 297
HEIGH, 42
HEINDALE, 376
HEISE, 356
Helen,133
Helena, 133
HELMSLEY, 349
HEMMETT, 50
HEMMING, 20, 177
HEMMINGS, 48, 65, 117
HEMMON, 155
HEMMONDS, 136, 240, 286, 306
HEMPSTEAD, 87, 98
HEMSLEY, 23, 47, 54, 73, 102, 113, 125, 143, 149, 189, 193, 202, 237, 284, 289, 292
HENDERSON, 3, 65, 67, 70, 122, 123, 215, 220, 233, 234, 283, 333, 342, 352, 374, 376
HENDY, 204, 294
Henrietta, 110, 129, 133, 153, 159, 169, 174, 221, 286
Henry, 101, 102, 103, 107, 114, 121, 122, 129, 130, 147, 153, 177, 181, 184, 188, 194, 217, 219, 281, 290, 292, 296
HENRY, 59, 63, 109, 118, 137, 152, 176, 179, 181, 188, 267, 277, 282, 285, 288, 292, 293
HENSLEY, 56
HEOMITAYO, 61
Hercules, 117, 121, 178
HERCULES, 100, 101, 178

HERLINE, 285
Hero, 130
HERON, 56
HEWLETT, 9, 10, 11, 16, 33, 43, 50, 57, 60, 61, 64, 66, 70, 104, 130, 132, 139, 178, 184, 212, 220, 236, 245, 250, 256, 259, 280, 286, 287, 288, 289, 293, 296
HEWS, 7
HIBBERT, 132, 220
HICKEY, 2, 46, 63, 73, 82, 87, 90, 98, 114, 138, 144, 152, 167, 188, 195, 197, 214, 234, 284, 285, 287
HIGGIN, 254
HILARIA, 246
Hill, 131
HILL, 37, 40, 47, 66, 75, 76, 104, 146, 163, 218, 282, 287, 291, 293, 324, 325, 356
HILL-RAVEN, 365
HINCKS, 74
HINEY, 36
HINKS, 2, 13, 20, 23, 52, 75, 100, 110, 164, 177, 261, 282, 285, 292, 295, 296
HOAR, 195, 257, 288
HOARE, 24, 27, 36, 39, 47, 67, 110, 125, 147, 148, 170, 221, 285, 286, 288, 289, 290, 291, 295
HOBSON, 368
HODDER, 35
HODGE, 76, 313
HODGSON, 87, 98
HODSON, 231
HOFFMAN, 58
HOFIUS, 87
HOGG, 256
Holland, 101
HOLLAND, 322
HOLME, 187, 253
HOLMES, 296, 324
HOLTON, 81, 98
HOME, 117, 126, 180, 206, 213, 287, 311, 312
HOMES, 220, 229
Honor, 100
HOOK, 40, 111, 293

395

HOOKER, 62
Hope, 301
HOPE, 49, 73, 116, 130, 216
HORN, 176, 290
HOSARIO, 297
HOSKIN, 37
HOSNER, 46
HOUSTON, 31
HOWARD, 37, 39, 43, 56, 60, 62, 153
HOWE, 179, 204
HOWELL, 331, 347, 361, 366
HUBBARD, 49
HUDSON, 253
HUGHES, 4, 7, 8, 24, 35, 37, 41, 42, 51,
   67, 71, 131, 142, 145, 155, 163, 191,
   208, 213, 230, 241, 266, 284, 294,
   331, 348, 359
HUGHMAN, 189
HUGHS, 3, 5, 33, 42, 48
HUGO, 28, 98
HULBERT, 31
HULL, 57
HULSE, 17, 24, 46, 47, 87, 98, 115, 125,
   193, 218, 286, 291, 296
HUMBLE, 293
HUME, 2, 16, 32, 59, 62, 65, 76, 82, 95,
   99, 116, 132, 136, 139, 143, 153, 166,
   178, 183, 191, 210, 215, 218, 232,
   244, 284, 285, 286, 287, 289, 291,
   292, 294, 295, 296, 297, 310, 311,
   328, 343
HUMES, 75, 184, 195, 241, 242, 250,
   263, 299, 301
HUNT, 2, 53, 71, 117, 124, 131, 152,
   170, 177, 180, 208, 212, 232, 283, 294
Hunter, 102, 117
HUNTER, 115, 233
HURN, 53
HURST, 198
HUSTA, 283
HYDE, 5, 19, 20, 21, 35, 49, 56, 57, 62,
   68, 74, 105, 117, 163, 180, 181, 192,
   201, 252, 263, 267, 275, 285, 286,
   288, 296, 299, 309, 314, 316, 320,
   321, 330, 337, 348, 354, 356

HYDE, FORBES & Co., 316, 330, 351,
   354, 361
HYDE & PETZOLD, 316
HYDE, PETZOLD & BETSON, 316
HYE, 286
HYMER, 46
IGLESIA, 69
ILES, 115, 117
IMAN, 320
IMPOTETO, 122
Infant, 103, 146, 148, 159, 162, 187, 201
Infant Girl, 117
INLET, 126
INNIS, 339, 341
Integrity, 10
Ireland, 108, 209
IRELAND, 367
IRVINE, 27
IRVING, 54
Isaac, 196, 292
Isabella, 98, 147
ISIDORE, 149, 178
ISLES, 302
J. B. C., 98
JACINTO, 337
Jack, 104, 107, 113, 114, 117, 121, 176,
   281
JACK, 220
Jackey, 107, 108, 121, 199
JACKSON, 7, 12, 19, 37, 58, 60, 87, 98,
   107, 132, 133, 139, 145, 182, 184,
   212, 213, 220, 234, 302, 307, 308, 341
Jacob, 7, 71, 100, 106, 121, 130, 184
JACOB, 146, 164, 300
JACOBO, 147
JACOBS, 56
JAHSEY, 4
JAMAICA, 220
Jamaica Jem, 132
Jamaica Robert, 69, 132
James, v, 12, 101, 102, 103, 111, 114,
   115, 116, 121, 127, 128, 132, 133,
   134, 138, 141, 146, 148, 153, 155,
   161, 169, 176, 180, 188, 205, 210,
   211, 212, 213, 219, 223, 274, 281, 290

JAMES, 32, 55, 71, 148, 149, 159, 237, 297, 347
James alias York, 121
JAMIESON, 63, 206, 299
JAMISON, 64
Jane, 69, 102, 103, 105, 111, 113, 117, 133, 142, 146, 156, 180, 188, 201, 208, 219, 224, 260, 263
JANE, 299
Jane Elizabeth, 138
Janet, 117, 133
Janette, 111, 117, 126, 161
JANNETT, 63
Jannette, 296
JANNETTE, 232
JARRATT, 224
JARRETT, 203
JAX, 72
JAY, 53
JAYE, 53, 65
JAYS, 192
JEAMES, 179
Jean, 117
Jeanie, 121
Jeannette, 268
JECKELL, 87, 98
JEFFERIES, 3
JEFFERS, 254
JEFFERSON, 9, 299
Jeffrey, 117, 122
JEFFREY, 48
JEFFREYS, 3, 87, 98, 143, 185, 195, 199, 203, 298, 299, 300, 301
JEFFRIES, 57, 68, 143, 151, 163, 164, 185, 186, 187, 288, 299, 306
Jem, 104, 117, 125, 126, 130, 161, 187, 218, 224
Jem Mondingo, 133
Jemima, 118
Jemmy, 102, 180, 183; old Jemmy, 115
JENKIN, 199
JENKINS, 37, 52, 74, 297, 301
JENKS, 39
JENNER, 33
JENNINGS, 56, 128, 192, 298, 305, 327, 343, 364, 370

JENNISON, 291
Jenny, 48, 102, 107, 108, 113, 114, 117, 127, 131, 138, 160, 161, 169, 180, 188, 211, 246
Jeoffry, 203
Jerry, 246
Jervis, 133
Jessie, 121
JESSOP, 302
Jessy, 103, 132, 219
JESTY, 351
Jewish Rites, 63
JEX, 87, 98, 236, 297
JEYES, 139
JEYS, 193
JICKSON, 290
Joanna, 142, 292
Jock, old, 102
Joe, 102, 105, 110, 111, 114, 121, 128, 129, 131, 133, 146, 177, 179, 188, 190, 211; Spanish Joe, 115
John, 11, 20, 30, 39, 53, 68, 100, 103, 104, 107, 111, 114, 115, 116, 121, 122, 125, 126, 128, 130, 131, 133, 142, 143, 146, 147, 153, 176, 181, 183, 184, 187, 188, 201, 203, 208, 210, 211, 218, 219, 220, 223, 246, 263, 266, 274, 290; old John, 111
JOHN, 18, 24, 71, 101, 189, 365
John (Mulatto), 132
John the Baptist, 204
Johnny, 103, 132, 161, 190
Johnson, 129, 130, 132, 221
JOHNSON, 2, 10, 25, 26, 28, 42, 44, 45, 51, 52, 53, 58, 64, 113, 118, 122, 131, 132, 146, 212, 220, 227, 270, 297, 298, 337
Johnston, 121
JOHNSTON, 88, 98, 109, 120, 127, 151, 216, 276, 285, 337, 344, 347, 351, 352
JOHNSTON & Co., 350, 356
JOHNSTONE, 99, 192, 278
JOINER, 302
Jonah, 146
Jonathan, 141

JONES, 3, 8, 10, 11, 12, 17, 21, 23, 24,
27, 31, 52, 54, 62, 73, 75, 77, 88, 102,
103, 110, 115, 116, 128, 131, 132,
133, 134, 136, 146, 147, 151, 163,
164, 174, 182, 183, 188, 192, 197,
210, 211, 219, 220, 226, 235, 242,
243, 256, 258, 276, 279, 297, 298,
299, 300, 301, 302, 317
JORDON, 301
Jose, 43, 44, 54, 56, 65, 112, 120, 130,
177, 224, 286
JOSE, 46, 51, 52, 65, 68, 144
JOSEFA, 167
JOSEFE, 146
Josep, 218
JOSEP, 46
JOSEPA, 57
Joseph, 10, 15, 41, 66, 74, 102, 115, 120,
125, 132, 136, 153, 161, 180, 183,
187, 192, 204, 219, 279, 284
JOSEPH, 12, 35, 46, 58, 72, 136, 175,
191, 209, 266, 299
JOSEPHA, 70
Josey, 121
Joshua, 121
JOYNER, 56, 297
Juan, 60
JUAN, 120, 228
Juana, 53, 263, 265, 272
Juanita, 155
Juba, 68, 133, 221
Juda Ann, 254
Judith, 39, 46, 152, 177
Judy, 133, 221
Jula, 218
Julia, 117, 201
Juliana, 116, 245
Julie, 281
JULITTE, 67
Julius, 132, 220
JUNE, 268
Jupiter, 52, 102, 132
Jury, 121, 316
KANE, 43, 312
KARR, 194
Kate, 109, 127, 133, 152, 153, 161, 177

Kato, 220
Katy, 204
KAUNTZ, 33
KEAN, 328
KEANE, 120
KEATH, 304
KECHA, 189
KEE, 98
KEEF, 219
KEEFE, v, 21, 103, 275, 303, 304
KEEFFE, 57, 302
KEENE, 60, 132, 133, 135, 156, 165,
201, 214, 220, 221, 258, 303, 304, 306
KEIF, 304
KEITH, 275, 303
KELLERMAN, 287
KELLEY, 304
Kelly, 123, 215
KELLY, 68, 77, 124, 215, 277, 303, 304
KELMUCO, 182
KEN..., 88
KENEDY, 242
KENNEDY, 6, 11, 12, 17, 88, 98, 110,
122, 195, 209, 236, 315
KENNEDY & Co., 367
KENNEDY & MONTGOMERY, 330
KENNER, 60
KENNY, 72
Kent, 133
KENT, 303
KENYON, 35, 47, 304
KERINA, 252
KETRUE, 272
KETTO, 271
KIDD, 104, 236
KIEF, 275, 304
KINDRED, 88, 99
King, 170, 292
KING, 37, 304
Kingsale, 132, 133
Kingston, 133
KINGSTON, 45
Kingstone, 221
KINGSTONE, 213
Kinsale, 220
Kitty, 101, 105, 113, 121, 140, 203

Knight, 116, 218
KNOT, 74
KNOTE, 21
KNOTH, 68, 9, 74, 220, 303, 353
KNOX, 13, 150, 303
KOLLER, 33
La BOY, 295
LA BRUCE, 233
La CROIX, 108, 109
La FLEUR, 306
La GRENADE, 272
La MONT, 248
La ROI, 65
La CASS, 45, see Le CAS, Le CASS
La CROIX, 203, see Le CROIX
LaCUSSAGNE, 63
LAFILLE, 30
LaFLEUR, 65
LAING, 62
LAMB, 2, 14, 15, 16, 30, 37, 53, 88, 99,
    101, 119, 125, 133, 134, 135, 140,
    141, 152, 156, 167, 179, 180, 186,
    189, 196, 197, 217, 220, 221, 261,
    277, 295, 299, 304, 306, 307, 308
LAMBERT, 169, 194, 211
LAMOIN, 256
LAMOINE, 375
LAMONT, 268
LAMOTE, 177
LaMOTTE, 63
LANG, 53
LANGDON, 52
LAPOT, 150
LARDNER, 356
LARIA, 31
LARNER, 356
LaROSE, 149
LAUGHTON, 56
Laurence, 61, 292
LAURIE, 180
LAVATER, 148
LAVIGNE, 233
LAVINE, 7
LAWES, 196
LAWLER, 307
LAWLESS, 112, 189, 307, 375

LAWNEYS, 242
Lawrence, 116, 212, 218, 290
LAWRIE, 42, 53, 59, 75, 77, 114, 117,
    118, 164, 193, 216, 225, 230, 267,
    275, 305, 306, 343, 376
LAWSON, 124, 317, 323, 376
LAWTON, 64, 88, 99
LAYA, 168
LAYARD, 40
Le BOIT, 336
LE BRUN, 329
Le CAS, 50, see La CASS
Le CASS, 47
Le CROIX, 28, 46, see La CROIX
LE CRUIT, 181
Le FOY, 41
Le GEYT, 126, 272, 343
Le MOIN, 365
LE ROY, 115
Leah, 107, 212
LEAH, 67
LEANDRO, 140
LEAVOR, 206
LEBRO, 25
LEBRUN, 344
LECKIE, 79, 311
LECRUIT, 276
LECUSE, 191
LEE, 24, 73, 151, 324
LeGEYT, 54, 74, 202, 352
LEIGH, 44, 81
Leith, 169, 211
LEMOIN, 256
LEMOINE, 149, 178
LeMONT, 206
LEMOTE, 177
Lenan, 190
Lennan, 100
LEON, 35
LEONA, 161, 291
Leonora, 128
LeROY, 195
LESLIE, 24, 88, 99
LESTER, 62, 209
LESTRANGE, 83
Letitia, 164

399

LEVEN, 169
LEVER, 88, 99
Lewis, 104, 117, 136, 218, 233
LEWIS, 2, 4, 10, 11, 16, 17, 18, 34, 62,
  66, 100, 138, 181, 224, 242, 267, 305,
  306, 308, 368
LEWREY, 33
LEY, 33
Leza, 269
LEZAYA, 39
LIBERTY, 67, 73
LIDDAL, 88, 89, 99
LIDDEL, 22
LIDDELL, 74, 189
LIDDLE, 281
LIGHT, 144
LIMPERT, 60
Limus, 131, 174
LIND, 34, 69, 306
Linder, 139
LINDO, 128, 192, 206, 210, 298, 307,
  308, 316
LINDORE, 206
LINDSAY, 5, 40, 89, 140, 203
LINE, 305
LINO, 162
LINSAY, 99
LINSEY, 33
LINTO, 45
LISTER, 62
LITTLE, 351
Little Jack, 132
LIVINGSTON, 39
LIVINGSTONE, 59
Lizzy, 125, 189
Llewellen, 108
Llewellyn, 187
LLEWELLYN, 89, 376
LOCARIO, 69
LOCK, 9, 38, 53, 218, 254, 305
LOCKWARD, 22, 27, 55, 89, 99, 104,
  345, 375
LOGAN, 36, 89
LOINSWORTH, 4, 5
LOMAN, 44

London, 58, 61, 100, 101, 102, 108, 114,
  132, 152, 177, 188, 204, 218
London Moco, 221
LONG, 59
Long Ben, 100
LONGSWORTH, 7, 10, 12, 14, 23, 25,
  36, 51, 72, 107, 115, 131, 144, 147,
  165, 169, 171, 179, 205, 212, 214,
  238, 306, 307, 339
LOPEZ, 28, 30, 46, 57, 90, 304, 329,
  334, 341, 344
LORAN, 244
LORD, 15, 109, 219, 288, 343
LOSANCA, 43
LOUI, 129
Louis, 117, 262
LOUIS, 19, 62, 129, 155, 163, 200, 259,
  269, 297
Louisa, 102, 114, 121, 177, 178
LOUIST, 267
Louiza, 188
LOVELL, 9, 100, 114, 165, 306
LOW, 206
LOWE, 7, 29, 165
LOWER, 313
LOWLY, 57
LOWRIE, 39, 139, 146, 150, 165, 211,
  216, 219, 226, 305, 307, 308, 336
LOWRY, 7, 134, 150, 287, 305
Lucas, 50, 54
LUCAS, 9, 28, 40, 54, 89, 99
Luckie, 102
LUCKIE, 305
Lucretia, 108, 113, 117, 120, 129, 181,
  211, 219, 279
Lucy, 104, 122, 128, 203, 218
LUIS, 74
LUKEFAST, 148
Lunnun, 120
LURGAN, 36
LYNCH, 57, 63, 67, 252, 280, 305
M'KENZIEs Point, 352
M'LENAN, 349
MABIALE, 165
MACALE, 75
MACBETH, 25

MACCA, 63
MACDELO, 270
MacDONALD, 89, 99, 150, 154, 314,
    318, 320, 323, 332, 333, 339, 353,
    359, 365, 374
Mack, 132
MACKAY, 27, 135, 204, 369
MACLACHLAN, 99
MacLARTY, 109
MacLEAN, 371
MADDOC, 72
MAGDALEN, 120, 281
MAGDELENE, 71
MAHONY, 28
MAIDEN, 77, 112
MAIN, 188, 233
Major, 140, 203
MAJOR, 59
MALACHI, 58
MALBRUCK, 257
MALETTE, 35
----MAN, 38
Mandingo, 221
Mandingo Harry, 114, 117, 188
Mangan, 121
Mangola Adam, 188
MANSANO, 36
Manuel, 69, 70, 73, 104, 199
MANUEL, 41, 68, 72, 104, 150, 201,
    252
Marcella, 286
MARCELLO, 52
March, 19, 100, 101, 108, 169, 190, 207
March, old, 147
MARCO, 68, 168, 282
Marcus, 121, 132, 187, 220
Margaret, 10, 101, 102, 103, 104, 110,
    123, 127, 133, 138, 160, 162, 169,
    174, 177, 192, 205, 210, 266, 290
MARI, 32
Maria, 42, 54, 71, 105, 115, 117, 121,
    122, 129, 130, 133, 139, 141, 147,
    155, 157, 164, 166, 170, 176, 177,
    184, 221, 263, 265, 278, 292
MARIA, 30, 40, 42, 50, 68, 125, 154,
    155, 288, 299

MARIAL, 168
Marie Eleanna, 98
MARIETTA, 299
Marina, 133, 201
Marinah, 111
Mark, 220
MARLOW, 35
Marriott, 177
Marshal, 133
MARSHAL, 36, 40
MARSHALL, 36
Martha, 161, 180
Martin, 121
MARTIN, 17, 24, 31, 38, 42, 44, 48, 54,
    104, 131, 132, 133, 144, 208, 220,
    221, 255, 284, 291, 311
Martina, 161
MARTINEZ, 48, 65
MARTINY, 63, 68, 90, 114, 347
Mary, 11, 73, 103, 105, 108, 113, 114,
    116, 117, 121, 124, 129, 132, 133,
    140, 147, 151, 153, 162, 166, 169,
    181, 188, 194, 203, 204, 207, 208,
    219, 223, 246, 262, 292, 293, 301
Mary Ann, 100, 110, 111, 121, 144, 174,
    184, 210, 268, 281, 283
Mary Anne, 130, 162
Mary Elizabeth, 98
Mary Frances, 121
Maryann, 269
Maryatt, 102
MASCALL, 135
MASKALL, 19, 29, 35, 63, 83, 90, 99,
    104, 106, 109, 111, 138, 143, 186,
    189, 195, 204, 210, 211, 262, 309,
    312, 314, 319, 325, 328, 333, 336,
    339, 350, 360, 365, 372, 374
MASKELL, 318
MASON, 50, 62, 90
MASSEY, 170, 205
MATHER, 15, 59
MATHIESON, 303
Matilda, 120, 292
MATTEA, 280
Matthew, 276
MAUD, 75

MAXWELL, 66
MAY, 326, 331, 356, 361, 366, 371, 373
MAYAN, 57
MAYBERRY, 280
MAYER, 262
MAZER, 5, 25
McARTHER, 55
McARTHY, 62, 71
McAULAY, 25, 52, 75, 116, 128, 130,
    147, 161, 210, 211, 224, 265, 310
McAULEY, 198
McBEAN, 50
McCAMBLY, 256
McCANTY, 247
McCLOUD, 244
McCOLLOCH, 73
McCOLLUCK, 21
McCULLOCH, 58, 143, 202
McCREA, 35
McDALY, 255
McDILLAM, 170
McDONALD, 5, 25, 43, 47, 66, 77, 79,
    89, 90, 105, 106, 187, 204, 253, 314,
    316, 317, 322, 332, 333, 339, 343,
    350, 352, 357, 365, 374
McEACHRAN, 90
McFOY, 178, 245
McGENNETT, 55
McGILL, 64
McGILLIVRAY, 72
McINNIS, 360
McINTYRE, 34
McKAW, 212
McKAY, 15, 35, 47, 111, 116, 171, 186,
    188, 219, 241, 310
McKEE, 107, 128, 144
McKENNY, 304
McKENZE, 2
McKENZIE,58, 75, 93,99, 151, 216
McKINLEY, 330, 331
McKINNEN, 113
McKINNEY, 84, 98, 111
McKINNON, 193, 349
McKINZEY, 193
McLachlan, 117, 180
McLARTY, 44

McLEAN, 14, 27, 50, 57, 72, 303, 311
McLELLAN, 131
McLENAN, 59, 129, 130, 195, 316, 323,
    328, 333, 336, 339, 360, 365, 374
McLENEN, 255
McLEOD, 74, 286
McLOUGHLIN, 43
McMANUS, 60, 63
McMILLAN, 26
McNAB, 77
McNISH, 4, 41, 47
McNIST, 32
McPHERSON, 49, 141, 170, 205, 296
McQUAY, 203
McRITCHEY, 27
McSWEANY, 90
McSWEENY, 57
McVIE, 2
McWHIRTER, 171
MEANEY, 247
MEANING, 294
MEANY, 3, 114, 137, 140, 195
MEATHER, 59
MEENY, 100
MEHAIR, 151
MEIGHAN, 2, 6, 17, 29, 35, 45, 49, 51,
    60, 64, 66, 79, 82, 87, 90, 108, 119,
    122, 128, 129, 131, 132, 143, 144,
    153, 154, 162, 164, 177, 179, 182,
    188, 190, 198, 203, 206, 212, 220,
    226, 233, 243, 258, 271, 277, 283,
    291, 294, 296, 298, 309, 310, 316, 339
MELBOURNE, 86
MELHADO, 90, 98
Mellago alias Robert, 121
Memba, 187, 188
MENDOZA, 62, 66
MENDS, 371
MENGAN, 271
METZGEN, 310
MENZIES, 10, 50, 55, 153, 272, 343,
    361
MERCEDES, 154
METCALF, 186, 334, 337, 341
METCALFE, 323, 338
Michael, 161

402

Michaela, a Spanish girl, 62
MIDCALF, 271
MIDDLEBURY, 51
Middleton, 100, 103, 104, 132, 199, 210, 219, 220
MIDDLETON, 21, 23, 24, 53, 61, 63, 112, 132, 133, 166, 214, 220, 317, 348
MILES, 19, 20, 27, 32, 54, 55, 56, 61, 136, 148, 162, 195, 196, 208, 270, 285
MILIANA, 167
MILIQUITA, 75
MILLAR, 6, 44, 225, 321
MILLER, 20, 33, 55, 71, 90, 108, 131, 203, 229
MILLERBROOK, 193
Milly, 176
Mimba, 107, 114, 133
Mingo, 104
MINNEY, 15
Mintin, 102
MITCHEL, 12, 49, 54, 66, 225
MITCHELL, 9, 130, 288
MIVETT, 203
Moca Jack, 114, 188
Moco Frank, 132, 220
Moco Jem, 180
Moco Peter, 133, 221
Moco Scotland, 114, 188
Moco Simon, 221
Modesta, 112
MOFFIT, 60
MOHEAR, 140
Moland, 123, 215
Moley, 124
MOLINA, 34, 148
Molly, 121, 125, 140, 169, 203, 246
Monday, 114, 117, 132, 141, 188, 190
MONDAY, 33, 60
Mondingo Tom, 133
Monemia, 116
MONGAN, 77
Mongola Adam, 114
Mongola Jack, 133
Monimia, 103
MONK, 34, 206
MONKS, 137

MONROE, 51
MONTALANO, 43
MONTE, 158
MONTGOMERY, 109, 313, 330, 343
MOODIE, 60, 134, 141
MOODY, 19, 36, 38, 57, 132, 133, 161, 165, 182, 205, 220, 221, 235, 300, 306, 311
MOON, 70
MOOR, 249
MOORE, 32, 165, 221
MOPPETT, 331, 351, 354, 356, 361, 366, 371, 373, 376
MORAVIA, 132, 220
MORAZON, 56, 320
MORE, 206
MORELL, 119
MORLAND, 8
Morgan, 100
MORGAN, 29, 30, 116, 147, 188
MORICE, 186
MORRELL, 27
Morris, 128, 213
MORRIS, 38, 47, 70, 74, 164, 260, 324
Morrison, 121
MORRISON, 72
Morton, 275
Moses, 101, 114, 292
MOULD, 28
MOULE, 45
MOWBRAY, 35
MOYER, 62, 73, 275
MOYERS, 38, 41
MUCKERSIE, 90
MUCKLEHANEY, 177, 194
MUCKLEHANY, 61, 102, 129, 152, 251
MUDIAN, 220
MULLINS, 54
Mundingo Prince, 117
Mungola Hazard, 117
Mungola Ned, 117
Mungola Prince, 117
MUNRO, 87, 98, 109
Muntucko, 117
Murphy, 130, 132, 184, 221
MURPHY, 50, 229

MURRAY, 44, 63, 91, 118, 296, 310, 365, 371
MUSINGE, 139
MUSLAAR, 43, 72, 122
MUSLAR, 368
MYCATA, 285
MYRES, 277
MYVETT, 52, 53, 69, 126, 127, 138, 166, 191, 297, 307
MYVITT, v
NACHULETT, 140
Nago Hazard, 117
NAIRN, 15
Nancy, 63, 102, 106, 108, 114, 121, 141, 152, 166, 170, 176, 177, 183, 187, 188, 209, 212, 246, 296, 298
Nanny, 104, 115, 128
NARCISSA, 52
Nathanael, 298
NEAL, 9, 12, 16, 20, 37, 41, 42, 62, 100, 105, 113, 121, 125, 136, 158, 164, 166, 174, 176, 187, 188, 194, 199, 206, 219, 228, 254, 272, 276, 292, 308, 310
Neale, 130
NEALE, 3, 62, 114, 134
NEALY, 157
Ned, 101, 108, 111, 133, 210, 217, 218, 221
NEEDHAM, 64
NEELE, 60
NEIL, 43, 66
NELLIN, 37
NELLING, 296
NELLIS, 14
Nelly, 107, 121, 125, 187
NELLY, 191, 278
Nelson, 101, 103, 104, 107, 108, 116, 117, 119, 121, 130, 131, 180, 184, 189, 210, 218, 260, 292, 322
NELSON, 72, 368
Neptune, 127, 130
NESBIT, 320
NETARIO, 150
NEVILLE, 74
New Liverpool, 72, 315, 359

New Liverpool Emigrant, 72
NEWMAN, 61, 136
NEWPORT, 5, 26, 79, 91, 110, 218, 371, 374, 376
NIASSA, 63
Nicholas, 25, 111, 117, 210
NICHOLAS, 32
NICHOLLS, 356, 367, 374
NICHOLS, 336, 351, 357
NICHOLSON, 22, 44, 91, 99, 100, 106, 146, 177, 189, 190, 204, 248, 252, 307, 343
NICKERSON, 357
NIVEN, 85
Noah, 28
NOAT, 4
NOBLE, 29
NOEL, 124, 196, 261, 284, 330
Nora, 114, 188
NORMAN, 47
Norns, 324
NORO, 115, 196
NORRISON, 31
NOTT, 26, 48, 303
November, 103, 130, 184, 219, 345
NOWELL, 3, 158
NUFIO, 66
NUGENT, 79, 246, 248
NUNN, 60
O'BRIEN, 7, 17, 24, 36, 75, 132, 224, 293, 295
O'CONNOR, 9, 12, 53, 166, 264, 272, 297
O'GEERY, 67
O'NEIL, 36
O'SAY, 43
OCHITA, 72
Ocro, 132
OFION, 158
OGLES, 144
Old George, 102
Old Jemmy, 115
Old Jock, 102
Old John, 111
Old March, 147
Old Simon, 117

Olive, 58, 110, 113, 179
Olivia, 133
ONGAY, 92, 99
ORD, 115, 218
ORFIL, 75
ORGILL, 75, 109, 144, 194
ORGLES, 194, 198
ORNANDEZ, 39
ORTEZ, 166
OSAFO, 167
Oscar, 262
OSCAR, 48
OSMAN, 40, 157, 158
OSWALD, 99
OTTLEY, 46
Otway, 59, 121, 132
OWEN, 97
OXBERRY, 320
OXEA, 35
OXLEY, 54
PABLO, 150, 265
PACUALLA, 150
PADDLE, 203
PADLE, 201
PAGE, 91, 99, 147
PALACIO, 267
Pallmall, 129
PALLOT, 354, 356, 361, 366
Palo, 115
Pamelia, 197
PANDI, 51, 160
PANDY, 167
PANGLOSS, 4
PANTALION, 125
PANTING, 64, 102, 110, 126, 148, 184, 202, 232, 235, 310, 343
PANTON, 226
Papa George, 117
Papa Quashie, 117, 180
PARDREN, 40
PAREOJEAN, 44
PARK, 70, 100
Parker, 114
PARKER, 21, 47, 72, 101, 117, 180, 181, 278
Parkes, 108

PARKES, 34, 307
PARKS, 3, 13, 16, 45, 107, 124, 146, 195
PARRY, 284
PASCAL, 74
Pascale, 43
PASLOW, 31, 40, 54, 62, 66, 79, 88, 91, 99, 107, 117, 132, 133, 140, 152, 167, 177, 180, 196, 197, 212, 220, 263
PASTON, 56
PATERSON, 35, 50
Patience 114, 115, 121, 130, 131, 133, 184, 188, 221
PATINETT, 52, 60, 131
PATNETT, 28, 300
PATRICIO, 167
Patrick, 130, 194
PATRONA, 63, 148
PATTEN, 69, 323, 362
PATTENETT, 208
PATTERSON, 194, 231
PATTIESON, 252
PATTINETT, 18, 19
PATTISON, 334, 337, 357
PATTNETT, 297
PATTON, 329
Patty, 102, 103, 118, 127, 177
PAUL, 40
Paulina, 246, 319
PAYNE, 283
PEACHEY, 210
PEACHY, 104
PEAR, 306
PEARCE, 78
PEARSON, 192
PEDDIE, 106, 177, 235
PEDERSON, 356, 361, 366
Pedro, 155
PEEBLES, 120, 176, 260, 277, 322, 343
Peggy, 43, 101, 102, 113, 123, 125, 130, 179, 184, 187
PENCER, 305
Penelope, 107, 188, 199
PEOQUINTO, 51
PEPPER, 127, 160
PEREZ, 167

PERRUE, 179
PERRY, 53, 71, 77, 106, 122, 177, 294
PETATLEY, 181
Peter, 65, 102, 103, 105, 108, 113, 114,
  120, 121, 130, 131, 132, 152, 153,
  163, 179, 184, 188, 211, 216, 219,
  246, 262, 266, 274
PETER, 7, 53, 150
PETERSGILL, 189
PETIE, 34
PETRANA, 72
Petrona, 129
PETSOLD, 226
PETTIT, 27
PETURINA, 140
PETZOLD, 45, 62, 67, 130, 171, 194,
  226, 246, 275, 281, 316, 321, 348, 374
Philime, 221
Philip, 100, 102, 129, 177
PHILIP, 45, 285
Philippe, 68
PHILIPS, 63, 372
PHILLIPS, 25, 40, 50, 91, 99, 136, 214,
  343, 349, 368
Phillis, 103, 113, 116, 119, 163, 207, 219
PHILON, 32
PHILPOTT, 312
Phoebe, 53, 102, 107, 117, 121, 131,
  147, 177
Phyllis, 121, 147, 155, 169
The PIASO, Spanish performers, 328
PICKET, 74
PICKETT, 236
PICKSTOCK, 47, 48, 79, 166, 170
PIERRE, 25, 43, 169
PIGG, 331
Pilotage rates, 358
PIMMELON, 74
PINDER, 4, 18, 19
PIPERSBURG, 20, 47, 167, 182, 191,
  259
PIRRONTIL, 39
PITKEITHLY, 320
PITKETHLY, 44, 45, 64, 111, 141, 181
PITT, 30, 60, 114, 139, 150, 163, 193,
  210, 252

PITTS, 2, 12, 13, 21, 31, 58, 122, 145,
  264, 280, 283
PITZOLD, 241
PLACIDO, 31
PLOWDEN, 24
POLLARD, 59
Polly, 101, 146
Pollydore, 220
Polydore, 104, 133, 210
POLYDORE, 2
Pompey, 51, 115, 133
POOL, 27
POOLE, 128, 140
Pope, 115, 179
POPHAM, 101, 178
Port Royal, 107, 119, 199
PORTAL, 40
PORTER, 16, 48, 64, 73, 193, 216
POTTAGE, 168, 312
POTTER, 53, 329, 330
POTTS, v, 6, 11, 13, 15, 19, 20, 22, 32,
  37, 46, 47, 52, 53, 57, 63, 75, 77, 78,
  79, 94, 101, 117, 127, 131, 132, 133,
  140, 167, 178, 180, 181, 188, 207,
  218, 220, 221, 231, 251, 280, 282,
  289, 295, 309, 323, 331, 343, 368, 376
POWEL, 25, 217
PRATT, 14, 125, 278, 282, 324
PREO, 157
Present, 102, 103, 177, 219
PRESTON, 69
PRIC, 71
PRICE, 36, 63, 71, 91, 99, 110, 117, 118,
  125, 128, 133, 134, 168, 179, 189,
  197, 217, 261, 281, 291
Primus, 52, 104, 210
Prince, 46, 102, 107, 110, 121, 127, 129,
  138, 177, 179, 183
Princess, 104, 133
PRIO, 8, 157
Priscilla, 58, 121
Providence, 167, 196
PROVIDENCE, 297
Prudence, 121, 133, 179, 221, 242
Prue, 113, 128
Punch, 114

406

PUPO, 101
PUPPO, 178
PURCELL, 94, 102, 107, 177
Qua, 48
Quaco, 133, 200
Qualm, 188
Quam, 114
Quamina, 115, 122, 129, 181, 206
Quamino, 105, 117
QUARTERMASTER, 51
Quasheba, 113
Quashee, 103
Quashie, 114, 117, 125, 130, 184, 190,
   219, 221, 224; Bony *[sic]* Quashie,
   117, Bonny Quashie, 180. Papa
   Quashie, 117, 180
QUASHIE, 180
QUAVE, 69
Quaw, 128, 132
Quawm, 132
Quawrm, 220
QUAYMAN, 145
QUILTER, 13, 46, 52, 63, 91, 99, 127,
   181, 189, 204
RABAN, 1, 18, 112, 189
RABATEAU, 55, 70, 113, 126, 134, 202
Rabian, 156
Rabien, 123
RABON, 203
RABOTEAU, 202, 232, 310, 317, 343
Rachael, 144, 156, 166, 284
Rachel, 102, 103, 113, 117, 174
RADCLIFFE, 34
RADFORD, 170, 205
RAEBON, 312
Rafiel, a Spaniard, 28
RAIN, 229
Ralph, 258
Ramin, 68
RAMON, 85
RAMONA, 147
Ramsay, 105
RAMSAY, 58, 82, 98, 106, 220, 320,
   343
RAN, 21
RAND, 182

RANN, 30, 38
Ratcliff, 177
RATCLIFF, 66
Ratcliffe, 102
RATHOMAN, 153
RAYBAN, 259
RAYBON, 16, 136, 168, 203, 312
RAYBUN, 174
RAYNE, 169
REBAN, 7
Rebecca, 103, 174, 219, 254
RECRUIT, 276
REDASS, 32
REDDING, 32
REDLYNCH, 93
REDUGEN, 101
REDUGIN, 178
REED, 228
REES, 320
REGALAER, 288
REMIE, 60, 188
REMMINGTON, 299
RENAU, 6
RENAUD, 110
RENEAU, 13, 17, 92, 99
RENNALS, 294
RENNIE, 299
RENNOW, 209
RENNY, 60
RENWICK, 99
RETIS, 46
REVEU, 363
REVEY, 253
REYES, 92, 99
REYNOLDS, 177
Rhoda, 125
Rhode, 187
RHODES, 351
RHYS, 67, 89, 92, 99, 128, 129, 376
RHYSE, 205, 376
RICALDE, 75
Richard, 99, 100, 102, 105, 107, 114,
   116, 121, 125, 128, 141, 147, 161,
   176, 183, 187, 188, 199, 204, 211,
   213, 218, 219, 292
RICHARDS, 69, 244

RICHARDSON, 68, 69, 128, 139, 140, 184, 212
Richmond, v, 101, 121, 124, 169, 178, 220
RIGHTON, 309
Rina, 117
RINTON, 42
ROBARTS, 36
Robert, 37, 102, 103, 113, 115, 116, 117, 119, 121, 125, 130, 132, 150, 152, 166, 169, 174, 184, 187, 199, 218, 219, 263, 269, 272
ROBERT, 15, 99, 216, 343
ROBERTA, 288
ROBERTS, 49, 116, 127, 181, 347
ROBERTSON, 64, 92, 93, 99, 139, 193, 216, 231, 310, 348
ROBERTSON & URQUHART, 354, 362, 364
Robin (Captain), 132
Robin Mandingo, 132
ROBINSON, v, 2, 8, 10, 12, 14, 17, 21, 22, 37, 50, 58, 61, 62, 92, 110, 121, 141, 145, 149, 154, 160, 168, 184, 202, 208, 217, 231, 236, 259, 266, 274, 289, 298, 300, 326, 368
ROBURN, 14, 15
Rochfort, 216
RODD, 48
Roderick, 102, 177
RODGERS, 206, 276, 323
Rodney, 36, 110, 132, 184, 220
RODRIGUES, 353
RODRIGUEZ, 30, 42, 92, 99, 339, 353
ROGERS, 28, 47, 55, 59, 61, 67, 126, 139, 201
ROMAN, 98
ROMARO, 69
Romeo, 101, 146, 188
ROSADO, 84, 92, 98, 99, 310
Rosanna, 117, 118, 142, 162
Rose, 54, 104, 105, 117, 125, 156, 159, 169, 187, 190, 206, 208, 210, 211, 217, 269
Rosella, 274
Rosette, 104, 121

ROSS, 40, 93, 99, 107, 127, 128, 133, 189, 197, 261
ROSWELL, 330, 334, 337, 344, 345
ROUQUE', 61
ROUQUIE, 324, 326, 351
ROVER, 117, 180
ROWLAND, 169
ROWLEY, 206
ROY, 12, 34
RUBEN, 70
RUBIO, 148
Ruffien, 70
Rum and Water, 102, 180
RUMBALL, 205
RUMBOD, 60
RUMBOLD, 60, 143
RUMFORD, 117, 180
Runaways, 101, 102, 104, 105, 106, 107, 108, 114, 117, 119, 121, 122, 127, 131, 133, 138, 139, 140, 146, 147, 150, 166, 169
RUNNALS, v, 81, 92, 99, 106, 171, 243, 285, 343
RUNNELS, 106, 187
Rushby, 300
RUST, 71
Ruth, 133
SAAR, 48
Sabina, 103, 117, 120, 133, 174, 176, 219, 221
SABIO, 115, 216
SABISTON, 354
SACKER, 91
SAFERY, 25
SALINE, 357
Sally, 120, 187, 193, 266, 285
SALLY, 228
Sally Jane, 225
Salome, 55
SALVADOR, 146, 147
Sam, 101, 104, 115, 121, 131, 138, 146, 161, 200, 278, 295
SAM, 75
Sambo, 125, 187
Samentee, 6
Sammy, 125, 187

Sampson, 107, 114, 116, 119, 161, 218, 274
SAMPSON, 192
Samson, 153
SAMSON, 47, 67
Samuel, 177
SANCHEZ, 22
Sancho, 56, 113, 119
SANCHO, 4, 119, 196, 260
SANDERS, 56
Sandy, 100, 114, 133, 188, 206
Sarah, 104, 105, 113, 115, 120, 130, 132, 133, 136, 138, 146, 153, 156, 169, 176, 184, 199, 207, 208, 211, 230, 254, 262, 266, 276
Sarah Ann, 218
Sarah Anne, 116, 254
Saraha, 218
SARRY, 64
SAUNDERS, 313
SAVAGE, 343, 354, 361
SAVERY, 11, 19, 30, 45, 50, 52, 213, 260
SAVIGNE, 196
SAVORY, 114, 123, 133, 139, 140, 168, 183, 184, 201, 214, 294
SAY, 140
SCHAISE, 92, 99, 159
SCHAW, 5
SCHRIEVER, 93
SCHURER, 93, 99
Scipio, 59, 130, 184, 224
Scotland, 107, 108, 129, 130, 141, 147, 181, 184, 199, 218
SCOTLAND, 40
SCOTT, 45, 72, 93, 99
SEAMAN, 88, 98
SEARLE, 82, 98
SEBASTIAN, 40, 298
SEBASTIANA, 167
Secundino, 67
SEDDON, 98, 356
SEDDONS, 51, 85, 147
SEGUNDE, 60
Segundo, 161
Selina, 169, 211

SELOSTINA, 282
SELWYN, 76
SEMPLES, 253
Seriaco, 120
SESTEN, 209
SEVERIA, 95
SHACKLING, 282
SHACLINE, 277
Shakespear, 114
Shakespeare, 188
SHAKESPEARE, 25
SHANKLIN, 28
SHARP, 50
SHAW, 4, 5, 32, 40, 59, 93, 99, 180, 322, 367
SHEA, 26
SHEDDEN, 361, 366, 371, 373, 376
SHEDDIN, 281
SHEDDON, 323
Shela, 292
SHEPARD, 53
SHERIFFS, 356
SHIEL, 104, 131, 199, 313, 331, 334, 373, 374
SHIEL & CARMICHAEL, 331, 334
SHORT, 233, 295
SIDDEN, 51
SIDDON, 41, 85
SIERS, 32
Sigario, 36
SILVA, 47
SILVERRIA, 59
Silvia, 147
Silvy, 183
SIMMONS, 153, 154, 181, 348
Simon, 14, 104, 114, 119, 131, 146, 147, 164, 176, 199, 210, 295; Old Simon, 117
SIMON, 45
SIMONS, 65
SIMPERT, 60
SIMPSON, 10, 11, 35, 337, 343, 344, 351
SIMSON, 247
SINCLAIR, 317, 324
SKINNER, 112

409

SLADE, 22
SLATER, 132, 220
Slave trade, 339, 344
Slavery, 330
SLESHER, 49
SLUSHER, 21, 43, 57, 146, 154, 168,
    189, 192, 211, 218, 274, 299
SMALE, 39, 84
SMALL, 49, 181, 282, 305
Smart, 104
SMART, 128
SMITH, v, 3, 4, 10, 11, 13, 19, 33, 36,
    40, 43, 45, 47, 50, 55, 58, 60, 64, 67,
    68, 69, 71, 104, 109, 110, 114, 118,
    119, 126, 127, 132, 133, 134, 135,
    137, 139, 144, 145, 153, 154, 161,
    163, 164, 168, 175, 184, 185, 187,
    190, 191, 198, 205, 208, 209, 215,
    220, 221, 230, 243, 245, 254, 257,
    261, 262, 271, 275, 278, 293, 294,
    298, 299, 304, 324, 330, 343, 351,
    361, 376
SMYTH, 79
SNELLING, 296
SNELLINGS, 106
SNODGRASS, 320, 325
SNOWDEN, 101, 178
SODEN, 325, 333, 339
Somerset, 125, 187
Sophia, 104, 116, 126, 130, 147, 153,
    184, 210, 218, 260, 261, 281
SOTO, 249
Spanish Joe, 115
SPARKES, 312
SPENCE, 49
SPENCER, 35, 37, 41, 57, 70, 98, 305
SPIKES, 72
SPINKS, 55
SPRAY, 66
SPROAT, 7, 49, 56, 59, 65, 71, 83, 137,
    145, 190, 219, 245, 270, 302
St John the Baptist, 106
ST. CROIX - see De ST. CROIX & Co.
St. GEO, 44
St. GERMAN, 50
St.VILLE, 50

Stafford, 132
STAFFORD, 36, 213
STAIN, 7, 18, 22, 59, 61, 64, 92, 112,
    121, 122, 129, 181, 190, 203, 207,
    208, 220, 224, 245, 275, 280, 293,
    306, 374
STAINE, 99, 132, 133
STAMFORD, 185
STANDFORD, 206
STANE, 7, 142
STANFORD, 126, 127, 161, 182, 213,
    226, 285, 287
STANN, 142
STANTON, 42, 325
Starvation in England, 371
Statira, 133, 153
Stella, 104, 133, 218
Stephen, 65, 142, 208
STEPHEN, 104
STEPHENS, 207, 229, 245, 327, 348,
    352, 373
Stepney, 114, 188, 309
STEVENS, 169, 347
STEWART, v, 29, 32, 46, 57, 72, 85,
    121, 122, 155, 156, 217, 322, 364,
    366, 367
STIBBINS, 33
STOBO, 109
STOCKDALE, 40
STOREY, 66
STRANGE, 266
STRANGEWAY, 65
STRANGEWAYS, 93
STRICKLAND, 67
STRUTT, 42
STUART, 93, 313, 343
SUART, 306
Success, 205
Sue, 103, 111, 113, 180
Sukey, 108, 146, 209
SULIMAN, 100
SULIVA, 35
SUNGA, 168
SUNTON, 44
SUPRIAN, 196
Susan, 107, 174, 290

410

Susanna, 60, 110
Susannah, 2, 118, 123, 133, 140, 203, 221, 290
Susannah Patience, 98
SUSMEIZEN, 56
Sutherland, 324
SUTHERLAND, 6, 49, 56, 105, 168, 169, 190, 195, 204, 213, 248, 263, 267
SUTTLE, 44, 60, 169
SWACEY, 2, 6
SWAN, 26, 38, 46, 168, 179
SWASEY, 6, 9, 35, 108, 109, 139, 182, 198, 209, 232, 288, 326, 343, 373
SWEASEY, 252
SWEENEY, 63
SWEET-ESCOTT, 93
Swift, 67
Sylvia, 103, 115, 121, 124, 133, 166, 219, 226
SYMMONDS, 210
SYMONS, 359, 362
Tabia, 132, 133, 220
Tabitha, 115, 218
TADD, 78
TAIT, 117, 180, 231
TALBOT, 162, 216
TALMADGE, 311
Tamias, 184
TATE, 3, 34, 35, 169
TATHAM, 85, 98
TAXAR, 186
Taylor, 104, 210
TAYLOR, 58, 61, 154, 155, 204, 205
Taylor Ben, 133
TEAKER, 237
Teenah, 246
Temple, 119
TEMPLES, 367
TENA, 46, 217
Tenah, 177, 224
TENAH, 238
TENCH, 236
Tenibo, 269
Tenius, 203
TENNER, 291
Teslar, 180

TEWKSBURY, 50
The Regatta, 373
Theresa, 133, 221
Thomas, 32, 41, 68, 71, 73, 102, 108, 116, 119, 121, 123, 128, 129, 130, 132, 133, 153, 169, 181, 183, 192, 197, 199, 207, 210, 211, 215, 218, 224, 256, 266, 269, 290, 296, 298, 300
THOMAS, 5, 39, 44, 61, 100, 154, 163, 180, 192, 229, 258
THOMPSON, 33, 145, 146, 150, 158, 169, 170, 190, 191, 203, 205, 231, 232, 243, 247, 286, 348
THOMSON, 14, 48, 53, 59, 65, 68, 93, 94, 99, 122, 263, 269, 317, 343
THORNTON, 94, 99
Three African Girls, 235
THURSTON, 94, 169, 206, 285
TIDDESLEY, 376
TILDESLEY, 314
TILDESLY, 70
TILLET, 8, 21, 94
TILLETT, v, 38, 45, 56, 64, 92, 94, 95, 98, 99, 102, 103, 113, 177, 179, 219, 227, 228, 237, 242, 261, 331
TILLOTE, 246
TILSTON, 312
TIMMERMAN, 213
TIMMONS, 151
TIMOTHY, 191
TINA, 54
Tinah, 152
TINAH, 143
TINKAM, 208
TINKER, 5, 266
TINKHAM, 131
Titus, 132
Toby, 103, 107, 117, 121, 130, 184, 199
TODD, 78
TOL, 75
TOLEDO, 85, 123, 323, 343, 351
Tom, 107, 108, 111, 117, 121, 128, 161, 218
Tom (aged), 100
Tom Eboe, 180
Tom Indian, 133

411

TOMLINS, 321
Tommy, 104, 117, 132, 161, 190
Toney, 129, 162, 181
TONEY, 29
TONOSTON, 136
TONSEND, 181
Tony, 301
TONY, 131
TOOLE, 70, 275
TOOTH, 7, 37, 47, 61, 129, 145, 194, 197, 374
Townsend, 117
TOWNSEND, 132, 133, 181, 220
TOWNSHEND, 171
TRAIL, 287
TRANWHO, 31
TRAP, 286
TRAPP, 6, 22, 30, 40, 49, 51, 70, 95, 99, 132, 143, 169, 170, 188, 197, 198, 211, 220, 260
Treaty, Guatemala & Central American States, 328
TROSINA, 159
TUCK, 302
TUCKBURY, 6
TUCKE, 16
TUCKER, 3, 12, 14, 22, 24, 32, 33, 39, 49, 54, 64, 70, 112, 118, 134, 136, 140, 142, 152, 169, 176, 184, 187, 199, 200, 207, 211, 212, 215, 245, 251, 252, 259, 288, 305
TUCKSY, 258
TUCKY, 214
TUKS, 246, 290
TULLY, 74
TUN, 152
TUNDO, 132
TURBULL, 31
TURNBULL, 3, 20, 26, 112, 189, 201, 249, 257, 310, 312, 343
TURNER, 59, 118
Tuslar, 102
TUSSEY, 43
TUTHILL, 335
TUTTY, 159
TUXEY, 148, 194, 277

TUXIE, 29
TWEENY, 1, 11, 57, 124, 125, 194
TWIGG, 74
TWISS, 320
Tyger Joe, 101
TYLER, 66, 112
UNARIA, 168
UNDERWOOD, 272
URQUHART, 132, 354, 362, 364, 367
USE, 126
USHER, 14, 22, 23, 27, 31, 33, 36, 49, 61, 64, 75, 78, 80, 94, 95, 98, 99, 107, 108, 115, 116, 131, 162, 174, 175, 179, 180, 192, 204, 205, 207, 212, 219, 242, 250, 269, 273, 283, 296, 303, 306, 310, 314, 316, 319, 323, 324, 326, 329, 330, 331, 332, 333, 334, 339, 343, 353, 374, 375, 376
UTER, 48, 57, 65, 103, 196, 267, 336, 343, 347
UTHER, 244
UTOR, 196
UVE, 139
VALANCY, 45
VALENCOURT, 89
Valentine, 125, 187
VALLROS, 248
VALPY, 63, 146, 178, 300
VASE, 126
VASQUEZ, 48, 310, 236
VAUGHAN, 39, 88, 119, 323, 324, 327, 330, 331, 334, 336, 342, 343, 346, 348, 349, 351, 352, 355, 357, 361, 367, 371, 372, 374
VAUGHN, 99
VENSEN, 267
Venture, 114, 188
VENTURE, 208
Venus, 65, 103, 105, 162, 219, 248
VERGES, 265
VERNEY, 51
VERNON, 3, 4, 39, 51, 53, 55, 114, 116, 117, 131, 135, 186, 199, 241, 247, 266, 283
Vick, 221

VICTORIA, 268
VIDEZ, 95, 99
VIELAJUS, 326, 338
Vincent, 167, 196
VINCENTE, 168
Violet, 101, 189
VISCADO, 39
VITTORIA, 65
VITTORINE, 19
Von OEHLHAFFEN, 91
WADDIE, 168
WADE, v, 62, 64, 73, 82, 92, 94, 96, 99,
    106, 130, 139, 165, 192, 242, 243, 343
Wages in England and Jamaica, 328
WAGGNER, 112, 113
WAGNER, 6, 10, 16, 32, 35, 36, 40, 58,
    96, 99, 136, 152, 155, 175, 176, 191,
    195, 199, 211, 214, 233, 263, 299
WAGNOR, 185
WAIGHT, 3, 20, 36, 59, 96, 109, 217
WAIGHT-GOLDING, 310
WAIR, 181
WAKEFIELD, 315
WALCOTT, 48
WALDON, 227
WALDRON, 4, 29, 42, 55, 104, 132,
    136, 141, 167, 178, 180, 182, 210,
    220, 227, 285
Walker, 100
WALKER, 51, 53, 66, 96, 99, 104, 132,
    220, 236, 313, 314, 316, 317, 319,
    323, 329, 332, 333, 335, 336, 339,
    350, 352, 358, 359, 367, 373, 374
WALL, 13, 36, 38, 49, 79, 96, 99, 101,
    117, 124, 128, 158, 171, 178, 180,
    204, 212, 215, 217, 355
WALLACE, 10, 186, 272, 362
WALLIS, 57, 247
WALLS, 368
WALSH, 91, 96, 99, 152, 177, 203, 349,
    357, 369, 372, 373, 374
WALSH & GOUGH, 373
Walter, 106, 204
WALTERS, 47, 56, 105, 106, 204
WALTON, 39, 228
WANSLEY, 33

WARBURTON, 49, 341
WARD, 262, 293
WARDLAW, 116, 210, 343
WARDLOW, 9, 56, 68, 97, 99, 310
WARIOR, 185
WARNER, 4
WARREN, 9, 13, 40, 62, 63, 120, 176,
    203, 264, 336, 357
WARRIER, 15
WARRIOR, 10, 11, 20, 58, 62, 113, 170,
    239, 304, 365
Warwick, 105, 184, 204
WATERS, 6, 229, 278
WATKINS, 261
WATSON, 132, 311, 354, 356, 361, 365,
    366, 371, 373, 376
WATTERS, 343
Wattle, 130
WEATHERALL, 312
WEATHERBY, 72, 217
WEBSTER, 298
WEDDALL, 313
WEDDY, 48
WEDLOCK, 211
WEELER, 177
WEIBELHAUSER, 62
WELCH, 326
WELLER, 320
WELSH, 33, 44, 67, 97, 99, 109, 210,
    252, 271, 312, 327, 329, 331, 335,
    336, 343, 344, 345
WELSH & GOUGH, 327, 331, 335, 345
Werna, 291
WEST, 313
WESTBY, 13, 16, 35, 37, 79, 213, 288,
    290, 300
WESTLAKE, 334
WETHERALL, 333
WETHERBY, 101
WHEELER, 61, 106
WHITE, v, 6, 22, 34, 45, 53, 54, 59, 61,
    78, 102, 103, 107, 109, 132, 139, 147,
    194, 217, 220, 232, 259, 275, 277
WHITEHEAD, 12, 52, 180
WHITING, 41

413

WHITNEY, 57, 74, 201, 314, 338, 343, 350
WHITTER, 45
WHYER, 179
WILD, 43
WILKINSON, 90
Will, 102, 153
Willberry, 163
William, 1, 10, 67, 69, 103, 104, 106, 107, 108, 114, 116, 117, 122, 125, 127, 128, 129, 132, 134, 140, 146, 147, 153, 176, 178, 187, 188, 190, 199, 203, 204, 205, 210, 219, 224, 234, 248, 266, 275, 290, 292, 293, 294, 296
WILLIAM, 1
WILLIAMS, 6, 13, 14, 15, 19, 41, 46, 48, 51, 53, 55, 59, 66, 67, 99, 112, 118, 119, 124, 127, 132, 148, 164, 170, 182, 189, 193, 194, 198, 213, 214, 228, 236, 238, 243, 253, 268, 277, 280, 291, 317, 325, 356
WILLIAMSON, 69, 97, 111, 188, 191, 343, 357, 362
WILLIS, 115, 218
WILLS, 64, 94, 97, 217, 316, 336
Willy, 147
WILSON, v, 11, 28, 32, 48, 54, 56, 75, 81, 97, 102, 109, 114, 153, 155, 168, 171, 177, 180, 188, 194, 201, 271, 312, 326, 356
WILY, 228, 343
WINCLE, 320
WINTER, 14, 16, 18, 39, 108, 124, 126, 133, 141, 170, 171, 179, 188, 204, 212, 225, 232, 258, 260, 277
WITEMAN, 97, 99
WODEHOUSE, 94
WOLDNAM, 200
WOLFENSTAN, 97, 99
WOLFENSTEIN, 58, 62

WOOD, 6, 29, 33, 42, 101, 113, 117, 123, 169, 174, 180, 201, 213, 373
WOODS, 12, 46, 97, 99, 144, 200, 317, 320, 327, 330, 343, 348, 357, 362, 367, 369, 372, 374
WOOLFRAY, 338
WOOLMAN, 67, 338
WORKMAN, 44
WORMEL, 75
WORSLEY, 26
WRIGHT, 4, 15, 26, 73, 75, 79, 99, 100, 101, 109, 178, 198
YALUPA, 40
YARBOROUGH, 306
YARBOUROUGH, 74
YARNESS, 10
YATE, 220
YATES, 133
YELA, 28
YISQUIBIS, 75
YNCLAN, 30
YNISTRELLA, 51
York, 121
YORK, 9
YOUNG, 2, 4, 5, 6, 9, 12, 13, 22, 23, 26, 31, 40, 41, 44, 48, 49, 62, 64, 73, 88, 97, 99, 100, 101, 102, 108, 132, 152, 154, 156, 171, 178, 179, 180, 182, 184, 190, 204, 209, 220, 229, 238, 239, 250, 272, 303, 305, 312, 314, 315, 319, 321, 323, 336, 349, 350, 351, 374, 375
YOUNG & TOLEDO, 323, 351
Younghal, 153

---oOo---

The lifeblood of Belize was trade, transported by ships. How many of the men who sailed from ports in the British Isles, the United States, and the islands of the Caribbean to Belize had wives and children in the settlement?

Please note that some vessels are described in more than one way - for example, the Victoria is shown as a brigand a brigantine. Search all categories for the vessel of interest. In many cases, the master (the captain) and the vessel's port of origin and/or its destination are mentioned.

Barques: *Addingham,* 354, 365, 361, 366, 371, 373; *Anteus.,* 23; *Arab,* 326; *Calcutta,* 58; *Caleb Angus,* 59; *Calista,* 354, 361; *Ceylon,* 66, 324, 326, 331, 353, 356, 361, 366, 371, 373, 376; *Duncan,* 334, 337, 344; *Egyptian,* 64; *Elizabeth & Jane,* 69, 324, 326, 330, 331, 334, 337, 344, 351, 353, 354, 356, 361; *Excellent,* 47; *Fair Arcadian,* 50, 17, 317, 323, 354; *Favourite,* 333, 334, 337, 344, 351, 354; *Hebe,* 64, 354, 357, 361, 367, 374; *Henry Angus,* 354; *Herald,* 54; *Hopewell,* 88; *La Bonne Mere (= Mere,),* 66, 316, 317. 331; *Lavinia,* 324, 334; *Lotus,* 61; *Mary,* 324, 334, 337; *McInroy,* 317; *Miriam & Jane,* 51; *Ocean,* 31; *Orestes,* 49, 50, *Orynthia,* 324, 347, 351, 354, 356, 361; *Othello,* 318, 371, 374; *Reliance,* 331, 347, 361, 366, 367, 374; *Sarah,* 319, 329; *Science,* 324, 366; *Wansbeck,* 324, 377, 344, 347, 351, 252, 364; *William,* 323; *William Shand,* 323.

Brigs: *Alert,* 324; 366; *Ann Mondel,* 347; *Ardent,* 331, 334, 337, 345, 354; *Ark,* 25; *Britannia,* 72; *Carib,* 357; *Carron,* 329, 330; *Catherine,* 43; *Davida Witton,* 59; *Dawn,* 28; *Europa,* 50, 324, 366; *Favorite,* 317, 320, 323, 347, 376; *Friendship,* 366, 376; *Hope,* 362, 365; brig *Inca,* 354, 366; *James Lyon,* 323, 348, 354, 361, 366, 371, 373, 376; *Janette Dunlop,* 33; *Joseph Hume,* 67, 329; *Lady Mary,* 337; *Lady Mary Fox,* 329; *Lois,* 60; *Lord Glenarm,* 351; *Lord Glenelg,* 337, 344; *Lord Lampton,* 324, 354; *Lyon,* 51; *M'Inroy,* 324; *Margaret,* 26, 27, 28, 330; *Mariner,* 30, 324, 334, 337, 344; *Mary,* 330, 334, 337, 344, 345; *Mary Ann,* 54, 324, 345, 347, 351; *Nestor,* 56; *Netreach,* 72; *Papaneau,* 350, 351, 354, 356; *Penelope,* 70, 71; *Rose,* 341; *Rosella,* 351; *Shannon,* 331, 361; *Susan,* 54; *Tallyrand,* 351, 355, 356, 361, 367; *Texas,* 327; *Trinidad,* 324, 361; *Vapois,* a Spanish Brig, 39; *Victoria,* 326, 366; *Victory,* 351; *Visiter or Visitor,* 331, 351, 354, 356, 361, 366, 371, 373, 376; *William Henry Angas,* 361, 366, 371, 373; *Worthington,* 344; *Wyoming,* 326, 327

Brigantines: *Alice,* 69; *James Lyon,* 356; *Patsey B. Blount,* 356, 361, 366; *Victoria,* 331, 356, 361, 367, 373; *Victory,* 371.

Cutter: *Elizabeth,* 58; Seaman of the *Elizabeth,* 44.

Draggers or Droghers: *Alicia,* 349; *Alice,* 329; *Eliza,* 54, 72, 329, 337, 351; John Inglis, 329, 337; *Reform,* 317.

Ships of the Royal Navy:
  H. M. Brig of War *Buzzard*, 344.
  H. M. Brigs *Pilot*, 320; *Ringdove*, 364, 366; *Serpent*, 373, 376.
  H. M. Packet *Express*, 330; *Hope*, 320, 354; *Lapwing*, 361; *Pandora*, 339, 341;
    Pickle, 321; *Pigeon*, 347; *Swift*, 326.
  H. M. Ship *Blossom*, 81, 97; *Comus*, 73; *Hyacinth*, 85; *Harlequin*, 327; *Leopard*, 81.

Slave ships: *La Amistad*, 344; *Clara and Eagle*, 327; *Rodeur*, 363; *St. Leon*, 363;
  Sierra Del Pilar, 322; *Wyoming, Clara,* and *Eagle,* 344.

Schooners: *Albion*, 349; *Alert*, 326; *Crusader*, 318; Schooner *Custer Braxton*, 71;
  Fifeshire, 374; *Government Schooner*, 55; *Guatemala Packet*, 329, 344, 354; *Henry*,
  54; *Hope*, 354, 356; *Isabella,* 53; *Morning Star*, 326, 329, 371; *November*, 356, 361;
  Rolls, 317; *Rosella*, 329, 367; *San Pedro*, 329; *Sylph*, 348; *Water Witch*, 345
  William Wallace, 344, 345, 373.

Ships: *Admiral Moorsom or Moorsome,* 323, 334, 337, 338, 341; *Arab,* 351; *Calista*, 356,
  357, 366, 367, 371; *Cares*, 46; *Ceres*, 354, 356, 361, 366; *Glasgow*, 351; *Merlin*, 36;
  Minerva, 317, 320, 358; *Nautilus*, 25; *Stan Rumney*, 39; *Vanguard*, 354.

Steamer *Vera Cruz*, 329; *Vera Paz*, 315, 329, 334, 341, 344, 357, 360.

Shipping, category not shown: *Belmont*, 334; *Countess Durh*am, 366; *Crusader*, 366;
  Historian, 318; *Lilburn*, 334; *McInroy*, 324; *Norra*, 334; *Perseverence,* 324; *Redman*,
  366; *St. Croix*, 354; *Viceroy* of London, 93.

---o0o---

www.ingramcontent.com/pod-product-compliance
Lightning Source LLC
Chambersburg PA
CBHW072059040426
42334CB00041B/1357